Milestone Documents in American History

Exploring the Primary Sources
That Shaped America

Milestone Documents in American History

Exploring the Primary Sources That Shaped America

Volume 1: 1763 – 1823

Paul Finkelman
Editor in Chief

Bruce A. Lesh
Consulting Editor

Schlager Group

Milestone Documents in American History
Copyright © 2008 by Schlager Group Inc.

All rights reserved. No part of this book may be reproduced or utilized in any form or by any means, electronic or mechanical, including photocopying, recording, or by any information storage or retrieval systems, without permission in writing from the publisher. For information, contact:

Schlager Group Inc.
2501 Oak Lawn Avenue, Suite 245
Dallas, Tex. 75219
USA

You can find Schlager Group on the World Wide Web at
http://www.schlagergroup.com
http://www.milestonedocuments.com
Text and cover design by Patricia Moritz

Printed in the United States of America

10 9 8 7 6 5 4 3 2 1

ISBN: 978-0-9797758-0-2

This book is printed on acid-free paper.

Contents

Volume 1: 1763–1823

Volume 2: 1824–1887

Volume 3: 1888–1955

Volume 4: 1956–2003

Editorial and Production Staff

Copy Editors, Fact Checkers

Gerry Anders, Tracey Biscontini, Christa Gainor, Harrabeth Haidusek, Michael Holmes, Michael J. O'Neal, Susan Scharpf

Indexers

Judson Knight, Michael J. O'Neal

Imaging and Design

Patricia Moritz

Page Layout

Marco Di Vita

Schlager Group Editorial Staff

Andrea Betts, LaToya Stevenson, Leah Tieger, Kathy Wise

Managing Editor

Marcia Merryman-Means

Publisher

Neil Schlager

Publisher's Note

Welcome to *Milestone Documents in American History*, the inaugural publication of the Schlager Group imprint. Although we have produced dozens of titles for other reference publishers in the past decade, we have long dreamed of creating our own publications, ones crafted through our particular vision and perspective. This title represents the culmination of that dream.

This set also serves as the first offering in a larger series of volumes that we are calling "Milestone Documents." For some years now, primary sources have been at the forefront of history education at the high school and collegiate levels, and yet their coverage by reference publishers has been maddeningly spotty. Either they were relegated to the periphery of publications as "extra features," or they were offered up in large chunks with only the most basic of contextual analysis. Our goal with this set, as well as with upcoming titles in the "Milestone Documents" series, is to make the primary sources the star of the show and to offer students not just a plethora of full-text documents but something more useful still: informed, balanced, and engaging analysis written by trained and knowledgeable historians.

In this first publication and in the "Milestone Documents" series in general, we seek to live up to the highest editorial standards in the industry—comprehensiveness, first-rate writing, painstaking fact checking and editing, and terrific design. In an age when the information industry and the general public alike trumpet the dazzling capabilities of user-generated Web sites like Wikipedia, we believe that offering readers and librarians a traditional reference product built on informed scholarly judgment and professional editorial skills is more useful than ever. This is not to downplay the revolutionary role of the Internet in educating students about the past. In fact, throughout this publication readers will see references to our companion Web site, www.MilestoneDocuments.com. For now this site will include both free content (the full texts of the primary documents covered in this set) and premium content (aimed at students who do not have access to this publication through their libraries). Moving forward, we hope to augment the site with innovative new resources for students and educators alike. (Some of those resources may even take advantage of user-generated content.)

I thank the many people who have helped us to make this first Schlager Group publication a reality. Our advisory board of librarians and history educators was instrumental in helping us to hone the concept for this title. Paul Finkelman, the editor in chief and a renowned legal historian, crafted a superb, wide-ranging entry list and gathered a wonderful list of historians and other scholars to write for the publication. Bruce Lesh, the consulting editor, utilized his extensive experience as a history educator to write a compelling introductory essay, "Teaching with Primary Source Documents," and to compile eight incisive teacher-activity guides tied to the National History Standards. The employees at Salem Press, our distribution partner, have been unfailingly helpful. This publication was truly a collaborative enterprise, and it is richer for it.

We're excited about the upcoming titles in the series, which include the following:

- *Milestone Documents of American Leaders* (April 2009)
- *Milestone Documents in World History* (October 2009)
- *Milestone Documents of World Leaders* (April 2010)
- *Milestone Documents of World Religions* (October 2010)

In the meantime, we hope you enjoy this publication, and we look forward to a long and rewarding relationship with you.

Neil Schlager
Founder and President, Schlager Group
neil@schlagergroup.com

Advisers and Contributors

Editor in Chief

Paul Finkelman
President William McKinley Distinguished Professor of Law and Public Policy, Albany Law School (Albany, New York)

Consulting Editor

Bruce A. Lesh
Social Studies Department Chair, Franklin High School (Reisterstown, Maryland); Vice Chair, National Council for History Education

Advisory Board

Shelley Arlen
Chair, Collection Management Department, Smathers Library, University of Florida (Gainesville, Florida)

Ron Briley
Assistant Headmaster, Sandia Preparatory School (Albuquerque, New Mexico)

Ronald L. Burdick
Manager, History and Geography Department, Cleveland Public Library (Cleveland, Ohio)

William E. Fischer, Jr.
Senior Aerospace Science Instructor, Westland High School (Galloway, Ohio)

Erik France
History Teacher and Upper School Librarian, University Liggett School (Grosse Pointe, Michigan)

Patti Harrold
History Teacher, Edmond Memorial High School (Edmond, Oklahoma); Adjunct Professor, Friends University (Wichita, Kansas); Oklahoma State Coordinator, National Council for History Education

Joseph Labuda
Librarian, Pima Community College (Tucson, Arizona)

Barbara Lyons
Library Media Specialist, Wilton High School (Wilton, Connecticut)

Eric Novotny
Humanities Librarian, Pennsylvania State University (University Park, Pennsylvania)

James A. Percoco
History Teacher, West Springfield High School (Springfield, Virginia); History Educator in Residence, American University (Washington, D.C.)

Contributors

David Gray Adler
Idaho State University

Ginette Aley
University of Southern Indiana

Barry Alfonso
Independent Scholar, Pittsburgh, Pennsylvania

L. Diane Barnes
Youngstown State University

Kirk H. Beetz
Independent Scholar, Davis, California

Bradley G. Bond
Northern Illinois University

Ron Briley
Sandia Preparatory School

Stephen Burwood
State University of New York at Geneseo

J. Christopher Chamberlain
La Salle University

Henry L. Chambers, Jr.
University of Richmond School of Law

Stephen Clark
Albany Law School

Robert J. Cottrol
George Washington University

Thomas H. Cox
Sam Houston State University

Scott A. G. M. Crawford
Eastern Illinois University

Kristina E. Curry
Georgia State University

Michael Kent Curtis
Wake Forest University School of Law

Allan L. Damon
Horace Greeley High School (Ret.)

Donna M. DeBlasio
Youngstown State University

Christine Dee
Fitchburg State College

Marcia B. Dinneen
Bridgewater State College

Justus D. Doenecke
New College of Florida

Leigh Dyer
Charlotte Observer

Mark R. Ellis
University of Nebraska at Kearney

Lisa A. Ennis
University of Alabama at Birmingham

Paul Finkelman
Albany Law School

Caroline Fuchs
Mina Rees Library/CUNY Graduate Center

Tim Alan Garrison
Portland State University

Michael A. Genovese
Loyola Marymount University

G. Mehera Gerardo
Youngstown State University

Lewis L. Gould
University of Texas at Austin

Claudia B. Haake
La Trobe University

Martin Halpern
Henderson State University

Michael W. Handis
Graduate and University Center, City University of New York

Martin J. Hershock
University of Michigan-Dearborn

Michael Allen Holmes
Independent Scholar, Burlington, Vermont

James S. Humphreys
Lambuth University

John P. Kaminski
University of Wisconsin–Madison

Karen Linkletter
California State University, Fullerton

Jeff Littlejohn
Sam Houston State University

M. Philip Lucas
Cornell College

John W. Malsberger
Muhlenberg College

Gregory N. Mandel
Temple University—Beasley School of Law

Nicole Mitchell
University of Alabama at Birmingham

Sandy Moats
University of Wisconsin, Parkside

Gerard Molyneaux
La Salle University

Robert R. Montgomery
Independent Scholar, Newton, Massachusetts

Michael J. Mullin
Augustana College

Michael D. Murray
University of Missouri–St. Louis

Paul T. Murray
Siena College

Michael J. O'Neal
Independent Scholar, Moscow, Idaho

Alicia R. Ouellette
Albany Law School

Chester Pach
Ohio University

Lisa Paddock
Independent Scholar, Cape May County, New Jersey

Martha Pallante
Youngstown State University

Luca Prono
Independent Scholar, Bologna, Italy

John A. Ragosta
University of Virginia

Renee C. Redman
American Civil Liberties Union of Connecticut

Kristina L. Rioux
Loyola Marymount University

Alicia J. Rivera
University of California, Santa Barbara

Carey M. Roberts
Arkansas Tech University

Carl Rollyson
Baruch College, City University of New York

Michael T. Smith
McNeese State University

Bartholomew H. Sparrow
University of Texas at Austin

Stephen K. Stein
University of Memphis

R. S. Taylor Stoermer
University of Virginia

Mary E. Stuckey
Georgia State University

Lance J. Sussman
Reform Congregation Keneseth Israel

Cynthia J. W. Svoboda
Bridgewater State College

John R. Vile
Middle Tennessee State University

Randy Wagner
Independent Scholar, Vancouver, Washington

Jenny Wahl
Carleton College

Mark R. Wilson
University of North Carolina at Charlotte

Cary D. Wintz
Texas Southern University

Charles L. Zelden
Nova Southeastern University

Overview

Milestone Documents in American History represents a unique and innovative approach to history reference. Combining full-text primary sources with expert analysis, the 133 entries in the set comprise important and influential primary source documents from the Revolutionary era to the twenty-first century. While government and public documents make up the bulk of the documents in the collection, critical sources from private individuals are also are covered.

Organization

The set is organized chronologically in four volumes:

- Volume 1: 1763–1823
- Volume 2: 1824–1887
- Volume 3: 1888–1955
- Volume 4: 1956–2003

Within each volume, entries likewise are arranged chronologically by year.

Entry Format

Each entry in *Milestone Documents in American History* follows the same structure using the same standardized headings. The entries are divided into two main sections: analysis and document text. Following is the full list of entry headings:

- **Overview** gives a brief summary of the primary source document and its importance in history.
- **Context** places the document in its historical framework.
- **Time Line** chronicles key events surrounding the writing of the document.
- **About the Author** presents a brief biographical profile of the person or persons who wrote the document.
- **Explanation and Analysis of the Document** consists of a detailed examination of the document text, generally in section-by-section or paragraph-by-paragraph format.
- **Audience** discusses the intended audience of the document's author.
- **Impact** examines the historical influence of the document.
- **Questions for Further Study** proposes study questions for students.
- **Related Documents** features an annotated listing of related primary source documents.
- **Bibliography** lists articles, books, and Web sites for further research.
- **Essential Quotes** offers a selection of key quotes from the document and, in some cases, about the document
- **Glossary** defines important, difficult, or unusual terms in the document text.
- **Document Text** gives the actual text of the primary document.

Each entry features the byline of the scholar who wrote the analysis. Readers should note that in most entries the Document Text section includes the full text of the primary source document. In the case of some Supreme Court decisions, which generally contain several parts (majority opinion, concurring opinions, dissenting opinions) and which can be exceedingly lengthy, we were able to include only the full text of the majority opinion. In all such instances, readers can view the text of concurring and dissenting opinions at any of several free Internet sites.

Features

In addition to the text of the 133 entries, the set includes nearly 250 photographs and illustrations. The front matter of Volume 1 has two sections of interest to educators: "Teaching with Primary Source Documents" and "Teachers' Activity Guides." The latter comprises eight distinct guides, all of which are tied to the National History Standards and which make use of the documents covered in this set. Both sections were written by Consulting Editor Bruce A. Lesh. Rounding out the front matter are an "Introduction" to the set, written by Editor in Chief Paul Finkelman; a section of "Advisers and Contributors"; and a "Publisher's Note." At the end of Volume 4, readers will find a "List of Documents by Category" and a cumulative "Subject Index."

Acnowledgments

The full texts of Martin Luther King, Jr.'s "Letter from Birmingham Jail" and "I Have a Dream" Speech are reprinted by arrangement with The Heirs to the Estate of Martin Luther King Jr., c/o Writers House as agent for the proprietor New York, NY. Copyright 1963 Dr. Martin Luther King Jr.; Copyright renewed 1991 Coretta Scott King.

The full text of César Chávez's Commonwealth Address is reprinted by arrangement with the Cesar E. Chavez Foundation, TM/copyright 2007 the Cesar E. Chavez Foundation. www.chavezfoundation.org.

Questions

We welcome questions and comments about the set. Readers may address all such comments to the following address:

The Editor
MILESTONE DOCUMENTS IN AMERICAN HISTORY
Schlager Group Inc.
2501 Oak Lawn Avenue, Suite 245
Dallas, Texas 75219

Introduction

Milestone Documents in American History provides students and educators with a comprehensive, single source for the most important documents in the shaping of American society from the Revolution to the twenty-first century. These 133 full-text documents, which touch on politics, economics, science, race relations, gender equality, foreign policy, and religious liberty, allow students to fully explore their meaning and instructors to develop their own document-based projects.

We began by looking at the central documents in the National Archives. To those we added materials that were not generated by the national government, such as the writings of private citizens, papers connected to state governments, and speeches by politicians running for office. We supplemented this list with items reflecting the history of minority communities—particularly Native Americans, African Americans, and women—to give a more inclusive view of our nation's history.

Viewed in isolation, primary documents can be confusing and difficult to navigate. Older documents, in particular—from the founding period through the nineteenth century—often are written in archaic language using words with unusual meanings. The complex historical context in which these documents were formed may be unfamiliar to the younger reader. *Milestone Documents in American History* responds to these challenges with a variety of tools and materials. An introductory overview briefly defines each document's importance, while a section on context details its historical background. A timeline describes key events surrounding the writing of the document, and a section about the author offers a biographical profile of the writer or writers. Most important is the in-depth expert analysis of each document text, which is followed by sections describing the document's intended audience along with its historical impact and influence. A section of essential quotes singles out the document's key passages and, in some cases, highlights writings about the document. Next is an annotated listing of related primary documents and a bibliography to aid research. Questions for further study act as guideposts for study, challenging the student to look more closely at the issues surrounding each document. Rounding out the presentation is a glossary of important or unusual terms found in the document, followed by the full text of the document itself.

These diverse documents will elicit a variety of responses from the reader. The Declaration of Independence, Abraham Lincoln's Gettysburg Address, John F. Kennedy's Inaugural Address, and Martin Luther King, Jr.'s "I Have a Dream" Speech all underscore the power of language to convey ideas, stir emotions, and stimulate people to action. Reading these full-text documents will give students new insights into the power and beauty of language. Other documents—such as Supreme Court Chief Justice Roger Taney's majority opinion in *Dred Scott v. Sandford*, the Chinese Exclusion Act, or the Black Code of Mississippi passed after the Civil War—may trouble students as they contemplate the dark events of our history that, seen in retrospect, are shameful. Statutes such as the Act to Prohibit the Importation of Slaves, the Homestead Act, or the Sherman Antitrust Act will doubtless force students to read in a new way, as they start to sort out the complexities of lawmaking and begin to realize how difficult it is to set out on paper the rules for governing a society and developing social and economic policy. Other documents help the student grasp that the development of a nation is not always about politics or economics. Sometimes it is about understanding the world around us. Thomas Jefferson's Message to Congress about the Lewis and Clark Expedition and Thomas Edison's Patent Application for the Incandescent Light Bulb remind students that science and technology have played a key role in America's development.

Many of the documents in this collection proclaim the hope of America—what Americans have wanted their nation to achieve. George Washington's Farewell Address and Franklin D. Roosevelt's First Inaugural Address are prime examples of such documents. So, too, in another context, are several Supreme Court decisions, such as *Brown v. Board of Education*, *Miranda v. Arizona*, and the important but less well-known case of *Youngstown Sheet and Tube Co. v. Sawyer*. Other documents are eloquent pleas for social or economic change, among them, William Lloyd Garrison's First *Liberator* Editorial, the Seneca Falls Convention Declaration of Sentiments, Frederick Douglass's "Fourth of July" Speech, William Jennings Bryan's "Cross of Gold" Speech, and César Chávez's Commonwealth Address. Finally, the relevance and usefulness of historical inquiry are brought into focus with several documents that highlight momentous events and contentious issues of the twenty-first century: George W. Bush's Address to the Nation on September 11, 2001; the Bybee Torture Memo; and the Supreme Court decision in *Lawrence v. Texas*.

As with any publication of this nature, readers may quibble with our decision about which documents to include and which to leave out. Undoubtedly, there are numerous other primary sources that could be used to further explore the nation's past. We hope to offer a fundamental starting point—rather than a finish line—for historical analysis using primary source documents. We urge educators and students alike to continue their exploration with other primary sources not covered in this set.

With this collection we inaugurate a fresh approach to comprehending our nation's history. Understanding these historical documents and their context will prepare students to better appreciate the complexities of the twenty-first century.

Paul Finkelman
President William McKinley Distinguished Professor of Law and Public Policy
Albany Law School
Albany, New York

Teaching with Primary Source Documents

For some, it was the picture of a loved one in a military uniform, a diploma hanging on the wall, the box of dusty and dated clothing in the attic, or a discussion with an elder that opened up the past as an exciting, humbling, and intriguing field of study. Each of these items or events shares an evidentiary connection to ideas, events, and people in the past. These sources and others tell us about challenges overcome, goals achieved, and duties fulfilled as well as hobbies and trends that dominated the past. In addition, if studied carefully, these same items can inform us about fears, failures, and missed opportunities that came to define the history of a person, family, or a nation. Within the classroom, primary sources such as these can provide the texture, emotion, and complexity of the past that is often lost in textbooks. The pedagogical challenge for the classroom teacher is to find ways to incorporate historical sources into instruction in a manner that provides the texture while simultaneously meeting the demands of today's culture of assessment and accountability.

Source work—making use of historical sources to explain a historical question—has been the hallmark of professional historians since the turn of the twentieth century, and calls have been made for teachers to engage their students ever since that time. The last twenty years, however, have witnessed a resurgence of emphasis on the use of historical sources, especially primary sources, in the classroom. Tied to an explosion of research related to the ways in which history is learned and should be taught, there is new pedagogical emphasis on investigating the past through the same sources used by professionally trained historians. Simply providing students with a letter from Thomas Jefferson or a speech by Martin Luther King, Jr., however, does not ensure a successful experience with historical sources in the classroom. In order for students to effectively make use of historical sources, they must understand that these documents are more than simply a text on a page. Students must come to see historical sources as multidimensional, in that they not only are sources of "information" but also provide insight into the time period in which the source was created and the source's author. Gaining the most from historical sources in the classroom requires students to take several approaches.

First, the student must approach the study of history as a series of contextual questions that historians pose about the past and then set out to answer. Questions should be provocative and encourage investigation and discussion, be central to the curriculum needs of the teacher, and help deepen students' understanding of history as an interpretive discipline. Examples include these:

- How effective were the New Deal programs?
- What caused the Civil War?
- What impact did the Gulf of Tonkin incident have on America's involvement in Vietnam?

Central to the exploration of these questions is an analysis of the primary and secondary sources that provide information concerning the question. Once students see the past as a series of questions to be answered, the need for information—historical sources—becomes paramount to the debate over the answers.

Second, the student must gather a variety of historical sources and analyze them by asking the types of questions posed by historians:

- Who developed the source?
- What was the audience for the source?
- What was the purpose for creating the source?
- When, relative to the event/idea/individual under study, was the source created?
- What was the relationship between the source and the event/idea/individual being studied?

Thorough analysis of the information provided by the sources and the motivations of their creators, the context of the time being studied, and the consistency and inconsistencies within the historical record will allow students to develop a possible answer to the historical question being examined. The greater facility students have with approaching historical sources in a methodical and analytical manner, the more successful they will be in utilizing the information to address causality, multifaceted interpretations, and the complexity of deciphering the past. To gain facility with analyzing historical sources, students must practice applying and answering questions with every historical source they encounter.

Third, the student should apply the information derived from various sources to the historical question under discussion. To engage in the application of information to developing interpretations, they must be challenged to delve deeply into the source's background and to look for possible problems or contradictions:

- Areas where sources provide consistency of information
- Areas where sources are inconsistent
- Gaps in information
- Information about the source's author, the purpose for its creation, the intended audience, and other aspects that might affect the information's reliability

Once these questions are asked and answered, students can formulate an interpretation of the past—focused on answering the historical question being posed—and support their interpretation with information from the sources.

The use of historical sources, interpretive questions, and debate based on evidence has the potential to transform the history classroom from a didactic delivery of volumes of information to a conversation energized by the application of skills particular to the study of history, infused with the content that gives the discipline richness unlike any other. The documents contained within this collection provide students and teachers with the opportunity to explore questions about the past with the aid of treaties, maps, letters, contracts, legislative acts, public speeches, and other traces of the past. Careful use of these sources will allow students to delve into documents that provide a window on the causes and effects of major events and ideas—and the motivations of key individuals—in the American experience.

Bibliography

Barton, Keith C., and Linda S. Levstik. *Teaching History for the Common Good.* Mahwah, N.J.: Lawrence Erlbaum Associates, 2004.

Coventry, Michael, et al. "Ways of Seeing: Evidence and Learning in the History Classroom." *Journal of American History* 92, no. 4 (2006): 1371–1402.

Musbach, Joan. "Using Primary Sources in the Secondary Classroom." *OAH Magazine of History* 15, no. 4 (Summer 2001): 30–32.

Stearns, Peter N., Peter Seixas, and Sam Wineburg, eds. *Knowing, Teaching, and Learning History: National and International Perspectives.* New York: New York University Press, 2000.

VanSledright, Bruce. *In Search of America's Past: Learning to Read History in Elementary School.* New York: Teachers College Press, 2002.

———. "What Does It Mean to Think Historically and How Do You Teach It?" *Social Education* 68, no. 3 (2004): 230–233.

"Using Primary Sources." Wisconsin Historical Society "Turning Points" Web site. http://www.wisconsinhistory.org/turningpoints/primarysources.asp. Accessed on March 13, 2008.

"Using Primary Sources in the Classroom." Library of Congress "Learning Page" Web site. http://memory.loc.gov/learn/lessons/primary.html. Accessed on March 13, 2008.

"Using Primary Sources on the Web." American Library Association "Reference & User Services Association—History Section" Web site. http://www.lib.washington.edu/subject/History/RUSA/. Accessed on March 13, 2008.

Wineburg, Samuel S. *Historical Thinking and Other Unnatural Acts: Charting the Future of Teaching the Past.* Philadelphia: Temple University Press, 2001.

Bruce A. Lesh
Social Studies Department Chair
Franklin High School
Reisterstown, Maryland

Teachers' Activity Guides

The following activity guides correspond to the National History Standards as published by the National Center for History in the Schools. The documents in *Milestone Documents in American History* relate to most, though not all, of the eras and standards found in the National History Standards.

Era 3: Revolution and New Nation (1754–1820s)

Standard 1: The causes of the American Revolution, the ideas and interests involved in forging the Revolutionary movement, and the reasons for the American victory

Focus Question: Did the colonists have legitimate grievances against the English Crown?

- Provide students with one copy of the Virginia Declaration of Rights, the Declaration of Rights of the Stamp Act Congress, the Quartering Act, the Boston Non-Importation Agreement, the Declaration and Resolves of the First Continental Congress, the Intolerable Acts, Patrick Henry's "Liberty or Death" Speech, *Common Sense*, and the Declaration of Independence. (Students would have one document per person.)
- Instruct students to examine their documents and list all of the grievances made by the American colonists.
- Compile a class list of the grievances made by the colonists in each of the documents.
- Next, provide students with a copy of the Proclamation by the King for Suppressing Rebellion and Sedition and have them compare the colonists' grievances with those of the Crown. Have students speculate as to why the opinions of the documents would differ and how this might affect relations between England and its colonists.
- Use the information derived from the sources to create a class discussion on the legitimacy of the colonial rebellion.

Standard 2: The impact of the American Revolution on politics, economy, and society

Focus Question: Were liberties created, protected, extended, or suppressed as a result of the American Revolution?

- Provide student groups with copies of Pennsylvania: An Act for the Gradual Abolition of Slavery, the Northwest Ordinance, the Bill of Rights, the Alien and Sedition Acts, and An Act to Prohibit the Importation of Slaves. Ask students to examine the documents and determine whether civil liberties were created, protected, extended, or suppressed as a result of the Revolution.
- Ask students which other documents might be helpful in determining how widespread the creation, protection, extension, or suppression of liberties was in the two decades of post-Revolutionary America.

Standard 3: The institutions and practices of government as created during the Revolution and how they were revised between 1787 and 1815 to establish the foundation of the American political system based on the U.S. Constitution and Bill of Rights

Focus Question: Determine who had a greater influence over the policies of George Washington: Thomas Jefferson or Alexander Hamilton.

- Have students complete basic research on the background, personality, political beliefs, and position on the Bank of the United States held by either Thomas Jefferson or Alexander Hamilton.
- Provide students with copies of Jefferson's and Hamilton's Opinions on the Constitutionality of the Bank of the United States and have them list the arguments made by the person they researched (Jefferson or Hamilton) and the arguments made by his opponent.
- Allow students to represent either Jefferson or Hamilton in a debate over the Bank of the United States or to write a persuasive memo to President George Washington, arguing their position on the bank.
- Have students consult George Washington's Farewell Address for information that Washington might provide in response to his two most vocal advisers.

Era 4: Expansion and Reform (1801–1861)

Standard 1: U.S. territorial expansion between 1801 and 1861 and how it affected relations with external world powers and Native Americans

Focus Question: Did President Andrew Jackson overstep his constitutional authority by ordering the removal of the Indians from the American Southwest?

- Provide students with an introduction to the history of the colonial and American policies toward natives, including discussion of the "Six Civilized Nations" of the American Southwest.
- Provide students with copies of Andrew Jackson: On Indian Removal and ask them to identify five major reasons the president gives to justify the removal of the Indians.
- Instruct students to list other documents that would be useful in evaluating the impacts of and reactions to President Jackson's Indian removal policy.
- Have students analyze the documents they gathered and determine whether President Jackson overstepped his constitutional authority.

Standard 2: How the Industrial Revolution, increasing immigration, the rapid expansion of slavery, and the westward movement changed the lives of Americans and led toward regional tensions

Focus Question: Was westward expansion the sole cause of the Civil War?

- Instruct students to research and prepare mini-presentations on major writings of the 1850s including:
    - Compromise of 1850
    - Kansas-Nebraska Act
    - *Dred Scott v. Sandford*
- Discuss the impact these writings had on the sectional tensions within the country.
- Provide students with a copy of Abraham Lincoln's "House Divided" Speech. Have student volunteers read the speech aloud. As the speech is being read, students should identify the central arguments made by Abraham Lincoln.
- Discuss whether Lincoln feels that conflict is inevitable.

Standard 3: The extension, restriction, and reorganization of political democracy after 1800

No documents from our collection address this standard.

Standard 4: The sources and character of cultural, religious, and social reform movements in the antebellum period

Focus Question: How parallel were the antebellum complaints of women and African Americans?

- Provide students with background on William Lloyd Garrison, the Seneca Falls Convention, and Frederick Douglass.
- Divide students into groups of three and give each group William Lloyd Garrison's First *Liberator* Editorial, the Seneca Falls Convention Declaration of Sentiments, or Frederick Douglass's "Fourth of July" Speech. Have students analyze their document and list the complaints and demands made by the authors.
- Ask students to complete a Venn diagram comparing and contrasting the complaints and demands of antebellum African Americans and women.

Era 5: Civil War and Reconstruction (1850–1877)

Standard 1: The causes of the Civil War

Focus Question: Was the American civil War fought over slavery?

- Provide students with a copy of the South Carolina Declaration of Causes of Secession, Jefferson Davis's Inaugural Address to the Confederacy, or Abraham Lincoln's First Inaugural Address. Instruct students to list the reasons given by South Carolina, President Jefferson Davis, or President Abraham Lincoln as the causes of the Civil War.
- Compare and contrast the reasons provided in each document and discuss the degree to which the authors' sentiments support the contention that the war was fought over slavery.
- Direct students to gather other sources that support or counter the argument that the Civil War was fought to end slavery.
- Discuss the viewpoints provided by the new documents.

Standard 2: The course and character of the Civil War and its effect on the American people

Focus Question: Did the Emancipation Proclamation end slavery?

- Provide students with a copy of the Emancipation Proclamation and have them identify the stipulations for freeing the slaves.
- Have students defend or refute the following statement based on the information found in the Emancipation Proclamation: "In 1863, through the Emancipation Proclamation, President Abraham Lincoln freed the slaves."
- Have students investigate the reasons for the wording of the Emancipation Proclamation and determine the degree to which it should be held responsible for ending slavery.

Standard 3: How various Reconstruction plans succeeded or failed

Focus Question: How were the major successes of Reconstruction treated by southern governments and President Andrew Johnson?

- Introduce students to the basic issues and competing plans for Reconstruction of the Union at the conclusion of the Civil War.
- Have students examine the Thirteenth Amendment, the Fourteenth Amendment, and the Fifteenth Amendment to the U.S. Constitution and identify the changes for African Americans found in the documents.
- Provide students with the Black Code of Mississippi, the Civil Rights Act of 1866, and the Articles of Impeachment of Andrew Johnson and ask them to determine whether the states and President Andrew Johnson were attempting to uphold or overturn the changes generated by the Thirteenth, Fourteenth, and Fifteenth Amendments to the Constitution.
- Ask students to list other documents that might be useful in determining whether Reconstruction was a success or a failure.

Era 6: The Development of the Industrial United States (1870–1900)

Standard 1: How the rise of corporations, heavy industry, and mechanized farming transformed the American people

Focus Question: Was the invention of the light bulb a major turning point in world history?

- Provide students with Thomas Edison's Patent Application for the Incandescent Light Bulb. Ask students to identify the purpose of the document.
- Instruct students to create a web with all of the changes that would be generated by the invention and mass distribution of the light bulb. Prompt students to consider political, economic, and social changes that the light bulb might create.
- Discuss the changes generated from the mass production and distribution of the light bulb.
- Ask students to list other documents that help them determine whether the changes they listed actually happened.

Standard 2: Massive immigration after 1870 and how new social patterns, conflicts, and ideas of national unity developed among growing cultural diversity

Focus Question: To what degree were Chinese immigrants accepted into American society?

- Introduce students to the new immigrants of the 1880s–1920s.
- Distribute the Chinese Exclusion Act and have students identify the purpose of the legislation.
- Instruct students to find other primary sources that explain why the Chinese Exclusion Act was passed and why Chinese immigrants were initially welcomed but eventually excluded from entering the United States.

Standard 3: The rise of the American labor movement and how political issues reflected social and economic changes

No documents from our collection address this standard.

Standard 4: Federal Indian policy and U.S. foreign policy after the Civil War

Focus Question: Was the Dawes Severalty Act consistent or inconsistent with actions taken toward Indians?

- Have students conduct research on the American government's post–Civil War policies toward the Apache, Navajo, Sioux, Ute, Nez Percé, and other Native American tribes.
- Have groups make short presentations to the class outlining the methods utilized and the results of the American policies toward each tribe.
- Distribute copies of the Dawes Severalty Act and ask students to identify its elements.
- Discuss the degree to which the Dawes Severalty Act was a continuation or alteration of American policy toward Native Americans.

Era 7: The Emergence of Modern America (1890–1930)

Standard 1: How Progressives and others addressed problems of industrial capitalism, urbanization, and political corruption

Focus Question: How dramatic were the changes wrought by the Progressive movement?

- Instruct students to examine *Muller v. Oregon* and the Sixteenth, Seventeenth, and Nineteenth Amendments to the U.S. Constitution and identify the major changes represented by the documents.
- Review student analysis and place the changes represented by the documents along a continuum that ranges from dramatic changes to status quo.
- Instruct students to research other changes generated by the Progressive movement and to place these changes along the same continuum.
- Ask students which other documents might be useful in determining how dramatic were the changes generated by the Progressive movement.

Standard 2: The changing role of the United States in world affairs through World War I

Focus Question: Was the United States an imperialist power?

- Introduce the actions taken by European nations and Japan during the late nineteenth and early twentieth centuries regarding foreign policy and generate a definition of *imperialism*.
- Have students examine the Roosevelt Corollary to the Monroe Doctrine, Woodrow Wilson: Joint Address to Congress Leading to a Declaration of War against Germany, and Woodrow Wilson's Fourteen Points and list the motivations, limitations, and results of American involvement with the world.
- Have students determine whether the United States meets the definition of an imperialist power as exemplified by England, France, Germany, Italy, and Japan. Ask students to list other sources that might help better establish whether the United States should or should not be considered an imperialist power like other nations at the time.

Standard 3: How the United States changed from the end of World War I to the eve of the Great Depression.

No documents from our collection address this standard.

Era 8: The Great Depression and World War II (1929–1945)

Standard 1: The causes of the Great Depression and how it affected American society

No documents from our collection address this standard.

Standard 2: How the New Deal addressed the Great Depression, transformed American federalism, and initiated the welfare state

Focus Question: Why was 1936 a turning point for the New Deal?

- Have students read Franklin D. Roosevelt's Campaign Address at Madison Square Garden and list the arguments made by President Roosevelt.
- Divide students into two groups. Group 1 should research the successes of the New Deal between 1932 and 1936, and group 2 should research the failures of the New Deal between 1932 and 1936.
- Have students present their findings to the class and compare student research with the arguments made by President Roosevelt in his speech.
- Ask students why President Roosevelt's speech makes only selective use of the evidence about his first term in office. Have students discuss the benefits and problems of using a political speech as a historical source.

Era 9: Postwar United States (1945 to the early 1970s)

Standard 1: The economic boom and social transformation of the postwar United States

Focus Question: Did the postwar economic boom, as represented by the Servicemen's Readjustment Act (commonly called the GI Bill) and the Federal-Aid Highway Act, have a local impact?

- Distribute copies of the Servicemen's Readjustment Act and the Federal-Aid Highway Act. Have students identify the purposes, goals, and methods to reach the goals proposed in the legislation.
- Instruct students to interview grandparents, great-grandparents, or neighbors to elicit their memories concerning the GI Bill and the growth of American highways and on their associated benefits and problems.
- Discuss the benefits generated by these two landmark pieces of federal legislation.

Standard 2: How the cold war and conflicts in Korea and Vietnam influenced domestic and international politics

Focus Question: Did the Gulf of Tonkin Resolution expand or restrict presidential power?

- Distribute copies of the Gulf of Tonkin Resolution. Have students work in pairs to determine the impact on presidential power and the rationale for this change.
- Is the Gulf of Tonkin Resolution a declaration of war?
- Ask students to brainstorm a list of other documents that would be useful in determining reactions to and implications of the Gulf of Tonkin Resolution.
- Instruct students to gather these documents and determine whether the Gulf of Tonkin Resolution expanded or restricted presidential power.

Standard 3: Domestic policies after World War II

Focus Question: Why was Senator Joseph McCarthy censured by the United States Senate?

- Have students read Senate Resolution 301: Censure of Senator Joseph McCarty and list the charges brought against the senator.
- Ask students to generate a list of other documents that might be useful in determining whether the resolution accurately depicts the actions of Senator Joseph McCarthy.
- Instruct students to investigate the actions, beliefs, accomplishments, failures, criticisms, or supporters of Senator McCarthy.
- Share research findings and discuss the career of Senator McCarthy.
- Ask students to reread Senate Resolution 301 and determine whether the document accurately reflects the efforts of Senator McCarthy.
- Discuss the limitations to certain types of documents (congressional resolutions in this case) and why deeper research on a topic is necessary to paint a full historical picture.

Standard 4: The struggle for racial and gender equality and the extension of civil liberties

Focus Question: Did the changes generated by the civil rights revolution produce short-term or long-term changes?

- Provide students with one of the following documents: Executive Order 9981; *Brown v. Board of Education*; Executive Order 10730; Martin Luther King, Jr.'s "Letter from Birmingham Jail"; John F. Kennedy's Civil Rights Address; the Civil Rights Act of 1964; the Voting Rights Act of 1965; the Equal Rights Amendment; *Roe v. Wade*; or *Regents of the University of California v. Bakke*. Have students identify the change created by their document.
- Create a class timeline of the major events in the civil rights movement.
- Ask students to investigate one of the attempts at creating racial or gender equality and determine whether the effort was successful, met with resistance, or failed.
- Discuss the degree of success generated by the civil rights revolutions of the 1950s, 1960s, and 1970s.

Era 10: Contemporary United States (1968 to the present)

Standard 1: Recent developments in foreign and domestic politics

Focus Question: Did President Ronald Reagan increase or decrease cold war tensions with the Soviet Union?

- Direct students to gather information on the status of cold war relations between the United States and the Soviet Union from 1970 to 1980.
- Distribute copies of Ronald Reagan's "Evil Empire" Speech and ask students to identify the arguments made by President Reagan.
- Discuss whether the speech would have increased or decreased tensions between the Soviet Union and the United States.
- Instruct students to gather other documents that would help support or disprove their theory about President Reagan's impact on cold war relations with the Soviet Union.

Standard 2: Economic, social, and cultural developments in the contemporary United States

Focus Question: In what ways did the Supreme Court's decision in *Lawrence v. Texas* reflect the debates in the culture wars of the 1980s and 1990s?

- Instruct students to investigate the issues debated during the culture wars of the 1980s and 1990s and to classify them as political, social, or economic.
- Distribute copies of *Lawrence v. Texas* and ask students to determine the majority holding in the case and three reasons the Court's majority provided to substantiate its opinion.
- Ask students whether the decision in the case reflects the social, economic, or political issues of the culture wars.
- Ask students to brainstorm a list of other documents that would be useful in determining the reactions to and impacts of the Court's decision and have them gather these documents to analyze the reactions and impacts.

Milestone Documents in American History

Exploring the Primary Sources
That Shaped America

King George III (Library of Congress)

Proclamation of 1763

1763

"It will greatly contribute to the speedy settling of our said new Governments, that our loving Subjects should be informed of our Paternal care."

Overview

The Proclamation of 1763, issued October 7, 1763, by Great Britain's Board of Trade under King George III, represented an attempt to control settlement and trade on the western frontier of Britain's North American colonies. The proclamation essentially closed the Ohio Valley to settlement by colonists by defining the area west of the Appalachian Mountains as Indian land and declaring that the Indians were under the protection of the king. No settlement or land purchases were to be conducted there without the Crown's approval. The proclamation also defined four new colonies that Great Britain had won from France in the just-concluded Seven Years' War (1756–1763, known in its American manifestation as the French and Indian War). These colonies were Quebec (which in fact had long been settled), East and West Florida, and the island of Grenada.

The British hoped by this decree to prevent the conflicts between colonists and Indians that had played a part in the recent costly war and in fomenting a new Anglo-Indian war that had just broken out, today often called Pontiac's Rebellion (1763–1765) for the name of the Ottawa chief who was a principal leader on the Indian side. They also hoped to encourage settlement in the newly gained colonies while, at the same time, ending or at least controlling the seemingly endless westward stream of colonists, who in this and other respects had begun to appear too independent.

While most scholars have focused on its impact on Anglo-Indian relations along the frontier, it is important to remember that the proclamation suggested the permanency of British troops in colonial America. As the historian Fred Anderson has noted, "The Royal Proclamation of 1763 marked Britain's first effort to impose institutional form on the conquests, and the Grenville ministry's first attempt to outline a policy for the empire" (Anderson, p. 565).

Context

The context for the Proclamation of 1763 depended on one's location within the emerging British Empire. The act's implications differed according to whether the person considering it was within the chambers of Whitehall, residing in British North America, or living in an Indian community along the Appalachian divide. The proclamation transformed colonial-imperial land discussions and political relationships for the next decade. The edict challenged colonial conceptions about who "owned" the land and who should direct the settlement of it. The resulting salvos showed just how divergent colonial and imperial thoughts were regarding the future of North American settlement.

Even before Britain and France signed the Treaty of Paris in February of 1763, ending the Seven Years' War, English politicians had decided to reassess the imperial-colonial relationship. Many English officials believed that their North American colonies had shown an utter disregard for England's needs during the just-completed conflict. In military and economic matters the colonists had thought only of their self-interest, not Great Britain's. The result had been not only a major war but also a doubling of Britain's national debt—a direct consequence of colonial autonomy. The years preceding the war had seen tentative moves to impose a royal presence in North America, but they had not been enough. The war had shown just how independent the American colonies had become. Many a writer advised British officials to rethink and restructure their relationship with the American colonies. As the historian P. J. Marshall once noted, one "lesson of war for Britain's rulers was that empire required the effective exercise of authority"(Marshall, p. 89) Now Whitehall officials saw the postwar period as an opportunity to reassert parliamentary control over the colonies.

One area in which imperial officials were very proactive in their assertion of royal authority was Indian affairs. The Crown called representatives of several colonies to the meeting known as the Albany Congress of 1754 largely to address Indian land complaints, and the decision in 1755 to create an Indian superintendency system showed growing imperial concern about colonial autonomy regarding Indian relations. Nothing worried policy makers more than colonial efforts to expropriate Indian land, often illegally. Indeed, from London's perspective it was colonial claims to western lands and the colonists' insistence on settling these lands that had precipitated the Seven Years' War. The

Time Line

1754	■ Thomas Pownall writes an essay in which he proposes the colonization of the interior of North America with English settlements.
1755	■ Thomas Pownall revises his plan for English colonization of the North American interior, adding maps showing where he thought the western settlements should be located.
1758	■ General Jeffrey Amherst, the British commander in chief in North America, promises to remove British and French forts in the Ohio region once Britain defeats France.
1763	■ **May** Outbreak of Pontiac's Rebellion. ■ **October 7** The British Board of Trade issues the Proclamation of 1763.
1764	■ **July** The Board of Trade creates the "Plan for the Future Management of Indian Affairs."
1765	■ **July** Conferences are held concerning English possession of former French posts in the Ohio region.
1766	■ **July 25** The Oswego Peace Conference officially ends Pontiac's Rebellion.
1768	■ **November 5** The Treaty of Fort Stanwix is signed.
1774	■ **April–October** Lord Dunmore's War. ■ **June 22** Parliament passes the Quebec Act.

Crown might have hoped to forestall such a conflict, but it was unable to do so. And when the colonial conflict became an international conflict, imperial officials found they could not focus solely on their North American colonists, even if they had wanted to.

While the colonies thought only of the conquest of Canada, London officials needed to concern themselves with affairs in the Caribbean, Europe, Africa, and Asia. The result was a constant struggle between royal and colonial officials over the war in North America. Colonial governments complained about paying for the war while having no say in how it was prosecuted. The British statesman William Pitt's promise in 1758 to reimburse colonial regimes for the costs of the war solved some of the problems, but at a steep price; it contributed mightily to England's enormous debt crisis. Perhaps more important, the colonists' audacity to challenge London on both money and military matters revealed how much power colonial legislatures had assumed over the decades.

Once the war ended, the Board of Trade decided to assume powers previously exercised by the colonies and give these powers to royal officials. The Crown was not going to return to the pre-1754 status quo in colonial-imperial relations. Nowhere was this new assertion more obvious—and, from a colonial perspective, more dangerous—than in Parliament's decision regarding western lands. Known as the Proclamation of 1763, the act closed off the Ohio Valley to colonial settlement. Colonists and their governments had assumed that the victory over the French had offered them this region. The Proclamation of 1763 therefore marks the moment when colonists began "to reformulate their understanding of Britain" as a bastion of republican virtue and see it instead as a corrupt tyrannical regime (Shalev, p. 122).

In their reconception of England, colonists usually ignored their own actions regarding their Indian neighbors and the growing rift between the two peoples. London officials, however, did not. They remembered how colonial land greed had precipitated the war. Militarily this was important because England's strategy toward North America was predicated upon her Covenant Chain of Friendship with the Six Nations Iroquois. When Hendrick, a Mohawk spokesman, symbolically broke the chain in 1753, English policy makers were unprepared. One result of colonial actions had been that Indian agents such as William Johnson spent the first half of the Seven Years' War reestablishing Indian alliances rather than securing Indian allies to fight against the French. Many of the issues that Hendrick had raised were still unresolved at the end of the conflict.

Imperial officials, when looking at an enlarged territorial base and an economic crisis at home, knew that good Indian relations were cheaper to maintain than wars of conquest. Nevertheless, peaceful relations were going to be difficult if unrestricted colonial settlement of the West was allowed to continue. From Britain's perspective, this problem was compounded by the seeming indifference of the colonists. Many settlers, and not just veterans who had

www.milestonedocuments.com

been promised land for service, had begun moving into western Pennsylvania and the Ohio Valley. Fort Pitt (on the site of present-day Pittsburgh) served as more than "an imposing symbol of imperial presence and a threat to Indian independence" (Calloway, p. 55). It served as a beacon for squatters and settlers.

Complicating the situation were competing colonial territorial claims, such as the struggle between Pennsylvania and Connecticut over the Wyoming Valley. South Carolina and Georgia had their own territorial conflicts. The original charters extended beyond the Allegheny and Appalachian mountains, and now settlers used these charters to justify their western expansion. Making matters from the home government's viewpoint worse was the fact that settlement west of the mountains put the settlers beyond the geographic reach of both imperial and colonial officials. Rivers there flowed away from the Atlantic Ocean. Geography dictated that settlers turn their back on England and look toward the Ohio and Mississippi rivers for their future. Imperial officials knew that their enlarged empire required addressing this development.

The result of both Indian unhappiness and colonial movement was a decision by Whitehall officials to rethink colonial expansion. Britain's newly won lands in North America not only offered the Crown an opportunity to rein in this expansion—the cause of the war—but also offered an opportunity to remind the colonies of where ultimate power lay.

About the Author

Seemingly coming out of nowhere and issued to address a specific event, the Proclamation of 1763 actually had roots extending back nearly a decade. In 1754, when the Seven Years' War was just brewing, the British colonial statesman Thomas Pownall (1722–1805) wrote a proposal for colonizing the interior of North America with English settlements. He sent his essay, "Considerations on ye Means, Method, and Nature of Settling a Colony on Land South of Lake Erie" to his brother, John Pownall, then secretary for the Board of Trade (and the man responsible for writing the final Proclamation of 1763). Thomas Pownall later refined his proposals in his "Plan for New Settlements" (1755), and this time he included a map to illustrate where these western colonies should be located.

Pownall's "Plan" and his map are a blueprint for the future direction of Indian affairs. He proposed creating new colonies in the West, including one immediately south of Lake Erie in which the "New Proposed Government" was "to be taken out of the Province of N[ew] York & taken possession of & settled by military Townships" (Pownall, 1755, p. 2). The new western colony would be settled in an orderly fashion, by military men, under the direction of the Crown. He also proposed establishing a new colony south of Lake Erie. Instead of allowing colonists to settle either of the new colonies, Pownall suggested using retired military personnel, a suggestion later integrated into the Proclamation of 1763.

When Thomas Pownall drafted his proposals he made certain assumptions, and these assumptions influenced future British policy. One assumption was that the colonists would be more difficult to control the farther west they moved. Here geography, not Indian claims to the land, influenced Pownall's thinking. At the time of the proclamation's announcement, however, Indian land claims seemed just as important as geography. Another assumption was that the Indians and the colonists were unlikely to coexist peacefully. Interestingly, Pownall wanted a series of forts constructed on the borders of the Indian territory and the new colonies. They would serve a dual mission. First, they would stand as a reminder of British power. Second, they would protect the Indians from colonial land encroachment. In a later essay he went so far as to argue that colonial expansion should be confined "either by policy from home, or invasion of Indians abroad" (Pownall, 1764, p. 130). Perhaps this is why imperial officials did not require Jeffrey (sometimes spelled "Jeffery") Amherst, the British commander in chief in North America, to dismantle the former French forts, as he had promised the Indians he would in 1758.

When John Pownall drafted the Proclamation of 1763 he included many of his brother's ideas in the final draft, including the idea of military settlements to the west of existing colonies. For example, the proclamation promised discharged military personnel land grants ranging from fifty to five thousand acres, depending on one's rank. While the proclamation did not specify where those grants would be located, it was clear they would come from the Crown, not a colony. Thomas Pownall's writings to his brother provided a starting point when royal officials decided they needed to reconfigure imperial-colonial relations.

What began as a theoretical discussion became a necessity when news of "Pontiac's Rebellion" reached London. It was at this point that Thomas Pownall's thoughts about the necessity of dealing with Indian complaints took center stage. The outbreak of the war both prompted and allowed Charles Wyndham (the Earl of Egremont and the British secretary of state) and the Board of Trade to take action. A single document was prepared that not only addressed the integration of Britain's new territorial holdings into the empire but also sought to mollify her Indian inhabitants about the future. The result was the Proclamation of 1763.

Explanation and Analysis of the Document

The Proclamation of 1763 is a straightforward document that shows both the short-term and long-term policy positions of the imperial government.

It begins by defining its four newest colonies—Quebec, the two Floridas (East and West), and then Grenada. Listed first, Quebec's placement shows how royal officials saw the former French settlement as most important. It was the most settled of the North American colonies that England had secured at the Paris peace, and officials wanted to establish British colonial government there as quickly as possible. By clearly defining the province's eastern, western, and southern boundaries, the Crown superseded any territorial claims that one of its earlier colonies might have had to the land based on their original charters. The proclamation repudiated colonial charter claims of land "from sea to sea" (Jacobs, p. 10).

Imperial officials made clear their desire to see Quebec become the focus of population and territorial growth in 1774. The Quebec Act of that year made the land secured through the Seven Years' War a part of Quebec. Although English settlers accounted for only 5 percent of the colony's total population, the former French colony's boundary now stretched down the Ohio River into the very region where Virginians were engaged in a new war—Lord Dunmore's War—trying to secure it from the Shawnee and Delaware Indians. Integrated into the empire with the Proclamation of 1763, Quebec, and not Williamsburg or Philadelphia, would be where land patents were issued for the Ohio Valley.

After defining the new colonies, the Crown notifies its subjects about territorial readjustments. It annexes the "Islands of St. John's and Cape Breton, or Isle Royale, with the lesser Islands adjacent thereto" and places them under Nova Scotia's colonial government. One way to see this decision is as punishment of the Massachusetts Bay Colony for its parsimony during the Seven Years' War—after all, Massachusetts militiamen had regularly fought for and taken the island in previous conflicts with France, and Massachusetts officials, always interested in the fishing grounds to their north, might reasonably have assumed that governmental jurisdiction would be given to them. A more likely scenario, however, is that England was still dealing with the aftereffects of its earlier decision to exile the Acadians. By placing the islands under Nova Scotian control, the Crown probably believed it would limit Acadian unrest in Quebec should the exiles seek to return home.

The next portion of the document deals with a boundary dispute between Georgia and South Carolina. Here the Crown "annexed to our Province of Georgia all the Lands lying between the Rivers Alatamaha and St. Mary's." Whether this was intended to punish Carolina for the problems the Cherokee conflict of 1761 had created for the Crown is unknown. What is known is that Georgia at the time was smaller than South Carolina and its frontier was less extensive than South Carolina's. Thus the Crown could better regulate the expansion of that frontier, the very goal of the Proclamation of 1763.

Having dealt with territorial issues, the proclamation next sets out to create governments for the two Floridas and Quebec. Here the Crown showed its long-term policy objectives. To help the new colonies grow, the governors of Florida and Quebec were allowed to grant land so their populations might increase quickly. This growth promised to come on the very lands where existing colonies had hoped to settle their own people. Why, Americans wondered, were they being prevented from settling on lands their militias had won?

Having encouraged Quebec and Florida to create conditions that would lure new settlers, the proclamation then addresses a looming economic crisis—the return to England and retirement at half pay of some fifty thousand soldiers and several hundred officers. The proclamation promises servicemen who remain in America "Quantities of Lands" ranging in size from fifty acres for "every Private Man" to five thousand acres for a "Field Officer." The Crown hoped the offer not only would keep many veterans from returning but also would ensure an adequate reserve of soldiers should they be needed on the frontier of North America. In making the latter calculation, George III and his ministers were giving a nod to Thomas Pownall and his earlier essay, which had noted that military settlement would allow the British "to support our selves … against ye Western & French Indians." At the same time, Pownall observed, Britain would be "actually becoming possessed of ye Command of the Country" (Pownall, 1755, p. 4).

While the proclamation does not stipulate where the soldiers had to take their land, the assumption was that it would be in the territory given to Quebec. The reason for this is that immediately following the grants is a paragraph claiming it was "essential to our [England's] Interest" that lands of "the Several Nations or Tribes of Indians with whom We are connected … are reserved to them." In case the colonists and their governments missed this point, the paragraph concludes by saying that "no Governor or Commander in Chief" could grant any "Warrants of Survey" or pass "any Patents for Lands beyond the Bounds of their [current] respective Governments" until further notice was given. Moreover, those people who had "either willfully or inadvertently seated themselves upon any Lands … reserved to the said Indians" were to "remove themselves" forthwith. Colonists were also forbidden from "purchasing Lands of the Indians." For many colonists the rationale for fighting the Seven Years' War had disappeared.

The traditional independence of the colonies in Indian land purchases was at an end; the Crown, not colonial entities, would make all future land purchases. Henceforth, imperial officials would determine future colonial growth. This did not mean that purchases came to a complete end; Georgia officials secured more than 5,500,000 acres of land in three sessions between 1763 and 1775. Nevertheless, the prohibition of land purchases was the section of the proclamation that received the most attention from colonists and speculators.

Having, in their minds, brought unregulated western settlement to an end, Board of Trade members used the proclamation to restructure commerce with the Indians. If the proclamation promised a more organized settlement pattern, it also offered a more competitive economic environment. It opened the Indian trade to "all our subjects whatever," stipulating only that traders receive licenses from a colonial governor. This provision opened Pandora's box. Governors licensed almost any trader who applied for one, and soon traders swarmed the Indian country in pursuit of skins and profits. The proclamation created no mechanism for regulating such activities. As a result, trade now took place not only beyond the fort walls but also on the boundaries of Indian communities. Privy council members seem to have recognized the problems the proclamation had unintentionally created, since they later talked about creating regulations for the trade in correspondence with Indian Superintendent Sir William Johnson. Before regulations could be enacted, however, traders sought out new locales, including the recently created West Florida. For southern Indian groups such as the Choctaws, the decade following 1763 was one of profound social and economic change, and the "southern Indian trade became marked by disruption and violence" (Calloway, pp. 109–110).

In this new environment, the idea of separating Indians from colonists appealed to many southern Indian groups. Cherokee elders had long considered and used dividing lines when it came to conflict resolution. This approach had resolved at least one Cherokee-Creek conflict, and it was used in 1762 while negotiating the Cherokee War resolution. Both the Cherokee War and a change in colonial perceptions about the backcountry during the 1760s meant that negotiating some sort of demarcation became imperative, and this is what happened in the 1765–1767 period. Finally, the proclamation reserves land to the Crown not specifically given to East and West Florida or Quebec.

It is interesting to note what the proclamation did not do. It did not suspend the colonial charters and negate all existing colonial land claims. Nor did it propose to send more troops to America so that, as his secretary, Maurice Morgann, had suggested to William Petty, 2nd Earl of Shelburne, the president of the Board of Trade, the colonies might "now be surrounded by an army, navy, and by hostile tribes of Indians" (ctd. in Humphreys, pp. 247–248). What officials such as Egremont, Shelburne, and John Pownall were more interested in was figuring out how to combine the needs of imperial policy with the desires of colonists for western lands.

If the Seven Years' War made England the undisputed power of North America, the war left the Indians along the colonial frontier deeply worried. With the French gone, Creek and Seneca leaders could no longer play the British against the French. Headmen throughout the Eastern Woodlands found their ability to preserve their political autonomy threatened. No longer able to threaten aligning with the French, Indians in both the Southeast and Northeast found their traditional foreign policy strategies undermined. While it might be true that the English could provide the Indians with better goods than the French, it was also true that with English traders came settlers. Moreover, with French traders driven from the forest, at least temporarily, competition vanished, and prices rose.

At the same time, Jeffrey Amherst saw the end of the war as an opportunity to curtail Indian-related expenses. Worried more about political problems in England than about North America, he repeatedly warned Sir William Johnson about Johnson's lavish use of Indian gifts, arguing that "when men of what race soever behave ill, they must be punished but not bribed" (Long, pp. 180–182). Neolin, the Delaware prophet, spent the postwar years telling anyone who would listen that "this land where ye dwell I [the Master of Life] have made for you and not for others" (Stevens et al., vol. 6, p. 262). Neolin's words resonated. When Turtle Heart, a Delaware, met Captain Simeon Ecuyer during the siege of Fort Pitt, he told the commander that "this land is ours, and not yours" (Parkman, vol. 2, p. 23).

While contemporary writers expressed surprise at the outbreak of Pontiac's Rebellion in 1763, it should not have surprised them. When Fort Duquesne fell in 1758, the Indians of the region had warned the British that if Euro-Americans occupied the fort there "would be a great war" against them (Downes, pp. 93–95). Now, in 1763, not only did the forts remain, but Amherst also had curtailed Indian presents. The result was economic hardship for many Indian communities. Amherst's decision came at the very time when pent-up demand for British goods in North America's interior were greatest. At the same time, Indian groups found that their traditional foreign policy strategy no longer worked. With France defeated, there was no counterweight to Britain. These various streams—military retrenchment, colonial land-grabbing, and a new political reality—channeled their way toward violence in 1763, and though the war was never widespread or great in scope, it provided London officials with all the justification they needed to issue the Proclamation of 1763.

The proclaimed boundary line offered the Indians some hidden hope. Smallpox appeared in 1763. Generally blamed on Amherst on the evidence of his letter to Colonel Henry Bouquet during Pontiac's Rebellion about the possibility of giving the Indians blankets used by victims of the disease, the outbreak might simply have been the result of earlier epidemics introduced by soldiers and settlers moving throughout the interior. By separating Indians and colonizers, the proclamation offered an opportunity to end the ravages of disease.

Whatever the cause of the disease's outbreak, the Proclamation of 1763 offered the Indians an opportunity to see Amherst's earlier promise come to pass. Amherst had promised the Ohio Indians that he would destroy the forts built by the French once the war ended. He had not done so. The proclamation suggested that some forts were unnecessary to maintain while others would be transformed into centers of commerce, following the French rather than the English model. As the nineteenth-century historian William Poole noted, the proclamation promised to keep the Indians in "undisputed possession" of the land "between the Alleghanies [*sic*] and the Mississippi" (Poole, p. 687). If Pontiac's Rebellion had not brought the French back, it seemed to promise an end to unregulated colonial land encroachment.

Audience

The Crown aimed the Proclamation of 1763 at all residents of British North America and at policy makers in Eng-

www.milestonedocuments.com

Essential Quotes

"We have, with the Advice of our Said Privy Council, granted our Letters Patent, under our Great Seal of Great Britain, to erect, within the Countries and Islands ceded and confirmed to Us by the said Treaty, Four distinct and separate Governments, styled and called by the names of Quebec, East Florida, West Florida and Grenada."

(Paragraph 1)

"It will greatly contribute to the speedy settling of our said new Governments, that our loving Subjects should be informed of our Paternal care."

(Paragraph 8)

"We do further declare it to be Our Royal Will and Pleasure, for the present as aforesaid, to reserve under our Sovereignty, Protection, and Dominion, for the use of the said Indians, all the Lands and Territories not included within the Limits of Our said Three new Governments, or within the Limits of the Territory granted to the Hudson's Bay Company."

(Paragraph 13)

"[The proclamation is] a temporary expedien[t] to quiet the Minds of the Indians."

(George Washington, qtd. in Holton, p. 9)

land. It attempted to integrate into the enlarged British sphere both Indians and Euro-American colonists. To the colonists, however, it suggested that imperial officials blamed them, not the Indians, for the violence associated with Pontiac's Rebellion. For policy makers at home, the proclamation suggested a new imperial-colonial relationship that defined the limits of colonial autonomy and expansion.

South Carolina officials saw the proclamation as an opportunity "to make the backcountry safe enough to attract new immigrants" (Hatley, p. 182). Like many other colonists, Carolinians anticipated that the Crown would rescind the proclamation in the not-very-distant future. But the proclamation marked the beginning of a new understanding in Carolina. No longer was the frontier thought of in terms of the "Indian trade." Now the frontier became the focus of settlement. Farther north, George Washington expressed the hopes of many when he opined that the proclamation was "a temporary expedien[t] to quiet the Minds of the Indians" rather than a real change in policy (Holton, p. 9). He was mistaken, but what interested colonials heard in the proclamation was the promise of future settlement. They only hoped it would be under the Puritan influence, since the possibility of being placed under Georgian or Carolinian control presented its own problems, not the least of which centered on land practices and the Indian trade.

Residents in Quebec saw the proclamation as a continuation of French policy toward the Indians. The proclamation specifically cited the "great fraud and abuses" British colonial citizens had committed against the Indians, and how this had produced "great dissatisfaction" among the native peoples. French Indian policy had restricted trade to specific outposts and had forbidden settlers from purchasing land as individuals. The proclamation attempted to do these same things. New France had not experienced the Indian wars that periodically swept the British colonies. Many politicians saw this fact as proof of France's good relations with the Indians. In this sense, the proclamation promised Quebec and even Florida traders the status quo when it came to Indian policy.

While the government clearly aimed the proclamation at Indians and colonists alike, they were not the only audience. It was up to military commanders and Indian agents to bring the proclamation's promise to fruition, something they proved incapable of doing. Even William Johnson, Indian superintendent for the northern colonies, had put together a group of speculators known as the Illinois Company in hope of taking financial advantage of the new opportunities France's defeat created.

Impact

The Proclamation of 1763 is often credited with securing Indian friendship in the years to come. Besides such long-time Indian allies as the Mohawk, former French Indian allies such as the Ottawa sided with Britain during the Revolutionary War. The proclamation's recognition of Indian rights, when coupled with the actions of well-intentioned Indian agents, stood in stark contrast to the land avarice that western colonists from Virginia and Carolina showed.

For the original thirteen colonies, the proclamation contained some distressing items. It repudiated colonial charter claims of land "from sea to sea" (Jacobs, p. 10) The governors of Florida and Quebec were allowed to grant land so their populations might grow quickly. This growth promised to come on the very lands where existing colonies had hoped to settle their own people. The Indian trade was also transformed. Unlike the laissez-faire trade of earlier times, licenses were now to be required and the trade restricted to existing British outposts. Indian department officials and military personnel were authorized to seize and apprehend any person who disregarded any of the proclamation's edicts. Adding to this insult was the proclamation's placement of indigenous people within the empire. It made the Crown responsible for their protection. In the eyes of many, Indians and colonists now occupied the same legal space. This development occurred at the very time Indians, colonists, and British soldiers were fighting along the frontier.

It took five years and ten treaties, but the proclamation led to the creation of a continuous boundary from New York to the Gulf of Mexico. The two most important treaties regarding the Proclamation of 1763 were completed in 1768. John Stuart negotiated the Treaty of Hard Labor with the Cherokee in October of that year. Sir William Johnson completed his controversial negotiations with the northern Indians a month later in the Treaty of Fort Stanwix. Stuart's actions at Hard Labor were more in line with imperial expectations than were Johnson's. The southern Indian superintendent allowed the Cherokee to remain in control of the Kentucky region despite pressure from some of Virginia's leading men. Stuart's actions, however, were undermined by Johnson's scarcely a month later. At Stanwix, Johnson went well beyond his instructions to secure a boundary along the Ohio to the Great Kanawha River and then back to Chiswell's mines near the Virginia–North Carolina border. This arrangement would have kept Kentucky in Indian hands. Instead, Johnson secured Iroquois acquiescence to the Tennessee River, thereby opening up Kentucky to settlement. Stanwix alienated the western Indians and created tremendous discord between Pennsylvania and Virginia. By 1774 tensions reached such height that Virginia's governor, Lord Dunmore, sent his own representative to Pittsburgh with orders to bring the region under Virginian control.

In many ways the proclamation's audience was not supposed to read the document, but to hear it—from Indian agents and military officials. The proclamation's focus on Indian issues showed the imperial government's commitment to maintaining good Indian relations. As the Crown had done when it called the Albany Congress in 1754, it now put forward the proclamation in the hope that it would serve as a foundation for future negotiations involving Indian-colonial relations. While the proclamation became intertwined with Pontiac's Rebellion, the document clearly indicated that these relations were going to be placed on a new foundation.

A less obvious but harsh impact of the proclamation fell upon frontier squatters, many of whom were non-English-speaking Germans or anti-English Scotch-Irish. They first heard of the document from the soldiers assigned to remove them. Even officers who understood the reasoning behind such evictions grumbled about the duty to enforce them. Moreover, even when the army removed squatters, the families often returned the next season. In the end squatters found that the proclamation shielded them legally. Since no land titles could be issued, squatters settled on land indiscriminately. This does not mean that squatters came to accept the proclamation. They did not. What it did mean was that the proclamation offered protection to them when it came to clearing the land, even though it meant a legal limbo for them once they wanted to take title.

While squatters worked around the proclamation, the edict hurt one group of listeners particularly hard: the land speculators. Squatters could slip into the region and take up residence, but land companies could not. Speculators needed to obtain clear title to the land before they could sell it. The proclamation barred companies such as the Ohio Company of Virginia from renewing their earlier grants. As one lawyer commented, the proclamation was "a species of 'tyranny' that was 'sufficient to prevent the operations of the companies'" (Holton, p. 8).

The reference to tyranny was not simple rhetorical flourish. The proclamation served as a catalyst for a rethinking of what England stood for. The Seven Years' War had inspired a mass of literary works that likened the English-French conflict to Rome's struggle with Carthage. The British writer Horace Walpole, for example, said that victory made England "heirs apparent of the Romans" (Shalev, p. 115). Such comparisons did not enjoy long popularity in North America. The proclamation, when combined with the Sugar Act and Stamp Act, led colonists to recast the Roman metaphor. England became the corrupt and tyrannical Rome, the empire not the republic. The proclamation offered a new understand-

www.milestonedocuments.com

ing of England that eventually convinced the colonists that they were American rather British.

Related Documents

Pownall, Thomas. *The Administration of the Colonies*. London: J. Wilkie, 1764. Published anonymously at first, this book represented Pownall's call for a union of all British possessions on the basis of commercial interests.

Sullivan, James, et al., eds. *The Papers of Sir William Johnson*. 14 vols. Albany: University of the State of New York Press, 1921–1965. Johnson served as the British superintendent for Indian affairs from 1755 to 1774.

Bibliography

■ Articles

Curtis, Thomas D. "Land Policy: Precondition for the Success of the American Revolution." *American Journal of Economics and Sociology* 31, no. 2 (April 1972): 209–224.

Farrand, Max. "The Indian Boundary Line." *American Historical Review* 10, no. 4 (July 1905): 782–791.

Humphreys, R. A. "Lord Shelburne and the Proclamation of 1763." *English Historical Review* 49, no. 194 (April 1934): 241–264.

Lawson, Philip. "'Sapped by Corruption': British Governance of Quebec and the Breakdown of Anglo-American Relations on the Eve of Revolution." *Canadian Review of American Studies* 22, no. 3 (Winter 1991): 301–323.

Laub, C. Herbert. "British Regulation of Crown Lands in the West: The Last Phase, 1773–1775." *William and Mary Quarterly* 2nd series, 10, no. 1 (January 1930): 52–55.

Mullin, Michael J. "The Albany Congress and Colonial Confederation." *Mid-America* 72, no. 2 (April–July 1990): 93–105.

Shalev, Eran. "Empire Transformed: Britain in the American Classical Imagination, 1758–1783." *Early American Studies* 4, no. 1 (Spring 2006): 112–146.

Walton, F. P. Review of *The Administration of Justice under the Quebec Act, 1774*. *Journal of Comparative Legislation and International Law* 3rd series, 20, no. 4 (1938): 294–295.

■ Books

Anderson, Fred. *Crucible of War: The Seven Years' War and the Fate of Empire in British North America, 1754–1766*. New York: Alfred A. Knopf, 2000.

Calloway, Colin G. *The Scratch of a Pen: 1763 and the Transformation of North America*. New York: Oxford University Press, 2006.

Downes, Randolph C. *Council Fires on the Upper Ohio: A Narrative of Indian Affairs in the Upper Ohio Valley until 1795*. 1940. Reprint. Pittsburgh: University of Pittsburgh Press, 1994.

Hatley, Tom. *The Dividing Paths: Cherokees and South Carolinians through the Era of Revolution*. New York: Oxford University Press, 1993.

Hinderaker, Eric. *Elusive Empires: Constructing Colonialism in the Ohio Valley, 1673–1800*. New York: University of Cambridge Press, 1997.

Holton, Woody. *Forced Founders: Indians, Debtors, Slaves, and the Making of the American Revolution in Virginia*. Williamsburg, Va.: University of North Carolina Press, 1999.

Jacobs, Wilbur R. "British Indian Policies to 1783." In *Handbook of North American Indians*, Vol. 4: *History of Indian-White Relations*, ed. Wilcomb E. Washburn. Washington, D.C.: Smithsonian Institution, 1988.

Jones, Dorothy V. *License for Empire: Colonialism by Treaty in Early America*. Chicago: University of Chicago Press, 1982.

Long, J. C. *Lord Jeffery Amherst: A Soldier of the King*. New York: Macmillan, 1933.

Marshall, P. J. "Britain Defined by Its Empire." In *Major Problems in the Era of the American Revolution, 1760–1791: Documents and Essays*, 2nd ed. Richard D. Brown, ed. Boston: Houghton, Mifflin, 2000.

McNaught, Kenneth William Kirkpatrick. *The Pelican History of Canada*. New York: Penguin, 1976.

Parkman, Francis. *The Conspiracy of Pontiac and the Indian War after the Conquest of Canada*. 2 vols. 1870. Reprint. Lincoln: University of Nebraska Press, 1994.

Poole, William Frederick. "From the Treaty of Peace with France, 1763, to the Treaty of Peace with England, 1783." In *Narrative and Critical History of America*, Vol. 6, ed. Justin Winsor. Boston: Houghton, Mifflin, 1884–1889.

Sosin, Jack M. *Whitehall and the Wilderness: The Middle West in British Colonial Policy, 1760–1775*. Lincoln: University of Nebraska Press, 1961.

Stevens, Sylvester K., et al., eds. *The Papers of Henry Bouquet*. 6 vols. Harrisburg: Pennsylvania Historical Museum Commission, 1951–1984.

Surtees, Robert J. "Canadian Indian Policies." In *Handbook of North American Indians*. Vol 4: *History of Indian-White Relations*, ed. Wilcomb E. Washburn. Washington, D.C.: Smithsonian Institution, 1988.

Wickwire, Franklin B. *British Subministers and Colonial America, 1763–1783*. Princeton, N.J.: Princeton University Press, 1966.

Web Sites

The Quebec Act. The Avalon Project at Yale Law School Web site. http://www.yale.edu/lawweb/avalon/amerrev/parliament/quebec_act_1774.htm. Accessed on December 1, 2007.

—By Michael J. Mullin

www.milestonedocuments.com

Questions for Further Study

1. Discuss the role of the Proclamation of 1763 in Canada's historic development, and compare it with the Quebec Act of 1774. The latter act was considered by the colonies to be one of the hated Intolerable Acts. Was the vitriolic response to the Quebec Act on the part of the Protestant colonies a result of land envy or religion?

2. Indian groups generally sided with Britain when the Revolution started, in part because of the Proclamation of 1763. Would the Indians have had a better chance of holding on to their lands if the colonies had remained under British control rather than becoming independent?

Glossary

approbation	official approval
definitive treaty of peace	a reference to the Treaty of Paris of 1763, which ended the Seven Years' War
hereditaments	properties that could be inherited
quit-rents	land taxes imposed by the British authorities

Proclamation of 1763

By the King. A Proclamation. *George R.*

Whereas We have taken into Our Royal Consideration the extensive and valuable Acquisitions in America, secured to our Crown by the late *Definitive Treaty of Peace,* concluded at Paris, the 10th Day of February last; and being desirous that all Our loving Subjects, as well of our Kingdom as of our Colonies in America, may avail themselves with all convenient Speed, of the great Benefits and Advantages which must accrue therefrom to their Commerce, Manufactures, and Navigation, We have thought fit, with the Advice of our Privy Council, to issue this our Royal Proclamation, hereby to publish and declare to all our loving Subjects, that we have, with the Advice of our Said Privy Council, granted our Letters Patent, under our Great Seal of Great Britain, to erect, within the Countries and Islands ceded and confirmed to Us by the said Treaty, Four distinct and separate Governments, styled and called by the names of Quebec, East Florida, West Florida and Grenada, and limited and bounded as follows, viz.

First—The Government of Quebec bounded on the Labrador Coast by the River St. John, and from thence by a Line drawn from the Head of that River through the Lake St. John, to the South end of the Lake Nipissim; from whence the said Line, crossing the River St. Lawrence, and the Lake Champlain, in 45 Degrees of North Latitude, passes along the High Lands which divide the Rivers that empty themselves into the said River St. Lawrence from those which fall into the Sea; and also along the North Coast of the Baye des Chaleurs, and the Coast of the Gulph of St. Lawrence to Cape Rosieres, and from thence crossing the Mouth of the River St. Lawrence by the West End of the Island of Anticosti, terminates at the aforesaid River of St. John.

Secondly—The Government of East Florida. bounded to the Westward by the Gulph of Mexico and the Apalachicola River; to the Northward by a Line drawn from that part of the said River where the Chatahouchee and Flint Rivers meet, to the source of St. Mary's River, and by the course of the said River to the Atlantic Ocean; and to the Eastward and Southward by the Atlantic Ocean and the Gulph of Florida, including all Islands within Six Leagues of the Sea Coast.

Thirdly—The Government of West Florida, bounded to the Southward by the Gulph of Mexico, including all Islands within Six Leagues of the Coast, from the River Apalachicola to Lake Pontchartrain; to the Westward by the said Lake, the Lake Maurepas, and the River Mississippi; to the Northward by a Line drawn due East from that part of the River Mississippi which lies in 31 Degrees North Latitude, to the River Apalachicola or Chatahouchee; and to the Eastward by the said River.

Fourthly—The Government of Grenada, comprehending the Island of that name, together with the Grenadines, and the Islands of Dominico, St. Vincent's and Tobago, And to the end that the open and free Fishery of our Subjects may be extended to and carried on upon the Coast of Labrador, and the adjacent Islands, We have thought fit, with the advice of our said Privy Council to put all that Coast, from the River St. John's to Hudson's Streights, together with the Islands of Anticosti and Madelaine, and all other smaller Islands lying upon the said Coast, under the care and Inspection of our Governor of Newfoundland.

We have also, with the advice of our Privy Council, thought fit to annex the Islands of St. John's and Cape Breton, or Isle Royale, with the lesser Islands adjacent thereto, to our Government of Nova Scotia.

We have also, with the advice of our Privy Council aforesaid, annexed to our Province of Georgia all the Lands lying between the Rivers Alatamaha and St. Mary's.

And whereas it will greatly contribute to the speedy settling of our said new Governments, that our loving Subjects should be informed of our Paternal care, for the security of the Liberties and Properties of those who are and shall become Inhabitants thereof, We have thought fit to publish and declare, by this Our Proclamation, that We have, in the Letters Patent under our Great Seal of Great Britain, by which the said Governments are constituted, given express Power and Direction to our Governors of our Said Colonies respectively, that so soon as the state and circumstances of the said Colonies will admit thereof, they shall, with the Advice and Consent of the Members of our Council, summon and call General Assemblies within the said Governments respectively, in such Manner and Form as is used and directed in those Colonies and Provinces in America which are under our immediate Government: And We have also given Power to the said Governors, with the consent of our Said Councils, and the Representatives of the people, so to be summoned as aforesaid, to make, constitute, and ordain Laws, Statutes and Ordinances for the public peace, welfare and good government of our said colonies, and of the people and inhabitants thereof, as near as may be agreeable to the Laws of England, and under such regulations and restrictions as are used in other colonies; and in the mean time, and until such assemblies can be called as aforesaid, all persons inhabiting in, or resorting to our said colonies may confide in our royal protection for the enjoyment of the benefit of the Laws of our Realm of England; for which purpose, we have given power under our Great Seal to the Governors of our said colonies respectively, to erect and constitute, with the advice of our said Councils respectively, courts of Judicature and public justice within our said colonies, for the hearing and determining all causes, as well criminal as civil, according to Law and Equity, and, as near as may be, agreeable to the Laws of England, with liberty to all persons, who may think themselves aggrieved by the sentence of such courts, in all civil cafes, to appeal, under the usual limitations and restrictions, to us, in our Privy Council.

We have also thought fit, with the advice of our Privy Council as aforesaid, to give unto the Governors and Councils of our said Three new Colonies, upon the Continent full Power and Authority to settle and agree with the Inhabitants of our said new Colonies or with any other Persons who shall resort thereto, for such Lands. Tenements and Hereditaments, as are now or hereafter shall be in our Power to dispose of; and them to grant to any such Person or Persons upon such Terms, and under such moderate Quit-Rents, Services and Acknowledgments, as have been appointed and settled in our other Colonies, and under such other Conditions as shall appear to us to be necessary and expedient for the Advantage of the Grantees, and the Improvement and settlement of our said Colonies.

And Whereas, We are desirous, upon all occasions, to testify our Royal Sense and Approbation of the Conduct and bravery of the Officers and Soldiers of our Armies, and to reward the same, We do hereby command and impower our Governors of our said Three new Colonies, and all other our Governors of our several Provinces on the Continent of North America, to grant without Fee or Reward, to such reduced Officers as have served in North America during the late War, and to such Private Soldiers as have been or shall be disbanded in America, and are actually residing there, and shall personally apply for the same, the following Quantities of Lands, subject, at the Expiration of Ten Years, to the same Quit-Rents as other Lands are subject to in the Province within which they are granted, as also subject to the same Conditions of Cultivation and Improvement; viz.

- To every Person having the Rank of a Field Officer—5,000 Acres.
- To every Captain—3,000 Acres.
- To every Subaltern or Staff Officer—2,000 Acres.
- To every Non-Commission Officer—200 Acres.
- To every Private Man—50 Acres.

We do likewise authorize and require the Governors and Commanders in Chief of all our said Colonies upon the Continent of North America to grant the like Quantities of Land, and upon the same conditions, to such reduced Officers of our Navy of like Rank as served on board our Ships of War in North America at the times of the Reduction of Louisbourg and Quebec in the late War, and who shall personally apply to our respective Governors for such Grants.

And whereas it is just and reasonable, and essential to our Interest, and the Security of our Colonies, that the several Nations or Tribes of Indians with whom We are connected, and who live under our Protection, should not be molested or disturbed in the Possession of such Parts of Our Dominions and Territories as, not having been ceded to or purchased by Us, are reserved to them, or any of them, as their Hunting Grounds.—We do therefore, with the Advice of our Privy Council, declare it to be our Royal Will and Pleasure, that no Governor or Commander in Chief in any of our Colonies of Quebec, East Florida, or West Florida, do presume, upon any Pretence whatever, to grant Warrants of Survey, or pass any Patents for Lands beyond the Bounds of their respective Governments, as described in their Commissions: as also that no Governor or Commander in Chief in any of our other Colonies or Plantations in America do presume for the present, and until our further Pleasure be known, to grant Warrants of Survey or pass any Patent for lands beyond the heads of sources of any of the rivers which fall into the Atlantic Ocean from the West or North West; or upon any lands whatever, which not having been ceded to, or purchased by us, as aforesaid, are reserved to the said Indians, or any of them.

And We do further declare it to be Our Royal Will and Pleasure, for the present as aforesaid, to reserve under our Sovereignty, Protection, and Dominion, for the use of the said Indians, all the Lands and Territories not included within the Limits of Our said Three new Governments, or within the Limits of the Territory granted to the Hudson's Bay Company, as also all the Lands and Territories lying to the Westward of the Sources of the Rivers which fall into the Sea from the West and North West as aforesaid.

And We do hereby strictly forbid, on Pain of our Displeasure, all our loving Subjects from making any Purchases or Settlements whatever, or taking Possession of any of the Lands above reserved, without our especial leave and Licence for that Purpose first obtained.

And We do further strictly enjoin and require all Persons whatever who have either wilfully or inadvertently seated themselves upon any Lands within the Countries above described, or upon any other Lands which, not having been ceded to or purchased by Us, are still reserved to the said Indians as aforesaid, forthwith to remove themselves from such Settlements.

And whereas great Frauds and Abuses have been committed in purchasing Lands of the Indians, to the great Prejudice of our Interests, and to the great Dissatisfaction of the said Indians: In order, therefore, to prevent such Irregularities for the future, and to the end that the Indians may be convinced of our Justice and determined Resolution to remove all reasonable Cause of Discontent, We do, with the Advice of our Privy Council strictly enjoin and require, that no private Person do presume to make any purchase from the said Indians of any Lands reserved to the said Indians, within those parts of our Colonies where, We have thought proper to allow Settlement: but that, if at any Time any of the Said Indians should be inclined to dispose of the said Lands, the same shall be Purchased only for Us, in our Name, at some public Meeting or Assembly of the said Indians, to be held for that Purpose by the Governor or Commander in Chief of our Colony respectively within which they shall lie: And in case they shall lie within the limits of any proprietaries, conformable to such directions and instructions as we or they shall think proper to give for that purpose: and we do by the advice of our Privy Council, declare and enjoin, that the trade with the said Indians shall be free and open to all our subjects whatever; provided that every person who may incline to trade with the said Indians, do take out a licence for carrying on such trade, from the Governor or Commander in chief of any of our colonies respectively, where such person shall reside, and also give security to observe such regulations as we shall at any time think fit, by ourselves or commissaries, to be appointed for this purpose, to direct and appoint for the benefit of the said trade; and we do hereby authorize, enjoin and require the Governors and Commanders in chief of all our colonies respectively, as well those under our immediate government, as those under the government and direction of proprietaries, to grant such licences without fee or reward, taking especial care to insert therein a condition that such licence shall be void, and the security forfeited, in case the person to whom the same is granted shall refuse or neglect to observe such regulations as we shall think proper to prescribe as aforesaid.

And we do hereby authorize, enjoin, and require the Governors and Commanders in Chief of all our Colonies respectively, as well those under Our immediate Government as those under the Government and Direction of Proprietaries, to grant such Licences without Fee or Reward, taking especial Care to insert therein a Condition, that such Licence shall be void, and the Security forfeited in case the Person to whom the same is granted shall refuse or neglect to observe such Regulations as We shall think proper to prescribe as aforesaid.

And we do further expressly conjoin and require all Officers whatever, as well Military as those Employed in the Management and Direction of Indian Affairs, within the Territories reserved as aforesaid for the use of the said Indians, to seize and apprehend all Persons whatever, who standing charged with Treason, Misprisions of Treason, Murders, or other Felonies or Misdemeanors, shall fly from Justice and take Refuge in the said Territory, and to send them under a proper guard to the Colony where the Crime was committed of which they, stand accused, in order to take their Trial for the same.

Given at our Court, at St. James's the 7th. day of October, one thousand, seven hundred and sixty-three, in the third year of our reign.

GOD SAVE THE KING

Major General Thomas Gage, who was commander of British forces in America beginning in 1763, appealed to the Crown for the passage of the Quartering Act of 1765. (Library of Congress)

Quartering Act

1765

"Soldiers so quartered … shall be received and furnished with diet, and small beer, cyder, or rum mixed with water, by the owners."

Overview

The Quartering Act of 1765 was one of several laws enacted by the British Parliament during the ministry of George Grenville (1763–1765) that were meant to reduce England's war debt, raise revenues from the American colonies, and reshape Great Britain's imperial system. The act was an amendment to the annual Mutiny Act, which had regulated the British army since 1689. Through successive renewals it established rules governing every aspect of military life, from pay to quarters to punishments for desertion. The Quartering Act of 1765 was specifically directed to North America, where a small but costly army protected the western frontiers in the aftermath of Pontiac's Rebellion, an uprising of Native Americans in the Great Lakes region. The act required that the colonial legislatures pay for the quartering and feeding of these troops. In places where the Crown provided no barracks, the commander in chief of British forces (or his subordinate commanders) had the authority to requisition unoccupied houses and barns for the soldiers' use or to house the officers and men in public buildings, such as taverns or inns, at the expense of the colonial governments.

Unlike the riotous responses to the Grenville taxes—notably the Stamp Act of 1765—the colonial response to the Quartering Act was muted. In most instances the legislatures simply refused to appropriate the requested funds, and the military authority was powerless to respond. The colonists argued that the act's required expenditures were a direct tax that constitutionally could be levied only by their own assemblies. The Quartering Act was included in the abuses of power attributed to King George III of England in the Declaration of Independence. Restrictions on the quartering of troops survive in the Third Amendment of the Bill of Rights.

Context

On February 10, 1763, the Treaty of Paris ended the Seven Years' War, bringing to a close a half century of armed conflict between France and Great Britain. France was driven from Canada, England now controlled a vast region in North America that stretched southward from Newfoundland to Florida and inland to the Great Lakes and the Mississippi River, and the British Empire had more than doubled in size. The fifty years of warfare had cost Britain an estimated £130 million.

The peace negotiations were barely concluded when dissident Indians, aroused by the loss of their longtime French ally and fearful that English settlers would encroach on their lands, set the western frontier ablaze. Led by Pontiac, an Ottawa chief, six tribes raided English settlements in the Ohio River valley and western Pennsylvania between May and October 1763. All British forts but one west of Niagara were destroyed. Fort Detroit and Fort Pitt were under siege for several weeks, and hundreds of settlers were displaced, killed, or taken captive before the Native American tribes were subdued in mid-autumn.

In the aftermath of the Indian uprising the British government took steps to prevent a recurrence. On October 7 King George III promulgated the Proclamation of 1763, barring settlements beyond the Appalachians. At the same time the British government renewed an earlier decision to maintain a standing army in the colonies. On November 16, 1763, Major General Thomas Gage was named commander in chief of His Majesty's forces in North America. For the next twelve years from his headquarters, first in New York and later in Boston, Gage commanded more than ten thousand soldiers in stations scattered along the frontier at an annual cost of £350,000 or more. The heavily taxed Englishmen of the mother country believed the American colonists should bear some, if not all, of that burden.

Prime Minister Grenville agreed. On April 5, 1764, he sent Parliament the American Revenue Act, better known as the Sugar Act. It was the first law passed specifically to raise money from America for the Crown. He reorganized the customs service to enforce the mercantile laws the colonists regularly evaded and created an admiralty court in Halifax with jurisdiction over all the colonies. These and other reforms were aimed at reining in colonial governments that had become accustomed to a large measure of self-rule and parliamentary indifference.

Grenville's principal revenue law for America was the Stamp Act of March 22, 1765, which placed a tax on legal documents, newspapers, pamphlets, playing cards, and

Time Line

1628

■ **June 7**
The Petition of Right declares illegal standing armies in peacetime without Parliament's consent and the quartering of troops in private homes.

1689

■ **April 12**
In the first Mutiny Act, Parliament assumes responsibility for enforcing discipline within the army, reaffirming the civil control of the military.

1763

■ **February 10**
The Treaty of Paris ends the Seven Years' War, giving Canada, Florida, and certain West Indian islands to Great Britain.

■ **April 1**
George Grenville becomes England's prime minister and commits to reducing Britain's war debts.

■ **May 7–November 28**
Pontiac's Rebellion ravages the English colonial frontier.

■ **October 7**
The Proclamation of 1763 closes lands west of the Appalachians to further settlement.

1764

■ **April 5**
Parliament passes the Sugar Act to raise revenue from America.

1765

■ **March 22**
Parliament's Stamp Act, which places a direct tax on legal documents and newspapers, receives royal assent.

■ **March 24**
Parliament promulgates the Quartering Act for America.

■ **October 7–29**
Congress protests the stamp taxes as a violation of the colonial assemblies' taxing powers.

dice and was expected to bring in more than £100,000 annually to the royal Treasury. From the colonists' perspective, the law was a blatant assault on the taxing power of their representative assemblies, and riots, petitions, and protesting pamphlets swiftly followed.

While Grenville was occupied with these measures, General Gage wrote from New York asking for authority over governments that refused to appropriate funds to supply and house his troops and for powers to deal with deserters. The recently renewed Mutiny Act treated such matters but applied primarily to Britain. Gage asked that it be amended for use in America.

About the Author

The Quartering Act that emerged from Parliament on March 24, 1765, was primarily the work of three men: Welbore Ellis, the secretary at war; George Grenville, the prime minister; and Thomas Pownall, a member of Parliament. Without Grenville's knowledge, the initial draft was prepared by Ellis, who included Gage's request for authority to requisition private homes—an action expressly forbidden by the Petition of Right in 1628. Alerted to this constitutional violation, Grenville reworked the draft but failed to satisfy the House of Commons. He asked Pownall, a former colonial governor, to prepare a compromise proposal, which Parliament subsequently passed.

Of the three writers, the least known was Ellis. Born in Ireland on December 15, 1713, the son of the Protestant bishop of Kildare, Ellis served a total of thirty-four years in the House of Commons. He was first elected to Parliament in 1741 and returned there periodically, representing over time eight different boroughs. During the war years he opposed the government's receipt of any communications from the Continental Congress. He held a number of administrative posts, including secretary at war during Grenville's ministry. He was named colonial secretary in 1782, just before the colonies were lost. Returning to the House of Commons, he was given the honorary title of Father of the House in 1784 as the longest-sitting active member of Parliament. He died on February 2, 1802.

Grenville, the prime minister, was born in London on October 14, 1712. Educated at Eton and Oxford, he entered the Inner Temple and Lincoln's Inn, two of the Inns of Court, which held the exclusive right to train lawyers. He was admitted to the bar in 1735 and elected to Parliament in 1741. Three years later he joined the government as first lord of the admiralty. He was appointed a lord of the Treasury in June 1747 and served until March 1754. In the next decade he held three other administrative offices, some simultaneously. On April 1, 1763, he was named prime minister and began the tempestuous and unpopular tenure that produced unrest and opposition in the colonies and unease at home. Hardworking and moral, Grenville had few other virtues in his relationships with his colleagues and the public. He was unsympathetic to Gage's request for an amendment to the Mutiny Act in 1765, but under pressure from the king he reluctantly led the bill through Parliament. Grenville was dismissed by King George III on July 10, 1765, because of his failure to include the Queen Mother in a regency bill the king had requested following a brief spell of mental illness in June. Grenville died on November 13, 1770.

The only writer of the three to have lived in America was Pownall. Born in Lincolnshire, England, in 1722, he graduated from Trinity College, Cambridge, in 1743 and entered government service in the colonial office. A decade later he sailed to New York, where he remained for a year. During this time he attended the Albany Congress and met Benjamin Franklin, forming a lifelong friendship. In 1756 he was made governor of Massachusetts and four years later was appointed governor of South Carolina. He did not take office but returned instead to England to serve in Parliament, where he held a seat until 1781. In 1764 he published *Administration of the Colonies* based on his experiences in America. The popularity of the book and Pownall's reputation as an expert on America prompted Grenville to ask for his help with the Quartering Act. Consulting with Franklin, who was in London as a colonial agent, Pownall produced the final draft that Parliament approved. The author of ten books and many articles in *The Gentleman's Magazine*, he was a fellow of the Royal Academy. Pownall died in Bath on February 25, 1805.

Explanation and Analysis of the Document

The language of the Quartering Act of 1765 is legalese and reflects the lawyer's age-old habit of repeatedly cataloguing details to cover every possible condition or circumstance to ensure that there can be no doubt as to what the law requires. These repetitions of language are called boilerplate, and many of them are drawn from earlier versions of the Mutiny Act. Some of the words have meanings specific to the eighteenth century and now are archaic; others have different definitions in modern usage.

The first of two unnumbered paragraphs explains that the law will amend the recently passed Mutiny Act to make it applicable to the colonies in America. The second, longer paragraph describes the conditions in America that must be addressed by the amendment: The army will operate in areas where regular quarters for the troops are lacking. Carriages, wagons, horses, and oxen must be provided for the army's use on long marches. To meet these needs, the law authorizes a variety of civil officers, from the governor to local magistrates and constables, to respond to requests from the military to rent—at the colony's expense—as many public facilities as needed. In the absence of taverns, inns, or other public buildings, the civil authorities are required to rent uninhabited houses, barns, or outbuildings for the troops' use.

Section II limits the number of billets, or orders for housing, that may be issued to the number of soldiers present for duty; the commanding officers of troops on the march must give early notice in writing to local authorities so they can procure quarters for the troops.

Time Line

1766

■ **March 18**
Parliament repeals the Stamp Act but issues the Declaratory Act, which states that Parliament has the right to legislate for the colonies in all cases whatsoever.

1773

■ **December 16**
In the Boston Tea Party the Sons of Liberty dump 342 cases of tea into Boston Harbor to protest a new tax on tea.

1774

■ **March**
Parliament issues a new Quartering Act that reinforces and clarifies the amended Quartering Act of 1765.

1775

■ **July 6**
The Second Continental Congress issues a Declaration of the Causes and Necessity of Taking Up Arms.

1776

■ **July 4**
Congress issues the Declaration of Independence, which includes among its proofs of King George III's "tyranny and usurpations" the presence and forced quartering of a standing army in peacetime.

Section III warns that any officer who attempts to quarter his men in unlawful ways, or menaces or threatens any civil officer and is convicted before two justices of the peace on the sworn testimony of two witnesses, will be cashiered, or dismissed from military service. That punishment is subject to appeal within six months in any court having appellate jurisdiction. If any civilian can prove that he is housing a larger number of troops than his neighbors, he may appeal for relief to local court officers, who have the power to place the excess number elsewhere.

Section IV prohibits any military officer who is also a justice of the peace from executing any warrants with respect to the provisions of this act. Any such warrants are void.

Section V provides for feeding billeted officers and soldiers and for a daily ration of small beer, cider, or rum mixed with water, to be paid from their subsistence pay.

Section VI allows noncommissioned officers and their men to prepare their own meals, in which case the subsistence

www.milestonedocuments.com

Essential Quotes

"An act to amend and render more effectual, in his Majesty's dominions in America, an act passed in this present session of parliament, intituled, An act for punishing mutiny and desertion, and for the better payment of the army and their quarters."

(Opening lines)

"The commander in chief in America, or other officer under whose orders any regiment or company shall march, shall, from time to time, give, or cause to be given, … in writing, … to the respective governors of each province through which they are to march; in order that proper persons may be appointed and authorized … to take up and hire, if it shall be necessary, uninhabited houses, outhouses, barns, or other buildings, for the reception of such soldiers as the barracks and publick houses shall not be sufficient to contain or receive."

(Section II)

"The officers and soldiers so quartered and billeted as aforesaid (except such as shall be quartered in the barracks, and hired uninhabited houses, or other buildings as aforesaid) shall be received and furnished with diet, and small beer, cyder, or rum mixed with water, by the owners of the inns, livery stables, alehouses, victualling-houses, and other houses in which they are allowed to be quartered and billeted by this act; paying and allowing for the same the several rates herein after mentioned to be payable out of the subsistence-money, for diet and small beer, cyder, or rum mixed with water."

(Section V)

"And … the several persons who shall so take, hire, and fit up as aforesaid, such uninhabited houses, out-houses, barns, or other buildings, for the reception of the officers and soldiers, and who shall so furnish the same, and also the said barracks, with fire, candles, vinegar, and salt, bedding, utensils for dressing victuals, and small beer, cyder, or rum."

(Section VIII)

This cartoon shows Prime Minister George Grenville of Britain holding scales labeled "Debts" and "Savings." Among those in line to pay is a Native American woman representing America; she wears a sign labeled "taxation without representation." (Library of Congress)

www.milestonedocuments.com

money for meals will go directly to them and not the innkeepers or tavern owners. The latter will be paid for beverages (not exceeding five pints) and the use of utensils and salt.

Section VII requires civil officers to provide the military living in barracks or uninhabited houses, barns, and other outbuildings the utensils and supplies they may need to prepare their own meals, including fire, candles, vinegar, and salt. In addition, the civil officers are to supply beverages, bedding, and utensils.

Section VIII requires the colonies to reimburse with public funds all persons who hire or renovate uninhabited houses, barns, or other shelter for quartering troops and who also provide the billeted officers and men with bedding, utensils, beverages, candles, and other specified items.

Section IX warns that any officer taking a bribe from a property owner to avoid quartering troops on his property will be cashiered.

Section X authorizes officers to exchange men in already-rented quarters for others, provided the numbers of men remain the same.

Section XI states that any civil officer or property owner who fails to provide quarters or food to troops as requested by a commanding officer shall on conviction be fined up to £5 for every such offense and not less than forty shillings. Local magistrates are empowered to collect fines by the distress sale of the offender's property.

Section XII requires officers who receive subsistence money for whole regiments or individual companies to give notice to their troops and to various keepers of public houses where the troops are quartered that the money is available. Within four days the innkeepers and other renters may present their accounts for payment according to the schedule of listed daily rates by rank for diet and small beer and for straw and hay for the officers' horses. Any officer failing to distribute the proper money to each of his men will be cashiered on conviction.

Section XIII states that in cases where the subsistence money is not delivered on time to any officer or man, by accident or because he is on a march, the commanding officer is empowered to sign a certificate in lieu of payment for each such person and give the certificate to the creditor who, in turn, can present the certificate to the regimental paymaster for payment.

Section XIV requires various civil officers to keep a careful record of addresses and names of the owners of properties where troops are billeted to prevent abuses.

Section XV orders justices of the peace to execute warrants to meet the requests of commanding officers for carriages and drivers. If any town is unable to supply the requisite number, the order will apply in the next town and the next until the number is met.

Section XVI sets the rates for hiring wagons carrying twelve hundred pounds gross weight at seven pence sterling per mile. This is the New York rate, and other colonies are to set their rates in proportion to it. Other wagons and carriages are to be hired at rates adjusted to the weight of the vehicle. Drivers are to be paid daily for their work.

Section XVII limits the carrying weight of any hired vehicle to twelve hundred pounds.

Section XVIII requires that no wagon or carriage may travel more than a day's march if, within that time, the march reaches a place where new wagons or carriages may be hired. If no such place is within reach, then the hired vehicles must continue in service until they can be replaced.

Section XIX sets fines for various civil officers who refuse to execute the warrants of the justices of the peace for hiring wagons and carriages. The fine is a minimum of twenty shillings and a maximum of forty shillings for each offense, to be paid into the colony's treasury. Again, a distress sale of the offenders' possessions may be ordered if payment is not made.

Section XX provides a remedy for those occasions when troops are on the march and the army's rental allowance for carriages is less than the cost the various local civil officers have to pay to secure the vehicles. The civilians may pay a reasonable higher price for each carriage rented and secure repayment from the provincial or colonial government.

Section XXI requires that prior to taking wagons and oxen or carriages and horses on a long march beyond the town or village where they have been rented, the army will solicit two impartial persons to appraise their value. One of these people is chosen by the troops' commanding officer, and the other is chosen by the owners of the vehicles and animals. The appraisers will give to the officer and the owner written certificates attesting to the appraised value. Should any of the wagons, carriages, or animals be lost, damaged, or destroyed, the respective owners may, under oath, present the certificates and vouchers detailing the loss or destruction to the paymaster general of the military unit for payment at the appraised value.

Sections XXII and XXIII speak to one of the major problems General Gage faced in his command. These two provisions empower the civil authority to assist the military in apprehending deserters. Section XXII authorizes constables and other civil officers to arrest suspected deserters, bring them before a court officer, and jail them until they can be turned over to the military for trial. The jailers will be paid the full costs of maintaining the prisoners in jail, but none of the civil officers involved in the deserters' detention is entitled to a reward or fee for their capture.

Section XXIII levies a fine of £5 for each offense on any person who harbors or assists a deserter by providing shelter, giving him clothing, buying his weapon or other military gear, or otherwise abetting his escape. Each of these acts constitutes a separate offense. The fines will be paid under the warrant of a court officer on the oath of an informer and may be raised by a distress sale of the offender's property. A portion of the fine will go to the informer; the remainder will be turned over to the officer in whose unit the deserter serves. If the offender has insufficient property to pay the fines within four days of his conviction, the offender will be jailed for three months without bail or pardon or publicly whipped at the discretion of the court.

Section XXIV forbids any officer from breaking into any house without a warrant in search of a deserter in daytime. Any officer who enters or breaks into a dwelling or outbuilding in the night without a lawful warrant in search of deserters will be fined £20.

Section XXV reflects the continuing protection of the Petition of Right (1628), which prohibits bringing a civilian to trial by court-martial. The reference here is to civilian workers at forts and military encampments who may be accused of crimes in frontier areas far from local or colony courts. In such cases the commanding officer is authorized to arrest such persons, charge them under oath, and take them into custody and deliver them at "convenient speed" to the nearest civil magistrate in a settled area for trial in the appropriate colonial court, as if the alleged crime or offense had been committed within the jurisdiction of that court.

Section XXVI requires that all legal actions or complaints against any person or persons performing their duty under the act must be made in the principal court of record in the colony or province where the contested action took place. If the action happened in an unchartered or unorganized territory, such as the frontier, then legal proceedings must take place in the court of the colony next to that unorganized territory.

Section XXVII authorizes an officer leading troops to buy ferry passage for his men at half the ordinary rate charged to civilian passengers or to hire exclusive use of the ferry for himself and his men at half the ordinary rate for exclusive use. At crossings where there are no ferries, the officer is authorized to hire boats at half the ordinary rate.

Section XXVIII stipulates that all rents and other sums of money mentioned in the act and all forfeitures and penalties that arise from the enforcement of the act will be paid in lawful money at the rate of four shillings, eight pence sterling for a Spanish milled dollar—the world currency standard in the eighteenth century.

Section XXIX offers legal protections to any person or persons who may be sued as a consequence of doing their duty under the act, including triple damages from the plaintiffs for defense costs should the defendants be found not guilty or if the suit is dismissed or discontinued.

Section XXX states the act will be in force for two years from March 24, 1765, to March 24, 1767.

Audience

The Quartering Act was directed specifically to the commander in chief of His Majesty's forces in North America and his subordinate commanding officers, including the colonial officials who would be expected to enforce its provisions and, in the case of the provincial assemblies, to provide the requisite funds. General Gage received copies of the act at his headquarters in New York on August 1, 1765, and immediately dispatched them to every colonial governor from Nova Scotia to East and West Florida and to the commanding officers of some fifty troop stations or detachments as far west as the Mississippi. Since the act made it clear that compliance with the law was a civil matter, the colonial governors probably made copies of the law available to their colonial assemblies and to local officials, who were required to respond to the lawful requests of the military to provide requisitioned housing, meals, wagons, and other supplies as set forth in the act.

Impact

The colonists' responses to the Quartering Act differed according to their geographic location. Although the law extended to all of British North America, the newly established English colonies of Quebec, East Florida, and West Florida lacked both the economic resources and population to carry out its provisions. From the outset, barracks in these provinces were built and financed by the Crown, which met all other expenses as well. Among the thirteen older colonies the areas most affected were in the Middle Atlantic region, Massachusetts, and South Carolina, where more troops were based and where troop movements to the frontier were more common. The burden of supplying carriages, wagons, and quarters for troops on the march, for example, fell most heavily on New York, New Jersey, and Pennsylvania because they were the avenues through which soldiers from the north, west, and south would march to or from the frontier.

Compliance with the law was a civil matter, and the responsibility for its enforcement in any colony was divided among the governor and his council, the assembly, local civil authorities, and the courts of law. Without the consent of the assemblies, however, the law was virtually unenforceable because the military had no authority to compel them to impose the taxes necessary to its execution. In the run-up to the Revolution, compliance with the law was a matter of time and place. Pennsylvania and New Jersey (except on one occasion) were the most cooperative; the two colonies regularly voted the necessary funds for the troops, and neither attempted to evade its responsibilities.

By contrast, New York and, after 1768, Massachusetts hindered every effort at enforcement through evasions, subterfuge, and outright refusal. From time to time the New York assembly made partial funds available under pressure from Gage and the royal governor, but in Massachusetts the General Court (the legislature) stood firm, and Gage and his commanders were forced to rely on money from the king to house and supply their men.

The Quartering Act of 1765 was annually extended until 1769, when it was amended to provide a "local option" whereby a colonial or provincial law, if deemed satisfactory by Parliament, might be substituted for the original. This amended version was annually extended until June 2, 1774, when a new Quartering Act was promulgated as part of the Coercive Acts, or Intolerable Acts, intended to punish the people of Boston for the Boston Tea Party of December 16, 1773. Similarly to the 1765 act and its extensions, the new law added two specific clarifications of the provisions. The first established the right of the officer requesting quarters to select the geographic location where his troops would be billeted, thus preventing the government in Massachusetts from placing the troops on an island in Boston Harbor. The second provision amplified the first, stating that if no suitable barracks were made available at the request of an officer after twenty-four hours had passed, the officer was empowered to take possession of as many uninhabited houses, outbuildings, and barns as he needed for as long as he might need them. The officer would not need to wait for the appointment of a colonial official to undertake the hiring of the quarters. As in all the earlier acts, no private homes were included in the properties that might be requisitioned.

Despite the efforts of the British government to portray the Quartering Acts as assessing justifiable military expenses for the protection of the colonies, the colonists saw them as taxes imposed by Parliament in contravention of their charter and constitutional rights. Further, they saw the Quartering Acts as the lesser part of a larger tyranny: Parliament's posting to America a standing army in peacetime without the consent of the colonial legislatures. They viewed this as a standing army that had increasingly interfered with civil governments in New York and Massachusetts and elsewhere as the colonists opposed punitive measures, such as the Coercive Acts, that Parliament had no right to impose.

The quartering of troops and a standing army in peacetime hold a prominent place among the causes of conflict between the colonies and the mother country cited in the two principal documents the Continental Congress sent to Parliament and the Crown: the Declaration of the Causes

www.milestonedocuments.com

and Necessity of Taking Up Arms (July 6, 1775) and the Declaration of Independence (July 4, 1776). When Congress ordered the colonial governments to prepare for statehood by changing their English charters to constitutions, seven of the thirteen states initially included restrictions on the quartering of troops and a peacetime army; in time the other states added such restrictions as well. The continuing legacy of the Quartering Act of 1765 and its successors is the Third Amendment in the Bill of Rights, which carried limits on quartering troops into the Constitution in 1791.

Related Documents

Constitution of the United States, Analysis and Interpretation: Annotations of Cases Decided by the Supreme Court of the United States. Government Printing Office Web site. http://www.gpoaccess.gov/constitution. Accessed on December 13, 2007. The Third Amendment to the United States Constitution, which deals with the quartering of troops, is contained in the Annotated Constitution.

Engblom v. Carey, 677 F. 2d 957 (1982). University of Missouri School of Law Web site. http://www.law.umkc.edu/faculty/projects/ftrials/conlaw/engblom.html. Accessed on December 13, 2007. This case, brought by two corrections officers at a prison in New York State and decided in the United States Court of Appeals, Second Circuit, May 3, 1982, is the only case to date applying the Third Amendment.

Grenville Program (1764–1765). The Avalon Project at Yale Law School Web site. http://www.yale.edu/lawweb/avalon/18th.htm. Accessed on December 13, 2007. In addition to the Quartering Act, the Grenville Program (1764–1765) included the Currency Act, the Sugar Act, and the Stamp Act.

Intolerable Acts (1774). The Avalon Project at Yale Law School Web site. http://www.yale.edu/lawweb/avalon/18th.htm. Accessed on December 13, 2007. The Coercive Acts, or Intolerable Acts, of 1774 consisted of the Boston Port Bill, the Massachusetts Government Act, the Administration of Justice Act, the new Quartering Act, and the Quebec Act.

Morgan, Edmund Sears, ed. *Prologue to Revolution: Sources and Documents on the Stamp Act Crisis, 1764–1766.* 1959. Reprint. New York: W. W. Norton, 1973. This basic sourcebook on the Grenville Program contains sixty-five documents, ranging from the Sugar Act of 1764 to the Declaratory Act of 1766, as well as pamphlets, newspaper articles, and speeches from both American and British writers.

Morison, Samuel Eliot, ed. *Sources and Documents Illustrating the American Revolution, 1764–1788, and the Formation of the Federal Constitution.* New York: Galaxy Books, 1953. The documents include key laws from the Grenville program as well as the Coercive Acts, or Intolerable Acts, including the Quartering Act of 1774.

Perry, Richard L., ed. *Sources of Our Liberties: Documentary Origins of Individual Liberties in the United States Constitution and Bill of Rights.* Rev. ed. Buffalo, N.Y.: William S. Hein, 1990. Among the many documents are the Petition of Right (1628) and the several state constitutions drafted during the American Revolution that contained restrictions on standing armies in peacetime and the quartering of troops.

Bibliography

■ Articles

Bell, Tom W. "The Third Amendment: Forgotten but Not Gone." *William & Mary Bill of Rights Journal* 2, no. 1 (Spring 1993): 117–150.

Fields, William S., and David T. Hardy. "The Third Amendment and the Issue of the Maintenance of Standing Armies: A Legal History." *American Journal of Legal History* 35, no. 4 (October 1991): 393–431.

■ Books

Anderson, Fred. *Crucible of War: The Seven Years' War and the Fate of Empire in British North America, 1754–1766.* New York: Alfred A. Knopf, 2000.

Bullion, John L. *A Great and Necessary Measure: George Grenville and the Genesis of the Stamp Act, 1763–1765.* Columbia: University of Missouri Press, 1982.

Carter, Clarence E. "The Office of Commander in Chief: A Phase of Imperial Unity on the Eve of the Revolution." In *The Era of the American Revolution*, ed. Richard B. Morris. 1939. Reprint. New York: Harper & Row, 1965.

Morgan, Edmund S., and Helen M. Morgan, Helen M. *The Stamp Act Crisis: Prologue to Revolution.* Rev. ed. New York: Collier Books, 1963.

Shy, John. *Toward Lexington: The Role of the British Army in the Coming of the American Revolution.* Princeton, N.J.: Princeton University Press, 1965.

—By Allan L. Damon

Questions for Further Study

1. Compare and contrast the colonists' responses to the Stamp Act and the Quartering Act of 1765.

2. Do you agree or disagree with the U.S. Court of Appeals's application of the Third Amendment in *Engblom v. Carey* (1982)?

3. Imagine yourself as an eighteenth-century resident of western New York. To what degree would you support the Quartering Act of 1765?

www.milestonedocuments.com

Glossary

accoutrements	a soldier's equipment other than weapons or clothing
adjutant	a staff officer whose principal duty is to assist a superior
appraisement	estimation of value
billeting	housing or quartering troops under an official order (called a billet)
by distress	by a court ordered seizure of property to satisfy a debt
carriage	a four-wheeled vehicle or the portable equipment or baggage of an army
cashiered	dismissed from military service (usually for bad conduct)
chattels	personal, movable pieces of property (often a legal reference to animals or persons)
colour of this act	authority of this act
commissions officer of foot	commissioned officer of unmounted troops or infantry
common law courts	lower-level courts in the eighteenth-century English system that applied the common law, which is based on precedent, custom, and tradition rather than codified written law or statutes
commons	House of Commons in Parliament
constable	eighteenth-century term for a police officer
convey	transfer ownership
debarring	depriving, prohibiting, of forbidding
detachment	a unit separated from the main army for special duty
dominions	the lands or territories subject to the king's (or Parliament's) control
furniture	a soldier's personal belongings or military equipment
gaol	jail
house of correction	jail
intituled	entitled
ipso facto	by the fact itself; as a result

Glossary

lords spiritual and temporal	House of Lords in Parliament
magistrate	in eighteenth-century England, a synonym for justice of the peace
mainprize	legal responsibility for fulfillment of a contract or securing the release of a prisoner by bail or surety in anticipation of a trial
metheglin	spiced mead (an alcoholic drink made from fermented honey and water)
moiety	a half or one's portion of something
nonsuit	voluntarily withdrawn by a plaintiff, thus ending a lawsuit
outhouses	outbuildings adjacent to a house or dwelling
per diem	by the day; daily
plaint	complaint
pounds sterling	the basic monetary unit in Britain; in the eighteenth century the pound (£) was equal to twenty shillings or 240 pence
publick houses	inns or taverns
pursuant	in accordance with; proceeding from
quarter-master	a supply officer responsible for food, clothing, and equipment
regiment	about eight hundred officers and men, organized in ten companies and commanded by as many as six regimental officers; each company at full strength consisted of three officers, six noncommissioned officers, and seventy men
shilling	one-twentieth of a pound
small beer	beer with low or no alcoholic content
Spanish milled dollar	the English term for the Spanish 8 reales, which was the world money standard from the 1530s until the middle of the nineteenth century because the coin blanks containing silver were milled by machine in Mexico to a consistent size and weight. In eighteenth-century New York the milled dollar had a value of eight shillings; in Pennsylvania its value was seven shillings, six pence; and in England it was worth four shillings, six pence sterling.
tithingman	a peace officer, an underconstable
treble	triple
under his hand and seal	authorized by his signature
warrant	a legal order or writ authorizing an action (commonly search or seizure)

Document Text

Quartering Act of 1765

An act to amend and render more effectual, in his Majesty's dominions in America, an act passed in this present session of parliament, intituled, An act for punishing mutiny and desertion, and for the better payment of the army and their quarters.

WHEREAS in and by an act made in the present session of parliament, intituled, An act for punishing mutiny and desertion, and for the better payment of the army and their quarters; several regulations are made and enacted for the better government of the army, and their observing strict discipline, and for providing quarters for the army, and carriages on marches and other necessary occasions, and inflicting penalties on offenders against the same act, and for many other good purposes therein mentioned; but the same may not be sufficient for the forces that may be employed in his Majesty' dominions in America: and whereas, during the continuance of the said act, there may be occasion for marching and quartering of regiments and companies of his Majesty's forces in several parts of his Majesty's dominions in America: and whereas the publick houses and barracks, in his Majesty's dominions in America, may not be sufficient to supply quarters for such forces: and whereas it is expedient and necessary that carriages and other conveniences, upon the march of troops in his Majesty's dominions in America, should be supplied for that purpose: be it enacted by the King's most excellent majesty, by and with the advice and consent of the lords spiritual and temporal, and commons, in this present parliament assembled, and by the authority of the same, That for and during the continuance of this act, and no longer, it shall and may be lawful to and for the constables, tithingmen, magistrates, and other civil officers of villages, towns, townships, cities, districts, and other places, within his Majesty's dominions in America, and in their default or absence, for any one justice of the peace inhabiting in or near any such village, township, city, district or other place, and for no others; and such constables, tithingmen, magistrates, and other civil officers as aforesaid, are hereby required to quarter and billet the officers and soldiers, in his Majesty's service, in the barracks provided by the colonies; and if there shall not be sufficient room in the said barracks for the officers and soldiers, then and in such case only, to quarter and billet the residue of such officers and soldiers, for whom there shall not be room in such barracks, in inns, livery stables, ale-houses, victualling-houses, and the houses of sellers of wine by retail to be drank in their own houses or places thereunto belonging, and all houses of persons selling of rum, brandy, strong water, cyder or metheglin, by retail, to be drank in houses; and in case there shall not be sufficient room for the officers and soldiers in such barracks, inns, victualling and other publick alehouses, that in such and no other case, and upon no other account, it shall and may be lawful for the governor and council of each respective province in his Majesty's dominions in America, to authorize and appoint, and they are hereby directed and impowered to authorize and appoint, such proper person or persons as they shall think fit, to take, hire and make fit, and, in default of the said governor and council appointing and authorizing such person or persons, or in default of such person or persons so appointed neglecting or refusing to do their duty, in that case it shall and may be lawful for any two or more of his Majesty's justices of the peace in or near the said villages, town, townships, cities, districts, and other places, and they are hereby required to take, hire, and make fit for the reception of his Majesty's forces, such and so many uninhabited houses, outhouses, barns or other buildings, as shall be necessary, to quarter therein the residue of such officers and soldiers for whom there should not be rooms in such barracks and publick houses as aforesaid, and to put and quarter the residue of such officer and soldiers therein.

II. And it is hereby declared and enacted, That there shall be no more billets at any time ordered, than there are effective soldiers present to be quartered therein: and in order that this service may be effectually provided for, the commander in chief in America, or other officer under whose orders any regiment or company shall march, shall, from time to time, give, or cause to be given, as early notice as conveniently may be, in writing, signed by such commander or officer of their march, specifying their numbers and time of marching as near as may be, to the respective governors of each province through which they are to march; in order that proper per-

www.milestonedocuments.com

sons may be appointed and authorized, in pursuance of this act, to take up and hire, if it shall be necessary, uninhabited houses, outhouses, barns, or other buildings, for the reception of such soldiers as the barracks and publick houses shall not be sufficient to contain or receive.

III. And be it further enacted by the authority aforesaid, That if any military officer shall take upon himself to quarter soldiers, in any of his Majesty's dominions in America, otherwise than is limited and allowed by this act; or shall use or offer any menace or compulsion to or upon any justice of the peace, constable, tithingman, magistrate, or other civil officer before mentioned, in his Majesty's dominions in America, tending to deter and discourage any of them from performing any part of the duty hereby required or appointed; such military officer, for every such offence, being thereof convicted before any two or more of his Majesty's justices of the peace living within or near such villages, towns, townships, cities, districts or other places, by the oaths of two or more credible witnesses, shall be deemed and taken to be ipso facto cashiered, and shall be utterly disabled to have or hold any military employment in his Majesty's service, upon a certificate thereof being transmitted to the commander in chief in America; unless the said conviction shall be reserved upon an appeal brought, within six months, in the proper court for hearing appeals against convicting by justices of the peace: and in case any person shall find himself aggrieved, in that such constable, tithingman, magistrate, or other civil officer, shall have quartered or billeted in or upon his house a greater number of soldiers than he ought to bear in proportion to his neighbours, and shall complain thereof to one or more justice or justices of the peace of the village, town, township, city, district, or other place, where such soldiers are quartered, such justice or justices has or have hereby power to relieve such person, by ordering such and so many of the soldiers to be removed, and quartered upon such other person or persons, as they shall see cause; and such other person or persons shall be obliged to receive such soldiers accordingly.

IV. Provided also, and be it further enacted, That no justice or justices of the peace, having or executing any military office or commission in his Majesty's regular forces in America, may, during the continuance of this act, directly or indirectly, act or be concerned in the quartering, billeting or appointing any quarters, for any soldier or soldiers, according to the disposition made for quartering of any soldier or soldiers by virtue of this act (except where there shall be no other justice or justices of the peace) but that all warrants, acts, matters, or things, executed or appointed by such justice or justices of the peace for or concerning the same, shall be void; any thing in this act contained to the contrary notwithstanding.

V. Provided nevertheless, and it is hereby enacted, That the officers and soldiers so quartered and billeted as aforesaid (except such as shall be quartered in the barracks, and hired uninhabited houses, or other buildings as aforesaid) shall be received and furnished with diet, and small beer, cyder, or rum mixed with water, by the owners of the inns, livery stables, alehouses, victualling-houses, and other houses in which they are allowed to be quartered and billeted by this act; paying and allowing for the same the several rates herein after mentioned to be payable out of the subsistence-money, for diet and small beer, cyder, or rum mixed with water.

VI. Provided always, That in case any innholder, or other person, on whom any non-commission officers or private men shall be quartered by virtue of this act, in any of his Majesty's dominions in America (except on a march, or employed in recruiting, and likewise except the recruits by them raised, for the space of seven days at most, for such non-commission officers and soldiers who are recruiting, and recruits by them raised) shall be desirous to furnish such non-commission officers or soldiers with candles, vinegar, and salt, and with small beer or cyder, not exceeding five pints, or half a pint of rum mixed with a quart of water, for each man per diem, gratis, and allow to such non-commission officers or soldiers the use of fire, and the necessary utensils for dressing and eating their meat, and shall give notice of such his desire to the commanding officer, and shall furnish and allow the same accordingly; then, and in such case, the non-commission officers and soldiers so quartered shall provide their own victuals; and the officer to whom it belongs to receive, or that actually does receive, the pay and subsistence-money, for diet and small beer, to the non-commission officers and soldiers aforesaid, and not to the innholder or other person on whom such non-commission officers and soldiers are quartered; any thing herein contained to the contrary notwithstanding.

VII. And whereas there are several barracks in several places in his Majesty's said dominions in America, or some of them provided by the colonies, for the lodging and covering of soldiers in lieu of quarters, for the ease and convenience as well of the inhabitants of and in such colonies, as of the soldiers; it is

www.milestonedocuments.com

hereby further enacted, That all such officer and soldiers, so put and placed in such barracks, or hired uninhabited houses, out-houses, barns, or other buildings, shall, from time to time be furnished and supplied there by the persons to be authorized or appointed for that purpose by the governor and council of each respective province, or upon neglect or refusal of such governor and council in any province, then by two or more justices of the peace residing in or near such place, with fire, candles, vinegar, and salt, bedding, utensils for dressing their victuals, and small beer or cyder, not exceeding five pints, or half a pint of rum mixed with a quart of water, to each man, without paying any thing for the same.

VIII. And that the several persons who shall so take, hire, and fit up as aforesaid, such uninhabited houses, out-houses, barns, or other buildings, for the reception of the officers and soldiers, and who shall so furnish the same, and also the said barracks, with fire, candles, vinegar, and salt, bedding, utensils for dressing victuals, and small beer, cyder, or rum, as aforesaid, may be reimbursed and paid all such charges and expences they shall be put to therein, be it enacted by the authority aforesaid, That the respective provinces shall pay unto such person or persons all such sum or sums of money so by them paid, laid out, or expended, for the taking, hiring, and fitting up, such uninhabited houses, out-houses, barns, or other buildings, and for furnishing the officers and soldiers therein, and in the barracks, with fire, candles, vinegar, and salt, bedding, utensils for dressing victuals, and small beer, cyder, or rum, as aforesaid; and such sum or sums are hereby required to be raised, in such manner as the publick charges for the provinces respectively are raised.

IX. Provided always, and be it enacted by the authority aforesaid, That if any officer, within his Majesty's said dominions of America, shall take, or cause to be taken, or knowingly suffer to be taken, any money, of any person, for excusing the quartering of officers or soldiers, or any of them, in any house allowed by this act; every such officer shall be cashiered, and be incapable of serving in any military employment whatsoever.

X. And whereas some doubts may arise, whether commanding officers of any regiment or company, within his Majesty's said dominions in America, may exchange any men quartered in any village, town, township, city, district, or place, in his Majesty's said dominions in America, with another man quartered in the same place, for the benefit of the service; be it declared and enacted by the authority aforesaid, That such exchange as above mentioned may be made by such commanding officers respectively, provided the number of men do not exceed the number at that time billeted on such house or houses; and the constables, tithingmen, magistrates, and other chief officers of the villages, towns, townships, cities, districts, or other places where any regiment or company shall be quartered, are hereby required to billet such men so exchanged accordingly.

XI. And be it further enacted by the authority aforesaid, That if any constable, tithingman, magistrate, or other chief officer or person whatsoever, who, by virtue or colour of this act, shall quarter or billet, or be employed in quartering or billeting, any officers or soldiers, within his Majesty's said dominions in America, shall neglect or refuse, for the space of two hours, to quarter or billet such officers of soldiers, when thereunto required, in such manner as is by this act directed, provided sufficient notice be given before the arrival of such forces; or shall receive, demand, contract, or agree for, any sum or sums of money, or any reward whatsoever, for or on account of excusing, or in order to excuse, any person or persons whatsoever from quartering, or receiving into his, her, or their house or houses, any officer or soldier, or in case any victualler, or any other person within his Majesty's dominions in America, liable by this act to have any officer or soldier billeted or quartered on him or her, shall refuse to receive or victual any such officer or soldier so quartered or billeted upon him or her as aforesaid; or in case any person or persons shall refuse to furnish or allow, according to the directions of this act, the several things herein before directed to be furnished or allowed to officers and soldiers, so quartered or billeted on him or her, or in the barracks, and hired uninhabited houses, out-houses, barns or other buildings, as aforesaid, at the rate herein after mentioned; and shall be thereof convicted before one of the magistrates of any one of the supreme chief or principal common law courts of the colony where such offence shall be committed, either by his own confession, or by the oath of one or more credible witness or witnesses (which oath such magistrate of such court is hereby impowered to administrate) every such constable, tithingman, magistrate, or other chief officer or person so offending shall forfeit, for every such offence, the sum of five pounds sterling, or any sum of money not exceeding five pounds, nor less than forty shillings, as the said magistrate (before whom the matter shall be heard) shall in his discretion think fit; to be levied by distress and

Document Text

sale of the goods of the person offending, by warrant under the hand and seal of such magistrate before whom such offender shall be convicted, to be directed to a constable or other officer within the village, town, township, city, district, or other place, where the offender shall dwell; and shall direct the said sum of five pounds, or such other sum as shall be ordered to be levied in pursuance of this act as aforesaid, when levied, to be paid into the treasury of the province or colony where the offence shall be committed, to be applied towards the general charges of the said province or colony.

XII. And, that the quarters both of officers and soldiers, in his Majesty's said dominions in America, may hereafter be duly paid and satisfied, be it enacted by the authority aforesaid, That from and after the twenty fourth day of March, in the year one thousand seven hundred and sixty five, every officer to whom it belongs to receive, or that does actually receive, the pay or subsistence-money either for a whole regiment, or particular companies, or otherwise, shall immediately, upon each receipt of every particular sum which shall from time to time be paid, returned, or come to his or their hands, on account of pay or subsistence, give publick notice thereof to all persons keeping inns, or other places where officers or soldiers are quartered by virtue of this act: and shall also appoint the said innkeepers and others to repair to their quarters, at such times as they shall appoint for the distribution and payment of the said pay or subsistence money to the said officers or soldiers, which shall be within four days at farthest after receipt of the same as aforesaid, and the said innkeepers and other shall then and there acquaint such officer or officers with the accounts or debts (if any shall be) between them and the officers and soldiers so quartered in their respective houses; which account the said officer or officers are hereby required to accept of, and immediately pay the same, before any part of the said pay or subsistence be distributed either to the officers or soldiers; provided the accounts exceed not for a commissions officer of foot, being under the degree of a captain, for such officers diet and small beer per diem, one shilling, and if such officer shall have a horse or horses, for each horse or horses, for their hay and straw per diem, six pence, nor for one foot soldier's diet and small beer, cyder, or rum mixed as aforesaid, per diem, four pence: and if any officer or officers as aforesaid shall not give notice as aforesaid, and not immediately, upon producing such account stated, satisfy, content, and pay the same, upon complaint and oath made thereof by any two witnesses, before two of his Majesty's justices for the village, town, township, city, district, or other place where such quarters were (which oath such justices are hereby authorized and required to administer) the paymaster or paymasters of his Majesty's guards and garrisons, upon certificate of the said justices before whom such oath was made, of the sum due upon such accounts, an the persons to whom the same is owing, are hereby required and authorized to pay and satisfy the said sums out of the arrears due to the said officer or officers; upon penalty that such paymaster or paymasters shall forfeit their respective place or places of paymaster, and be discharged from holding the same for the future; and in case there shall be no arrears due to the said officer or officers, then the said paymaster or paymasters are hereby authorized and required to deduct the sums, he or they shall pay pursuant to the certificates of the said justices, out of the next pay or subsistence money of the regiment to which such officer or officers shall belong: and such officer or officers shall, for every such offence, or for neglecting to give notice of the receipt of such pay or subsistence money as aforesaid, be deemed and taken, and is hereby declared, to be ipso facto cashiered.

XIII. And, where it shall happen that the subsistence money due to any officer or soldier, within his Majesty's said dominions in America, shall, by occasion of any accident, not be paid to such officer or soldier, or such officer or soldier shall neglect to pay the same, so that quarters cannot be or are not paid as this act directs; and where any forces shall be upon their march, in his Majesty's dominions in America, so that no subsistence can be remitted to them to make payment as this act directs: or they shall neglect to pay the same; in every such case, it is hereby further enacted, That every such officer shall before his or their departure out of his or their quarters, where such regiment, troop, or company shall remain for any time whatsoever, make up the accounts with every person with whom such regiment or company shall have quartered, and sign a certificate thereof, and give the said certificate, so by him signed, to the party to whom such money is due, with the name of such regiment or company to which he or they shall belong, to the end the said certificate may be forthwith transmitted to the paymaster of his Majesty's guards and garrisons, who is hereby required immediately to make payment thereof to the person or persons to whom such money shall be due, to the end the same may be applied to such regiment or compa-

www.milestonedocuments.com

ny respectively; under pain as before in this act directed for nonpayment of quarters.

XIV. And, for better preventing abuses in quartering or billeting the soldiers in his Majesty's dominions in America, in pursuance of this act, be it further enacted by the authority aforesaid, That it shall and may be lawful to and for any one or more justices of the peace, or other officer, within their respective villages, towns, townships, cities, districts, or other places, in his Majesty's said dominions in America, by warrant or order under his or their hand and seal, or hands or seals, at any time or times during the continuance of this act, to require and command any constable, tithingman, magistrate, or other chief officer, who shall quarter or billet any soldiers in pursuance of this act, to give an account in writing unto the said justice or justices, or other officer requiring the same, of the number of officers and soldiers who shall be quartered or billeted by them and also the names of the house-keepers or persons upon whom, and the barracks and hired uninhabited houses, or other buildings as aforesaid, in which and where every such officer of soldiers shall be quartered or billeted, together with an account of the street or place where every such house-keeper or person dwells, and where every such barrack or hired uninhabited house or building is or are, and of the signs (if any) which belong to their houses; to the end that it may appear to the said justice or justices; or other officer, where such officers or soldiers are quartered or billeted, and that he or they may thereby be the better enabled to prevent or punish all abuses in the quartering or billeting them.

XV. And be it further enacted by the authority aforesaid, That for the better and more regular provision of carriages for his Majesty's forces in their marches, or for their arms, clothes, or accoutrements, in his Majesty's said dominions in America, all justices of the peace within their several villages, town, townships, cities, districts, and places, being duly required thereunto by an order from his Majesty, or the general of his forces, or of the general commanding, or the commanding officer there shall, as often as such order is brought and shewn unto one or more of them, by the quarter-master, adjutant, or other officer of the regiment, detachment, or company, so ordered to march, issue out his or their warrants to the constables, tithingmen, magistrates, or other officers of the villages, towns, townships, cities, districts, and other places, from, through, near, or to which such regiment, detachment, or company, shall be ordered to march, requiring them to make such provision for carriages, with able men to drive the same, as shall be mentioned in the said warrant: allowing them reasonable time to do the same, that the neighbouring parts may not always bear the burthen: and in case sufficient carriages cannot be provided within any such village, town, township, city, district, or other place, then the next justice, or justices of the peace of the village, town, township, city, district, or other place, shall, upon such order as aforesaid being brought or shewn to one or more of them, by any of the officers as aforesaid, issue his or their warrants to the constables, tithingman, magistrate, or other officers, of such next village, town, township, city, district, or other place, for the purposes aforesaid, to make up such deficiency; and such constable, tithingman, magistrate, or other officer, shall order or appoint such person or persons, having carriages, within their respective villages, towns, townships, cities, districts, or other places, as they shall think proper to provide and furnish such carriages and men, according to the warrant aforesaid; who are hereby required to provide and furnish the same accordingly.

XVI. And be it further enacted, That the pay or hire for a New York wagon, carrying twelve hundred pounds gross weight, shall be seven pence sterling for each mile; and for every other carriage in that and every other colony in his Majesty's said dominions in America, in the same proportion; and at or after the same rate or price for what weight every such other carriage shall carry; and that the first day's pay or hire for every such carriage, shall be paid down by such officer to such constable, tithingman, magistrate, or other civil officer, who shall get or procure such carriages, for the use of the owner or owners thereof; and the pay or hire for every such carriage after the first day, shall be paid every day, from day to day, by such officer as aforesaid, into the hands of the driver or drivers of such carriages respectively, until such carriages shall be discharged from such service, for the use of the owner and owners thereof.

XVII. Provided always, and be it further enacted, That no such wagon, cart, or carriage, impressed by authority of this act, shall be liable or obliged, by virtue of this act, to carry above twelve hundred weight; any thing herein contained to the contrary notwithstanding.

XVIII. Provided also, That no such wagon, cart, or carriage, shall be obliged to travel more than one day's march, if, within that time, they shall arrive at any other place where other carriages may be procured; but, in case other sufficient carriages cannot be procured, then such carriages shall be obliged to continue in the service till they shall arrive at such village, town, township, city, district, or other place, where proper and sufficient carriages, for the service of the forces, may be procured.

XIX. And be it further enacted by the authority aforesaid, That if any constable, tithingman, magistrate, or other civil officer, within his Majesty's dominions in America, shall willfully neglect or refuse to execute such warrants of the justices of the peace, as shall be directed unto them for providing carriages as aforesaid; or if any person or persons appointed by such constable, tithingman, magistrate, or other civil officer, to provide or furnish any carriage and man, shall refuse or neglect to provide the same, or any other person or persons whatsoever shall willfully do any act or thing whereby the execution of the said warrants shall be delayed, hindered, or frustrated; every such constable, tithingman, magistrate, civil officer, or other person so offending, shall, for every such offence, forfeit any sum not exceeding forty shillings sterling, no less than twenty shillings, to be paid into the treasury of the province where any such offence shall be committed; to be applied towards the aforesaid contingent charges of the province: and all and every such offence or offences, and all and every other offence or offences, in this act mentioned, and not otherwise provided, shall and may be inquired of, heard, and fully determined, by two of his majesty's justices of the peace dwelling in or near the village, town, township, city, district, or place, where such offence shall be committed; who have hereby power to cause the said penalty to be levied by distress and sale of the offenders goods and chattels, rendering the overplus (if any) to the owner.

XX. And whereas the allowance hereby provided, for the payment of the carriages that may be necessary in the marching of troops, may not be a sufficient compensation for the same, to satisfy the constables, tithingmen, magistrates, and other civil officer, their charges and expences therein; for remedy whereof, be it further enacted by the authority aforesaid, That the constables, tithingmen, magistrates, and civil officers, procuring such carriages, shall pay a reasonable expence or price for every carriage so procured; and that every such constable, tithingman, magistrate, civil officer, or other person, shall be repaid what he or they shall so expend, together with his or their own charges and expences attending the same, by the province or colony where the same shall arise.

XXI. Provided always, and be it further enacted by the authority aforesaid, That where it shall be necessary to take wagons or other carriages for long marches, beyond the settlements, an appraisement shall be made of the value of such horses and carriages, at the time of the taking them up to be employed in such marches beyond the settlements, by two indifferent persons, one to be chosen by the commanding officer of such forces, and the other by the owner of such cattle or carriages; a certificate of which appraisement shall be given to the owner or owners of such cattle or carriages respectively: and in case any of the cattle or carriages, so taken up for such service, shall in the execution thereof, be lost or destroyed; that then and in every such case, upon producing the said certificate and proper vouchers upon oath of such loss or destruction, to the paymaster general of his majesty's guards and garrisons, the said paymaster shall, and he is hereby required to pay to the respective owners of such cattle or carriages, the sums specified, in such certificates and vouchers, to be the value of such cattle or carriages so lost or destroyed.

XXII. And whereas several soldiers, being duly enlisted in his Majesty's service, do often desert such service; for remedy whereof, be it further enacted by the authority aforesaid, That it shall and may be lawful to and for the constable, tithingman, magistrate, or other civil officer, of the village, town, township, city, district, or place, within the said dominions in America, where any person, who may be reasonably suspected to be such a deserter, shall be found, to apprehend, or cause him to be apprehended; and to cause such person to be brought before any justice of the peace or other chief magistrate living in or near such village, town, township, city, district, or place, who hath hereby power to examine such suspected person; and if by his confession, or testimony of one or more witness or witnesses upon oath, or the knowledge of such justice of the peace, or other magistrate, it shall appear, or be found, that such suspected person is a lifted soldier, and ought to be with the regiment or company to which he belongs, such justice of the peace or other magistrate shall forthwith cause him to be conveyed to the gaol of the village, town, township, city, district, county, or place where he shall be found, or to the house of correction or other publick prison in such village, town, township, city, district, county, or place, where such deserter shall be apprehended, and transmit an account thereof to the commander in chief of his Majesty's forces in the said dominions in America, or to the commanding officer of the forces posted nearest to such justice or justices, or other magistrate or magistrates, for the time being, to the end that such person may be proceeded against according to law: and the gaoler or keeper of such gaol, house of correction, or prison, shall receive the full subsistence of such deserter or deserters during the time that he or they shall continue in his custody for the maintenance of such deserter or deserters: but shall not be intitled to any fee or reward on account of the imprisonment of such deserter or deserters; any law, usage, or custom to the contrary notwithstanding.

XXIII. Provided always, That if any person shall harbour, conceal, or assist, any deserter for his Majesty's service within his Majesty's said dominions in America, knowing him to be such, the person so offending, shall forfeit for every such offence, the sum of five pounds; or if any person shall knowingly detain, buy or exchange, or otherwise receive, any arms, clothes, caps, or other furniture belonging to the King, from any soldier or deserter, or any other person, upon any account or pretence whatsoever, within his Majesty's dominions in America, or cause the colour of such clothes to be changed; the person so offending shall forfeit, for every such offence, the sum of five pounds; and upon conviction upon the oath of one or more credible witness or witnesses, before any of his Majesty's justices of the peace, the said respective penalties of five pounds, and five pounds, shall be levied by warrant under the hands of the said justice or justices of the peace, by distress and sale of the goods and chattels of the offenders; one moiety of the said first-mentioned penalty of five pounds to be paid to the informer, by whose means such deserter shall be apprehended; and one moiety of the said last mentioned penalty of five pounds to be paid to the informer; and the residue of the said respective penalties to be paid to the officer to whom any such deserter or soldier did belong: and in case any such offenders, who shall be convicted as aforesaid, of harbouring or assisting any such deserter or deserters, or having knowingly received any arms, clothes, caps, or other furniture belonging to the King; or having caused the colour of such clothes to be changed, contrary to the intent of this act, shall not have sufficient goods and chattels, whereon distress may be made, to the value of the penalties recovered against him for such offence, or shall not pay such penalties within four days after such conviction; then, and in such case, such justice of the peace shall and may, by warrant under his hand and seal, commit such offender to the common gaol, there to remain, without bail or mainprize, for the space of three months, or cause such offender to be publickly whipt, at the discretion of such justice.

XXIV. And be it further enacted, That no commission officer shall break open any house, within his Majesty's dominions in America, to search for deserters, without a warrant from a justice of the peace, and in the day-time; and that every commission officer who shall, in the night, or without warrant from one or more of his Majesty's justices of the peace (which said warrants the said justice or justices are hereby impowered to grant) forcibly enter into, or break open, the dwelling-house or out-houses of any person whatsoever under pretence of searching for deserters, shall, upon due proof thereof, forfeit the sum of twenty pounds.

XXV. And whereas several crimes and offenses have been and may be, committed by several person, not being soldiers, at several forts or garrisons, and several other places within his Majesty's dominions in America, which are not within the limits or jurisdiction of any civil government there hitherto established; and which crimes and offenses are not properly cognizable or triable and punishable, by a court-martial, but by the civil magistrate; by means whereof several great crimes and offenses may go unpunished, to the great scandal of government; for remedy whereof, be it further enacted by the authority aforesaid, That from and after the twenty fourth day of March, one thousand seven hundred and sixty five, and for so long afterwards as this act shall continue in force, if any person or persons, not being a soldier or soldiers, do or shall commit any crime or crimes, or offence or offenses, in any of the said forts, garrisons, or places, within his Majesty's dominions in America, which are not within the limits or jurisdiction of any civil government hitherto established, it shall and may be lawful for any person or persons to apprehend such offender or offenders, and to carry, him, her, or them, before the commanding officer for the time being of his Majesty's forces there; and such offender being charged upon oath in writing, before the said commanding officer, and which oath the said commanding officer is hereby impowered to administer, that then, and in every such case, the said commanding officer shall receive and take into his custody, and safely keep, every such offender, and shall convey and deliver, or cause to be conveyed and delivered, with all convenient speed, every such offender to the civil magistrate of the next adjoining province, together with the cause of his or her detainer, to be committed and dealt with by such

www.milestonedocuments.com

civil magistrates or magistrate according to law; and every such civil magistrate is hereby commanded and required to commit every such offender, that he or she may be dealt with according to law; and in every such case, it shall and may be lawful to prosecute and try every such offender in the court of such province or colony, where crimes and offenses of the like nature are usually tried, and where the same would be properly tried in case such crime or offence had been committed within the jurisdiction of such court, and such crime shall and may be alleged to be committed within the jurisdiction of such court; and such court shall and may proceed therein to trial, judgment, and execution, in the same manner as if the such crime or offence had been really committed within the jurisdiction of such court; any law, usage, custom, matter, or thing, whatsoever to the contrary notwithstanding,

XXVI. And be it further enacted by the authority aforesaid, That every bill, plaint, action, or suit, against any person or persons, for any act, matter, or thing, to be acted or done in pursuance of this act, or the said other in part recited act, in any of his Majesty' dominions in America, shall be brought and prosecuted in and before some principal court of record in the colony where such matter or thing shall be done or committed; and in case the same shall not be done or committed within the jurisdiction of any such court, then in the court of the colony next to the place where the same shall be done and committed, and in no other court whatsoever.

XXVII. And be it further enacted by the authority aforesaid, That where any troops or parties upon command have occasion in their march, in any of his Majesty's dominions in America, to pass regular ferries, it shall and may be lawful for the commanding officer either to pass over with his party as passenger, or to hire the ferry-boat entire to himself and his party, debarring others for that time in his option; and in case he shall chuse to take passage for himself and party as passengers he shall only pay for himself and for each person, officer, or soldier, under his command, half of the ordinary rate payable by single persons at any such ferry; and in case he shall hire the ferry-boat for himself and party, he shall pay half of the ordinary rate for such boat or boats; and in such places where there are no regular ferries, but that all passengers hire boats at the rate they can agree for, officers with or without parties are to agree for boats at the rates that other persons do in the like cases.

XXVIII. And be it further enacted by the authority aforesaid, That all sum and sums of money mentioned in this act, and all penalties and forfeitures whatsoever to be incurred or forfeited for any offence, cause, matter, or thing whatsoever, to be done, committed, or omitted to be done in his Majesty's colonies and dominions in America, contrary to the true intent and meaning of this act, shall be, and shall be paid and forfeited in lawful money of the colony or place where the same shall be forfeited or become due, at the rate of four shillings and eight pence sterling money for a Spanish milled dollar, and not otherwise.

XXIX. And be it further enacted by the authority aforesaid, That if any action, bill, plaint, or suit, shall be brought or commenced against any person or persons for any act, matter, or thing, done or acted in pursuance of this act, that it shall and may be lawful to and for all and every person or persons so sued to plead thereto the general issue that he or they are not guilty, and to give the special matter in evidence to the jury who shall try the cause; and if the verdict therein shall pass for the defendant or defendants, or the plaintiff or plaintiffs therein shall become nonsuit, or suffer a discontinuance, or by any other means judgment therein shall be given for the defendants or defendant therein; that in every such case the justice or justices, or other judge or judges of the court in which such action shall be brought; shall by force and virtue of this act allow unto such defendant or defendants his or their treble costs, which he or they shall have sustained, or be put to, by reason of the defence of such suit, for which cost such defendant and defendants shall have the like remedy as in other cases where costs are by the law given to defendants.

XXX. And be it further enacted by the authority aforesaid, That this act and every thing herein contained, shall continue and be in force in all his Majesty's dominions in America, from the twenty fourth day of March, in the year one thousand seven hundred and sixty five, until the twenty fourth day of March in the year of our Lord one thousand seven hundred and sixty seven.

Benjamin Franklin led the effort to have the British Parliament repeal the unpopular Stamp Act. (Library of Congress)

Declaration of Rights of the Stamp Act Congress

1765

"It is inseparably essential to the freedom of a people, and the undoubted right of Englishmen, that no taxes be imposed on them, but with their own consent."

Overview

The Stamp Act Congress was convened on October 7, 1765, to address the passage of the Stamp Act by Parliament on March 8, 1765. The congress's delegates responded to the act on October 19, 1765, by approving a Declaration of Rights (including fourteen resolutions) and several petitions denying Parliament's authority to tax the thirteen colonies. The Stamp Act Congress and its resolutions helped lead to the act's repeal in March 1766. They also led the colonists to focus on the idea of constitutional limitations on parliamentary authority, a concept that contributed to the American Revolution.

The Stamp Act required that anything formally written or printed must appear on stamped paper dispensed by English agents. This was a visible and pervasive tax, which was imposed by Parliament to help pay the great debts the English incurred while protecting their colonies during the French and Indian War (1754–1763). The stamp duties triggered outrage among the American colonists. They maintained that taxes were gifts to the king that could be offered only through a body that represented them. Since the colonists were not represented in Parliament, either actually or virtually, they believed that Parliament had no authority to impose the stamp tax on the colonies. In their minds, the stamp duties represented a confiscation of their property, since they had not given their consent to a parliamentary power to lay taxes.

Context

Faced with massive debts incurred in the French and Indian War, Great Britain sought means of raising revenue in the American colonies, which, in their view, were the beneficiary of England's generous military action. In 1763 George Grenville, the first lord of the treasury and the chancellor of the exchequer, began hatching a series of legislative measures that would impose taxes on the colonists to satisfy England's financial needs. In April 1764 Parliament passed the Sugar Act, also known as the American Revenue Act, which levied a tax on molasses, an imported commodity in New England. Lord Grenville made it clear that the measure was a tax, designed to raise money for England. The American colonists were still seething over the Sugar Act, which they considered an illegal tax, when they were hit with the Stamp Act duties in 1765. Some colonies responded by passing nonimportation acts, economic boycotts that they hoped would pressure England to abandon the Sugar Act. At the same time, the British expanded the jurisdiction of the vice admiralty courts to try those who interfered with revenue laws. These courts did not employ juries. As a consequence, the colonists were shocked by what they considered a violation of their ancient rights as Englishmen to trial by jury.

The passage of the Stamp Act was thus immersed in a cauldron of anger and protest. The American colonists sniffed conspiracy against their liberties. They resented the measure as a violation of their rights as Englishmen, for it had been long held in Great Britain that taxes were a gift, to be offered by a body that represented the people. Those who lived in England, the colonists explained, could be taxed by Parliament precisely because they enjoyed representation. But those in the American colonies were not represented in Parliament. Thus they were being taxed without their consent, a violation not only of their rights as subjects of the Crown but also of their natural rights as men. Taxing their property without their consent amounted to blatant confiscation.

In response to the Stamp Act, the Massachusetts Assembly, at the suggestion of James Otis, sent an invitation to the other colonial assemblies to participate in a meeting in New York City to discuss the colonies' options. The resulting Stamp Act Congress determined to issue a Declaration of Rights and to petition the king, the House of Commons, and the House of Lords for relief. They sought repeal of the act. In the American colonies' first display of national unity, the Stamp Act Congress approved fourteen resolutions that sought to define constitutional principles and limitations on parliamentary authority and complained of the economic pain inflicted on the colonies by the stamp duties.

Above all, the congress sought repeal of the Stamp Act. In this pursuit they were aided by merchants in London,

Time Line

1763

■ The French and Indian War ends, with Great Britain deeply concerned about the massive debt incurred in protecting its American colonies.

■ **September 30 and October 10**
George Grenville, the British prime minister, considers the possibility of a stamp tax but finds the proposals unsatisfactory.

1764

■ **April 5**
Parliament passes the Sugar Act, also known as the American Revenue Act.

1765

■ **March 8**
Parliament approves the Stamp Act, which receives royal assent on March 22 and comes into effect on November 1. The fifteenth resolution asserts Parliament's authority to tax the colonies.

■ **March 13**
The Stamp Act is transmitted to the Massachusetts Assembly.

■ **May 17**
George Grenville meets with colonial agents to discuss the sums of money that ought to be generated from the Stamp Act.

■ **May 29**
Patrick Henry delivers a speech to the Virginia House of Burgesses introducing resolutions against the Stamp Act, including one denying Parliament's authority to tax the colonies.

■ **May 30**
The Virginia House of Burgesses approves Henry's resolutions by one vote.

■ **June 8**
The Massachusetts Assembly, at the suggestion of James Otis, sends a circular to the other colonial assemblies inviting them to attend a meeting that will become known as the Stamp Act Congress.

who acknowledged their dependence on robust trade with the colonists and pushed for the act's repeal in the House of Commons. Taxes on the colonists that resulted in fewer purchases of English goods spelled trouble for English merchants. Violence, too, marred the process. In response to the Stamp Act, a group of angry colonists organized themselves into the Sons of Liberty for the purpose of opposing and protesting the stamp duties. They pillaged the homes of those who would serve as tax collectors and generally intimidated and dissuaded Loyalists from enforcing the act.

The Stamp Act Congress, caught in the clutches of a great national crisis, was forced to choose between acquiescence or confrontation. It chose confrontation. In this, it gave vent to ideas and concepts that had lain dormant, awaiting an occasion for articulation. When the chance came, the congress rejected Parliament's authority to tax the American colonists. This assertion of the colonists' rights placed the colonies on a path that changed history.

About the Author

The journal of the Stamp Act Congress provides no hint as to the delegate or delegates who wrote the initial draft of the convention's Declaration of Rights, the document that provided the foundation for the petitions to the king and Parliament in which the colonists sought relief from the Stamp Act. This was by design; discussions and debates among the twenty-seven delegates could be more candid if their remarks were not published, and, given the sensitive nature of the deliberations, the delegates preferred anonymity. The assertion of limits on parliamentary authority, including denial of authority to levy taxes, might invite retribution.

Knowledge of the congress's work is drawn mainly from fragmentary accounts in diaries, the delegates' letters, newspaper accounts and pamphlets that bear close resemblance to the petitions, and resolves issued by the convention. It is a safe bet that John Dickinson, a brilliant pamphleteer and an acute theorist from Pennsylvania, produced the first draft of the resolutions. The collection of his papers includes a paper in his handwriting that provides "the original Draft of the Resolves of the first Congress held at New York in the year 1765" (Weslager, p. 139).

Explanation and Analysis of the Document

The immediate result of the Stamp Act Congress lay in the petitions and resolves sent to the king, the House of Commons, and the House of Lords. The congress was seeking relief from the Stamp Act duties through nonenforcement of its provisions and, ideally, through its appeal. The resolutions reflect the colonists' deeply held views of their rights and the limits of parliamentary authority. The act itself provoked, for many, the first serious and sustained consideration of constitutional principles, an intellectual and political undertaking that would continue through the American Revolution and beyond. The first eight resolutions reflect the emphatic, unqualified view of the congress that Parliament has no constitutional authority to tax the colonies. The next four resolutions complain about the financial impact of the taxes. The final two resolutions assert the right of the colonists to petition the king, the Commons, and the Lords and the duty to seek repeal of the act and other legislative measures that have encroached upon American commerce.

Resolutions I and II speak of the duties of the colonists as subjects of the Crown. The first resolution provides that the colonists owe "due subordination" to Parliament. That obligation implies a recognition of Parliament's authority to make laws governing the entire empire, but that sweeping authority is limited, according to the colonists, who contend that the power to legislate does not include the power to tax, a point emphasized in the sixth resolution.

The assertion in the second resolution that the colonists are "entitled" to the rights and liberties enjoyed by "natural born subjects" aims at reminding English readers that their rights are not less substantial than those of their peers in the kingdom. Implicit in this reminder is the concept that taxes may be imposed only by a body that represents the taxpayer. Since the colonists are not represented in Parliament, that body may not levy taxes upon them. In addition, all of the other rights possessed by English subjects, including trial by jury, are enjoyed by the colonists.

In the third resolution, the Stamp Act Congress provides that "it is inseparably essential to the freedom of a people" and the "undoubted right of Englishmen" that taxes may not be levied without their consent. This resolution emphasizes two key points. First, taxes are a gift, founded on the willingness and approval of the people. The term *consent* is critical. If the people are not represented in Parliament, which the colonists contend they are not, then they cannot give their consent to be taxed. Rather, the tax imposed by Parliament represents a confiscation of their property. Second, the right to grant one's consent is not merely the "undoubted right of Englishmen" but also essential to a free people. Here the congress is drawing upon the rights of men, often characterized as natural rights. The third resolution, then, broadens the argument about Parliament's taxing power and denies it in terms that are universal. The appeal to natural rights became a powerful weapon and motivating argument for the colonists, a commonplace in their battles with Great Britain over the next decade.

The themes of representation and consent color the fourth and fifth resolutions. The congress emphasizes in the fourth resolution that the colonists "are not" and "cannot be" represented in Parliament. It should be clear to all, Americans and English alike, that the colonists do not enjoy any actual representation; they did not vote for candidates who stood for election. The dispute between the two sides centered on the issue of whether the colonies enjoyed virtual representation. Great Britain maintained that even though the colonists did not elect their own representatives, they were nonetheless virtually represented, since Parliament represents everyone within the empire. Accordingly, the colonists were represented and could be taxed.

Time Line

1765

- **October 7**
  The Stamp Act Congress convenes in New York City. Twenty-seven delegates from nine colonies attend, including Timothy Ruggles of Massachusetts, who is elected the chair of the proceedings.

- **October 19**
  The Stamp Act Congress approves the Declaration of Rights with fourteen resolutions, including the denial of parliamentary authority to tax the colonies.

- **October 25**
  The Stamp Act Congress is adjourned.

1766

- **March 18**
  Parliament repeals the Stamp Act in the face of pressure from merchants in England and the American colonies. The Declaratory Act is passed by Parliament for the purpose of taxing the colonies.

The colonists rejected the concept of virtual representation. Those living in England did not share the colonists' interests. The colonists emphasized actual representation, which could occur only if they had the opportunity to elect their representatives. For a time, some leading thinkers, including James Otis, considered the idea of pushing for actual representation in Parliament, but this pursuit was wisely discouraged by others. It was observed that even if the colonists sent delegates to London, they would be outnumbered, outmaneuvered, and unable to assert any real influence. They also would be at the mercy of Parliament's taxing power because they would be unable to argue that they were being taxed without representation or their consent. It was more effective, the members of the congress believed, to be in a position to argue that the Stamp Act was unconstitutional because the colonists were not represented.

Having established in the fourth resolution that the colonists are not represented in Parliament, the congress asserts in the fifth resolution that "no taxes" may be "constitutionally imposed on them, but by their respective legislatures." The concept of consent, the sheet anchor of the Declaration of Independence and republicanism itself, is repeatedly brandished by the congress. Without the consent of the governed, taxation is illegitimate and unconstitutional.

The Stamp Act Congress draws a distinction between legislation and taxation. In the sixth resolution, the congress complains that Parliament may not tax the colonists, since taxes are a gift that may be granted by the represen-

www.milestonedocuments.com

Handwritten notes by Benjamin Franklin grace the margins of a bound pamphlet on the Stamp Act. (AP Photo/Joseph Kaczmarek)

tatives of the people who offer the gift. Since Parliament does not represent the colonists, it would be "unreasonable" and in violation of the British Constitution for Parliament to assume it may give the property of the colonists to the king.

England's decision to extend the jurisdiction of the vice admiralty courts to prosecutions of acts that violated the revenue laws, including the Stamp Act, generated great anxiety and anger among the colonists. In the seventh and eighth resolutions, the Stamp Act Congress reiterates the right to trial by jury and the threat that the admiralty courts pose to that right. The right to trial by jury was regarded as an ancient liberty. The right to be tried by one's peers plumbed the depths of English legal history. In the admiralty courts, there was no jury. As a consequence, the congress asserts that trial in the admiralty courts deprives colonists of an "inherent and invaluable right" guaranteed to every British subject.

To make matters worse, the Stamp Act duties were enforceable by the vice admiralty courts, which were originally established to handle disputes between merchants and seamen. In these courts, there was no trial by jury, so a refusal to abide by the Stamp Act provisions could result in a prosecution in which a colonist would not be tried by his peers. This feature, the colonists maintained, would violate their right under the British Constitution to a jury trial. As the colonists surveyed these programs and policies, it became increasingly clear to them that their liberty was being threatened.

The remaining resolutions reflect the assertions of the Stamp Act Congress that the stamp duties, like other revenue laws, threaten the livelihood, the financial well-being, and the liberty, security, and happiness of the colonists. The congress was clever and correct in observing that the Stamp Act would hurt British merchants as well, since, as explained in the eleventh resolution, the restrictions would hinder the ability of the colonists to purchase goods manufactured in England. The implied threat, backed by nonimport agreements in various colonies, was aided by British merchants' appeals to the House of Commons to repeal the Stamp Act for the reasons asserted by the congress.

The Stamp Act Congress's combination of legal and constitutional arguments, supported by eminently practical concerns that reflected the impact of the stamp duties on the colonies, created a powerful and persuasive case for repeal. The innovative thinking that colors the resolutions invited further exploration among the colonists and paved

Essential Quotes

"That His Majesty's liege subjects in these colonies, are entitled to all the inherent rights and liberties of his natural born subjects within the kingdom of Great-Britain."

(Second Resolution)

"That it is inseparably essential to the freedom of a people, and the undoubted right of Englishmen, that no taxes be imposed on them, but with their own consent, given personally, or by their representatives."

(Third Resolution)

"That the only representatives of the people of these colonies, are persons chosen therein by themselves, and that no taxes ever have been, or can be constitutionally imposed on them, but by their respective legislatures."

(Fifth Resolution)

"That the late Act of Parliament … for granting and applying certain Stamp Duties …have a manifest tendency to subvert the rights and liberties of the colonists."

(Eighth Resolution)

"[He] hoped that the power and sovereignty of Parliament, over every part of the British dominions, for the purpose of raising or collecting any tax, would never be disputed."

(George Grenville, qtd. in Morgan, p. 76)

"It is my opinion that this kingdom has no right to lay a tax upon the colonies.… Taxation is no part of the governing or legislative power."

(William Pitt, qtd. in Morgan, p. 342)

"The general execution of the stamp-act would be impracticable, without occasioning more mischief than it was worth, by totally alienating the affections of the Americans, and thereby lessening their commerce."

(Benjamin Franklin to his son, William, November 9, 1765; qtd. in Vaughan, p. 21)

www.milestonedocuments.com

the way for additional claims of violations of constitutional rights, which resounded throughout the colonies in the run-up to the Revolutionary War.

Audience

The Stamp Act Congress had as its principal targets the king, the House of Lords, and the House of Commons, each of which it had petitioned to repeal the Stamp Act. By passing its petitions and resolutions, the congress hoped to persuade Great Britain that the Stamp Act was unconstitutional and repressive. In asserting the unconstitutionality of the duties, the congress was speaking the language of English law and constitutionalism: No Englishman may be taxed without his consent. Since the colonists believed that they were not represented by Parliament, that body could hardly lay claim to authority to tax the colonies. The legal argument proceeded beyond the assertions of English law; it advanced the doctrine of natural rights and its core element of consent, an adroit maneuver that invoked universal themes. In its claim that the stamp duties were harsh and repressive, the congress wisely pitched its argument to an audience that understood practical financial matters—English merchants. The Stamp Act Congress found influential allies in British shopkeepers, manufacturers, and businessmen, all of whom relied on the Americans as valuable customers.

The Stamp Act Congress had an additional, if somewhat secondary, audience in the American colonists. The congress exercised care and caution in protecting the petitions and resolutions from the public eye before transmitting them to Great Britain, in fear that public release would suggest to the British that the aim of the congress was to appeal to the people rather than to seek relief from the king and Parliament. The congress's Declaration of Rights did enjoy great currency throughout the colonies, with colonial legislatures embracing the resolutions and adopting some of their own. The resolutions, moreover, were eminently quotable and were invoked by men up and down the coast who were outraged by the Stamp Act and, in their own ways, protested the duties imposed by the measure.

The Stamp Act Congress enjoyed another audience that it could not contemplate at that juncture: the future. The congress was highly influential in uniting American colonists and speaking a constitutional language that would become pivotal in asserting rights and liberties and demanding limitations on parliamentary power. Those arguments lit the way for American leaders to confront Great Britain over the next decade.

Impact

The immediate impact of the Stamp Act Congress within the colonies may be measured by the way in which the colonies embraced it and honored those who had labored to produce the petitions and resolutions that confronted British tyranny. Delegates from six of the nine colonies that had participated in the proceedings signed the Declaration of Rights in New York. Delegates from three of the colonies—New York, Connecticut, and Georgia—lacked the authority to sign until they had presented the petitions to their respective assemblies. Once this was done, those three legislative bodies quickly passed their own resolves to support the Stamp Act Congress. In South Carolina, members of the legislature were so impressed with the extraordinary work of their delegates that they sought approval to commission paintings of them to be hung inside the Commons House.

Four colonies were not represented at the congress: Georgia, New Hampshire, North Carolina, and Virginia. Georgia moved immediately to approve the congress's work and authorized the speaker of the house to forward its petitions to the king and Parliament. The failure of New Hampshire to send delegates to the convention met with stinging criticism, but it was quickly overcome when the house lent its enthusiastic approval by signing the documents and appointing its own lobbyists to win the support of the Crown and Parliament. Two colonies, North Carolina and Virginia, took no action on the petitions and resolutions of the congress. In each instance, their respective governors, loathe to incur the wrath of Britain, dissolved their assemblies and thus prevented action by those eager to support the work of the congress. By the time the assemblies had returned, the executives were able to explain to the legislators that the Stamp Act had been repealed and that their grievances had been satisfied. Accordingly, there was no need for any action.

The rousing effect on colonists of the congress's assertion of limits on parliamentary authority, including the rights of the colonies to be free of taxes imposed by Parliament and the early discussion of constitutional principles, had little influence in England and probably had no impact on the decision to repeal the Stamp Act. The assertion of constitutional rights, so emphatically stated in the congress's petitions and resolutions, did stir opposition in Parliament on matters of authority and rights; these issues dominated the relations between Great Britain and America for much of the next decade. But the repeal of the act mostly was attributable to complaints by merchants about its financial impact—on England.

English merchants felt the stinging effects of the Stamp Act and exercised their influence through petitions to Parliament to terminate legislation that, they firmly believed, would drive them to ruin. They were keenly aware of the great importance of trade with the North American colonies. The organization by colonial leaders that produced nonimportation agreements, first in response to the Sugar Act and then in reaction to the Stamp Act, inflicted considerable damage on British businesses. Financial failure for merchants in England was on the horizon; this was talk that Parliament could understand. The central problem that leaders faced in repealing the act, however, was the fear of appearing weak in the face of colonial opposition. Repealing the act would represent a victory for the Stamp Act Congress, vindication for the violence perpetrated by the Sons of Liberty against British stamp distributors, and, most important, subversion of Parliament's assertion of a right to tax the colonies. If the British government relented on the power to tax, how could it proceed with any subsequent tax measures? How would it raise much-needed revenue?

When Parliament repealed the Stamp Act in 1766, it endeavored to save face by passing the Declaratory Act, which, to members in the Commons and the Lords, asserted Parliament's right to tax the colonies. But the Declaratory Act was ambiguous on precisely that point. The legislation affirmed Parliament's authority to make laws and statutes binding the colonists "in all cases whatever." The phrase meant, in the minds of members, that the legislative power encompassed the taxing power. Americans were left to wonder whether England had finally accepted their claim of a distinction between the legislative and taxing powers, or whether England was continuing to assert that the legislative power encompassed the taxing power. It would not be long before the colonists had their answer and the two sides were headed to war.

Related Documents

The Declaration of Independence. The Avalon Project at Yale Law School Web site. http://www.yale.edu/lawweb/avalon/declare.htm. Accessed on December 17, 2007. This document from July 4, 1776, should be examined for its statements about consent of the governed, limited government, governmental legitimacy and natural rights, and themes and concepts that bear on the work of the Stamp Act Congress.

The Declaratory Act. The Avalon Project at Yale Law School Web site. http://www.yale.edu/lawweb/avalon/amerrev/parliament/declaratory_act_1766.htm. Accessed on December 17, 2007. Parliament agreed to repeal the Stamp Act in 1766 on the condition that the Declaratory Act would be passed. As the act continued to assert Parliament's right to levy taxes on the colonies, its passage incited further tension between England and the colonies and moved the two toward war.

Pickering, Danby, ed. *The Statutes at Large from Magna Carta to the End of the Eleventh Parliament of Great Britain*, vol. 26. Cambridge, U.K.: Cambridge University Press, 1762–1869. The Avalon Project at Yale Law School Web site. http://www.yale.edu/lawweb/avalon/amerrev/parliament/sugar_act_1764.htm. Accessed on December 17, 2007. This volume includes the 1764 Sugar Act, which was a revision of the 1733 Sugar and Molasses Act. The taxes imposed by this act inspired some American colonies to engage in nonimportation agreements as a reaction to what they considered a parliamentary abuse of power.

Townshend Revenue Act. The Avalon Project at Yale Law School Web site. http://www.yale.edu/lawweb/avalon/amerrev/parliament/townsend_act_1767.htm. Accessed on December 17, 2007. Passed by Parliament on June 29, 1767, the many parts of this act provided further fuel to the animosity between England and the American colonies. The Townshend Revenue Act taxed various products imported by the colonies, including paper, tea, lead, and glass. The colonists responded with the famous rejection "No taxation without representation," which was first used by Jonathan Mayhew in a 1750 sermon in Boston.

Bibliography

■ Articles

Gipson, Lawrence Henry. "The Great Debate in the Committee of the Whole House of Commons on the Stamp Act, as Reported by Nathaniel Ryder." *Pennsylvania Magazine of History and Biography* 86, no. 1 (1962): 10–41.

Laprade, William T. "The Stamp Act in British Politics." *American Historical Review* 35, no. 4 (1930): 735–757.

■ Books

Morgan, Edmund S. *The Birth of the Republic, 1763–1789*. Chicago: University of Chicago Press, 1977.

Morgan, Edmund S., and Helen M. Morgan. *The Stamp Act Crisis: Prologue to Revolution*. New York: Collier Books, 1963.

Vaughan, Alden T., ed. *Chronicles of the American Revolution*. New York: Grosset and Dunlap, 1965.

Weslager, Clinton A. *The Stamp Act Congress*. Newark: University of Delaware Press, 1976.

■ Web Sites

"Stamp Act Congress—1765." USHistory.org Web site. http://www.ushistory.org/declaration/related/sac65.htm. Accessed on December 17, 2007.

—By David Gray Adler

www.milestonedocuments.com

Questions for Further Study

1. Great Britain and the American colonies were sharply divided on the question of whether the power of legislation entailed the authority to tax. Review the legal arguments proffered by each side and determine which had the better argument. What accounts for the wide divergence of views on this issue?

2. One of the critical issues that arose out of the Stamp Act controversy was the question of consent. In your view, were the colonists represented in Parliament? Why or why not? In your view, what is the utility of virtual, as opposed to actual, representation?

3. The Stamp Act Congress asserted, on behalf of the colonists, not merely their rights as Englishmen but also their rights as men. In drawing on the concept of natural rights, the congress hoped to bolster its assertions about liberty. In your view, is the doctrine of natural rights persuasive? Why or why not? What role did natural rights play in the unfolding crisis between Great Britain and the American colonies?

4. The petitions and resolutions of the Stamp Act Congress were part of what has been characterized as an American journey—an intellectual and political undertaking that seized the world's attention and transformed thinking about republicanism. In the scheme of things, what importance would you assign to the contributions of the Stamp Act Congress?

Glossary

burthensome	burdensome
courts of Admiralty	courts that exercise jurisdiction over all maritime matters
liege	subordinate
specie	money

Document Text

Declaration of Rights of the Stamp Act Congress

The members of this Congress, sincerely devoted, with the warmest sentiments of affection and duty to His Majesty's Person and Government, inviolably attached to the present happy establishment of the Protestant succession, and with minds deeply impressed by a sense of the present and impending misfortunes of the British colonies on this continent; having considered as maturely as time will permit the circumstances of the said colonies, esteem it our indispensable duty to make the following declarations of our humble opinion, respecting the most essential rights and liberties of the colonists, and of the grievances under which they labour, by reason of several late Acts of Parliament.

I. That His Majesty's subjects in these colonies, owe the same allegiance to the Crown of Great-Britain, that is owing from his subjects born within the realm, and all due subordination to that august body the Parliament of Great Britain.

II. That His Majesty's liege subjects in these colonies, are entitled to all the inherent rights and liberties of his natural born subjects within the kingdom of Great-Britain.

III. That it is inseparably essential to the freedom of a people, and the undoubted right of Englishmen, that no taxes be imposed on them, but with their own consent, given personally, or by their representatives.

IV. That the people of these colonies are not, and from their local circumstances cannot be, represented in the House of Commons in Great-Britain.

V. That the only representatives of the people of these colonies, are persons chosen therein by themselves, and that no taxes ever have been, or can be constitutionally imposed on them, but by their respective legislatures.

VI. That all supplies to the Crown, being free gifts of the people, it is unreasonable and inconsistent with the principles and spirit of the British Constitution, for the people of Great-Britain to grant to His Majesty the property of the colonists.

VII. That trial by jury is the inherent and invaluable right of every British subject in these colonies.

VIII. That the late Act of Parliament, entitled, An Act for granting and applying certain Stamp Duties, and other Duties, in the British colonies and plantations in America, etc., by imposing taxes on the inhabitants of these colonies, and the said Act, and several other Acts, by extending the jurisdiction of the courts of Admiralty beyond its ancient limits, have a manifest tendency to subvert the rights and liberties of the colonists.

IX. That the duties imposed by several late Acts of Parliament, from the peculiar circumstances of these colonies, will be extremely burthensome and grievous; and from the scarcity of specie, the payment of them absolutely impracticable.

X. That as the profits of the trade of these colonies ultimately center in Great-Britain, to pay for the manufactures which they are obliged to take from thence, they eventually contribute very largely to all supplies granted there to the Crown.

XI. That the restrictions imposed by several late Acts of Parliament, on the trade of these colonies, will render them unable to purchase the manufactures of Great-Britain.

XII. That the increase, prosperity, and happiness of these colonies, depend on the full and free enjoyment of their rights and liberties, and an intercourse with Great-Britain mutually affectionate and advantageous.

XIII. That it is the right of the British subjects in these colonies, to petition the King, Or either House of Parliament.

Lastly, That it is the indispensable duty of these colonies, to the best of sovereigns, to the mother country, and to themselves, to endeavour by a loyal and dutiful address to his Majesty, and humble applications to both Houses of Parliament, to procure the repeal of the Act for granting and applying certain stamp duties, of all clauses of any other Acts of Parliament, whereby the jurisdiction of the Admiralty is extended as aforesaid, and of the other late Acts for the restriction of American commerce.

www.milestonedocuments.com

Boston Non-Importation Agreement

1768

"We will not, from and after the 1st of January 1769, import into this province any tea, paper, glass, or painters colours."

Overview

In a town meeting in Boston, merchants and traders agreed to boycott goods that were subject to England's Townshend Revenue Act until the duties (taxes) imposed on those goods were repealed. Some critical supplies, such as salt, hemp, and duck, were exempt from the boycott. Some sixty merchants signed the Boston Non-Importation Agreement on August 1, 1768, and within two weeks, all but sixteen of Boston's shopkeepers, traders, and merchants had joined the effort. Tradesmen and craftsmen soon joined the cause, since the protest would encourage their business. Within weeks and months, most of the major cities and many of the colonies subscribed to the non-importation movement. As in other areas, Boston led the way in fomenting opposition and protest to Parliament's taxing measures.

Context

The Boston Non-Importation Agreement of 1768 reflected the heated debate between the American colonists and Great Britain over the issue of Parliament's authority to tax the colonies. Initially an effort undertaken by merchants and traders to protest the passage by Parliament of the Townshend Revenue Act, which imposed new duties on goods imported by the colonists, the agreement to refuse to import those items until the duties were repealed ignited similar protests up and down the eastern seaboard.

Essentially a boycott, the non-importation agreements reflected the latest colonial response to the claim by Parliament of authority to levy taxes on the colonies. The repeal of the Stamp Act had seemingly curbed the antagonism, but that proved fleeting when Parliament quickly passed the Declaratory Act, which reaffirmed its assertion of taxing power. The Townshend Revenue Act, which imposed duties on a variety of goods, including tea, paper, glass, salt, coal, and fishhooks, among many others, represented an exercise of this broad authority. Unlike the Stamp Act, which triggered outrage in the colonies with its stated goal of raising revenue to pay the debt incurred during the French and Indian War, the purpose of the Townshend Revenue Act was to raise funds to provide for the maintenance and salaries of judges and governors. The act was met initially with acquiescence, but it soon produced a storm of protest and indignation among the colonists.

The implementation of the Townshend Revenue Act on November 20, 1767, drew virtually no criticism in the colonies. Some feared that opposition to the duties might inspire the violence and riots that marked the opposition to the Stamp Act. Others sought to avoid offending Great Britain. It was observed, moreover, that the colonists could hardly protest these duties when they had acquiesced in the duties imposed a year earlier by the Molasses Act. Benjamin Franklin tried to maintain the distinction between the authority of Parliament to levy external taxes, though not internal ones, which would dictate acquiescence. In the end, the absence of objection was likely attributable to the fact that the Townshend duties applied to a relatively small number of colonists, principally merchants and traders, unlike the Stamp Act taxes, which applied to tens of thousands of people. Opposition and protest, particularly in the form of non-importation agreements, might never have emerged had it not been for the fiery writings of John Dickinson and his famous "Letters from a Farmer."

Dickinson's letters to newspapers, each signed "A Farmer," were possibly more influential than any contemporary political document other than Thomas Paine's *Common Sense*. In reaction to the Townshend Revenue Act, Dickinson penned twelve weekly letters that were published initially in the *Pennsylvania Chronicle* in early December of 1767 and in more than two dozen additional papers throughout the colonies. Dickinson, a bright and talented attorney and an acute political theorist, argued that the duties were unconstitutional because Parliament lacked authority to tax the colonists, who were not represented in that body and, consequently, had not consented to be taxed. He therefore denied any distinction between external and internal taxes, although he was careful to avoid criticizing Franklin. He drew attention to the impact of the duties on the colonists, who, he asserted, would be "enslaved" by Great Britain. If England could forbid the colonists from engaging in manufacturing enterprises and require them to purchase all goods from the mother coun-

Time Line

1766

■ **March**
Parliament repeals the Stamp Act and passes the Declaratory Act. The Declaratory Act reiterates the authority of Parliament to govern the colonies in every respect, and implies the authority to impose taxes on the colonists.

■ **April**
Parliament renews the Quartering Act, which requires colonies to support British troops quartered in colonial America.

■ **June**
Parliament passes the Molasses Act, which levies taxes on colonial imports of molasses.

■ **September**
British customs officials are authorized, pursuant to writs of assistance, to search colonists' homes for contraband.

■ **December**
The New York Assembly refuses to allocate funds in support of the Quartering Act.

1767

■ **June 29**
Parliament passes the Townshend Revenue Act. The measure is to take effect in November.

■ **June**
Parliament passes the New York Restraining Act, which suspends the assembly's authority to pass laws until it authorizes funds to support British troops quartered in the colonies, as required by the Quartering Act.

■ **June**
The New York Assembly capitulates and approves funding in accord with the terms of the Quartering Act.

■ **December**
The first of John Dickinson's "Letters from a Farmer" is published in the *Pennsylvania Chronicle*. It assails the Townshend Act.

try, at a cost and tax determined by England alone, they would lose all their independence. Among other arguments and tactics, he challenged those "defeatist colonists," who would refrain from opposition because they were not yet "strong enough." The measures imposed by England, he claimed, would only become more frequent and more stringent with the passage of time.

Dickinson's letters helped to unite the American colonies. He wrote to James Otis of Massachusetts to warn of the danger to the colonists' liberties posed by the Townshend duties. Otis, in response, urged the Massachusetts House of Representatives to take action, initially by petitioning the king.

The Townshend Act was merely the most recent affront. The Stamp Act had triggered significant resistance because of its threats to the colonists' cherished right of consent. The Declaratory Act, passed on the heels of the rescission of the Stamp Act, renewed Parliament's claim to tax the colonists, a claim that the colonists bitterly rejected. The New York Restraining Act suspended the authority of the New York Assembly until it appropriated funds to support the Quartering Act, which required the colonies to provide money to support English troops quartered in America. The colonists resented these measures as encroaching on their rights to representation and consent and to tax themselves. The Townshend duties were particularly galling. Not only were they designed to raise revenue, but they also aimed to raise revenue to support and maintain the offices and salaries of judges and governors who, before the passage of this act, were paid colonial legislatures. The Townshend Act, therefore, represented a broad assault on the liberties of the colonists. To make matters worse, it approved general writs of assistance, which authorized searches for contraband in the homes of colonists.

The Boston Non-Importation Agreement reflected the boiling anger of colonists, offended by what they perceived to be deep threats to their political and economic liberties. The agreement, if not always faithfully followed, provided an occasion for intercolonial union in opposing and protesting Great Britain's measures. They reflected earlier boycott efforts aimed at the effects of the Stamp Act. As a consequence, the non-importation agreements represented a continuation of resistance tactics, and they afforded an opportunity to the colonists to contemplate their loss of confidence in English rule. Great Britain's colonial policy was under siege, and the opportunities for repairing the strained relations became more and more remote.

About the Author

It is not possible to identify the author or authors of the Boston Non-Importation Agreement of August 1, 1768. Some sixty merchants and traders signed the agreement on the day of its adoption. The agreement was perhaps inspired by the widely read and influential newspaper letters authored by a "Farmer," known to be John Dickinson, a lawyer in Pennsylvania, whose powers of analysis exposed the frailties of the Townshend Revenue Act duties, which were the object of protest. Dickinson's influence may be seen sequentially. After authoring the first of his protest letters, he wrote to James Otis, a member of the Massachusetts House of Representatives, to complain about the violation of colonial liberties wrought by the Townshend Act. Otis was moved to act and led the assembly in the passage of a petition to the king to protest the Townshend duties. That petition persuaded other colonial assemblies to follow suit, and soon the city of Boston approved the Non-Importation Agreement.

Explanation and Analysis of the Document

The Boston Non-Importation Agreement is a relatively brief, straightforward statement of intent to boycott goods and products subject to duties imposed by the Townshend Revenue Act. The agreement, signed by sixty "Merchants and Traders in the Town of Boston," signals the intention of its signers to refrain from purchasing various products and supplies until the duties are repealed by Parliament. The bold authors stated that "we will not, from and after the 1st of January 1769, import into this province any tea, paper, glass, or painters colours, until the act imposing duties on those articles shall be repealed." Further, the signers agreed not to import "any kind of goods or merchandize from Great Britain … from the 1st of January 1769, to the 1st of January 1770, except salt, coals, fish hooks and lines, hemp, and duck bar lead and shot, woolcards and card wire."

It is difficult to imagine a more lean statement of a city's policy. Unadorned by moving, passionate, and transcendent lines like those found in the Declaration of Independence, and lacking the fiery rhetoric of works from the pens of writers such as Patrick Henry and James Otis, the Non-Importation Agreement is marked by its simplicity. It was, in a word, a business agreement, and, as such, it did not require elegance and peroration. Its aim was emphatic.

The decision to employ a boycott, a time-tested method of obtaining changes and concessions, reflected several factors. First, it expressed the views of the Boston signers that the duties were burdensome. The taxes did not impose a burden on tens of thousands of colonists, as had the Stamp Act, but it was a burden nonetheless on merchants, traders, and shopkeepers. Second, it gave vent to the increasing frustration of businessmen caused by the increased restrictions on colonial trade. Third, the restrictions were snuffing out the prospects of merchants to enjoy prosperity. In short, they viewed the restrictions as harassing and intended, by design, to shackle colonial aspirations. Fourth, it reflected the emphatic belief, among a growing number of colonists, and most recently given persuasive articulation by John Dickinson, that Parliament lacked authority to tax the colonists. Indeed, as Dickinson and others had argued, the imposition of taxes violated the constitutional rights of the American colonists as English subjects. Fifth, the offense against their rights, not merely in the form of taxation but also manifested in the threat to their independence to determine the support and salaries of local judges and governors, suggested a broad conspiracy against their liberties.

Time Line

1768

- **January–May**
  Dickinson's letters are published throughout the colonies and arouse opposition to the Townshend duties.
- **February**
  The Massachusetts House of Representatives approves resolutions denying the authority of Parliament to tax the colonists and invites other colonial assemblies to do the same.
- **June–December**
  Most of the colonial assemblies pass resolutions denying a parliamentary power to tax the colonies.
- **August 1**
  Sixty Boston merchants and traders sign the Boston Non-Importation Agreement.
- **August–September**
  New York adopts a non-importation agreement.

1770

- **March**
  The Townshend Revenue Act is partially repealed. The tax on tea remains.
- **July–September**
  Non-importation agreements in various colonial cities are partially repealed to harmonize with England's action.

www.milestonedocuments.com

Audience

The Boston Non-Importation Agreement was aimed directly at Parliament. The purpose of the agreement was to persuade Parliament to repeal the Townshend Act duties, and until members did repeal the act, the many goods that were subjected to its taxes would not be imported by Boston merchants and traders. The Boston businessmen were, of course, shrewd enough to believe that their English counterparts would have an interest in persuading Parliament to repeal the act as a means of preventing damage to colonial trade, which was an important facet of their economic welfare. As such, the traders, merchants, and shopkeepers in England formed a target of the Non-Importation Agreement.

Essential Quotes

"We will not send for or import from Great Britain, either upon our own account, or upon commission, this fall, any other goods than what are already ordered for the fall supply."

(Paragraph 2)

"We will not, from and after the 1st of January 1769, import into this province any tea, paper, glass, or painters colours, until the act imposing duties on those articles shall be repealed."

(Paragraph 6)

"If we can find no relief from this infamous situation … we may bow down our necks, with all the stupid serenity of servitude, to any drudgery, which our lords and masters shall please to command."

(John Dickinson, qtd. in Knollenberg, p. 52)

The American population represented an audience for the Boston agreement as well. The announcement of a boycott of British goods would enjoy a greater prospect for success if the boycott were embraced not only in Boston but also in New England and throughout the colonies. As a business document, the agreement was intended to engender support among merchants, traders, shopkeepers, craftsmen, and others who would, in one way or another, enjoy the fruits of a successful boycott. As a political document, its aim was wide, and it was intended to be a model worthy of emulation by leaders throughout the colonies who harbored the same interests and concerns that motivated those who signed the agreement.

Impact

The statement in the Non-Importation Agreement that the boycott would endure until the Townshend duties were repealed marks a firm intent to redraw the terms of trade between Great Britain and the American colonies. In a word, it represented a new contract. As a political stance, it was sure to anger members of Parliament, which it did. Members in the House of Commons expressed frustration that the colonists denied the taxing authority of Parliament. As an economic policy, it was clever. After all, the best leverage the colonists possessed was to place pressure on English merchants and traders, who relied on trade with the colonists. The threat of an interruption to that trade, or a policy that weakened that market, was sure to upset the business community in England. The Stamp Act had had that effect, of course, and English merchants and traders had brought pressure on Parliament to repeal the measure precisely because it had a damaging effect on trade with the colonies.

Accordingly, the Boston merchants might have expected similar results when they signed the Non-Importation Agreement. The results, however, were not what they expected. English merchants did not rush to Parliament to lobby for the repeal of the Townshend Act. They were not moved to action in part because there was a prevalent feeling inside the business community that colonial merchants had not exhibited gratitude to their English counterparts for their role in the repeal of the Stamp Act. But the more important factor in explaining the failure of Englishmen to oppose the Townshend duties lay in the colonists' failure to exert their leverage.

If the colonists' principal means of bringing pressure to bear lay in their adherence to the Non-Importation Agreement, their failure to adhere to it undermined their leverage, or what leverage they may have had. The imports by Boston merchants and traders were reduced, almost by half, in the wake of the Non-Importation Agreement. Yet that meant that there was still sufficient trading activity with English merchants. Moreover, the failure of other port cities in New England to adhere to the agreement further undermined the leverage that colonists might have had. That lack of fidelity marred the efforts of non-importation agreement throughout the colonies.

If the agreement was not a particularly important factor in the repeal of the Townshend Act, it did nonetheless enjoy and portend political success. The combined efforts to fashion political unity in Boston and elsewhere sent a strong message to England. The colonists were growing confident in their ability to organize for change. And change is a matter of degree. The willingness of the colonists to assert their interests and their rights in a more assertive manner was likely to continue. And the level of assertion, sparked by the writings of men like John Dickinson, was likely to embolden others and, eventually, a nation. The agreements, if not immediately successful, were a major entry in the growing parade of colonial opposition and protest that would not be denied.

Parliament partially repealed the Townshend Act on April 12, 1770. It maintained, of course, the claim of parliamentary authority to tax the colonies. The decision to rescind the measure may have reflected in part the protests of the colonists, but in truth the Non-Importation Agreement was not very successful. Adherence to the boycott was undermined by self-interest, smuggling, and loopholes. Some leaders, including John Hancock, violated the agreements. Hancock, for example, permitted captains of his ships to transport goods that were prohibited by the agreement. It is true that for the year in which the Boston agreement was in force, imports were cut in half. Other ports enjoyed somewhat better records, while others were less faithful. New York enjoyed the best record. The repeal of the Townshend duties was more likely attributable to the ministry's opposition, which was grounded in the long-standing policy of Great Britain to promote its manufacturing, trade, and exports. The partial repeal led some colonies to partially repeal their non-importation agreement. In the volatile world of Great Britain's relations with colonial America, the path to war was only temporarily delayed.

Related Documents

Declaratory Act, 1766, 6 Geo. III, c. 12. In *The Statutes at Large from Magna Charta to the End of the Eleventh Parliament of Great Britain*, ed. Danby Pickering. Cambridge, U.K.: J. Bentham, 1762–1807. In this act, Parliament declared that it had authority to legislate on all matters, a decision that implied the authority to tax the colonists.

Dickinson, John. "Letters from a Farmer." In *The Writings of John Dickinson*, ed. Paul Leicester Ford, vol. I., pp. 277–406. Philadelphia: Historical Society of Pennsylvania, 1895. These letters are important to understanding the political and constitutional thought of the colonists.

Stamp Act, 1765, 5 Geo. III, c. 12. In *The Statutes at Large from Magna Charta to the End of the Eleventh Parliament of Great Britain*, ed. Danby Pickering. Cambridge, U.K.: J. Bentham, 1762–1807. The Stamp Act was designed to raise revenue through the imposition of "stamp fees" on all formal—and most printed—documents. Virtually everything printed was required to appear on special stamped paper shipped from London and dispersed by agents in America.

Townshend Revenue Act, 1767, 7 Geo. III, c. 46. In *The Statutes at Large from Magna Charta to the End of the Eleventh Parliament of Great Britain*, ed. Danby Pickering. Cambridge, U.K.: J. Bentham, 1762–1807. In this act, Parliament applied a tax on most colonial imports.

Bibliography

■ Books

Knollenberg, Bernhard. *Growth of the American Revolution: 1766–1775*. New York: Free Press, 1975.

Maier, Pauline. *From Resistance to Revolution: Colonial Radicals and the Development of American Opposition to Britain, 1765–1776*. New York: Alfred A. Knopf, 1972.

Miller, John C. *Origins of the American Revolution*. Stanford, Calif.: Stanford University Press, 1959.

Morgan, Edmund S. *The Birth of the Republic, 1763–89*, rev. ed. Chicago: University of Chicago Press, 1977.

—By David Gray Adler

www.milestonedocuments.com

Questions for Further Study

1. Did the unwillingness of all Boston traders and merchants to adhere to the Boston Non-Importation Agreement reflect an inherent weakness in large-scale efforts to employ boycotts as an economic and political tool? If so, how might the Boston merchants have successfully opposed the Townshend duties?

2. In your view, were John Dickinson's "Letters from a Farmer" as influential as Tomas Paine's *Common Sense*? How would you compare the influence of the two documents?

3. Given the context of the times, when Boston passed the Non-Importation Agreement, do you believe that there was a realistic way of forestalling the American Revolution? That is, was the impasse between the two sides on the question of Parliament's taxing authority unbridgeable?

Glossary

card wire	very fine steel wire used in a brush for the purpose of combing cotton wool
duck bar lead and shot	a bar of lead converted into shot for hunting ducks
hemp	the tough, coarse fiber of the cannabis plant used to make cordage or ropes, especially for ropes used in the rigging of ships
woolcards	wire-toothed brushes, similar to a dog brush, used to disentangle textile fiber; especially used for carding wool

Boston Non-Importation Agreement

August 1, 1768

The merchants and traders in the town of Boston having taken into consideration the deplorable situation of the trade, and the many difficulties it at present labours under on account of the scarcity of money, which is daily increasing for want of the other remittances to discharge our debts in Great Britain, and the large sums collected by the officers of the customs for duties on goods imported; the heavy taxes levied to discharge the debts contracted by the government in the late war; the embarrassments and restrictions laid on trade by several late acts of parliament; together with the bad success of our cod fishery, by which our principal sources of remittance are like to be greatly diminished, and we thereby rendered unable to pay the debts we owe the merchants in Great Britain, and to continue the importation of goods from thence; We, the subscribers, in order to relieve the trade under those discouragements, to promote industry, frugality, and economy, and to discourage luxury, and every kind of extravagance, do promise and engage to and with each other as follows:

First, That we will not send for or import from Great Britain, either upon our own account, or upon commission, this fall, any other goods than what are already ordered for the fall supply.

Secondly, That we will not send for or import any kind of goods or merchandize from Great Britain, either on our own account, or on commissions, or any otherwise, from the 1st of January 1769, to the 1st of January 1770, except salt, coals, fish hooks and lines, hemp, and duck bar lead and shot, wool-cards and card wire.

Thirdly, That we will not purchase of any factor, or others, any kind of goods imported from Great Britain, from January 1769, to January 1770.

Fourthly, That we will not import, on our own account, or on commissions or purchase of any who shall import from any other colony in America, from January 1769, to January 1770, any tea, glass, paper, or other goods commonly imported from Great Britain.

Fifthly, That we will not, from and after the 1st of January 1769, import into this province any tea, paper, glass, or painters colours, until the act imposing duties on those articles shall be repealed.

In witness whereof, we have hereunto set our hands, this first day of August, 1768.

www.milestonedocuments.com

This drawing from 1774, titled "The able doctor, or, America swallowing the bitter draught," shows Lord North forcing tea down the throat of a figure representing America. (Library of Congress)

Intolerable Acts

1774

"Dangerous commotions and insurrections have been fomented and raised in the town of Boston."

Overview

As a direct response to the Boston Tea Party, the British ministry during the early months of 1774 brought before Parliament a string of bills that became known in the American colonies as the Intolerable Acts or the Coercive Acts. Within a year, the British government's attempt to enforce the legislation had developed into the conflict that became the Revolutionary War.

The Intolerable Acts closed the port of Boston, altered the government of the Massachusetts Bay Colony to centralize British authority, allowed for British officials accused of crimes to be tried in another colony or in England, and sanctioned the billeting of British troops in unused buildings. The British ministry considered the acts as crucial to restoring Parliament's authority in the colonies. Americans perceived them as arbitrary and unreasonable attacks on fundamental British rights. Among the Intolerable Acts, Americans included another bill, the Quebec Act, because it protected the Roman Catholic Church in Canada, established a royally appointed rather than an elected legislative assembly, and placed in Canada's jurisdiction much of the western territory that Americans hoped to exploit.

Word of the Intolerable Acts led to an outbreak of public anger throughout British America, including the Caribbean, and ultimately resulted in the creation of the First Continental Congress by delegates from the thirteen colonies. The Congress insisted on the immediate and unconditional repeal of the offending legislation. Its members' primary achievement was the adoption of the Continental Association, an agreement to ban immediately the importation of British goods and, if the Americans' demands were not met within a year, to halt the exportation of goods to Britain. To enforce the Association, the Congress directed the election of local committees of inspection throughout the colonies.

Faced with the demands of the Congress and confronted by the practical impossibility of enforcing the legislation in Massachusetts Bay, the British ministry settled on a military response. Lord Dartmouth, the cabinet minister responsible for the American colonies, ordered Lieutenant General Thomas Gage, the royal governor of Massachusetts Bay, to confiscate a store of arms kept at Concord. The resulting engagements at Lexington and Concord proved to be the opening shots of the American Revolution.

Context

In May 1773 the British ministry piloted through Parliament the Tea Act, intended to rescue from imminent collapse the East India Company and its many investors. The legislation exempted the company from the import duties on tea brought into England and reexported to America. To British imperial policy makers, as well as America's friends in Parliament, the measure seemed neither novel nor politically dangerous. To help the East India Company dispose of its massive surplus of tea, then moldering in warehouses throughout London, the bill substantially lowered the commodity's price while retaining a small duty. It also gave the East India Company the authority to choose the American merchants to whom it would consign the tea. With one negligible bill, British ministers believed that they would save the company and increase revenues to the treasury through the reduced duty and the increased consumption by Americans of a more affordable product, while at the same time subtly reinforcing Parliament's right to lay external taxes on the colonies.

No one in London foresaw, however, the enemies the Tea Act would create. British policy makers failed to appreciate the degree to which radical American politicians would exploit the bill as a thinly veiled attempt to secure colonial submission to the principle of parliamentary taxation. They also failed to recognize the political hazard created by a measure that would undercut and possibly drive out of business those merchants who made fortunes by smuggling cheap Dutch tea into the colonies. In ports up and down the Atlantic coast, radical politicians and angry merchants found common cause in opposing the Tea Act.

In the summer of 1773 the East India Company put the plan into action when it dispatched shipments of tea to four major colonial ports—Charleston, Philadelphia, New York, and Boston. When the ships reached New York and Philadelphia, they were turned back by colonists who

Time Line

1773

■ **May 10**
Parliament passes the Tea Act, allowing the East India Company a monopoly to sell its surplus tea to the American colonies at a reduced duty.

■ **December 16**
Boston radicals throw the Boston Tea Party, dumping 352 casks of East India Company tea into the harbor in protest of the Tea Act.

1774

■ **January 13**
The *Virginia Gazette* reports the destruction of the tea in Boston Harbor.

■ **January 27**
British ministers in London receive first official word of the Boston Tea Party.

■ **February 19**
The British cabinet decides that parliamentary action is necessary to establish authority in Boston.

■ **March 31**
Parliament passes the first of the Intolerable Acts, the Boston Port Act, closing the port of Boston as of June 1.

■ **May 16**
The Virginia Assembly receives confirmation of the Boston Port Act.

■ **May 17**
Rhode Island issues a call for a "general congress" to coordinate an intercolonial response to the Intolerable Acts.

■ **May 20**
Parliament passes the second and third of the Intolerable Acts, the Massachusetts Government Act and the Administration of Justice Act.

■ **May 26**
Virginia's royal governor dissolves the Virginia Assembly for setting a day of fasting and prayer on June 1 to show support for Bostonians.

■ **June 2**
Parliament passes the Quartering Act.

refused to allow the tea to land. In Charleston the tea was unloaded, but the tax was not paid. In Boston, however, Massachusetts Bay's governor, Thomas Hutchinson, believed that the landing of the tea was a necessary demonstration of parliamentary sovereignty. Once it became clear that Boston's radicals would not allow the tea off the company's three ships, Hutchinson intended to invoke a law that authorized him forcibly to unload the cargo of any ship in the harbor that failed to pay the import taxes within three weeks. At the same time he refused to grant permission for the company's three ships to leave. On the evening of December 16, when Samuel Adams learned of Hutchinson's final refusal to release the ships, he turned to the large crowd that had gathered at the Old South Meeting House and declared that they could do nothing more to save the country. Almost immediately, a group of men disguised as Mohawk warriors assembled outside and proceeded to Boston Harbor, where they boarded the ships and systematically dumped overboard 352 casks of tea worth £10,000.

When news of the destruction of the tea reached Britain, the actions of the Boston radicals were almost universally condemned. Even among America's friends in London, there were few who would condone the blatant ruin of private property, especially in response to a law that had actually made tea more affordable for Americans. Some colonial leaders, such as George Washington and Benjamin Franklin, thought that the Bostonians had gone too far. In no other American city had radicals acted with such harmful consequences.

The people of Boston and Massachusetts Bay, therefore, were clearly isolated as the driving force of American resistance to British authority. Imperial policy makers were eager to settle the issue of sovereignty underlying the claims of American radicals that Parliament had no right to rule for them. When an effort by moderate British ministers to find a way to enforce the laws and punish Boston under existing authority failed, the cabinet decided that the matter should be settled by Parliament. The shift in focus from the Crown to the legislature of the kingdom dramatically transformed the issues at stake, making a collision between British and American perceptions of constitutional supremacy inevitable.

About the Author

Though each of the Intolerable Acts was introduced and managed through the House of Commons by Frederick North (1732–1792), second Earl of Guilford, as George III's prime minister, it is impossible to identify the author(s) of the individual pieces of legislation.

Explanation and Analysis of the Document

The Intolerable Acts were four separate pieces of legislation adopted by Parliament in 1774 in response to the

Boston Tea Party: the Boston Port Act, the Massachusetts Government Act, the Administration of Justice Act, and the Quartering Act. Even though it was not related to the events in Boston, a fifth act, the Quebec Act, was often included by American radicals as one of the Intolerable Acts.

◆ The Boston Port Act (March 31, 1774)

The only one of the Intolerable Acts intended solely as a punitive measure, the Boston Port Act was designed "to discontinue, in such manner, and for such time … the landing and discharging, lading or shipping, of goods, wares, and merchandise, at the town, and within the harbour, of Boston." It also declares "that the officers of his Majesty's customs should be forthwith removed" from Boston to Salem. The preamble justifies the legislation in breathless, hyperbolic terms, claiming that "dangerous commotions and insurrections" had been "fomented and raised … by divers ill-affected persons, to the subversion of his Majesty's government, and to the utter destruction of the publick peace." Boston is described as being wracked with "commotions and insurrections" that led to the seizure and destruction of "certain valuable cargoes of teas, being the property of the East India Company." Consequently, "the present condition of the said town and harbour" has rendered it a place where "the commerce of his Majesty's subjects cannot be safely carried on … nor the customs payable to his Majesty duly collected."

The act's opening clause is its most sweeping. Effective June 1, 1774, it prohibits anyone in or around Boston Harbor from loading or unloading "any goods, wares, or merchandise whatsoever" to or from any ship. Nothing could be transported by water out of the city to the colony's trading partners, whether in another country or another part of Massachusetts Bay, nor could any stores enter the port. (The act did not apply to overland transportation through the narrow neck that connects Boston with the mainland.) The penalty, however, for anyone who wanted to test Parliament's newfound mettle hardly matched the overheated rhetoric in the preamble. Instead of a threat of criminal prosecution, which one might reasonably expect for those who dared to destroy Boston's public peace, the sanction was strikingly equitable, providing an economic punishment for an economic infraction. Intrepid captains who sought to flaunt the ban did so "upon pain of the forfeiture" of whatever goods they were attempting to move, along with the "boat, lighter, ship, or vessel or other bottom into which the same shall be taken, and of the guns, ammunition, tackle, furniture, and stores, in or belonging to the same."

Clauses II and III of the bill also attempt to curtail any effort to skirt the act's prohibition. The latter section raises the stakes somewhat for Bostonians who participated in an attempt to ship merchandise or assisted someone who did. It sets the penalty for getting caught at triple the value of the goods seized, together with the forfeiture of "the vessels and boats, and all the horses, cattle, and carriages, whatsoever made use of in the shipping, unshipping, landing, removing, carriage, or conveyance of any of the aforesaid goods, wares, and merchandise." Clause III moves from the shore to ships, placing any vessel "seen hovering" in Boston Harbor "or within one league from the said bay" on notice that a Royal Navy ship of war or a customs officer had new authority to "compel such ship or vessel to depart to some other port or harbour." Although government officials were vaguely empowered to "use such force for that purpose as shall be found necessary," potential malefactors were given notice that they had six hours to clear out of Boston, facing forfeiture of their vessels and everything on board if they failed to heed the directive.

The act's fourth provision lists those items excluded from the ban on shipping. Military stores and anything intended for official purposes were exempt, as was "any fuel or victual brought coastwise from any part of the continent of America, for the necessary use and sustenance of the inhabitants of the said town of Boston" so long as the ships were furnished with a pass and searched by customs officials for contraband. Also, any vessels that arrived in Boston Harbor by May 31, the day before the act's effective date, could engage in their intended business provided that they left within a fortnight.

Clause V addresses the potential for corruption among those enforcing the legislation. It explicitly removes the prosecution of "all seizures, penalties, and forfeitures, inflicted by this act" from the jurisdiction of any provincial

Time Line

1774

- **June 22** Parliament passes the Quebec Act.
- **August 8** Thomas Jefferson's *Summary View of the Rights of British America* is published in Williamsburg.
- **September 5** First Continental Congress meets in Philadelphia.
- **October 20** The Congress adopts the Continental Association, a non-importation agreement to take effect December 1, 1774, and to be enforced by local committees of inspection.

1775

- **January 23** Parliament debates petitions calling for reconciliation with the American colonies.
- **February 9** Parliament declares Massachusetts in a state of rebellion.
- **April 19** Battles of Lexington and Concord occur.

www.milestonedocuments.com

The Boston Tea Party of 1773, depicted here, led directly to four of the five Intolerable Acts passed by the British Parliament in 1774. (Library of Congress)

officer who might feel inclined to go soft on defendants who also happened to be their neighbors. It gives the responsibility to almost everyone else with a title or access to someone with one, including

> any admiral, chief commander, or commissioned officer, of his Majesty's fleet, or ships of war, or by the officers of his Majesty's customs, or some of them, or by some other person deputed or authorised, by warrant from the lord high treasurer, or the commissioners of his Majesty's treasury for the time being, and by no other person whatsoever.

Nevertheless, such officers were not themselves beyond suspicion. The stiffest penalty for an infraction created by any of the Intolerable Acts was reserved for any among the authorities who "shall, directly or indirectly, take or receive any bribe or reward, to connive at such lading or unlading" or who helped someone else evade the act's penalties. A fine of £500—a substantial sum equal to half the typical annual salary for a royal governor—per offense and permanent disbarment from the offender's post, whether civil or military, awaited anyone who accepted such inducements. On the other hand, the penalty for attempting to bribe such an official was set at a comparatively mild £50.

The sixth and seventh provisions deal with more mundane administrative matters. The former clause stipulates that the recovery or prosecution of fines and penalties under the act would be determined by two older acts of Parliament, one passed in 1764 that governed the sugar trade between Britain and the Caribbean colonies, and the other enacted in 1768, entitled "An act for the more easy and effectual recovery of the penalties and forfeitures inflicted by the acts of parliament relating to the trade or revenues of the British colonies and plantations in America." The Boston Port Act's seventh condition addresses consignment and charter arrangements, declaring "utterly void" as of June 1 all bills of lading and consignment contracts to carry goods "to or from the said town of Boston, or any part of the bay or harbour thereof."

The bill's eighth provision establishes the conditions by which Bostonians could rehabilitate themselves in the eyes of the empire. If the Privy Council, along with the Crown, determined that "peace and obedience to the laws" were restored in Massachusetts Bay, then the king or the Privy Council had the authority to adjust the act's reach by establishing "open places, quays, and wharfs" within Boston Harbor, free of all commercial restrictions. According to Clause IX, individuals who used wharves that remained closed, however, were subject to the forfeitures set for illegal shipping elsewhere in the bill.

It would take more than good behavior for commercial normalcy to return to Boston. Parliament was not about to let the recent riotous events in New England be forgotten. Clause X forbids the king from doing anything to open the port or any wharves, creeks, or quays until

> full satisfaction hath been made by or on behalf of the inhabitants of the said town of Boston to the united company of merchants of England trading to the East Indies, for the damage sustained by the said company by the destruction of their goods sent to the said town of Boston.

The legislation also aimed to take care of Crown officers whose property had been destroyed or damaged in the unrest, setting as a final condition for withdrawal of the act "that reasonable satisfaction hath been made to the officers of his Majesty's revenue, and others, who suffered by the riots and insurrections" of the previous year.

◆ The Massachusetts Government Act (May 20, 1774)

The preamble to the Massachusetts Government Act, by far the longest and most threatening to colonial constitutional sensibilities of the Intolerable Acts, declares that the government established by charter in 1691, by which one province—Massachusetts Bay—was created out of several small colonies, was fundamentally flawed. Among the charter's imperially problematic components was the provision that allowed for the annual election by the provincial assembly of a twenty-eight-member panel that would sit as the upper body of the legislature and act as an advisory council to the governor. Unfortunately, the preamble opines, "the said method of electing such counsellors … hath, by repeated experience, been found to be extremely ill adapted to the plan of government established" in the province "and hath been so far from contributing … to the maintenance of the just subordination to, and conformity with, the laws of Great Britain." The practice of electing the upper body in Massachusetts Bay

> had the most manifest tendency to obstruct, and, in great measure, defeat, the execution of the laws; to weaken the attachment of his Majesty's well-disposed subjects in the said province to his Majesty's government, and to encourage the ill-disposed among them to proceed even to acts of direct resistance to, and defiance of, his Majesty's authority.

It "accordingly happened that an open resistance to the execution of the laws hath actually taken place in the town of Boston," an event, the preamble implies, that everyone should have seen coming as the inevitable product of an insidious constitutional defect.

The effective section of the act provides a remedy amounting to a political coup de grâce. In the bill's first two provisions, Parliament declares that the section of the charter of 1691 "which relates to the time and manner of electing the assistants or counsellors … is hereby revoked and made void and of none effect." Henceforth, "the offices of all counsellors and assistants … shall be thereunto nominated and appointed by his Majesty," to follow that practice employed in several of the other colonies, such as Virginia. Clauses III to VI grant to the governor alone, without consent of the council, the power to appoint all judges, the attorney general, sheriffs, and other court officers in the province and to remove them without the consent of the council (except for sheriffs).

www.milestonedocuments.com

Clause VII places unprecedented new limits on local authority by curtailing the frequency and purview of New England's troublesome town meetings. Because "a great abuse has been made of the power of calling [town meetings], and the inhabitants have, contrary to the design of their institution, been misled to treat upon matters of the most general concern, and to pass many dangerous and unwarrantable resolves," no town meeting other than the single annual session could be called without written permission of the governor. Moreover, matters eligible for the consideration of annual town meetings were limited to choosing local officials and representatives to the assembly; "no other matter shall be treated of at such meetings."

The remainder of the act, Clauses VIII through XXIV, covers matters relating to the administration of the courts, the most serious of which was the alteration in Clause VIII in the manner of electing juries. The act claims that local election of jurors "affords occasion for many evil practices, and tends to pervert the free and impartial administration of justice." Consequently, juries were no longer to be elected but were to be chosen by the sheriff of each county. Clauses IX through XIX specify the process by which future jurors would be selected and summoned, while the final provisions set out the types of cases for which juries could be employed and their costs.

◆ The Administration of Justice Act (May 20, 1774)

The Administration of Justice Act was designed to improve law and order in the province. In doing so, it employs perhaps the most inflammatory and aggressive language found in any of the Intolerable Acts, even though it and the Quartering Act were the only acts intended to be temporary. The Administration of Justice Act claims that the Bostonians had, in fact, attempted "to throw off the authority of the parliament of Great Britain" with "an actual and avowed resistance, by open force." Being allowed to go "uncontrouled and unpunished, in defiance of his Majesty's authority, and to the subversion of all lawful government" led to "the present disordered state" of Massachusetts Bay, requiring parliamentary action. Furthermore, the act declares that provincial officials accused of stepping beyond the boundaries of the law should not be "liable to be brought to trial for the same before persons who do not acknowledge the validity of the laws."

Clause I, therefore, was designed to ensure that colonial malefactors were adequately punished for their transgressions and that provincial officials were not criminally charged for merely unpopular actions. It grants to the governor's discretion, but with the consent of the council, the option to send those accused to be tried "in some other of his Majesty's colonies, or in Great Britain" should the governor find "that an indifferent trial cannot be had within the said province."

Clauses II through VII cover the procedures to be followed in trials removed to other jurisdictions. All witnesses were required to be transported to appear in court for trials, wherever they were held, with their costs covered by the colony (Clause II). While the witnesses were gone from Massachusetts Bay, they were protected from any judicial action that otherwise could be commenced against them (Clause III). Clause IV allows the governor to grant bail to provincial officials, such as magistrates or justices of the peace, who had been accused of a capital crime if the act occurred "either in the execution of his duty as a magistrate, for the suppression of riots, or in the support of the laws of revenue." Furthermore, officials who were accused could postpone all action taken against them by signaling their intent to apply to the governor for removal of the proceedings to another jurisdiction (Clause V). The sixth and seventh provisions establish that trials held in other colonies or in Great Britain "shall thereupon proceed in like manner, to all intents and purposes, as if the offence had been committed in such place" as regards questions of trial procedure, law, and appeal. If, for example, the trial were to be removed to Britain, the offense could be treated as if it "had been committed in the county of Middlesex, or in any other county of that part of Great Britain called England." Clause VIII limits the duration of the legislation, setting forth that "every clause, provision, regulation, and thing, herein contained, shall ... be, and continue in force, for and during the term of three years."

◆ The Quartering Act (June 2, 1774)

The Quartering Act, the briefest of all, was an effort to improve housing options for British troops stationed in America. It seeks to address colonial doubts about "whether troops can be quartered otherwise than in barracks" if barracks were already provided for them by provincial and local authorities. According to the act, however, often troops had to be at a distance from their barracks and required other housing. Clauses I and II of the act, therefore, clarify the authority of commanding officers to use the then-existing law (the Quartering Act of 1765) to billet soldiers in empty houses, barns, and other outbuildings should colonial officials fail to do so within twenty-four hours of such a request for housing. Officers were also required to make "a reasonable allowance" to the owners of such buildings for their use. Contrary to Patriot rhetoric, it did not grant commanding officers the authority to impose troops on private homes. In fact, the Quartering Act of 1765 established stiff penalties, including immediate and permanent removal from the service, for any officer who attempted to do so. The final clause states that the act would remain in force until March 1776, a duration of less than two years.

◆ The Quebec Act (June 22, 1774)

Because of its timing, passing not a month after the Quartering Act, and provisions that seemed designed to inflame colonial sensibilities (both of which were entirely coincidental), the Quebec Act was considered by American radicals as one of the Intolerable Acts. In fact, the Quebec Act was a pragmatic, though perhaps imperially myopic, approach to the massive administrative problems posed by Great Britain's acquisition of the extensive territory of Catholic, French-speaking Quebec, along with the thinly populated wilderness beyond the Saint Lawrence River valley.

The first paragraph expands the boundaries of the Province of Quebec established in 1763 up the Saint Lawrence Valley, down the western edge of Pennsylvania, and along the Ohio River to the Mississippi. The next two paragraphs, however, stipulate that Quebec's new borders would affect neither the existing limits of any other British American province or those property rights granted in the land that fell within the new jurisdiction.

Paragraphs 4 through 11 recognize the political and legal problems posed by the absorption into the British Empire of more than sixty-five thousand people "professing the Religion of the Church of *Rome*, and enjoying an established Form of Constitution and System of Laws, by which their Persons and Property had been protected, governed, and ordered, for a long Series of Years." The fourth paragraph "revoked, annulled, and made void" all the laws and rules that formed Quebec's existing civil government, while the fifth guarantees to Roman Catholics and their clergy the rights to practice their religion, subject to the supremacy of the British Crown. To guard against the possibility that Catholic priests might look to the authority of the Vatican before they turned to Whitehall or become an invidious fifth column in North America, paragraphs 7 and 8 require clergy to pledge to *"be faithful, and bear true Allegiance to His Majesty King George"* and to do their utmost *"to disclose and make known to His Majesty, His Heirs and Successors, all Treasons, and traitorous Conspiracies, and Attempts ... against Him, ... renouncing all Pardons and Dispensations from any Power or Person whomsoever to the Contrary."* Paragraphs 11 through 14 cover property rights more fully, retaining in force the existing French civil law for property and civil rights as well as the customs that determined inheritance. English law, on the other hand, having "been sensibly felt by the Inhabitants [of Quebec], from an Experience of more than Nine Years, during which it has been uniformly administered," would govern criminal affairs.

The provisions that sanction the practice of Catholicism and a French civil law system that did not hold property rights as sacrosanct, as did the English, raised concerns among many American Patriots. The remainder of the legislation's clauses exacerbated matters by appearing to justify radical arguments that imperial officials intended to deprive colonists of their representative assemblies. Paragraph 15 states that "at present [it is] inexpedient to call an Assembly" and vests all legislative authority in the hands of a council appointed by the Crown, with the advice of the Privy Council. Unlike its colonial brethren, Quebec's coun-

Essential Quotes

"Dangerous commotions and insurrections have been fomented and raised in the town of Boston, in the province of Massachuset's [sic] Bay, in New England, by divers ill-affected persons, to the subversion of his Majesty's government, and to the utter destruction of the publick peace, and good order of the said town."

(Preamble, Boston Port Act)

"The persons so annually elected, hath, for some time past, been such as had the most manifest tendency to obstruct, and, in great measure, defeat, the execution of the laws; to weaken and, in great measure, defeat, the execution of the laws; to weaken the attachment of his Majesty's well-disposed subjects in the said province to his Majesty's government, and to encourage the ill-disposed among them to proceed even to acts of direct resistance to, and defiance of, his Majesty's authority; And it hath accordingly happened that an open resistance to the execution of the laws hath actually taken place in the town of Boston."

(Preamble, Massachusetts Government Act)

"In the present disordered state of the said province, it is of the utmost importance to the general welfare thereof, and to the re-establishment of lawful authority throughout the same, that neither the magistrates acting in support of the laws, nor any of his Majesty's subjects aiding and assisting them therein, or in the suppression of riots and tumults, raised in opposition to the execution of the laws and statutes of this realm, should be discouraged from the proper discharge of their duty."

(Preamble, Administration of Justice Act)

www.milestonedocuments.com

cil had no authority to levy province-wide taxes, but paragraph 16 stipulates that it could authorize the inhabitants of towns or districts to assess their own rates "for the Purpose of making Roads, erecting and repairing publick Buildings, or for any other Purpose respecting the local Convenience and Oeconomy of such Town or District." In another departure from colonial legislative practice, the next two paragraphs establish tighter standards for royal review of Quebec's provincial ordinances, stipulating that all laws disallowed by the Crown would be void retroactively from their moment of passage (whereas most colonial laws struck down in Whitehall were void from the date of denial), while any law regarding religion or that provided for a punishment of more than three months' imprisonment (roughly the amount of time it took for messages to travel from Quebec to London and back again) required prior Crown approval.

Audience

Although the clear target of the Intolerable Acts was Boston and Massachusetts Bay, the audience of the legislation included every potential radical or oppositional figure in the British world. The dramatic alteration of the Massachusetts charter and constitution, for example, was a deliberate display of the supremacy of Parliament within the British Empire, a serious lesson to be learned by all of the colonies, from Ireland to Barbados. Should the legislation succeed in bringing Boston to heel, no disaffected upstarts, especially those in the ostensibly self-reliant polities on the Atlantic seaboard, could legitimately claim sovereignty and authority derived from any source outside of Westminster.

Impact

The response of Lord North's ministry and the British parliament to the Boston Tea Party was unprecedented. Legislation included the closure of Boston's port, changes to the colony's government, and substantial alterations to its judicial system. These changes appeared to policy makers in Whitehall and Westminster as just the kind of sweeping yet decisive action needed to restore harmony and calm to British America.

It seems clear today that Lord North and his ministers were wrong in almost every way. In fact, the Intolerable Acts appear to have been carefully designed to justify every radical argument about the rampant corruption that had eaten away the heart of the glorious British constitution, turning its institutions into tools of tyranny. The Massachusetts Government Act attacked a colonial charter, the foundational instrument of government cherished by many colonists as the bulwark of their own liberty and property. The Administration of Justice Act threatened the sacred, ancient right of trial by jury, raising the specter of secret courts and illegal condemnations. The Boston Port Act required vessels of the Royal Navy sent from one British port to engage in what many saw as an act of civil war by blockading another British port, though one in America. The Quebec Act resurrected traditional fears of popish plots and Jesuitical schemes to undermine Protestantism by protecting the Catholic Church in Canada, while it also struck at more banal, but no less potent concerns held by land speculators who saw the source of their future wealth—western land—vanishing into a distant and "foreign" jurisdiction. Nearly every colonial fear was given form in these acts.

Along with miscalculation was an almost complete lack of practical foresight on the part of the British ministry. Parliament showed that it could pass the Intolerable Acts, but whether it could enforce them remained in question. Moreover, the Massachusetts Government Act, unlike the others, could be enforced in only two ways: through cooperation or by force. Because cooperation was unlikely, force became inevitable. Even so, it took almost a year before Lord North's government attempted to turn the language of the legislation into real punishment for Boston. During the delay, the explicit threat posed to the other colonies by the Intolerable Acts generated a flurry of activity in all of the colonies to defend themselves.

This growing sense of a common threat created a wellspring of support for Massachusetts Bay and a sense of solidarity that had never before existed in British America. In every colony and in defiance of royal governors, calls went out for a halt to trade with Britain and the convening of a congress. The attack upon the Massachusetts charter, in particular, shook each colony's sense of the security of its liberties. Virginia's role in rallying to the cause of Boston as the cause of America was especially important, perceived as Virginia was on both sides of the Atlantic as the steadiest and most loyal colony in the British world. Despite the dissolution of the assembly by a tendentious governor, Virginia's political leaders—moderates and radicals alike—met on their own to establish a ban on British imports and to join the clamor for a continental congress. Thomas Jefferson articulated the radical view of the dispute in his *Summary View of the Rights of British America*, arguing that the only connection that existed, or that had ever existed, between the colonies and Britain was in the person of the sovereign; there had never been a place in that relationship for Parliament. Throughout the summer of 1774 committees and conventions met in each colony to elect delegates to a general congress and spell out their goals and hopes for its work.

The most important product of the First Continental Congress that met in September 1774 was the adoption of the Continental Association. The agreement called for the immediate repeal of a list of parliamentary acts and brandished non-importation and nonexportation as the weapons with which they would fight for the repeal. The Association directed towns and counties in every colony to establish committees of inspection that would enforce the trade restrictions. These committees, in no small way, formed the basis of the government that would grow out of the Revolution.

Related Documents

Boyd, Julian P., Lyman H. Butterfield, and Mina R. Bryan, eds. *The Papers of Thomas Jefferson*, Vol. 1: *1760–1776*. Princeton, N.J.: Princeton University Press, 1950. This collection includes the text of Jefferson's *Summary View of the Rights of British America*, the clearest statement of the radical Patriot perception of the empire in the wake of the Intolerable Acts.

Ford, Worthington Chauncey, ed. *Journals of the Continental Congress, 1774–1789*, Vol. 1: *1774*. Washington, D.C.: Government Printing Office, 1904. Volume 1 describes the Continental Association, the coordinated intercolonial response to the Intolerable Acts.

Bibliography

■ Books

Ammerman, David. *In the Common Cause: American Response to the Coercive Acts of 1774*. Charlottesville: University of Virginia Press, 1974.

Brown, Richard D. *Revolutionary Politics in Massachusetts: The Boston Committee of Correspondence and the Towns, 1772–1774*. Cambridge, Mass: Harvard University Press, 1970.

Cogliano, Francis D. *Revolutionary America, 1763–1815: A Political History*. New York: Routlege, 1999.

Donoughue, Bernard. *British Politics and the American Revolution: The Path to War, 1773–1775*. New York: St. Martin's Press, 1964.

Griffin, Patrick N. *American Leviathan: Empire, Nation, and Revolutionary Frontier*. New York: Hill and Wang, 2007.

Marston, Jerrilyn Greene. *King and Congress: The Transfer of Political Legitimacy, 1774–1776*. Princeton, N.J.: Princeton University Press, 1987.

Thomas, Peter D. G. *Tea Party to Independence: The Third Phase of the American Revolution, 1773–1776*. New York: Oxford University Press, 1991.

Tucker, Robert W., and David C. Hendrickson. *The Fall of the First British Empire: Origins of the War of American Independence*. Baltimore, Md.: Johns Hopkins University Press, 1982.

—By R. S. Taylor Stoermer

www.milestonedocuments.com

Questions for Further Study

1. Consider each of the Intolerable Acts. Were any of them justified? Standing alone, would any one act likely have elicited a sense of common purpose among the American colonies sufficient to link their causes with the cause of Massachusetts Bay? Why or why not?

2. Compare the Intolerable Acts with earlier instances in which Parliament legislated for the colonies. Were the measures truly unprecedented? If so, what accounts for the dramatic change in British policy? If not, why did the Americans perceive the acts as constitutional innovations?

3. What were the enduring lessons of such punitive legislation? Has the U.S. Congress or the British parliament enacted anything similar since 1774?

4. What role did the press play in transmitting information about the events surrounding the Intolerable Acts? Was the information communicated accurately?

Glossary

cocket	official seal; shipper's clearance; customs duty
de Talibus Circumstantibus	taking whoever happens to be standing around
gaol	jail
letters patent	an open document issued by a monarch or a government conferring a patent or another right
messuages	homes and their immediate outbuildings
Oyer and Terminer	a court authorized to hear certain criminal cases
sign manual	the signature of the monarch
Venire Facias	a writ issued by an official of the court summoning prospective jurors
videlicet	to wit
wharfinger	an owner or keeper of a wharf

Document Text

Intolerable Acts

Boston Port Act

March 31, 1774

An act to discontinue, in such manner, and for such time as are therein mentioned, the landing and discharging, lading or shipping, of goods, wares, and merchandise, at the town, and within the harbour, of Boston, in the province of Massachuset's Bay, in North America.

WHEREAS dangerous commotions and insurrections have been fomented and raised in the town of Boston, in the province of Massachuset's Bay, in New England, by divers ill-affected persons, to the subversion of his Majesty's government, and to the utter destruction of the publick peace, and good order of the said town; in which commotions and insurrections certain valuable cargoes of teas, being the property of the East India Company, and on board certain vessels lying within the bay or harbour of Boston, were seized and destroyed: And whereas, in the present condition of the said town and harbour, the commerce of his Majesty's subjects cannot be safely carried on there, nor the customs payable to his Majesty duly collected; and it is therefore expedient that the officers of his Majesty's customs should be forthwith removed from the said town: May it please your Majesty that it may be enacted; and be it enacted by the King's most excellent majesty, by and with the advice and consent of the lords spiritual and temporal, and commons, in this present parliament assembled, and by the authority of the same, That from and after the first day of June, one thousand seven hundred and seventy-four, it shall not be lawful for any person or persons whatsoever to lade put, or cause or procure to be laden or put, off or from any quay, wharf, or other place, within the said town of Boston, or in or upon any part of the shore of the bay, commonly called The Harbour of Boston, between a certain headland or point called Nahant Point, on the eastern side of the entrance into the said bay, and a certain other headland or point called Alderton Point, on the western side of the entrance into the said bay, or in or upon any island, creek, landing place, bank, or other place, within the said bay or headlands, into any ship, vessel, lighter, boat, or bottom, any goods, wares, or merchandise whatsoever, to be transported or carried into any other country, province or place whatsoever, or into any other part of the said province of the Massachuset's Bay, in New England; or to take up, discharge, or lay on land, or cause or procure to be taken up, discharged, or laid on land, within the said town, or in or upon any of the places aforesaid, out of any boat, lighter, ship, vessel, or bottom, any goods, wares, or merchandise whatsoever, to be brought from any other country, province, or place, or any other part of the said province of the Massachuset's Bay in New England, upon pain of the forfeiture of the said goods, wares, and merchandise, and of the said boat, lighter, ship, or vessel or other bottom into which the same shall be taken, and of the guns, ammunition, tackle, furniture, and stores, in or belonging to the same: And if any such goods, wares, or merchandise, shall, within the said town, or in any the places aforesaid, be laden or taken in from the shore into any barge, hoy, lighter, wherry, or boat, to be carried on board any ship or vessel coming in and arriving from any other country or province, or other part of the said province of the Massachuset's Bay in New England, such barge, hoy, lighter, wherry, or boat, shall be forfeited and lost.

II. And be it further enacted by the authority aforesaid, That if any warfinger, or keeper of any wharf, crane, or quay, of their servants, or any of them, shall take up or land, or knowingly suffer to be taken up or landed, or shall ship off, or suffer to be waterborne, at or from any of their said wharfs, cranes, or quays, any such goods, wares, or merchandise; in every such case, all and every such wharfinger, and keeper of such wharf, crane, or quay, and every person whatever who shall be assisting, or otherwise concerned in the shipping or in the loading or putting on board any boat, or other vessel for that purpose, or in the unshipping such goods, wares, and merchandise, or to whose hands the same shall knowingly come after the loading, shipping, or unshipping thereof, shall forfeit and lose treble the value thereof, to be computed at the highest price which such sort of goods, wares, and merchandise, shall bear at the place where such offence shall be committed, together with the vessels and boats, and all the horses, cattle, and carriages, whatsoever made

www.milestonedocuments.com

use of in the shipping, unshipping, landing, removing, carriage, or conveyance of any of the aforesaid goods, wares, and merchandise.

III. And be it further enacted by the authority aforesaid, That if any ship or vessel shall be moored or lie at anchor, or be seen hovering within the said bay, described and bounded as aforesaid, or within one league from the said bay so described, or the said headlands, or any of the islands lying between or within the same, it shall and may be lawful for any admiral, chief commander, or commissioned officer, of his Majesty's fleet or ships of war, or for any officer of his Majesty's customs, to compel such ship or vessel to depart to some other port or harbour, or to such station as the said officer shall appoint, and to use such force for that purpose as shall be found necessary: And if such ship or vessel shall not depart accordingly, within six hours after notice for that purpose given by such person as aforesaid, such ship or vessel, together with all the goods laden on board thereon, and all the guns, ammunition, tackle, and furniture, shall be forfeited and lost, whether bulk shall have been broken or not.

IV. Provided always, That nothing in this act contained shall extend, or be construed to extend, to any military or other stores for his Majesty's use, or to the ships or vessels whereon the same shall be laden, which shall be commissioned by, and in the immediate pay of, his Majesty, his heirs or successors; nor to any fuel or victual brought coastwise from any part of the continent of America, for the necessary use and sustenance of the inhabitants of the said town of Boston, provided the vessels wherein the same are to be carried shall be duly furnished with a cocket and let-pass, after having been duly searched by the proper officers of his Majesty's customs at Marblehead, in the port of Salem, in the said province of Massachuset's Bay; and that some officer of his Majesty's customs be also there put on board the said vessel, who is hereby authorized to go on board, and proceed with the said vessel, together with a sufficient number of persons, properly armed, for his defence, to the said town or harbour of Boston; nor to any ships or vessels which may happen to be within the said harbour of Boston on or before the first day of June, one thousand seven hundred and seventy four, and may have either laden or taken on board, or be there with intent to load or take on board, or to land or discharge any goods, wares, and merchandise, provided the said ships and vessels do depart the said harbour within fourteen days after the said first day of June, one thousand seven hundred and seventy-four.

V. And be it further enacted by the authority aforesaid, That all seizures, penalties, and forfeitures, inflicted by this act, shall be made and prosecuted by any admiral, chief commander, or commissioned officer, of his Majesty's fleet, or ships of war, or by the officers of his Majesty's customs, or some of them, or by some other person deputed or authorised, by warrant from the lord high treasurer, or the commissioners of his Majesty's treasury for the time being, and by no other person whatsoever: And if any such officer, or other person authorised as aforesaid, shall, directly or indirectly, take or receive any bribe or reward, to connive at such lading or unlading, or shall make or commence any collusive seizure, information, or agreement for that purpose, or shall do any other act whatsoever, whereby the goods, wares, or merchandise, prohibited as aforesaid, shall be suffered to pass, either inwards or outwards, or whereby the forfeitures and penalties inflicted by this act may be evaded, every such offender shall forfeit the sum of five hundred pounds for every such offence, and shall become incapable of any office or employment, civil or military; and every person who shall give, offer, or promise, any such bribe or reward, or shall contract, agree, or treat with any person, so authorised as aforesaid, to commit any such offence, shall forfeit the sum of fifty pounds.

VI. And be it further enacted by the authority aforesaid, That the forfeitures and penalties inflicted by this act shall and may be prosecuted, sued for, and recovered, and be divided, paid, and applied, in like manner as other penalties and forfeitures inflicted by any act or acts of parliament, relating to the trade or revenues of the British colonies or plantations in America, are directed to be prosecuted, sued for, or recovered, divided, paid, and applied, by two several acts of parliament, the one passed in the fourth year of his present Majesty, (intituled, An act for granting certain duties in the British colonies and plantations in America; for continuing, amending, and making perpetual, an act passed in the sixth year of the reign of his late majesty King George the Second, intituled, An act for the better securing and encouraging the trade of his Majesty's sugar colonies in America: for applying the produce of such duties, and of the duties to arise by virtue of the said act, towards defraying the expences of defending, protecting, and securing, the said colonies and plantations; for explaining an act made in the twenty-fifth year of the reign of King Charles the Second, intituled, An act for the encouragement of the Greenland and Eastland trades, and for the

Document Text

better securing the plantation trade; and for altering and disallowing several drawbacks on exports from this kingdom, and more effectually preventing the clandestine conveyance of goods to and from the said colonies and plantations, and improving and securing the trade between the same and Great Britain;) the other passed in the eighth year of his present Majesty's reign, (intituled, An act for the more easy and effectual recovery of the penalties and forfeitures inflicted by the acts of parliament relating to the trade or revenues of the British colonies and plantations in America.)

VII. And be it further enacted by the authority aforesaid, That every charter party bill of loading, and other contract for consigning shipping, or carrying any goods, wares, and merchandize whatsoever, to or from the said town of Boston, or any part of the bay or harbour thereof, described as aforesaid, which have been made or entered into, or which shall be made or entered into, so long as this act shall remain in full force, relating to any ship which shall arrive at the said town or harbour, after the first day of June, one thousand seven hundred and seventy-four, shall be, and the same are hereby declared to be utterly void, to all intents and purposes whatsoever.

VIII. And be it further enacted by the authority aforesaid, That whenever it shall be made to appear to his Majesty, in his privy council, that peace and obedience to the laws shall be so far restored in the said town of Boston, that the trade of Great Britain may safely be carried on there, and his Majesty's customs duly collected, and his Majesty, in his privy council, shall adjudge the same to be true, it shall and may be lawful for his Majesty, by proclamation, or order of council, to assign and appoint the extent, bounds, and limits, of the port or harbour of Boston, and of every creek or haven within the same, or in the islands within the precincts thereof; and also to assign and appoint such and so many open places, quays, and wharfs, within the said harbour, creeks, havens, and islands, for the landing, discharging, lading, and shipping of goods, as his Majesty, his heirs or successors, shall judge necessary and expedient; and also to appoint such and so many officers of the customs therein as his Majesty shall think fit, after which it shall be lawful for any person or persons to lade or put off from, or to discharge and land upon, such wharfs, quays, and places, so appointed within the said harbour, and none other, any goods, wares, and merchandise whatever.

IX. Provided always, That if any goods, wares, or merchandize, shall be laden or put off from, or discharged or landed upon, any other place than the quays, wharfs, or places, so to be appointed, the same, together with the ships, boats, and other vessels employed therein, and the horses, or other cattle and carriages used to convey the same, and the person or persons concerned or assisting therein, or to whose hands the same shall knowingly come, shall suffer all the forfeitures and penalties imposed by this or any other act on the illegal shipping or landing of goods.

X. Provided also, and it is hereby declared and enacted, That nothing herein contained shall extend, or be construed, to enable his Majesty to appoint such port, harbour, creeks, quays, wharfs, places, or officers in the said town of Boston, or in the said bay or islands, until it shall sufficiently appear to his Majesty that full satisfaction hath been made by or on behalf of the inhabitants of the said town of Boston to the united company of merchants of England trading to the East Indies, for the damage sustained by the said company by the destruction of their goods sent to the said town of Boston, on board certain ships or vessels as aforesaid; and until it shall be certified to his Majesty, in council, by the governor, or lieutenant governor, of the said province, that reasonable satisfaction hath been made to the officers of his Majesty's revenue, and others, who suffered by the riots and insurrections above mentioned, in the months of November and December, in the year one thousand seven hundred and seventy-three, and in the month of January, in the year one thousand seven hundred and seventy-four.

XI. And be it further enacted by the authority aforesaid, That if any action or suit shall be commenced, either in Great Britain or America, against any person or persons, for any thing done in pursuance of this act of parliament, the defendant or defendants, in such action or suit, may plead the general issue, and give the said act, and the special matter, in evidence, at any trial to be had thereupon, and that the same was done in pursuance and by the authority of this act: and if it shall appear so to have been done, the jury shall find for the defendant or defendants; and if the plaintiff shall be nonsuited, or discontinue his action, after the defendant or defendants shall have appeared: or if judgment shall be given upon any verdict or demurrer, against the plaintiff, the defendant or defendants shall recover treble costs, and have the like remedy for the same, as defendants have in other cases by law.

Document Text

Massachusetts Government Act

May 20, 1774

An act for the better regulating the government of the province of the Massachuset's Bay, in New England.

WHEREAS by letters patent under the great seal of England, made in the third year of the reign of their late majesties King William and Queen Mary, for uniting, erecting, and incorporating, the several colonies, territories, and tracts of land therein mentioned, into one real province, by the name of Their Majesties Province of the Massachuset's Bay, in New England; whereby it was, amongst other things, ordained and established, That the governor of the said province should, from thenceforth, be appointed and commissionated by their Majesties, their heirs and successors: It was, however, granted and ordained, That, from the expiration of the term for and during which the eight and twenty persons named in the said letters patent were appointed to be the first counsellors or assistants to the governor of the said province for the time being, the aforesaid number of eight and twenty counsellors or assistants should yearly, once in every year, for ever thereafter, be, by the general court or assembly, newly chosen: And whereas the said method of electing such counsellors or assistants, to be vested with the several powers, authorities, and privileges, therein mentioned, although conformable to the practice theretofore used in such of the colonies thereby united, in which the appointment of the respective governors had been vested in the general courts or assemblies of the said colonies, hath, by repeated experience, been found to be extremely ill adapted to the plan of government established in the province of the Massachuset's Bay, by the said letters patent herein-before mentioned, and hath been so far from contributing to the attainment of the good ends and purposes thereby intended, and to the promoting of the internal welfare, peace, and good government of the said province, or to the maintenance of the just subordination to, and conformity with, the laws of Great Britain, that the manner of exercising the powers, authorities, and privileges aforesaid, by the persons so annually elected, hath, for some time past, been such as had the most manifest tendency to obstruct, and, in great measure, defeat, the execution of the laws; to weaken and, in great measure, defeat, the execution of the laws; to weaken the attachment of his Majesty's well-disposed subjects in the said province to his Majesty's government, and to encourage the ill-disposed among them to proceed even to acts of direct resistance to, and defiance of, his Majesty's authority; And it hath accordingly happened that an open resistance to the execution of the laws hath actually taken place in the town of Boston, and the neighbourhood thereof, within the said province: And whereas it is, under these circumstances, become absolutely necessary, in order to the preservation of the peace and good order of the said province, the protection of his Majesty's well-disposed subjects therein resident, the continuance of the mutual benefits arising from the commerce and correspondence between this kingdom and the said province, and the maintaining of the just dependance of the said province upon the crown and parliament of Great Britain, that the said method of annually electing the counsellors or assistants of the said province should no longer be suffered to continue but that the appointment of the said counsellors or assistants should henceforth be put upon the like footing as is established in such other of his Majesty's colonies or plantations in America, the governors whereof are appointed by his Majesty's commission, under the great seal of Great Britain: Be it therefore enacted by the King's most excellent Majesty, by and with the advice and consent of the lords spiritual and temporal, and commons, in this present parliament assembled, and by the authority of the same, That from and after the first day of August, one thousand seven hundred and seventy-four, so much of the charter, granted by their majesties King William and Queen Mary to the inhabitants of the said province of the Massachuset's Bay, in New England, and all and every clause, matter, and thing, therein contained, which relates to the time and manner of electing the assistants or counsellors for the said province, be revoked, and is hereby revoked and made void and of none effect; and that the offices of all counsellors and assistants, elected and appointed in pursuance thereof, shall from thenceforth cease and determine: And that, from and after the said first day of August, one thousand seven hundred and seventy-four, the council, or court of assistants of the said province for the time being, shall be composed of such of the inhabitants or proprietors of lands within the same as shall be thereunto nominated and appointed by his Majesty, his heirs and successors, from time to time, by warrant under his or their signet or sign manual, and with the advice of the privy council, agreeable to the practice now used in respect to the appointment of counsellors in such of his Majesty's other colonies in

www.milestonedocuments.com

Document Text

America, the governors whereof are appointed by commission under the great seal of Great Britain: provided, that the number of the said assistants or counsellors shall not, at any one time, exceed thirty-six, nor be less than twelve.

II. And it is hereby further enacted, That the said assistants or counsellors, so to be appointed as aforesaid, shall hold their offices respectively, for and during the pleasure of his Majesty, his heirs or successors; and shall have and enjoy all the powers, privileges, and immunities, at present held, exercised, and enjoyed, by the assistants or counsellors of the said province, constituted and elected, from time to time, under the said charter, (except as herein-after excepted); and shall also, upon their admission into the said council, and before they enter upon the execution of their offices respectively, take the oaths, and make, repeat, and subscribe, the declarations required, as well by the said charter as by any law or laws of the said province now in force, to be taken by the assistants or counsellors who have been so elected and constituted as aforesaid.

III. And be it further enacted by the authority aforesaid, That from and after the first day of July, one thousand seven hundred and seventy-four, it shall and may be lawful for his Majesty's governor for the time being of the said province, or, in his absence, for the lieutenant-governor, to nominate and appoint, under the seal of the province, from time to time, and also to remove, without the consent of the council, all judges of the inferior courts of common pleas, commissioners of Oyer and Terminer, the attorney general, provosts, marshals, justices of the peace, and other officers to the council or courts of justice belonging; and that all judges of the inferior courts of common pleas, commissioners of Oyer and Terminer, the attorney general, provosts, marshals, justices, and other officers so appointed by the governor, or, in his absence, by the lieutenant-governor alone, shall and may have, hold, and exercise, their said offices, powers, and authorities, as fully and completely, to all intents and purposes, as any judges of the inferior courts of common pleas, commissioners of Oyer and Terminer, attorney general, provosts, marshals, or other officers, have or might have done heretofore under the said letters patent, in the third year of the reign of their late majesties King William and Queen Mary; any law, statute, or usage, to the contrary notwithstanding.

IV. Provided always, and be it enacted, That nothing herein contained shall extend, or be construed to extend, to annul or make void the commission granted before the said first day of July, one thousand seven hundred and seventy-four, to any judges of the inferior courts of common pleas, commissioners of Oyer and Terminer, the attorney general, provosts, marshals, justices of the peace, or other officers; but that they may hold and exercise the same, as if this act had never been made, until the same shall be determined by death, removal by the governor, or other avoidance, as the case may happen.

V. And be it further enacted by the authority aforesaid, That, from and after the said first day of July, one thousand seven hundred and seventy-four, it shall and may be lawful for his Majesty's governor, or, in his absence, for the lieutenant-governor for the time being of the said province, from time to time, to nominate and appoint the sheriffs without the consent of the council, and to remove such sheriffs with such consent, and not otherwise.

VI. And be it further enacted by the authority aforesaid, That, upon every vacancy of the officers of chief justice and judges of the superior court of the said province, from and after the said first day of July, one thousand seven hundred and seventy-four, the governor for the time being, or, in his absence, the lieutenant-governor, without the consent of the council, shall have full power and authority to nominate and appoint the persons to succeed to the said offices; who shall hold their commissions during the pleasure of his Majesty, his heirs and successors; and that neither the chief justice or judges appointed before the said first day of July, one thousand seven hundred and seventy-four, nor those who shall hereafter be appointed pursuant to this act, shall be removed, unless by the order of his Majesty, his heirs or successors, under his or their sign manual.

VII. And whereas, by several acts of the general court, which have been from time to time enacted and passed within the said province, the freeholders and inhabitants of the several townships, districts, and precincts, qualified, as is therein expressed, are authorised to assemble together, annually, or occasionally, upon notice given, in such manner as the said acts direct, for the choice of select men, constables, and other officers, and for the making and agreeing upon such necessary rules, orders, and bye laws, for the directing, managing, and ordering, the prudential affairs of such townships, districts, and precincts, and for other purposes: and whereas a great abuse has been made of the power of calling such meetings, and the inhabitants have, contrary to the design of their institution, been misled to treat upon matters of the most general concern, and to pass many dangerous

Document Text

and unwarrantable resolves: for remedy whereof, be it enacted, That from and after the said first day of August, one thousand seven hundred and seventy-four, no meeting shall be called by the select men, or at the request of any number of freeholders of any township, district, or precinct, without the leave of the governor, or, in his absence, of the lieutenant-governor, in writing, expressing the special business of the said meeting, first had and obtained, except the annual meeting in the months of March or May, for the choice of select men, constables, and other officers, or except for the choice of persons to fill up the offices aforesaid, on the death or removal of any of the persons first elected to such offices, and also, except any meeting for the election of a representative or representatives in the general court; and that no other matter shall be treated of at such meetings, except the election of their aforesaid officers or representatives, nor at any other meeting, except the business expressed in the leave given by the governor , or, in his absence, by the lieutenant-governor.

VIII. And whereas the method at present used in the province of Massachuset's Bay in America, of electing persons to serve on grand juries, and other juries, by the freeholders and inhabitants of the several towns, affords occasion for many evil practices, and tends to pervert the free and impartial administration of justice: for remedy whereof, be it further enacted by the authority aforesaid, That, from and after the respective times appointed for the holding of the general sessions of the peace in the several counties within the said province, next after the month of September, one thousand seven hundred and seventy-four, the jurors to serve at the superior courts of judicature, courts of assize, general gaol delivery, general sessions of the peace, and inferior court of common pleas, in the several counties within the said province, shall not be elected, nominated, or appointed, by the freeholders and inhabitants of the several towns within the said respective counties nor summoned or returned by the constables of the said towns; but that, from thenceforth, the jurors to serve at the superior courts of judicature, courts of assize, general gaol delivery, general sessions of the peace, and inferior court of common pleas within the said province, shall be summoned and returned by the sheriffs of the respective counties within the said province; and all writs of Venire Facias, or other process or warrants to be issued for the return of jurors to serve at the said courts, shall be directed to the sheriffs of the said counties respectively, any law, custom, or usage, to the contrary notwithstanding.

IX. Provided always, and be it further enacted by the authority aforesaid, That wherever the sheriff of any country shall happen to be a party, or interested or related to any party of person interested in any prosecution or suit depending in any of the said courts; that then in such case, the writ of Venire Facias, of other process or warrant for the summoning and return of a jury, for the trial of such prosecution or suit, shall be directed to, and executed by, the coroner of such county; and in case such coroner shall be also a party, or interested in, or related to, the Venire Facias, or other process or warrant, for the summoning and return of a jury for the trial of such prosecution or suit shall be directed to, and executed by, a proper and indifferent person, to be appointed for that purpose by the court wherein such prosecution or suit shall be depending.

X. And that all sheriffs may be the better informed of persons qualified to serve on juries at the superior courts of judicature, courts of assize, general gaol delivery, general sessions of the peace, and inferior court of common pleas, within the said province, be it further enacted by the authority aforesaid, That the constables of the respective towns, within the several counties of the said province, shall, at the general sessions of the peace to be holden for each county, next after the month of September in every year, upon the first day of the said sessions, return and deliver to the justices of the peace, in open court, a true life, in writing, of the names and places of abode of all persons within the respective towns for which they serve, or the districts thereof, qualified to serve upon juries, with their titles and additions, between the age of one and twenty years and the age of seventy years; which said justices or any two of them, at the said sessions in the respective counties, shall cause to be delivered a duplicate of the aforesaid lists, by the clerk of the peace of every country, to the sheriffs, or their deputies, within ten days after such session; and cause each of the said lists to be fairly entered into a book by the clerk of the peace, to be by him provided, and kept for that purpose amongst the records of the said court; and no sheriff shall impanel or return any person or persons to serve upon any grand jury, petit jury, whatsoever, in any of the said courts that shall not be named or mentioned in such list: and, to prevent a failure of justice, through the neglect of constables to make such returns of persons qualified to serve on juries, as in and by this act is directed, the clerks of the peace of the said several counties are hereby required and commanded, twenty days at least next

www.milestonedocuments.com

Document Text

before the month of September, yearly, and every year, to issue forth precepts or warrants, under their respective hands and seals, to the respective constables of the several towns within the said respective counties, requiring them, and every of them, to make such return of persons qualified to serve upon juries as hereby respectively directed; and every constable failing at any time to make and deliver such return to the justices in open court, as aforesaid, shall forfeit and incur the penalty of five pounds sterling to his Majesty, and his successors: to be recovered by bill, plaint, or information, to be prosecuted in any of the courts aforesaid; and, in order that the constables may be the better enabled to make complete lists of all persons qualified to serve on juries, the constables of the several towns shall have free liberty, at all seasonable times, upon request by them made to any officer or officers, who shall have in his or their custody any book or account of rates or taxes on the freeholder or inhabitants within such respective towns, to inspect the same, and take from thence the names of such persons qualified to serve on juries, dwelling within the respective, towns for which such lists are to be given in and returned pursuant to this act; and shall, in the month of September, yearly, and every year, upon two or more Sundays, fix upon the door of the church, chapel, and every other publick place of religious worship within their respective precincts, a true and exact list of all such persons intended to be returned to the said general sessions of the peace, as qualified to serve on juries, pursuant to the directions of this act; and leave at the same time a duplicate of such list with the town clerk of the said place, perused by the freeholder and inhabitants thereof, to the end that notice may be given of persons duly qualified who are omitted, or of persons inserted by mistake who ought to be omitted out of such lists; and it shall and may be lawful to and for the justices, at the general sessions of the peace to which the said lists shall be so returned, upon due proof made before them of any person or persons duly qualified to serve on juries being omitted in such lists, or of any person or persons being inserted therein who ought to have been omitted, to order his or their name or names to be inserted or struck out, as the case may require: and in case any constable shall wilfully omit, out of such list, any person or persons, whose name or names ought to be inserted, or shall wilfully insert any person or persons who ought to be omitted, every constable so offending, shall, for every person so omitted or inserted in such list, contrary to the true intent and meaning of this act, be fined by the said justices, in the said general sessions of the peace, in the sum of forty shillings sterling.

XI. Provided always, and be it enacted by the authority aforesaid, That in case default shall at any time hereafter be made, by any constable or constables, to return lists of persons qualified to serve on juries within any of the said towns to the said court of general sessions of the peace; then, and in such case, it shall be lawful for the sheriff of the county, in which such default shall be made, to summon and return to the several courts aforesaid, or any of them, such and so many persons dwelling in such towns, or the districts thereof, qualified to serve on juries, as he shall think fit to serve on juries at such respective courts; any thing herein contained to the contrary thereof in any-wise notwithstanding.

XII. And be it further enacted by the authority aforesaid, That every summons of any person, to serve upon any of the juries at the said courts, or any of them, shall be made by the sheriff, or other person, ten days at the least before the holding of every such court; and in case any jurors, so to be summoned, be absent from the usual place of his habitation at the time of such summons, notice of such summons shall be given, by leaving a note, in writing, under the hand of such sheriff, or person, containing the contents thereof, at the dwelling-house of such juror, with some person inhabiting in the same

XIII. Provided always, and be it further enacted by the authority aforesaid, That in case a sufficient number of persons qualified to serve on juries shall not appear at the said courts, or any of them, to perform the service of grand or petit jurors; that then, and in such case, it shall be lawful for the said court to issue a writ or precept to the sheriff, requiring him to summon a sufficient number of other persons qualified to serve on juries, immediately to appear at such court, to fill up and compleat the number of jurors to serve at such court; and such persons are hereby required to appear and serve as jurors at the said courts accordingly.

XIV. And be it further enacted by the authority aforesaid, That no person who shall serve as a juror, at any of the said courts, shall be liable to serve again as a juror at the same court, or any other of the courts aforesaid, for the space of three years then next following; except upon special juries.

XV. And, in order that sheriffs may be informed of the persons who have served as jurors, it is hereby further enacted by the authority, aforesaid, that every sheriff shall prepare and keep a book, or register, wherein. the names of all such persons who have

www.milestonedocuments.com

served as jurors, with their additions and places of abode, and the times when, and the courts in which they served, shall be alphabetically entered and registered; which books or registers shall, from time to time, be delivered over to the succeeding sheriff of the said county; within ten days after he shall enter upon his office; and every juror, who shall attend and serve at any of the courts aforesaid, may at the expiration of the time of holding every such court, upon, application to the sheriff, or his deputy, have a certificate immediately, gratis, from the sheriff, or his deputy, testifying such his attendance and service; which said certificate the said sheriff, or his deputy, is required to give to every such juror.

XVI. And be it further enacted by the authority aforesaid, That if, by reason of challenges, or otherwise, there shall not be a sufficient number of jurors for the trial of any prosecution for any misdemeanour, or any action depending in any of the said courts; then, and in such case, the jury shall be filled up de Talibus Circumstantibus, to be returned by the sheriff, unless he be a party, or interested or related to any party or person interested in such prosecution or action; and, in any of which cases, to be returned by the coroner, unless he be a party, or interested or related to any party or person interested in such prosecution or action; and, in any of these cases, to be returned by a proper and indifferent person, to be appointed by the court for that purpose.

XVII. And be it further enacted by the authority aforesaid, That in case any person summoned to serve upon the grand or petit jury, at any of the courts aforesaid, or upon the jury in any prosecution, action, or suit, depending in any of the said courts, shall not appear and serve at the said courts, according to the said summons, (not having any reasonable excuse to be allowed by the judges or justices at such court), he shall be fined by the judges or justices of such court in any sum not exceeding the sum of ten pounds, nor less than twenty shillings sterling.

XVIII. And be it further enacted by the authority aforesaid, That every sheriff, or other officer, to whom the Venire Facias, or other process or warrant, for the trial of causes, or summoning of juries, shall be directed, shall, upon his return of every such writ, or other process or warrant, (unless in cases where a special jury shall be struck by order or rule of court, pursuant to this act), annex a pannel to the said writ, or process, or warrant, containing the christian and surnames, additions, and places of abode, of a competent number of jurors, named in such lists, which number of jurors shall not be less than twenty-four, nor more than forty-eight, without direction of the judges or justices of such court or session, or one of them, who are hereby respectively impowered and required, if he or they see cause, by order, under his or their respective hand or hands, to direct a greater number; and then such number as shall be so directed shall be the number to be returned to serve on such jury.

XIX. And be it further enacted by the authority aforesaid, That for the trials of all actions or suits depending in any of the said courts, the name of each and every person who shall be summoned and returned as aforesaid, with his addition, and the place of his abode, shall be written in several and distinct pieces of parchment, or paper, being all as near as may be of equal size and bigness. and shall be delivered unto the officer to be appointed by the court for that purpose, by the sheriff, under sheriff, or some agent of his; and shall, by direction and care of such officer, be rolled up all as near as may be, in the same manner, and put together in a box or glass to be provided for that purpose; and when any cause shall be brought on to be tried, some indifferent person, by direction of the court, may and shall, in open court, draw out twelve of the said parchments or paper, one after another; and if any of the persons, whose names shall be so drawn, shall not appear, or shall be challenged, and such challenge allowed, then such person shall proceed to draw other parchments or papers from the said box, till twelve indifferent persons shall be drawn; which twelve indifferent persons being sworn shall be the jury to try the said cause: and the names of the persons so drawn and sworn shall be kept apart by themselves in some other box or glass, to be kept, for that purpose, till such jury shall have given in their verdict and the same is recorded, or until such jury shall, by consent of the parties, or leave of the court, be discharged; and then the same names shall be rolled up again, and returned to the former box or glass, there to be kept, with the other names remaining at that time undrawn, and so toties quoties, as long as any cause remains then to be tried.

XX. And be it further enacted by the authority aforesaid, That it shall and may be lawful to and for the superior court of assize, and court of common pleas upon motion made on behalf of his Majesty, his heirs or successors, or on the motion of any prosecutor or defendant, in any indictment or information for any misdemeanor depending, or to be brought or prosecuted in the said court, or on the motion of any plaintiff or plaintiffs, defendant or defendants, in any action, cause, or suit whatsoever, depending, or to be brought and carried on in the said court, and the said court, is hereby authorized and required, upon motion as aforesaid, in any of the cases before mentioned, to order and appoint a jury to be struck for the trial of any issue joined in any of the said cases, and triable by a jury of twelve men, by such officer of the said court as the court shall appoint; and for that purpose the sheriff, or his deputy, shall attend such officer with the duplicate of the lists of persons qualified to serve on juries; and such officer shall thereupon take down, in writing, from the said duplicate, the names of forty-eight persons qualified to serve on juries, with their additions, and places of abode, a copy whereof shall forthwith be delivered to the prosecutors or plaintiffs, their attornies or agents, and another copy thereof to the defendants, their attornies or agents, in such prosecutions and causes; and the said officer of the court aforesaid shall, at a time to be fixed by him for that purpose, strike out the names of twelve of the said persons, at the nomination of the prosecutors or plaintiffs, their attornies or agents, and also the names of twelve others of the said persons, at the nomination of the said defendants in such prosecutions and suits; and the twenty-four remaining persons shall be struck and summoned, and returned to the said court as jurors, for the trial of such issues.

XXI. Provided always, That in case the prosecutors or plaintiffs, or defendants, their attornies or agents, shall neglect or refuse to attend the officer at the time fixed for striking the names of twenty-four persons as aforesaid, or nominate the persons to struck out; then, and in such case, the said officer shall, and he is hereby required to strike out the names of such number of the said persons as such prosecutors or plaintiffs, or defendants, might have nominated to be struck out.

XXII. And be it further enacted, That the person or party who shall apply for such special jury as aforesaid, shall not only bear and pay the fees for striking such jury, but shall also pay and discharge all the expences occasioned by the trial of the cause by such special jury, and shall not have any further or other allowance for the same, upon taxation of costs, than such person or party would be intitled unto in case the cause had been tried by a common jury, unless the judge, before whom the cause is tried, shall, immediately after the trial, certify, in open court, under his hand, upon the back of the record, that the same was a cause proper to be tried by a special jury.

XXIII. And be it further enacted by the authority aforesaid, That, in all actions brought in any of the said courts, where it shall appear to the court in which such actions are depending, that it will be proper and necessary that the jurors who are to try the issues in any such actions, should have the view of the messuages, lands, or place in question, in order to their better understanding the evidence that will be given upon the trial of such issues; in every such case the respective courts in which such actions shall be depending may order the jury to the place in question, who then and there shall have the matters in question shewn them by two persons to be appointed by the court; and the special costs of all such views as allowed by the court, shall, before the trial, be paid by the party who moved for the view, (the adverse party not consenting thereto); and shall, at the taxation of the bill of costs, have the same allowed him, upon his recovering judgement in such trial; and upon all views with the consent of parties, ordered by the court, the costs thereof, as allowed by the court, shall, before trial, be equally paid by the said parties; and in the taxation of the bill of costs, the party recovering judgement shall have the sum by him paid allowed to him; any law, usage, or custom, to the contrary notwithstanding.

XXIV. And be it further enacted by the authority aforesaid, That if any action shall be brought against any sheriff, for what he shall do in execution, or by virtue of this act, he may plead the general issue, and give the special matter in evidence; and if a verdict shall be found for him, he shall recover treble costs.

Administration of Justice Act

May 20, 1774

An act for the impartial administration of justice in the cases of persons questioned for any acts done by them in the execution of the law, or for the suppression of riots and tumults, in the province of the Massachuset's Bay, in New England.

WHEREAS in his Majesty's province of Massachuset's Bay, in New England, an attempt hath lately been made to throw off the authority of the parliament of Great Britain over the said province, and an actual and avowed resistance, by open force, to the execution of certain acts of parliament, hath been suffered to take place, uncontrouled and unpunished, in defiance of his Majesty's authority, and to the subversion of all lawful government whereas, in the present disordered state of the said province, it is of the utmost importance to the general welfare thereof, and to the re-establishment of lawful authority throughout the same, that neither the magistrates acting in support of the laws, nor any of his Majesty's subjects aiding and assisting them therein, or in the suppression of riots and tumults, raised in opposition to the execution of the laws and statutes of this realm, should be discouraged from the proper discharge of their duty, by an apprehension, that in case of their being questioned for any acts done therein, they may be liable to be brought to trial for the same before persons who do not acknowledge the validity of the laws, in the execution thereof, or the authority of the magistrate in the support of whom, such acts had been done: in order therefore to remove every such discouragement from the minds of his Majesty's subjects, and to induce them, upon all proper occasions, to exert themselves in support of the public peace of the provinces, and of the authority of the King and parliament of Great Britain over the same; be it enacted by the King's most excellent majesty, by and with the advice and consent of the lords spiritual and temporal, and commons, in this present parliament assembled, and by the authority of the same, That if any inquisition or indictment shall be found, or if any appeal shall be sued or preferred against any person, for murder, or other capital offence, in the province of the Massachuset's Bay, and it shall appear, by information given upon oath to the governor, or, in his absence, to the lieutenant-governor of the said province, that the fact was committed by the person against whom such inquisition or indictment shall be found, or against whom such appeal shall be sued or preferred, as aforesaid, either in the execution of his duty as a magistrate, for the suppression of riots, or in the support of the laws of revenue, or in acting in his duty as an officer of revenue, or in acting under the direction and order of any magistrate, for the suppression of riots, or for the carrying into effect the laws of revenue, or in aiding and assisting in any of the cases aforesaid: and if it shall also appear, to the satisfaction of the said governor, or lieutenant-governor respectively, that an indifferent trial cannot be had within the said province, in that case, it shall and may be lawful for the governor, or lieutenant-governor, to direct, with the advice and consent of the council, that the inquisition, indictment, or appeal, shall be tried in some other of his Majesty's colonies, or in Great Britain; and for that purpose, to order. the person against whom such inquisition or indictment shall be found, or against whom such appeal shall be sued or preferred, as aforesaid, to be sent, under sufficient custody, to the place appointed for his trial, or to admit such person to bail, taking a recognizance, (which the said governor, or, in his absence, the lieutenant-governor, is hereby authorised to take), from such person, with sufficient sureries, to be approved of by the said governor, or, in his absence, the lieutenant-governor, in such sums of money as the said governor or, in his absence, the lieutenant-governor, shall deem reasonable for the personal appearance of such person, if the trial shall be appointed to be had in any other colony, before the governor, or lieutenant-governor, or commander in chief of such colony; and if the trial shall be appointed to be had in Great Britain, then before his Majesty's court of King's Bench, at a time to be mentioned in such recognizances; and the governor, or lieutenant-governor, or commander in chief of the colony where such trial shall be appointed to be had, or court of King's Bench, where the trial is appointed to be had in Great Britain, upon the appearance of such person, according to such recognizance, or in custody, shall either commit such person, or admit him to bail, until such trial; and which the said governor, or lieutenant-governor, or commander in chief, and court of King's Bench, are hereby authorised and impowered to do.

II. And, to prevent a failure of justice, from the want of evidence on the trial of any such inquisition, indictment or appeal, be it further enacted, That the governor, or, in his absence, the lieutenant-governor, shall, and he is hereby authorised and required, to bind in recognizances to his Majesty all such witnesses as the prosecutor or person against whom such inquisition or indictment shall be found, or appeal sued or preferred, shall desire to attend the trial of the said inquisition, indictment, or appeal, for their personal appearance, at the time and place of such trial, to give evidence: and the said governor, or in his absence, the lieutenant-governor, shall thereupon appoint a reasonable sum to be allowed for the expences of every such witness, and shall thereupon give to each witness a certificate, in writing, under his hand and seal, that such witness has entered into a recognizance to give evidence, and specifying the sum allowed for his expenses and the collector and collectors of the customs, or one of them, within the said province, upon the delivery of such certificate, are, and is hereby authorised and required, forthwith to pay to such witness the sum specified therein for his expences.

III. And be it further enacted by the authority aforesaid, That all prosecutors and witnesses, who shall be

www.milestonedocuments.com

under recognizances to appear in any of his Majesty's colonies in America, or in Great Britain, in pursuance of this art, shall be free from all arrests and restraints, in any action or suit to be commenced against them during their going to such colony, or coming to Great Britain, and their necessary stay and abiding there, on occasion of such prosecution, and returning again to the said province of the Massachusset's Bay.

IV. And be it further enacted by the authority aforesaid, That all and every his Majesty's, justices of the peace, and other justices and coroners, before whom any person shall be brought, charged with murder, or other capital crime, where it shall appear by proof, on oath, to such justices or coroners, that the fact was committed by such person, either in the execution of his duty as a magistrate, for the suppression of riots, or in the support of the laws of revenue, or in acting in his duty as an officer of revenue, or in acting under the direction and order of any magistrate, for the suppression of riots, or for the carrying into effect the laws of revenue, or in aiding and assisting in any of the cases aforesaid, are hereby authorized and required to admit every such person to brought before him or them, as aforesaid, to bail; any law, custom, or usage, to the contrary thereof in any-wise notwithstanding.

V. And be it further enacted by the authority aforesaid, That where it shall be made appear to the judges or justices of any court, within the said province of Massachuset's Bay, by any person, against whom any inquisition or indictment shall be found, or appeal sued or preferred for murder, or other capital crime, that the fact was committed by such person, either in the execution of his duty as a magistrate, for the suppression of riots, or in the support of the laws of revenue, or in acting in his duty as an officer of revenue, or in acting under the direction and order of any magistrate, for the suppression of riots, or for the carrying into effect the laws of revenue, or in aiding and assisting in any of the cases aforesaid, and that he intends to make application to the governor, or lieutenant-governor of the said province, that such inquisition, indictment, or appeal, may be tried in some other of his Majesty's colonies, or in Great Britain, the said judges or justices are hereby authorised and required to adjourn or postpone the trial of such inquisition, indictment, or appeal, for a reasonable time, and admit the person to bail, in order that he may make application to the governor, or lieutenant-governor, for the purpose aforesaid.

VI. And be it further enacted, That the governor, or, in his absence, the lieutenant governor, if he shall direct the trial to be had in any other of his Majesty's colonies, shall transmit the inquisition, indictment, or appeal, together with recognizances of the witnesses, and other recognizances, under the seal of the province, to the governor, or lieutenant-governor, or commander in chief of such other colony, who shall immediately issue a commission of Oyer and Terminer, and deliver, or cause to be delivered, the said inquisition, indictment, or appeal, with the said recognizances to the chief justice, and such other persons as have usually been commissioners of Oyer and Terminer, justices of assize, or general gaol delivery there; who shall have power to proceed upon the said inquisition, indictment, or appeal, as if the same had been returned, found, or preferred before them; and the trial shall thereupon proceed in like manner, to all intents and purposes, as if the offence had been committed in such place: and in case the governor, or, in his absence the lieutenant-governor, shall direct the trial to be had in Great Britain, he shall then transmit the inquisition, indictment or appeal; together with the recognizances, of the witnesses, and other recognizances, under the seal of the province to one of Majesty's principal secretaries of state, who shall deliver, or cause to be delivered, the same, to the master of the crown office to be filed of record in the court of King's Bench, and the inquisition, indictment, or appeal, shall be tried and proceeded upon, in the next term, or at such other time as the court shall appoint, at the bar of the court of King's Bench, in like manner to all intents and purposes, as if the offence had been committed in the county of Middlesex, or in any other county of that part of Great Britain called England, where the court of King's Bench shall fit, or else before such commissioners, and in such county, in that part of Great Britain called England, as shall be assigned by the King's majesty's commission, in like manner and form to all intents and purposes, as if such offence had been committed in the same county where such inquisition, indictment, or appeal, shall be so tried.

VII. And be it enacted by the authority aforesaid, That in case, on account of any error or defect in any indictment, which, in virtue or under the authority of this act, shall be transmitted to any other colony, or to Great Britain, the same shall be quashed, or judgement thereon arrested, or such indictment adjudged bad upon demurrer, it shall and may be lawful to prefer a new indictment or indictments against the person or persons accused in the said colony, to which such indictment, so quashed or adjudged bad shall have been transmitted, or before the grand jury of any county in Great Britain, in case such former indictment shall have been transmitted to Great Britain, in the same manner as could be done in case the party accused should return to the place where the offence was committed; and the grand jury and petty jury of such other colony or county in Great Britain shall have power to find and proceed upon such indictment or indictments, in the same manner as if the offence, by such indictment or indictments charged, had been committed within the limits of the colony or county for which such juries shall respectively be impanelled to serve.

VIII. And be it further enacted by the authority aforesaid, That this act, and every clause, provision, regulation, and thing, herein contained, shall commence and take effect upon the first day of June, one thousand seven hundred and seventy-four; and be, and continue in force, for and during the term of three years.

Quartering Act

June 2, 1774

An act for the better providing suitable quarters for officers and soldiers in his Majesty's service in North America.

WHEREAS doubts have been entertained, whether troops can be quartered otherwise than in barracks, in case barracks have been provided sufficient for the quartering of all officers and soldiers within any town, township, city, district, or place, within his Majesty's dominions in North America: And whereas it may frequently happen, from the situation of such barracks, that, if troops should be quartered therein, they would not be stationed where their presence may be necessary and required: be it therefore enacted by the King's most excellent majesty, by and with the advice and consent of the lords spiritual and temporal, and commons, in this present parliament assembled, and by the authority of the same, That, in such cases, it shall and may be lawful for the persons who now are, or may be hereafter, authorised be law, in any of the provinces within his Majesty's dominions in North America, and they are hereby respectively authorised, impowered, and directed, on the requisition of the officer who, for the time being, has the command of his Majesty's forces in North America, to cause any officers or soldiers in his Majesty's service to be quartered and billetted in such manner as is now directed by law, where no barracks are provided by the colonies.

II. And be it further enacted by the authority aforesaid, That if it shall happen at any time that any officers or soldiers in his Majesty's service shall remain within any of the said colonies without quarters, for the space of twenty-four hours after such quarters shall have been demanded, it shall and may be lawful for the governor of the province to order and direct such and so many uninhabited houses, out-houses, barns, or other buildings, as he shall think necessary to be taken, (making a reasonable allowance for the same), and make fit for the reception of such officers and soldiers, and to put and quarter such officers and soldiers therein, for such time as he shall think proper.

III. And be it further enacted by the authority aforesaid, That this act, and every thing herein contained, shall continue and be in force, in all his Majesty's dominions in North America, until the twenty-fourth day of March, one thousand seven hundred and seventy-six.

Quebec Act

June 22, 1774

An Act for making more effectual Provision for the Government of the Province of *Quebec* in *North America*.

Whereas His Majesty, by His Royal Proclamation, bearing Date the Seventh Day of *October*, in the Third Year of His Reign, thought fit to declare the Provisions which had been made in respect to certain Countries, Territories, and Islands in *America*, ceded to His Majesty by the definitive Treaty of Peace, Concluded at *Paris* on the Tenth Day of *February*, One thousand seven hundred and sixty-three: And whereas, by the Arrangements made by the said Royal Proclamation, a very large Extent of Country, within which there were several Colonies and Settlements of the Subjects of *France*, who claimed to remain therein under the Faith of the said Treaty, was left, without any Provision being made for the Administration of Civil Government therein; and certain Parts of the Territory of *Canada*, where sedentary Fisheries had been established and carried on by the Subjects of *France*, Inhabitants of the said Province of *Canada*, Under Grants and Concessions from the Government thereof, were annexed to the Government of *Newfoundland*, and thereby subjected to regulations inconsistent with the Nature of such Fisheries: May it therefore please Your most Excellent Majesty that it may be enacted; and be it

www.milestonedocuments.com

enacted by the King's most Excellent Majesty, by and with the Advice and Consent of the Lords Spiritual and Temporal, and Commons, in this present Parliament assembled, and by the Authority of the same, That all the Territories, Islands, and Countries in *North America*, belonging to the Crown of *Great Britain*, bounded on the South by a Line from the Bay of *Chaleurs*, along the High Lands which divide the Rivers that empty themselves into the River *Saint Lawrence* from those which fall into the Sea, to a Point in Forty-five Degrees of Northern Latitude, on the Eastern Bank of the River *Connecticut*, until, in the same Latitude, it meets the River *Saint Lawrence*; from thence up the Eastern Bank of the said River to the Lake *Ontario*; thence through the Lake *Ontario*, and the River commonly called *Niagara*; and thence along by the Eastern and Southeastern Bank of Lake *Erie*, following the said Bank, until the same shall be intersected by the Northern Boundary, granted by the Charter of the Province of *Pennsylvania*, in case the same shall be so intersected; and from thence along the the said Northern and Western Boundaries of the said Province, until the said Western Boundary strike the *Ohio*: But in case the said Bank of the said Lake shall not be found to be so intersected, then following the said Bank until it shall arrive at that Point of the said Bank which shall be nearest to the North-western Angle of the said Province of *Pennsylvania*, and thence, by a right Line, to the said North-western Angle of the said Province; and thence along the Western Boundary of the said Province, until it strike the River *Ohio*; and along the Bank of the said River, Westward, to the Banks of the *Mississippi*, and Northward to the Southern Boundary of the Territory granted to the Merchants Adventurers of *England*, trading to *Hudson's Bay*; and also all such Territories, Islands, and Countries, which have, since the Tenth of *February*, One thousand seven hundred and sixty-three, been made Part of the Government of *Newfoundland*, be, and they are hereby, during His Majesty's Pleasure, annexed to, and made Part and Parcel of, the Province of *Quebec*, as created and established by the said Royal Proclamation of the Seventh of *October*, One thousand seven hundred and sixty-three.

Provided always, That nothing herein contained, relative to the Boundary of the Province of *Quebec*, shall in anywise affect the Boundaries of any other Colony.

Provided always, and be it enacted, That nothing in this Act contained shall extend, or be construed to extend, to make void, or to vary or alter any Right, Title, or Possession, derived under any Grant, Conveyance, or otherwise howsoever, of or to any Lands within the said Province, or the Provinces thereto adjoining; but that the same shall remain and be in Force, and have Effect, as if this Act had never been made.

And Whereas the Provisions, made by the said Proclamation, in respect to the Civil Government of the said Province of *Quebec*, and the Powers and Authorities given to the Governor and other Civil Officers of the said Province, by the Grants and Commissions issued in consequence thereof, have been found, upon Experience, to be inapplicable to the State and Circumstances of the said Province, the Inhabitants whereof amounted, at the Conquest, to above Sixty-five thousand Persons professing the Religion of the Church of *Rome*, and enjoying an established Form of Constitution and System of Laws, by which their Persons and Property had been protected, governed, and ordered, for a long Series of Years, from the First Establishment of the said Province of *Canada*; be it therefore further enacted by the Authority aforesaid, That the said Proclamation, so far as the same relates to the said Province of *Quebec*, and the Commission under the Authority whereof the Government of the said Province is at present administered, and all and every the Ordinance and Ordinances made by the Governor and Council of *Quebec* for the Time being, relative to the Civil Government and Administration of Justice in the said Province, and all Commissions to Judges and other Officers thereof, be, and the same are hereby revoked, annulled, and made void, from and after the First Day of *May*, One thousand seven hundred and seventy-five.

And, for the more perfect Security and Ease of the Minds of the Inhabitants of the said Province, it is hereby declared, That His Majesty's Subjects, professing the Religion of the Church of *Rome* of and in the said Province of *Quebec*, may have, hold, and enjoy, the free Exercise of the Religion of the Church of *Rome*, subject to the king's Supremacy, declared and established by an Act, made in the First Year of the Reign of Queen *Elizabeth*, over all the Dominions and Countries which then did, or there-after should belong, the Imperial Crown of this Realm; and that the Clergy of the said Church may hold, receive, and enjoy, their accustomed Dues and Rights, with respect to such persons only as shall profess the said Religion.

Provided nevertheless, That it shall be lawful for His Majesty, His Heirs or Successors, to make such Provision out of the rest of the said accustomed

Document Text

Dues and Rights, for the Encouragement of the Protestant Religion, and for the Maintenance and Support of a Protestant Clergy within the said Province, as he or they shall, from Time to Time, think necessary and expedient.

Provided always, and be it enacted, That no Person, professing the Religion of the Church of *Rome*, and residing in the said Province, shall be obliged to take the Oath required by the said Statute passed in the First Year of the Reign of Queen *Elizabeth*, or any other Oaths substituted by any other Act in the Place thereof; but that every such Person who, by the said Statute is required to take the Oath therein mentioned, shall be obliged, and is hereby required, to take and subscribe the following Oath before the Governor, or such other Person in such Court of Record as His Majesty shall appoint, who are hereby authorized to administer the same; *videlicet*,

I A. B. *do sincerely promise and swear, That I Will be faithful, and bear true Allegiance to His Majesty King* GEORGE, *and him will defend to the utmost of my Power, against all traiterous Conspiracies, and Attempts whatsoever, which shall be made against His Person, Crown, and Dignity; and I will do my utmost Endeavour to disclose and make known to His Majesty, His Heirs and Successors, all Treasons, and traiterous Conspiracies, and Attempts, which I shall know to be against Him, or any of Them; and all this I do swear without any Equivocation, mental Evasion, or secret Reservation, and renouncing all Pardons and Dispensations from any Power or Person whomsoever to the Contrary.*

So HELP ME GOD.

And every such Person, who shall neglect or refuse to take the said Oath before mentioned, shall incur and be liable to the same Penalties, Forfeitures, Disabilities, and Incapacities, as he would have incurred and been liable to for neglecting or refusing to take the Oath required by the said Statute passed in the First Year of the Reign of Queen *Elizabeth*.

And be it further enacted by the Authority aforesaid, That all His Majesty's *Canadian* Subjects, within the Province of *Quebec*, the religious Orders and Communities only excepted, may also hold and enjoy their Property and Possessions, together with all Customs and Usages relative thereto, and all other their Civil Rights, in as large, ample, and beneficial Manner, as if the said Proclamation, Commissions, Ordinances, and other Acts and Instruments, had not been made, and as may consist with their Allegiance to His Majesty, and Subjection to the Crown and Parliament of *Great Britain*; and that in all Matters of Controversy, relative to Property and Civil Rights, Resort shall be had to the Laws of *Canada*, as the Rule for the Decision of the same; and all Causes that shall hereafter be instituted in any of the Courts of Justice, to be appointed within and for the said Province, by His Majesty, His Heirs and Successors, shall, with respect to such Property and Rights, be determined agreeably to the said Laws and Customs of *Canada*, until they shall be varied or altered by any Ordinances that shall, from Time to Time, be passed in the said Province by the Governor, Lieutenant Governor, or Commander in Chief, for the Time being, by and with the Advice and Consent of the Legislative Council of the same, to be appointed in Manner herein-after mentioned.

Provided always, That nothing in this Act contained shall extend, or be construed to extend, to any Lands that have been granted by His Majesty, or shall hereafter be granted by His Majesty, His Heirs and Successors, to be holden in free and common Soccage.

Provided also, That it shall and may be lawful to and for every Person that is Owner of any Lands, Goods, or Credits, in the said Province, and that has a Right to alienate the said Lands, Goods, or Credits, in his or her Life-time, by Deed of Sale, Gift, or otherwise, to devise or bequeath the same at his or her Death, by his or her last Will and Testament; any Law, Usage, or Custom, heretofore or now prevailing in the Province, to the Contrary hereof in any-wise notwithstanding; such Will being executed, either according to the Laws of Canada, or according to the Forms prescribed by the Laws of *England*.

And Whereas the Certainty and Lenity of the Criminal Law of *England*, and the Benefits and Advantages resulting from the Use of it, have been sensibly felt by the Inhabitants, from an Experience of more than Nine Years, during which it has been uniformly administered; be it therefore further enacted by the Authority aforesaid, That the same shall continue to be administered, and shall be observed as Law in the Province of *Quebec*, as well in the Description and Quality of the Offence as in the Method of Prosecution and Trial; and the Punishments and Forfeitures thereby inflicted to the Exclusion of every other Rule of Criminal Law, or Mode of Proceeding thereon, which did or might prevail in the said Province before the Year of our Lord One thousand seven hundred and sixty-four; any Thing in this Act to the Contrary thereof in any Respect notwithstanding; subject nevertheless to such Alterations and Amendments as the Governor, Lieutenant-governor, or Com-

www.milestonedocuments.com

Document Text

mander in Chief for the Time being, by and with the Advice and Consent of the legislative Council of the said Province, hereafter to be appointed, shall, from Time to Time, cause to be made therein, in Manner herein-after directed.

And Whereas it may be necessary to ordain many Regulations for the future Welfare and good Government of the Province of *Quebec*, the Occasions of which cannot now be foreseen, nor, without much Delay and Inconvenience, be provided for, without intrusting that Authority, for a certain Time, and under proper Restrictions, to Persons resident there: And whereas it is at present inexpedient to call an Assembly; be it therefore enacted by the Authority aforesaid, That it shall and may be lawful for His Majesty, His Heirs and Successors, by Warrant under His or Their Signet or Sign Manual, and with the Advice of the Privy Council, to constitute and appoint a Council for the Affairs of the Province of *Quebec*, to consist of such Persons resident there, not exceeding Twenty-three, nor less than Seventeen, as His Majesty, His Heirs and Successors, shall be pleased to appoint; and, upon the Death, Removal, or Absence of any of the Members of the said Council, in like Manner to constitute and appoint such and so many other Person or Persons as shall be necessary to supply the Vacancy or Vacancies; which Council, so appointed and nominated, or the major Part thereof, shall have Power and Authority to make Ordinances for the Peace, Welfare, and good Government, of the said Province, with the Consent of His Majesty's Governor, or, in his Absence, of the Lieutenant-governor, or Commander in Chief for the Time being.

Provided always, That nothing in this Act contained shall extend to authorise or impower the said legislative Council to lay any Taxes or Duties within the said Province, such Rates and Taxes only excepted as the Inhabitants of any Town or District within the said Province may be authorised by the said Council to assess, levy, and apply, within the said Town or District, for the Purpose of making Roads, erecting and repairing publick Buildings, or for any other Purpose respecting the local Convenience and Oeconomy of such Town or District.

Provided also, and be it enacted by the Authority aforesaid, That every Ordinance so to be made, shall, within Six Months, be transmitted by the Governor, or, in his Absence, by the Lieutenant-governor, or Commander in Chief for the Time being, and laid before His Majesty for His Royal Approbation; and if His Majesty shall think fit to disallow thereof, the same shall cease and be void from the Time that His Majesty's Order in Council thereupon shall be promulgated at *Quebec*.

Provided also, That no Ordinance touching Religion, or by which any Punishment may be inflicted greater than Fine or Imprisonment for Three Months, shall be of any Force or Effect, until the same shall have received His Majesty's Approbation.

Provided also, That no Ordinance shall be passed at any Meeting of the Council where less than a Majority of the whole Council is present, or at any Time except between the First Day of *January* and the First Day of *May*, unless upon some urgent Occasion, in which Case every Member thereof resident at *Quebec*, or within Fifty Miles thereof, shall be personally summoned by the Governor, or, in his Absence, by the Lieutenant-governor, or Commander in Chief for the Time being, to attend the same.

And be it further enacted by the Authority aforesaid, That nothing herein contained shall extend, or be construed to extend, to prevent or hinder His Majesty, His Heirs and Successors, by His or Their Letters Patent under the Great Seal of *Great Britain* from erecting, constituting, and appointing, such Courts of Criminal, Civil, and Ecclesiastical Jurisdiction within and for the said Province of *Quebec*, and appointing, from Time to Time, the Judges and Officers thereof, as His Majesty, His Heirs and Successors, shall think necessary and proper for the Circumstances of the said Province.

Provided always, and it is hereby enacted, That nothing in this Act contained shall extend, or be construed to extend, to repeal or make void, within the said Province of *Quebec*, any Act or Acts of the Parliament of *Great Britain* heretofore made, for prohibiting, restraining, or regulating, the Trade or Commerce of His Majesty's Colonies and Plantations in *America*; but that all and every the said Acts, and also all Acts of Parliament heretofore made concerning or respecting the said Colonies and Plantations, shall be, and are hereby declared to be, in Force, within the said Province of *Quebec*, and every Part thereof.

Finis.

gion, laws, and liberties, may not be subverted; upon which appointment and direction, the said delegates being now assembled in a full and free representation[1] of these Colonies, taking into their most serious consideration the best means for attaining the ends aforesaid, do, in the first place, (as their ancestors in like cases have usually done,) for vindicating and asserting their rights and liberties, declare—

1. That the power of making laws for ordering or regulating the internal polity of these Colonies, is, within the limits of each Colony, respectively and exclusively vested in the Provincial Legislature of such Colony; and that all statutes for ordering or regulating the internal polity of the said Colonies, or any of them, in any manner or in any case whatsoever, are illegal and void.

at these arbitrary proceedings of parliament and administration, have severally elected, constituted, and appointed deputies to meet and sit in general congress, in the city of Philadelphia, in order to obtain such establishment, as that their religion, laws, and liberties may not be subverted:

Whereupon the deputies so appointed being now assembled, in a full and free representation of these Colonies, taking into their most serious consideration, the best means of attaining the ends aforesaid, do, in the first place, as Englishmen, their ancestors in like cases have usually done, for asserting and vindicating their rights and liberties, declare,

That the inhabitants of the English Colonies in North America, by the immutable laws of nature, the principles of the English constitution, and the several charters or compacts, have the following Rights:

Resolved, N. C. D. 1. That they are entitled to life, liberty, & property, and they have never ceded to any sovereign power whatever, a right to dispose of either without their consent.

The Declaration and Resolves of the First Continental Congress (Library of Congress)

Declaration and Resolves of the First Continental Congress

1774

"The inhabitants of the English colonies in North-America ... are entitled to life, liberty and property."

Overview

The Declaration and Resolves of the First Continental Congress, adopted on October 14, 1774, is the Continental Congress's most important proclamation of principles and demonstrates the widening gap between the American colonists and their English motherland. Issued roughly six months before fighting broke out between the colonists and the British at Lexington and Concord, the document reflects the colonies' continued attempts to remain loyal to the Crown while disputing the authority, or sovereignty, of Parliament to legislate for or tax the colonies without their representation.

The grievances that Congress articulates in its Declaration and Resolves repeat the complaints of the Stamp Act Congress and foreshadow those that the Second Continental Congress repeats and embellishes in the Declaration of Independence. The Declaration and Resolves expresses special concern over British taxation, perceived abuses of the judicial system, the continued presence of the British army in North America, and English recognition of Catholicism in Canada. Whereas Thomas Jefferson would phrase the Declaration of Independence almost solely in terms of the rights of man (natural rights), the Declaration and Resolves continues to express the colonists' beliefs that they were, as English citizens, entitled to the same rights as other Englishmen; the colonists also continued to rely on the rights that they thought the king had guaranteed them in the charters authorizing the establishment of the colonies.

Context

Tension had been building between the thirteen North American colonies since the end of the Seven Years' War in 1763, through which Britain had secured Canada. Ending a period of neglect that Britain had pursued in the colonies before the war, England increased the presence of its troops in America during this conflict and thought that it was appropriate to tax the colonies for the armies' continuing expenses. British leaders thought that their legislature, Parliament, represented all English citizens, including those who had settled in America, and could thus exercise sovereignty over them. Americans increasingly rejected this view, known as "virtual representation," for "actual representation," under which Parliament could represent only areas that had elected representatives. Since American colonists were not properly represented in Parliament, Patriots concluded that Parliament could neither legislate for nor tax the colonies—functions that should be therefore reserved for colonial assemblies.

Britain challenged this assumption when it began enacting a series of revenue measures, beginning with the Sugar Act (1764) and culminating in the Stamp Act (1765). In Virginia, Patrick Henry introduced a resolution, adopted by the House of Burgesses, asserting that only it had the right to tax its citizens. Massachusetts issued a call that resulted in the convocation of representatives from nine of the thirteen colonies at the Stamp Act Congress in October, 1765. This congress petitioned for the laws' repeal and resolved not to import items subject to such taxes. The petition, along with mob action in the streets and a change of ministries in Britain, led Parliament to repeal the Stamp Act. At the same time, however, Parliament asserted through the Declaratory Act (1766) that it still had taxing power. Later, with the adoption of the Townshend Revenue Act in 1767, Parliament enacted new duties. These duties, together with vigorous methods of collection and the continued presence of British troops in American colonies, provided additional sources of friction, such as the actions of a mob that led to the so-called Boston Massacre of March 5, 1770, in which frightened British troops fired into a crowd, killing five people.

In time, the British repealed all of their taxes except for a token tax on tea. Continued colonial concern over this assertion of parliamentary sovereignty led colonial Patriots, dressed as Indians, to toss English tea into Boston Harbor. The British retaliated with a series of measures known as the Coercive Acts (or Intolerable Acts), which included shutting down Boston Harbor. The Virginia House of Burgesses, meeting in Richmond, expressed support for the Bostonians. As in the earlier Stamp Act crisis, colonists sent representatives, this time to Philadelphia, to articulate their grievances and consider collective action.

Like the Stamp Act Congress that had preceded it, the First Continental Congress was convened to articulate the

Time Line

1754	■ The Seven Years' War begins.
1763	■ **February 10** Treaty of Paris is signed, ending Seven Years' War; with the end of the war, Britain stopped its policy of "salutary [beneficial] neglect" of colonial affairs.
1764	■ **April 5** The British Parliament adopts the Sugar Act.
1765	■ **March 22** Parliament adopts the Stamp Act, to go into effect on November 1. ■ **May 15** Parliament adopts the Quartering Act, obligating colonies to pay for the support of troops. ■ **October 19** The Stamp Act Congress, meeting in New York City, adopts the Declaration of Rights.
1766	■ **March 18** Parliament repeals the Stamp Act but adopts the Declaratory Act.
1767	■ **June 29** Parliament adopts the Townshend Revenue Act, taxing a variety of colonial goods.
1770	■ **March 5** Parliament repeals most of the Townshend Revenue Act; five colonists are killed by British gunfire in the so-called Boston Massacre.
1773	■ **April 27** Parliament adopts the Tea Act, partly in an attempt to aid the East India Company. ■ **December 16** Boston Tea Party destroys British tea.

colonists's grievances against Parliament. The Massachusetts House of Representatives issued the call on June 17, 1774, for a meeting in Philadelphia for which two states had already made preparations. In time, fifty-five delegates, from all colonies except Georgia, sent representatives to meet in Carpenter's Hall, near the Pennsylvania State House, or Independence Hall.

As with the Stamp Act Congress, each colony had a single vote. Congress chose Virginia's Peyton Randolph, chairman of that colony's House of Burgesses, as its president, and Charles Thomson of Pennsylvania as its secretary. Other notable delegates included John and Samuel Adams of Massachusetts; Roger Sherman and Silas Deane of Connecticut; John Jay of New York; William Livingston of New Jersey; John Dickinson of Pennsylvania; Caesar Rodney of Delaware; Samuel Chase of Maryland; Richard Henry Lee, George Washington, Patrick Henry, Benjamin Harrison, and Edmund Pendleton of Virginia; and John Rutledge of South Carolina. The delegates created two committees. One committee, composed of two delegates from each colony, was commissioned to prepare a statement of colonial rights, their infringements, and the means of redressing them. The second committee, consisting of one representative from each colony, was commissioned to report on laws affecting colonial trade and manufacturing. Meanwhile, John Sullivan of New Hampshire prepared the first draft of the Declaration and Resolves.

Historians often divide members of the convention into moderate (conservative) delegates like John Jay of New York and Joseph Galloway of Pennsylvania, who were desperately trying to maintain ties to the mother country, and radicals like John and Samuel Adams and Patrick Henry, who already seemed determined to seek independence. Radicals gained the upper hand in authoring the Declaration and Resolves of the First Congress, yet the document called for peaceful resistance rather than armed force.

Explanation and Analysis of the Document

The Declaration and Resolves begins with six introductory paragraphs. These are followed by ten numbered resolutions, two more paragraphs of explanation, another multiparagraph resolution specifically targeting British laws that Congress considered unconstitutional, and a summary conclusion.

◆ Seven Introductory Paragraphs

The first paragraph conveys the colonists' perception that the end of the Seven Years' War had changed the way the British Parliament treated the colonies. At that time, Congress believed Parliament ceased enacting measures simply designed to regulate the trade of its empire and began imposing taxes to collect revenue. Although Britain did not have a single written document designated as a constitution, it had established regularized understandings and procedures that the colonists thought Parliament was now violating and that Americans therefore labeled unconstitutional. Congress registered special concern over the expansion of jurisdiction of admiralty courts, which they thought undermined traditional freedoms that England's system of common, or judge-made, law had provided.

Congress continues to express concern about admiralty courts in the second paragraph. It points out that judges of such courts depended on the king for their offices and salaries. Moreover, such courts could try Americans for their offenses outside their own colony and, indeed, in England itself, where they were far less likely to receive a sympathetic hearing.

The third paragraph focuses on the immediate catalyst of Congress, namely, the Parliament's adoption of three of the statutes commonly referred to (although not here) as the Intolerable Acts. These laws, which Parliament largely adopted in reaction to the Boston Tea Party, respectively halted commerce in Boston, rearranged its government, and provided for the suppression of riotous assemblies. The third paragraph also focuses on the Quebec Act, a separate law that had allowed for the establishment of the Roman Catholic Church in Canada at a time when all North American colonies to the south were predominately Protestant. This law also left Canada without effective representative government.

Paragraph 4 denounces Britain's dissolution of colonial assemblies and what Congress regarded as its contempt for colonial petitions. At a time when English law operated according to the legal fiction that "the king can do no wrong" and when Congress was holding out hope that the king would respond positively to its grievances against Parliament, Congress specifically blamed "his Majesty's ministers of state" for this reception rather than the king himself.

Although Congress was designated as "continental," most delegates probably continued to think of themselves as Englishmen or as citizens of their individual colonies (or both) rather than as Americans. Paragraph 5 accordingly lists the twelve colonies in attendance by name, much as the preamble to the Articles of Confederation (proposed in 1777 and ratified in 1781) would do; by contrast, the preamble of the U.S. Constitution, which created a stronger national government, refers to "We the People of the United States" rather than listing states individually. In paragraph 5 of the Declaration and Resolves, Congress expresses its purpose as that of preventing the subversion of colonial "religion, laws, and liberties."

Paragraph 6 further focuses on colonial rights, which it describes as having three sources. These are "the immutable laws of nature, the principles of the English constitution, and the several charters or compacts." The colonists' first claim, which appears to have been its most radical and controversial, rests on natural rights; these subsequently became the primary foundation for the Declaration of Independence, which the Second Continental Congress adopted in July 1776. The second claim indicates that those who adopted the resolution very much continued to view themselves as British subjects, entitled to all rights—including the principle of "no taxation without representation"—of those citizens who lived within Great Britain

Time Line

1774

- **June 1**
  Britain closes Boston Harbor under authority of the Boston Port Bill.
- **June 17**
  Massachusetts calls for a continental congress to meet in Philadelphia.
- **June 22**
  The Quebec Act recognizes the Roman Catholic Church in Canada and continues to leave Canada without representative government.
- **Summer**
  James Wilson authors *Considerations on the Nature and Extent of the Legislative Authority of the British Parliament,* and Thomas Jefferson authors *A Summary View of the Rights of British America.*
- **September 5**
  The First Continental Congress begins meeting.
- **September 17**
  Massachusetts delegation presents Congress with the Suffolk County Resolutions.
- **September 28**
  Joseph Galloway proposes a plan of union between Britain and the colonies that somewhat resembles the later English commonwealth system but which Congress rejects.
- **October 14**
  Congress issues its Declaration and Resolves.
- **October 20**
  Congress issues the Continental Association, providing for nonimportation and nonconsumption of British goods.
- **October 26**
  The First Continental Congress adjourns.

1775

- **April 19**
  Fighting breaks out between colonial and British soldiers at Lexington and Concord.

www.milestonedocuments.com

Time Line

1776

- **January 9**
Thomas Paine publishes *Common Sense*, questioning the colonists' continued allegiance to the English king.

- **July 2**
The Second Continental Congress agrees to a resolution for independence, offered the previous month by Richard Henry Lee.

- **July 4**
The Second Continental Congress adopts a modified version of Thomas Jefferson's Declaration of Independence.

itself. Congress rests its third claim, which arguably most closely approximates North Americans' later reliance on state and national constitutions, on rights that the colonists traced to the charters the king had issued when the New World was first colonized.

◆ The Numbered Resolutions

Congress indicates that its resolutions had been adopted N.C.D. This abbreviation of the Latin *nemine contradicente* means "no one contradicting" and thus indicates that the states had adopted the resolutions unanimously.

The Declaration of Independence would refer in its opening paragraph to the rights of "life, liberty, and the pursuit of happiness." In a similar but not identical fashion, the first numbered resolution of the Declaration and Resolves refers to the rights, often associated with the English social-contract philosopher John Locke (1632–1704), of "life, liberty and property." Locke had argued that such rights were inalienable. Similarly, Congress observes that it had never "ceded," or granted, authority over these rights to "any foreign power" to "dispose" of them without their consent.

Lest Britain argue that the colonists had forfeited their rights when they moved to the New World, the second resolution indicates the congressional belief that the colonists brought their rights with them when they immigrated to America. This was consistent with arguments that Thomas Jefferson had made in the summer of 1774 in *A Summary View of the Rights of British America*. Whereas the second resolution focuses on the rights that colonists possessed when they immigrated, the third resolution argues that they and their descendants continued to possess such rights consistent with "their local and other circumstances." The sixth resolution reiterates that colonial rights included the "benefit of such of the English statutes, as existed at the time of their colonization; and which they have, by experience, respectively found to be applicable to their several local and other circumstances."

Consistent with both English and American views of the importance of republican, or representative, government, the fourth and longest resolution (apparently designed chiefly by John Adams of Massachusetts and James Duane of New York) identifies the "right in the people to participate in their legislative council" as fundamental to "English liberty, and ... all free government." Without using the term, this resolution further outlines the American view of actual representation, which stressed that citizens had to elect representatives to representative assemblies before such bodies could tax them. As the dispute with Britain progressed, most Americans acknowledged, as Congress does in this paragraph, that the king presided over the entire empire and that royal vetoes of colonial legislation and parliamentary attempts to regulate "external commerce" were thus justified. Congress just as heartily rejects the imposition of "every idea of taxation internal or external, for raising a revenue on the subjects, in America, without their consent." Although this resolution does not specifically say so, most Americans traced the principle of "no taxation without representation" to the Magna Carta, an agreement with his barons that King John had signed in 1215 and that subsequently became one of the landmarks of English and American liberties. Congress argues that only its own colonial assemblies had the power to legislate for or to enact direct taxes upon them.

The fifth resolution ties American grievances over the content of parliamentary legislation to the means that Britain used to enforce it. English citizens were justly proud of their system of common law, which developed from precedents accumulated over time by independent judges who were largely free of royal domination. Trial by jurymen from a person's own vicinity, or vicinage, was an especially valuable right that Americans feared was being taken from them by the transference of trials to admiralty courts, in which such a right was not recognized as it would later be in state constitutions and in the Sixth and Seventh Amendments of the U.S. Constitution.

Resolutions 6 and 7 attempt to reinforce common-law protections by appeals to English laws that had been in effect at the time of North American colonization and to royal charters and colonial codes. Colonists continued to insist that they were bound to England not by allegiance to Parliament, in which they were not represented, but by allegiance to the king, who held the empire together and who had signed the colonial charters. In a phrase that the First Amendment to the U.S. Constitution would later echo, Congress affirms in Resolution 8 its "right peaceably to assemble, consider of their grievances, and petition the king." It dismisses all attempts to deny such rights as illegal.

Contemporary theorists known as republicans, who constituted an important strand of colonial thinking, stressed the obligations of citizens to maintain free government. Republicans promoted militia service but feared professional armies, especially those composed of mercenaries, who might have interests separate from and hearts less sympathetic toward those they were commissioned to defend. Resolution 9 accordingly argues that such standing armies, like taxes, were illegal, short of consent as expressed through colonial assemblies.

This French engraving depicts the First Continental Congress in session in Philadelphia in 1774. (Library of Congress)

Resolution 10 stresses the need for "the constituent branches of the legislature" to be "independent of each other." It accordingly protests the role of royal councils in exercising legislative powers, arguably presaging later arguments for separating the powers of government into separate legislative, executive, and judicial branches.

In a subsequent paragraph, Congress reiterates both the "indubitable [undeniable] rights and liberties" of itself and its "constituents," albeit focusing chiefly on "representatives in their several provincial legislature[s]." Perhaps anticipating the much broader list of colonial grievances that the Declaration of Independence later articulated, Congress further observes that it was passing over other grievances from "an ardent desire, that harmony and mutual intercourse of affection and interest may be restored." Although this language sounds conciliatory, Congress charges that British actions, taken as a whole, demonstrate "a system formed to enslave America." Observing the manner in which British laws since the Seven Years' War had asserted new powers over the colonies, members of the First Continental Congress, like those of the Second Continental Congress that followed, perceived a broader design inimical to colonial liberties. Significantly, in objecting to the operation of admiralty courts in its next resolution, Congress refers at one point to the violation of "ancient limits."

◆ Final Resolution

In a summary resolution, Congress identifies the acts that the British Parliament had adopted and needed to repeal in order to restore "harmony." These include a variety of revenue acts as well as laws that permitted the deprivation of jury trials, exempted prosecutors from liability for baseless prosecutions, permitted trials outside the colonies, closed down Boston Harbor, and otherwise altered colonial governments.

One result of the Seven Years' War had been British acquisition of Canada, which had been largely settled by French-speaking people, who were predominately Roman Catholic. In attempting to reconcile Canadians to British rule, Britain had recognized the Catholic religion in the Quebec Act of 1774. The thirteen colonies to the south feared and objected to such recognition. At a time when much of Europe had been torn apart by wars between Catholics and Protestants, Congress observes the danger of "so total a dissimilarity of religion, law and government … of the neighboring British colonies" and reminds the British that their own assistance in the form of "blood and treasure" had helped conquer North America from the French. Despite such complaints, on October 26, 1774, Congress

John Jay was a key moderate delegate at the First Continental Congress. (AP Photo/Robert Fridenberg)

www.milestonedocuments.com

John Sullivan of New Hampshire prepared the first draft of the Declaration and Resolves of the First Continental Congress. (AP Photo/Robert Fridenberg)

adopted a letter to the inhabitants of Quebec soliciting their support in the controversy with England. Moreover, when the Second Continental Congress later drafted the Articles of Confederation, it included a clause that would have allowed Canada to join the new association without further action on the part of the former British colonies.

Congress followed with condemnations of the laws requiring colonies to quarter British troops and to host a standing army without colonial consent.

◆ The Final Paragraph

In time, the accumulation of colonial grievances against the British led to war, but in October 1774 Congress continued to hope for a restoration of "that state, in which both countries found happiness and prosperity." Its Declaration and Resolves thus ends with three forceful but peaceful measures. The first is "to enter into a non-importation, non-consumption, and non-exportation agreement or association." The second is "to prepare an address to the people of Great-Britain, and a memorial to the inhabitants of British America." And the third is to "to prepare a loyal address to his majesty, agreeable to resolutions already entered into." Congress had already agreed to a nonimportation agreement. Congress approved an address to the English people on October 21, 1774, and a petition to the king later that month.

Audience

The final paragraph of the Declaration and Resolves indicates that Congress was addressing at least three audiences. At a time when sentiment in America was still split between Loyalists, who wanted to remain loyal to England, and Patriots, who were beginning to think that the colonies might in time have to declare their independence, Congress was seeking to assure the former that it was proceeding cautiously according to established forms and the latter that it was adequately defending their liberties.

By evoking their rights as English citizens, the colonists also sought to appeal to public opinion within Britain. The colonists hoped that British citizens who cherished the protections of common law and the principle of no taxation without representation would recognize that a threat to liberty in the colonies was also a threat to their own. Significantly, some members of Parliament were sympathetic to colonial arguments that it had no right to tax them.

Congress continued to adhere to the idea, increasingly becoming something of a legal fiction, that the colonies could maintain their allegiance to the English king without recognizing the sovereignty of Parliament. The members of Congress still hoped that the king would reward their loyalty by protecting the liberties they thought they were advancing. In the concluding paragraph of the Declaration and Resolves, Congress does not specifically address Parliament, presumably because it did not recognize Parliament's authority over the colonies. Instead, Congress appeals to the king against Parliament—whereas in the Declaration of Independence, Congress, disappointed with the king's response, would direct most of its grievances against his actions.

Although it mixed appeals for natural rights with appeals from the rights of English citizens and the authority of royal charters, the Declaration and Resolves, unlike the Declaration of Independence, does not otherwise appeal to the sentiments of all humankind or to the citizens or sovereigns of other nations. Members of Congress had little reason to believe that appeals to their rights as English citizens would resonate in nations that did not recognize similar rights. Congress was not calling for war, but had it been doing so its emphasis on common-law rights and on the rights of Protestants was hardly likely to secure foreign allies.

Impact

Although Congress regarded this document as conciliatory, the British regarded it as but another in a line of incessant complaints from the colonists. Adhering to the doctrine of virtual representation, the British continued to assert that Parliament had authority to legislate on behalf of the colonies. Many British leaders further regarded colonial attempts to distinguish between internal and external legislation as inconsistent or ill conceived. King George III and his key ministers persuaded Parliament to appropriate increased funds for British troops in North America and sent secret orders telling the troops to squelch colonial

Essential Quotes

"The good people of the several colonies … justly alarmed at these arbitrary proceedings of parliament and administration, have severally elected, constituted, and appointed deputies to meet, and sit in general Congress, in the city of Philadelphia, in order to obtain such establishment, as that their religion, laws, and liberties, may not be subverted."

(Paragraph 5)

"That the inhabitants of the English colonies in North-America, by the immutable laws of nature, the principles of the English constitution, and the several charters or compacts, have the following RIGHTS."

(Paragraph 6)

"They are entitled to life, liberty and property: and they have never ceded to any foreign power whatever, a right to dispose of either without their consent."

(Paragraph 7)

"The foundation of English liberty, and of all free government, is a right in the people to participate in their legislative council: and as the English colonists are not represented, and from their local and other circumstances, cannot properly be represented in the British parliament, they are entitled to a free and exclusive power of legislation in their several provincial legislatures, where their right of representation can alone be preserved, in all cases of taxation and internal polity, subject only to the negative of their sovereign, in such manner as has been heretofore used and accustomed."

(Paragraph 10)

"They have a right peaceably to assemble, consider of their grievances, and petition the king."

(Paragraph 14)

www.milestonedocuments.com

opposition. Parliament further responded to American plans of nonimportation and nonconsumption by restricting colonial trade.

The outbreak of fighting at Lexington and Concord the following April as well as the publication of Thomas Paine's *Common Sense* in January 1776 undermined colonial allegiance to the English king. On August 23, 1775, George III issued the Proclamation for Suppressing Rebellion and Sedition against the colonies. The colonists responded in July 1776 with the Declaration of Independence, and fighting expanded into full-scale war.

The Declaration and Resolves continues to be of value. The document articulates the views of American Patriots at a critical point in their history. It also points to more timeless principles of natural rights and representative government that Americans later incorporated in both state and federal constitutions.

Related Documents

Dickinson, John. *Letters from a Farmer in Pennsylvania: To the Inhabitants of the British Colonies*. Their Own Words Web site. http://deila.dickinson.edu/theirownwords/title/0004.htm. Accessed on July 8, 2007. First published in 1767 and 1768 and then reprinted in 1774, this series of letters by a colonial moderate shows how even such individuals took issue with British revenue acts.

Jefferson, Thomas. "A Summary View of the Rights of British America." Colonial Williamsburg Web site. http://www.history.org/Almanack/life/politics/sumview.cfm. Accessed on July 8, 2007. This work shows Thomas Jefferson's views of American rights at the time of the First Continental Congress.

Jensen, Merrill, ed. *Tracts of the American Revolution, 1763–1776*. Indianapolis, Ind.: Hackett Pub. Co., 2003. This book contains tracts and pamphlets from the end of the Seven Years' War to the writing of the Declaration of Independence.

Seabury, Samuel. *Letters of a Westchester Farmer, 1774–1775*. New York: Da Capo Press, 1970. Project Canterbury Web site. http://anglicanhistory.org/usa/seabury/farmer/. Accessed on July 9, 2007. This pamphlet contains four essays by a prominent Loyalist clergyman essentially taking the British side of the issues and questioning the work of the First Continental Congress.

Smith, Paul H., ed. *Letters of Delegates to Congress, 1774–1789*. Washington: Library of Congress, 1976–2000. This work contains contemporary letters of the individuals who were involved in the decision making in the early Congresses.

Wilson, James. "Considerations on the Nature and Extent of the Legislative Authority of the British Parliament." East Tennessee State University History Department Web site. http://www.etsu.edu/cas/history/docs/parlimentauth.htm. Accessed on July 9, 2007. This work presents the developing colonial view that Parliament did not have the right to legislate for or impose taxes upon the colonies.

Bibliography

■ Articles

Johnson, Richard R. "'Parliamentary Egotisms': The Clash of Legislatures in the Making of the American Revolution." *Journal of American History* 74 (September 1987): 338–362.

Lovejoy, David S. "'Rights Imply Equality': The Case against Admiralty Jurisdiction in America, 1764–1776." *William and Mary Quarterly* 3rd ser., 16 (October 1959): 459–484.

Morgan, Edmund S. "Colonial Ideas of Parliamentary Power, 1764–1766." *William and Mary Quarterly* 3rd ser., 5 (July 1948): 311–341.

Slaughter, Thomas P. "The Tax Man Cometh: Ideological Opposition to Internal Taxes, 1760–1790." *William and Mary Quarterly* 3rd ser., 41 (October 1984): 566–591.

■ Books

Bowling, Kenneth R., and Donald R. Kennon, eds. *Inventing Congress: Origins and Establishment of the First Federal Congress*. Athens: Ohio University Press, 1999.

Burnett, Edmund Cody. *The Continental Congress*. Westport, Conn.: Greenwood Press, 1975.

Gammon, C. L. *The Continental Congress: America's Forgotten Government*. Baltimore, Md.: Publish America, 2005.

Ford, Worthington Chauncey, ed. *Journals of the Continental Congress, 1774–1789*, Volume 1: *1774*. New York: Johnson Reprint Corporation, 1968.

Martin, James K. *In the Course of Human Events: An Interpretative Exploration of the American Revolution*. Arlington Heights, Ill.: AHM Publishing Corporation, 1979.

Morgan, Edmund S. *The Birth of the Republic, 1763–89*, rev. ed. Chicago: University of Chicago Press, 1992.

Rakove, Jack N. *The Beginnings of National Politics: An Interpretative History of the Continental Congress*. Baltimore, Md.: Johns Hopkins University Press, 1979.

■ Web Sites

"Congress: Proceedings of the First Continental Congress." ushistory.org Web site.
http://www.ushistory.org/declaration/related/congress.htm. Accessed on July 8, 2007.

"Documents from the Continental Congress and the Constitutional Convention, 1774–1789." Library of Congress "American Memory" Web site.
http://memory.loc.gov/ammem.collections/continental/. Accessed on July 8, 2007.

—By John R. Vile

Questions for Further Study

1. The Declaration and Resolves draws upon three sources of rights. Identify these sources. Which do you think was the strongest? Which appeal do you think would have the greatest impact in America? In England? In the rest of the world? Explain.

2. The Declaration and Resolves indicates a fundamental difference in understanding between American and British views of representation. Consider the strengths and weaknesses of the doctrines of actual representation and virtual representation. How, if at all, do you think that contemporaries might have applied these rival doctrines of representation to women or to slaves?

3. Much of the Declaration of Independence consists of a list of colonial grievances against the English king. Examining this list of grievances, what, if any, overlap do you find with those listed in the earlier Declaration and Resolves?

4. Ultimately, the English king refused to accept colonial grievances. Imagine that you are an adviser to King George III and you have just received a copy of the Declaration and Resolves of the First Continental Congress. What would you advise him to do? What problems do you anticipate with Parliament if the king accepts the legitimacy of colonial grievances? What do you anticipate will happen if the king rejects these grievances? Do you see any middle path between these two options?

5. Imagine that the king and Parliament have considered colonial grievances and have agreed on principle to accept colonial representation in Parliament. How do you think this agreement in principle might have been implemented? Do you think this would have resolved the controversy between the colonies and the British? What problems do you anticipate might derive from such an agreement? What do you think would be the best way to solve them? Would you anticipate that Parliament might one day move from England to the United States? Explain.

6. Read the first ten amendments to the U.S. Constitution (the Bill of Rights). Which of these rights appear to be foreshadowed by the Declaration and Resolves? Are there provisions in the Bill of Rights that appear to contradict arguments in the Resolves? Does the Declaration and Resolves articulate any important rights that did not find their way into the Bill of Rights?

Glossary

common law	the system of law, developed in England and transported in large part to the American colonies, based chiefly on the accumulation of judicial precedents
courts of admiralty	non-common-law courts, typically instituted to try violations of the law on the high seas, which the British used in America to try individuals believed to be guilty of evading duties or smuggling
ceded	given to another
duties	tariffs, or taxes, levied on imported goods

www.milestonedocuments.com

Glossary

English constitution	not a single written document but a series of accepted practices thought to protect the rights of all citizens
indemnify	to protect against legal penalty or loss
immutable	unchangeable
indubitable	indisputable; not to be doubted
laws of nature	God-given principles that the colonists thought provided a basis for their rights
N.C.D.	an abbreviation of the Latin *nemine contradicente*, meaning "no one contradicting" and thus representing unanimity
memorial	petition
negative of their sovereign	power of the English king to veto acts of colonial legislation
peers	fellow citizens
redress	aid or remedy
royal charters	outlines of rights made by the English king that allowed for the settlements of most American colonies
treasons and misprisions	rebellion or malfeasance, typically directed at a king
vicinage	vicinity, or area where one lives

Document Text

Declaration and Resolves of the First Continental Congress

October 14, 1774

Whereas, since the close of the last war, the British parliament, claiming a power, of right, to bind the people of America by statutes in all cases whatsoever, hath, in some acts, expressly imposed taxes on them, and in others, under various presences, but in fact for the purpose of raising a revenue, hath imposed rates and duties payable in these colonies, established a board of commissioners, with unconstitutional powers, and extended the jurisdiction of courts of admiralty, not only for collecting the said duties, but for the trial of causes merely arising within the body of a county:

And whereas, in consequence of other statutes, judges, who before held only estates at will in their offices, have been made dependant on the crown alone for their salaries, and standing armies kept in times of peace: And whereas it has lately been resolved in parliament, that by force of a statute, made in the thirty-fifth year of the reign of King Henry the Eighth, colonists may be transported to England, and tried there upon accusations for treasons and misprisions, or concealments of treasons committed in the colonies, and by a late statute, such trials have been directed in cases therein mentioned:

And whereas, in the last session of parliament, three statutes were made; one entitled, "An act to discontinue, in such manner and for such time as are therein mentioned, the landing and discharging, lading, or shipping of goods, wares and merchandise, at the town, and within the harbour of Boston, in the province of Massachusetts-Bay in New England"; another entitled, "An act for the better regulating the government of the province of Massachusetts-Bay in New England"; and another entitled, "An act for the impartial administration of justice, in the cases of persons questioned for any act done by them in the execution of the law, or for the suppression of riots and tumults, in the province of the Massachusetts-Bay in New England"; and another statute was then made, "for making more effectual provision for the government of the province of Quebec, etc." All which statutes are impolitic, unjust, and cruel, as well as unconstitutional, and most dangerous and destructive of American rights:

And whereas, assemblies have been frequently dissolved, contrary to the rights of the people, when they attempted to deliberate on grievances; and their dutiful, humble, loyal, and reasonable petitions to the crown for redress, have been repeatedly treated with contempt, by his Majesty's ministers of state:

The good people of the several colonies of New-Hampshire, Massachusetts-Bay, Rhode Island and Providence Plantations, Connecticut, New-York, New-Jersey, Pennsylvania, Newcastle, Kent, and Sussex on Delaware, Maryland, Virginia, North-Carolina and South-Carolina, justly alarmed at these arbitrary proceedings of parliament and administration, have severally elected, constituted, and appointed deputies to meet, and sit in general Congress, in the city of Philadelphia, in order to obtain such establishment, as that their religion, laws, and liberties, may not be subverted: Whereupon the deputies so appointed being now assembled, in a full and free representation of these colonies, taking into their most serious consideration, the best means of attaining the ends aforesaid, do, in the first place, as Englishmen, their ancestors in like cases have usually done, for asserting and vindicating their rights and liberties, DECLARE,

That the inhabitants of the English colonies in North-America, by the immutable laws of nature, the principles of the English constitution, and the several charters or compacts, have the following RIGHTS:

Resolved, N.C.D. 1. That they are entitled to life, liberty and property: and they have never ceded to any foreign power whatever, a right to dispose of either without their consent.

October, 1774 67

gion, laws, and liberties, may not be subverted; upon which appointment and direction, the said delegates being now assembled in a full and free representation[1] of these Colonies, taking into their most serious consideration the best means for attaining the ends aforesaid, do, in the first place, (as their ancestors in like cases have usually done,) for vindicating and asserting their rights and liberties, declare—

1. That the power of making laws for ordering or regulating the internal polity of these Colonies, is, within the limits of each Colony, respectively and exclusively vested in the Provincial Legislature of such Colony; and that all statutes for ordering or regulating the internal polity of the said Colonies, or any of them, in any manner or in any case whatsoever, are illegal and void.

at these arbitrary proceedings of parliament and administration, have severally elected, constituted, and appointed deputies to meet and sit in general congress, in the city of Philadelphia, in order to obtain such establishment, as that their religion, laws, and liberties may not be subverted:

Whereupon the deputies so appointed being now assembled, in a full and free representation of these Colonies, taking into their most serious consideration, the best means of attaining the ends aforesaid, do, in the first place, as Englishmen, their ancestors in like cases have usually done, for asserting and vindicating their rights and liberties, declare,

That the inhabitants of the English Colonies in North America, by the immutable laws of nature, the principles of the English constitution, and the several charters or compacts, have the following Rights:

Resolved, N. C. D. 1. That they are entitled to life, liberty, & property, and they have never ceded to any sovereign power whatever, a right to dispose of either without their consent.

[1] "Q. If the Colonies should not be named?"—*Marginal note.*

www.milestonedocuments.com

Document Text

Resolved, N.C.D. 2. That our ancestors, who first settled these colonies, were at the time of their emigration from the mother country, entitled to all the rights, liberties, and immunities of free and natural-born subjects, within the realm of England.

Resolved, N.C.D. 3. That by such emigration they by no means forfeited, surrendered, or lost any of those rights, but that they were, and their descendants now are, entitled to the exercise and enjoyment of all such of them, as their local and other circumstances enable them to exercise and enjoy.

Resolved, 4. That the foundation of English liberty, and of all free government, is a right in the people to participate in their legislative council: and as the English colonists are not represented, and from their local and other circumstances, cannot properly be represented in the British parliament, they are entitled to a free and exclusive power of legislation in their several provincial legislatures, where their right of representation can alone be preserved, in all cases of taxation and internal polity, subject only to the negative of their sovereign, in such manner as has been heretofore used and accustomed: But, from the necessity of the case, and a regard to the mutual interest of both countries, we cheerfully consent to the operation of such acts of the British parliament, as are bonfide, restrained to the regulation of our external commerce, for the purpose of securing the commercial advantages of the whole empire to the mother country, and the commercial benefits of its respective members; excluding every idea of taxation internal or external, for raising a revenue on the subjects, in America, without their consent.

Resolved, N.C.D. 5. That the respective colonies are entitled to the common law of England, and more especially to the great and inestimable privilege of being tried by their peers of the vicinage, according to the course of that law.

Resolved, N.C.D. 6. That they are entitled to the benefit of such of the English statutes, as existed at the time of their colonization; and which they have, by experience, respectively found to be applicable to their several local and other circumstances.

Resolved, N.C.D. 7. That these, his Majesty's colonies, are likewise entitled to all the immunities and privileges granted and confirmed to them by royal charters, or secured by their several codes of provincial laws.

Resolved, N.C.D. 8. That they have a right peaceably to assemble, consider of their grievances, and petition the king; and that all prosecutions, prohibitory proclamations, and commitments for the same, are illegal.

Resolved, N.C.D. 9. That the keeping a standing army in these colonies, in times of peace, without the consent of the legislature of that colony, in which such army is kept, is against law.

Resolved, N.C.D. 10. It is indispensably necessary to good government, and rendered essential by the English constitution, that the constituent branches of the legislature be independent of each other; that, therefore, the exercise of legislative power in several colonies, by a council appointed, during pleasure, by the crown, is unconstitutional, dangerous and destructive to the freedom of American legislation.

All and each of which the aforesaid deputies, in behalf of themselves, and their constituents, do claim, demand, and insist on, as their indubitable rights and liberties, which cannot be legally taken from them, altered or abridged by any power whatever, without their own consent, by their representatives in their several provincial legislature.

In the course of our inquiry, we find many infringements and violations of the foregoing rights, which, from an ardent desire, that harmony and mutual intercourse of affection and interest may be restored, we pass over for the present, and proceed to state such acts and measures as have been adopted since the last war, which demonstrate a system formed to enslave America.

Resolved, N.C.D. That the following acts of parliament are infringements and violations of the rights of the colonists; and that the repeal of them is essentially necessary, in order to restore harmony between Great Britain and the American colonies, viz.

The several acts of Geo. III. ch. 15, and ch. 34.-5 Geo. III. ch. 25.-6 Geo. ch. 52.-7 Geo. III. ch. 41 and ch. 46.-8 Geo. III. ch. 22. which impose duties for the purpose of raising a revenue in America, extend the power of the admiralty courts beyond their ancient limits, deprive the American subject of trial by jury, authorize the judges certificate to indemnify the prosecutor from damages, that he might otherwise be liable to, requiring oppressive security from a claimant of ships and goods seized, before he shall be allowed to defend his property, and are subversive of American rights.

Also 12 Geo. III. ch. 24, intituled, "An act for the better securing his majesty's dockyards, magazines, ships, ammunition, and stores," which declares a new offence in America, and deprives the American subject of a constitutional trial by jury of the vicinage, by authorizing the trial of any person, charged with the committing any offence described in the said act, out of the realm, to be

Document Text

indicted and tried for the same in any shire or county within the realm.

Also the three acts passed in the last session of parliament, for stopping the port and blocking up the harbour of Boston, for altering the charter and government of Massachusetts-Bay, and that which is entitled, "An act for the better administration of justice, etc."

Also the act passed in the same session for establishing the Roman Catholic religion, in the province of Quebec, abolishing the equitable system of English laws, and erecting a tyranny there, to the great danger (from so total a dissimilarity of religion, law and government) of the neighboring British colonies, by the assistance of whose blood and treasure the said country was conquered from France.

Also the act passed in the same session, for the better providing suitable quarters for officers and soldiers in his majesty's service, in North-America.

Also, that the keeping a standing army in several of these colonies, in time of peace, without the consent of the legislature of that colony, in which such army is kept, is against law.

To these grievous acts and measures, Americans cannot submit, but in hopes their fellow subjects in Great Britain will, on a revision of them, restore us to that state, in which both countries found happiness and prosperity, we have for the present, only resolved to pursue the following peaceable measures: 1. To enter into a non-importation, non-consumption, and non-exportation agreement or association. 2. To prepare an address to the people of Great-Britain, and a memorial to the inhabitants of British America: and 3. To prepare a loyal address to his majesty, agreeable to resolutions already entered into.

www.milestonedocuments.com

Patrick Henry shown in an undated portrait. (AP Photo)

Patrick Henry's "Liberty or Death" Speech

1775

"I know not what course others may take; but as for me, give me liberty or give me death!"

Overview

On March 23, 1775, Patrick Henry delivered his famous "Give me liberty or give me death" speech to a meeting of the Virginia House of Burgesses being held at St. John's Church in Richmond. A renowned orator, Henry was speaking out of more than a decade of opposition to the British Crown, which he viewed as usurping the rights of American colonists. As he arose to speak, he understood that several of his fellow burgesses were not yet prepared to accept the idea of revolution. While acknowledging their reservations about such a drastic course of action, he framed the debate as a question of freedom or slavery. It was too late to talk of peace when the war, in his view, had already begun with the Crown's massing of its military forces. His speech elevated public discourse far beyond mere protests against the British Crown or even the upholding of the colonists' rights as British subjects. Henry's words became famous because he suggested that what was at stake was the very identity of free citizens.

Context

In May 1774, John Murray, the 4th Earl of Dunmore and the British governor of the Virginia Colony, dissolved Virginia's colonial assembly because of its participation in the Committees of Correspondence (groups organized by colonists to obtain advance knowledge of acts of Parliament that had an impact on the American colonies). Believing that the governor's act was an effort to curb colonial self-government, Henry began in November 1774 to organize a volunteer militia in his home county of Hanover. Clearly he was moving toward a position of armed opposition to the British Crown. Both Governor Dunmore and Henry also were responding to the actions of other colonies, especially Massachusetts, which as early as 1773 had initiated its own Committee of Correspondence. The question was how far colonists were prepared to venture in asserting and defending their rights.

Some members of the Virginia House of Burgesses considered Henry's views extreme. They were prepared to defend colonial rights, but they balked at the idea of military resistance to acts of Parliament. Henry's resolutions submitted to the House of Burgesses affirming not only the colony's right to raise a militia but the urgent need to do so alarmed many of his colleagues. They believed that a negotiated settlement could be reached with the mother country, provided that the colonists acted with discretion and moderation. To Henry, such temporizing only weakened the rights he was attempting to preserve. While caution and prudence might seem the wisest course, in fact it would doom the colonies to servitude. Great Britain was already taking measures that showed it had little interest in recognizing colonial rights, Henry pointed out to the burgesses. He believed the moderates were no longer responding to the reality of the situation, which was one of crisis.

It was time for immediate and decisive action. Henry's powerful speech in March 1775 acknowledged his colleagues' concerns about the consequences of open resistance to royal authority, but he was asserting that the time for compromise had already elapsed and that the threat to liberty was so grave that calls for conciliation were no longer beneficial. The choice he described was stark: The colonists had to assert their rights with force. To do otherwise was not merely to accept the status quo but also to acquiesce to a diminution of liberty that would result in nothing less than slavery. Henry believed that moderation was not an option because the status quo was an illusion; colonial self-government had already eroded to a point that made it impossible for the colonists to retrieve their rights from royal authority.

Henry's appeal constituted an alarm and a call to the individual conscience. He was uniting his interpretation of recent history with his own demand for liberty. What made his speech so powerful was his willingness not merely to urge a radical course of action but also to say that it was vitally necessary for his fellow colonists and that he was willing to risk his own life in pursuit of their common desire for freedom.

About the Author

Patrick Henry was born in Hanover County, Virginia, on May 29, 1736, and died in Charlotte County, Virginia, on

Time Line

1736	■ **May 29** Henry is born in Hanover County, Virginia.
1760	■ Henry begins his law practice.
1765	■ Henry is elected to the Virginia House of Burgesses. ■ **May 30** Henry begins his campaign against the Stamp Act recently enacted by Parliament. ■ **November 1** The Stamp Act, a direct tax levied on American colonists for items such as legal documents, commercial contracts, newspapers, wills, and pamphlets, takes effect in the colonies.
1769	■ Henry is admitted to the Virginia Colony's highest judicial body, the General Court.
1774	■ **May** Virginia's royal governor dismisses the colonial assembly. ■ **September–October** The First Continental Congress convenes in Philadelphia.
1775	■ **March** Henry urges the arming of the Virginia militia. ■ **March 23** Henry delivers his famous "Give me liberty or give me death" speech to the Virginia House of Burgesses at St. John's Church, Richmond. ■ **May 10** First meeting of the Second Continental Congress.
1776	■ Henry briefly serves as the commander in chief of Virginia's armed forces. ■ **June 29** Virginia constitution is adopted by members of the colonial House of Burgesses.

June 6, 1799. Coming from a family of moderate means, Henry first worked in a country store and then as a farmer. Then he read law—a common practice in the eighteenth century before the establishment of law schools—and was admitted to the Virginia Bar in 1760. He soon established a formidable reputation in the courtroom based on his electrifying addresses to juries. One of Henry's early court cases challenged the English Crown's authority to overturn a law passed by the Virginia assembly. Although he lost his case, Henry became a popular colonial leader, lauded for his belief in the colonists' constitutional rights.

When he was elected to the Virginia House of Burgesses in 1765, Henry again earned plaudits for his speech making. He became so outraged over the Stamp Act—which he deemed taxation without representation, since the colonists had not been consulted and had not given their consent to the measure—that he proposed that the Virginia Assembly should declare itself independent. The incensed Henry even issued a threat to the British monarchy, warning King George III to heed the examples of previous rulers who had lost their lives to usurpers.

Now aligned with a radical faction that included Thomas Jefferson, Henry joined a number of burgesses calling for a Virginia constitutional convention and a continental congress—his response to the royal governor's dissolution of the colonial assembly in 1774. As a delegate to the First and Second Continental Congresses (1774–1775), he called for the arming of a militia—the first step, he openly announced, in a war he deemed inescapable. His uncompromising posture is expressed in his most famous statement from his speech in March 1775: "I know not what course others may take; but as for me, give me liberty or give me death!"

Henry's passionate commitment to individual liberty made him a keen supporter of the American Revolution and the Articles of Confederation, a document that ceded sovereign authority to the states. As an Antifederalist, he opposed the ratification of the U.S. Constitution, arguing that it endowed the central (federal) government with too much power. He feared that the rights of individual citizens might be imperiled in a federal system that made the states subordinate. Henry rejected efforts to make him part of the newly formed U.S. government, although in 1799 he consented in deference to President George Washington's request to run as a Federalist for a Virginia state senate seat. Henry won but died before taking office.

While Henry's stirring words ensured his place in American history, the measure of the man and his accomplishments has vexed historians, who decry the paucity of documents and records of his life, the need to rely on hearsay about reactions to his speeches, and the fact that he did not take a prominent part in the battles of the Revolution or in the newly formed government of the United States. Jefferson worked with Henry but concluded that his fellow Virginian was a demagogue with little interest in government itself. Yet Henry was elected to five terms as his state's governor and was famous for inspiring men of all classes and ways of life, insisting on the rights of the common man, the reduction of taxes, relief for the poor, and expansion of the money supply to assist a broad spectrum of Americans.

Explanation and Analysis of the Document

When Patrick Henry began speaking on March 23, 1775, he understood that while his calls for militant action against the British Crown enjoyed considerable support, many of his fellow burgesses still questioned the wisdom of a direct confrontation with the king and Parliament. Quite aside from a sense of loyalty to the mother country, which many of the burgesses continued to espouse with diminishing enthusiasm, Virginia and the other colonies faced the world's greatest empire. Great Britain had vanquished France in the Seven Years' War (1756–1763), and the idea of a band of colonists emerging victorious from a war with a world power seemed doubtful to a considerable number of Virginians. How other colonies would react to a call to arms also remained a problem. Certainly Massachusetts could be counted on, but Pennsylvania, for example, continued to be dominated by a political elite that resisted demands for direct and immediate action against the royal government.

Thus Henry's first sentence directs a compliment at his opposition. Not only are those who disagree with him able men, but he also admires their patriotism. Henry accords due respect to the opinions that diverge from his own. This rhetorical ploy disarms precisely those in the audience who are eager to disagree with the speaker. Giving time to his opposition strengthens Henry's case—or at least provides a moment for him to suggest that just as he has listened carefully to their views, it is now time to listen to his. Henry, with a well-known reputation for radicalism, thus begins his speech in the mildest, most engaging way to address the concerns of those dissenting from his views.

Henry's second sentence begins with a truism: Different men think differently. Again, this manner of expression delays the moment when members of the audience might begin to challenge his views. Then, shifting to a personal mode, Henry refers to himself, noting that his views are the opposite of what others have just expressed, and precisely because of that fact he must "speak forth my sentiments freely and without reserve." The topic of Henry's speech is his craving for liberty, which he emphasizes by using the word *freely* and discussing the notion that a man should be able to speak "without reserve." Henry's speech thus becomes the personification of his ideas: a free man speaking freely who means no disrespect to those who think otherwise. The first two sentences exhibit a man keenly desirous of maintaining the decorum of the assembly, taking issue with certain opinions by expressing his own, as is inevitable among groups of different men.

The fourth sentence again puts off the matter of Henry's views for another instant so that he can recognize the questing (an inquiry as to what should be done about the British Crown's suppression of American rights) as one of

Time Line

1776	■ **July 6** Henry is sworn in as Virginia's first governor.
1788	■ **June 25** Virginia ratifies the U.S. Constitution.
1799	■ **June 6** Henry dies shortly after his election to the Virginia state senate.

"awful moment to this country." The words that follow are only justifiable because so much is at stake. This is a defining moment, which now (in the fifth sentence) Henry heralds in dramatic terms: The choice is "freedom or slavery." By adding "for my own part," Henry not only acknowledges that this is his personal opinion but also indicates that he is compelled to take responsibility for what he is about to say. To do anything less would not do justice to the "magnitude of the subject," which can be grasped only through the "freedom of the debate." The final sentences of the first paragraph come full circle, with Henry pointing out that by expressing his views, he is as patriotic as his opponents. All sides of an argument must be heard in order to remain faithful to one's country and God. For Henry to suppress his own beliefs would, in effect, be an act of treason and of disloyalty to the "Majesty of Heaven, which I revere above all earthly kings." The final sentence in the first paragraph concludes by putting the British monarch in his place by reminding Henry's fellow burgesses that their ultimate loyalty must be to the Creator, the first cause of all life. Without challenging the moderates and those who regard him as a firebrand, Henry nevertheless suggests that his radicalism is founded on universal principles that cannot be overturned by any lesser authority than God.

Henry's second, shorter paragraph begins with another truism: how natural it is to avoid painful truths and rely on "illusions of hope." He buttresses this notion of illusions with an allusion to classical mythology, to the siren that led men astray by creating beautiful fantasies masking an ugly reality. This use of mythology contains an implied criticism of the moderates, who have not drawn such a picture of "awful moment." However, Henry seeks not to alienate but to overcome his opposition, so he then shifts to a series of questions. Rather than declaring that wise men are not deceived by fantasies, he asks what such men should do in the "great and arduous struggle for liberty." *Great* here means both "important" and "good," suggesting that the quest for freedom requires courage and determination. Rather than telling the burgesses what to think, he asks them to consider the matter as he does. Shifting to a biblical allusion, he poses another question about the

www.milestonedocuments.com

A drawing depicting Patrick Henry's famous speech to the Virginia Assembly in 1775 (Library of Congress)

"numbers of those, who, having eyes, see not, and, having ears, hear not, the things which so nearly concern their temporal salvation." Are men blinding themselves to the truth of Henry's difficult quest? The question is pointed but not nearly as inflammatory as using a sentence to directly accuse his opponents of willful blindness. In referencing his "anguish of spirit," Henry acknowledges that his position causes him suffering, but he affirms it is better to "know the whole truth, to know the worst, and to provide for it." This broad argument contains an indirect allusion to preparing for war, including the raising and arming of a militia. Repeating "for my part" indicates that Henry is standing alone, relying on his own conscience and intelligence. He again undermines his opposition by moving attention toward his own heroic posture, which he defines as the prudent position by using the word *provide*. That word purposely downplays the strong action that Henry advocates.

The short second paragraph is followed by two paragraphs in which Henry gathers up the experience of the colony's last decade (beginning in 1765, when he delivered his defiant attack on the Stamp Act). The only way to gauge the future is by assessing the past, which leads Henry to reject the counsel of those who believe they can negotiate better terms with the British ministry. Henry suggests that the British ministry's purposes are insidious, that the royal government is gradually eroding the colonists' rights while depending on their love of the mother country. He believes that all romantic notions of the ties between Great Britain and America should be dismissed: "Suffer not yourselves to be betrayed with a kiss." Britain's warlike actions belie its professions of love; instead of the reconciliation of two peoples, the ministry's aim is to subdue its colonial subjects. The huge size of the military expedition sent out to the colonies ought to convince the colonists that they are regarded as the enemy. At this point, presenting old arguments to Britain to halt the movement of its armies and navies would only be a form of self-deception. Then, in two hammer-blow sentences, Henry dispatches the efforts of a decade: No amount of pleading, begging, and bowing has moved the king to intervene on the colonists' behalf; indeed, the monarch has spurned their love. Henry works up a scene of shame in which the colonists have allowed themselves to be the victims of a tyrannical government. They can recover their dignity only by abandoning spurious reasons to hope.

Essential Quotes

"Suffer not yourselves to be betrayed with a kiss."

(Paragraph 4)

"We have petitioned; we have remonstrated; we have supplicated; we have prostrated ourselves before the throne, and have implored its interposition to arrest the tyrannical hands of the ministry and Parliament. Our petitions have been slighted; our remonstrances have produced additional violence and insult; our supplications have been disregarded; and we have been spurned, with contempt, from the foot of the throne!"

(Paragraph 4)

"The battle, sir, is not to the strong alone; it is to the vigilant, the active, the brave."

(Paragraph 5)

"Our chains are forged! Their clanking may be heard on the plains of Boston! The war is inevitable—and let it come! I repeat it, sir, let it come."

(Paragraph 5)

"I know not what course others may take; but as for me, give me liberty or give me death!"

(Paragraph 6)

www.milestonedocuments.com

Henry reaches the crescendo of this paragraph when he boldly declares his solution to all these years of shame: In order to be free, the colonists must fight.

Having declared his support for war, Henry now confronts in the fifth paragraph the concern that the colonies do not have the strength to fight an empire. He argues that the colonists can only become weaker if they delay their declaration of war. Hope has become a phantom, which Henry pictures as the colonists lying supinely on their backs, unable to take decisive action. Liberty, Henry assures his fellow burgesses, is a "holy cause" and will draw millions to its defense. The idea of freedom is invincible, Henry asserts. God is just, and right is on the colonists' side. They will be fighting for the destiny of their nation, and there will be friends to help, perhaps an allusion to American hopes that the French would side against the British. The coming battle will reward the brave and the watchful—those who have given up hope in British fairness and integrity. It is too late for any other choice: Any retreat at this point would mean submitting to the Crown's power and thus to slavery. Shifting again to vivid imagery, Henry announces, "Our chains are forged! Their clanking may be heard on the plains of Boston! The war is inevitable—and let it come! I repeat it, sir, let it come." From initially expressing due deference to his opponents, Henry has moved to an uncompromising, radical, and vehement call for war, rousing his fellow burgesses to embrace the inevitable conflict and to do so with enthusiasm.

The brief concluding paragraph subsides for a sentence, as Henry recovers from the outburst at the end of the fourth paragraph. In a quieter voice he states that there is no point in pursuing the matter, as the time for excusing or rationalizing the British ministry's actions and the negative role of the monarch is over. Some still cry for peace, but the war has actually begun, Henry insists, returning to his vehemence. Colonists are already on the field of battle, he notes, alluding to the clashes between the royal government and colonists in Boston. Henry asks his fellow burgesses: Is life precious at any cost, at the cost of freedom? Is a life of slavery preferable to death? Then, shifting the responsibility from them to himself, Henry concludes in one of the most powerful and famous declarations in American history: "I know not what course others may take; but as for me, give me liberty or give me death!"

Audience

Henry's immediate audience was his fellow burgesses. He had been preparing for more than two years to give his "liberty or ... death" speech, which was based on his experiences forming a local voluntary militia and meeting with other colonists, especially in Massachusetts, who also saw that British measures to stifle dissent would soon quash their ability to assert or defend their rights.

Henry was not speaking merely as a legislator—or even to those in other colonies—but to history itself. His earlier speeches had invoked the fate of other tyrants who had impeded the course of human liberty. He took his stand on the human need for freedom. It was this appeal to universal rights that he helped spread throughout the colonies, thus shrinking the audience for those still seeking a less extreme resolution of the conflicts between the colonies and the mother country.

Henry also was delivering an ultimatum to royal authority in the colonies. He would not accept any half measures where liberty was concerned. Challenging the royal governor's authority, he made it clear that he based his actions not on narrow legal lines but on what he considered the very nature of a free man. Life itself was not worth living if submission to the Crown meant the abrogation of fundamental human rights.

Impact

Henry's speech had a profound and stirring impact on everyone who heard it. For years, men would recollect his words and their reactions. To say that it was the most powerful speech ever delivered in Virginia's House of Burgesses is an understatement. The speech's historic significance was recognized immediately. One burgess supposedly said that he wanted to be buried on the spot.

One account described a hushed assembly hanging on Henry's every word. Even Henry's opponents admitted how moved they were by his words. Edmund Randolph, for example, attributed a religious intensity to Henry's address, declaring, "The British King was lying prostrate from the thunder of heaven" (Beeman, p. 66). Thus Henry's words became not merely his own but virtually a kind of divine judgment on the actions of the British Crown. Henry himself, in that moment, seemed a prophet, speaking as "man was never known to speak before," Randolph claimed (Beeman, p. 66). Henry had made a contribution not only to the colonial cause but also to the cause of humankind.

The practical impact of Henry's speech took the form of approving his resolution that the colony arm itself and send delegates to the Second Continental Congress. Jefferson later acknowledged that Henry's bold words had solidified the elite of colonial leaders, bolstering them in their determination to reject overweening royal authority. Henry's boldness also affected new leaders in colonies like Pennsylvania, where the elite had resisted radicalism.

While Henry's words inspired his fellow colonists, they prompted royal authorities to increase military measures, so that by April 18, 1775, British troops were sent to Lexington and Concord, Massachusetts. Governor Dunmore secured Virginia's supply of gunpowder and even threatened to free all slaves who were willing to fight for the British Crown. The result, however, was to strengthen the forces of radicalism and to make Henry's words even more apposite. In retrospect, Henry's speech took on an air of inevitability, as if he were the first to describe a state of affairs—a drive for liberty—that no power on earth could restrain. Thus many of the retrospective accounts of Henry's speech must be viewed in the context of the events that later seemed to confirm his rousing convictions.

Related Documents

"Articles of Confederation." National Archives "Our Documents" Web site. http://www.ourdocuments.gov/doc.php?doc=3. Accessed on December 4, 2007. The first attempt to form a national government.

"Constitution of the United States." National Archives "Our Documents" Web site. http://www.ourdocuments.gov/doc.php?doc=9. Accessed on December 4, 2007. The Constitution of 1787 replaced the Articles of Confederation as the nation's governing document.

"Declaration of Independence." National Archives "Our Documents" Web site. http://www.ourdocuments.gov/doc.php?doc=2. Accessed on December 4, 2007. Thomas Jefferson wrote the bulk of this 1776 declaration.

"Lee Resolution." National Archives "Our Documents" Web site. http://www.ourdocuments.gov/doc.php?doc=1. Accessed on December 4, 2007. On June 7, 1776, Richard Henry Lee of Virginia introduced a resolution in the Second Continental Congress proposing independence for the American colonies.

Bibliography

■ Books

Beeman, Richard R. *Patrick Henry: A Biography*. New York: McGraw-Hill, 1974.

Mayer, Henry. *A Son of Thunder: Patrick Henry and the American Republic*. New York: Franklin Watts, 1986.

Mayo, Bernard. *Myths and Men: Patrick Henry, George Washington, Thomas Jefferson*. Athens: University of Georgia Press, 1959.

Meade, Robert D. *Patrick Henry*. 2 vols. Philadelphia: Lippincott, 1957–1969.

Willison, George F. *Patrick Henry and His World*. Garden City, N.Y.: Doubleday, 1969.

■ Web Sites

"Patrick Henry." Independence Hall Association ushistory.org Web site.
http://www.ushistory.org/declaration/related/henry.htm". Accessed on December 4, 2007.

Red Hill Patrick Henry National Memorial Web site.
http://www.redhill.org/. Accessed on December 4, 2007.

—By Carl Rollyson

www.milestonedocuments.com

Questions for Further Study

1. Compare Henry's "Give me liberty or give me death" speech with the resolution that Richard Henry Lee submitted to the Second Continental Congress on June 7, 1776. How did the Congress's deliberations coincide with Henry's stirring call for liberty?

2. Compare Henry's comments on the British Crown and his statements about liberty with those in the Declaration of Independence.

3. How did Henry's beliefs in liberty later clash with certain provisions of the U.S. Constitution? Why was it so difficult for him to accept the idea of a federal government? Why did he find the Articles of Confederation more satisfactory?

Glossary

awful	enormously important, extremely shocking, or so impressive as to inspire awe
extentuate	to lessen the seriousness of a mistake or wrongdoing
insidious	slowly and subtly harmful or destructivc
irresolution	the state of being unsure and unable to make decisions
remonstrated	reasoned or pleaded forcefully
supplicated	begged

Document Text

Patrick Henry's "Liberty or Death" Speech

No man thinks more highly than I do of the patriotism, as well as abilities, of the very worthy gentlemen who have just addressed the house. But different men often see the same subject in different lights; and, therefore, I hope it will not be thought disrespectful to those gentlemen if, entertaining as I do opinions of a character very opposite to theirs, I shall speak forth my sentiments freely and without reserve. This is no time for ceremony. The question before the house is one of awful moment to this country. For my own part, I consider it as nothing less than a question of freedom or slavery; and in proportion to the magnitude of the subject ought to be the freedom of the debate. It is only in this way that we can hope to arrive at the truth, and fulfill the great responsibility which we hold to God and our country. Should I keep back my opinions at such a time, through fear of giving offense, I should consider myself as guilty of treason towards my country, and of an act of disloyalty toward the Majesty of Heaven, which I revere above all earthly kings.

Mr. President, it is natural to man to indulge in the illusions of hope. We are apt to shut our eyes against a painful truth, and listen to the song of that siren till she transforms us into beasts. Is this the part of wise men, engaged in a great and arduous struggle for liberty? Are we disposed to be of the numbers of those who, having eyes, see not, and, having ears, hear not, the things which so nearly concern their temporal salvation? For my part, whatever anguish of spirit it may cost, I am willing to know the whole truth, to know the worst, and to provide for it.

I have but one lamp by which my feet are guided, and that is the lamp of experience. I know of no way of judging of the future but by the past. And judging by the past, I wish to know what there has been in the conduct of the British ministry for the last ten years to justify those hopes with which gentlemen have been pleased to solace themselves and the House. Is it that insidious smile with which our petition has been lately received?

Trust it not, sir; it will prove a snare to your feet. Suffer not yourselves to be betrayed with a kiss. Ask yourselves how this gracious reception of our petition comports with those warlike preparations which cover our waters and darken our land. Are fleets and armies necessary to a work of love and reconciliation? Have we shown ourselves so unwilling to be reconciled that force must be called in to win back our love? Let us not deceive ourselves, sir. These are the implements of war and subjugation; the last arguments to which kings resort. I ask gentlemen, sir, what means this martial array, if its purpose be not to force us to submission? Can gentlemen assign any other possible motive for it? Has Great Britain any enemy, in this quarter of the world, to call for all this accumulation of navies and armies? No, sir, she has none. They are meant for us: they can be meant for no other. They are sent over to bind and rivet upon us those chains which the British ministry have been so long forging. And what have we to oppose to them? Shall we try argument? Sir, we have been trying that for the last ten years. Have we anything new to offer upon the subject? Nothing. We have held the subject up in every light of which it is capable; but it has been all in vain. Shall we resort to entreaty and humble supplication? What terms shall we find which have not been already exhausted? Let us not, I beseech you, sir, deceive ourselves. Sir, we have done everything that could be done to avert the storm which is now coming on. We have petitioned; we have remonstrated; we have supplicated; we have prostrated ourselves before the throne, and have implored its interposition to arrest the tyrannical hands of the ministry and Parliament. Our petitions have been slighted; our remonstrances have produced additional violence and insult; our supplications have been disre-

Document Text

garded; and we have been spurned, with contempt, from the foot of the throne! In vain, after these things, may we indulge the fond hope of peace and reconciliation.

There is no longer any room for hope. If we wish to be free—if we mean to preserve inviolate those inestimable privileges for which we have been so long contending—if we mean not basely to abandon the noble struggle in which we have been so long engaged, and which we have pledged ourselves never to abandon until the glorious object of our contest shall be obtained—we must fight! I repeat it, sir, we must fight! An appeal to arms and to the God of hosts is all that is left us! They tell us, sir, that we are weak; unable to cope with so formidable an adversary. But when shall we be stronger? Will it be the next week, or the next year? Will it be when we are totally disarmed, and when a British guard shall be stationed in every house? Shall we gather strength but irresolution and inaction? Shall we acquire the means of effectual resistance by lying supinely on our backs and hugging the delusive phantom of hope, until our enemies shall have bound us hand and foot? Sir, we are not weak if we make a proper use of those means which the God of nature hath placed in our power. The millions of people, armed in the holy cause of liberty, and in such a country as that which we possess, are invincible by any force which our enemy can send against us. Besides, sir, we shall not fight our battles alone. There is a just God who presides over the destinies of nations, and who will raise up friends to fight our battles for us. The battle, sir, is not to the strong alone; it is to the vigilant, the active, the brave. Besides, sir, we have no election. If we were base enough to desire it, it is now too late to retire from the contest. There is no retreat but in submission and slavery! Our chains are forged! Their clanking may be heard on the plains of Boston! The war is inevitable—and let it come! I repeat it, sir, let it come.

It is in vain, sir, to extenuate the matter. Gentlemen may cry, Peace, Peace—but there is no peace. The war is actually begun! The next gale that sweeps from the north will bring to our ears the clash of resounding arms! Our brethren are already in the field! Why stand we here idle? What is it that gentlemen wish? What would they have? Is life so dear, or peace so sweet, as to be purchased at the price of chains and slavery? Forbid it, Almighty God! I know not what course others may take; but as for me, give me liberty or give me death!

www.milestonedocuments.com

Frederick, Lord North (Library of Congress)

Proclamation by the King for Suppressing Rebellion and Sedition

1775

"We ... command all our Officers ... to disclose and make known all treasons and traitorous conspiracies which they shall know to be against us, our crown and dignity."

Overview

By the summer of 1775, conditions in the British colonies in North America had reached a near frenzy. After twelve years of increasing tensions, rebellious colonists, who now believed that a conspiracy existed to deprive them of their rights as Englishmen, openly took up arms against the mother country. After the April 19, 1775, skirmishes at Lexington and Concord, their war of words and harassment mutated into one where the weapons were rifles and artillery. George III, urged by his advisers, felt it necessary to make a statement expressing his displeasure and the lack of tolerance for such rebellious actions. While independence from Great Britain was not an option openly discussed, the Proclamation by the King for Suppressing Rebellion and Sedition certainly moved colonists farther along that path. Many saw it as a declaration of war. It was evidence that the conspiracy against the colonists had reached the highest levels of the government and was not limited to colonial governors and Parliament. Both sides had engaged in brinkmanship and crossed the line; there was now little or no chance of reconciliation.

George III, king of Great Britain and Ireland, had been reared in the English courts and possessed a fairly sophisticated grasp of English power politics. However, neither he nor his advisers from their vantage point in England could fully grasp the machinations and nuances of colonial politics as his subjects in North America played them. George III was capable, careful, and deliberate in his actions but probably lacked the imagination and the information necessary to grasp the tortuous nature of colonial affairs. Caught up in their debate and factional struggles, colonial politicians also failed to comprehend the larger picture and their place within the empire. Most concerned themselves with colonial rivalries and obsessed over the slights and accomplishments of those on the same side of the Atlantic Ocean.

Context

Since 1763 British colonists in North America had become increasing convinced of a conspiracy based in the mother country to constrain their traditional rights and privileges. In the minds of North Americans this translated into the maintenance of the status quo. Following the Peace of Paris and the abdication of French holdings on the North American continent, the British government found itself with a huge war debt and the enormous cost of controlling its vast empire. It appeared logical to those in the higher ranks of the British ruling circles that North American colonists help pay the price for their new security and prosperity. The colonists did not agree, and the more rebellious and discontent took action to counter changes in British policies. Actions such as the Proclamation of 1763, the Currency Act, the Sugar Act, and the posting of ships of the British Admiralty off North American coasts made colonists suspicious. They met the Stamp Act of 1765 with active resistance in the forms of constitutional protests, media campaigns, and mob actions. Simultaneously, parties on both sides of the ocean grew increasingly out of touch with the realities of their opposition. Subsequent crises occurred when Parliament tried to enforce legislation such as the Townshend Revenue Act and Tea Act in 1768 and 1773, respectively. With each crisis, the tactics and the costs dramatically escalated. Nonimportation and extralegal embargoes on taxed goods joined earlier methods of resistance. When the Massachusetts faction led by Samuel and John Adams dumped 342 chests of tea into the harbor on the night of December 16, 1773, they not only defeated their chief rival Thomas Hutchinson, the colonial governor, but also brought down the wrath of the king and Parliament.

The next year, 1774, saw a further escalation in the tensions between the colonies and the mother country and between various colonial factions. Miscalculations and misunderstandings continued to grow on both sides of the Atlantic. The British possessed somewhat contradictory images of their colonial subjects. In one vision, they perceived all colonists in the light of ungrateful children balking at assuming the responsibilities of mature adults within the empire. Others persisted in believing that the problems in the colonies were localized in New England—in Massachusetts specifically—and could be solved by making an example of that colony and its leaders. The colonists, too, suffered from several misapprehensions. While nearly all colonial politicians shared a belief that a conspiracy existed

Time Line

1763

■ **February 10**
The Treaty of Paris ending the Seven Years' War, or Great War for Empire, is signed, radically changing British expectations of North American colonists and signaling the growth of tensions between the two opponents.

■ **October 7**
The Proclamation of 1763 becomes public knowledge and closes the Ohio Territory to organized colonization and frustrated colonial land speculators and settlers.

1765

■ **March 22**
The Stamp Act is the first concerted move by Parliament to extend its authority over the colonists and alleviate their debts and tax burdens at home by placing an excise tax on printed goods; this causes the first organized protests in the colonies.

1766

■ **March 18**
The Declaratory Act, authored by the British statesman Edmund Burke, is issued in response to the repeal of the Stamp Act to reestablish parliamentary authority over the colonies.

1767

■ **June 29**
The Townshend Revenue Act, more commonly known as the Townshend Duties, an excise tax on imported goods aimed at relieving the continuing British economic woes, is passed; colonists resist with force and nonimportation.

1770

■ **March 5**
In the so-called Boston Massacre, British soldiers kill five colonists in an urban riot; this is seen by colonists as further proof of conspiracy.

1773

■ **December 16**
Boston Tea Party occurs, and rebel colonists dressed as Native Americans dump tea belonging to the nearly bankrupt British East India Company into the harbor.

to deprive them of their rights and privileges, they were far from agreement on how to regain them; they agreed on the cause and its origins but not on the remedy. The spectrum ran from the liberal Joseph Galloway of Pennsylvania, an accommodationist who felt the breach could be mended through compromise and negotiation, to the radical Samuel Adams of Massachusetts and Patrick Henry of Virginia, who felt that armed resistance was the solution to regaining their lost privileges. Additionally, the repeal of the Stamp Act and the majority of the Townshend duties gave colonial leaders a false sense of their importance and power within the empire. For example, political leaders in Great Britain felt that the implementation of the Coercive Acts (or Intolerable Acts) in the spring of 1774 would punish wrongdoers and send a strong warning to like-minded or sympathetic colonials. In North America, however, those acts, along with the Quebec Act, an unrelated body of legislation to reorganize former French territories into a more manageable holding, discredited conservatives, alienated moderates, and vindicated radicals. When the Continental Congress, an extralegal body of delegates from all colonies except Georgia, met in September of that year, the accommodationists found their position a difficult one. Their only major contribution to the discussion, Thomas Galloway's Plan of Union, narrowly went down in defeat, while the body endorsed the radicals' Declaration and Resolves of the First Continental Congress, the Suffolk Resolves, and the development of the Continental Association to enforce nonimportation and nonconsumption of British goods.

The Continental Congress's last action before dissolving proved ominous; it declared a second meeting to convene May 25, 1775, if relations with the mother country continued to deteriorate. By the deadline, covert hostilities and constitutional protests had given way to armed rebellion. In the aftermath of the initial encounters at Lexington and Concord on April 19, 1775, the Second Continental Congress had to declare a rationale for the rebellion. Reconciliationists proposed the Declaration of the Causes and Necessity of Taking Up Arms as an olive branch. Discussions about independence on the part of the radicals were at least temporarily stymied. While the delegates debated the purpose of the conflict, the fighting continued. On June 17, 1775, the British, commanded by General Thomas Gage and led by General William Howe, broke the siege of British troops in Boston by dislodging rebel forces from their strongholds on Bunker Hill and Breed's Hill. The British won the day but at an enormous cost of over 40 percent of their troops; 1,054 were killed or wounded. George III and Parliament faced the same dilemma as the colonists—What was the purpose of their war?

About the Author

George III, king of the United Kingdom and Ireland and king of Hanover, was born in 1738 to Frederick Louis, Prince of Wales, and Augusta of Saxe-Gotha. His birth at the Duke of Norfolk's residence in Saint James's Square had particular significance, since he was the first Prince of Wales born in England since Charles II before the English Revolution of the 1640s. The British had a difficult time embracing a king they perceived as a German. Reports of George III's abilities as a student varied widely from claims of retardation to keen aptitude for his studies. The most reasonable assessment appears to be that he had above-average intelligence, but not brilliance, and that he was shy, reserved, and socially backward. The death of his father in 1750 left George III in an unenviable position: a minor having to negotiate the twisted paths of the English court and the assumption of his father's duties as the Prince of Wales. While he was a minor, George III remained part of his mother's household and entered into one of his most significant relationships, that with John Stuart, the 3rd Earl of Bute. Named groom of the robe, Stuart served as adviser, mentor, and confidant to the young prince.

Shortly after George III reached majority, two events occurred that had a profound effect on his career and personal life. In 1760 George II, George III's grandfather, died and left him as his heir. In his twentieth year, George III became king of the United Kingdom and Ireland as well as king of Hanover, a hereditary German holding. After a protracted search for a suitable wife, on September 8, 1761, George III married Charlotte, princess of Mechlenburg-Streiltz at Saint James's Palace. Two weeks later Great Britain witnessed their coronation at Westminster Abbey. Observers characterized the court that they established, primarily at Buckingham Palace, as temperate, respectable, and prizing formality and procedure. George III's siblings and offspring proved to be less sober and frequently engaged in activities that the king found uncomfortable and which often led to strained relations. The tendencies of both his sibling and his offspring toward debt and unfortunate personal misalliances, within and outside the bonds of matrimony, created considerable anxiety and familial estrangements.

George III's political life was equally strained. The first decade of his tenure saw seven prime ministers. The revolving ministries operated most notably under George Grenville; Charles Watson-Wentworth, 2nd Marquess of Rockingham; and the elder William Pitt (later Lord Chatham). Until the appointment of Frederick North, 2nd Earl of Guilford, in 1770 factions formed and fell with nearly annual regularity. George III also eventually severed his close ties to Lord Bute but had no one to replace him. Lord North and the younger William Pitt came closest to filling the void left by Bute's fall from grace. George III's reactions to troubles in North America were colored by his desires to eliminate factional politics and to maintain order. George III's reaction to the escalation to arms in North America was predictable. As an eighteenth-century monarch, he saw suppression of the rebellion as his only viable option.

George III ruled Great Britain and her empire for sixty years. While the American rebellion and the eventual loss of the North American colonies caused some damage to his reputation, his subsequent alliance with the younger William Pitt, and his strong opposition to the French Revolution and the Napoleonic conquest made him extremely popular. His political opposition, primarily Whigs, frequently criticized George III for overstepping the constitutional boundaries established by the Glorious Revolution of 1688. He was, however, fairly circumspect in his actions for an eighteenth-century ruler. One final factor, illness, had a profound impact on George III's long reign. His contemporaries believed that their king suffered from periodic bouts of insanity, during which he raved, ranted, and needed physical restraint. Medical historians today contend that George III suffered from porphyria, an inherited homological disorder causing intermittent bouts of acute pain, paralysis, personality changes, and general neurological damage. George III's first confirmed attack occurred in 1788–1789, although the mental breakdown he suffered during the Stamp Act crisis in 1765 may have been related. He fell ill again in 1801, but then stabilized for nine years. After 1810 his condition worsened, and he never fully recovered. He eventually lost his hearing and his sight. Although his people waited for his recovery, in 1811 Parliament confirmed

Time Line

1774

- **March 31–June 22**
  The Coercive Acts (Intolerable Acts) and Quebec Act are enacted in hopes of suppressing rebellious colonists.
- **September 5–October 26**
  Continental Congress meets in Philadelphia, where colonial leaders discuss their plight and initiate a plan of action.

1775

- **April 19**
  The shots fired at Lexington and Concord mark the beginning of armed rebellion in the colonies.
- **May 25**
  Second Continental Congress meets for the second time in Philadelphia.
- **June 17**
  The British win the Battle of Bunker Hill, but it is, at best, a Pyrrhic victory.
- **August 23**
  Proclamation by the King for Suppressing Rebellion and Sedition is issued by George III.

1776

- **July 4**
  The Declaration of Independence is issued by the Second Continental Congress.

www.milestonedocuments.com

his oldest son, George, as Prince Regent. George III died in confinement on January 29, 1820. His legacy is a mixed one. British historians interpret his reign as one characterized by sedate competency occasionally blighted by periods of instability. U.S. historians have generally vilified him in terms akin to Thomas Paine's "Royal Brute."

Explanation and Analysis of the Document

The Proclamation by the King for Suppressing Rebellion and Sedition is a relatively short document issued on August 23, 1775, in the aftermath of the eruption of armed hostilities in North American colonies late that spring. Given the distance and the time it took for news to reach Great Britain from the Americas, news of Lexington, Concord and Bunker Hill was fresh in the minds of the author and his first audiences. In his proclamation, George III describes who the guilty parties were and what crimes they had committed. He continues by explaining who had the authority to suppress the wrongdoers and concludes with what their remedies might be.

George III opens his declaration with a description of those who had been led into rebellion. In the first section he cautions North American colonists not be led astray by "dangerous and ill designing men." He continues reminding his colonial subjects that they owe much to the mother country. The British armies and admiralty had guaranteed their safety. British funding had paid for their development and had laid the foundations for their prosperity. Implicit in his caution is what the loss of the support might cost the colonists.

The second statement in the document illustrates the unlawful and ungrateful actions of the rebels. George III carefully lays out the progression of the colonials' wrongdoing. He begins by pointing out the public disturbances, heckling, mob action, and rioting promoted by the instigators. The rebels' interference with trade and commerce, nonimportation and boycott, and their restraint of those loyal souls wishing to continue their trade with great Britain also comes under scrutiny and criticism. Finally, George III points out that the guilty parties have stockpiled arms and ammunitions and have resorted to armed rebellion to resist the authority of the Crown.

In the third segment George III identifies the perpetrators of the rebellion. He contends that "divers wicked and desperate persons" had promoted and aided the escalation to violence through their correspondence, advice, and funding. These instigators were those he truly condemned because they understood what they were doing. They might have led lesser persons astray.

The second paragraph of the document is the longest and most involved; it also changes the focus from what had gone wrong and who was to blame toward what could be done about rebellious colonists. In the initial part of the statement, George III warns those who are wavering in their loyalty to the Crown that ignorance and fear of reprisal are not acceptable excuses for failure to defend that institution. He promises to protect those who maintain faith with him. George III explains that he and his advisers, most probably Lord North, had issue the proclamation to assure loyal citizens and all officers of the Crown that the suppression of the rebellion is their duty. He suggests that their obligations include actively defending the empire, exposing its enemies and their conspiracies, and bringing traitors to justice.

The final sections detail the appropriate actions of those remaining loyal to the Crown. George III orders all British officeholders, those in the military and civilian branches, and ordinary subjects to be vigilant and watchful for signs of collaboration with the enemy as well as to identify those individuals openly engaging in traitorous or seditious behavior. To stress this, he warns them that the law requires them to cooperate. Information regarding treasonous or seditious behaviors should be transmitted in the most expeditious fashion to the proper authorities. Those authorities would in turn make sure that those engaging in treasonous behavior received full and proper punishments.

Audience

The Proclamation by the King for Suppressing Rebellion and Sedition was authored with three particular audiences in mind: the members of Great Britain's political elite, the general population of Great Britain, and the American colonists. For each of these groups the intent of the document differed. For his political allies and his opposition, the work contained an explanation of the course of action that George III and his ministers intended to pursue. He hoped to appear strong and decisive to his critics—primarily the Whigs—and to provide his supporters—the Tories—with a ground that they could defend. George III intended that the British public read his message as a patriotic rallying cry. He wanted and needed their support to suppress the rebellion. They provided the funding and men to pursue the conflict. By stating that the colonists' actions were treasonous, he anticipated deflecting their growing frustrations over Britain's economic problems toward the American colonists. Georges III's edict had a twofold purpose for his American audience. He wished to identify what construed treason and who engaged in those activities. The work put those individuals and groups on notice: If one persists, he or she will be hunted and punished. To those remaining loyal to the Crown and to those wavering in their allegiances, his meaning was clear: If one cooperates and acts in defense of the Crown, he or she has nothing to fear.

In the proclamation, George III also made a statement in reference to its style and language. Both were weighty and serious and both carried the force of law. While twenty-first-century readers might find the language and style obtuse and obscure, George III's eighteenth-century audiences would have clearly understood the language and style. The format of the statement was a commonly accepted one; George III addresses his audiences, states the problem, and defines its solution. North American colonists

Essential Quotes

> *"After various disorderly acts committed in disturbance of the public peace, to the obstruction of lawful commerce, and to the oppression of our loyal subjects carrying on the same; have at length proceeded to open and avowed rebellion, by arraying themselves in a hostile manner, to withstand the execution of the law, and traitorously preparing, ordering and levying war against us."*
>
> (Paragraph 1)

> *"And whereas, there is reason to apprehend that such rebellion hath been much promoted and encouraged by the traitorous correspondence, counsels and comfort of divers wicked and desperate persons within this realm."*
>
> (Paragraph 1)

> *"We do accordingly strictly charge and command all our Officers, as well civil as military, and all others our obedient and loyal subjects, to use their utmost endeavors to withstand and suppress such rebellion, and to disclose and make known all treasons and traitorous conspiracies which they shall know to be against us, our crown and dignity."*
>
> (Paragraph 2)

www.milestonedocuments.com

were familiar with this constitutional construct and adopted it as their own. The Declaration of Independence offers a prime example of their adaptation.

Impact

The Proclamation by the King for Suppressing Rebellion and Sedition had a different impact on each of George III's audiences. For those engaging in the highest levels of British politics, George III's statement provided further evidence of their opinions concerning his leadership and its effectiveness. His supporters found a firmness of purpose and direction in his words, while his opposition saw evidence of his intractable nature and failure to compromise. Similarly to George III, both sides viewed the document through the lens of an eighteenth-century elite who practiced the politics of convenience and factional loyalty. The statement not only served to define the position of the Crown but also functioned as fodder for discussion and debate. The British public was much less discriminating in its interpretations. Their reading of the document was filtered by the popular press. In fact, given the low literacy rates in Great Britain, most of their understanding came by word of mouth. For them, the proclamation was a call to arms and a sacrifice in protection of the empire. George III and his advisers hoped to deflect the public from their misery and to create a common cause.

Colonists digested the edict differently. First, more colonists could read, and they subjected the proclamation to individual and group scrutiny. In that sense, they read the document as the British elites would rather than as the general British public would. Rather than absorbing it as propaganda, colonists felt that the proclamation spoke and applied to each of them. Conservatives—those hoping to reform from within—perceived it as a warning and a call for reconciliation. Radicals—those seeing rebellion as the only way to secure their freedoms—took it as a declaration of war. All colonists felt the need to respond. George III felt the declaration was the first step in solving his problems in North America. He failed to realize that issuing the proclamation raised the stakes and forced colonists to choose sides. In the process, the moderates and undecided were forced from the middle and leaned more toward rebellion.

Related Documents

George III, king of Great Britain and Ireland. "Proclamation of 1763." ushistory.org Web site. http://www.ushistory.org/declaration/related/proc63.htm. Accessed on September 27, 2007. This document was the first in a series that convinced British colonists in North America of a conspiracy between the Parliament and the king to restrict colonists' rights and liberties.

Jefferson, Thomas. "The Declaration of Independence." ushistory.org Web site. http://www.ushistory.org/declaration/document/index.htm. Accessed on September 27, 2007. Written by Thomas Jefferson, this declaration is the fruition of the American blending of British constitutional law and Enlightenment thought.

Bibliography

■ Books

Bailyn, Bernard. *Ideological Origins of the American Revolution*. Cambridge, Mass.: Belknap Press, 1977.

Brown, Richard D. *The Strength of a People: The Idea of an Informed Citizenry in America, 1650–1870*. Chapel Hill: University of North Carolina Press, 1996.

Hallahan, William H. *The Day the Revolution Began, 19 April 1775*. New York: Harper Collins, 2001.

Maier, Pauline. *American Scripture: Making the Declaration of Independence*. New York: Vintage Books, 1998.

Martin, James Kirby. *In the Course of Human Events: An Interpretive Exploration of the American Revolution*. Arlington Heights, Ill.: Harlan Davidson, Inc., 1979.

Wright, Esmond. *Fabric of Freedom, 1763–1800*, rev. ed. New York: Hill and Wang, 1978.

Wood, Gordon. *The Radicalism of the American Revolution*. New York: Vintage Books, 1993.

■ Web Sites

"The Age of George III." A Web of English History Web site. http://www.historyhome.co.uk/c-eight/18chome.htm. Accessed on September 5, 2007.

"Declaration of Causes and Necessity for Taking Up Arms, July 6, 1775." The Library of Congress "American Memory" Web site. http://memory.loc.gov/cgi-bin/query/r?ammem/hlaw:@field(DOCID+@lit(jc00254)). Accessed on December 11, 2007.

"The Declaration of Independence." ushistory.org Web site. http://www.ushistory.org/declaration/index.htm. Accessed on September 5, 2007.

"Historic Royal Speeches and Writings: George III (1760–1820)." The British Monarchy Web site. http://www.royal.gov.uk/files/pdf/georgeiii.pdf. Accessed on September 6, 2007.

—By Martha Pallante

Questions for Further Study

1. Compare and contrast Proclamation by the King for Suppressing Rebellion and Sedition with the Declaration of Independence. How are the documents structured? Do they share any similarities in language or in form? What were the intents of each author? On what legal foundations are they based? What rights does each claim to protect?

2. Why do British colonists in North America read the proclamation so differently from their British counterparts? In what ways does this difference characterize the lack of understanding that existed on both sides of the Atlantic Ocean?

3. What factors constrained George III's response to the colonists' actions? Which are constitutional in nature? Which are parts of the mind-set typical of an eighteenth-century ruler? In your opinion, as an eighteenth-century monarch, could George III have acted in any other way?

4. If you were a landed gentleman and minor officeholder in Massachusetts in late 1775 and undecided about which side in the debate over the rebellion you favored, how might you have reacted to George III's proclamation? What pressures might your neighbors, some conservative and some radical, have applied to sway your opinion?

Glossary

comfort	aid or encouragement
condign	in accordance with what is deserved
crown	the monarchy
designing	engaging in hostile planning or crafty scheming
dignity	honor owed the king
divers	an indefinite amount; more than one
dominions	territories or colonies subject to a ruler
plantations	settlements in a new country or region; colonies
Privy Council	body of officials and dignitaries chosen by the British monarch and serving as an advisory body or council to the Crown
Royal Proclamation	official public announcement or edict; the king's edict
thereunto	besides; in addition to
to apprehend	to come to know; to lay hold of with understanding
whereas	legal preamble used to introduce a declaration, affirmation, or command

www.milestonedocuments.com

Proclamation by the King for Suppressing Rebellion and Sedition

August 23, 1775

Whereas many of our subjects in divers parts of our Colonies and Plantations in North America, misled by dangerous and ill designing men, and forgetting the allegiance which they owe to the power that has protected and supported them; after various disorderly acts committed in disturbance of the public peace, to the obstruction of lawful commerce, and to the oppression of our loyal subjects carrying on the same; have at length proceeded to open and avowed rebellion, by arraying themselves in a hostile manner, to withstand the execution of the law, and traitorously preparing, ordering and levying war against us: And whereas, there is reason to apprehend that such rebellion hath been much promoted and encouraged by the traitorous correspondence, counsels and comfort of divers wicked and desperate persons within this realm:

FREDERICK lord NORTH.

To the end therefore, that none of our subjects may neglect or violate their duty through ignorance thereof, or through any doubt of the protection which the law will afford to their loyalty and zeal, we have thought fit, by and with the advice of our Privy Council, to issue our Royal Proclamation, hereby declaring, that not only all our Officers, civil and military, are obliged to exert their utmost endeavors to suppress such rebellion, and to bring the traitors to justice, but that all our subjects of this Realm, and the dominions thereunto belonging, are bound by law to be aiding and assisting in the suppression of such rebellion, and to disclose and make known all traitorous conspiracies and attempts against us our crown and dignity; and we do accordingly strictly charge and command all our Officers, as well civil as military, and all others our obedient and loyal subjects, to use their utmost endeavors to withstand and suppress such rebellion, and to disclose and make known all treasons and traitorous conspiracies which they shall know to be against us, our crown and dignity; and for that purpose, that they transmit to one of our principal Secretaries of State, or other proper officer, due and full information of all persons who shall be found carrying on correspondence with, or in any manner or degree aiding or abetting the persons now in open arms and rebellion against our Government, within any of our Colonies and Plantations in North America, in order to bring to condign punishment the authors, perpetrators, and abetters of such traitorous designs.

Given at our Court at St. James's the twenty-third day of August, one thousand seven hundred and seventy-five, in the fifteenth year of our reign.

God save the King.

COMMON SENSE;

ADDRESSED TO THE

INHABITANTS

OF

AMERICA,

On the following intereſting

SUBJECTS.

I. Of the Origin and Deſign of Government in general, with conciſe Remarks on the Engliſh Conſtitution.

II. Of Monarchy and Hereditary Succeſſion.

III. Thoughts on the preſent State of American Affairs.

IV. Of the preſent Ability of America, with ſome miſcellaneous Reflections.

Man knows no Maſter ſave creating HEAVEN,
Or thoſe whom choice and common good ordain.

THOMSON.

The title page of Thomas Paine's Common Sense, *published in 1776* (Library of Congress)

Common Sense

1776

"We have it in our power to begin the world over again."

Overview

By the close of 1775, after years of antagonism between the American people and the British government, not a single patriot had stepped forth to passionately argue the case for refusing the control of the empire centered across the Atlantic Ocean. The first patriot to speak out for this cause was Thomas Paine, who presented his ideas in the pamphlet *Common Sense*. The pamphlet was first published and distributed in Philadelphia, Pennsylvania, on January 9, 1776—nine months after the first clash between American and British soldiers in Lexington and Concord, Massachusetts. Six months after the publication of *Common Sense*, the Continental Congress formally issued Thomas Jefferson's *Declaration of Independence*, and the Revolutionary War officially began.

Paine was, in fact, an Englishman who had been in North America for only about a year when he wrote *Common Sense*. As such he was perhaps in a good position to understand the illegitimacy and absurdity of his home country's rule in the New World. Americans were angered by excesses in taxation; extensive restriction on trade; and the many recent atrocities inflicted on them by British troops ("Redcoats"), such as the slaying of five civilians in the Boston Massacre of 1770. Nevertheless, separation from Britain simply was not widely discussed as an option until the publication of *Common Sense*.

Context

With the end of the Seven Years' War in 1763, antagonism between the American colonies and their governing nation across the Atlantic gradually grew too great to be ignored. Perhaps the most widespread grievance among colonists was that they did not enjoy the same general rights as did the citizens who lived in Great Britain. When Patrick Henry famously demanded either "liberty" or "death" in 1775, after the incidents at Lexington and Concord, he wished for his fellow colonists not independence but simply equal rights as English citizens. In July of that year, the Continental Congress tried to end hostilities and seek reconciliation by extending the Olive Branch Petition to the king of England. The king, however, declined to receive the petition, and to demonstrate his authority he issued a Proclamation for the Suppression of Rebellion and Sedition against the colonies.

Thus, frustration with and resentment over the rule of the British was nearly universal in America by 1776, but a consensus regarding the most appropriate way for the colonies to proceed was not. There had been conflicts, occasionally violent, but the majority of the American population desired only greater liberty within the existing political structure, not a complete dismantling of it. Most Americans saw England as a loving, if stern and unfair, parent, and many colonists rejected the notion of independence for fear of demonstrating ingratitude and irrationality.

The citizens of the various colonies, meanwhile, found themselves in a range of circumstances. While Virginia and Massachusetts, in particular, were suffering economically because of imperial policies, other colonies—such as New York, Pennsylvania, and South Carolina—were flourishing. Certain colonies even bore rivalries with each other, such as over the delineations of borders. Many people believed that only the continued oversight of the "mother" country could sustain any unity among the religiously and socially diverse American populace. Indeed, few people had envisioned any alternate form of government; in some circles *democracy* was simply another word for "mob rule."

About the Author

Thomas Paine was born in Thetford, England, in 1737, and largely lived in the working-class world in which he was raised, despite his elementary education and marked intelligence. He served for two years aboard one of the many privateers operating as both merchant and pirate ships during the Seven Years' War with France, thus gaining a degree of experience in combat among common men. Upon returning to England, Paine began his own corset-making business and attempted to start a family, but his first wife died after only a year of marriage, perhaps while giving birth to the couple's premature infant. Paine remarried but separated from his second wife after several years. Following these setbacks, he gained work as a tax collector, a position he later

Time Line

1763

■ **February 10**
Treaty of Paris signed, ending Seven Years' War, essentially opening hostility between Americans and British.

1770

■ **March 5**
Boston Massacre; five colonists are killed.

1773

■ **December 16**
Boston Tea Party.

1775

■ **April 19**
First shots fired between Redcoats and Patriots at Lexington and Concord, Massachusetts; after that, fighting continues intermittently throughout colonies.

■ **March 23**
Patrick Henry delivers famed "liberty" speech to Virginia House of Burgesses.

■ **July 5**
Second Continental Congress issues Olive Branch Petition, seeking reconciliation with the British Crown.

■ **July 6**
Congress also issues Declaration of the Causes and Necessity of Taking Up Arms, offering justification for military resistance in the name of liberty (though not necessarily independence).

■ **August 23**
King George III issues Proclamation by the King for Suppressing the Rebellion and Sedition against colonies.

1776

■ **January 9**
Common Sense is published.

■ **June 7**
Virginia's Richard Henry Lee offers a resolution for independence to the Continental Congress.

■ **July 2**
Lee's resolution is approved.

■ **July 4**
Continental Congress issues Thomas Jefferson's Declaration of Independence.

lost for failing to perform adequately. Nevertheless, he was later rehired and served for seven years before being fired again after petitioning (in vain) the British Parliament for higher salaries for those in his line of work. In his petition, *Case of the Officers of Excise*, he commented at length on the unjust discrepancies between the lives of the rich and the poor—the poor being especially numerous in that era.

While traveling in England's dissident circles, Paine made the acquaintance of the American statesman Benjamin Franklin, who wrote him letters of introduction to take with him upon his eventual move to America. Paine reached America on November 30, 1774. When he arrived, however, he was suffering from illness, perhaps typhus, and needed to spend a month and a half recovering. After another month and a half, Paine was already writing for the *Pennsylvania Magazine*, through which he became moderately known after penning a polemic against slavery. Some of America's greatest minds began pressuring Paine to address the worsening relationship between Britain and its overseas colonies. Benjamin Franklin had previously urged Paine to write a current history of the grievances between the Americans and the British. Then Benjamin Rush, another antislavery advocate, suggested that Paine write something that could stir the colonists to consider separation from the mother country. Paine set to work on such a project and published *Common Sense* on January 9, 1776. Just six months later, America declared its independence.

Paine, meanwhile, would spend his remaining years engaged in many pursuits, and would receive mixed reviews from critics. Through the Revolutionary War he served in various political offices while bolstering national morale by producing some sixteen *Crisis* papers and a number of other publications. (The first issue of *Crisis*, published in December 1776, opens with the legendary words, "These are the times that try men's souls.") Afterward, Paine sailed to France, where he published essays supporting the workers' movement in Britain; lambasting much of Christianity, which led to his being branded and despised as an atheist; and even criticizing the first president of the United States, George Washington, which further ruined Paine's reputation in the country he had helped usher into existence. Paine finally returned to America in 1802, moving to a farm awarded him by New York State for his wartime services. Lacking family and abusing alcohol, he died with few remaining assets to his name on June 8, 1809.

Explanation and Analysis of the Document

◆ Introduction

In the introduction of *Common Sense*, Paine effectively establishes the incendiary tone that he would employ throughout the pamphlet. Of note here is his opening admission to professing ideas that were not necessarily popular; cleverly, he remarks that his ideas were "not *yet* sufficiently fashionable," implying that no others had considered the issues as fully as he does within the pamphlet. He labels the people of America "sufferers" and "grievously oppressed," immediately assuring all common citizens that he was sympathetic toward their collective plight. Paine expresses his intent to focus on ideas, not men, and thus establishes his relative objectivity. Also, in referring to the "cause of America" as "the cause of all mankind," he lends his work enormous gravity, which was perhaps of great value in justifying the vehemence of his arguments.

◆ "Of the Origin and Design of Government in General, with Concise Remarks on the English Constitution"

Paine opens the first main section of his pamphlet by delineating the differences between the notions of "society" and "government," with the former termed a "blessing" and the latter "a necessary evil." He details the manner in which a small society would develop into a larger one, eventually entailing the institution of a representative government. This government, Paine notes, is only virtuous in that it precisely serves the interests of *all* the community's people. This opening strain of philosophical thought serves to prepare unschooled readers especially for the logical discrediting of British monarchical rule.

Many of Paine's notions are presented in scientific, particularly biological, terms. In paragraph 4 he makes one of his first references to Newtonian mechanics, which Sir Isaac Newton (1642–1727) had formulated less than a century earlier and which could thus still be invoked with a fair impact on the popular consciousness. In paragraph 5 Paine uses a simple but effective analogy comparing the shelter of government to that of a tree. He then refers to man's "natural right." Indeed, throughout the text, Paine draws on natural metaphors and uses the words *nature* and *natural* with the utmost positive connotations, reflecting the fact that in the colonial era the relationship between humans and nature was still very strong.

In paragraphs 7–13 Paine sets about first denouncing governmental tyranny and then demonstrating that, though well disguised, the British government was a symbol of such tyranny. In paragraph 14 Paine notes that the monarchy and the House of Lords, "by being hereditary, are independent of the People." Thus, as he noted earlier and would expound upon later, only in being *selected* by the people can those who govern truly *represent* the people. His analysis of the purported "checking" of power in the monarchical system in paragraphs 15–21 was perhaps carefully read by those who drew up the U.S. Constitution, with its emphasis on adequate true checks and balances. Paine dismisses the monarchy as "a mere absurdity" in paragraph 18, and in fact his intent in *Common Sense* is largely destructive; he was well aware that he would not have to devise the new government to come in order to convince the people of the inaptness of the one they were then living under.

In paragraphs 21–25 Paine reiterates that no government that is directed by a ruler who inherited his position (such as a king) can offer the people true and just representation. In paragraph 23 Paine refers to "the fate of Charles the First," who, after long conflict with Parliament, both through legal struggles and civil wars, was beheaded in 1649; Paine's point is that even this incident did not lead subsequent English monarchs to act with increased moral virtue.

◆ "Of Monarchy and Hereditary Succession"

In this section Paine focuses further on the illegitimacy of monarchical rule under any circumstances. In paragraphs 1–3 he laments the fact that kings ever came into existence at all, positing that they have been the ultimate cause of most wars. In paragraph 4 he introduces religion to the discussion, referring to "government by kings" as "the most prosperous invention the Devil ever set on foot for the promotion of idolatry."

Throughout the opening paragraphs of this section, Paine invokes the Bible, the lessons of which would have struck chords with common men of the time. For instance, in paragraphs 5–8 Paine introduces a general conception of the nature of kings, as drawn from biblical readings. In paragraph 9 he refers to the story of Gideon, as found in Judges 8:22–23. In that story, Gideon pointedly refuses the kingship offered him by the people of Israel, noting that only God can rule over man. In paragraph 10 Paine invokes discussion from I Samuel 8:6–22 and I Samuel 12:13–19. He refers to "the idolatrous customs of the Heathens," raising the question of the difference between idolizing "gods" that are manifestations of nature and idolizing kings and priests, who are merely other men. At the end of paragraph 10 he states, "Monarchy in every instance is the popery of government," the word *popery* being related to the Roman Catholic pope. (The majority of Americans during Paine's era, being Protestants, would not have recognized the "authority" of the pope as legitimate.) At the end of paragraph 11, when Paine asserts that nature makes a mockery of monarchy by often "giving mankind an *ass for a lion*," he is simply pointing out that many of the rulers of England had inherited their positions despite obvious imbecility.

In paragraph 12 Paine notes that even if people choose a first king, they are unjustly constraining their descendants to the rule of that king's descendants. He then points out in paragraph 13 that even if a king long ago came to power by unjust means, the monarchy could later deceive the people regarding its origins. (When Paine suggests in paragraph 13 that an unjustly throned king might invent for himself a "Mahomet-like" tale, he is referring to Muhammad, the Prophet and founder of Islam, who gained followers and fought for his religion during the sixth and seventh centuries.)

In paragraphs 14–25 through the end of the section, Paine comments specifically on the questionable origins and deeds of the English monarchy, adding generalized asides throughout. As referred to in paragraph 14, William the Conqueror, the illegitimate son of the duke of Normandy (thus, as far as Paine is concerned, a "French bastard"), established the long-running English monarchy in 1066 after invading England and killing King Harold in the Battle of Hastings. The conflicts referred to in paragraphs 20–21, collectively known as the Wars of the Roses (1455–1485), illustrate the violence that could arise in a system in which the hereditary passing of rule could be dis-

www.milestonedocuments.com

Thomas Paine shown in an engraving from 1793 (Library of Congress)

rupted. (Sir William Meredith, from paragraph 24, was a member of Parliament in England.)

◆ "Thoughts on the Present State of American Affairs"

In paragraphs 1–5 of this section Paine introduces his extended polemic analyzing the American situation, through which he repeatedly concludes that the wisest course of action would be for the colonies to declare and fight for independence. Indeed, in publishing *Common Sense*, Paine sought both to stir emotion and to ensure that every relevant nuance of the situation was understood by every potential citizen of the envisioned nation. (The reference in paragraph 3 is to Henry Pelham, a British politician; Paine mentions him simply to illustrate the vice of shortsightedness.)

In paragraphs 5–8 Paine denounces the possibility of America's maintaining any sort of union with Great Britain, first noting in paragraph 7 that the commercial ties between the two countries are meaningless. As mentioned in paragraph 9, Hanover, in modern Germany, was linked to England but was taken by the French in the Seven Years' War; Paine's point is that maintaining exclusive association with a country at war with others would only unnecessarily broaden the extent of that war. In paragraphs 10–14 Paine seeks to discredit the familial ties that many colonists certainly felt with their "parent" country. A commonality between England and America to which Paine makes no reference, perhaps strategically, is the English language; indeed, the working classes especially might have dwelled on the importance of a shared mother tongue had Paine mentioned it at all.

In paragraphs 15–19 Paine argues that America's security would not be enhanced through its ties with Great Britain; on the contrary, he believes America would only find itself dragged unnecessarily into the empire's conflicts. In paragraph 19 Paine links the European discovery of America in 1492 to the Protestant Reformation, which essentially began in 1517 when Martin Luther created a set of theses regarding the role of the Roman Catholic Church. Luther's revolutionary stance predictably resulted in increased persecution by papal authorities. Paine posits that God himself perhaps meant for the North American continent to serve as a "sanctuary" from the persecution in Europe.

In paragraphs 20–27 Paine emphasizes that the avoidance of a revolution at that time would be an irresponsibly shortsighted and cowardly delaying of the inevitable. He describes Boston, Massachusetts, as a "seat of wretchedness" in paragraph 22. After the Boston Tea Party, when disguised patriots destroyed imported tea, the British Parliament punished the entire state by closing the Boston port, decimating trade and rapidly impoverishing residents. Paine believed that all Americans were morally obligated to defend themselves, their families, and their countrymen against such tyranny. The 1765 Stamp Act, referred to in paragraph 27, imposed unpopular taxes on newspapers and other documents. It was repealed in 1766, which provided the Revolutionary movement with some momentum, but in 1767 a number of alternate taxes were imposed. These, too, were later repealed in 1770—except for the tax on tea, which brought about the Boston Tea Party.

In paragraphs 28–37 Paine asserts that the American colonies had grown to the point where dependence on Great Britain was a hindrance to smooth governmental functioning. Frederick North, well known as Lord North and mentioned in paragraph 32, was the British prime minister from 1770 to 1782. The "millions … expended," then, refers to resources lost not only through the paying of taxes imposed by the Parliament headed by North but also through the organizational activity undertaken by Americans in efforts to gain the repeal of many of the laws North had enacted. Later in that paragraph, Paine notes the "folly" of paying "a Bunker-hill price" for anything; he refers to the Battle of Bunker Hill, a 1775 conflict in which British redcoats sustained massive losses while subduing rebel troops during the Siege of Boston. The reference to the King's "negative" in paragraph 34 means the monarch's ability to veto any legislation proposed by the colonists. Above all, Paine notes in paragraph 36 that the British Parliament would only ever enact laws affecting America in Britain's interest, not in America's interest.

In paragraphs 38–41 Paine again comments on military matters, noting that engaging in war then would be the only sure way to avoid the continual future loss of life. In hopes of quelling people's fears regarding not just conflict but also the nation's unknown future, in paragraphs 42–48 Paine discusses possibilities regarding the government that would take shape after the overthrow of British rule. He pointedly declares that he does not mean for his word to be the last. Thus, in opening debate regarding the

Essential Quotes

"The cause of America is in a great measure the cause of all mankind."

(Introduction)

"Nature disapproves [hereditary monarchy], otherwise she would not so frequently turn it into ridicule, by giving mankind an ass for a lion.*"*

(Of Monarchy and Hereditary Succession, Paragraph 11)

"I offer nothing more than simple facts, plain arguments, and common sense."

(Thoughts on the Present State of American Affairs, Paragraph 1)

"There is something very absurd, in supposing a continent to be perpetually governed by an island."

(Thoughts on the Present State of American Affairs, Paragraph 29)

"We have it in our power to begin the world over again."

(Appendix to the Third Edition, Paragraph 15)

shape of the government to come, he subtly leaves as a foregone conclusion the idea that independence would soon be gained. (The reference in paragraph 48 is to the Italian Giacinto Dragonetti who wrote *Treatise of Virtues and Rewards*, which first appeared in England in 1769; Dragonetti is invoked simply for being, as Paine notes, a "wise observer on governments.") Paine concludes this section in paragraph 49 by noting that only God and the law will be "King."

"Massanello" (correctly, Masaniello), from paragraph 50, was an Italian fisherman who led a revolt in Naples in 1647 and executed some 1,500 people before his own assassination. Paine mentions him to stress that the rational formation of a republic would far better serve the people than a coup, which might only bring about more tyranny. In paragraphs 51–53 Paine concludes his analysis of the American situation with a fairly impassioned plea for the overthrow of oppression.

◆ "Of the Present Ability of America: With Some Miscellaneous Reflections"

In this section Paine discusses the "ripeness or fitness of the continent for independence" in quantitative and qualitative terms, definitively stating in paragraph 2 that the time for action was the present. In paragraphs 4–15 Paine offers detailed discussion on the advantages the colonies would reap in amassing a naval force; he cites financial figures and dismisses the negative aspects of incurring debt while producing this navy. The privateer *Terrible*, discussed in paragraph 11, was in fact a ship whose crew Paine would have joined as a young man had his father not dissuaded him; Paine might have perished, as did most of the ship's crew, in a battle with a French ship. In paragraphs 13–14 Paine dismisses the notion that the British would ever offer America sufficient military protection. Paine goes on to cite America's abundance of military resources (paragraph 16) and its yet-unoccupied land (paragraph 17) as additional national assets.

Paine proceeds to remark on various aspects of the possibility of independence. In paragraphs 18–20 he posits that America's youth was a reason for, not against, going to war, as the populace was then energetic and ambitious. In paragraph 21 he mentions the need to avoid being subdued by a conqueror, and in paragraph 22 he advocates freedom of religion. In paragraphs 23–26 he revisits notions regarding the government to come, mentioning a continental charter and equal representation through a congress. The episode discussed in paragraph 24 was one in which certain state assembly politicians concocted a resolution instructing their

www.milestonedocuments.com

delegates to the Continental Congress to not support separation from Britain. (Charles Wolfran Cornwall, mentioned in paragraph 26, was speaker of the House of Commons in the government headed by Lord North.)

In this section's conclusion, paragraphs 27–33, which constituted the original conclusion to the entire pamphlet, Paine simply summarizes certain points and reiterates his contention that the only rational option for the colonies was to declare independence.

◆ "Appendix to the Third Edition"

Paine attached the "Appendix" beginning with the second edition to address the fact that a speech by King George III, in which the monarch condemned all acts of resistance carried out by the colonists, appeared in Pennsylvania on the day that *Common Sense* was first distributed. By and large, Paine uses this section to demonstrate that many of his contentions were proved accurate by the king's words, which he characterizes as "wilful audacious libel against the truth, the common good, and the existence of mankind." In fact, much of the text in paragraphs 1–5 is devoted to personal criticism of the king. Sir John Dalrymple, mentioned in paragraph 4, wrote several political works similar to "The Address of the People of England to the Inhabitants of America"; the author of that work argues that the king should be thanked for the repeal of the Stamp Act since he did not prevent those proceedings. Paine dismisses this praise of the king as "idolatry."

In paragraphs 6–19 Paine effectively reiterates points that he made throughout the original text in favor of independence over reconciliation. While somewhat repetitive, Paine was perhaps especially wise to condense his thoughts in closing to solidify his ideas in the minds of readers. The "last war" referred to in paragraph 8 was the Seven Years' War of the 1750s and 1760s, which pitted numerous European nations against one another and even expanded to the American colonies in the form of the French and Indian War. The letter lambasted in paragraph 12, written by William Smith and signed by the New York colonial governor William Tryon, urged the New York assembly to fully consider reconciliation with Britain. Through paragraphs 15–19 Paine endeavors to convey to his readers the full gravity of the American situation; indeed, by the time the colonists read, "The birthday of a new world is at hand," they had in all likelihood already been swayed by Paine's monumental arguments.

Audience

Common Sense was written with an enormous audience in mind: the entire population of North America. By virtue of his life experience, Paine was attuned to the inclinations and desires of both the upper and lower classes, and his pamphlet proved successful largely because of his intent and ability to communicate with the masses. While the tone may seem excessively academic to the modern reader, elongated grammatical constructions were standard in the eighteenth century; thus, in its time, *Common Sense* was considered exceptionally accessible.

With regard to content, Paine catered to common men in part by focusing more on ideas and general concepts than on legislative or political specifics. When he offers formulations regarding the possible shape of the new American government, he does so vaguely and briefly so as not to alienate the less educated with technicalities. Many of his references were to the Bible, with which most any literate person would have been familiar in that era. Further, Thomas Wendel notes, "Paine's genius lies in his earthy metaphors and in the rapier thrust of his epigrammatic style, a style that at times rises to apostrophic grandeur" (p. 20). Indeed, in *Common Sense*, Paine makes frequent references to nature and the natural order, strengthening the connections that common men, many of whom were farmers, would have felt with his ideas. Overall, forgoing scholarly objectivity, Paine argues quite vehemently that America had no reasonable course to follow but that which would bring about immediate separation from Great Britain.

Impact

Revealing why *Common Sense* would prove so important, Benjamin Rush noted before its publication, "When the subject of American independence began to be agitated in conversation, I observed the public mind to be loaded with an immense mass of prejudice and error relative to it" (Liell, p. 55). This was unsurprising, given that most of the dialogue regarding possible political action was produced by and directed only toward the elite. Circulation and readership of periodicals was low and, most relevantly, limited to the most learned classes. Thus, the common man may have had no more knowledge of the truth behind recent occurrences other than what could be propagated by word of mouth, which one would expect to be slow and fairly circumspect.

Common Sense was first published anonymously, as Paine believed that the pamphlet would bear more of an impact if readers understood that it was not being distributed for any one person's personal gain; he truly wished only that his ideas would become every colonist's ideas. Philadelphia proved an ideal launching pad for the pamphlet, as that city was the most populous in the colonies as well as the most politically active—and indeed, among the elite the pamphlet was rapidly devoured and digested. Within days laypeople and congressional delegates alike were passing the text and their opinions of it to friends, and within a month the pamphlet's third edition was being published.

The relevance of the emergence of *Common Sense* can perhaps be most readily understood in considering its publication statistics:

At a time when the most widely circulated colonial newspapers were fortunate if they averaged two thousand sales per week, when the average pamphlet was printed in one or two editions of perhaps a few thousand copies, *Common Sense* went through 25 editions and reached literally hundreds of thousands of readers in the single year of 1776.

Indeed, estimates hold that, by year's end, some 500,000 copies were in circulation among a population of only 2.5 million, of which perhaps one-fourth were slaves and largely illiterate. By contrast, in the twenty-first century, if 10 million copies of a given book are published, with America's population near 300 million, the book is considered extraordinarily successful. (These figures perhaps also reflect the characters of the people occupying the region in the respective eras; in the twenty-first century, of course, citizens are far more likely to receive political "wisdom" from television programs.)

Ultimately, with the general populace and the elite alike swayed by Paine's arguments, a political tide in favor of revolution rapidly swept through the nation. Modern historians are virtually unanimous in saying that *Common Sense* played a major role in spurring the colonists to revolution. Harvey J. Kaye offers a succinct description of the pamphlet's impact in *Thomas Paine and the Promise of America*: "Whatever its originality in idea and language, *Common Sense* was radically original in appeal and consequence. Whether it changed people's minds or freed them to speak their minds, it pushed them—not all of them, but vast numbers of them—to revolution" (p. 50). Even contemporary observers, however, were well aware of the pamphlet's importance. In *Thomas Paine: Apostle of Freedom*, Jack Fruchtman, Jr., cites the words of John Adams: "Without the pen of the author of *Common Sense*, the sword of Washington would have been raised in vain" (p. 78).

Related Documents

Butterfield, L.H., ed. *The Letters of Benjamin Rush*. 2 vols. Princeton, N.J.: Princeton University Press, 1951. Rush played a major role in encouraging Paine to write the pamphlet that would spark the American Revolution. Included in this work is correspondence with Paine himself as well as with Benjamin Franklin, who had served to introduce the two men.

———. *The Diary and Autobiography of John Adams*. 4 vols. Cambridge, Mass.: Belknap Press, 1961. Adams, while himself a fierce patriot, was firmly opposed to many of Paine's notions with regard to the shape the new nation ought to take. Most of Adams's views, including those regarding Paine, can be found in this collection.

Foner, Philip Sheldon, ed. *The Complete Writings of Thomas Paine*. New York: Citadel Press, 1945. Paine himself wrote a number of other pamphlets and essays aside from *Common Sense* and the aforementioned *Crisis* papers. These other works included *The Rights of Man* (2 parts, 1791 and 1792), in which Paine again deconstructs the English monarchy and offers a defense for the French Revolution, and *The Age of Reason* (2 parts, 1794 and 1795), in which he denounces religious institutions as a whole while endorsing belief in God. Foner's edition of Paine's writings has been widely used by historians.

Smyth, Albert Henry, ed. *The Writings of Benjamin Franklin*. 10 vols. New York: Macmillan, 1905–1907. Franklin essentially discovered Paine in dissident circles in England, as evinced by a number of letters in this weighty collection.

Bibliography

Books

Bailyn, Bernard. *The Ideological Origins of the American Revolution*. Cambridge, Mass.: Belknap Press, 1967.

Bodnar, John E. *Remaking America: Public Memory, Commemoration, and Patriotism in the Twentieth Century*. Princeton, N.J.: Princeton University Press, 1991.

Foner, Eric. *Tom Paine and Revolutionary America*. New York: Oxford University Press, 1976.

Fruchtman, Jack, Jr. *Thomas Paine: Apostle of Freedom*. New York: Four Walls Eight Windows, 1994.

Hawke, David Freedman. *Benjamin Rush: Revolutionary Gadfly*. Indianapolis, Ind.: Bobbs-Merrill, 1971.

Kaye, Harvey J. *Thomas Paine and the Promise of America*. New York: Hill and Wang, 2005.

Liell, Scott. *Forty-six Pages: Thomas Paine, "Common Sense," and the Turning Point to American Independence*. Philadelphia: Running Press, 2003.

Locke, John. *Two Treatises of Government*, ed. Peter Laslett. New York: Cambridge University Press, 1988.

Nelson, Craig. *Thomas Paine: Enlightenment, Revolution, and the Birth of Modern Nations*. New York: Viking, 2006.

Paine, Thomas. *Political Writings*, ed. Bruce Kuklick. New York: Cambridge University Press, 1989.

Wendel, Thomas, ed. *Thomas Paine's Common Sense: The Call to Independence*. Woodbury, N.Y.: Barron's Educational Series, 1975.

Web Sites

"Thomas Paine." ushistory.org Web site.
http://www.ushistory.org/paine/. Accessed on May 4, 2007.

Thomas Paine National Historical Association Web site.
http://www.thomaspaine.org/. Accessed on May 4, 2007.

"Thomas Paine Papers." William L. Clements Library, University of Michigan Web site.
http://www.clements.umich.edu/Webguides/NP/Paine.html. Accessed on May 4, 2007.

"Thomas Paine Papers." American Philosophical Association Web site.
http://www.amphilsoc.org/library/mole/p/paine.pdf. Accessed on January 24, 2008.

—By Michael Allen Holmes

www.milestonedocuments.com

Questions for Further Study

1. The overall impact of *Common Sense* has been likened to that of the 1848 publication of *The Communist Manifesto*, in which Karl Marx and Friedrich Engels heralded the possibility of bringing about a classless society. Compare and contrast the two documents, focusing on any *one* of the aspects considered in this chapter (for example, Context, Author, Audience, and so on).

2. Paine makes several statements regarding national debt, perhaps most notably, "A national debt is a national bond; and when it bears no interest, is in no case a grievance" and "as we are running the next generation into debt, we ought to do the work of it, otherwise we use them meanly and pitifully." Reflect on the American national debt in the modern era. How was the situation in the late eighteenth century different from that of the twenty-first century? Do Paine's remarks bear relevance in the modern era? What would Paine say about the present situation?

3. Paine notes, "The present time, likewise, is that peculiar time which never happens to a nation but once, viz., the time of forming itself into a government." Answer *one* of the following two questions: (a) If the opportunity arose to alter whatever aspects of the American government seemed to need alteration, as slightly or drastically as necessary, what would you suggest be changed? (b) If you could oversee the inception of an entirely *new* country according to your own ideals, in the location of your choosing (be it real or imaginary), what form would your government take?

4. As previously discussed, in *Common Sense,* Paine makes frequent reference to "nature" and "natural law," which was perhaps especially wise given the connections that existed between the human being and nature in the Revolutionary era. How has that relationship changed over the two and a quarter centuries since? Would references to "natural law" bear as much weight for modern Americans? What ideological concepts might instead touch modern Americans most deeply? That is, if one sought to persuade the vast majority of Americans with regard to some revolutionary concept, what notions might a polemicist most widely draw upon?

5. Means of communication have greatly evolved since the eighteenth century, most dramatically in the decades following the conception of the Internet. Discuss the effectiveness and social implications of modern forms of mass communication, including newspapers, books, television, film, e-mail, and Web sites (as well as any alternate media of relevance). Conclude by discussing the implications of this vast array of communicative options regarding the propagation of ideas throughout the masses. Would a revolutionary such as Paine have found disseminating his ideas more or less difficult in the modern era?

Glossary

apostate	one who abandons loyalty to
avarice	greed
barrister	type of lawyer, specifically one who pleads cases in an English court
bowers	shelters, such as from the canopies of trees
capricious	impulsive; impetuous
cavilings	small, inconsequential objections
convulsions	violent disturbances
countenance	moral support
credulous	inclined to believe
disaffection	the loss of affection for
encomium	wholehearted praise
execration	denunciation; assertion that something is evil
extirpate	exterminate
felicity	happiness
Felo de se	literally, "evildoer with respect to oneself"; something that causes its own destruction
fidelity	loyalty
gradation	change in small amounts
impregnable	secure from invasion
jesuitically	manipulatingly through language
junto	assembly of people with a common purpose
papistical	Roman Catholic; that is, in reference to the role of the pope, authoritarian
pecuniary	fiscal
prepossession	attitude previously formed
prudence	essentially, common sense with respect to government or management
putative	generally supposed
reciprocal	equally exchanged
remissness	neglect; laxity
Rubicon	a boundary that, when crossed, commits the person to a certain course
sanguine	optimistic
sophist	one who uses reason falsely or deceptively
specious	having deceptive allure
sycophant	one who flatters and serves those in power for personal gain
toryism	loyalty to the Crown
variance	discord; antagonism
viz.	namely
wherefore	thus, one can conclude that

www.milestonedocuments.com

Document Text

COMMON SENSE

Perhaps the sentiments contained in the following pages, are not *yet* sufficiently fashionable to procure them general favour; a long habit of not thinking a thing *wrong*, gives it a superficial appearance of being *right*, and raises at first a formidable outcry in defense of custom. But the tumult soon subsides. Time makes more converts than reason. As a long and violent abuse of power, is generally the Means of calling the right of it in question (and in Matters too which might never have been thought of, had not the Sufferers been aggravated into the inquiry) and as the King of England hath undertaken in his *own right*, to support the parliament in what he calls *theirs*, and as the good people of this country are grievously oppressed by the combination, they have an undoubted privilege to inquire into the pretensions of both, and equally to reject the usurpation of either. In the following sheets, the author hath studiously avoided every thing which is personal among ourselves. Compliments as well as censure to individuals make no part thereof. The wise, and the worthy, need not the triumph of a pamphlet; and those whose sentiments are injudicious, or unfriendly, will cease of themselves unless too much pains are bestowed upon their conversion. The cause of America is in a great measure the cause of all mankind. Many circumstances hath, and will arise, which are not local, but universal, and through which the principles of all Lovers of Mankind are affected, and in the Event of which, their Affections are interested. The laying a Country desolate with Fire and Sword, declaring War against the natural rights of all Mankind, and extirpating the Defenders thereof from the Face of the Earth, is the Concern of every Man to whom Nature hath given the Power of feeling; of which Class, regardless of Party Censure, is the *author*.

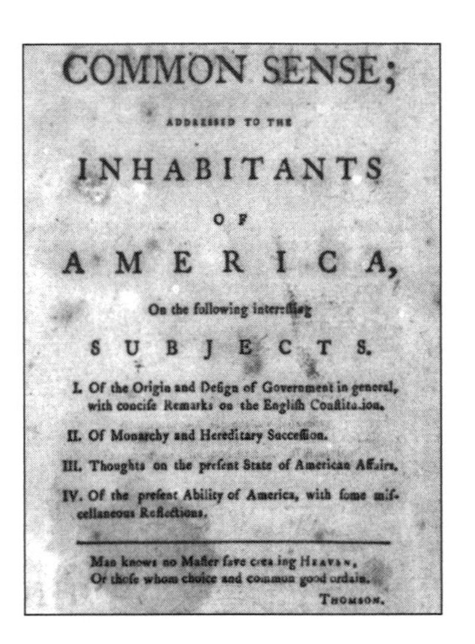
COMMON SENSE;
ADDRESSED TO THE
INHABITANTS
OF
AMERICA,
On the following interesting
SUBJECTS.
I. Of the Origin and Design of Government in general, with concise Remarks on the English Constitution.
II. Of Monarchy and Hereditary Succession.
III. Thoughts on the present State of American Affairs.
IV. Of the present Ability of America, with some miscellaneous Reflections.

Man knows no Master save creating HEAVEN,
Or those whom choice and common good ordain.
THOMSON.

P. S. The Publication of this new Edition hath been delayed, with a View of taking notice (had it been necessary) of any Attempt to refute the Doctrine of Independance: As no Answer hath yet appeared, it is now presumed that none will, the Time needful for getting such a Performance ready for the Public being considerably past. Who the Author of this Production is, is wholly unnecessary to the Public, as the Object for Attention is the *doctrine itself*, not the *man*. Yet it may not be unnecessary to say, That he is unconnected with any Party, and under no sort of Influence public or private, but the influence of reason and principle.

Philadelphia, February 14, 1776

Of the Origin and Design of Government in General, with Concise Remarks on the English Constitution

Some writers have so confounded society with government, as to leave little or no distinction between them; whereas they are not only different, but have different origins. Society is produced by our wants, and government by our wickedness; the former promotes our happiness *positively* by uniting our affections, the latter *negatively* by restraining our vices. The one encourages intercourse, the other creates distinctions. The first is a patron, the last a punisher.

Society in every state is a blessing, but Government, even in its best state, is but a necessary evil; in its worst state an intolerable one: for when we suffer, or are exposed to the same miseries *by a government*, which we might expect in a country *without government*, our calamity is heightened by reflecting that we furnish the means by which we suffer. Government, like dress, is the badge of lost innocence; the palaces of kings are built upon the ruins of the bowers of paradise. For were the impulses of conscience clear, uniform and irresistibly obeyed, man would need no other lawgiver; but that not being the case, he finds it necessary to surrender up a part of his property to furnish means for the protection of the rest; and this he is induced to do by the same prudence which in every other case advises him, out of two evils to choose the least. Wherefore, security being the true design and end of government, it unanswerably follows that whatever form thereof appears most likely to ensure it to us, with the least expense and greatest benefit, is preferable to all others.

In order to gain a clear and just idea of the design and end of government, let us suppose a small number of persons settled in some sequestered part of the earth, unconnected with the rest; they will then represent the first peopling of any country, or of the world. In this state of natural liberty, society will be their first thought. A thousand motives will excite them thereto; the strength of one man is so unequal to his wants, and his mind so unfitted for perpetual solitude, that he is soon obliged to seek assistance and relief of another, who in his turn requires the same. Four or five united would be able to raise a tolerable dwelling in the midst of a wilderness, but one man might labour out the common period of life without accomplishing any thing; when he had felled his timber he could not remove it, nor erect it after it was removed; hunger in the mean time would urge him to quit his work, and every different want would call him a different way. Disease, nay even misfortune, would be death; for, though neither might be mortal, yet either would disable him from living, and reduce him to a state in which he might rather be said to perish than to die.

Thus necessity, like a gravitating power, would soon form our newly arrived emigrants into society, the reciprocal blessings of which would supercede, and render the obligations of law and government unnecessary while they remained perfectly just to each other; but as nothing but Heaven is impregnable to vice, it will unavoidably happen that in proportion as they surmount the first difficulties of emigration, which bound them together in a common cause, they will begin to relax in their duty and attachment to each other: and this remissness will point out the necessity of establishing some form of government to supply the defect of moral virtue.

Some convenient tree will afford them a State House, under the branches of which the whole Colony may assemble to deliberate on public matters. It is more than probable that their first laws will have the title only of Regulations and be enforced by no other penalty than public disesteem. In this first parliament every man by natural right will have a seat.

But as the Colony encreases, the public concerns will encrease likewise, and the distance at which the members may be separated, will render it too inconvenient for all of them to meet on every occasion as at first, when their number was small, their habitations near, and the public concerns few and trifling. This will point out the convenience of their consenting to leave the legislative part to be managed by a select number chosen from the whole body, who are supposed to have the same concerns at stake which those have who appointed them, and who will act in the same manner as the whole body would act were they present. If the colony continue encreasing, it will become necessary to augment the number of representatives, and that the interest of every part of the colony may be attended to, it will be found best to divide the whole into convenient parts, each part sending its proper number: and that the *elected* might never form to themselves an interest separate from the *electors*, prudence will point out the propriety of having elections often: because as the *elected* might by that means return and mix again with the general body of the *electors* in a few months, their fidelity to the public will be secured by the prudent reflection of not making a rod for themselves. And as this frequent interchange will establish a common interest with every part of the community, they will mutually and naturally support each other, and on this, (not on the unmeaning name of king,) depends the *strength of government, and the happiness of the governed.*

Here then is the origin and rise of government; namely, a mode rendered necessary by the inability of moral virtue to govern the world; here too is the design and end of government, viz. Freedom and security. And however our eyes may be dazzled with show, or our ears deceived by sound; however prejudice may warp our wills, or interest darken our understanding, the simple voice of nature and reason will say, 'tis right.

I draw my idea of the form of government from a principle in nature which no art can overturn, viz. that the more simple any thing is, the less liable it is to be disordered, and the easier repaired when disordered; and with this maxim in view I offer a few remarks on the so much boasted constitution of England. That it was noble for the dark and slavish times in which it was erected, is granted. When the world was overrun with tyranny the least remove therefrom was a glorious rescue. But that it is imperfect, subject to convulsions, and incapable of producing what it seems to promise is easily demonstrated.

Absolute governments, (tho' the disgrace of human nature) have this advantage with them, they are simple; if the people suffer, they know the head from which their suffering springs; know likewise the remedy; and are not bewildered by a variety of caus-

www.milestonedocuments.com

Document Text

es and cures. But the constitution of England is so exceedingly complex, that the nation may suffer for years together without being able to discover in which part the fault lies; some will say in one and some in another, and every political physician will advise a different medicine.

I know it is difficult to get over local or long standing prejudices, yet if we will suffer ourselves to examine the component parts of the English Constitution, we shall find them to be the base remains of two ancient tyrannies, compounded with some new Republican materials.

First. — The remains of Monarchical tyranny in the person of the King.

Secondly. — The remains of Aristocratical tyranny in the persons of the Peers.

Thirdly. — The new Republican materials, in the persons of the Commons, on whose virtue depends the freedom of England.

The two first, by being hereditary, are independent of the People; wherefore in a *constitutional sense* they contribute nothing towards the freedom of the State.

To say that the constitution of england is an *union* of three powers, reciprocally *checking* each other, is farcical; either the words have no meaning, or they are flat contradictions.

First. — That the King it not to be trusted without being looked after; or in other words, that a thirst for absolute power is the natural disease of monarchy.

Secondly. — That the Commons, by being appointed for that purpose, are either wiser or more worthy of confidence than the Crown.

But as the same constitution which gives the Commons a power to check the King by withholding the supplies, gives afterwards the King a power to check the Commons, by empowering him to reject their other bills; it again supposes that the King is wiser than those whom it has already supposed to be wiser than him. A mere absurdity!

There is something exceedingly ridiculous in the composition of Monarchy; it first excludes a man from the means of information, yet empowers him to act in cases where the highest judgment is required. The state of a king shuts him from the World, yet the business of a king requires him to know it thoroughly; wherefore the different parts, by unnaturally opposing and destroying each other, prove the whole character to be absurd and useless.

Some writers have explained the English constitution thus: the King, say they, is one, the people another; the Peers are a house in behalf of the King, the commons in behalf of the people; but this hath all the distinctions of a house divided against itself; and though the expressions be pleasantly arranged, yet when examined they appear idle and ambiguous; and it will always happen, that the nicest construction that words are capable of, when applied to the description of something which either cannot exist, or is too incomprehensible to be within the compass of description, will be words of sound only, and though they may amuse the ear, they cannot inform the mind: for this explanation includes a previous question, viz. *How came the king by a power which the people are afraid to trust, and always obliged to check*? Such a power could not be the gift of a wise people, neither can any power, *which needs checking*, be from God; yet the provision which the constitution makes supposes such a power to exist.

But the provision is unequal to the task; the means either cannot or will not accomplish the end, and the whole affair is a Felo de se: for as the greater weight will always carry up the less, and as all the wheels of a machine are put in motion by one, it only remains to know which power in the constitution has the most weight, for that will govern: and tho' the others, or a part of them, may clog, or, as the phrase is, check the rapidity of its motion, yet so long as they cannot stop it, their endeavours will be ineffectual: The first moving power will at last have its way, and what it wants in speed is supplied by time.

That the crown is this overbearing part in the English constitution needs not be mentioned, and that it derives its whole consequence merely from being the giver of places and pensions is self-evident; wherefore, though we have been wise enough to shut and lock a door against absolute Monarchy, we at the same time have been foolish enough to put the Crown in possession of the key.

The prejudice of Englishmen, in favour of their own government, by King, Lords and Commons, arises as much or more from national pride than reason. Individuals are undoubtedly safer in England than in some other countries: but the will of the king is as much the law of the land in Britain as in France, with this difference, that instead of proceeding directly from his mouth, it is handed to the people under the formidable shape of an act of parliament. For the fate of Charles the First hath only made kings more subtle—not more just.

Wherefore, laying aside all national pride and prejudice in favour of modes and forms, the plain truth is that *it is wholly owing to the constitution of the people, and not to the constitution of the government* that the crown is not as oppressive in England as in Turkey.

An inquiry into the *constitutional errors* in the English form of government, is at this time highly necessary; for as we are never in a proper condition of doing justice to others, while we continue under the influence of some leading partiality, so neither are we capable of doing it to ourselves while we remain fettered by any obstinate prejudice. And as a man who is attached to a prostitute is unfitted to choose or judge of a wife, so any prepossession in favour of a rotten constitution of government will disable us from discerning a good one.

Of Monarchy and Hereditary Succession

Mankind being originally equals in the order of creation, the equality could only be destroyed by some subsequent circumstance: the distinctions of rich and poor may in a great measure be accounted for, and that without having recourse to the harsh ill-sounding names of oppression and avarice. Oppression is often the *consequence*, but seldom or never the *means* of riches; and tho' avarice will preserve a man from being necessitously poor, it generally makes him too timorous to be wealthy.

But there is another and great distinction for which no truly natural or religious reason can be assigned, and that is the distinction of men into *kings* and *subjects*. Male and female are the distinctions of nature, good and bad the distinctions of Heaven; but how a race of men came into the world so exalted above the rest, and distinguished like some new species, is worth inquiring into, and whether they are the means of happiness or of misery to mankind.

In the early ages of the world, according to the scripture chronology there were no kings; the consequence of which was, there were no wars; it is the pride of kings which throws mankind into confusion. Holland, without a king hath enjoyed more peace for this last century than any of the monarchical governments in Europe. Antiquity favours the same remark; for the quiet and rural lives of the first Patriarchs have a snappy something in them, which vanishes when we come to the history of Jewish royalty.

Government by kings was first introduced into the world by the Heathens, from whom the children of Israel copied the custom. It was the most prosperous invention the Devil ever set on foot for the promotion of idolatry. The Heathens paid divine honours to their deceased kings, and the Christian World hath improved on the plan by doing the same to their living ones. How impious is the title of sacred Majesty applied to a worm, who in the midst of his splendor is crumbling into dust!

As the exalting one man so greatly above the rest cannot be justified on the equal rights of nature, so neither can it be defended on the authority of scripture; for the will of the Almighty as declared by Gideon, and the prophet Samuel, expressly disapproves of government by Kings.

All anti-monarchical parts of scripture, have been very smoothly glossed over in monarchical governments, but they undoubtedly merit the attention of countries which have their governments yet to form. "Render unto Cesar the things which are Cesar's" is the scripture doctrine of courts, yet it is no support of monarchical government, for the Jews at that time were without a king, and in a state of vassalage to the Romans.

Near three thousand years passed away, from the Mosaic account of the creation, till the Jews under a national delusion requested a king. Till then their form of government (except in extraordinary cases where the Almighty interposed) was a kind of Republic, administered by a judge and the elders of the tribes. Kings they had none, and it was held sinful to acknowledge any being under that title but the Lord of Hosts. And when a man seriously reflects on the idolatrous homage which is paid to the persons of kings, he need not wonder that the Almighty, ever jealous of his honour, should disapprove a form of government which so impiously invades the prerogative of Heaven.

Monarchy is ranked in scripture as one of the sins of the Jews, for which a curse in reserve is denounced against them. The history of that transaction is worth attending to.

The children of Israel being oppressed by the Midianites, Gideon marched against them with a small army, and victory thro' the divine interposition decided in his favour. The Jews, elate with success, and attributing it to the generalship of Gideon, proposed making him a king, saying, "Rule thou over us, thou and thy son, and thy son's son." Here was temptation in its fullest extent; not a kingdom only, but an hereditary one; but Gideon in the piety of his soul replied, "I will not rule over you, neither shall my son rule over you. *the Lord shall rule over you.*" Words need not be more explicit: Gideon doth not decline the honour, but denieth their right to give it; neither

www.milestonedocuments.com

Document Text

doth he compliment them with invented declarations of his thanks, but in the positive style of a prophet charges them with disaffection to their proper Sovereign, the King of Heaven.

About one hundred and thirty years after this, they fell again into the same error. The hankering which the Jews had for the idolatrous customs of the Heathens, is something exceedingly unaccountable; but so it was, that laying hold of the misconduct of Samuel's two sons, who were intrusted with some secular concerns, they came in an abrupt and clamorous manner to Samuel, saying, "Behold thou art old, and they sons walk not in thy ways, now make us a king to judge us like all the other nations." And here we cannot observe but that their motives were bad, viz. that they might be *like* unto other nations, i. e. the Heathens, whereas their true glory lay in being as much *unlike* them as possible. "But the thing displeased Samuel when they said, give us a King to judge us; and Samuel prayed unto the Lord, and the Lord said unto Samuel, hearken unto the voice of the people in all that they say unto thee, for they have not rejected thee, but they have rejected me, *that I should not reign over them*. According to all the works which they have done since the day that I brought them up out of Egypt even unto this day, wherewith they have forsaken me, and served other Gods: so do they also unto thee. Now therefore hearken unto their voice, howbeit, protest solemnly unto them and show them the manner of the King that shall reign over them," i.e. not of any particular King, but the general manner of the Kings of the earth whom Israel was so eagerly copying after. And notwithstanding the great distance of time and difference of manners, the character is still in fashion. "And Samuel told all the words of the Lord unto the people, that asked of him a King. And he said, This shall be the manner of the King that shall reign over you. He will take your sons and appoint them for himself for his chariots and to be his horsemen, and some shall run before his chariots" (this description agrees with the present mode of impressing men) "and he will appoint him captains over thousands and captains over fifties, will set them to ear his ground and to reap his harvest, and to make his instruments of war, and instruments of his chariots, And he will take your daughters to be confectionaries, and to be cooks, and to be bakers" (this describes the expense and luxury as well as the oppression of Kings) "and he will take your fields and your vineyards, and your olive yards, even the best of them, and give them to his servants. And he will take the tenth of your seed, and of your vineyards, and give them to his officers and to his servants" (by which we see that bribery, corruption, and favouritism, are the standing vices of Kings) "and he will take the tenth of your men servants, and your maid servants, and your goodliest young men, and your asses, and put them to his work: and he will take the tenth of your sheep, and ye shall be his servants, and ye shall cry out in that day because of your king which ye shell have chosen, *and the Lord will not hear you in that day."* This accounts for the continuation of Monarchy; neither do the characters of the few good kings which have lived since, either sanctify the title, or blot out the sinfulness of the origin; the high encomium of David takes no notice of him *officially as a king*, but only as a *man* after God's own heart. "Nevertheless the people refused to obey the voice of Samuel, and they said, Nay, but we will have a king over us, that we may be like all the nations, and that our king may judge us, and go out before us and fight our battles." Samuel continued to reason with them but to no purpose; he set before them their ingratitude, but all would not avail; and seeing them fully bent on their folly, he cried out, "I will call unto the Lord, and he shall send thunder and rain" (which was then a punishment, being in the time of wheat harvest) "that ye may perceive and see that your wickedness is great which ye have done in the sight of the Lord, *in asking you a king*. So Samuel called unto the Lord, and the Lord sent thunder and rain that day, and all the people greatly feared the Lord and Samuel. And all the people said unto Samuel, Pray for thy servants unto the Lord thy God that we die not, for *we have added unto our sins this evil, to ask a king."* These portions of scripture are direct and positive. They admit of no equivocal construction. That the Almighty hath here entered his protest against monarchical government is true, or the scripture is false. And a man hath good reason to believe that there is as much of kingcraft as priestcraft in withholding the scripture from the public in popish countries. For monarchy in every instance is the popery of government.

To the evil of monarchy we have added that of hereditary succession; and as the first is a degradation and lessening of ourselves, so the second, claimed as a matter of right, is an insult and imposition on posterity. For all men being originally equals, no one by birth could have a right to set up his own family in perpetual preference to all others for ever, and tho' himself might deserve some decent degree of honours of his contemporaries, yet his descen-

www.milestonedocuments.com

dants might be far too unworthy to inherit them. One of the strongest natural proofs of the folly of hereditary right in Kings, is that nature disapproves it, otherwise she would not so frequently turn it into ridicule, by giving mankind an *ass for a lion*.

Secondly, as no man at first could possess any other public honors than were bestowed upon him, so the givers of those honors could have no power to give away the right of posterity, and though they might say "We choose you for our head," they could not without manifest injustice to their children say "that your children and your children's children shall reign over ours forever." Because such an unwise, unjust, unnatural compact might (perhaps) in the next succession put them under the government of a rogue or a fool. Most wise men in their private sentiments have ever treated hereditary right with contempt; yet it is one of those evils which when once established is not easily removed: many submit from fear, others from superstition, and the more powerful part shares with the king the plunder of the rest.

This is supposing the present race of kings in the world to have had an honorable origin: whereas it is more than probable, that, could we take off the dark covering of antiquity and trace them to their first rise, we should find the first of them nothing better than the principal ruffian of some restless gang, whose savage manners of pre-eminence in subtilty obtained him the title of chief among plunderers; and who by increasing in power and extending his depredations, overawed the quiet and defenseless to purchase their safety by frequent contributions. Yet his electors could have no idea of giving hereditary right to his descendants, because such a perpetual exclusion of themselves was incompatible with the free and restrained principles they professed to live by. Wherefore, hereditary succession in the early ages of monarchy could not take place as a matter of claim, but as something casual or complemental; but as few or no records were extant in those days, the traditionary history stuff'd with fables, it was very easy, after the lapse of a few generations, to trump up some superstitious tale conveniently timed, Mahomet-like, to cram hereditary right down the throats of the vulgar. Perhaps the disorders which threatened, or seemed to threaten, on the decease of a leader and the choice of a new one (for elections among ruffians could not be very orderly) induced many at first to favour hereditary pretensions; by which means it happened, as it hath happened since, that what at first was submitted to as a convenience was afterwards claimed as a right.

England since the conquest hath known some few good monarchs, but groaned beneath a much larger number of bad ones: yet no man in his senses can say that their claim under William the Conqueror is a very honourable one. A French bastard landing with an armed Banditti and establishing himself king of England against the consent of the natives, is in plain terms a very paltry rascally original. It certainly hath no divinity in it. However it is needless to spend much time in exposing the folly of hereditary right; if there are any so weak as to believe it, let them promiscuously worship the Ass and the Lion, and welcome. I shall neither copy their humility, nor disturb their devotion.

Yet I should be glad to ask how they suppose kings came at first? The question admits but of three answers, viz. either by lot, by election, or by usurpation. If the first king was taken by lot, it establishes a precedent for the next, which excludes hereditary succession. Saul was by lot, yet the succession was not hereditary, neither does it appear from that transaction that there was any intention it ever should. If the first king of any country was by election, that likewise establishes a precedent for the next; for to say, that the right of all future generations is taken away, by the act of the first electors, in their choice not only of a king but of a family of kings for ever, hath no parallel in or out of scripture but the doctrine of original sin, which supposes the free will of all men lost in Adam; and from such comparison, and it will admit of no other, hereditary succession can derive no glory. for as in Adam all sinned, and as in the first electors all men obeyed; as in the one all mankind were subjected to Satan, and in the other to sovereignty; as our innocence was lost in the first, and our authority in the last; and as both disable us from re-assuming some former state and privilege, it unanswerably follows that original sin and hereditary succession are parallels. Dishonourable rank! inglorious connection! yet the most subtle sophist cannot produce a juster simile.

As to usurpation, no man will be so hardy as to defend it; and that William the Conqueror was an usurper is a fact not to be contradicted. The plain truth is, that the antiquity of English monarchy will not bear looking into.

But it is not so much the absurdity as the evil of hereditary succession which concerns mankind. Did it ensure a race of good and wise men it would have the seal of divine authority, but as it opens a door to the *foolish*, the *wicked*, and the *improper*, it hath in it the nature of oppression. Men who look upon themselves born to reign, and others to obey, soon

Document Text

grow insolent. Selected from the rest of mankind, their minds are early poisoned by importance; and the world they act in differs so materially from the world at large, that they have but little opportunity of knowing its true interests, and when they succeed in the government are frequently the most ignorant and unfit of any throughout the dominions.

Another evil which attends hereditary succession is, that the throne is subject to be possessed by a minor at any age; all which time the regency acting under the cover of a king have every opportunity and inducement to betray their trust. The same national misfortune happens when a king worn out with age and infirmity enters the last stage of human weakness. In both these cases the public becomes a prey to every miscreant who can tamper successfully with the follies either of age or infancy.

The most plausible plea which hath ever been offered in favor of hereditary succession is, that it preserves a nation from civil wars; and were this true, it would be weighty; whereas it is the most barefaced falsity ever imposed upon mankind. The whole history of England disowns the fact. Thirty kings and two minors have reigned in that distracted kingdom since the conquest, in which time there has been (including the revolution) no less than eight civil wars and nineteen Rebellions. Wherefore instead of making for peace, it makes against it, and destroys the very foundation it seems to stand upon.

The contest for monarchy and succession, between the houses of York and Lancaster, laid England in a scene of blood for many years. Twelve pitched battles besides skirmishes and sieges were fought between Henry and Edward. Twice was Henry prisoner to Edward, who in his turn was prisoner to Henry. And so uncertain is the fate of war and the temper of a nation, when nothing but personal matters are the ground of a quarrel, that Henry was taken in triumph from a prison to a palace, and Edward obliged to fly from a palace to a foreign land; yet, as sudden transitions of temper are seldom lasting, Henry in his turn was driven from the throne, and Edward re-called to succeed him. The parliament always following the strongest side.

This contest began in the reign of Henry the Sixth, and was not entirely extinguished till Henry the Seventh, in whom the families were united. Including a period of 67 years, viz. from 1422 to 1489.

In short, monarchy and succession have laid (not this or that kingdom only) but the world in blood and ashes. 'Tis a form of government which the word of God bears testimony against, and blood will attend it.

If we enquire into the business of a King, we shall find that in some countries they may have none; and after sauntering away their lives without pleasure to themselves or advantage to the nation, withdraw from the scene, and leave their successors to tread the same idle round. In absolute monarchies the whole weight of business civil and military lies on the King; the children of Israel in their request for a king urged this plea, "that he may judge us, and go out before us and fight our battles." But in countries where he is neither a Judge nor a General, as in England, a man would be puzzled to know what *is* his business.

The nearer any government approaches to a Republic, the less business there is for a King. It is somewhat difficult to find a proper name for the government of England. Sir William Meredith calls it a Republic; but in its present state it is unworthy of the name, because the corrupt influence of the Crown, by having all the places in its disposal, hath so effectually swallowed up the power, and eaten out the virtue of the House of Commons (the Republican part in the constitution) that the government of England is nearly as monarchical as that of France or Spain. Men fall out with names without understanding them. For 'tis the Republican and not the Monarchical part of the Constitution of England which Englishmen glory in, viz. the liberty of choosing an House of Commons from out of their own body—and it is easy to see that when Republican virtues fail, slavery ensues. Why is the constitution of England sickly, but because monarchy hath poisoned the Republic; the Crown hath engrossed the Commons.

In England a King hath little more to do than to make war and giveaway places; which, in plain terms, is to empoverish the nation and set it together by the ears. A pretty business indeed for a man to be allowed eight hundred thousand sterling a year for, and worshipped into the bargain! Of more worth is one honest man to society, and in the sight of God, than all the crowned ruffians that ever lived.

Thoughts on the Present State of American Affairs

In the following pages I offer nothing more than simple facts, plain arguments, and common sense: and have no other preliminaries to settle with the reader, than that he will divest himself of prejudice and prepossession, and suffer his reason and his feelings to determine for themselves that he will put on,

www.milestonedocuments.com

or rather that he will not put off, the true character of a man, and generously enlarge his views beyond the present day.

Volumes have been written on the subject of the struggle between England and America. Men of all ranks have embarked in the controversy, from different motives, and with various designs; but all have been ineffectual, and the period of debate is closed. Arms as the last resource decide the contest; the appeal was the choice of the King, and the Continent has accepted the challenge.

It hath been reported of the late Mr. Pelham (who tho' an able minister was not without his faults) that on his being attacked in the House of Commons on the score that his measures were only of a temporary kind, replied, *"they will last my time."* Should a thought so fatal and unmanly possess the Colonies in the present contest, the name of ancestors will be remembered by future generations with detestation.

The Sun never shined on a cause of greater worth. 'Tis not the affair of a City, a County, a Province, or a Kingdom; but of a Continent—of at least one-eighth part of the habitable Globe. 'Tis not the concern of a day, a year, or an age; posterity are virtually involved in the contest, and will be more or less affected even to the end of time, by the proceedings now. Now is the seed-time of Continental union, faith and honour. The least fracture now will be like a name engraved with the point of a pin on the tender rind of a young oak; the wound would enlarge with the tree, and posterity read in it full grown characters.

By referring the matter from argument to arms, a new era for politics is struck—a new method of thinking hath arisen. All plans, proposals, &c. prior to the nineteenth of April, i.e. to the commencement of hostilities, are like the almanacks of the last year; which tho' proper then, are superceded and useless now. Whatever was advanced by the advocates on either side of the question then, terminated in one and the same point, viz. a union with Great Britain; the only difference between the parties was the method of effecting it; the one proposing force, the other friendship; but it hath so far happened that the first hath failed, and the second hath withdrawn her influence.

As much hath been said of the advantages of reconciliation, which, like an agreeable dream, hath passed away and left us as we were, it is but right that we should examine the contrary side of the argument, and enquire into some of the many material injuries which these Colonies sustain, and always will sustain, by being connected with and dependant on Great Britain. To examine that connection and dependance, on the principles of nature and common sense, to see what we have to trust to, if separated, and what we are to expect, if dependant.

I have heard it asserted by some, that as America has flourished under her former connection with Great Britain, the same connection is necessary towards her future happiness, and will always have the same effect. Nothing can be more fallacious than this kind of argument. We may as well assert that because a child has thrived upon milk, that it is never to have meat, or that the first twenty years of our lives is to become a precedent for the next twenty. But even this is admitting more than is true; for I answer roundly that America would have flourished as much, and probably much more, had no European power taken any notice of her. The commerce by which she hath enriched herself are the necessaries of life, and will always have a market while eating is the custom of Europe.

But she has protected us, say some. That she hath engrossed us is true, and defended the Continent at our expense as well as her own, is admitted; and she would have defended Turkey from the same motive, viz.—for the sake of trade and dominion.

Alas! we have been long led away by ancient prejudices and made large sacrifices to superstition. We have boasted the protection of Great Britain, without considering, that her motive was *interest* not *attachment*; and that she did not protect us from *our enemies* on *our account*; but from *her enemies* on *her own account*, from those who had no quarrel with us on any *other account*, and who will always be our enemies on the *same account*. Let Britain waive her pretensions to the Continent, or the Continent throw off the dependance, and we should be at peace with France and Spain, were they at war with Britain. The miseries of Hanover last war ought to warn us against connections.

It hath lately been asserted in parliament, that the Colonies have no relation to each other but through the Parent Country, i.e. that Pennsylvania and the Jerseys and so on for the rest, are sister Colonies by the way of England; this is certainly a very roundabout way of proving relationship, but it is the nearest and only true way of proving enmity (or enemyship, if I may so call it.) France and Spain never were, nor perhaps ever will be, our enemies as *Americans*, but as our being the *subjects of Great Britain*.

But Britain is the parent country, say some. Then the more shame upon her conduct. Even brutes do not devour their young, nor savages make war upon their families. Wherefore, the assertion, if true, turns

Document Text

to her reproach; but it happens not to be true, or only partly so, and the phrase *parent or mother country* hath been jesuitically adopted by the King and his parasites, with a low papistical design of gaining an unfair bias on the credulous weakness of our minds. Europe, and not England, is the parent country of America. This new World hath been the asylum for the persecuted lovers of civil and religious liberty from *every part* of Europe. Hither have they fled, not from the tender embraces of the mother, but from the cruelty of the monster; and it is so far true of England, that the same tyranny which drove the first emigrants from home, pursues their descendants still.

In this extensive quarter of the globe, we forget the narrow limits of three hundred and sixty miles (the extent of England) and carry our friendship on a larger scale; we claim brotherhood with every European Christian, and triumph in the generosity of the sentiment.

It is pleasant to observe by what regular gradations we surmount the force of local prejudices, as we enlarge our acquaintance with the World. A man born in any town in England divided into parishes, will naturally associate most with his fellow parishioners (because their interests in many cases will be common) and distinguish him by the name of *neighbor*; if he meet him but a few miles from home, he drops the narrow idea of a street, and salutes him by the name of *townsman*; if he travel out of the county and meet him in any other, he forgets the minor divisions of street and town, and calls him *countryman*, i.e. *countyman*; but if in their foreign excursions they should associate in France, or any other part of *Europe*, their local remembrance would be enlarged into that of *Englishmen*. And by a just parity of reasoning, all Europeans meeting in America, or any other quarter of the globe, are *countrymen*; for England, Holland, Germany, or Sweden, when compared with the whole, stand in the same places on the larger scale, which the divisions of street, town, and county do on the smaller ones; Distinctions too limited for Continental minds. Not one third of the inhabitants, even of this province, [Pennsylvania], are of English descent. Wherefore, I reprobate the phrase of Parent or Mother Country applied to England only, as being false, selfish, narrow and ungenerous.

But, admitting that we were all of English descent, what does it amount to? Nothing. Britain, being now an open enemy, extinguishes every other name and title: and to say that reconciliation is our duty, is truly farcical. The first king of England, of the present line (William the Conqueror) was a Frenchman, and half the peers of England are descendants from the same country; wherefore, by the same method of reasoning, England ought to be governed by France.

Much hath been said of the united strength of Britain and the Colonies, that in conjunction they might bid defiance to the world. But this is mere presumption; the fate of war is uncertain, neither do the expressions mean anything; for this continent would never suffer itself to be drained of inhabitants, to support the British arms in either Asia, Africa, or Europe.

Besides, what have we to do with setting the world at defiance? Our plan is commerce, and that, well attended to, will secure us the peace and friendship of all Europe; because it is the interest of all Europe to have America a free port. Her trade will always be a protection, and her barrenness of gold and silver secure her from invaders.

I challenge the warmest advocate for reconciliation to show a single advantage that this continent can reap by being connected with Great Britain. I repeat the challenge; not a single advantage is derived. Our corn will fetch its price in any market in Europe, and our imported goods must be paid for buy them where we will.

But the injuries and disadvantages which we sustain by that connection, are without number; and our duty to mankind at large, as well as to ourselves, instruct us to renounce the alliance: because, any submission to, or dependance on, Great Britain, tends directly to involve this Continent in European wars and quarrels, and set us at variance with nations who would otherwise seek our friendship, and against whom we have neither anger nor complaint. As Europe is our market for trade, we ought to form no partial connection with any part of it. It is the true interest of America to steer clear of European contentions, which she never can do, while, by her dependance on Britain, she is made the makeweight in the scale of British politics.

Europe is too thickly planted with Kingdoms to be long at peace, and whenever a war breaks out between England and any foreign power, the trade of America goes to ruin, *because of her connection with Britain*. The next war may not turn out like the last, and should it not, the advocates for reconciliation now will be wishing for separation then, because neutrality in that case would be a safer convoy than a man of war. Every thing that is right or reasonable pleads for separation. The blood of the slain, the weeping voice of nature cries, *'tis time to part*. Even the distance at which the Almighty hath placed England and America is a strong and natural proof that

Document Text

the authority of the one over the other, was never the design of Heaven. The time likewise at which the Continent was discovered, adds weight to the argument, and the manner in which it was peopled, encreases the force of it. The Reformation was preceded by the discovery of America: As if the Almighty graciously meant to open a sanctuary to the persecuted in future years, when home should afford neither friendship nor safety.

The authority of Great Britain over this continent, is a form of government, which sooner or later must have an end: And a serious mind can draw no true pleasure by looking forward, under the painful and positive conviction that what he calls "the present constitution" is merely temporary. As parents, we can have no joy, knowing that this government is not sufficiently lasting to ensure any thing which we may bequeath to posterity: And by a plain method of argument, as we are running the next generation into debt, we ought to do the work of it, otherwise we use them meanly and pitifully. In order to discover the line of our duty rightly, we should take our children in our hand, and fix our station a few years farther into life; that eminence will present a prospect which a few present fears and prejudices conceal from our sight.

Though I would carefully avoid giving unnecessary offence, yet I am inclined to believe, that all those who espouse the doctrine of reconciliation, may be included within the following descriptions. Interested men, who are not to be trusted, weak men who *cannot* see, prejudiced men who will not see, and a certain set of moderate men who think better of the European world than it deserves; and this last class, by an ill-judged deliberation, will be the cause of more calamities to this Continent than all the other three.

It is the good fortune of many to live distant from the scene of present sorrow; the evil is not sufficiently brought to their doors to make them feel the precariousness with which all American property is possessed. But let our imaginations transport us a few moments to Boston; that seat of wretchedness will teach us wisdom, and instruct us for ever to renounce a power in whom we can have no trust. The inhabitants of that unfortunate city who but a few months ago were in ease and affluence, have now no other alternative than to stay and starve, or turn out to beg. Endangered by the fire of their friends if they continue within the city and plundered by the soldiery if they leave it, in their present situation they are prisoners without the hope of redemption, and in a general attack for their relief they would be exposed to the fury of both armies.

Men of passive tempers look somewhat lightly over the offences of Great Britain, and, still hoping for the best, are apt to call out, "Come, come, we shall be friends again for all this." But examine the passions and feelings of mankind: bring the doctrine of reconciliation to the touchstone of nature, and then tell me whether you can hereafter love, honour, and faithfully serve the power that hath carried fire and sword into your land? If you cannot do all these, then are you only deceiving yourselves, and by your delay bringing ruin upon posterity. Your future connection with Britain, whom you can neither love nor honour, will be forced and unnatural, and being formed only on the plan of present convenience, will in a little time fall into a relapse more wretched than the first. But if you say, you can still pass the violations over, then I ask, hath your house been burnt? Hath your property been destroyed before your face? Are your wife and children destitute of a bed to lie on, or bread to live on? Have you lost a parent or a child by their hands, and yourself the ruined and wretched survivor? If you have not, then are you not a judge of those who have. But if you have, and can still shake hands with the murderers, then are you unworthy the name of husband, father, friend or lover, and whatever may be your rank or title in life, you have the heart of a coward, and the spirit of a sycophant.

This is not inflaming or exaggerating matters, but trying them by those feelings and affections which nature justifies, and without which, we should be incapable of discharging the social duties of life, or enjoying the felicities of it. I mean not to exhibit horror for the purpose of provoking revenge, but to awaken us from fatal and unmanly slumbers, that we may pursue determinately some fixed object. It is not in the power of Britain or of Europe to conquer America, if she do not conquer herself by *delay* and *timidity*. The present winter is worth an age if rightly employed, but if lost or neglected, the whole continent will partake of the misfortune; and there is no punishment which that man will not deserve, be he who, or what, or where he will, that may be the means of sacrificing a season so precious and useful.

It is repugnant to reason, to the universal order of things to all examples from former ages, to suppose, that this continent can longer remain subject to any external power. The most sanguine in Britain does not think so. The utmost stretch of human wisdom cannot, at this time, compass a plan short of separation, which can promise the continent even a year's security. Reconciliation is *now* a falacious dream.

www.milestonedocuments.com

Document Text

Nature hath deserted the connexion, and Art cannot supply her place. For, as Milton wisely expresses, "never can true reconcilement grow where wounds of deadly hate have pierced so deep."

Every quiet method for peace hath been ineffectual. Our prayers have been rejected with disdain; and only tended to convince us, that nothing flatters vanity, or confirms obstinacy in Kings more than repeated petitioning—and noting hath contributed more than that very measure to make the Kings of Europe absolute: Witness Denmark and Sweden. Wherefore, since nothing but blows will do, for God's sake, let us come to a final separation, and not leave the next generation to be cutting throats, under the violated unmeaning names of parent and child.

To say, they will never attempt it again is idle and visionary, we thought so at the repeal of the stamp act, yet a year or two undeceived us; as well may we suppose that nations, which have been once defeated, will never renew the quarrel.

As to government matters, it is not in the power of Britain to do this continent justice: The business of it will soon be too weighty, and intricate, to be managed with any tolerable degree of convenience, by a power, so distant from us, and so very ignorant of us; for if they cannot conquer us, they cannot govern us. To be always running three or four thousand miles with a tale or a petition, waiting four or five months for an answer, which when obtained requires five or six more to explain it in, will in a few years be looked upon as folly and childishness—There was a time when it was proper, and there is a proper time for it to cease.

Small islands not capable of protecting themselves, are the proper objects for kingdoms to take under their care; but there is something very absurd, in supposing a continent to be perpetually governed by an island. In no instance hath nature made the satellite larger than its primary planet, and as England and America, with respect to each other, reverses the common order of nature, it is evident they belong to different systems: England to Europe, America to itself.

I am not induced by motives of pride, party, or resentment to espouse the doctrine of separation and independance; I am clearly, positively, and conscientiously persuaded that it is the true interest of this continent to be so; that every thing short of *that* is mere patchwork, that it can afford no lasting felicity,—that it is leaving the sword to our children, and shrinking back at a time, when, a little more, a little farther, would have rendered this continent the glory of the earth.

As Britain hath not manifested the least inclination towards a compromise, we may be assured that no terms can be obtained worthy the acceptance of the continent, or any ways equal to the expense of blood and treasure we have been already put to.

The object, contended for, ought always to bear some just proportion to the expense. The removal of North, or the whole detestable junto, is a matter unworthy the millions we have expended. A temporary stoppage of trade, was an inconvenience, which would have sufficiently ballanced the repeal of all the acts complained of, had such repeals been obtained; but if the whole continent must take up arms, if every man must be a soldier, it is scarcely worth our while to fight against a contemptible ministry only. Dearly, dearly, do we pay for the repeal of the acts, if that is all we fight for; for in a just estimation, it is as great a folly to pay a Bunker-hill price for law, as for land. As I have always considered the independancy of this continent, as an event, which sooner or later must arrive, so from the late rapid progress of the continent to maturity, the event could not be far off. Wherefore, on the breaking out of hostilities, it was not worth the while to have disputed a matter, which time would have finally redressed, unless we meant to be in earnest; otherwise, it is like wasting an estate on a suit at law, to regulate the trespasses of a tenant, whose lease is just expiring. No man was a warmer wisher for reconciliation than myself, before the fatal nineteenth of April 1775, but the moment the event of that day was made known, I rejected the hardened, sullen tempered Pharaoh of England for ever; and disdain the wretch, that with the pretended title of *Father of His People*, can unfeelingly hear of their slaughter, and composedly sleep with their blood upon his soul.

But admitting that matters were now made up, what would be the event? I answer, the ruin of the continent. And that for several reasons.

First. The powers of governing still remaining in the hands of the king, he will have a negative over the whole legislation of this continent. And as he hath shewn himself such an inveterate enemy to liberty, and discovered such a thirst for arbitrary power; is he, or is he not, a proper man to say to these colonies, *"You shall make no laws but what I please."* And is there any inhabitant in America so ignorant, as not to know, that according to what is called the *present constitution*, that this continent can make no laws but what the king gives it leave to; and is there any man so unwise, as not to see, that (considering what has happened) he will suffer no law to be made here, but such as suit *his* purpose. We may be as effectually enslaved by the want of laws in America, as by submitting to laws made for us in England. After matters are made up (as it is called) can there be any doubt, but the whole power of the crown will be exerted, to keep this continent as low and humble as possible? Instead of going forward we shall go backward, or be perpetually quarrelling or ridiculously petitioning.—We are already greater than the king wishes us to be, and will he not hereafter endeavour to make us less? To bring the matter to one point. Is the power who is jealous of our prosperity, a proper power to govern us? Whoever says *No* to this question is an *independant*, for independancy means no more, than, whether we shall make our own laws, or, whether the king, the greatest enemy this continent hath, or can have, shall tell us, *"there shall be no laws but such as I like."*

But the king you will say has a negative in England; the people there can make no laws without his consent. In point of right and good order, there is something very ridiculous, that a youth of twenty-one (which hath often happened) shall say to several millions of people, older and wiser than himself, I forbid this or that act of yours to be law. But in this place I decline this sort of reply, though I will never cease to expose the absurdity of it, and only answer, that England being the King's residence, and America not so, make quite another case. The king's negative *here* is ten times more dangerous and fatal than it can be in England, for *there* he will scarcely refuse his consent to a bill for putting England into as strong a state of defence as possible, and in America he would never suffer such a bill to be passed.

America is only a secondary object in the system of British politics, England consults the good of *this* country, no farther than it answers her *own* purpose. Wherefore, her own interest leads her to suppress the growth of *ours* in every case which doth not promote her advantage, or in the least interferes with it. A pretty state we should soon be in under such a second-hand government, considering what has happened! Men do not change from enemies to friends by the alteration of a name: And in order to shew that reconciliation *now* is a dangerous doctrine, I affirm, *that it would be policy in the king at this time, to repeal the acts for the sake of reinstating himself in the government of the provinces*; in order that *he may accomplish by craft and subtility, in the long run, what he cannot do by force and violence in the short one*. Reconciliation and ruin are nearly related.

Secondly. That as even the best terms, which we can expect to obtain, can amount to no more than a temporary expedient, or a kind of government by guardianship, which can last no longer than till the colonies come of age, so the general face and state of things, in the interim, will be unsettled and unpromising. Emigrants of property will not choose to come to a country whose form of government hangs but by a thread, and who is every day tottering on the brink of commotion and disturbance; and numbers of the present inhabitants would lay hold of the interval, to dispose of their effects, and quit the continent.

But the most powerful of all arguments, is, that nothing but independance, i. e. a continental form of government, can keep the peace of the continent and preserve it inviolate from civil wars. I dread the event of a reconciliation with Britain now, as it is more than probable, that it will followed by a revolt somewhere or other, the consequences of which may be far more fatal than all the malice of Britain.

Thousands are already ruined by British barbarity; (thousands more will probably suffer the same fate.) Those men have other feelings than us who have nothing suffered. All they *now* possess is liberty, what they before enjoyed is sacrificed to its service, and having nothing more to lose, they disdain submission. Besides, the general temper of the colonies, towards a British government, will be like that of a youth, who is nearly out of his time; they will care very little about her. And a government which cannot preserve the peace, is no government at all, and in that case we pay our money for nothing; and pray what is it that Britain can do, whose power will be wholly on paper, should a civil tumult break out the very day after reconciliation? I have heard some men say, many of whom I believe spoke without thinking, that they dreaded an independance, fearing that it would produce civil wars. It is but seldom that our first thoughts are truly correct, and that is the case here; for there are ten times more to dread from a patched up connexion than from independance. I make the sufferers case my own, and I protest, that were I driven from house and home, my property destroyed, and my circumstances ruined, that as a man, sensible of injuries, I could never relish the doctrine of reconciliation, or consider myself bound thereby.

The colonies have manifested such a spirit of good order and obedience to continental government, as is sufficient to make every reasonable person easy and happy on that head. No man can assign

www.milestonedocuments.com

Document Text

the least pretence for his fears, on any other grounds, that such as are truly childish and ridiculous, viz. that one colony will be striving for superiority over another.

Where there are no distinctions there can be no superiority, perfect equality affords no temptation. The republics of Europe are all (and we may say always) in peace. Holland and Swisserland are without wars, foreign or domestic: Monarchical governments, it is true, are never long at rest; the crown itself is a temptation to enterprizing ruffians at *home*; and that degree of pride and insolence ever attendant on regal authority, swells into a rupture with foreign powers, in instances, where a republican government, by being formed on more natural principles, would negotiate the mistake.

If there is any true cause of fear respecting independance, it is because no plan is yet laid down. Men do not see their way out—Wherefore, as an opening into that business, I offer the following hints; at the same time modestly affirming, that I have no other opinion of them myself, than that they may be the means of giving rise to something better. Could the straggling thoughts of individuals be collected, they would frequently form materials for wise and able men to improve into useful matter.

Let the assemblies be annual, with a President only. The representation more equal. Their business wholly domestic, and subject to the authority of a Continental Congress.

Let each colony be divided into six, eight, or ten, convenient districts, each district to send a proper number of delegates to Congress, so that each colony send at least thirty. The whole number in Congress will be least 390. Each Congress to sit and to choose a president by the following method. When the delegates are met, let a colony be taken from the whole thirteen colonies by lot, after which, let the whole Congress choose (by ballot) a president from out of the delegates of *that* province. In the next Congress, let a colony be taken by lot from twelve only, omitting that colony from which the president was taken in the former Congress, and so proceeding on till the whole thirteen shall have had their proper rotation. And in order that nothing may pass into a law but what is satisfactorily just, not less than three fifths of the Congress to be called a majority.—He that will promote discord, under a government so equally formed as this, would have joined Lucifer in his revolt.

But as there is a peculiar delicacy, from whom, or in what manner, this business must first arise, and as it seems most agreeable and consistent that it should come from some intermediate body between the governed and the governors, that is, between the Congress and the people, let a *continental conference* be held, in the following manner, and for the following purpose.

A committee of twenty-six members of Congress, viz. two for each colony. Two members for each House of Assembly, or Provincial Convention; and five representatives of the people at large, to be chosen in the capital city or town of each province, for, and in behalf of the whole province, by as many qualified voters as shall think proper to attend from all parts of the province for that purpose; or, if more convenient, the representatives may be chosen in two or three of the most populous parts thereof. In this conference, thus assembled, will be united, the two grand principles of business, *knowledge* and *power*. The members of Congress, Assemblies, or Conventions, by having had experience in national concerns, will be able and useful counsellors, and the whole, being impowered by the people, will have a truly legal authority.

The conferring members being met, let their business be to frame a *continental charter*, or Charter of the United Colonies; (answering to what is called the Magna Charta of England) fixing the number and manner of choosing members of Congress, members of Assembly, with their date of sitting, and drawing the line of business and jurisdiction between them: (Always remembering, that our strength is continental, not provincial:) Securing freedom and property to all men, and above all things, the free exercise of religion, according to the dictates of conscience; with such other matter as is necessary for a charter to contain. Immediately after which, the said Conference to dissolve, and the bodies which shall be chosen comformable to the said charter, to be the legislators and governors of this continent for the time being: Whose peace and happiness, may God preserve, Amen.

Should any body of men be hereafter delegated for this or some similar purpose, I offer them the following extracts from that wise observer on governments *Dragonetti*. "The science" says he "of the politician consists in fixing the true point of happiness and freedom. Those men would deserve the gratitude of ages, who should discover a mode of government that contained the greatest sum of individual happiness, with the least national expense."

—"Dragonetti on virtue and rewards."

Document Text

But where says some is the King of America? I'll tell you Friend, he reigns above, and doth not make havoc of mankind like the Royal Brute of Britain. Yet that we may not appear to be defective even in earthly honors, let a day be solemnly set apart for proclaiming the charter; let it be brought forth placed on the divine law, the word of God; let a crown be placed thereon, by which the world may know, that so far as we approve as monarchy, that in America *the law is King*. For as in absolute governments the King is law, so in free countries the law *ought* to be King; and there ought to be no other. But lest any ill use should afterwards arise, let the crown at the conclusion of the ceremony be demolished, and scattered among the people whose right it is.

A government of our own is our natural right: And when a man seriously reflects on the precariousness of human affairs, he will become convinced, that it is infinitely wiser and safer, to form a constitution of our own in a cool deliberate manner, while we have it in our power, than to trust such an interesting event to time and chance. If we omit it now, some, Massanello may hereafter arise, who laying hold of popular disquietudes, may collect together the desperate and discontented, and by assuming to themselves the powers of government, may sweep away the liberties of the continent like a deluge. Should the government of America return again into the hands of Britain, the tottering situation of things, will be a temptation for some desperate adventurer to try his fortune; and in such a case, what relief can Britain give? Ere she could hear the news, the fatal business might be done; and ourselves suffering like the wretched Britons under the oppression of the Conqueror. Ye that oppose independance now, ye know not what ye do; ye are opening a door to eternal tyranny, by keeping vacant the seat of government. There are thousands, and tens of thousands, who would think it glorious to expel from the continent, that barbarous and hellish power, which hath stirred up the Indians and Negroes to destroy us, the cruelty hath a double guilt, it is dealing brutally by us, and treacherously by them.

To talk of friendship with those in whom our reason forbids us to have faith, and our affections wounded through a thousand pores instruct us to detest, is madness and folly. Every day wears out the little remains of kindred between us and them, and can there be any reason to hope, that as the relationship expires, the affection will increase, or that we shall agree better, when we have ten times more and greater concerns to quarrel over than ever?

Ye that tell us of harmony and reconciliation, can ye restore to us the time that is past? Can ye give to prostitution its former innocence? Neither can ye reconcile Britain and America. The last cord now is broken, the people of England are presenting addresses against us. There are injuries which nature cannot forgive; she would cease to be nature if she did. As well can the lover forgive the ravisher of his mistress, as the continent forgive the murders of Britain. The Almighty hath implanted in us these unextinguishable feelings for good and wise purposes. They are the guardians of his image in our hearts. They distinguish us from the herd of common animals. The social compact would dissolve, and justice be extirpated from the earth, or have only a casual existence were we callous to the touches of affection. The robber, and the murderer, would often escape unpunished, did not the injuries which our tempers sustain, provoke us into justice.

O ye that love mankind! Ye that dare oppose, not only the tyranny, but the tyrant, stand forth! Every spot of the old world is overrun with oppression. Freedom hath been hunted round the globe. Asia, and Africa, have long expelled her.—Europe regards her like a stranger, and England hath given her warning to depart. O! receive the fugitive, and prepare in time an asylum for mankind.

Of the Present Ability of America: With Some Miscellaneous Reflections

I have never met with a man, either in England or America, who hath not confessed his opinion, that a separation between the countries would take place one time or other: And there is no instance in which we have shown less judgment, than in endeavoring to describe, what we call, the ripeness or fitness of the continent for independence.

As all men allow the measure, and vary only in their opinion of the time, let us, in order to remove mistakes, take a general survey of things, and endeavor if possible to find out the *very* time. But I need not go far, the inquiry ceases at once, for the *time hath found us*. The general concurrence, the glorious union of all things, proves the fact.

'Tis not in numbers but in unity that our great strength lies: yet our present numbers are sufficient to repel the force of all the world. The Continent hath at this time the largest body of armed and disciplined men of any power under Heaven: and is just arrived at that pitch of strength, in which no single

www.milestonedocuments.com

Document Text

colony is able to support itself, and the whole, when united, is able to do any thing. Our land force is more than sufficient, and as to Naval affairs, we cannot be insensible that Britain would never suffer an American man of war to be built, while the Continent remained in her hands. Wherefore, we should be no forwarder an hundred years hence in that branch than we are now; but the truth is, we should be less so, because the timber of the Country is every day diminishing, and that which will remain at last, will be far off or difficult to procure.

Were the Continent crowded with inhabitants, her sufferings under the present circumstances would be intolerable. The more seaport-towns we had, the more should we have both to defend and to lose. Our present numbers are so happily proportioned to our wants, that no man need be idle. The diminution of trade affords an army, and the necessities of an army create a new trade.

Debts we have none: and whatever we may contract on this account will serve as a glorious memento of our virtue. Can we but leave posterity with a settled form of government, an independent constitution of its own, the purchase at any price will be cheap. But to expend millions for the sake of getting a few vile acts repealed, and routing the present ministry only, is unworthy the charge, and is using posterity with the utmost cruelty; because it is leaving them the great work to do, and a debt upon their backs from which they derive no advantage. Such a thought's unworthy a man of honour, and is the true characteristic of a narrow heart and a piddling politician.

The debt we may contract doth not deserve our regard if the work be but accomplished. No nation ought to be without a debt. A national debt is a national bond; and when it bears no interest, is in no case a grievance. Britain is oppressed with a debt of upwards of one hundred and forty millions sterling, for which she pays upwards of four millions interest. And as a compensation for her debt, she has a large navy; America is without a debt, and without a navy; yet for the twentieth part of the English national debt, could have a navy as large again. The navy of England is not worth at this time more than three millions and a half sterling.

The first and second editions of this pamphlet were published without the following calculations, which are now given as a proof that the above estimation of the navy is a just one. See Entic's "Naval History," Intro., p. 56.

The charge of building a ship of each rate, and furnishing her with masts, yards, sails, and rigging, together with a proportion of eight months boatswain's and carpenter's sea-stores, as calculated by Mr. Burchett, Secretary to the navy.

For a ship of 100 guns,	35,553 £
90	29,886
80	23,638
70	17,785
60	14,197
50	10,606
40	7,558
30	5,846
20	3,710

And hence it is easy to sum up the value, or cost, rather, of the whole British navy, which, in the year 1757, when it was at its greatest glory, consisted of the following ships and guns.

Ships	Guns	Cost of One	Cost of All
6	100	35,553 £	213,318 £
12	90	29,886	358,632
12	80	23,638	283,656
43	70	17,785	764,755
35	60	14,197	496,895
40	50	10,605	424,240
45	40	7,558	340,110
58	20	3,710	215,180
85 sloops, bombs, and fireships,			
one with another at		2,000	170,000
Cost,			3,266,786 £
Remains for guns,			233,214
Total,			3,500,000 £

No country on the globe is so happily situated, or so internally capable of raising a fleet as America. Tar, timber, iron, and cordage are her natural produce. We need go abroad for nothing. Whereas the Dutch, who make large profits by hiring out their ships of war to the Spaniards and Portuguese, are obliged to import most of the materials they use. We ought to view the building a fleet as an article of commerce, it being the natural manufactory of this country. 'Tis the best money we can lay out. A navy when finished is worth more than it cost: And is that nice point in national policy, in which commerce and protection are united. Let us build; if we want them not, we can sell; and by that means replace our paper currency with ready gold and silver.

In point of manning a fleet, people in general run into great errors; it is not necessary that one-fourth part should be sailors. The Terrible privateer, captain

Document Text

Death, stood the hottest engagement of any ship last war, yet had not twenty sailors on board, though her complement of men was upwards of two hundred. A few able and social sailors will soon instruct a sufficient number of active landsmen in the common work of a ship. Wherefore we never can be more capable of beginning on maritime matters than now, while our timber is standing, our fisheries blocked up, and our sailors and shipwrights out of employ. Men of war, of seventy and eighty guns, were built forty years ago in New England, and why not the same now? Ship building is America's greatest pride, and in which she will, in time, excel the whole world. The great empires of the east are mainly inland, and consequently excluded from the possibility of rivalling her. Africa is in a state of barbarism; and no power in Europe hath either such an extent of coast, or such an internal supply of materials. Where nature hath given the one, she hath withheld the other; to America only hath she been liberal to both. The vast empire of Russia is almost shut out from the sea; wherefore her boundless forests, her tar, iron and cordage are only articles of commerce.

In point of safety, ought we to be without a fleet? We are not the little people now which we were sixty years ago; at that time we might have trusted our property in the streets, or fields rather, and slept securely without locks or bolts to our doors and windows. The case is now altered, and our methods of defence ought to improve with our increase of property. A common pirate, twelve months ago, might have come up the Delaware, and laid the city of Philadelphia under contribution for what sum he pleased; and the same might have happened to other places. Nay, any daring fellow, in a brig of fourteen or sixteen guns, might have robbed the whole Continent, and carried off half a million of money. These are circumstances which demand our attention, and point out the necessity of naval protection.

Some perhaps will say, that after we have made it up with Britain, she will protect us. Can they be so unwise as to mean that she will keep a navy in our harbors for that purpose? Common sense will tell us that the power which hath endeavoured to subdue us, is of all others the most improper to defend us. Conquest may be effected under the pretence of friendship; and ourselves, after a long and brave resistance, be at last cheated into slavery. And if her ships are not to be admitted into our harbours, I would ask, how is she going to protect us? A navy three or four thousand miles off can be of little use, and on sudden emergencies, none at all. Wherefore if we must hereafter protect ourselves, why not do it for ourselves? Why do it for another?

The English list of ships of war is long and formidable, but not a tenth part of them are at any time fit for service, numbers of them are not in being; yet their names are pompously continued in the list; if only a plank be left of the ship; and not a fifth part of such as are fit for service can be spared on any one station at one time. The East and West Indies, Mediterranean, Africa, and other parts, over which Britain extends her claim, make large demands upon her navy. From a mixture of prejudice and inattention we have contracted a false notion respecting the navy of England, and have talked as if we should have the whole of it to encounter at once, and for that reason supposed that we must have one as large; which not being instantly practicable, has been made use of by a set of disguised Tories to discourage our beginning thereon. Nothing can be further from truth than this; for if America had only a twentieth part of the naval force of Britain, she would be by far an over-match for her; because, as we neither have, nor claim any foreign dominion, our whole force would be employed on our own coast, where we should, in the long run, have two to one the advantage of those who had three or four thousand miles to sail over before they could attack us, and the same distance to return in order to refit and recruit. And although Britain, by her fleet, hath a check over our trade to Europe, we have as large a one over her trade to the West Indies, which, by laying in the neighborhood of the Continent, lies entirely at its mercy.

Some method might be fallen on to keep up a naval force in time of peace, if we should judge it necessary to support a constant navy. If premiums were to be given to merchants to build and employ in their service ships mounted with twenty, thirty, forty, or fifty guns (the premiums to be in proportion to the loss of bulk to the merchant), fifty or sixty of those ships, with a few guardships on constant duty, would keep up a sufficient navy, and that without burdening ourselves with the evil so loudly complained of in England, of suffering their fleet in time of peace to lie rotting in the docks. To unite the sinews of commerce and defence is sound policy; for when our strength and our riches play into each other's hand, we need fear no external enemy.

In almost every article of defence we abound. Hemp flourishes even to rankness so that we need not want cordage. Our iron is superior to that of other countries. Our small arms equal to any in the world. Cannon we can cast at pleasure. Saltpetre and gun-

www.milestonedocuments.com

powder we are every day producing. Our knowledge is hourly improving. Resolution is our inherent character, and courage hath never yet forsaken us. Wherefore, what is it that we want? Why is it that we hesitate? From Britain we can expect nothing but ruin. If she is once admitted to the government of America again, this Continent will not be worth living in. Jealousies will be always arising; insurrections will be constantly happening; and who will go forth to quell them? Who will venture his life to reduce his own countrymen to a foreign obedience? The difference between Pennsylvania and Connecticut, respecting some unlocated lands, shows the insignificance of a British government, and fully proves that nothing but Continental authority can regulate Continental matters.

Another reason why the present time is preferable to all others is, that the fewer our numbers are, the more land there is yet unoccupied, which, instead of being lavished by the king on his worthless dependents, may be hereafter applied, not only to the discharge of the present debt, but to the constant support of government. No nation under Heaven hath such an advantage as this.

The infant state of the Colonies, as it is called, so far from being against, is an argument in favour of independence. We are sufficiently numerous, and were we more so we might be less united. 'Tis a matter worthy of observation that the more a country is peopled, the smaller their armies are. In military numbers, the ancients far exceeded the moderns; and the reason is evident, for trade being the consequence of population, men became too much absorbed thereby to attend to anything else. Commerce diminishes the spirit both of patriotism and military defence. And history sufficiently informs us that the bravest achievements were always accomplished in the nonage of a nation. With the increase of commerce England hath lost its spirit. The city of London, notwithstanding its numbers, submits to continued insults with the patience of a coward. The more men have to lose, the less willing are they to venture. The rich are in general slaves to fear, and submit to courtly power with the trembling duplicity of a spaniel.

Youth is the seed-time of good habits as well in nations as in individuals. It might be difficult, if not impossible, to form the Continent into one government half a century hence. The vast variety of interests, occasioned by an increase of trade and population, would create confusion. Colony would be against colony. Each being able would scorn each other's assistance; and while the proud and foolish gloried in their little distinctions the wise would lament that the union had not been formed before. Wherefore the present time is the true time for establishing it. The intimacy which is contracted in infancy, and the friendship which is formed in misfortune, are of all others the most lasting and unalterable. Our present union is marked with both these characters; we are young, and we have been distressed; but our concord hath withstood our troubles, and fixes a memorable era for posterity to glory in.

The present time, likewise, is that peculiar time which never happens to a nation but once, viz., the time of forming itself into a government. Most nations have let slip the opportunity, and by that means have been compelled to receive laws from their conquerors, instead of making laws for themselves. First, they had a king, and then a form of government; whereas the articles or charter of government should be formed first, and men delegated to execute them afterwards; but from the errors of other nations let us learn wisdom, and lay hold of the present opportunity—*to begin government at the right end*.

When William the Conqueror subdued England, he gave them law at the point of the sword; and, until we consent that the seat of government in America be legally and authoritatively occupied, we shall be in danger of having it filled by some fortunate ruffian, who may treat us in the same manner, and then, where will be our freedom? where our property?

As to religion, I hold it to be the indispensable duty of government to protect all conscientious professors thereof, and I know of no other business which government hath to do therewith. Let a man throw aside that narrowness of soul, that selfishness of principle, which the niggards of all professions are so unwilling to part with, and he will be at once delivered of his fears on that head. Suspicion is the companion of mean souls, and the bane of all good society. For myself, I fully and conscientiously believe that it is the will of the Almighty that there should be a diversity of religious opinions among us. It affords a larger field for our Christian kindness; were we all of one way of thinking, our religious dispositions would want matter for probation; and on this liberal principle I look on the various denominations among us to be like children of the same family, differing only in what is called their Christian names.

In page [97] I threw out a few thoughts on the propriety of a Continental Charter (for I only presume to offer hints, not plans) and in this place I take the liberty of re-mentioning the subject, by observing that a charter is to be understood as a bond of solemn obligation, which the whole enters into, to support the right of every separate part, whether of religion, professional freedom, or property. A firm bargain and a right reckoning make long friends.

I have heretofore likewise mentioned the necessity of a large and equal representation; and there is no political matter which more deserves our attention. A small number of electors, or a small number of representatives, are equally dangerous. But if the number of the representatives be not only small, but unequal, the danger is increased. As an instance of this, I mention the following: when the petition of the associators was before the House of Assembly of Pennsylvania, twenty-eight members only were present; all the Bucks county members, being eight, voted against it, and had seven of the Chester members done the same, this whole province had been governed by two counties only; and this danger it is always exposed to. The unwarrantable stretch likewise, which that house made in their last sitting, to gain an undue authority over the delegates of that province, ought to warn the people at large how they trust power out of their own hands. A set of instructions for their delegates were put together, which in point of sense and business would have dishonoured a school-boy, and after being approved by a few, a very few, without doors, were carried into the house, and there passed *in behalf of the whole colony*; whereas, did the whole colony know with what ill will that house had entered on some necessary public measures, they would not hesitate a moment to think them unworthy of such a trust.

Immediate necessity makes many things convenient, which if continued would grow into oppressions. Expedience and right are different things. When the calamities of America required a consultation, there was no method so ready, or at that time so proper, as to appoint persons from the several houses of assembly for that purpose; and the wisdom with which they have proceeded hath preserved this Continent from ruin. But as it is more than probable that we shall never be without a *congress*, every well wisher to good order must own that the mode for choosing members of that body deserves consideration. And I put it as a question to those who make a study of mankind, whether representation and election is not too great a power for one and the same body of men to possess? When we are planning for posterity, we ought to remember that virtue is not hereditary.

It is from our enemies that we often gain excellent maxims, and are frequently surprised into reason by their mistakes. Mr. Cornwall (one of the Lords of the Treasury) treated the petition of the New York Assembly with contempt, because *that* house, he said, consisted but of twenty-six members, which trifling number, he argued, could not with decency be put for the whole. We thank him for his involuntary honesty.

To *conclude*, however strange it may appear to some, or however unwilling they may be to think so, matters not, but many strong and striking reasons may be given to show that nothing can settle our affairs so expeditiously as an open and determined declaration for independence. Some of which are,

First. — It is the custom of Nations, when any two are at war, for some other powers, not engaged in the quarrel, to step in as mediators, and bring about the preliminaries of a peace; But while America calls herself the subject of Great Britain, no power, however well disposed she may be, can offer her mediation. Wherefore, in our present state we may quarrel on for ever.

Secondly. — It is unreasonable to suppose that France or Spain will give us any kind of assistance, if we mean only to make use of that assistance for the purpose of repairing the breach, and strengthening the connection between Britain and America; because, those powers would be sufferers by the consequences.

Thirdly. — While we profess ourselves the subjects of Britain, we must, in the eyes of foreign nations, be considered as Rebels. The precedent is somewhat dangerous to their peace, for men to be in arms under the name of subjects; we, on the spot, can solve the paradox; but to unite resistance and subjection requires an idea much too refined for common understanding.

Fourthly. — Were a manifesto to be published, and despatched to foreign Courts, setting forth the miseries we have endured, and the peaceful methods which we have ineffectually used for redress; declaring at the same time that not being able longer to live happily or safely under the cruel disposition of the British Court, we had been driven to the necessity of breaking off all connections with her; at the same time, assuring all such Courts of our peaceable disposition towards them, and of our desire of entering into trade with them; such a memorial would produce more good effects to this Continent than if a ship were freighted with petitions to Britain.

Under our present denomination of British subjects, we can neither be received nor heard abroad; the custom of all Courts is against us, and will be so, until by an independence we take rank with other nations.

www.milestonedocuments.com

Document Text

These proceedings may at first seem strange and difficult, but like all other steps which we have already passed over, will in a little time become familiar and agreeable; and until an independence is declared, the Continent will feel itself like a man who continues putting off some unpleasant business from day to day, yet knows it must be done, hates to set about it, wishes it over, and is continually haunted with the thoughts of its necessity.

Appendix to the Third Edition

Since the publication of the first edition of this pamphlet, or rather, on the same day on which it came out, the king's speech made its appearance in this city. Had the spirit of prophecy directed the birth of this production, it could not have brought it forth at a more seasonable juncture, or at a more necessary time. The bloody-mindedness of the one, shows the necessity of pursuing the doctrine of the other. Men read by way of revenge. And the speech, instead of terrifying, prepared a way for the manly principles of independence.

Ceremony, and even silence, from whatever motives they may arise, have a hurtful tendency when they give the least degree of countenance to base and wicked performances, wherefore, if this maxim be admitted, it naturally follows, that the king's speech, *is* being a piece of finished villany, deserved and still deserves, a general execration, both by the Congress and the people.

Yet, as the domestic tranquillity of a nation, depends greatly on the chastity of what might properly be called *national manners*, it is often better to pass some things over in silent disdain, than to make use of such new methods of dislike, as might introduce the least innovation on that guardian of our peace and safety. And, perhaps, it is chiefly owing to this prudent delicacy, that the king's speech hath not before now suffered a public execution. The speech, if it may be called one, is nothing better than a wilful audacious libel against the truth, the common good, and the existence of mankind; and is a formal and pompous method of offering up human sacrifices to the pride of tyrants.

But this general massacre of mankind, is one of the privileges and the certain consequences of kings, for as nature knows them not, they know not her, and although they are beings of our own creating, they know not us, and are become the gods of their creators. The speech hath one good quality, which is, that it is not calculated to deceive, neither can we, even if we would, be deceived by it. Brutality and tyranny appear on the face of it. It leaves us at no loss: And every line convinces, even in the moment of reading, that he who hunts the woods for prey, the naked and untutored Indian, is less savage than the king of Britain. Sir John Dalrymple, the putative father of a whining jesuitical piece, fallaciously called, "The address of the people of England to the inhabitants of America," hath perhaps from a vain supposition that the people here were to be frightened at the pomp and description of a king, given (though very unwisely on his part) the real character of the present one: "But," says this writer, "if you are inclined to pay compliments to an administration, which we do not complain of (meaning the Marquis of Rockingham's at the repeal of the Stamp Act) it is very unfair in you to withhold them from that prince, by whose NOD ALONE they were permitted to do any thing." This is toryism with a witness! Here is idolatry even without a mask: And he who can calmly hear and digest such doctrine, hath forfeited his claim to rationality an apostate from the order of manhood and ought to be considered as one who hath not only given up the proper dignity of man, but sunk himself beneath the rank of animals, and contemptibly crawls through the world like a worm.

However, it matters very little now what the king of England either says or does; he hath wickedly broken through every moral and human obligation, trampled nature and conscience beneath his feet, and by a steady and constitutional spirit of insolence and cruelty procured for himself an universal hatred. It is now the interest of America to provide for herself. She hath already a large and young family, whom it is more her duty to take care of, than to be granting away her property to support a power who is become a reproach to the names of men and christians, whose office it is to watch the morals of a nation, of whatsoever sect or denomination ye are of, as well as ye who are more immediately the guardians of the public liberty, if ye wish to preserve your native country uncontaminated by European corruption, ye must in secret wish a separation. But leaving the moral part to private reflection, I shall chiefly confine my further remarks to the following heads:

First, That it is the interest of America to be separated from Britain.

Secondly, Which is the easiest and most practicable plan, *reconciliation or independence*? with some occasional remarks.

Document Text

In support of the first, I could, if I judged it proper, produce the opinion of some of the ablest and most experienced men on this continent: and whose sentiments on that head, are not yet publicly known. It is in reality a self-evident position: for no nation in a state of foreign dependence, limited in its commerce, and cramped and fettered in its legislative powers, can ever arrive at any material eminence. America doth not yet know what opulence is; and although the progress which she hath made stands unparalleled in the history of other nations, it is but childhood compared with what she would be capable of arriving at, had she, as she ought to have, the legislative powers in her own hands. England is at this time proudly coveting what would do her no good were she to accomplish it; and the continent hesitating on a matter which will be her final ruin if neglected. It is the commerce and not the conquest of America by which England is to be benefited, and that would in a great measure continue, were the countries as independent of each other as France and Spain; because the specious errors of those who speak without reflecting. And among the many which I have heard, the following seems the most general, viz. that had this rupture happened forty or fifty years hence, instead of now, the continent would have been more able to have shaken off the dependence. To which I reply, that our military ability, at this time, arises from the experience gained in the last war, and which in forty or fifty years' time, would be totally extinct. The continent would not, by that time, have a quitrent reserved thereon will always lessen, and in time will wholly support, the yearly expense of government. It matters not how long the debt is in paying, so that the lands when sold be applied to the discharge of it, and for the execution of which the Congress for the time being will be the continental trustees.

I proceed now to the second head, viz. Which is the easiest and most practicable plan, reconciliation or independence; with some occasional remarks.

He who takes nature for his guide, is not easily beaten out of his argument, and on that ground, I answer generally that independence being a single simple line, contained within ourselves; and reconciliation, a matter exceedingly perplexed and complicated, and in which a treacherous capricious court is to interfere, gives the answer without a doubt.

The present state of America is truly alarming to every man who is capable of reflection. Without law, without government, without any other mode of power than what is founded on, and granted by, courtesy. Held together by an unexampled occurrence of sentiment, which is nevertheless subject to change, and which every secret enemy is endeavoring to dissolve. Our present condition is, Legislation without law; wisdom without a plan; a constitution without a name; and, what is strangely astonishing, perfect independence contending for dependence. The instance is without a precedent, the case never existed before, and who can tell what may be the event? The property of no man is secure in the present un-braced system of things. The mind of the multitude is left at random, and seeing no fixed object before them, they pursue such as fancy or opinion presents. Nothing is criminal; there is no such thing as treason, wherefore, every one thinks himself at liberty to act as he pleases. The Tories would not have dared to assemble offensively, had they known that their lives, by that act, were forfeited to the laws of the state. A line of distinction should be drawn between English soldiers taken in battle, and inhabitants of America taken in arms. The first are prisoners, but the latter traitors. The one forfeits his liberty, the other his head.

Notwithstanding our wisdom, there is a visible feebleness in some of our proceedings which gives encouragement to dissensions. The continental belt is too loosely buckled: And if something is not done in time, it will be too late to do any thing, and we shall fall into a state, in which neither reconciliation nor independence will be practicable. The king and his worthless adherents are got at their old game of dividing the continent, and there are not wanting among us printers who will be busy in spreading specious falsehoods. The artful and hypocritical letter which appeared a few months ago in two of the New York papers, and likewise in two others, is an evidence that there are men who want both judgment and honesty.

It is easy getting into holes and corners, and talking of reconciliation: But do such men seriously consider how difficult the task is, and how dangerous it may prove, should the continent divide thereon? Do they take within their view all the various orders of men whose situation and circumstances, as well as their own, are to be considered therein? Do they put themselves in the place of the sufferer whose all is already gone, and of the soldier, who hath quitted all for the defence of his country? If their ill-judged moderation be suited to their own private situations only, regardless of others, the event will convince them that "they are reckoning without their host."

Put us, say some, on the footing we were in the year 1763: To which I answer, the request is not now in the power of Britain to comply with, neither will she propose it; but if it were, and even should be

www.milestonedocuments.com

Document Text

granted, I ask, as a reasonable question, By what means is such a corrupt and faithless court to be kept to its engagements? Another parliament, nay, even the present, may hereafter repeal the obligation, on the pretence of its being violently obtained, or unit wisely granted; and, in that case, Where is our redress? No going to law with nations; cannon are the barristers of crowns; and the sword, not of justice, but of war, decides the suit. To be on the footing of 1763, it is not sufficient, that the laws only be put in the same state, but, that our circumstances likewise be put in the same state; our burnt and destroyed towns repaired or built up, our private losses made good, our public debts (contracted for defence) discharged; otherwise we shall be millions worse than we were at that enviable period. Such a request, had it been complied with a year ago, would have won the heart and soul of the continent, but now it is too late. "The Rubicon is passed." Besides, the taking up arms, merely to enforce the repeal of a pecuniary law, seems as unwarrantable by the divine law, and as repugnant to human feelings, as the taking up arms to enforce obedience thereto. The object, on either side, doth not justify the means; for the lives of men are too valuable to be cast away on such trifles. It is the violence which is done and threatened to our persons; the destruction of our property by an armed force; the invasion of our country by fire and sword, which conscientiously qualifies the use of arms: and the instant in which such mode of defence became necessary, all subjection to Britain ought to have ceased; and the independence of America should have been considered as dating its era from, and published by, the first musket that was fired against her. This line is a line of consistency; neither drawn by caprice, nor extended by ambition; but produced by a chain of events, of which the colonies were not the authors.

I shall conclude these remarks, with the following timely and well-intended hints. We ought to reflect, that there are three different ways by which an independency may hereafter be effected, and that one of those three, will, one day or other, be the fate of America, viz. By the legal voice of the people in Congress; by a military power, or by a mob: It may not always happen that our soldiers are citizens, and the multitude a body of reasonable men; virtue, as I have already remarked, is not hereditary, neither is it perpetual. Should an independency be brought about by the first of those means, we have every opportunity and every encouragement before us, to form the noblest, purest constitution on the face of the earth. We have it in our power to begin the world over again. A situation, similar to the present, hath not happened since the days of Noah until now.

The birthday of a new world is at hand, and a race of men, perhaps as numerous as all Europe contains, are to receive their portion of freedom from the events of a few months. The reflection is awful, and in this point of view, how trifling, how ridiculous, do the little paltry cavilings of a few weak or interested men appear, when weighed against the business of a world.

Should we neglect the present favorable and inviting period, and independence be hereafter effected by any other means, we must charge the consequence to ourselves, or to those rather whose narrow and prejudiced souls are habitually opposing the measure, without either inquiring or reflecting. There are reasons to be given in support of independence which men should rather privately think of, than be publicly told of. We ought not now to be debating whether we shall be independent or not, but anxious to accomplish it on a firm, secure, and honorable basis, and uneasy rather that it is not yet began upon. Every day convinces us of its necessity. Even the Tories (if such beings yet remain among us) should, of all men, be the most solicitous to promote it; for as the appointment of committees at first protected them from popular rage, so, a wise and well established form of government will be the only certain means of continuing it securely to them. Wherefore, if they have not virtue enough to be *Whigs*, they ought to have prudence enough to wish for independence.

In short, independence is the only bond that tie and keep us together. We shall then see our object, and our ears will be legally shut against the schemes of an intriguing, as well as cruel, enemy. We shall then, too, be on a proper footing to treat with Britain; for there is reason to conclude, that the pride of that court will be less hurt by treating with the American States for terms of peace, than with those, whom she denominates "rebellious subjects," for terms of accommodation. It is our delaying in that, encourages her to hope for conquest, and our backwardness tends only to prolong the war. As we have, without any good effect therefrom, withheld our trade to obtain a redress of our grievances, let us now try the alternative, by independently redressing them ourselves, and then offering to open the trade. The mercantile and reasonable part of England, will be still with us; because, peace, with trade, is preferable to war without it. And if this offer be not accepted, other courts may be applied to.

On these grounds I rest the matter. And as no offer hath yet been made to refute the doctrine con-

Document Text

tained in the former editions of this pamphlet, it is a negative proof, that either the doctrine cannot be refuted, or, that the party in favor of it are too numerous to be opposed. *wherefore*, instead of gazing at each other with suspicious or doubtful curiosity, let each of us hold out to his neighbor the hearty hand of friendship, and unite in drawing a line, which, like an act of oblivion, shall bury in forgetfulness every former dissension. Let the names of Whig and Tory be extinct; and let none other be heard among us, than those of a good citizen, an open and resolute friend, and a virtuous supporter of the *rights of mankind*, and of the *free and independent States of America*.

www.milestonedocuments.com

George Mason's first draft of the Virginia Declaration of Rights (The Library of Virginia)

Virginia Declaration of Rights

1776

"All men are by nature equally free and independent, and have certain inherent rights."

Overview

The basis of the Bill of Rights (1791), an addendum to the U.S. Constitution, the Virginia Declaration of Rights was written by the colony's George Mason in 1776. Disturbed by various attempts by the British parliament to govern the behavior of the American colonists, Mason drafted the Virginia Declaration of Rights. This document asserts the colonists' basic rights to life, liberty, and property. The document essentially justifies the colonists' quest for independence. Once the Virginia Declaration of Rights was approved, copies of the document made their way to all of the colonies and to the Continental Congress itself. Other colonial governments quickly followed Virginia's example, drafting similar versions of the document. In writing the Declaration of Independence, Thomas Jefferson relied heavily on Mason's work. Many of Mason's ideas expressed in the Virginia Declaration of Rights found their way into the later U.S. Bill of Rights and France's Declaration of the Rights of Man and of the Citizen.

Context

After the British passed the Stamp Act in 1763, Mason and other Virginians, including Patrick Henry and Richard Henry Lee, were outraged. The historian Dumas Malone notes that despite America's famed Patrick Henry and George Washington, it was "Mason who was the dean of the intellectual rebels in Virginia" (Rutland, 1961, p. xiv). In the spring of 1766 Mason wrote a letter to the *London Public Ledger* denying treason on the behalf of the colonists who had rebelled against the parliamentary acts. Signing his letter "A Virginia Planter," Mason declared that the American colonists "were tired of being treated as a schoolmaster would handle unruly boys" (Rutland, 1961, p. 34).

In response to the British Revenue Act of 1767 and the Townshend Revenue Act, Mason drafted the Non-Importation Resolves, which his friend George Washington introduced to the House of Burgesses. Though the Virginia governor dissolved the House of Burgesses before the body could adopt the resolves, members of the group gathered at the nearby Raleigh Tavern and voted in favor of them.

Many, including Washington, encouraged Mason to accept an appointment to the House of Burgesses. Mason steadfastly refused the position. He did, however, draft a set of twenty-four resolves in July 1774. Known as the Fairfax Resolves, the document outlined the rights of the American colonists. In the Fairfax Resolves, Mason asserted that as citizens of the British colonies, the colonists should be afforded the same rights as Englishmen. He went on to say that if those rights were denied them, they "were justified in resorting to extralegal devices" (Rutland, 1961, p. 40).

When Mason's Virginia Declaration of Rights was introduced to the Virginia Convention, several men found fault with the opening line, which asserts that all men are created free and independent. They claimed that such was not the case, as slaves were not free and independent. The delegates argued about the slavery issue for four days, delaying discussion about the rest of the document. By the time the group approved the document on June 12, 1776, six more items had been added to Mason's ten.

Passing through the Virginia Convention, the Virginia Declaration of Rights was soon read throughout the colonies and in the Continental Congress. By the end of 1776 five states had drafted similar declarations of rights, modeled almost verbatim on Mason's document.

Though a "bill of rights" was not included in the new Constitution drafted by the Constitutional Convention, Richard Henry Lee of the Continental Congress attempted to amend the document by including a declaration of rights. Lee proved unsuccessful, but several other delegates to the Congress agreed that without a declaration of rights, more problems had been created than solved.

About the Author

Mason was born in Fairfax County, Virginia, in 1725 to George and Ann Mason. Mason's father died when Mason was just ten years old. Without a father, Mason spent much of his childhood with his uncle John Mercer, a lawyer, poring over his uncle's law books, including Giles Jacob's *Every Man His Own Lawyer*.

Time Line

1774

■ **July 18**
Mason writes the Fairfax Resolves, declaring the colonists' rights. The document also encourages colonists to boycott British goods until their rights are acknowledged.

1776

■ **May 6**
The Virginia Convention assembles in Williamsburg and votes in favor of instructing the colony's delegates to the Continental Congress to advocate for declaring independence from England.

■ **May 14**
The Virginia Convention appoints a committee to draft a declaration of rights.

■ **May 20–26**
Mason and a committee from the Virginia Convention draft the Virginia Declaration of Rights.

■ **June 12**
Virginia Declaration of Rights is adopted by the Virginia Constitutional Convention.

■ **June 11–28**
Thomas Jefferson relies heavily on the Virginia Declaration of Rights when he writes the country's Declaration of Independence.

1787

■ **June 8**
James Madison uses the Virginia Declaration of Rights while drafting the Bill of Rights, the first ten amendments to the U.S. Constitution.

■ **September 25**
Congress passes the Bill of Rights.

1789

■ **August 26**
France's Marquis de Lafayette draws upon Mason's Virginia Declaration of Rights for his Declaration of the Rights of Man and of the Citizen during the French Revolution.

1791

■ **December 15**
The United States officially adopts the Bill of Rights.

Never attending college, Mason instead became a wealthy planter and married Ann Eilbeck on April 4, 1750. Soon after, Mason built a new home, which he called Gunston Hall, on more than 5,000 acres of land situated on the Northern Neck of the Potomac River. Aside from an area filled with deer, most of the family's land was devoted to growing wheat, corn, and tobacco. Mason quickly became a respected businessman in the county and was sought out for legal advice as well. By his thirtieth birthday, Mason had begun serving as a justice of the peace for Fairfax County.

Devastated when his wife died in March 1773, Mason was brought out of his melancholy by the Boston Tea Party in December of that year. After he wrote the Fairfax Resolves in 1774, Mason was called on to accept a seat in the House of Burgesses. Though Mason refused the position, he did accept a post on the county's safety committee and was responsible for ferreting out local merchants who imported British goods. During this time, Mason also became the head of the local militia, the Fairfax Independent Company. He was also asked to be one of Virginia's delegates to the Continental Congress, but he denied this appointment as well.

He did, however, attend the Virginia Convention of 1776, filling the seat vacated by George Washington, who had resigned to become commander in chief of the Continental army. It was here that Mason drafted his Virginia Declaration of Rights. The historian Dumas Malone believes that

> more than any other single American, except possibly Thomas Jefferson, whom in some sense he anticipated, George Mason may be regarded as the herald of the new era; and in our own age, when the rights of individual human beings are being challenged by totalitarianism around the world, men can still find inspiration in his noble words. (Rutland, 1961, p. x)

In April 1780, at fifty-four years old, Mason married Sarah Brent. Now a member of the Constitutional Convention charged with drafting the Constitution, Mason and two others had the dissenting vote. Mason especially wanted the new constitution to include a bill of rights. Others felt this unnecessary, since the proposed constitution would not repeal the documents of individual states. Mason refused to sign the newly drafted Constitution.

Returning to his home and suffering from ill health, Mason essentially retreated from politics, declining a seat in the Senate after the death of Senator William Grayson. Mason died at Gunston Hall on October 7, 1792.

Explanation and Analysis of the Document

Drawing on the Enlightenment ideals of John Locke, the English Bill of Rights of 1689, and the Magna Carta, the Virginia Declaration of Rights contains sixteen articles. The first nine articles pertain to the basic principles of a free republic. The following seven articles deal with the rights of individuals.

Essential Quotes

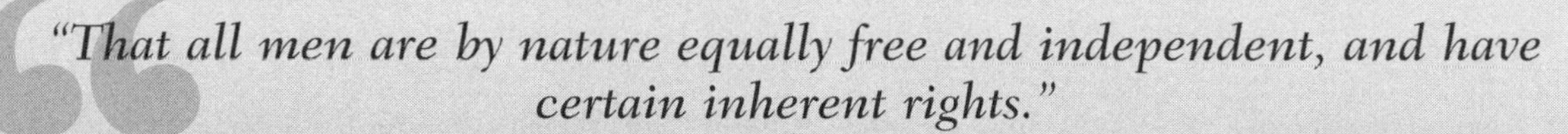

"That all men are by nature equally free and independent, and have certain inherent rights."

(Section I)

"That all power is vested in, and consequently derived from, the people."

(Section II)

"Whenever any government shall be found inadequate or contrary ... a majority of the community hath an indubitable, unalienable, and indefeasible right to reform, alter or abolish it, in such manner as shall be judged most conducive to the public weal."

(Section III)

"That the legislative and executive powers of the state should be separate and distinct from the judicative."

(Section V)

"That the freedom of the press is one of the great bulwarks of liberty and can never be restrained but by despotic governments."

(Section XII)

"That the people have a right to uniform government."

(Section XIV)

www.milestonedocuments.com

Section I declares that free men are entitled to life, liberty, and property in addition to their happiness and safety. These "inherent" rights cannot be denied.

Section II states that a government's power is vested with the people. Public officials are the servants of the people and get their authority from the people.

Section III maintains that a government is established for the benefit of its citizens. Section III also states that the best government is that which produces "the greatest degree of happiness and safety." In addition, the people have the right to abolish or reform the government if it is not fulfilling its duties.

Section IV affirms that no one is entitled to compensation or privileges. It also says that public offices are not to be hereditary.

Section V avows that the legislative, executive, and judicial branches of government should be separate from one another. In addition, regular elections should be held for positions in the legislative and executive branches.

Section VI maintains that all elections should be free and that all men should have the right to vote. This section goes on to say that men cannot be taxed without their consent and that their property cannot be taken for public use without their consent.

Section VII declares that abolishing laws or enforcing laws without the consent of the people is detrimental to their rights.

Section VIII says that an individual has the right to know the crime of which he has been accused and to know his accuser. It also states that a man is entitled to a trial by a jury of his peers and that he cannot be forced to provide evidence against himself.

Section IX also deals with the judicial process. This section asserts that one's bail or fines should not be excessive, nor should cruel and unusual punishments be inflicted.

Section X maintains that general warrants for the search and seizure of one's home should not be allowed without sufficient evidence.

Section XI states that in disputes of property or between individuals, there should be a trial by jury.

Section XII champions the freedom of the press as "one of the greatest bulwarks of liberty" and asserts that it should never be restricted.

Section XIII maintains that a nation should be defended by a well-trained militia. During peacetime, however, standing armies should be avoided.

Section XIV states that the people of Virginia have the right to a regular government and that no separate or independent government should be established.

Section XV maintains that government and liberty are preserved by adhering to "justice, moderation, temperance, frugality, and virtue."

Section XVI states that men are allowed to practice any religion and that citizens should be tolerant of one another.

Audience

As much for the members of the Virginia Convention and the citizens of Virginia, Mason wrote the Virginia Declaration of Rights for all American colonists. Like his contemporaries Patrick Henry, James Madison, and Thomas Jefferson, among others, Mason was outraged at the actions of the British parliament. He fully believed that all men were created equal and independent. The first American document of its kind, the Virginia Declaration of Rights appealed to what most Virginians considered their fundamental rights.

Impact

Of the Virginia Declaration of Rights, the British historian John Acton said:

"It was from America that the plain ideas that men ought to mind their own business, and that the nation is responsible to Heaven for the acts of the State—ideas long locked in the breast of solitary thinkers and hidden among Latin folios—burst forth like a conqueror upon the world they were destined to transform, under the title of the Rights of Man.... In this way the politic hesitancy of European statesmanship was at last broken down; and the principle gained ground, that a nation can never abandon its fate to an authority it cannot control" (pp. 55–56).

As soon as the Virginia Convention approved Mason's draft of the Virginia Declaration of Rights in June 1776, copies of the document were distributed up and down the seaboard. Five other colonies had composed similar documents by the end of the year. By 1780 eight more states had drafted documents declaring the individual rights of their citizens.

Many of the ideas found in Mason's text also made their way into Thomas Jefferson's draft of the Declaration of Independence. In 1791 the principles listed in Mason's document became the basis for the Bill of Rights, the first ten amendments to the U.S. Constitution. Both the 1789 French Declaration of the Rights of Man and of the Citizen and the 1948 United Nations Declaration of Human Rights contain elements of the Virginia Declaration of Rights. The Mason biographer Rutland writes, "The Virginia Declaration of Rights expanded the conception of the personal rights of citizens as no other document before its adoption had done" (1955, p. 40).

Related Documents

Anzenberger, Joseph F., ed. *The Gunston Hall Collection of the Papers of George Mason*. Lorton, Va.: Gunston Hall, 1980. This book contains the collection of Mason's papers, including correspondence and land deeds, housed at his home, Gunston Hall.

Dunn, Terry K., ed. *The Recollections of John Mason: George Mason's Son Remembers His Father and Life at Gunston Hall*. Marshall, Va.: EPM Publications, 2004. This work recounts the memories of Mason's son John.

Mason, George. *The Objections of the Hon. George Mason to the Proposed Federal Constitution: Addressed to the Citizens of Virginia*. Printed by Thomas Nicholas, 1787. First published in 1787, this pamphlet consists of Mason's reasons for opposing the Constitution.

———. *The Fairfax Resolves*. Fairfax, Va.: Board of Regents, Gunston Hall, 1974. This work is a copy of the Fairfax Resolves printed during the document's bicentennial celebration.

Rutland, Robert A., ed. *The Papers of George Mason, 1725–1792*. Chapel Hill: University of North Carolina Press, 1970. This work contains Mason's collected papers and correspondence.

Bibliography

■ Articles

Bailey, Kenneth P. "George Mason, Westerner." *William and Mary College Quarterly*, 2nd ser., 23, no. 4 (1943): 409–417.

Bernstein, Mark. "'The Necessity of Refusing My Signature.'" *American History* 41, no. 4 (2006): 50–55.

Dreisbach, Daniel L. "George Mason's Pursuit of Religious Liberty in Revolutionary Virginia." *Virginia Magazine of History and Biography* 108, no. 1 (2000): 5–44.

Moore, R. Walton. "George Mason, The Statesman." *William and Mary College Quarterly*, 2nd ser., 13, no. 1 (1933): 10–17.

Morison, Samuel Eliot. "Prelude to Independence: The Virginia Resolutions of May 15, 1776." *William and Mary Quarterly*, 3rd ser., 8, no. 4 (1951): 483–492.

Scott, James Brown. "George Mason." *Virginia Law Register* 12, no. 9 (1927): 556–561.

———. "George Mason: Remarks at the Celebration of the One Hundred and Fiftieth Anniversary of the Adoption of the Virginia Bill of Rights, Williamsburg, June 12, 1926." *William and Mary College Quarterly*, 2nd ser., 7, no. 1 (1927): 17–20.

Wallenstein, Peter. "Flawed Keepers of the Flame: The Interpreters of George Mason." *Virginia Magazine of History and Biography* 102, no. 2 (1994): 229–270.

■ Books

Acton, John. *History of Freedom and Other Essays*. London: Macmillan, 1907.

Broadwater, Jeff. *George Mason, Forgotten Founder*. Chapel Hill: University of North Carolina Press, 2006.

Cohen, Martin B., ed. *Federalism: The Legacy of George Mason*. Fairfax, Va.: George Mason University Press, 1988.

Davidow, Robert P., ed. *Natural Rights and Natural Law: The Legacy of George Mason*. Fairfax, Va.: George Mason University Press, 1986.

The George Mason Lectures: Honoring the Two Hundredth Anniversary of the Virginia Declaration of Rights, Adopted by the Virginia Convention, June 12, 1776. Williamsburg, Va.: Colonial Williamsburg Foundation, 1976.

Haynes, Charles C., et al. *First Freedoms: A Documentary History of First Amendment Rights in America*. Oxford, U.K.: Oxford University Press, 2006.

Henri, Florette. *George Mason of Virginia*. New York: Crowell-Collier Press, 1971.

Miller, Helen Hill. *George Mason, Constitutionalist*. Gloucester, Mass.: P. Smith, 1966.

———. *George Mason, Gentleman Revolutionary*. Chapel Hill: University of North Carolina Press, 1975.

Pacheco, Josephine F., ed. *The Legacy of George Mason*. Fairfax, Va.: George Mason University Press, 1983.

Rowland, Kate Mason. *The Life of George Mason, 1725–1792*. New York: Putnam, 1892.

Rusk, Dean. *Mason and Jefferson Revisited: An Address on the Occasion of the Celebration of the Prelude to Independence at the Eighteenth-Century Capital, Williamsburg, Virginia, May 28, 1966*. Williamsburg, Va.: Colonial Williamsburg, 1966.

Rutland, Robert Allen. *The Birth of the Bill of Rights, 1776–1791*. Chapel Hill: University of North Carolina Press, 1955.

———. *George Mason, Reluctant Statesman*. Williamsburg, Va.: Colonial Williamsburg, 1961.

Shumate, T. Daniel, ed. *The First Amendment: The Legacy of George Mason*. Fairfax, Va.: George Mason University Press, 1985.

When Virginia Joined the Union: A Backward Look at the Powerful Prophecy of Men Who Foresaw in 1788 the Trend of Events in 1963. Richmond: Virginia Commission on Constitutional Government, 1963.

■ Web Sites

"The Virginia Declaration of Rights." Constitution Society Web site. http://www.constitution.org/bcp/virg_dor.htm. Accessed on October 25, 2007.

"The Virginia Declaration of Rights." National Center for Public Policy Research Web site. http://www.nationalcenter.org/VirginiaDeclaration.html. Accessed on October 25, 2007.

"The Virginia Declaration of Rights." American Treasures of the Library of Congress Web site. http://www.loc.gov/exhibits/treasures/trt006.html. Accessed on October 25, 2007.

—By Nicole Mitchell

www.milestonedocuments.com

Questions for Further Study

1. Compare and contrast the Virginia Declaration of Rights, the French Declaration of the Rights of Man and of the Citizen, and the U.S. Bill of Rights. What are some similarities? What are some differences?

2. Read the letter from "A Virginia Planter" that was published in the *London Public Ledger*. What does it have in common with Mason's other writings? Does the letter hint at some of Mason's later ideas? Why or why not?

3. Mason and several others attempted to persuade the Constitutional Convention to include elements of the Virginia Declaration of Rights in the new Constitution. Why did they fail? What was different with the later Bill of Rights?

4. Look at the United Nations Declaration of Human Rights. What does this document have in common with Mason's Virginia Declaration of Rights?

5. The Mason biographer Robert Allen Rutland calls Mason a "reluctant statesman." Though Mason wrote the Virginia Declaration of Rights, he allowed someone else to introduce the document to the Virginia House of Burgesses, and he continually refused to serve in political roles. What are some other reasons why Rutland believes Mason to be a "reluctant statesman"? What does Rutland mean by this term?

Glossary

amenable	accountable and answerable to; liable and legally responsible to
bulwarks	defenses or safeguards; supports or protection
burthens	an old form of the word *burdens*: something that is carried; loads or responsibilities
compact	a contract or an agreement between two or more people
descendible	able to be transferred by inheritance
despotic	tyrannical
dictates	guiding principles
divest	strip, take away, or deprive of
emoluments	payments for one's services
forbearance	patience, tolerance, or self-control
indefeasible	unable to be annulled or voided
indubitable	unquestionable; unable to be doubted
injurious	harmful or detrimental
judicative	having the ability to judge
maladministration	poor or inefficient management; corrupt or incompetent administration
subordination	subservience or subjection to another
suffrage	the right to vote
temperance	moderation; self-restraint; avoidance of excess
trained to arms	prepared for battle; instructed in the use of weapons
trustees	persons appointed to manage or govern
unalienable	unable to be surrendered, transferred, or given to another
vicinage	region or vicinity
weal	well-being or happiness; welfare of the community

Document Text

Virginia Declaration of Rights

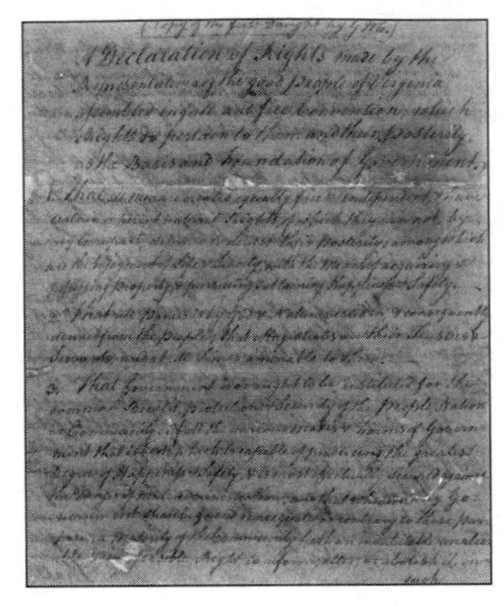
A Declaration of Rights made by the

◆ **Section I**

That all men are by nature equally free and independent, and have certain inherent rights, of which, when they enter into a state of society, they cannot, by any compact, deprive or divest their posterity; namely, the enjoyment of life and liberty, with the means of acquiring and possessing property, and pursuing and obtaining happiness and safety.

◆ **Section II**

That all power is vested in, and consequently derived from, the people; that magistrates are their trustees and servants, and at all times amenable to them.

◆ **Section III**

That government is, or ought to be, instituted for the common benefit, protection, and security of the people, nation or community; of all the various modes and forms of government that is best, which is capable of producing the greatest degree of happiness and safety and is most effectually secured against the danger of maladministration; and that, whenever any government shall be found inadequate or contrary to these purposes, a majority of the community hath an indubitable, unalienable, and indefeasible right to reform, alter or abolish it, in such manner as shall be judged most conducive to the public weal.

◆ **Section IV**

That no man, or set of men, are entitled to exclusive or separate emoluments or privileges from the community, but in consideration of public services; which, not being descendible, neither ought the offices of magistrate, legislator, or judge be hereditary.

◆ **Section V**

That the legislative and executive powers of the state should be separate and distinct from the judicative; and, that the members of the two first may be restrained from oppression by feeling and participating the burthens of the people, they should, at fixed periods, be reduced to a private station, return into that body from which they were originally taken, and the vacancies be supplied by frequent, certain, and regular elections in which all, or any part of the former members, to be again eligible, or ineligible, as the laws shall direct.

◆ **Section VI**

That elections of members to serve as representatives of the people in assembly ought to be free; and that all men, having sufficient evidence of permanent common interest with, and attachment to, the community have the right of suffrage and cannot be taxed or deprived of their property for public uses without their own consent or that of their representatives so elected, nor bound by any law to which they have not, in like manner, assented, for the public good.

◆ **Section VII**

That all power of suspending laws, or the execution of laws, by any authority without consent of the representatives of the people is injurious to their rights and ought not to be exercised.

◆ **Section VIII**

That in all capital or criminal prosecutions a man hath a right to demand the cause and nature of his accusation to be confronted with the accusers and witnesses, to call for evidence in his favor, and to a speedy trial by an impartial jury of his vicinage, without whose unanimous consent he cannot be found guilty, nor can he be compelled to give evidence against himself; that no man be deprived of his liberty except by the law of the land or the judgement of his peers.

◆ **Section IX**

That excessive bail ought not to be required, nor excessive fines imposed; nor cruel and unusual punishments inflicted.

Document Text

◆ Section X

That general warrants, whereby any officer or messenger may be commanded to search suspected places without evidence of a fact committed, or to seize any person or persons not named, or whose offense is not particularly described and supported by evidence, are grievous and oppressive and ought not to be granted.

◆ Section XI

That in controversies respecting property and in suits between man and man, the ancient trial by jury is preferable to any other and ought to be held sacred.

◆ Section XII

That the freedom of the press is one of the greatest bulwarks of liberty and can never be restrained but by despotic governments.

◆ Section XIII

That a well regulated militia, composed of the body of the people, trained to arms, is the proper, natural, and safe defense of a free state; that standing armies, in time of peace, should be avoided as dangerous to liberty; and that, in all cases, the military should be under strict subordination to, and be governed by, the civil power.

◆ Section XIV

That the people have a right to uniform government; and therefore, that no government separate from, or independent of, the government of Virginia, ought to be erected or established within the limits thereof.

◆ Section XV

That no free government, or the blessings of liberty, can be preserved to any people but by a firm adherence to justice, moderation, temperance, frugality, and virtue and by frequent recurrence to fundamental principles.

◆ Section XVI

That religion, or the duty which we owe to our Creator and the manner of discharging it, can be directed by reason and conviction, not by force or violence; and therefore, all men are equally entitled to the free exercise of religion, according to the dictates of conscience; and that it is the mutual duty of all to practice Christian forbearance, love, and charity towards each other.

www.milestonedocuments.com

IN CONGRESS. JULY 4, 1776.

unanimous Declaration of the thirteen united States of America.

The Declaration of Independence (National Archives and Records Administration)

Declaration of Independence

1776

"These united Colonies are, and of Right ought to be Free and Independent States."

Overview

To the modern student of history, the revolutionary break by the American colonies from Great Britain may seem as inevitable as it was necessary. But in the 1770s, that was not the common perception. The initial effort by the framers of the American system of government was not to separate from Great Britain and form a new government but to be accepted by Great Britain as an equal partner—to be given the rights and responsibilities of full British citizenship. Early efforts to secure such acceptance met with contempt and refusal, and by 1776 the Founding Fathers were forced to make a choice: subservience or revolution.

When the Founders eventually came to the conclusion that independence was their only option, they felt, as men of the Enlightenment, in the Age of Reason, that they were bound by honor to declare to the world the reasons for their radical act. The Continental Congress thus selected a committee of five men to draft a statement calling for independence. That committee—consisting of Thomas Jefferson, John Adams, Benjamin Franklin, Robert R. Livingston, and Roger Sherman—surprisingly chose the thirty-four-year-old Virginian Thomas Jefferson to write the first draft of what would become the Declaration of Independence. These men could hardly have imagined the full impact their handiwork would have, for in modern times the Declaration of Independence is one of the most read and honored documents produced by the revolutionaries of that age. It is a document that has had a profound impact not only on that revolutionary generation but also on future generations.

Context

In 1774 the American colonies established the First Continental Congress. This Congress first met in Philadelphia from September 5 to October 26 of that year, with the chief goal of settling the dispute with Britain, not separating from the motherland. The Congress passed resolutions aimed at gaining certain political and economic rights and presented the request to the king of England.

King George III, however, refused to grant the requests made by the colonies. The colonies thus agreed to form another congress, but on April 19, 1775, even before the Second Continental Congress could meet, fighting broke out at Lexington and Concord, Massachusetts, between colonial minutemen and British troops. Several colonial minutemen were killed, and the losses inflamed the passions of the colonists and put additional pressure on the Congress to become bolder. When the Second Continental Congress met on May 10, 1775, the delegates were more radicalized and inclined toward revolution. George Washington was named commander of the fledging militia, and war seemed a possibility.

By later in the mid-1770s the colonists had grown impatient with British intransigence. Efforts at accommodation had failed utterly, as the colonial efforts to persuade the British to accept the American colonies as a full part of the British government were soundly rejected. The colonists felt they had no choice but to revolt against Great Britain.

The case for revolution was starkly established by the pamphleteer Thomas Paine, who in January 1776 published his famous broadside *Common Sense*. In that brief but powerfully argued pamphlet, Paine boldly articulates both the need for revolutionary fervor and the intellectual underpinnings for what would indeed become the American Revolution. Such ideas had been percolating in the colonies for several decades, and Paine demonstrated a talent for articulating the revolutionary sentiment in a manner that proved both compelling and convincing.

Paine largely made the case for independence using language accessible to the average citizen, attacking the British monarchy and inciting the colonists to separate: "Everything that is right, pleads for separation. The blood of the slain, the weeping voice of nature cried, 'Tis time to part'" (Paine, p. 30). *Common Sense* created a firestorm. Over 120,000 copies of the pamphlet were sold in the first three months of publication alone—the equivalent of nearly 20 million in the modern-day United States. Roughly one in every thirteen adult colonists owned a copy, with most citizens who lacked a copy reading someone else's. To Paine, the king of England was "the Royal Brute of Great Britain" (p. 43). In America, Paine asserted, "the law is

Time Line

1773

■ **December 16**
The colonies respond to taxation without representation by staging the Boston Tea Party.

1774

■ **September 5**
Delegates of the First Continental Congress meet in Philadelphia, eventually agreeing to send grievances to King George III.

1775

■ **April 19**
British and American soldiers exchange fire in the towns of Lexington and Concord, Massachusetts.

■ **May 10**
The Second Continental Congress begins meeting in Philadelphia.

■ **June 17**
The Battle of Bunker Hill takes place.

1776

■ **January 10**
Thomas Paine's *Common Sense* is published.

■ **June 7**
Delegate Richard Henry Lee presents the Lee Resolution, a motion urging the Continental Congress to declare independence from Great Britain.

■ **June 11**
Congress selects a committee to draft a declaration of independence. Thomas Jefferson, John Adams, Benjamin Franklin, Roger Sherman, and Robert R. Livingston are appointed.

■ **June 12–27**
Thomas Jefferson creates several drafts of the declaration. After he presents a final draft to the declaration committee, other members make minor revisions.

■ **June 28**
The committee's draft of the Declaration of Independence is submitted to Congress.

king" (p. 43). Paine called for the colonies to declare their independence and establish a republic.

Last-ditch efforts to repair the breach with Britain failed, and on July 4, 1776, the Continental Congress issued the Declaration of Independence. Thus, with the impact of *Common Sense* being followed shortly by the Declaration of Independence, a wave of revolutionary sentiment swept the colonies. Reconciliation was no longer possible; becoming a full part of England was not an option. The only choice was revolution.

About the Author

Thomas Jefferson, the principal author of the Declaration of Independence, is considered by many to be the greatest person the United States has ever produced. A true Renaissance man, Jefferson was a statesman, author, politician, philosopher, diplomat, inventor, scientist, and much more.

Tall for his time, at six feet, two inches, with sandy red hair, hazel eyes, and a weak speaking voice, Jefferson was both loathed and loved by his contemporaries. The *Connecticut Courant*, a Federalist newspaper, warned voters prior to the election of 1800 that if Jefferson were to be named president, "Murder, robbery, rape, adultery, and incest will all be openly taught and practiced, the air will be rent with the cries of the distressed, the soil will be soaked with blood, and the nation black with crimes" (qtd. in Kamber, p. 15). When Jefferson indeed gained the nation's highest office, he demonstrated a desire to democratize and remove the pomp from the presidency, to bring it in line with more republican manners. He did away with bowing, replacing this regal custom with the more egalitarian handshake. Jefferson also abolished the weekly levee, ended formal state dinners, and abandoned Washington's custom of making personal addresses to Congress (although this may have been due as much to Jefferson's weak speaking voice as to his particular inclinations). This practice continued until 1913 and the presidency of Woodrow Wilson.

Jefferson in fact exerted increased influence over Congress. Employing the president's power as party leader, Jefferson used a variety of means to press his agenda in the legislature while respecting the constitutional prerogatives of Congress. He lobbied key party leaders, drafted bills for his congressional supporters to introduce, authorized party members to act as his spokesman in Congress, lobbied legislators at social gatherings in the White House, and had cabinet members work closely with the legislature. Jefferson's use of his political party was an innovation in presidential leadership. It was an exercise of extra-constitutional power, but one he deemed necessary to make the Constitution operate effectively. Jefferson's methods allowed him to build a strong presidency, responsive to the majority will of the people, as expressed through the political party.

Jefferson's great success in dealing with Congress was matched by equally impressive failures in his dealings with the judiciary. While Congress was controlled by Jefferson's

Republican Party (a predecessor of the modern Democratic Party), the courts were in Federalist hands. During Jefferson's first term, the Supreme Court issued a direct challenge to the presidency in *Marbury v. Madison* (1803), the famous "midnight judges" case, in which the court established the doctrine of judicial review. Prior to that time, the branch of the federal government that would be the final arbiter of the Constitution was not certain.

One of the most pressing challenges to Jefferson's minimalist view of government came during the Louisiana Purchase controversy. An opportunity presented itself for the United States to double its size for a relatively low cost, as France was willing to sell the territory of Louisiana to the United States. The negotiations were delicate, and Jefferson wished to seize the moment—but nowhere did the Constitution authorize the acquisition of territory by the president or the federal government. Jefferson indeed believed that the purchase required a constitutional amendment, and he went so far as to draft an amendment to give the government the power to acquire the Louisiana Purchase. "The Constitution has made no provision for our holding foreign territory," he admitted (Ford, vol. 8, p. 244).

Ultimately, grand opportunity outweighed constitutional questions, as Jefferson decided to change his tune. Fearing that delay might jeopardize the deal, Jefferson concluded that "the less we say about constitutional difficulties respecting Louisiana the better, and that what is necessary for surmounting them must be done" in silence (Ford, vol. 8, p. 245). For $15 million—a mere three cents per acre—Jefferson acquired the Louisiana Purchase from France.

Time Line

1776

■ **July 2**
The Continental Congress votes to declare the independence of the United States of America. Representatives from all thirteen colonies except New York vote in favor of the motion for independence. Congress then begins to revise the committee's draft of the declaration.

■ **July 4**
Congress adopts the final Declaration of Independence. John Hancock, president of the Continental Congress, orders the congressional printer to print 200 broadsides of the declaration.

■ **July 6**
The Declaration of Independence reaches the American public for the first time with its publication in the *Pennsylvania Evening Post.*

■ **July 9**
New York finally accepts Congress's motion to declare independence at the New York state convention.

■ **July 19**
Wishing to communicate the now-unanimous consent of all thirteen colonies to declare independence, Congress orders the Declaration of Independence to be signed by all congressional representatives.

www.milestonedocuments.com

Explanation and Analysis of the Document

On July 4, 1776, Jefferson's amended draft of a document declaring independence from Great Britain was presented to the Continental Congress for a vote. This Declaration of Independence was a powerful statement of principle and high purpose. It was also a call to revolution. While the majority of the document consists of an exhaustive list of grievances against the British king, the driving creed can be found in the brief but powerful opening. An utterly amazing revolutionary document, it will ever be read and honored by lovers of liberty around the world. To the contrary, in his diary entry dated July 4, 1776, King George III of England wrote, "Nothing of importance this day" (Spalding, p. 215). As every American knows, the Fourth of July marks the anniversary of the founding of the United States of America. It was a monumental day and a monumental event; it was the beginning of a new nation.

One can hardly help but be moved by the inspiring words of the Declaration of Independence. The appeal to reason, the bold language and even bolder message, the call to arms, and the proclamation of universal rights all leave the reader reeling with democratic fervor. The language is concise, clear, to the point, and dripping with powerful prose and even more powerful imagery. From the preamble to the last resounding phrases, the men of the United States of America's founding era wrote a declaration for the ages.

◆ Introduction and Preamble

Although the primary aim of the Declaration of Independence is to declare the independence of the United States, its related aims include the delivery of a compelling argument for the legitimacy of America's right to independence, to thus set the United States on an honorable foundation. In a letter to Henry Lee written nearly fifty years after his drafting the Declaration of Independence, Thomas Jefferson remarked that the purpose of the document was "not to find out new principles, or new arguments, never before thought of … but to place before mankind the common sense of the subject, in terms so plain and firm as to command their assent, and to justify ourselves in the independent stand we are compelled to take" (Thomas Jefferson to Henry Lee, May 8, 1825; http://www.ashbrook.org/constitution/henry_lee.html).

Thomas Jefferson holding and pointing to the Declaration of Independence (Library of Congress)

The introduction of the Declaration of Independence begins, "When in the Course of human events, it becomes necessary for one people to dissolve the political bands which have connected them with another." In the immediate opening, the focus is placed not on "the causes that impel them to the separation" but on "the Course of human events"—and moreover, not on the United States but on the broader "one people." Within the preamble, the focus will likewise be on universal principles, not on particular events.

In conveying that the document shall address the standard by which any "one people" in "the Course of human events" may wish to declare independence, the introduction to the Declaration of Independence establishes the structure of the argumentation to follow. If the objective standard of the right to independence is accepted, and if the American states are found to have met this standard due to suffered injustices, the Declaration of Independence shall be found to present a compelling argument for the sovereignty of the United States of America.

Much of the phrasing and argumentation of the Declaration of Independence is rooted in Enlightenment ideology. Two particular elements of thought from the Age of Reason are crucial to understanding this document. First, according to Enlightenment thinkers, certain natural laws or fundamental principles are understood to exist. Furthermore, man is able to know natural laws by unaided human reason. As Jefferson claims, natural laws are "self-evident." Human beings cannot alter or change the laws of nature but rather are participants in natural design; as the Declaration of Independence claims, the laws of nature are not determined by human beings but are created by "Nature's God." Most significant is Jefferson's claim that natural laws have the following ethical implications for human beings: "that all men are created equal, that they are endowed by their Creator with certain unalienable Rights, that among these are Life, Liberty and the pursuit of Happiness."

Second, many Enlightenment thinkers, including the framers, subscribed to a certain genealogy of political life. According to this theory, prior to the invention of government, there existed a prepolitical state. In this state, termed the "state of nature," natural rights were not equally protected in the strife of all against all. Government was then created by the consent of member peoples for the protection of natural rights. As such, the authority of any government rests in the hands of its political leaders only by virtue of the consent of the people. Thus, authority should ultimately be understood to rest in the hands of the ruled.

Enlightenment thinkers held that because the laws of nature are both irrevocable and universal, they can be appealed to as a consistent standard by which to judge the laws of governments, sometimes termed "positive law." When positive law infringes upon man's natural rights, citizens have a right to rebel against the injurious forces of government. Within the Declaration of Independence, Jefferson refers to rebellion as not just a right but also a fundamental duty. Respect for natural law compels action to protect its principles and to avoid chaos and instability. At the same time, however, Jefferson promotes caution. He writes, "Governments long established should not be changed for light and transient causes." Some sufferings are to be tolerated for the greater good of social order; however, as Jefferson and the other Founding Fathers observed, the British Crown had violated the natural rights of the American colonists with a "train of abuses and usurpations, pursuing invariably the same Object." As the Declaration of Independence concludes, the once-unifying force of British rule had operated against the interests of its colonial subjects, severing the colonists from their rights as human beings and violating the principles of its own authority.

In expressing that the American people wished to establish a sovereign government, the Declaration of Independence communicates the founding principles of the new nation. The United States of America would be structured in reaction to the unfavorable aspects of British law. Unlike Great Britain, the United States would protect the natural rights of human beings by "laying its foundation on such principles"—the laws of nature—"and organizing its powers in such form, as to them shall seem most likely to effect their Safety and Happiness."

A drawing showing the signing of the Declaration of Independence, July 4, 1776 (Library of Congress)

www.milestonedocuments.com

◆ Indictment

The portion of the Declaration of Independence containing the colonist's many grievances against King George III provides evidence in support of the preamble's claim that the United States has a legitimate right to independence, as compelled by significant injury. Here, the universal focus of the preamble is abandoned in favor of a sharper focus on the practical facts that obliged the United States to declare separation. The indictment occupies a considerable portion of the written text of the document, supporting the claim of repeated injuries and usurpations.

At the time of the drafting of the Declaration of Independence, American complaints against the British Crown were well known. Among the colonists, some were compelled to raise these complaints following lived experiences of political oppression. Others then came to know of these complaints from widespread sources of report, including insurrectionary political pamphlets. In fact, the historical contexts of some of the events alluded to in the Declaration's list of grievances remain less known to modern students of history.

One such grievance states that the king refused to grant the colonies greater representation in Parliament despite the increasing population in the colonies. In 1767, under George III, eighteen Massachusetts laws for the establishment of new townships went ignored by the British Crown. Given the means of the era, expanding the colonies without developing new towns would have been difficult. Modes of transportation were limited, such that political representatives could not feasibly maintain contact with constituents in farther locations. Thus, new towns were needed in order to provide all citizens with access to political representation.

Another grievance addresses efforts made by the King to hinder immigration to the colonies, making reference to the royal Proclamation of 1763. This was a proclamation issued by King George III following Great Britain's acquisition of French territory in North America. The proclamation forbade colonists of the thirteen colonies from settling or buying land west of the Appalachians and gave the Crown a monopoly on land bought from Native Americans. The proclamation angered the colonists, since these were lands that they had helped fight for in the French and Indian War. Furthermore, many colonists had already settled in this area.

Another grievance refers to the brand of "mock Trial" received by British officials stationed in the colonies in accord with the Administration of Justice Act of 1774. The Administration of Justice Act granted a change of venue to another British colony or to Great Britain in trials of officials charged with crimes stemming from their enforcement of the law or suppression of riots. The purpose of this act was to ensure that the trials in question would be more conducive to the Crown than they would have been if held in the colonies, owing to the prejudices of local juries.

Although "cutting off our Trade with all parts of the world" appears as a general complaint, it specifically refers to the Boston Port Act of 1774. The Boston Port Act was a response to the Boston Tea Party; it outlawed the use of the port of Boston for "landing and discharging, loading or shipping, of goods, wares, and merchandise" until such time as restitution was made to the king's treasury and to the East India Company for damages suffered.

Another grievance admonishes the king "for abolishing the free System of English Laws in a neighbouring Province, establishing therein an Arbitrary government, and enlarging its Boundaries so as to render it at once an example and fit instrument for introducing the same absolute rule into these Colonies." This grievance is a reference to the Quebec Act of 1774, which expanded British territory to include modern-day Illinois, Indiana, Michigan, Ohio, Wisconsin, and parts of Minnesota. The colonists denounced the act for establishing procedures of governance in this territory. The act also guarantees the free practice of the Roman Catholic faith in these lands, such that it was also denounced for giving preference to Catholicism.

One further grievance charges the King with the grave crimes of "taking away our Charters, abolishing our most valuable Laws, and altering fundamentally the Forms of our Governments." This complaint refers to the Massachusetts Government Act of 1774. In the wake of the Boston Tea Party, Parliament launched a legislative offensive against Massachusetts to punish its errant behavior. British officials realized that part of their inability to control the colony was rooted in the highly independent nature of local government there. The Massachusetts Government Act effectively abrogated the colony's charter and provided for an unprecedented amount of royal control. Severe limits were placed on the powers of town meetings, the essential ingredient of American self-government. Under the Massachusetts Government Act, most elective offices in the colony were to be filled with royal appointees, not with popularly elected officials.

◆ Denunciation and Conclusion

The denunciation of the British Crown appears in the Declaration of Independence only after the conditions justifying the Revolution have been shown, in the indictment against the king. The denunciation conveys the Founding Fathers' disappointment that their attempts at rectifying injustices had thus far been unsuccessful. The list of grievances contained in the document would not be the British Crown's first clue to the colonists' discontent. As the denunciation claims,

> We have warned them from time to time of attempts by their legislature to extend an unwarrantable jurisdiction over us. We have reminded them of the circumstances of our emigration and settlement here. We have appealed to their native justice and magnanimity, and we have conjured them by the ties of our common kindred to disavow these usurpations, which, would inevitably interrupt our connections and correspondence.

The last paragraph of the document includes the assertion that "these United Colonies are, and of Right ought to be Free and Independent States." For the purpose of making this declaration clear, the conclusion provides a short enumeration of the rights of free and independent states: "They have full Power to levy War, conclude Peace, contract Alliances, establish Commerce, and to do all other Acts and Things which Independent States may of right do." In becoming a sovereign nation, the United States would not only enjoy these rights but would also equally respect those of other nations.

Finally, the conclusion of the Declaration of Independence contains the first clear answer to the question, under whose authority was the document written? Here, it is claimed that the "Representatives of the united States of America, in General Congress" are the spokespersons behind this announcement to the British Crown. This claim of authority together with the fifty-six appending signatures indeed sends a powerful message. On behalf of an emerging American politic, powerful through its unanimity, the inspiring words of the Declaration of Independence pronounce guiding and universal principles as well as the historic event of American independence.

Audience

The Declaration of Independence essentially had three audiences: the American colonists, the British government, and the people of the world. In declaring the states' independence, the Continental Congress first sought to persuade as many colonists as possible to take part in the Revolution. Taking on the most powerful nation in the world was an enormous risk, and the chances for success seemed quite slim. This aspect of the document reveals an obvious narrow self-interest, but the Revolution was also to be fought for timeless and universal principles. No revolution can be successful without a significant portion of the population backing the rebels, and uncertainty remained regarding just how much support could be mustered for the revolt against Great Britain. In that sense, the Declaration of Independence was one grand piece of recruiting propaganda aimed at inspiring the people to take up arms against the British. As such, it indeed proved quite effective.

The Declaration of Independence was, of course, also aimed at the British government—but it was likewise aimed at the British people. Some sympathy for the American cause could be found both in the Parliament and among the British people, and the colonists were waging a

Essential Quotes

"When in the Course of human events, it becomes necessary for one people to dissolve the political bands which have connected them with another, and to assume among the powers of the earth, the separate and equal station to which the Laws of Nature and of Nature's God entitle them, a decent respect to the opinions of mankind requires that they should declare the causes which impel them to the separation."

(Introduction)

"We hold these truths to be self-evident, that all men are created equal, that they are endowed by their Creator with certain unalienable rights, that among these are Life, Liberty, and the pursuit of Happiness.—That to secure these rights, Governments are instituted among Men, deriving their just powers from the consent of the governed,—That whenever any Form of Government becomes destructive of these ends, it is the Right of the People to alter or to abolish it, and to institute new Government, laying its foundation on such principles and organizing its powers in such form, as to them shall seem most likely to effect their Safety and Happiness."

(Preamble)

"Prudence, indeed, will dictate that Governments long established should not be changed for light and transient causes; and accordingly all experience hath shewn, that mankind are more disposed to suffer, while evils are sufferable, than to right themselves by abolishing the forms to which they are accustomed. But when a long train of abuses and usurpations, pursuing invariably the same Object evinces a design to reduce them under absolute Despotism, it is their right, it is their duty, to throw off such Government, and to provide new Guards for their future security."

(Preamble)

"We, therefore, the Representatives of the united States of America, in General Congress, Assembled, appealing to the Supreme Judge of the world for the rectitude of our intentions, do, in the Name, and by Authority of the good People of these Colonies, solemnly publish and declare, That these United Colonies are, and of Right ought to be Free and Independent States."

(Conclusion)

www.milestonedocuments.com

battle for British public opinion as much as they were informing the government of Great Britain that they were declaring independence.

Finally, the Declaration of Independence was aimed at a worldwide audience. The framers were men of the Enlightenment—often referred to as the Age of Reason—and felt compelled to make the case for revolution to an audience of like-minded persons who might be persuaded that, indeed, their cause was just and their goals admirable. Believing that honorable men would rally to the cause of freedom, the Founding Fathers sought to make their case against the British government and for the rights for which they were fighting.

Impact

The Declaration of Independence had a profound impact in its age and far beyond its time. Along with Thomas Paine's *Common Sense*, the Declaration of Independence was a rousing call to arms at a time when armed insurrection against British rule was not yet a certainty. Jefferson's magnificent document all but sealed the fate of revolution.

While the immediate impact of the Declaration of Independence was felt primarily in colonial America, the long-term impact has been much broader, if harder to measure. The document's creed has been invoked to justify revolutions in Africa, Asia, Latin America, and elsewhere. Widely read and oft cited, the Declaration remains one of the most influential political documents ever penned by an American.

Related Documents

"Boston Port Act." ushistory.org Web site. http://www.ushistory.org/declaration/related/bpb.htm. Accessed on January 24, 2008. The Boston Port Act outlawed the use of Boston Harbor for external trade, a complaint cited in the Declaration of Independence.

"Constitution of the United States." National Archives "Our Documents" Web site. http://www.ourdocuments.gov/doc.php?doc=9. Accessed on December 21, 2007. The U.S. Constitution, the supreme law of the United States of America, was adopted by the Constitutional Convention on September 17, 1787. The Constitution served to define the United States as a nation, completing the aim of national sovereignty first achieved in the Declaration of Independence.

Locke, John. *Second Treatise of Government*. The second part of Locke's *Two Treatises of Government*, first published in 1689, was highly influential on the American founders. Herein, Locke formulates that according to natural law, governments are made legitimate by the consent of the governed.

Paine, Thomas. *Common Sense*. New York: Bantam Books, 2004. A political pamphlet published anonymously by Paine in 1776, *Common Sense* advocated a declaration of independence by the American colonies and quickly sparked a popular revolutionary movement. Paine's arguments for independence would later find resonance in the Declaration of Independence.

Bibliography

■ Books

Ford, Paul Leicester, ed. *The Writings of Thomas Jefferson*. 10 vols. New York: Knickerbocker Press, 1892–1897.

Kamber, Victor. *Poison Politics: Are Negative Campaigns Destroying Democracy?* New York: Perseus Publishing, 2003.

Larson, Edward J., and Michael P. Winship. *The Constitutional Convention: A Narrative History; From the Notes of James Madison*. New York: Modern Library, 2005.

Liell, Scott. *46 Pages: Thomas Paine,* Common Sense, *and the Turning Point to American Independence*. Philadelphia: Running Press, 2003.

Samples, John, ed. *James Madison and the Future of Limited Government*. Washington, D.C.: Cato Institute, 2002.

Spalding, Matthew. *The Founders' Almanac: A Practical Guide to the Notable Events, Greatest Leaders and Most Eloquent Words of the American Founding*. Washington, D.C.: Heritage Foundation, 2002.

■ Web Sites

"The Constitution of the United States." The Avalon Project at Yale Law School Web site.
http://www.yale.edu/lawweb/avalon/usconst.htm. Accessed on August 8, 2007.

"Declaration of Independence." National Archives "Charters of Freedom" Web site.
http://www.archives.gov/national-archives-experience/charters/declaration.html. Accessed on August 8, 2007.

Jefferson, Thomas. "Letter to Henry Lee." Ashbrook Center for Public Affairs at Ashland University Web site.
http://www.ashbrook.org/constitution/henry_lee.html. Accessed on December 21, 2007.

"The Rough Draft of the Declaration of Independence." From Revolution to Reconstruction Web site.
http://www.let.rug.nl/usa/D/1776-1800/independence/doitj.htm. Accessed on August 8, 2007.

—By Michael A. Genovese and Kristina L. Rioux

Questions for Further Study

1. The ideas that animated the American Revolution claim to be universally applicable. "We hold these truths," notes the Declaration of Independence, "to be self-evident, that all men are created equal." Today, in the West at least, we have expanded our definition of "all men" to include all persons. But this idea is not universally embraced. There are still governments that do not accept the "all" to include women, and some states have religious qualifications for full citizenship. Some social and political movements, fundamentalism in particular, flatly reject the "universal" values promoted in the Declaration of Independence. What reasons do governments give for not treating citizens equally? Would the Founding Fathers consider any of these reasons to be valid?

2. The preamble justifies rebellion with the following claim: "But when a long train of abuses and usurpations, pursuing invariably the same Object evinces a design to reduce them under absolute Despotism, it is their right, it is their duty, to throw off such Government, and to provide new Guards for their future security." What sorts of activities reduce a government to absolute despotism? What sorts are to be tolerated? How can one determine the difference?

3. The conclusion of the Declaration of Independence enumerates the rights of the United States: "as Free and Independent States, they have full Power to levy War, conclude Peace, contract Alliances, establish Commerce, and to do all other Acts and Things which Independent States may of right do." What are some other rights that might have been included? Are the rights enumerated in this section of the Declaration of Independence of greater importance than others? Defend your position.

www.milestonedocuments.com

Glossary

abdicated	renounced or relinquished a throne, right, power, claim, responsibility, or the like
absolved	freed from guilt or blame or their consequences
acquiesce	to assent tacitly; to submit or comply silently or without protest
Appropriations	authorizations by a lawmaking body for money to be paid from the treasury for a specific use
Arbitrary	done by individual will or judgment rather than by law or statute
Arethren	fellow members; brothers
Charters	documents issued by a sovereign or state outlining the conditions under which a corporation, colony, city, or other body is organized and defining its rights and privileges
consanguinity	the state of being related by blood or common ancestors or of being closely related or linked
convulsions	violent acts of turmoil; agitations
divine Providence	the foreseeing care and guidance of God or nature over the creatures of the earth
evinces	shows clearly; makes evident or manifest
formidable	of great strength; forbidding

Glossary

kindred	community
magnanimity	the quality of being generous
perfidy	deliberate breach of faith or trust; treachery
Quartering	housing for soldiers
sufferance	suffering; misery
usurpations	acts of usurping; wrongful or illegal encroachments, infringements, or seizures

Document Text

Declaration of Independence

IN CONGRESS, July 4, 1776.

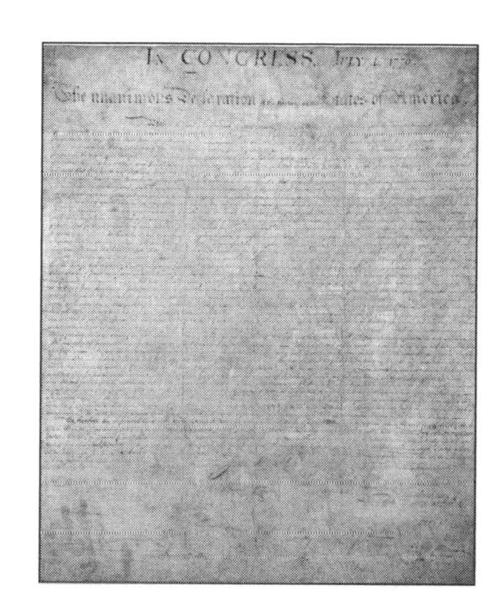

The unanimous Declaration of the thirteen united States of America,

When in the Course of human events, it becomes necessary for one people to dissolve the political bands which have connected them with another, and to assume among the powers of the earth, the separate and equal station to which the Laws of Nature and of Nature's God entitle them, a decent respect to the opinions of mankind requires that they should declare the causes which impel them to the separation.

We hold these truths to be self-evident, that all men are created equal, that they are endowed by their Creator with certain unalienable Rights, that among these are Life, Liberty and the pursuit of Happiness.—That to secure these rights, Governments are instituted among Men, deriving their just powers from the consent of the governed,—That whenever any Form of Government becomes destructive of these ends, it is the Right of the People to alter or to abolish it, and to institute new Government, laying its foundation on such principles and organizing its powers in such form, as to them shall seem most likely to effect their Safety and Happiness. Prudence, indeed, will dictate that Governments long established should not be changed for light and transient causes; and accordingly all experience hath shewn, that mankind are more disposed to suffer, while evils are sufferable, than to right themselves by abolishing the forms to which they are accustomed. But when a long train of abuses and usurpations, pursuing invariably the same Object evinces a design to reduce them under absolute Despotism, it is their right, it is their duty, to throw off such Government, and to provide new Guards for their future security.—Such has been the patient sufferance of these Colonies; and such is now the necessity which constrains them to alter their former Systems of Government. The history of the present King of Great Britain is a history of repeated injuries and usurpations, all having in direct object the establishment of an absolute Tyranny over these States. To prove this, let Facts be submitted to a candid world.

• He has refused his Assent to Laws, the most wholesome and necessary for the public good.

• He has forbidden his Governors to pass Laws of immediate and pressing importance, unless suspended in their operation till his Assent should be obtained; and when so suspended, he has utterly neglected to attend to them.

• He has refused to pass other Laws for the accommodation of large districts of people, unless those people would relinquish the right of Representation in the Legislature, a right inestimable to them and formidable to tyrants only.

• He has called together legislative bodies at places unusual, uncomfortable, and distant from the depository of their public Records, for the sole purpose of fatiguing them into compliance with his measures.

• He has dissolved Representative Houses repeatedly, for opposing with manly firmness his invasions on the rights of the people.

• He has refused for a long time, after such dissolutions, to cause others to be elected; whereby the Legislative powers, incapable of Annihilation, have returned to the People at large for their exercise; the State remaining in the mean time exposed to all the dangers of invasion from without, and convulsions within.

• He has endeavoured to prevent the population of these States; for that purpose obstructing the Laws for Naturalization of Foreigners; refusing to pass others to encourage their migrations hither, and raising the conditions of new Appropriations of Lands.

• He has obstructed the Administration of Justice, by refusing his Assent to Laws for establishing Judiciary powers.

www.milestonedocuments.com

Document Text

• He has made Judges dependent on his Will alone, for the tenure of their offices, and the amount and payment of their salaries.

• He has erected a multitude of New Offices, and sent hither swarms of Officers to harrass our people, and eat out their substance.

• He has kept among us, in times of peace, Standing Armies without the Consent of our legislatures.

• He has affected to render the Military independent of and superior to the Civil power.

• He has combined with others to subject us to a jurisdiction foreign to our constitution, and unacknowledged by our laws; giving his Assent to their Acts of pretended Legislation: For Quartering large bodies of armed troops among us: For protecting them, by a mock Trial, from punishment for any Murders which they should commit on the Inhabitants of these States: For cutting off our Trade with all parts of the world: For imposing Taxes on us without our Consent: For depriving us in many cases, of the benefits of Trial by Jury: For transporting us beyond Seas to be tried for pretended offences For abolishing the free System of English Laws in a neighbouring Province, establishing therein an Arbitrary government, and enlarging its Boundaries so as to render it at once an example and fit instrument for introducing the same absolute rule into these Colonies: For taking away our Charters, abolishing our most valuable Laws, and altering fundamentally the Forms of our Governments: For suspending our own Legislatures, and declaring themselves invested with power to legislate for us in all cases whatsoever.

• He has abdicated Government here, by declaring us out of his Protection and waging War against us.

• He has plundered our seas, ravaged our Coasts, burnt our towns, and destroyed the lives of our people.

• He is at this time transporting large Armies of foreign Mercenaries to compleat the works of death, desolation and tyranny, already begun with circumstances of Cruelty & perfidy scarcely paralleled in the most barbarous ages, and totally unworthy the Head of a civilized nation.

• He has constrained our fellow Citizens taken Captive on the high Seas to bear Arms against their Country, to become the executioners of their friends and Brethren, or to fall themselves by their Hands.

• He has excited domestic insurrections amongst us, and has endeavoured to bring on the inhabitants of our frontiers, the merciless Indian Savages, whose known rule of warfare, is an undistinguished destruction of all ages, sexes and conditions.

In every stage of these Oppressions We have Petitioned for Redress in the most humble terms: Our repeated Petitions have been answered only by repeated injury. A Prince whose character is thus marked by every act which may define a Tyrant, is unfit to be the ruler of a free people.

Nor have We been wanting in attentions to our Brittish brethren. We have warned them from time to time of attempts by their legislature to extend an unwarrantable jurisdiction over us. We have reminded them of the circumstances of our emigration and settlement here. We have appealed to their native justice and magnanimity, and we have conjured them by the ties of our common kindred to disavow these usurpations, which, would inevitably interrupt our connections and correspondence. They too have been deaf to the voice of justice and of consanguinity. We must, therefore, acquiesce in the necessity, which denounces our Separation, and hold them, as we hold the rest of mankind, Enemies in War, in Peace Friends.

We, therefore, the Representatives of the united States of America, in General Congress, Assembled, appealing to the Supreme Judge of the world for the rectitude of our intentions, do, in the Name, and by Authority of the good People of these Colonies, solemnly publish and declare, That these United Colonies are, and of Right ought to be Free and Independent States; that they are Absolved from all Allegiance to the British Crown, and that all political connection between them and the State of Great Britain, is and ought to be totally dissolved; and that as Free and Independent States, they have full Power to levy War, conclude Peace, contract Alliances, establish Commerce, and to do all other Acts and Things which Independent States may of right do. And for the support of this Declaration, with a firm reliance on the protection of divine Providence, we mutually pledge to each other our Lives, our Fortunes and our sacred Honor.

To all to whom these Presents shall come, we the undersigned Delegates of the States affixed to our Names send greeting. Whereas the Delegates of the United States of America in Congress assembled did on the fifteenth day of November in the Year of our Lord One Thousand Seven Hundred and Seventy seven, and in the Second Year of the Independence of America agree to certain articles of Confederation and perpetual Union between the States of Newhampshire, Massachusetts-bay, Rhodeisland and Providence Plantations, Connecticut, New York, New Jersey, Pennsylvania, Delaware, Maryland, Virginia, North Carolina, South Carolina and Georgia in the Words following, viz. "Articles of Confederation and perpetual Union between the States of Newhampshire, Massachusetts-bay, Rhodeisland and Providence Plantations, Connecticut, New-York, New-Jersey, Pennsylvania, Delaware, Maryland, Virginia, North-Carolina, South-Carolina and Georgia.

Article I. The Stile of this confederacy shall be "The United States of America."

Article II. Each state retains its sovereignty, freedom and independence, and every Power, Jurisdiction and right, which is not by this confederation expressly delegated to the United States, in Congress assembled.

Article III. The said states hereby severally enter into a firm league of friendship with each other, for their common defence, the security of their Liberties, and their mutual and general welfare, binding themselves to assist each other, against all force offered to, or attacks made upon them, or any of them, on account of religion, sovereignty, trade, or any other pretence whatever.

Article IV. The better to secure and perpetuate mutual friendship and intercourse among the people of the different states in this union, the free inhabitants of each of these states, paupers, vagabonds and fugitives from Justice excepted, shall be entitled to all privileges and immunities of free citizens in the several states; and the people of each state shall have free ingress and regress to and from any other state, and shall enjoy therein all the privileges of trade and commerce, subject to the same duties, impositions and restrictions as the inhabitants thereof respectively, provided that such restriction shall not extend so far as to prevent the removal of property imported into any state, to any other state of which the Owner is an inhabitant; provided also that no imposition, duties or restriction shall be laid by any state, on the property of the united states, or either of them.

If any Person guilty of, or charged with treason, felony, or other high misdemeanor in any state, shall flee from Justice, and be found in any of the united states, he shall upon demand of the Governor or executive power, of the state from which he fled, be delivered up and removed to the state having jurisdiction of his offence.

Full faith and credit shall be given in each of these states to the records, acts and judicial proceedings of the courts and magistrates of every other state.

Article V. For the more convenient management of the general

The Articles of Confederation (National Archives and Records Administration)

Articles of Confederation

1777

"The Articles thereof shall be inviolably observed by the States we respectively represent, and ... the Union shall be perpetual."

Overview

The Articles of Confederation, sometimes called the Articles of Confederation and Perpetual Union, was the first constitution of the United States and the American colonies' first successful attempt to form a unified government. The colonies' different interests and Great Britain's hesitance to see a unified colonial structure had sabotaged previous attempts for union. The Declaration of Independence made it imperative that some type of union be created, not only to coordinate the Revolutionary War but also to create a single state to deal with foreign nations whose assistance the country needed.

The Articles of Confederation set up a government that united the states through a confederate legislature—the Congress of the Confederation (the successor to the Second Continental Congress). The Confederation, however, had only certain powers given to it; all other powers were reserved for the states. Individual colonies wanted to retain their sovereignty and looked suspiciously at a continental government that could possibly usurp their powers. As a result, the Articles formed a confederation in which each state retained its own power over its citizens, transport, industries, and so forth, and the Confederation government was given only certain specific powers such as foreign affairs. This created a loose federal organization of states in perpetual alliance with one another.

Context

At the end of the French and Indian War in 1763, the differences between the American colonies and Great Britain intensified. With the British treasury empty from the war, the British government sought to recuperate monetary losses by making the colonies pay taxes for their own defense while the colonials insisted that taxation without representation was unlawful. With the French threat removed, many colonists questioned why Great Britain was so involved in colonial affairs; the colonies could run their own affairs without British interference.

Several attempts at colonial union were made. In 1754 the meeting of the Albany Congress resulted in the Albany Plan of Union, which was never enacted or accepted. In 1774 Joseph Galloway, delegate from Pennsylvania, presented to the First Continental Congress his own plan of union for the colonies, but again nothing was done. In 1775 Benjamin Franklin, from Pennsylvania, also tried to interest the Congress in a union, and he wrote his version of the Articles of Confederation. No action was taken.

Two groups dominated colonial political thinking. The radicals—primarily small farmers, teachers, craftsmen, and the landless—believed in direct democracy: the control of the citizenry over the government. Only small political units could be directly controlled by the people, so the radicals believed in the colonial governments' power as the supreme authority. In addition, many radicals sought a change in the social and political order: redistribution of land, the payment of higher taxes by well-off people, and so forth. A strong, central government was not desirable because it would be too far removed from the control of the people. In contrast, the conservatives were large landowners, merchants, ship owners, and lawyers who wanted the repeal of repressive British laws; many did not want to see, at least in the beginning, the end of British rule. They believed in a strong central government for the colonies—Great Britain was the original central authority—and they did not want any change in the social order. In effect, the conservatives feared direct, democratic control embodied in the revolutionary state legislatures, and they looked to a strong central government to curb the power of the states to protect personal property and the rights of the wealthy.

By 1776, however, it became clear to most conservatives that rapprochement with Great Britain was impossible. A union between the colonies became necessary, therefore, not only to coordinate the war with Britain but also to serve as the contact between the colonies and the Spanish and French governments, from whom the colonies sought support. While debating the Declaration of Independence, the Second Continental Congress set up a commission to create a plan for union. John Dickinson of Pennsylvania and Delaware headed the committee to draft the Articles of Confederation. Dickinson wrote the draft that was later

Time Line

1763	■ **February 10** The Treaty of Paris, sometimes called the Peace of Paris, is signed, ending the French and Indian War.
1776	■ **January** Thomas Paine's *Common Sense* is published; it explains in lay terms the reasons for independence. ■ **June 12** A committee headed by John Dickinson and created by the Continental Congress drafts the Articles of Confederation. ■ **July 4** The Declaration of Independence is approved by the Second Continental Congress. ■ **July 12** Debates on the Articles of Confederation begin in the Second Continental Congress.
1777	■ **November 15** The Second Continental Congress accepts the Articles of Confederation; the document is sent to the colonies for ratification.
1781	■ **March 1** The last colony, Maryland, ratifies the Articles of Confederation, thereby creating the first national government of the United States of America.
1782	■ The Bank of North America (the first modern bank of the United States) opens.
1783	■ **June 21** Mutinous soldiers hold the Confederation Congress hostage in Philadelphia. ■ **September 23** The Treaty of Paris ends the Revolutionary War.
1786	■ **August** Shays's Rebellion erupts in Massachusetts.

debated in Congress. The finished version of the Articles, which was ratified and went into effect on March 1, 1781, came from Dickinson's draft.

About the Author

John Dickinson, known as the "Penman of the Revolution," was born on the Croisadore, his family's estate near the village of Trappe in Talbot County, Maryland, on November 8, 1732. His father, Samuel Dickinson, was a prosperous farmer. His mother, Mary (Cadwalader) Dickinson, was his father's second wife. In 1740 the family moved to Kent County, Delaware. John was educated there by private tutors until 1750, when he went to Philadelphia to study law with John Moland.

In 1753 Dickinson went to London to study law at Middle Temple. After returning to Philadelphia, Dickinson became a prominent lawyer from 1757 to 1760. Dickinson then entered public life, serving in the Assembly of the Lower Counties (as Delaware was known at the time) as a speaker. In 1762 Dickinson won a seat in the Pennsylvania Assembly, and he was reelected in 1764. He quickly became the assembly's leader of the conservatives and gained notoriety for his defense of the proprietary governor against the faction led by Benjamin Franklin.

Dickinson's influential pamphlet *The Late Regulations Respecting the British Colonies* advocated pressuring British merchants to have the Stamp Act repealed. As a result, the Pennsylvania Assembly sent Dickinson as a representative to the Stamp Act Congress in 1765, and he drafted its resolutions. In 1767 and 1768 Dickinson wrote a series of newspaper articles called *Letters from a Farmer in Pennsylvania, to the Inhabitants of the British Colonies*, which circulated throughout the colonies; the articles attacked British taxation and advocated resistance to all unjust laws. Dickinson always remained optimistic, however, that a peaceful resolution could be found. Because of his *Letters*, Dickinson was given an honorary LLD from the College of New Jersey, which was later known as Princeton University.

Dickinson continued to criticize British policy. In 1768 he attacked the Townshend Revenue Act, which the British established to collect duties to pay the salaries of royal officials in the colonies. Dickinson advocated resistance through nonimportation and nonexportation agreements on British goods.

In 1770 Dickinson married the daughter of wealthy merchant Isaac Norris, Mary Norris, with whom he had two daughters: Sally and Maria. In 1771 Dickinson was reelected to the Pennsylvania Assembly, where he drafted a petition to the king that was approved. Dickinson's belief in nonviolence, however, led to the decline in his popularity. In 1774 Dickinson chaired the Philadelphia Committee of Correspondence and briefly served in the First Continental Congress as a Pennsylvania representative.

Throughout 1775 Dickinson continued to write to the British government for a redress of colonial grievances, but he was slowly drawn into the Revolutionary fray. While

Dickinson served in the Second Continental Congress from 1775 to 1776, he drew up the Declaration of the Causes and Necessity of Taking Up Arms. He voted against the Declaration of Independence in 1776 and refused to sign it. Dickinson nonetheless entered the army to fight the British. He declined to serve in the Congress and resigned from the Pennsylvania Assembly.

Dickinson headed the congressional committee to draft the Articles of Confederation from 1776 to 1777. He authored the draft of the Articles that was debated in the Congress. Delaware sent Dickinson to the Continental Congress from 1779 to 1780 as a delegate. In 1781 Dickinson served as the president of Delaware's Supreme Executive Council. Dickinson moved back to Philadelphia and served as the president of Pennsylvania from 1782 to 1785. He represented Delaware at the Annapolis Convention in 1786.

Although he was in poor health, Dickinson was sent by Delaware to the Constitutional Convention in 1787, where he argued against the U.S. Constitution. He nonetheless authorized his friend and fellow delegate George Read to sign his name to the Constitution and advocated its ratification by writing a series of letters under the pen name "Fabius." Dickinson soon withdrew from public life and wrote on politics. In 1801 his works were published in two volumes. He died on February 14, 1808, in Wilmington, Delaware, and was buried in the Friends Burial Ground. Dickinson College, chartered in 1783, in Carlisle, Pennsylvania, was named in his honor.

Time Line

1787

- **May 25–September 17** The Constitutional Convention meets in Philadelphia.
- **July 13** The Confederation Congress passes the Northwest Ordinance.

1788

- **July 25** The former secretary to the Confederation Congress turns over all official records.

1789

- **April 30** George Washington is inaugurated as the president of the United States in New York City.

Explanation and Analysis of the Document

To understand the Articles of Confederation as accepted by the Continental Congress, one must compare Dickinson's draft and the final version. On June 12, 1776, the Continental Congress created a committee consisting of several lawyers to draft the Articles of Confederation. Dickinson was viewed as the leader. The conservatives who served on the committee were Dickinson, Edward Rutledge, Robert R. Livingston, Francis Hopkinson, Thomas Stone, Joseph Hewes, Button Gwinnett, and Thomas Nelson. Thomas McKean, who was radical in his desire for independence despite being conservative in all other political leanings, also served. Roger Sherman and Josiah Bartlett served as moderates, between radical and conservative. Stephen Hopkins and Samuel Adams—John Adams's cousin—were the only true radicals serving on the committee.

This conservative-dominated committee wrote a document that created a confederation in name only. Merrill Jensen noted:

> The Dickinson draft, while by no means as explicit as the Constitution of 1787, made the constitution of the central government the standard by which the rights, powers, and duties of the states were to be measured. Congress was theoretically, if not practically, the supreme authority. In contrast, the final draft of the Articles of Confederation was a pact between thirteen sovereign states which agreed to delegate certain powers for specific purposes, while they retained all powers not expressly delegated by them to the central government. (1970, p. 130)

Dickinson's language in the draft was that of a lawyer: He used phrases and terms that have multiple meanings from a legal viewpoint, and a layperson would not realize the legal meanings. He was extremely precise in what he wrote. His exactness of language caused Rutledge to comment in a letter to the statesman and jurist John Jay that the Articles occupied "the Vice of his [Dickinson's] Productions to a considerable Degree; I mean the Vice of Refining too much" (Jensen, 1970, p. 127).

The committee's debates over the Articles are not recorded. The debate over Dickinson's draft in the radical-controlled Continental Congress, however, is recorded in that body's proceedings. Dickinson's draft has twenty articles, whereas the accepted document has thirteen articles. The final document's language is rewritten; much of the legal phrasing is eliminated or rewritten. After a preamble of greetings, the document's full title is given as "The Articles of Confederation and perpetual Union between the states of New Hampshire, Massachusetts-bay, Rhode Island and Providence Plantations, Connecticut, New York, New Jersey, Pennsylvania, Delaware, Maryland, Virginia, North Carolina, South Carolina and Georgia."

Article I fixes "The United States of America" as the name of the new nation, establishing it as the official name of the country. This name is used in the closing paragraph—the only time in the entire document—of the Declaration of Independence, where the representatives of the colonies who signed the Declaration are called the representatives of the United States of America.

www.milestonedocuments.com

Article II, which was Article III in Dickinson's draft, defines the powers of the states with respect to the Confederation. All power is reserved to the states, and the states give only certain powers to the Congress of the Confederation. In effect, there is no balance of powers between the Confederation and the state governments; the state governments remain the ultimate power in the new country, and the Confederation government's powers are strictly limited to those enumerated in the Articles, which assign it a subservient role to the governments of the states.

Article III, which was Article II in Dickinson's draft, establishes the "firm league of friendship" between the states for their mutual defense and protection from those outside the Confederation who might seek to destroy their freedoms and liberties. The Articles do not create or allow, however, a standing federal army of the United States. In time of war, officers appointed by the Congress of the Confederation would command all state militias and armies. The Congress would declare war and call on the states to raise an army to defend the United States or to suppress internal strife, as would be the case in Shays's Rebellion in Massachusetts. The states would not always answer Congress's call to arms—again, as would be the case in Shays's Rebellion—which presented a serious weakness to the Confederation.

Article IV extends the same rights and privileges to all citizens when they travel to other states within the Confederation. It also guarantees transit free of harassment or restriction from state to state as well as protection for visiting citizens under the laws of each state as though that citizen were from that state. In addition, it recognizes the legitimacy of the proceedings of the magistrates and courts of all states, and it ensures extradition, at the request of state authorities, of any criminals who have fled to escape arrest.

Article IV establishes the idea of dual citizenship—one being a citizen of both a state and the United States—a concept that would later be built upon by the Constitutional Convention of 1787. Under the Articles however, such a concept had no meaning. Each state viewed itself as a community of people, and only the leaders of a community could exert control over the people. The United States government had no jurisdiction over individual citizens of the states, since this would imply the collapse of the existing communities. Therefore, the Confederation had no authority to act upon the citizens of the states, except in cases where state citizens were serving in the Confederation military. The Confederation could act only upon the state governments, not on the people. Article IV, to the colonials, meant a reciprocal type of citizenship—citizens of one state are guaranteed the same rights and protections as citizens of any state they visit. Being a United States citizen was an alien concept.

Article V deals with the states' representation in the Congress of the Confederation. The article requires each state to have no fewer than two and no more than seven delegates at any time. The process by which delegates are selected is reserved for state legislatures to decide; states have the right to recall delegates and send others in their place. Each state has one vote in the Congress, which is to meet on the first Monday of every November. The article sets delegates' term limits and the prohibition that none could hold any other Confederation office while serving as a delegate. States are responsible for caring for their delegates while they serve in Congress. Delegates are also assured freedom of speech when in Congress and protected from arrest (except for treason, felony, or breech of the peace) by states through which they travel on their way to and from attendance in Congress.

States could send no less than two and no more than seven delegates to the Continental Congress. Each state had one vote. Several instances are recorded where a state's delegates split evenly, therefore nullifying the ability of the state to vote. It was not unheard of for riders to be sent to the state to bring back an absentee or alternate delegate. Only with this delegate could the tie be broken and the state's vote registered.

Lengthy debates resulted in the "one state, one vote" unicameral legislature that the accepted document codifies. Representation based on state population had been suggested, but smaller states opposed it based on the fear that larger states would dominate the Confederation. The southern states insisted that their representation include their slaves, who were not citizens and had no rights. Northern states opposed this since it would swell southern states' representation. The congressional representation problem would create a crisis in the Constitutional Convention of 1787, which was resolved only by compromise and by the creation of the bicameral Congress that Americans know today.

Article VI prohibits any state from sending embassies to foreign countries or entering into treaties or alliances with them. Foreign relations is strictly reserved for the Confederation government. In addition, no United States public servant can accept a position or title from a foreign government, nor can the government of the United States bestow any title of nobility. States are prohibited from collecting duties on foreign imports that might interfere with treaties the United States has or would have with Spain or France. States are prohibited from having standing armies and navies in times of peace except a number as determined by the United States for the defense of the state or its trade. States, however, are required to keep their militias trained, armed, and prepared. States cannot engage in war without Congress's permission unless the state is attacked or has advanced warning of an attack and Congress cannot be consulted ahead of time. States have to wait for a declaration of war from the United States before granting commissions to vessels of war or letters of marque and to attack only the foreign nation with whom the United States is at war.

Article VII stipulates that the legislature of a state will appoint the officers with the rank of colonel and below of any army that state raises. The Congress of the Confederation would appoint generals. This was in keeping with the tradition established during the Revolution whereby Congress appointed George Washington commander in chief of the colonial forces as well as all the other generals that fought the war. Responsibility of raising and maintaining the army is the sole responsibility of the state that originally creates it.

Article VIII deals with expenses of war and those for the common defense and welfare of the United States. A common treasury is to be established and used to pay for said expenses. Each state pays into the common treasury, which is based on the value of a state's land (granted or surveyed), buildings, and so forth. The Congress is responsible for periodically directing the reestimation of the states' property values. State legislatures levy and collect taxes due to the United States in a time frame agreed to by Congress.

This article's problem is that the United States has no recourse in collecting money that states owe it. It is assumed that the states' good conduct would ensure that money due to the United States would be collected by the date set. In many cases, the states would neglect this article, and Congress would have little or no money with which to run the country.

Article IX, the largest of the Articles, reserves Congress's right to determine the condition of peace and war. Sending and receiving embassies and entering into treaties and alliances with foreign powers are reserved for Congress. The United States, however, cannot make any commercial treaty with a foreign power that restricts a state from imposing the same tax to foreign goods and commerce that the foreign nation imposes on the state. Congress also decides war prizes captured on land and sea and issues letters of marque and reprisal in times of peace. Congress would establish courts appointed to dispose of said prizes; members of Congress cannot serve as judges in these courts.

States can ask Congress to become involved in land disputes between states, but only as a last resort. The Articles did not give Congress authority over the western lands, which delayed ratification. These western lands were located between the Appalachian Mountains and the Mississippi River. Even before the end of the Revolutionary War, many people believed that Great Britain would give this land to the new nation. Also, since many of the boundaries set by colonial charters were vague and overlapped in many cases, some colonies viewed parts of the western lands as part of their states. Virginia's charter of 1609, for example, set vague colony boundaries. The Virginians considered territories east of the Mississippi River as land given to them by their charter. If the Mississippi River were meant to be Virginia's boundary, the colony could claim all land that today is Tennessee, Kentucky, Ohio, and western Pennsylvania.

Even before the new nation won independence, land disputes threatened to tear it apart. Dickinson's draft gave Congress full control to settle western territories but did not explain how to do it. Article IX in the accepted document fails to give authority to Congress over the western lands unless the conflicted states ask for Congress's assistance in resolving the dispute. The obtuse procedure that Congress would use to settle disputed boundaries is discussed in Article IX. However, the procedure by which Congress would resolve disputed western lands is not detailed.

Although Article IX also gives Congress authority to regulate the value of the Confederation and the states' coins—no national currency is established. Responsibility for equity in the exchange rates of all the states' currencies is

John Dickinson wrote the draft of the Articles of Confederation that was debated in Congress. (Library of Congress)

assigned to the Confederation. Congress regulates trade, manages Native American affairs, creates and regulates state post offices, collects postal duties, appoints naval officers, and makes army and navy rules and regulations and directs their operations.

Article IX also establishes a "Committee of the States" to run the Confederation while Congress is not in session. Each state appoints one delegate to the committee, which can appoint others to posts that are necessary to run the Confederation government. The committee chooses a president to serve a yearly term; no president can serve more than one term in three years. The committee ascertains needed funds to run the Confederation and can borrow money and issue bills of credit. The article regulates how to draft and equip a navy and the way each state should raise a number of soldiers proportionate to the white population. The committee's president is the de facto president of the United States. He serves as head of government, meets foreign embassies, and has a ceremonial role. The Confederation's president is a legislator; he serves in the Congress of the Confederation, as did those he appoints to executive positions. The president and his staff need to carry out not only their executive duties but also their legislative duties.

www.milestonedocuments.com

Dickinson's draft created a "Council of State," which was headed by a president. Congress would have chosen the president and his officers, and the council would have continued to function when Congress was in session. The council could summon Congress while not in session if warranted and could prepare items for Congress's debate. The council was in charge of U.S. armed forces while Congress was not in session. Like the committee, the council would not be above Congress; unlike the committee, the council would be independent of Congress.

The Congress of the Confederation needs a majority vote of nine states—or a two-thirds majority, which today is needed to override a presidential veto—to pass legislation or do business. A simple majority to pass legislation is not considered enough—most states have to agree to pass legislation. The Congress can adjourn at any time and can meet anywhere in the United States. Congress's proceedings are to be published regularly, excluding anything of a secretive nature. Copies of recorded congressional debates and votes would be available to delegates and state legislatures.

Article X gives the Committee of the States the power to act in the name of Congress when Congress is not in session. It also gives the committee any additional powers that Congress (with a nine states majority) decides to invest in it.

Article XI allows Canada to enter the Confederation on the footing of a state. Congress does not have to approve Canada's joining. Otherwise, at least nine states must approve the admission of a colony to the United States. The Northwest Ordinance of 1787, in addition to the Ordinance of 1784 and Land Ordinance of 1785, set up the process by which states could be admitted.

Article XII recognizes all debts created by Congress in executing the duties of the Confederation. Payment of all these debts by the United States is pledged. The United States has no way to ensure the states' prompt payment to the national treasury. In many cases, the Confederation would lack the proper funds.

Article XIII calls on member states to honor the Articles and uphold the decisions made by the Congress. It is again reiterated that the Confederation is perpetual. Only Congress can make changes or amendments to the existing Articles and only by a nine-state majority vote, as stated in Article X; changes approved by Congress must then be ratified by the state legislatures before the changes could become law.

The Articles end by declaring that the delegates approve and call for the ratification of the document. All questions and problems of the Confederation are to be resolved by Congress, which is the supreme authority in all Confederation matters. The states are called upon to abide by the Articles; the union is again called perpetual.

Audience

To fully understand Dickinson's draft of the Articles, one needed legal training or at least a high degree of education. Literate people could understand most of the document, but the legal phrases and jargon have different, hidden meanings that could be lost on the general reader. In contrast, the adopted Articles of Confederation is written in straightforward language with a quite plain meaning. The language does not have hidden meanings.

The Articles would have been read by many different people throughout the colonies. Copies of the final document were made and sent to all state assemblies for ratification. From there, copies were circulated at the pleasure of the state legislatures. The Virginia legislature, for example, reviewed and debated the Articles without making the document public. Massachusetts, in contrast, printed 250 copies of the Articles and sent them to the towns for review and comment.

Impact

The Articles of Confederation made the United States of America a nation. Whereas all other attempts at colonial unification had failed, the Articles created a government that could direct the American Revolution and be represented in Spanish and French courts. Thirteen states would no longer be seeking freedom; the United States of America would request aid, and, as such, one large nation would negotiate with foreign powers the terms of financial agreements, loans, and military assistance. France would recognize and assist the United States of America in the American Revolution.

With the end of the Revolution, however, the radicals' interests in a national government faded. The defeated British were expected to withdraw from forts on western lands, which the Treaty of Paris (1783) ceded to the United States. (The United States did not force full British compliance until the War of 1812.) Independence had been achieved. The radicals were concerned with state legislatures and local government, embodied in the states. As time went on, the Congress of the Confederation found it harder to get the states to pay what they owed into the national treasury and to send enough delegates for Congress to have a quorum to conduct Confederation business.

Even in 1783 Congress lacked the funds to pay veterans of the Continental army. On June 21 mutinous Pennsylvania soldiers surrounded the Pennsylvania State House in Philadelphia and refused to let the legislators leave until they promised to pay them. The crisis was averted when the soldiers became drunk and distracted, and the legislators were able to escape without serious incident. The Congress of the Confederation, however, never again met in Philadelphia.

Shays's Rebellion, which erupted in western Massachusetts in August 1786, was far more serious. Because of an economic downturn, small farmers were facing foreclosures and debt proceedings while still trying to pay high taxes. Daniel Shays and other local leaders organized hundreds of armed men, who forced the closing of several courthouses; they even forced the Massachusetts Supreme Court in Springfield to adjourn. The governor of Massachusetts sent an urgent request to the Congress of the

Essential Quotes

"The said States hereby enter into a firm league of friendship with each other, for their common defense, the security of their liberties, and their mutual and general welfare, binding themselves to assist each other, against all force offered to, or attacks made upon them, or any of them, on account of religion, sovereignty, trade, or any other pretense whatever."

(Article III)

"If any person guilty of, or charged with, treason, felony, or other high misdemeanor in any State, shall flee from justice, and be found in any of the United States, he shall, upon demand of the Governor or executive power of the State from which he fled, be delivered up and removed to the State having jurisdiction of his offense."

(Article IV)

"Freedom of speech and debate in Congress shall not be impeached or questioned in any court of place out of Congress, and the members of Congress shall be protected in their persons from arrests or imprisonments, during the time of their going to and from, and attendance on Congress, except for treason, felony, or breach of the peace."

(Article V)

"When land forces are raised by any State for the common defense, all officers of or under the rank of colonel, shall be appointed by the legislature of each State respectively, by whom such forces shall be raised, or in such manner as such State shall direct, and all vacancies shall be filled up by the State which first made the appointment."

(Article VII)

"And we do further solemnly plight and engage the faith of our respective constituents, that they shall abide by the determination of the United States in Congress assembled, on all questions, which by the said Confederation are submitted to them. And that the Articles thereof shall be inviolably observed by the States we respectively represent, and that the Union shall be perpetual."

(Article XIII)

Confederation for U.S. troops to be sent to help put down the rebels and restore order. Congress requested troops be sent to Massachusetts; the Confederation lacked the funds to pay for such an army, and the states simply ignored Massachusetts' plea. Shays's Rebellion eventually ended in February 1787 when Massachusetts forces finally defeated Shays at Petersham without help.

The solution to the western land problems was resolved in the Confederation through three land acts, adopted by Congress in 1784, 1785, and 1787, that finally settled the western boundaries of landless states and set up the process by which these territories were administered. Along with the two previous ordinances (1784 and 1785), the Northwest Ordinance addressed the area of the Northwest Territory (also known as the Old Northwest) and created a blueprint for how public lands would be surveyed and divided into smaller parcels of land. In addition, the ordinances directed how local and regional governments were created, how each town had public lands for schools, how the territory would be represented in Congress, and how and when these territories could enter the Union. The Northwest Ordinance outlawed slavery in the Northwest Territory. The land ordinances also ensured that new states would enter the Union on an equal footing with the original states and not be inferior in status to them.

Spain, a potentially hostile state that controlled the mouth of the Mississippi River at New Orleans, served as a bottleneck for farmers living in the western lands. The Mississippi was the natural way for the farmers to move their crops to market, but the United States had no commercial treaty with Spain over usage of the Mississippi. Some farmers, seeking to use the river, went so far as to swear allegiance to the crown of Spain so that their crops could go to New Orleans. As a result, the Annapolis Convention met in September 1786 to discuss these and other commercial problems. Five states attended, and it was resolved that the Articles had to be revised to solve the problems of national commerce.

The conservatives saw their chance. In 1787 the Congress of the Confederation created a committee to revise or amend the Articles of Confederation. Most of the delegates were conservatives (the radicals boycotted or simply had no interest). This committee, now known as the Constitutional Convention of 1787, secretly and illegally drafted the current U.S. Constitution, thereby creating a new form of government, although most of the Articles were rewritten and incorporated into the Constitution. It can also be said, in retrospect, that the Constitution of 1787 closed the gaps in the Articles of Confederation and eliminated the weaknesses, to create a functional federal government for the United States.

The Articles of Confederation did give the United States a strong start as a new nation. The Articles, however, never mentioned or addressed slavery and did not create a federal judiciary. The Constitution of 1787 discussed slavery and set up the checks and balances of the three branches of the federal government.

Under the Articles, the United States reduced its Revolutionary War debt by more than half, diffused the disputes over the western lands ceded by Great Britain, settled how new states would enter the Union, and allowed the creation of the first national banking system in the United States. The Congress of the Confederation held its first debates at the new national capital.

Related Documents

Boyd, Julian P., Lyman H. Butterfield, and Mina R. Bryan, eds. *The Papers of Thomas Jefferson*, Vol. 1: *1760–1776*. Princeton: Princeton University Press, 1950. Thomas Jefferson's influence on the development of democracy in the United States should not be underestimated. His thoughts on government, views of the events taking place during his lifetime, and belief in the United States are discussed. Jefferson's ideas on the Articles of Confederation are recorded.

"Constitution of the United States." National Archives "Charters of Freedom" Web site. http://www.archives.gov/national-archives-experience/charters/constitution.html. Accessed on October 7, 2007. The U.S. Constitution, successor to the Articles, incorporated the Articles and expanded the power of the federal government to set up the current three branches and the checks-and-balances system. The progression of American political thought is evident from the Declaration of Independence through the Articles and into the Constitution.

"Declaration of Independence." National Archives "Charters of Freedom" Web site. http://www.archives.gov/national-archives-experience/charters/declaration_transcript.html. Accessed on October 7, 2007. Thomas Jefferson's draft of the Declaration of Independence was reworked in its final form and adopted by the Continental Congress on July 4, 1776. The Articles of Confederation was the next logical step in the progression of American political thought after the Declaration and illustrates why the Articles emphasized the power of the states over the limited powers of the Confederation government.

Ford, Worthington Chauncey, Gaillard Hunt, John Clement Fitzpatrick, et al., eds. *Journals of the Continental Congress, 1774–1789*. Washington, D.C.: Government Printing Office, 1904–1937. The thirty-four volumes created by the Continental (and Confederation) Congress are the record of all the debates, votes, and motions made. The debates of the committee that created the Dickinson draft of the Articles of Confederation are not recorded. The debates over Dickinson's draft in the Continental Congress, which reduced the articles from twenty to thirteen and rewrote and rephrased the document, are recorded here.

Madison, James. *Notes of Debates in the Federal Convention of 1787*. Athens: Ohio University Press, 1984. These are the proceedings of the committee that wrote the Constitution. The thoughts and beliefs of the delegates as they worked out a new type of government and debated on why the federal system under the Articles did not work and why changes were necessary are recorded here.

Madison, James, Alexander Hamilton, and John Jay. *The Federalist Papers*. New York: Pocket Books, 2004. Madison, Hamilton, and Jay wrote a series of articles published in American papers and collected in *The Federalist* to generate support for the adoption of the U.S. Constitution. They explain why the Articles of Confederation was abandoned for an entirely new type of government.

Bibliography

■ Articles

Cain, Michael J., and Keith L. Dougherty. "Suppressing Shays' Rebellion: Collective Action and Constitutional Design under the Articles of Confederation." *Journal of Theoretical Politics* 11, no. 2 (April 1999): 233–260.

Lienesch, Michael. "Historical Theory and Political Reform: Two Perspectives on Confederation Politics." *Review of Politics* 45, no. 1 (January 1983): 94–115.

Lutz, Donald S. "The Articles of Confederation as the Background to the Federal Republic." *Publius* 20, no. 1 (Winter 1990): 55–70.

McCormick, Richard P. "Ambiguous Authority: The Ordinances of the Confederation Congress, 1781–1789." *American Journal of Legal History* 41, no. 4 (October 1997): 411–439.

Payne, Samuel B. "The Iroquois League, the Articles of Confederation, and the Constitution." *William and Mary Quarterly* 53, no. 3 (July 1996): 605–620.

Rakove, Jack. "The Legacy of the Articles of Confederation." *Publius* 12, no. 4 (Autumn 1982): 45–66.

■ Books

Berkin, Carol. *A Brilliant Solution: Inventing the American Constitution*. New York: Harcourt, 2002.

Burnett, Edmund C. *The Continental Congress*. New York: Macmillian, 1941.

Flower, Milton E. *John Dickinson: Conservative Revolutionary*. Charlottesville: University of Virginia Press, 1983.

Hoffert, Robert W. *A Politics of Tensions: The Articles of Confederation and American Political Ideas*. Niwot: University Press of Colorado, 1992.

Jensen, Merrill. *The New Nation: A History of the United States during the Confederation, 1781–1789*. New York: Knopf, 1950.

———. *The Articles of Confederation: An Interpretation of the Social-Constitutional History of the American Revolution, 1774–1781*. Madison: University of Wisconsin Press, 1970.

Main, Jackson T. *The Antifederalists: Critics of the Constitution, 1781–1788*. Chapel Hill: University of North Carolina Press, 1961.

Manley, John F., and Kenneth M. Dolbeare, eds. *The Case against the Constitution: From the Antifederalists to the Present*. Armonk, N.Y.: M. E. Sharpe, 1987.

■ Web Sites

"American Confederation." The James Madison Center Web site. http://www.jmu.edu/madison/center/main_pages/madison_archives/constit_confed/confederation/confederation.htm. Accessed on October 29, 2007.

"Articles of Confederation." The Avalon Project at Yale Law School Web site. http://www.yale.edu/lawweb/avalon/artconf.htm. Accessed on January 24, 2008.

—By Michael W. Handis

Questions for Further Study

1. What were the specific powers granted to the United States in the Articles of Confederation?

2. Dickinson's draft of the Articles of Confederation created a "Council of State," but the accepted document created a "Committee of the States." Compare these two bodies.

3. Compare Dickinson's draft of the Articles of Confederation and the final draft adopted by the Continental Congress. Why were changes made to Dickinson's draft?

4. Compare the Articles of Confederation and the U.S. Constitution. How did the writers of the Constitution address the perceived problems in the Articles?

www.milestonedocuments.com

Glossary

Articles	statements or paragraphs in a document or constitution that regulate the running of a government
confederation	an association of independent states, the central government of which can make recommendations to the different states but cannot interfere in their internal affairs and does not have authority over the individual states' citizens
constituents	people represented by an elected official
executive	the department in a government that enforces laws and is responsible for handling specific responsibilities, such as foreign affairs and collecting taxes
legislature	body of elected officials that write and pass laws
marque or reprisal, letters of	authorizations from a leader or state allowing the pirating of a foreign country's ships, goods, and so forth, usually issued during a time of war

Document Text

Articles of Confederation

To all to whom these Presents shall come, we the undersigned Delegates of the States affixed to our Names send greeting.

Articles of Confederation and perpetual Union between the states of New Hampshire, Massachusetts-bay Rhode Island and Providence Plantations, Connecticut, New York, New Jersey, Pennsylvania, Delaware, Maryland, Virginia, North Carolina, South Carolina and Georgia.

◆ I.

The Stile of this Confederacy shall be

"The United States of America".

◆ II.

Each state retains its sovereignty, freedom, and independence, and every power, jurisdiction, and right, which is not by this Confederation expressly delegated to the United States, in Congress assembled.

◆ III.

The said States hereby severally enter into a firm league of friendship with each other, for their common defense, the security of their liberties, and their mutual and general welfare, binding themselves to assist each other, against all force offered to, or attacks made upon them, or any of them, on account of religion, sovereignty, trade, or any other pretense whatever.

◆ IV.

The better to secure and perpetuate mutual friendship and intercourse among the people of the different States in this Union, the free inhabitants of each of these States, paupers, vagabonds, and fugitives from justice excepted, shall be entitled to all privileges and immunities of free citizens in the several States; and the people of each State shall free ingress and regress to and from any other State, and shall enjoy therein all the privileges of trade and commerce, subject to the same duties, impositions, and restrictions as the inhabitants thereof respectively, provided that such restrictions shall not extend so far as to prevent the removal of property imported into any State, to any other State, of which the owner is an inhabitant; provided also that no imposition, duties or restriction shall be laid by any State, on the property of the United States, or either of them.

If any person guilty of, or charged with, treason, felony, or other high misdemeanor in any State, shall flee from justice, and be found in any of the United States, he shall, upon demand of the Governor or executive power of the State from which he fled, be delivered up and removed to the State having jurisdiction of his offense.

Full faith and credit shall be given in each of these States to the records, acts, and judicial proceedings of the courts and magistrates of every other State.

◆ V.

For the most convenient management of the general interests of the United States, delegates shall be annually appointed in such manner as the legislatures of each State shall direct, to meet in Congress on the first Monday in November, in every year, with a power reserved to each State to recall its delegates, or any of them, at any time within the year, and to send others in their stead for the remainder of the year.

No State shall be represented in Congress by less than two, nor more than seven members; and no person shall be capable of being a delegate for more than three years in any term of six years; nor shall any person, being a delegate, be capable of holding any office under the United States, for which he, or

www.milestonedocuments.com

another for his benefit, receives any salary, fees or emolument of any kind.

Each State shall maintain its own delegates in a meeting of the States, and while they act as members of the committee of the States.

In determining questions in the United States in Congress assembled, each State shall have one vote.

Freedom of speech and debate in Congress shall not be impeached or questioned in any court or place out of Congress, and the members of Congress shall be protected in their persons from arrests or imprisonments, during the time of their going to and from, and attendence on Congress, except for treason, felony, or breach of the peace.

◆ VI.

No State, without the consent of the United States in Congress assembled, shall send any embassy to, or receive any embassy from, or enter into any conference, agreement, alliance or treaty with any King, Prince or State; nor shall any person holding any office of profit or trust under the United States, or any of them, accept any present, emolument, office or title of any kind whatever from any King, Prince or foreign State; nor shall the United States in Congress assembled, or any of them, grant any title of nobility.

No two or more States shall enter into any treaty, confederation or alliance whatever between them, without the consent of the United States in Congress assembled, specifying accurately the purposes for which the same is to be entered into, and how long it shall continue.

No State shall lay any imposts or duties, which may interfere with any stipulations in treaties, entered into by the United States in Congress assembled, with any King, Prince or State, in pursuance of any treaties already proposed by Congress, to the courts of France and Spain.

No vessel of war shall be kept up in time of peace by any State, except such number only, as shall be deemed necessary by the United States in Congress assembled, for the defense of such State, or its trade; nor shall any body of forces be kept up by any State in time of peace, except such number only, as in the judgement of the United States in Congress assembled, shall be deemed requisite to garrison the forts necessary for the defense of such State; but every State shall always keep up a well-regulated and disciplined militia, sufficiently armed and accoutered, and shall provide and constantly have ready for use, in public stores, a due number of filed pieces and tents, and a proper quantity of arms, ammunition and camp equipage.

No State shall engage in any war without the consent of the United States in Congress assembled, unless such State be actually invaded by enemies, or shall have received certain advice of a resolution being formed by some nation of Indians to invade such State, and the danger is so imminent as not to admit of a delay till the United States in Congress assembled can be consulted; nor shall any State grant commissions to any ships or vessels of war, nor letters of marque or reprisal, except it be after a declaration of war by the United States in Congress assembled, and then only against the Kingdom or State and the subjects thereof, against which war has been so declared, and under such regulations as shall be established by the United States in Congress assembled, unless such State be infested by pirates, in which case vessels of war may be fitted out for that occasion, and kept so long as the danger shall continue, or until the United States in Congress assembled shall determine otherwise.

◆ VII.

When land forces are raised by any State for the common defense, all officers of or under the rank of colonel, shall be appointed by the legislature of each State respectively, by whom such forces shall be raised, or in such manner as such State shall direct, and all vacancies shall be filled up by the State which first made the appointment.

◆ VIII.

All charges of war, and all other expenses that shall be incurred for the common defense or general welfare, and allowed by the United States in Congress assembled, shall be defrayed out of a common treasury, which shall be supplied by the several States in proportion to the value of all land within each State, granted or surveyed for any person, as such land and the buildings and improvements thereon shall be estimated according to such mode as the United States in Congress assembled, shall from time to time direct and appoint.

The taxes for paying that proportion shall be laid and levied by the authority and direction of the legislatures of the several States within the time agreed upon by the United States in Congress assembled.

◆ IX.

The United States in Congress assembled, shall have the sole and exclusive right and power of determining on peace and war, except in the cases mentioned in the sixth article—of sending and receiving ambassadors—entering into treaties and alliances, provided that no treaty of commerce shall be made whereby the legislative power of the respective States shall be restrained from imposing such imposts and duties on foreigners, as their own people are subjected to, or from prohibiting the exportation or importation of any species of goods or commodities whatsoever—of establishing rules for deciding in all cases, what captures on land or water shall be legal, and in what manner prizes taken by land or naval forces in the service of the United States shall be divided or appropriated—of granting letters of marque and reprisal in times of peace—appointing courts for the trial of piracies and felonies commited on the high seas and establishing courts for receiving and determining finally appeals in all cases of captures, provided that no member of Congress shall be appointed a judge of any of the said courts.

The United States in Congress assembled shall also be the last resort on appeal in all disputes and differences now subsisting or that hereafter may arise between two or more States concerning boundary, jurisdiction or any other causes whatever; which authority shall always be exercised in the manner following. Whenever the legislative or executive authority or lawful agent of any State in controversy with another shall present a petition to Congress stating the matter in question and praying for a hearing, notice thereof shall be given by order of Congress to the legislative or executive authority of the other State in controversy, and a day assigned for the appearance of the parties by their lawful agents, who shall then be directed to appoint by joint consent, commissioners or judges to constitute a court for hearing and determining the matter in question: but if they cannot agree, Congress shall name three persons out of each of the United States, and from the list of such persons each party shall alternately strike out one, the petitioners beginning, until the number shall be reduced to thirteen; and from that number not less than seven, nor more than nine names as Congress shall direct, shall in the presence of Congress be drawn out by lot, and the persons whose names shall be so drawn or any five of them, shall be commissioners or judges, to hear and finally determine the controversy, so always as a major part of the judges who shall hear the cause shall agree in the determination: and if either party shall neglect to attend at the day appointed, without showing reasons, which Congress shall judge sufficient, or being present shall refuse to strike, the Congress shall proceed to nominate three persons out of each State, and the secretary of Congress shall strike in behalf of such party absent or refusing; and the judgement and sentence of the court to be appointed, in the manner before prescribed, shall be final and conclusive; and if any of the parties shall refuse to submit to the authority of such court, or to appear or defend their claim or cause, the court shall nevertheless proceed to pronounce sentence, or judgement, which shall in like manner be final and decisive, the judgement or sentence and other proceedings being in either case transmitted to Congress, and lodged among the acts of Congress for the security of the parties concerned: provided that every commissioner, before he sits in judgement, shall take an oath to be administered by one of the judges of the supreme or superior court of the State, where the cause shall be tried, 'well and truly to hear and determine the matter in question, according to the best of his judgement, without favor, affection or hope of reward': provided also, that no State shall be deprived of territory for the benefit of the United States.

All controversies concerning the private right of soil claimed under different grants of two or more States, whose jurisdictions as they may respect such lands, and the States which passed such grants are adjusted, the said grants or either of them being at the same time claimed to have originated antecedent to such settlement of jurisdiction, shall on the petition of either party to the Congress of the United States, be finally determined as near as may be in the same manner as is before presecribed for deciding disputes respecting territorial jurisdiction between different States.

The United States in Congress assembled shall also have the sole and exclusive right and power of regulating the alloy and value of coin struck by their own authority, or by that of the respective States—fixing the standards of weights and measures throughout the United States—regulating the trade and managing all affairs with the Indians, not members of any of the States, provided that the legislative right of any State within its own limits be not infringed or violated—establishing or regulating post offices from one State to another, throughout all the United States, and exacting such postage on the papers passing through the same as may be requisite to defray the expenses of the said office—appointing all officers of the land forces, in the service of the United States, excepting regimental officers—

www.milestonedocuments.com

Document Text

appointing all the officers of the naval forces, and commissioning all officers whatever in the service of the United States—making rules for the government and regulation of the said land and naval forces, and directing their operations.

The United States in Congress assembled shall have authority to appoint a committee, to sit in the recess of Congress, to be denominated 'A Committee of the States', and to consist of one delegate from each State; and to appoint such other committees and civil officers as may be necessary for managing the general affairs of the United States under their direction—to appoint one of their members to preside, provided that no person be allowed to serve in the office of president more than one year in any term of three years; to ascertain the necessary sums of money to be raised for the service of the United States, and to appropriate and apply the same for defraying the public expenses—to borrow money, or emit bills on the credit of the United States, transmitting every half-year to the respective States an account of the sums of money so borrowed or emitted—to build and equip a navy—to agree upon the number of land forces, and to make requisitions from each State for its quota, in proportion to the number of white inhabitants in such State; which requisition shall be binding, and thereupon the legislature of each State shall appoint the regimental officers, raise the men and cloath, arm and equip them in a solid-like manner, at the expense of the United States; and the officers and men so cloathed, armed and equipped shall march to the place appointed, and within the time agreed on by the United States in Congress assembled. But if the United States in Congress assembled shall, on consideration of circumstances judge proper that any State should not raise men, or should raise a smaller number of men than the quota thereof, such extra number shall be raised, officered, cloathed, armed and equipped in the same manner as the quota of each State, unless the legislature of such State shall judge that such extra number cannot be safely spread out in the same, in which case they shall raise, officer, cloath, arm and equip as many of such extra number as they judeg can be safely spared. And the officers and men so cloathed, armed, and equipped, shall march to the place appointed, and within the time agreed on by the United States in Congress assembled.

The United States in Congress assembled shall never engage in a war, nor grant letters of marque or reprisal in time of peace, nor enter into any treaties or alliances, nor coin money, nor regulate the value thereof, nor ascertain the sums and expenses necessary for the defense and welfare of the United States, or any of them, nor emit bills, nor borrow money on the credit of the United States, nor appropriate money, nor agree upon the number of vessels of war, to be built or purchased, or the number of land or sea forces to be raised, nor appoint a commander in chief of the army or navy, unless nine States assent to the same: nor shall a question on any other point, except for adjourning from day to day be determined, unless by the votes of the majority of the United States in Congress assembled.

The Congress of the United States shall have power to adjourn to any time within the year, and to any place within the United States, so that no period of adjournment be for a longer duration than the space of six months, and shall publish the journal of their proceedings monthly, except such parts thereof relating to treaties, alliances or military operations, as in their judgement require secrecy; and the yeas and nays of the delegates of each State on any question shall be entered on the journal, when it is desired by any delegates of a State, or any of them, at his or their request shall be furnished with a transcript of the said journal, except such parts as are above excepted, to lay before the legislatures of the several States.

◆ X.

The Committee of the States, or any nine of them, shall be authorized to execute, in the recess of Congress, such of the powers of Congress as the United States in Congress assembled, by the consent of the nine States, shall from time to time think expedient to vest them with; provided that no power be delegated to the said Committee, for the exercise of which, by the Articles of Confederation, the voice of nine States in the Congress of the United States assembled be requisite.

◆ XI.

Canada acceding to this confederation, and adjoining in the measures of the United States, shall be admitted into, and entitled to all the advantages of this Union; but no other colony shall be admitted into the same, unless such admission be agreed to by nine States.

◆ XII.

All bills of credit emitted, monies borrowed, and debts contracted by, or under the authority of Congress, before the assembling of the United States, in pursuance of the present confederation, shall be deemed and considered as a charge against the United States, for payment and satisfaction whereof the said United States, and the public faith are hereby solemnly pleged.

◆ XIII.

Every State shall abide by the determination of the United States in Congress assembled, on all questions which by this confederation are submitted to them. And the Articles of this Confederation shall be inviolably observed by every State, and the Union shall be perpetual; nor shall any alteration at any time hereafter be made in any of them; unless such alteration be agreed to in a Congress of the United States, and be afterwards confirmed by the legislatures of every State.

And Whereas it hath pleased the Great Governor of the World to incline the hearts of the legislatures we respectively represent in Congress, to approve of, and to authorize us to ratify the said Articles of Confederation and perpetual Union. Know Ye that we the undersigned delegates, by virtue of the power and authority to us given for that purpose, do by these presents, in the name and in behalf of our respective constituents, fully and entirely ratify and confirm each and every of the said Articles of Confederation and perpetual Union, and all and singular the matters and things therein contained: And we do further solemnly plight and engage the faith of our respective constituents, that they shall abide by the determinations of the United States in Congress assembled, on all questions, which by the said Confederation are submitted to them. And that the Articles thereof shall be inviolably observed by the States we respectively represent, and that the Union shall be perpetual.

In Witness whereof we have hereunto set our hands in Congress. Done at Philadelphia in the State of Pennsylvania the ninth day of July in the Year of our Lord One Thousand Seven Hundred and Seventy-Eight, and in the Third Year of the independence of America.

Agreed to by Congress 15 November 1777. In force after ratification by Maryland, 1 March 1781

www.milestonedocuments.com

Treaty of Fort Pitt

1778

"A perpetual peace and friendship shall from henceforth take place."

Overview

On September 17, 1778, the United States of America signed its first known formal treaty with an Indian nation, the Delawares, giving a signal of mutual recognition and friendship. This treaty was concluded at Fort Pitt, Pennsylvania, and provided for an alliance between the United States and the Delawares. The treaty's final article (Article VI) stated that Indians friendly to the United States would be permitted to form a state of the Union, with the Delawares at their head, subject to certain conditions. It is not clear whether the United States was planning to honor this treaty clause, especially since the Continental Congress still lacked a constitution and did not have the legal power to create a new state. However, the fact that such a treaty was even made indicated the status and influence accorded to the Delaware Indians in spite of the decline of their numerical strength. The negotiation and signing of the Treaty of Fort Pitt also reflected the need of the United States for allies and the military importance of the native nations.

In spite of this treaty, during the War of Independence the Americans repeatedly failed to keep their promises to support their Delaware allies. The British, however, did better by their Native American supporters. Consequently, some of the Delawares decided to side with the English, thus abandoning their allegiance to the United States and to the treaty the U.S. government had shown little inclination or ability to honor. Nonetheless, the treaty is reflective of the power relations in North America at the time and shows that the newly created United States considered Native American nations as sovereign entities.

Context

The document was created when the United States, still embroiled in the War of Independence, entered into negotiations and subsequently a treaty with the Delawares at Fort Pitt on September 17, 1778. At this time the colonial period and British rule were coming to an end, but independence had not yet been secured. The United States thus was in need of allies and was striving to limit the number of their potential enemies.

The colonial rivalry between England and France in North America, which had most recently manifested in the French and Indian War between 1754 and 1763, had ended with the Treaty of Paris of 1763 and the loss of the better part of the French empire. This had left Great Britain the predominant power in North America. In the wake of this conflict, antagonism soon grew between the American colonies and the imperial center. Through the royal Proclamation of 1763 Britain sought to curb the westward expansion of the colonists and thereby preserve the peace with the Indians and avoid costly confrontation with the native populations. Westward expansion thus was hindered by Britain as well as by the Indian occupation of the lands in question. Possibly encouraged by the temporary quality of the language of the proclamation, however, the colonists often refused to accept this artificial dividing line and intruded onto Native American lands in spite of it, making illegal purchases or simply taking lands.

These recurring intrusions eventually contributed to the outbreak of Pontiac's Rebellion (or War) in 1763. Even though the Indian alliance under Pontiac was initially very successful, Britain eventually prevailed in this conflict, and English forces put down the so-called rebellion. Partly as a result of this recent military clash with Indians, Britain adopted the opinion that the colonies should contribute to the costs of the war and also to those of the army of which, according to the British view, the colonists were the main beneficiaries. This, among other issues, led to an argument over taxes and eventually contributed to the debate over taxation without representation, as for instance in the debates surrounding the Stamp Act of 1765 (repealed in 1766) and the Tea Act of 1773. The latter resulted in the Boston Tea Party of 1773, in which colonists, some of them disguised as American Indians, threw tea into the harbor.

Colonial opposition to British policies and disobediences like these led to a gradual transfer of power from the king's government to the colonists through a series of conflicts beginning in the 1760s. In 1774 the First Continental Congress convened at Philadelphia in opposition to the Coercive Acts (or Intolerable Acts), as the colonists called a series of laws made by Great Britain, and it also adopted a colonial bill of rights. Britain turned to force to repress the colonies, as for instance in armed confrontations at

Time Line

1754–1763

- The French and Indian War, called the Seven Years' War in Europe, pitches Britain and France against one another in a colonial North American setting.

1763

- **February 10**
The Treaty of Paris is signed, ending the French and Indian War between Britain and France; France loses the better part of its empire.

- **October 7**
The royal Proclamation of 1763 makes land purchases beyond a fixed boundary line illegal; the attempt is to establish peaceful relations with Native Americans living in that area and thus to forestall costly wars with American Indians.

1763–1766

- Pontiac's War (also known as Pontiac's Conspiracy or Pontiac's Rebellion) takes place. The event is a struggle by an alliance of Native Americans against European encroachment under the leadership of the Ottawa chief Pontiac.

1768

- **November 5**
The Treaty of Fort Stanwix arranges for native land cessions in an attempt to establish a new boundary line between Native Americans and settlers, as the latter have moved beyond the line established by the royal Proclamation of 1763.

1774

- The First Continental Congress convenes at Philadelphia in opposition to British policies regarding the colonies.

1776

- **January 10**
The pamphlet entitled *Common Sense*, authored by Thomas Paine, is published, giving voice to the grievances of the colonies against Britain.

- **July 4**
The Declaration of Independence is approved by the Continental Congress.

Lexington and Concord, and eventually declared that it considered the colonies to be in rebellion. The colonies could defend themselves militarily only by calling on a third power, France, and by trying to persuade Indians either to join the colonists' cause against Britain or at least to remain neutral in the conflict. However, to pursue an alliance with France, the colonies first had to declare their independence, as France's interest was to reduce the British Empire rather than to save or rebuild it. Such practical considerations, as well as the general mood captured and expressed in the 1776 publication of Thomas Paine's pamphlet *Common Sense*, eventually led the Continental Congress to consider declaring the colonies independent, and it approved the Declaration of Independence on July 4, 1776.

American chances to win an outright war with Britain seemed slim at best. British military might was far superior to anything the colonies could have expected to muster as the latter were seriously lacking in manpower. To persuade more colonists to enlist into the Continental army, land had to be promised to those who stayed for the duration of the war. Military fortunes at first rested firmly with the British forces but, later on and especially farther inland, turned to the Americans. As a result of the improved military performance of the Continental army, in February 1778 France decided to side openly with the colonies against its former imperial rival, Britain, and thus significantly strengthened the colonies militarily.

It was in September of the same year that the United States signed the Fort Pitt treaty with the Delawares. This treaty, the first known treaty between the United States and a Native American nation, reflected the continued need of the United States for allies as well as its desire to keep other tribes, like the Delawares, neutral. The Continental Congress tried to attract native allies or at least to avoid having American Indian tribes join the British enemy forces, which might have swung the fortunes of the war and thus of the colonies. The Delawares, the so-called grandfather tribe of the Northeast, were considered important allies even though they had come under the partial control of the Iroquois Confederacy (also known as the Six Nations or the Haudenosaunee). They had already begun, however, to extract themselves from this confederacy. The 1778 treaty with the United States, and especially its promise of a creation of an Indian state of the Union with the Delawares at its head, is reflective of just how important Indians were in military and political matters during this period. Similar to the situation during the heyday of colonial competition between France and England, once again there was a fierce competition for Native American allies, only now it was the United States and Britain who were competing.

Because the Continental Congress still lacked a constitution, it did not have the power to create new states, and it is therefore doubtful that the country intended to fulfill the somewhat qualified promises made to the Delawares. It is possible that the primary objectives were to gain safe passage through Delaware territory, to concentrate the Delaware warriors in one place, and to secure Delaware neutrality and that the promises made to the Delawares were merely supposed to provide the necessary incentive to make them agree to these objectives.

Only when Great Britain was increasingly losing its military advantage and saw the colonies enter into an alliance with France did the country become more conciliatory and offer to repeal a number of laws. By this time it was too late, however, as the colonies were by then firmly set on achieving their independence. When the British general Charles Cornwallis surrendered at Yorktown in October 1781 Britain initiated peace negotiations, having become tired of a costly war that seemed to lead nowhere and where the tide of military fortune was increasingly turning against British forces. Peace and American independence from Britain were secured in the 1783 Treaty of Paris. In this document Britain also ceded lands to the United States, some of which were subsequently sold off to meet war-related debts. Through this land cession, American settlements also came to expand.

About the Author

In the Treaty of Fort Pitt, the United States is represented by Andrew Lewis and Thomas Lewis, commissioners for the United States, and the Delawares by Captain White Eyes; Captain John Kill Buck, Jr.; and Captain Pipe, identified as chief men of the Delaware nation. As it was the product of some negotiation, it is likely that all of these men as well as others had a part in authoring the treaty, even though the written version of the treaty probably was more the product of the delegates of the United States than those of the Delawares. It is also probable that Colonel George Morgan, a United States agent for Indian affairs at Fort Pitt, would have been involved in making the treaty or at least in the preliminaries to it and that he and White Eyes (also known by his Delaware name of Koquethagechton, or "that which is put near the head") had a significant influence, especially on Article VI of the document.

The Delawares initially were neutral in the War of Independence, even though the Moravian missionaries (members of a Protestant Christian denomination) living among some of them were sympathetic to the Americans and their cause. Captain Pipe (also known as Kogieschquanoheel, or "causer of daylight"), however, was leaning toward the British side, as he believed that the Americans were scheming for Delaware lands. The Delawares were thus divided, but White Eyes, who wielded considerable influence within the tribe and was a personal friend to Colonel Morgan's, held firmly to the neutrality of the tribe, resisting efforts by Wyandots and members of the Six Nations/Haudenosaunee/Iroquois to bring the Delawares over to the British side.

The United States itself was sending mixed signals, and the changing allegiances among Europeans may have been confusing to the Indians. At first the Continental Congress had assured the Indians that the conflict was just a family dispute of which they did not have to take any notice, but later both the English and the Americans attempted to win over the Indians. The United States arranged for a meeting at Fort Pitt in 1778 because the Americans wanted to move against Fort Detroit. To do this they would have to move their forces through Delaware territory, but they were unwilling to do so without guarantees that they would be unopposed. The commissioners realized that other tribes would interpret this as the abandonment of neutrality by the Delawares, something that could put them in considerable danger from tribes who were allied with the British. It was possibly in an attempt to persuade the Delawares to agree to this danger that the commissioners felt compelled to offer certain incentives. The document signed on September 17, 1778, provided for an extensive alliance between the United States and the Delawares, gave U.S. troops free passage, and arranged for the construction of a fort to protect the tribe. Most important, Article VI of the treaty permitted the Delawares the creation of a fourteenth state of the Union with a representation in Congress, albeit subject to the approval of Congress.

It appears, however, that the commissioners were unwilling to take any risks and resorted to additional methods besides offering special incentives to reach the desired agreement. Colonel Morgan reported that liquor was distributed and that treaty clauses were misrepresented delib-

Time Line

1778	**■ September 17** The Treaty of Fort Pitt is signed between the United States of America and the Delaware Indians.
1783	**■ September 3** The Treaty of Paris between Britain and the United States ends the American War of Independence (1775–1783), gains the former colonies' independence from Britain, and arranges for English land cessions.
1785	**■ January 21** In the Treaty of Fort McIntosh between the U.S. government and representatives of the Wyandot, Delaware, Chippewa, and Ottawa nations, the latter cede claims to Ohio lands.
1787	**■ July 13** The Northwest Ordinance allows for U.S. westward expansion by the admission of new states, but it also promises fair treatment to Native Americans and never to take their lands without their consent.

www.milestonedocuments.com

erately in the translations. Some Delawares later asserted that the document had not been written down correctly and did not conform to what they had been told during the negotiations. Nonetheless, White Eyes, who had probably been one of the main proponents of the American cause, offered his services as a guide for the American troops. He reportedly died of smallpox on the march. In a letter to Congress, however, Colonel Morgan stated that White Eyes had been murdered, although in his correspondence he did not disclose the reasons or the circumstances of the death of his friend.

Explanation and Analysis of the Document

The treaty with the Delawares of 1778 includes six articles.

Article I: The very brief first article of the treaty ends all hostilities between the signatories and arranges for forgiveness of past ones.

Article II: The second article calls for perpetual peace and friendship between the contracting parties. It furthermore obliges the United States and the Delawares to come to one another's aid should one of them be engaged in a just and necessary war and to lend such assistance in due proportion to their abilities. This article also obligates each party to the treaty to send the other a warning should it discover any planned hostilities against the other.

Article III: This article refers specifically to the War of Independence and portrays the outcome of this war as having a great importance on the peace and security of the two parties to the treaty. It specifically requires the Delaware nation to permit U.S. forces free passage through their country as well as guidance. The Delawares are obligated to supply the troops with corn, meat, horses, and other things, and the commanding officers are obliged to reimburse them for the full value of these items. In this article the Delawares also agree to send as many of their best warriors as they can spare to join the American troops. To secure the protection of old men, women, and children during the absence of these warriors, the United States consents to build, pay for, and adequately garrison a fort.

Article IV: Through this article the two undersigned parties agree that neither of them should punish the infractions made by the other party's citizens but instead should secure the offender and submit him to a fair trial by judges or juries of both parties and in accordance with their laws. This arrangement was supposed to be clarified later on by Congress with the assistance of the Delawares. Both parties also agree not to harbor any enemies of the other but to secure and deliver them.

Article V: This article talks about the confederation entered into by the Delaware nation and the United States and obligates the United States to supply the Delawares with clothing, utensils, and implements of war as far as this may be in the states' power. The fifth article also arranges for fair trade between the two parties.

Article VI: The sixth article of the treaty discusses the attempts of enemies of the United States to persuade the Indians that the United States is intent on appropriating the Indians' lands. In this article, the United States guarantees the Delawares and their heirs their complete territorial rights as long as the Delaware nation remains a friend of the United States. The two signatories further agree that in the future other tribes could be invited to join the United States as a state with the Delawares at its head and with a representation in Congress, should this be in the interest of both parties. However, this last arrangement is specifically stated to be subject to the approval of Congress.

Audience

The written version of the Treaty of Fort Pitt was intended primarily for the U.S. government. It secured concessions from the Delawares that benefited the United States and that were noted in a manner deemed appropriate for the purpose. Given the subsequent complaints by the Delawares, however, it appears as if the version of the treaty translated to them during the negotiations at Fort Pitt, at least in some aspects, differed significantly from the written version. The intention of this oral version of the treaty appears to have been to secure Delaware approval of U.S. demands. One could thus say that there were two treaties, and each had a different audience.

Impact

With White Eyes's death while serving as a guide for American troops, the United States lost its main ally among the Delawares. The United States subsequently failed to live up to the promises it had made to the Delawares in the 1778 treaty. Although a fort, named Fort Laurens, was constructed to protect the Delawares, it was never garrisoned sufficiently to fulfill its purpose, something that the Delawares fully realized. They had also been told that the Americans would take Fort Detroit, but repeated attempts by various commanding officers failed to achieve this goal, and the Delawares continued to feel threatened by the relative proximity of this British post. They would furthermore have come under increasing pressure by other tribes owing to the supposed abandonment of their former neutrality.

In April 1779 Colonel Morgan arranged for Delaware leaders to meet with representatives of the Continental Congress to inform them about the misinterpretations of the treaty and the many promises that had not been kept. Instead of addressing their demands, however, American representatives merely asked them to be patient. On this occasion they met with George Washington, the commander in chief of the American army, who told them the king of France had promised help to the Americans, implying that the promises to the Delawares would soon be delivered. During the severe winter of 1779–1780, however, the Delawares were in dire need of food and clothing, but the United States once again failed to make good on its promise of aid. The mood in the Delaware council finally turned, and it decided

Essential Quotes

"That a perpetual peace and friendship shall from henceforth take place."

(Article II)

"The United States do engage to guarantee to the aforesaid nation of Delawares, and their heirs, all their territorial rights in the fullest and most ample manner, as it hath been bounded by former treaties, as long as they the said Delaware nation shall abide by, and hold fast the chain of friendship now entered into."

(Article VI)

"And it is further agreed on between the contracting parties should it for the future be found conducive for the mutual interest of both parties to invite any other tribes who have been friends to the interest of the United States, to join the present confederation, and to form a state whereof the Delaware nation shall be the head, and have a representation in Congress: Provided, nothing contained in this article to be considered as conclusive until it meets with the approbation of Congress."

(Article VI)

www.milestonedocuments.com

to ally with the English instead. This had repercussions for the peaceful members of the tribe who continued to live under the guardianship of Moravian missionaries. On March 8, 1782, American militiamen committed a massacre against peaceful Moravian Delawares at Gnadenhutten, Ohio, in retaliation for Delaware raids. Fifty-six adults and thirty-four children were beaten to death and scalped, a decision the militia had made in council. The Delawares had made the decision to switch their allegiance at a time when the military tide was turning in favor of the Americans. When it became obvious that the colonists would win the war, some of the Delawares left the United States for Canada, and others left for Spanish territory.

The lands ceded through the Treaty of Paris of 1783, which ended the War of Independence and secured the United States' independence from Britain, were in parts occupied by Indian nations who had been ignored in the negotiations. In 1783 thirty-five of these tribes, including some Delawares, united in defense against growing intrusions into their lands. The United States, however, believed it had acquired these lands by conquest and through the Treaty of Paris, and it considered all Indian rights to the lands in question to have been extinguished. Attempting to settle the undecided and volatile situation, in the Treaty of Fort McIntosh of 1785 the Delaware, Wyandot, and a few other nations entered into an agreement with the United States against the wishes of the other tribes of the alliance. They agreed to cede lands and to put themselves under the protection of the United States. The remaining tribes of the alliance later renounced this treaty and insisted that the terms of the 1768 Treaty of Fort Stanwix be met, which had established the Ohio River as a boundary line between whites and Indians. Although the first Indian treaties signed after the end of the Revolution until about 1786 asserted the United States' rights to land by virtue of conquest, in the face of native responses the United States determined that military conflicts with Indians would become unavoidable if this policy continued and that this would incur costs far higher than paying compensation for the recently confiscated lands and the abandonment of the new land policy. Through the passage of the 1787 Northwest Ordinance the United States instead proclaimed the intent to observe the utmost good faith toward the Indians and declared that it would acquire their lands only with their consent.

This new policy was reflected in the treaties the United States entered into with Indians, but treaties increasingly described the lands retained by the Indians rather than the ones to be ceded. Furthermore, treaties with the United States became the primary method of acquiring Indian lands, since, under the new Constitution, only the federal government had the power to acquire Indian land. As Indian military power increasingly waned, however, attitudes toward Indian nations began to shift, and the market in preemption rights also contributed to this development.

This new perception eventually was incorporated into the law through a number of cases, most notably *Fletcher v. Peck* (1810), *Johnson v. M'Intosh* (1823), and the so-called Cherokee Nation Cases of 1831 and 1832. Lindsay G. Robertson, in *Conquest by Law: How the Discovery of America Dispossessed Indigenous Peoples of Their Lands*, has determined that

> Chief Justice John Marshall devised the discovery doctrine in 1823 as a means of shoring up the claims of Virginia militia bounty warrant holders to lands in the southwestern corner of the State of Kentucky. The weapon he thus forged for his former colleagues in arms was seized by expansionist Georgians and wielded against Native Americans throughout the eastern United States. The reformulation of the doctrine he engineered in *Worcester v. Georgia* proved impossible to sustain. *Johnson* was too important to removal. In 1835, Jackson appointees took control of Marshall's court and revived the *Johnson* formulation. (p. 142)

The legacy of these decisions and the way they influenced the relationship between the United States and Native American nations endure to this day, and little remains of the times when Native Americans were parties to treaties with the United State and powerful military allies or opponents. The Delawares, the first tribe to sign a formal treaty with the United States of America, lost their federal recognition in 2005."

Related Documents

Cherokee Nation v. Georgia, 30 U.S. 1, 5 Pet. 1, 8 L.Ed. 25 (1831). The Cherokee nation applied for an injunction against the state of Georgia, but the Supreme Court under John Marshall refused to hear the case on the grounds that the Cherokees were not a foreign nation but rather a "domestic dependent nation"; therefore the Court had no jurisdiction.

"Constitution of the United States." National Archives "Charters of Freedom" Web site. http://www.archives.gov/national-archives-experience/charters/constitution_transcript.html. Accessed on October 21, 2007. Rather than revising the Articles of Confederation, the Federal Convention in 1787 in Philadelphia decided to compose a new document, eventually resulting in the Constitution.

"Declaration of Independence." National Archives "Charters of Freedom" Web site. http://www.archives.gov/national-archives-experience/charters/declaration_transcript.html. Accessed on October 21, 2007. The Declaration of Independence was drafted by Thomas Jefferson and lists certain rights and convictions as well as a host of grievances against the king of England, including inciting insurrections by the "merciless Indian Savages."

Johnson v. M'Intosh, 21 U.S. 543, 5 L.Ed. 681, 8 Wheat. 543 (1823). The case under Chief Justice Marshall had to evaluate the legitimacy of two competing claims of right to the same land; one was rooted in a purchase from Indians, the other in one from the U.S. government. Even though Indians were not party to the case, it eventually directly affected their rights to the sale of their lands and more.

Worcester v. Georgia, 31 U.S. 515, 6 Pet. 515, 8 L.Ed. 483 (1832). Possibly realizing the damages done by his previous rulings, in this decision Chief Justice Marshall held that the Cherokees constituted a nation with distinct sovereign powers, but this failed to save the Cherokees from removal.

Bibliography

■ Articles

Haake, Claudia: "Identity, Sovereignty, and Power: The Cherokee-Delaware Agreement of 1867, Past and Present." *American Indian Quarterly* 26, no. 3 (2002): 418–435.

■ Books

Adams, Richard C. *Legends of the Delaware Indians and Picture Writing*, ed. Deborah Nichols. Syracuse, N.Y.: Syracuse University Press, 1997.

Banner, Stuart. *How the Indians Lost Their Land: Law and Power on the Frontier*. Cambridge, Mass.: Belknap Press, 2005.

Baylin, Bernard. *The Ideological Origins of the American Revolution*. Cambridge, Mass.: Belknap Press, 1992.

Deloria, Vine, Jr., and Raymond J. DeMallie, eds. *Documents of American Indian Diplomacy: Treaties, Agreements, and Conventions, 1775–1979*. Norman: University of Oklahoma Press, 1999.

Haake, Claudia B. *The State, Removal and Indigenous Peoples in the United States and Mexico, 1620–2000*. New York: Routledge, 2007.

Horsman, Reginald. *Expansion and American Indian Policy, 1783–1812*. East Lansing: Michigan State University Press, 1967.

———. *The Origins of Indian Removal, 1815–1824*. East Lansing: Michigan State University Press, 1970.

Kappler, Charles J., ed. *Indian Affairs: Laws and Treaties*. 2 vols. Washington, D.C.: Government Printing Office, 1904.

Newcomb, William W. Jr. *The Culture and Acculturation of the Delaware Indians*. Ann Arbor: University of Michigan Press, 1956.

Robertson, Lindsay G. *Conquest by Law: How the Discovery of America Dispossessed Indigenous Peoples of Their Lands*. Oxford, U.K.: Oxford University Press, 2005.

Seed, Patricia. *Ceremonies of Possession in Europe's Conquest of the New World, 1492–1640*. Cambridge, U.K.: University of Cambridge Press, 1995.

———. *American Pentimento: The Invention of Indians and the Pursuit of Riches*. Minneapolis: University of Minnesota Press, 2001.

Wallace, Anthony F. C. *King of the Delawares: Teedyuscung, 1700–1763*. Philadelphia: University of Pennsylvania Press, 1949.

Washburn, Wilcomb E., ed. *The American Indian and the United States: A Documentary History*. 4 vols. New York: Random House, 1973.

Weslager, Clinton A. *The Delaware Indians: A History*. New Brunswick, N.J.: Rutgers University Press, 1972.

White, Richard. *The Middle Ground: Indians, Empires, and Republics in the Great Lakes Region, 1650–1815*. New York: Cambridge University Press, 1991.

■ **Web Sites**

D'Errico, Peter. "American Indian Sovereignty: Now You See It, Now You Don't." Inaugural lecture at the American Indian Civics Project at Humboldt State University, Arcata, Calif., October 24, 1997. University of Massachusetts Amherst Web site.
http://www.umass.edu/legal/derrico/nowyouseeit.html. Accessed on October 10, 2007.

—By Claudia B. Haake

www.milestonedocuments.com

Questions for Further Study

1. Compare and contrast the attitudes toward American Indians as they can be found in the Declaration of Independence, the United States Constitution, and the 1778 Treaty of Fort Pitt. How is the relationship between the United States of America and Native American nations portrayed in these documents?

2. How did the relationship between Native Americans and the United States change between the Treaty of Fort Pitt in 1778 and the Treaty of Paris in 1783? What brought about this change, and how did it affect the Indians?

3. Compare the legal relationship between the United States and Native Americans as reflected in the Treaty of Fort Pitt and in *Cherokee Nation v. Georgia* (1831). How does this reflect on power relations in North America?

Glossary

emolument	advantage or compensation
extirpate	destroy or exterminate
garrisoned	staffed with soldiers, as at a military post
timeous	timely; soon

Document Text

Treaty of Fort Pitt

Articles of agreement and confederation, made and, entered; into by, Andrew and Thomas Lewis, Esquires, Commissioners for, and in Behalf of the United States of North-America of the one Part, and Capt. White Eyes, Capt. John Kill Buck, Junior, and Capt. Pipe, Deputies and Chief Men of the Delaware Nation of the other Part.

◆ Article I.

That all offences or acts of hostilities by one, or either of the contracting parties against the other, be mutually forgiven, and buried in the depth of oblivion, never more to be had in remembrance.

◆ Article II.

That a perpetual peace and friendship shall from henceforth take place, and subsist between the contracting: parties aforesaid, through all succeeding generations: and if either of the parties are engaged in a just and necessary war with any other nation or nations, that then each shall assist the other in due proportion to their abilities, till their enemies are brought to reasonable terms of accommodation: and that if either of them shall discover any hostile designs forming against the other, they shall give the earliest notice thereof that timeous measures may be taken to prevent their ill effect.

◆ Article III.

And whereas the United States are engaged in a just and necessary war, in defence and support of life, liberty and independence, against the King of England and his adherents, and as said King is yet possessed of several posts and forts on the lakes and other places, the reduction of which is of great importance to the peace and security of the contracting parties, and as the most practicable way for the troops of the United States to some of the posts and forts is by passing through the country of the Delaware nation, the aforesaid deputies, on behalf of themselves and their nation, do hereby stipulate and agree to give a free passage through their country to the troops aforesaid, and the same to conduct by the nearest and best ways to the posts, forts or towns of the enemies of the United States, affording to said troops such supplies of corn, meat, horses, or whatever may be in their power for the accommodation of such troops, on the commanding officer's, &c. paying, or engageing to pay, the full value of whatever they can supply them with. And the said deputies, on the behalf of their nation, engage to join the troops of the United States aforesaid, with such a number of their best and most expert warriors as they can spare, consistent with their own safety, and act in concert with them; and for the better security of the old men, women and children of the aforesaid nation, whilst their warriors are engaged against the common enemy, it is agreed on the part of the United States, that a fort of sufficient strength and capacity be built at the expense of the said States, with such assistance as it may be in the power of the said Delaware Nation to give, in the most convenient place, and advantageous situation, as shall be agreed on by the commanding officer of the troops aforesaid, with the advice and concurrence of the deputies of the aforesaid Delaware Nation, which fort shall be garrisoned by such a number of the troops of the United States, as the commanding officer can spare for the present, and hereafter by such numbers, as the wise men of the United States in council, shall think most conducive to the common good.

◆ Article IV.

For the better security of the peace and friendship now entered into by the contracting parties, against all infractions of the same by the citizens of either party, to the prejudice of the other, neither party shall proceed to the infliction of punishments on the citizens of the other, otherwise than by securing the offender or offenders by imprisonment, or any other competent means, till a fair and impartial trial can be had by judges or juries of both parties, as near as can be to the laws, customs and usages of the contracting parties and natural justice. The mode of such trials to be hereafter fixed by the wise men of the United States in Congress assembled, with the assistance of such deputies of the Delaware nation, as may be appointed to act in concert with them in adjusting this matter to their mutual liking. And it is further agreed between the parties aforesaid, that neither shall entertain or give countenance to the enemies of the other, or protect in their respective states, criminal fugitives, servants or slaves, but the same to apprehend, and secure and deliver to the State or States, to which such enemies, criminals, servants or slaves respectively belong.

◆ Article V.

Whereas the confederation entered into by the Delaware nation and the United States, renders the first dependent on the latter for all the articles of clothing, utensils and implements of war, and it is judged not only reasonable, but indispensably necessary, that the aforesaid Nation be supplied with such articles from time to time, as far as the United States may have it in their power, by a well-regulated trade, under the conduct of an intelligent, candid agent, with an adequate salary, one more influenced by the love of his country, and a constant attention to the duties of his department by promoting the common interest, than the sinister purposes of converting and binding all the duties of his office to his private emolument: Convinced of the necessity of such measures, the Commissioners of the United States, at the earnest solicitation of the deputies aforesaid, have engaged in behalf of the United States, that such a trade shall be afforded said nation conducted on such principles of mutual interest as the wisdom of the United States in Congress assembled shall think most conducive to adopt for their mutual convenience.

◆ Article VI.

Whereas the enemies of the United States have endeavored, by every artifice in their power, to possess the Indians in general with an opinion, that it is the design of the States aforesaid, to extirpate the Indians and take possession of their country to obviate such false suggestion, the United States do engage to guarantee to the aforesaid nation of Delawares, and their heirs, all their territorial rights in the fullest and most ample manner, as it hath been bounded by former treaties, as long as they the said Delaware nation shall abide by, and hold fast the chain of friendship now entered into. And it is further agreed on between the contracting parties should it for the future be found conducive for the mutual interest of both parties to invite any other tribes who have been friends to the interest of the United States, to join the present confederation, and to form a state whereof the Delaware nation shall be the head, and have a representation in Congress: Provided, nothing contained in this article to be considered as conclusive until it meets with the approbation of Congress. And it is also the intent and meaning of this article, that no protection or countenance shall be afforded to any who are at present our enemies, by which they might escape the punishment they deserve.

In witness whereof, the parties have hereunto interchangeably set their hands and seals, at Fort Pitt, September seventeenth, anno Domini one thousand seven hundred and seventy-eight.

Andrew Lewis, [L. S.]
Thomas Lewis, [L. S.]
White Eyes, his x mark, [L. S.]
The Pipe, his x mark, [L. S.]
John Kill Buck, his x mark, [L. S.]
In presence of—
Lach'n McIntosh, brigadier-general, commander the Western Department.
Daniel Brodhead, colonel Eighth Pennsylvania Regiment,
W. Crawford, collonel,
John Campbell,
John Stephenson,
John Gibson, colonel Thirteenth Virginia Regiment,
A. Graham, brigade major,
Lach. McIntosh, jr., major brigade,
Benjamin Mills,
Joseph L. Finley, captain Eighth Pennsylvania Regiment,
John Finley, captain Eighth Pennsylvania Regiment.

www.milestonedocuments.com

An Act for the gradual Abolition of Slavery

When we contemplate our Abhorrence of that Condition to which the Arms and Tyranny of Great Britain were exerted to reduce us; when we look back on the Variety of Dangers to which we have been exposed, and how miraculously our Wants in many Instances have been supplied and our Deliverances wrought, when even Hope and human fortitude have become unequal to the Conflict; we are unavoidably led to a serious and grateful Sense of the manifold Blessings which we have undeservedly received from the hand of that Being from whom every good and perfect Gift cometh. Impressed with these Ideas we conceive that it is our duty, and we rejoice that it is in our Power, to extend a Portion of that freedom to others, which hath been extended to us; and a Release from that State of Thraldom, to which we ourselves were tyrannically doomed, and from which we have now every Prospect of being delivered. It is not for us to enquire, why, in the Creation of Mankind, the Inhabitants of the several parts of the Earth, were distinguished by a difference in Feature or Complexion. It is sufficient to know that all are the

The Pennsylvania Gradual Abolition Act (The Pennsylvania State Archives)

Pennsylvania: An Act for the Gradual Abolition of Slavery

1780

"It is sufficient to know that all are the work of an Almighty Hand."

Overview

On March 1, 1780, with the Revolution still raging and its outcome in doubt, the Pennsylvania legislature became the first legislature in history to take steps to abolish slavery. Pennsylvania's Act for the Gradual Abolition of Slavery is both idealistic and practical. It tries to balance the idea of liberty, which was at the heart of the Revolution, with the founding generation's deep respect for private property. The law also recognizes the significance of race in both the creation of slavery and the perpetuation of discrimination against former slaves. Eventually four other states and a Canadian province—Connecticut (1784), Rhode Island (1784), New York (1799), New Jersey (1804), and Upper Canada (present-day Ontario) (1794)—adopted similar laws to end slavery. Thus the Pennsylvania law became a model for how places with slavery ended the institution. These places accomplished what no other societies before them had: the peaceful eradication of slavery.

Unlike the ending of slavery in the rest of the United States, the Pennsylvania law took into account the need to provide some equality and protection for former slaves. It also recognized that masters had a property interest in their slaves. While the American Revolutionaries used the rhetoric of liberty throughout their struggle, they also persistently acknowledged and argued for the right of property. Thomas Jefferson's famous language from the Declaration of Independence—that all people are entitled to "life, liberty and the pursuit of happiness"—is a paraphrase of John Locke's trinity of "life, liberty and property" from his *Two Treatises of Government* (1690), and almost all white Americans accepted that property was essential to liberty.

Context

When the American Revolution began in 1775, slavery was legal in all of the thirteen colonies. In New England, where the war started, some masters allowed their male slaves to enlist to fight for both their liberty and the liberty of the new nation. In the first battles in Massachusetts—at Lexington and Concord and then at Bunker Hill—a few blacks, such as Salem Poor and Peter Salem, distinguished themselves in battle. When the slaveholding George Washington took command of the Revolutionary Army based outside of Boston, he was shocked to see armed and uniformed blacks in the ranks of the militias from New England. Initially Washington demanded that these black soldiers be mustered out of the army; within a few months, impressed by their skill and courage and desperate for any soldiers, Washington changed his mind and welcomed black soldiers. By the end of the war one of his favorite units was the First Rhode Island Infantry, even though about half the soldiers in that unit had been slaves when the war began. Washington quickly came to admire the dedication of those black soldiers who fought for their own liberty—and that of their families—as well as for the independence of the new nation.

Eventually thousands of slaves gained freedom for themselves and their families through military service, but these individual emancipations did not solve the great problem of slavery in the new nation. At the time of the Revolution, slavery presented the first great—and for a long time the most enduring—contradiction in American history. The Declaration of Independence asserts, "All men are created equal" and have a right to "life, liberty and the pursuit of happiness." This language seems to condemn slavery. But the man who wrote these words, Thomas Jefferson, owned about 150 slaves at the time, and by the end of his life he owned more than two hundred slaves. The English literary figure Samuel Johnson pointedly asked during the Revolution, "How is it that we hear the loudest yelps for liberty among the drivers of negroes?" (qtd. in Murphy, p. 437).

In the South most Americans tried to ignore the issue of slavery, although hundreds if not thousands of individual southerners privately freed their slaves during and after the Revolution. Most famously, Washington provided for the freedom of all of his slaves when he died in 1799. The less famous, but still significant South Carolina Revolutionary Henry Laurens freed his slaves during his lifetime. Indeed, during and after the Revolution as many as fifty thousand southern slaves were freed by their owners, but this hardly made a dent in the overall southern slave population,

Time Line

1688	■ **February** Germantown Quakers issue first protest against slavery in the new world.
1737	■ Benjamin Lay publishes *All Slave-Keepers That Keep the Innocent in Bondage, Apostates Pretending to Lay Claim to the Pure and Holy Christian Religion.*
1754	■ John Woolman publishes *Some Considerations on the Keeping of Negroes.*
1758	■ Philadelphia Yearly Meeting of the Society of Friends (Quakers) officially urges all Quakers to emancipate their slaves.
1762	■ Anthony Benezet publishes *A Short Account of That Part of Africa Inhabited by the Negroes.*
1772	■ Benezet publishes *Some Historical Account of Guinea.*
1773	■ Benjamin Rush publishes *An Address to the Inhabitants of the British Settlements in America, upon Slave-Keeping.*
1775	■ **April** First antislavery society in America is organized in Philadelphia, calling itself the Society for the Relief of Free Negroes Unlawfully Held in Bondage. ■ **April 19** Battles of Lexington and Concord in Massachusetts ignite the American Revolution.
1776	■ **July 4** Continental Congress meeting in Philadelphia issues the Declaration of Independence.

which numbered more than one million when the Revolution ended.

In the North, social and economic factors led to greater opposition to slavery. The religious background of many northerners—Quakers, Congregationalists, Methodists, and Baptists—led to significant opposition to slavery in Pennsylvania and New England. This contrasted with the dominance of Anglican/Episcopalian leadership in the South. Antislavery sentiment was particular strong in Pennsylvania, where Quakers and other pietists had long opposed slavery, as did freethinkers like Benjamin Franklin and Benjamin Rush.

Opposition to slavery in Pennsylvania was rooted, to a great extent, in the state's religious heritage. Pennsylvania took the lead in ending slavery in part because Quakers, Mennonites, and other members of pietistic faiths were among the earliest opponents of slavery in America. In February 1688, Quakers in Germantown, Pennsylvania, issued a resolution that sets out "the reasons why we are against the traffic of men-body." The resolution notes the revulsion Europeans had for the thought of being enslaved by Turks and then argues, "Now, though they are black, we cannot conceive there is more liberty to have them slaves" than it is for the Turks to enslave white Europeans. The resolution also argues that slavery violates the fundamental tenets of Christianity: "There is a saying, that we should do to all men like as we will be done ourselves; making no difference of what generation, descent, or colour they are." Finally, the Germantown Quakers argue that slavery in effect violates the commandment against adultery, because "separating wives from their husbands, and giving them to others," as slave traders did, was the equivalent of sanctioning adultery. The resolution specifically singles out fellow Quakers in Pennsylvania who "here handel men as they handel there the cattle" (Hall et al., pp. 55–56). This seemed particularly wrong because the Quakers had been persecuted for their beliefs in Europe and some were now persecuting men for their color.

The Germantown resolution set the tone for religious antislavery protests in Pennsylvania. Soon Quakers throughout the colony were asserting that blacks were equal to whites and thus could not be enslaved. Other Quakers, however, argued that slavery was sanctioned by the Bible and that the only obligation of Christians was to treat slaves humanely and to teach them the Gospel. This issue divided many Quaker meetings. By the mid-1700s, however, almost all Quakers accepted the idea that slavery was wrong. In 1737 Benjamin Lay published *All Slave-Keepers That Keep the Innocent in Bondage, Apostates Pretending to Lay Claim to the Pure and Holy Christian Religion*. The book was printed by Benjamin Franklin; it is likely that in setting the type for this book (and, in fact, helping Lay organize his notes), Franklin began to understand the deep problem that slavery presented for a just society. Eventually Franklin became a vigorous opponent of slavery and the president of the Pennsylvania Society for the Abolition of Slavery. With its pretentious title and aggressive attacks on slaveholding, Lay's book antagonized many people. But it also stimulated opposition to slavery and led to the emergence of John Woolman as the first significant antislavery activist in Pennsylvania. He was soon joined by his fellow Quaker Anthony Benezet in a vigorous and mostly successful campaign to convince Quakers that slavery was wrong.

By the eve of the Revolution, a significant percentage of the people in Pennsylvania believed slavery was morally wrong. This understanding extended beyond Quakers. In 1773 the respected physician and soon-to-be patriot leader Benjamin Rush (who had been influenced by Benezet) published *An Address to the Inhabitants of the British Settlements in America, upon Slave-Keeping.* Rush argued for racial equality on medical grounds and against slavery. Three years later Rush, along with Franklin, signed the Declaration of Independence. In 1775 Thomas Paine, a recent migrant to Philadelphia, published an essay attacking slavery. He soon became the most famous pamphleteer of the Revolution, writing the classic *Common Sense* (1776) and *The American Crisis* (1776–1783). Paine's essay against slavery appeared in a Philadelphia newspaper on the very eve of the Revolution. Paine asked "with what consistency or decency" would the Americans complain that the British king was trying to enslave them, "while they hold so many hundred thousands in slavery" (qtd. in Zilversmit, p. 96). In April 1775, less than a week before the first battles of the Revolution, ten men in Philadelphia organized the Society for the Relief of Free Negroes Unlawfully Held in Bondage. This was the first antislavery organization in the Americas or in England, and its establishment confirmed Philadelphia's status as the center of antislavery thought and action. Quakers led the movement, but Presbyterians like Rush and deists like Franklin and Paine were also vitally concerned about the problem of slavery and slaveholding.

Ironically, while the Revolution brought opponents of slavery like Rush, Paine, and Franklin into the political mainstream, it undermined the political significance of the Quakers, who were the most antislavery group in the new state. Many Quakers sympathized with the British, and those who did not refused to take up arms because they were pacifists. Thus, during the Revolution, Quakers saw their political power erode. However, by this time, opposition to slavery was not confined to the Quakers. In 1779 George Bryan, a Presbyterian member of the new state legislature, proposed legislation to end slavery in Pennsylvania. His bill received an enthusiastic reception, although some opposition came from those who feared free blacks and those who owned slaves. In January 1780 more than 60 percent of the state legislators voted to pass Bryan's bill. The law came into effect on March 1, 1780.

About the Author

The 1780 act was proposed by George Bryan, a member of the Pennsylvania legislature. Like most pieces of

Time Line

1780

- **March 1**
Pennsylvania legislature passes the Gradual Abolition Act.

- **June 15**
Massachusetts Constitution declares all people are born "free and equal."

1781

- Massachusetts courts rule that the new constitution has ended slavery in the state.

1783

- **September 3**
American Revolution ends with the signing of the Treaty of Paris.

1784

- Rhode Island and Connecticut both pass gradual abolition acts based on the Pennsylvania law.

1787

- **May 25–September 17**
Constitutional Convention meets in Philadelphia and includes a number of provisions protecting slavery in the Constitution.

- **July 13**
Congress meeting under the Articles of Confederation in New York passes the Northwest Ordinance, banning slavery in the territories that later become the states of Ohio, Indiana, Illinois, Michigan, Wisconsin, and parts of Minnesota.

1788

- **March 29**
Pennsylvania legislature passes supplement to Gradual Abolition Act.

1793

- **February 12**
Congress passes the first federal fugitive slave law.

1799

- **March 29**
New York passes a gradual abolition act based on the Pennsylvania law.

www.milestonedocuments.com

Time Line

1804	■ **February 15** New Jersey passes a gradual abolition act based on the Pennsylvania law.
1808	■ **January 1** Congress officially bans the African slave trade.
1820	■ Missouri Compromise allows slavery in Missouri but bans it north and west of Missouri.
1827	■ **July 4** New York frees all remaining slaves in the state.

legislation, it has no single author. Legislators altered and amended the act as it went through committees and was read on the floor of the legislature. Bryan is considered the father of the law. Born in Dublin, Ireland, Bryan came to Philadelphia when he was about twenty years old. He practiced law, became a Patriot leader, and was a devout Presbyterian whose religious values influenced his opposition to slavery. Before the Revolution, Bryan was a delegate to the Stamp Act Congress (October 1765), and from 1777 to 1779 he served on the Supreme Executive Council of the state, usually as the council's vice president but for a time as the president, which was the equivalent of being the governor of the state. In 1779 he was elected to the state assembly, where he immediately proposed the Gradual Abolition Act. Shortly after passage of the act he became a judge.

Explanation and Analysis of the Document

The 1780 Gradual Abolition Act was part of the social and political revolution associated with the rebellion that led to American independence. Emancipation dovetailed with the stated claims of the American Revolutionaries, and structurally the 1780 act resembles the Declaration of Independence. Each has a two-paragraph preamble, which sets out the document's purpose. The Declaration is not a statute but rather a series of statements justifying independence. The 1780 act, as a statute, becomes less dramatic after the preamble, because it must explain how emancipation is to work.

In addition to this structural resemblance to the Declaration of Independence, the statute can be seen as a legislative implementation of the Declaration. That document asserts, "We hold these truths to be self-evident, that all men are created equal, that they are endowed by their Creator with certain unalienable rights, that among these are life, liberty, and the pursuit of happiness." Clearly, slavery was incompatible with these ideals.

◆ Section 1

The Pennsylvania legislature surely understood the relationship of slavery to the Declaration, thus the author notes that slavery "deprived" slaves "of the common blessings that they were by nature entitled to." Beyond this, the preamble ignores the general assertions of liberty in the Declaration, and it instead focuses on the specific harms of slavery and the relationship of slavery to the Revolution. Equally intriguing is the deistic approach to this issue.

The preamble (Section 1) begins by noting the difficulties of the Revolution. In comparison with subsequent wars—especially the U.S. Civil War and the massive conflicts of the twentieth century—the approximately 4,500 military deaths in the Revolution seem relatively small in number. But for the emerging American states these were painful losses that affected communities across the new nation. The Revolution was costly in treasure and blood, and the people of Pennsylvania understood that. By 1780 they also knew that even though the war was not over, it was likely that sooner or later they would gain independence. For five years they had held off the greatest military power in the world. The horrible and bloody struggle for independence leads to another parallel with the Declaration.

In the Declaration, Thomas Jefferson avoided any reference to a particular faith or even to the generally shared notions of what today might be called a Judeo-Christian tradition or shared views of the Bible. Thus, Jefferson used phrases like "their creator" and "nature's God" when making claims to liberty based on natural law. Similarly, the authors of the 1780 act marveled at the accomplishment of independence and, while not specifying any particular faith or religion, ascribed their success to Divine Providence. The opening sentence of the preamble to the statute reflects the secular religiosity of the age. The Pennsylvania legislators came from a variety of religious backgrounds and had no interest in asserting allegiance to a particular faith or sect. At the same time, they understood a sense of Divine Providence. Thus, the statute's preamble later refers to the "Almighty Hand" in explaining the differences among the races. Faith, but not denomination, church, or sect, is important to the legislators, but only as it reflects and supports their larger social goal.

This goal, of course, is ending slavery. The statute's authors assert they have no more right to own slaves than England has a right to rule them. This is surely the logic of the Revolution and a logic that had been discussed in Pennsylvania and elsewhere since the early 1770s. Just as the Americans in 1776 (in the Declaration of Independence) felt they had to explain to the world why they were rebelling against England, so too did the Pennsylvania legislators have to explain why they were taking the radical step of ending slavery. The natural law arguments in the preamble of the Declaration ("We hold these truths to be self-evident …") were not sufficient to convince the world or even a significant number of Americans that a rebellion was necessary. Thus the Congress, in 1776, asserted in the Declaration that "a decent respect to the opinions of mankind requires that they should declare the causes which impel them to the separation." This led to a long list of reasons for the rebellion that constituted the bulk of the Declaration of Independence.

While not explicitly stating it the way the Declaration does, the Pennsylvania statute follows the same logic. Having asserted the moral argument for emancipation, the legislators turned to defusing arguments against it while elaborating the reasons for the law. First the 1780 preamble explains that there is a moral obligation to bring freedom to slaves, just as the colonists are being delivered from English rule. However, many Americans doubted that blacks were like white people and even deserved freedom. The Pennsylvania legislature dismissed this, using an argument that appealed to both religion and science: "It is not for us to enquire why, in the creation of mankind, the inhabitants of the several parts of the earth were distinguished by a difference in feature or complexion. It is sufficient to know that all are the work of an Almighty Hand."

The legislature simply refused to be drawn into a debate over race. All men were created by "the Almighty Hand" and thus no person had a right to question the reasons why some had a different skin color. Indeed, because the "Almighty Hand" had delivered Pennsylvania from British tyranny, the legislature felt an obligation to help deliver others from bondage.

◆ Section 2

Having dealt with the race issue, the legislators reminded readers about the horrors of slavery. Section 2 of the act, which is a second preamble, sets out what became one of the most powerful arguments against slavery: It leads to "an unnatural separation and sale of husband and wife from each other and from their children; an injury, the greatness of which can only be conceived by supposing that we were in the same unhappy case." Few people in Pennsylvania, at least, could argue against the idea that separating families was deeply immoral. The last part of this sentence is also a blow against racial thinking. By suggesting that white Pennsylvanians could understand the suffering of slaves only by "supposing that we were in the same unhappy case," the legislators in effect asked whites to imagine they were black slaves.

Having asserted why the act was proper, the legislature then turned to the far more difficult task of setting out how slavery in the state should be terminated. This was not easy. Even as they condemned slaveholding, the legislators knew they could not simply take property away from those who owned it. If the Revolution was about liberty, it was also about property. Indeed, the key slogan of the period before the Revolution, "Taxation without representation is tyranny," underscored the extent to which this was a revolution of middle-class property owners who believed that liberty and property went hand in hand.

◆ Section 3

There was no perfect answer to the problem of how to give freedom to one person without taking property away from someone else. In the end, the Pennsylvania legislature solved the problem by not, in fact, freeing anyone while still ensuring a relatively speedy end to all slavery in the state. The legislature provided that all slaves living in the state would remain slaves for the rest of their lives or for as long as their masters chose to keep them in bondage. For all the rhetoric of liberty in the preamble, *no one* actually gained his or her freedom under the law. Therefore no one in the state could complain that he or she had lost property under the law.

What, then, did the law accomplish? The key provision is Section 3 of the act, which asserts that every child born in Pennsylvania after the passage of the act, even if the child of slave woman, would be born free. Since the status of slavery passed through the mother, the ultimate result was obvious. As the existing slaves died off there would be no new slaves to replace them. Quite literally, slavery would soon die out in Pennsylvania. This provision is reinforced by Section 10 of the law, which prohibits anyone from bringing slaves into the state except on temporary visits.

◆ Section 5

Section 5 of the law requires that all slaveholders register each slave with a local court, giving the slave's name, age, and gender. Each registration would be accompanied by a two-dollar fee—not a large sum, but enough money to make some master try to avoid paying it. Any blacks not registered under this provision by November 1, 1780, were considered free people. The Pennsylvania courts interpreted these rules strictly. In *Wilson v. Belinda* (1817) the Pennsylvania Supreme Court ruled that the slave woman Belinda, then about forty years old, was free because in 1780 her master had neglected to list her gender on the registration form. The master clearly believed the name *Belinda* could indicate only a female, but the court disagreed. The registration had to be accurate to prevent fraud, and a strict interpretation of the law favored freedom. In *Respublica v. Blackmore* (1797) the court ruled that slaves owned by citizens of Pennsylvania could not be registered if they were not living in Pennsylvania at the time the act went into effect. In this case Blackmore lost her slaves because she and her husband had not brought them into the state before the law went into effect; merely owning them in Maryland was not sufficient.

The registration process, the generally hostile climate toward slavery in the state, and the dislocations of the Revolution clearly had an effect on slaveholding. In 1765, a decade before the Revolution began, there were about fourteen hundred slaves in Philadelphia and one hundred free blacks out of a total population of twenty-four hundred. By 1790 Philadelphia had about 28,500 people, but fewer than four hundred of them were slaves, and about two thousand were free blacks. In the rest of the state the process of emancipation was slower but still significant. Before the Revolution almost all of the blacks in Pennsyl-

www.milestonedocuments.com

vania were slaves. By 1790 there were more than 6,500 free blacks in the state and just 3,700 slaves. A decade later there were just seventeen hundred slaves and more than fourteen thousand free blacks in the state. By 1820 there were only about two hundred slaves in the state but more than thirty thousand free blacks. In forty years slavery in Pennsylvania had all but disappeared.

◆ Section 4 and Sections 6 to 14

The ending of slavery was not, however, a simple factor of letting slavery die out. The legislators understood that slavery was a complex institution, with many human issues in what was a very inhumane system. The status of the children of slaves posed a serious problem for the gradual abolition process. Under slavery, masters had a huge financial interest in the children of their slave women. Every child born to a slave woman was a financial asset. The child of a slave woman born under a gradual abolition scheme became a financial liability. The child would be born free, and the master, as the owner of the mother, would have to pay to raise the child. Furthermore, general society would face a growing population of children of former slaves who would have few skills and might become burdens on the entire society.

The legislators understood that if the children of slaves were not trained and educated for freedom they would not succeed in a free society. To solve this problem, the legislature used two tactics. First the law declares that the children of slave women, while born free, would be subject to an indenture until age twenty-eight. This would enable the master to recover the full cost of raising such children and actually give the masters a decent profit on each child. Modern economists have estimated that masters were handsomely compensated for raising the children of slaves if they kept them as servants until age twenty-eight. During this indenture period, masters were required to educate their black servants and prepare them for freedom. There was a strong incentive for doing so, because, under Section 6 of the law, masters were financially responsible for any blacks who could not take care of themselves. However, if masters freed their servants before age twenty-eight, they were not responsible for them. This incentive, combined with the growing public hostility toward slavery, probably accounts for the steep decline of slavery and bondage in Philadelphia. However, in the rural areas of the state, especially along the Maryland and Virginia border, slaveholding lingered into the first two decades of the nineteenth century.

The act also allows free blacks, including those indentured until age twenty-eight, to testify against their masters or any other white person. This was an enormously important step in guaranteeing equal justice for blacks in the state. As indentured servants, the children of slave women had a number of legal rights and protections, and this provision of the law allowed them to vindicate those rights. This provision also served as a warning to masters not to abuse or mistreat the children of their female slaves, who would one day be free.

When Pennsylvania passed its abolition act, slavery was legal in all of the thirteen new states. Pennsylvania's goal was not to make war with its neighbors. Thus the 1780 act contains a number of provisions to protect the interests of out-of-state slaveholders, such as allowing visitors to bring slaves into the state for up to six months. This provision led to controversies, as opponents of slavery tried to manipulate the law to free slaves who had not yet been in the state for six months. Just as the courts were strict on the registration procedures, so too were they strict on this provision. The courts rejected the argument that the six months could be cumulative, asserting that it had to be one continuous six-month period, unless there was a fraudulent attempt to evade the law by moving a slave back and forth across the border on a regular basis. Similarly, when abolitionists claimed that six lunar months would satisfy the law, the court summarily rejected the freedom suit. In another attempt to ensure sectional harmony, the 1780 act allows masters to recover runaway slaves who escaped into Pennsylvania. Seven years before the Constitutional Convention provided for the return of fugitive slaves, Pennsylvania did so.

The act also allows members of Congress and other government officials, as well as foreign ambassadors, to keep slaves indefinitely in the state. At the time, Philadelphia was the nation's capital, and this rule was absolutely necessary for national harmony. Even after the capital had moved to Washington, the courts held that congressmen could move slaves into the state for indefinite periods of time. During the War of 1812, Langdon Cheves, a congressman from South Carolina, stayed in Philadelphia with his slaves for more than six months, and the state supreme court upheld his right to do so. However, when Pierce Butler, another southerner, stayed in the state after his term expired, he lost his slave.

Audience

This act was aimed at the people of Pennsylvania. Slave owners needed to understand that if they wanted to hold on to their slaves, they had to fulfill all of the requirements of the new statute. Judges and lawyers needed to understand just what those requirements were. In addition, like the Declaration of Independence, this act was aimed at a larger public opinion. The preamble, in particular, was an appeal to "a decent respect to the opinions of mankind" and was designed to convince Americans as well as Europeans that slavery was wrong and that the people of Pennsylvania took seriously the ideology of the American Revolution. In a sense, the first two paragraphs of the law provide an answer to Samuel Johnson's query "How is it that we hear the loudest yelps for liberty among the drivers of negroes?" In Pennsylvania, the demands for liberty were now coming from people who would no longer tolerate slavery.

Impact

The Pennsylvania Gradual Abolition Act of 1780 was the first of its kind in the modern world. Never before had

Essential Quotes

"When we look back on the variety of dangers to which we have been exposed, and how miraculously our wants in many instances have been supplied, ... when even hope and human fortitude have become unequal to the conflict; we are unavoidably led to a serious and grateful sence of the manifold blessings which we have undeservedly received from the hand of that Being from whom every good and perfect gift cometh."

(Section 1)

"It is not for us to enquire why, in the creation of mankind, the inhabitants of the several parts of the earth were distinguished by a difference in feature or complexion. It is sufficient to know that all are the work of an Almighty Hand."

(Section 1)

"We find in the distribution of the human species, that the most fertile as well as the most barren parts of the earth are inhabited by men of complexions different from ours, and from each other; from whence we may reasonably, as well as religiously, infer, that He who placed them in their various situations, hath extended equally his care and protection to all, and that it becometh not us to counteract his mercies."

(Section 1)

www.milestonedocuments.com

a slaveholding jurisdiction taken steps to end human bondage. Never before had slave owners acquiesced in the end of slavery. The law was not passed unanimously, and after it was passed, there was a backlash led by slave owners, who campaigned against those legislators who had supported abolition. In 1781 a new legislature considered a bill to repeal or modify the law. The bill failed, in part because of petitions and protests by blacks, who actively worked to keep their recently acquired freedom. The rapid decline of slaveholding, especially in Philadelphia, guaranteed that the 1780 law would not be undone. On the contrary, in 1788 the legislature passed an elaborate act to close some loopholes in the law and further protect free blacks, indentured blacks, and slaves.

The twenty-eight-year indenture was far too long, and masters profited too much from it, while the children of slave women were forced to give a substantial number of their productive years to their mothers' owners. Otherwise the act was a valiant and mostly successful pioneering effort to dismantle slavery. In 1784 Rhode Island and Connecticut passed similar laws, as did New York in 1799 and New Jersey in 1804. In 1794 Upper Canada also passed a similar law. All of these statutes had shorter indentures for the children of slave women. On the other hand, some did not give blacks as many legal rights as the Pennsylvania law. In the end, these differences were not nearly as important as the general direction of all these laws. Without riots, rebellions, or great social upheaval, these places brought about an end to slavery and started on a path that led to a freed North. All of these states eventually sped up the abolition process by either freeing all slaves or at least (as in New Jersey) turning them into indentured servants with legal protections as rights. On July 4, 1827, New York, having previously passed a gradual abolition act, became the first state to fully end slavery. By 1850 there were no slaves in any of these states, although in New Jersey there were still a few hundred former slaves who had become indentured servants.

Blacks did not gain full legal equality in most of the North, and everywhere they faced social inequality. The Pennsylvania law did not anticipate segregation or the depth of white hostility to freed blacks. For all its flaws, the law was a remarkable first step on the road to fulfilling the promise of the Revolution and the Declaration of Independence, that America would become a nation where all people could exercise their "unalienable rights" to "life, liberty, and the pursuit of happiness."

Related Documents

"Declaration of Independence." National Archives "Our Documents" Web site. http://www.ourdocuments.gov/doc.php?doc=2. Accessed on December 21, 2007. The Declaration is the founding document of American society and sets out basic principles of liberty. The Pennsylvania act was an implementation of those principles.

An Act to Explain and Amend an Act Entitled "An Act for the Gradual Abolition of Slavery." 13 Stat. Penn. 52 (1788). http://www.palrb.us/statutesatlarge/17001799/1788/0/act/1345.pdf. Accessed on January 25, 2008. This law, passed by the Pennsylvania legislature on March 29, 1788, closed some loopholes in the 1780 act and made it far more difficult for masters to bring slaves into the state or evade the provisions of the 1780 law. For example, under the 1788 law slaves of migrants became free immediately if the master "intended" to move to the state, thus denying them the six months' right of transit for actual visitors. This law also prohibited masters of the children of slave women from taking them out of the state if they were pregnant, so their children might be born in slave states.

An Act for the Gradual Abolition of Slavery. In *Laws of the State of New York,* vol. 3. Albany, N.Y.: Charles R. and George Webster, 1800. http://www.courts.state.ny.us/history/pdf/lemmon/L1799%20ch62.pdf. Accessed on January 25, 2008. This New York law, passed in 1799, was similar to the Pennsylvania act of 1780. It differed from the Pennsylvania law in that the female children of slave women only had to serve until age twenty-five. The law also allowed masters from other states to bring their slaves into New York for nine months, rather than the six months allowed in Pennsylvania. New York had considerably more slaves than Pennsylvania, and opposition to any emancipation in the state was stronger.

Bibliography

■ Articles

Fogel, Robert W., and Stanley L. Engerman. "Philanthropy at Bargain Prices: Notes on the Economics of Gradual Emancipation." *Journal of Legal Studies* 3, no. 2 (1974): 377–401.

■ Books

Finkelman, Paul. *An Imperfect Union: Slavery, Federalism, and Comity*. Chapel Hill: University of North Carolina Press, 1981.

Hall, Kermit, Paul Finkelman, and James W. Ely, Jr. *American Legal History: Cases and Materials.* 3rd ed. New York: Oxford University Press, 2000.

Murphy, Arthur. *The Works of Samuel Johnson, LL.D.* 2 vols. New York: Arthur V. Blake, 1838.

Nash, Gary B. *Forging Freedom: The Formation of Philadelphia's Black Community, 1720–1840*. Cambridge, Mass.: Harvard University Press, 1988.

Nash, Gary B., and Jean R. Soderlund. *Freedom by Degrees: Emancipation in Pennsylvania and Its Aftermath*. New York: Oxford University Press, 1991.

Zilversmit, Arthur. *The First Emancipation*. Chicago: University of Chicago Press, 1967.

—By Paul Finkelman

Questions for Further Study

1. What reasons does the legislature give for ending slavery in the state?

2. What were the procedures that a master had to fulfill in order to keep slaves owned before March 1, 1780?

3. Can you think of any ways in which masters might have avoided the law in order to get the most value out of their slaves?

4. What other provisions would you have wanted in this law if you were a slave or the child of a slave?

Glossary

covenant	contract or agreement between two or more people
indenture	contract under which a laborer (an indentured servant) agrees to work for someone (a master) for a specific term of years, after which time the master is usually required to give the former servant money or goods to start out in life as a free person.

www.milestonedocuments.com

Pennsylvania: An Act for the Gradual Abolition of Slavery

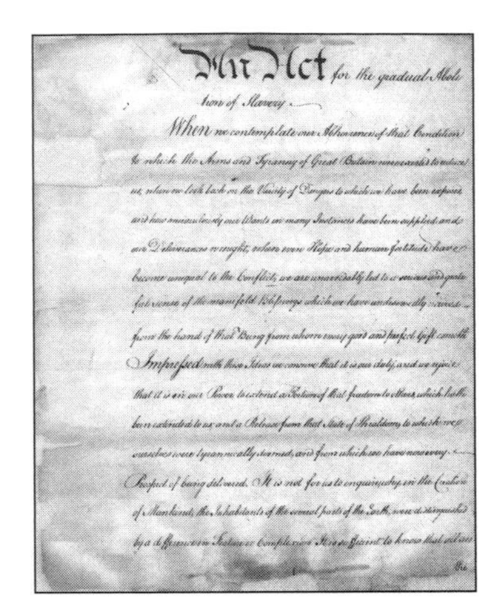
An Act for the gradual Abolition of Slavery.

WHEN we contemplate our abhorrence of that condition to which the arms and tyranny of Great Britain were exerted to reduce us; when we look back on the variety of dangers to which we have been exposed, and how miraculously our wants in many instances have been supplied, and our deliverances wrought, when even hope and human fortitude have become unequal to the conflict; we are unavoidably led to a serious and grateful sence of the manifold blessings which we have undeservedly received from the hand of that Being from whom every good and perfect gift cometh. Impressed with there ideas, we conceive that it is our duty, and we rejoice that it is in our power to extend a portion of that freedom to others, which hath been extended to us; and a release from that state of thraldom to which we ourselves were tyrannically doomed, and from which we have now every prospect of being delivered. It is not for us to enquire why, in the creation of mankind, the inhabitants of the several parts of the earth were distinguished by a difference in feature or complexion. It is sufficient to know that all are the work of an Almighty Hand. We find in the distribution of the human species, that the most fertile as well as the most barren parts of the earth are inhabited by men of complexions different from ours, and from each other; from whence we may reasonably, as well as religiously, infer, that He who placed them in their various situations, hath extended equally his care and protection to all, and that it becometh not us to counteract his mercies. We esteem it a peculiar blessing granted to us, that we are enabled this day to add one more step to universal civilization, by removing as much as possible the sorrows of those w ho have lived in undeserved bondage, and from which, by the assumed authority of the kings of Great Britain, no effectual, legal relies could be obtained. Weaned by a long course of experience from those narrower prejudices and partialities we had imbibed, we find our hearts enlarged with kindness and benevolence towards men of all conditions and nations; and we conceive ourselves at this particular period extraordinarily called upon, by the blessings which we have received, to manifest the sincerity of our profession, and to give a Substantial proof of our gratitude.

◆ Section 2.

And whereas the condition of those persons who have heretofore been denominated Negro and Mulatto slaves, has been attended with circumstances which not only deprived them of the common blessings that they were by nature entitled to, but has cast them into the deepest afflictions, by an unnatural separation and sale of husband and wife from each other and from their children; an injury, the greatness of which can only be conceived by supposing that we were in the same unhappy case. In justice therefore to persons So unhappily circumstanced, and who, having no prospect before them whereon they may rest their sorrows and their hopes, have no reasonable inducement to render their service to society, which they otherwise might; and also in grateful commemoration of our own happy deliverance from that state of unconditional submission to which we were doomed by the tyranny of Britain.

◆ Section 3.

Be it enacted, and it is hereby enacted, by the representatives of the freeman of the commonwealth of Pennsylvania, in general assembly met, and by the authority of the same, That all persons, as well Negroes and Mulattoes as others, who shall be born within this state from and after the passing of this act, shall not be deemed and considered as servants for life, or slaves; and that all servitude for life, or slavery of children, in consequence of the slavery of their mothers, in the case of all children born within this state, from and after the passing of this act as aforesaid, shall be, and hereby is utterly taken away, extinguished and for ever abolished.

www.milestonedocuments.com

◆ Section 4.

Provided always, and be it further enacted by the authority aforesaid, That every Negro and Mulatto child born within this state after the passing of this act as aforesaid (who would, in case this act had not been made, have been born a servent for years, or life, or a slave) shall be deemed to be and shall be by virtue of this act the servant of such person or his or her assigns, who would in such case have been entitled to the service of such child, until such child shall attain unto the age of twenty eight years, in the manner and on the conditions whereon servants bound by indenture for sour years are or may be retained and holder; and shall be liable to like correction and punishment, and entitled to like relies in case he or she be evilly treated by his or her master or mistress, and to like freedom dues and other privileges as servants bound by indenture for sour years are or may be entitled, unless the person to whom the service of any such child shall belong shall abandon his or her claim to the same; in which case the overseers of the poor of the city, township or district respectively, where such child shall be So abandoned, shall by indenture bind out every child so abandoned, as an apprentice for a time not exceeding the age herein before limited for the service of such children.

◆ Section 5.

And be it further enacted by the authority aforesaid, That every person, who is or shall be the owner of any Negro or Mulatto slave or servant for life or till the age of thirty one years, now within this state, or his lawful attorney, shall on or before the said first day of November next deliver or calm to be delivered in writing to the clerk of the peace of the county, or to the clerk of the court of record of the city of Philadelphia, in which he or she shall respectively inhabit, the name and surname and occupation or profession of such owner, and the name of the county and township, district or ward wherein he or she resideth; and also the name and names of any such slave and slaves, and servant and servants for life or till the age of thirty one years, together with their ages and sexes severally and respectively set forth and annexed, by such person owned or statedly employed and then being within this state, in order to ascertain and distinguish the slaves and servants for life, and till the age of thirty one years, within this state, who shall be such on the said first day of November next, from all other persons; which particulars shall by said clerk of the sessions asked clerk of the said city court be entered in books to be provided for that purpose by the said clerks; and that no Negro or Mulatto, now within this state, shall from and after the said first day of November, be deemed a slave or servant for life, or till the age of thirty one years, unless his or her name shall be entered as aforesaid on such record, except such Negro and Mulatto slaves and servants as are herein after excepted; the said clerk to be entitled to a see of two dollars for each slave or servant so entered as aforesaid from the treasurer of the county, to be allowed to him in his accounts.

◆ Section 6.

Provided always, That any person, in whom the ownership or right to the service of any Negro or Mulatto shall be vested at the passing of this act, other than such as are herein before excepted, his or her heirs, executors, administrators and assigns, and all and every of them severally shall be liable to the overseers of the poor of the city, township or district to which any such Negro or Mulatto shall become chargeable, for such necessary expence, with costs of suit thereon, as such overseers may be put to, through the neglect of the owner, master or mistress of such Negro or Mulatto; notwithstanding the name and other descriptions of such Negro or Mulatto shall not be entered and recorded as aforesaid; unless his or her master or owner shall before such slave or servant attain his or her twenty eighth year execute and record in the proper county a deed or instrument, securing to such slave or or servant his or her freedom.

◆ Section 7.

And be it further enacted by the authority aforesaid, That the offences and crimes of Negroes and Mulattoes, as well slaves and servants as freemen, shall be enquired of, adjudged, corrected and punished in like manner as the offences and crimes of the other inhabitants of this state are and shall be enquired of, adjudged, corrected and punished, and not otherwise; except that a slave shall not be admitted to bear witness against a freeman.

◆ Section 8.

And be it further enacted by the authority aforesaid, That in all cases wherein sentence of death shall be pronounced against a slave, the jury before whom he or she shall be tried, shall appraise and declare the value of such slave; and in case such sentence be executed, the court shall make an order on

Document Text

the state treasurer, payable to the owner for the same and for the costs of prosecution; but case of remission or mitigation, for the costs only.

◆ Section 9.

And be it further enacted by the authority aforesaid, That the reward for taking up runaway and absconding Negro and Mulatto slaves and servants, and the penalties for enticing away, dealing with, or harbouring, concealing or employing Negro and Mulatto slaves and servants, shall be the same, and shall be recovered in like manner as in case of servants bound for sour years.

◆ Section 10.

And be it further enacted by the authority aforesaid, That no man or woman of any nation or colour, except the Negroes or Mulattoes who shall be registered as aforesaid, shall at any time hereafter be deemed, adjudged, or holden within the territories of this commonwealth as slaves or servants for life, but as free men and free women; except the domestic slaves attending upon delegates in congress from the other American states, foreign ministers and consuls, and persons passing through or sojourning in this state, and not becoming resident therein; and seamen employed in ships not belonging to any inhabitant of this state, nor employed in any ship owned by any such inhabitant. Provided such domestic slaves be not aliened or sold to any inhabitants nor (except in the case of members of congress, foreign ministers and consuls) retained in this state longer than six months.

◆ Section 11.

Provided always; And be it further enacted by the authority aforesaid, That this act or any thing in it contained shall not give any relies or shelter to any absconding or runaway Negro or Mulatto slave or servant, who has absented himself or shall absent himself from his or her owner, master or mistress residing in any other state or country, but such owner, master or mistress shall have like right and aid to demand, claim and take away his slave or servant, as he might have had in case this act had not been made: And that all Negro and Mulatto slaves now owned and heretofore resident in this state, who have absented themselves, or been clandestinely carried away, or who may be employed abroad as seamen and have not returned or been brought back to their owners, masters or mistresses, before the passing of this act, may within five years be registered as effectually as is ordered by this act concerning those who are now within the state, on producing such slave before any two justices of the peace, and satisfying the said justices by due proof of the former residence, absconding, taking away, or absence of such slaves as aforesaid; who thereupon shall direct and order the said slave to be entered on the record as aforesaid.

◆ Section 12.

And whereas attempts maybe made to evade this act, by introducing into this state Negroes and Mulattoes bound by covenant to serve for long and unreasonable terms of years, is the same be not prevented.

◆ Section 13.

Be it therefore enacted by the authority aforesaid, That no covenant of personal servitude or apprenticeship whatsoever shall be valid or binding on a Negro or Mulatto for a longer time than seven years, unless such servant or apprentice were at the commencement of such servitude or apprenticeship under the age of twenty one years; in which case such Negro or Mulatto may be holden as a servant or apprentice respectively, according to the covenant, as the case shall be, until he or she shall attain the age of twenty eight years, but no longer.

◆ Section 14.

And be it further enacted by the authority aforesaid, That an act of assembly of die province of Pennsylvania, passed in the year one thousand Seven hundred and five, intitled, "an Act for the trial of Negroes;" and another act of assembly of the said province, passed in the year one thousand seven hundred and twenty five, intitled, "An Act for the better regulating of Negroes in this province;" and another act of assembly of the said province, passed in the year one thousand seven hundred and sixty one, intitled, .. "An Act for laying a duty on Negro and Mulatto slaves imported into this province;" and also another act of assembly of the said province, passed in the year one thousand seven hundred and seventy three, inititled, "An Act making perpetual an Act laying a duty on Negro and Mulatto slaves imported into this province, and for laying an additional duty said slaves," shall be and are hereby repealed, annulled and made void.

John Bayard, Speaker

Enabled into a law at Philadelphia, on Wednesday, the first day of March, A.D. 1780

Thomas Paine, clerk of the general assembly.

[1785 July]

To the Honorable the General Assembly of the Commonwealth of Virginia

A Memorial and Remonstrance.

We the subscribers, citizens of the said commonwealth, having taken into serious consideration, a Bill printed by order of the last Session of General assembly, e Bill establishing a provision for Teachers of the Christian Religion," and conceiving that the same if finally armed with the sanctions of a law, will be a dangerous abuse of power, are bound as faith -bers of a free State to remonstrate against it, and to declare the reasons by which we are determined. We remonstrate against the said Bill.

1. Because we hold it for a fundamental and undeniable truth "that Religion or the duty which we owe to our Creator and the manner of discharging it, can be dire -ly by reason and conviction, not by force or violence." The Religion then of every man must be left to the conviction and conscience of every man; and it is the right of every man to exercise it as may dictate. This right is in its nature an unalienable right. It is unalienable, because the opinions of men, depending only on the evidence contemplated by their own minds cannot follow the dicta of other men: It is unalienable also, because what is here a right towards men, is a duty towards the Creator. It is the duty of every man to render to the Creator such homage and such only as he bel to be acceptable to him. This duty is precedent, both in order of time and in degree of obligation, to the claims of Civil Society. Before any man can be considered as a member of Civil Society, he must be consi as a subject of the Governour of the Universe: And if a member of Civil Society, who enters into any subordinate Association, must always do it with a reservation of his duty to the General Authority; much mo must every man who becomes a member of any particular Civil Society, do it with a saving of his allegiance to the Universal Sovereign. We maintain therefore that in matters of Religion, no mans right abridged by the institution of Civil Society and that Religion is wholly exempt from its cognizance. True it is, that no other rule exists, by which any question which may divide a Society, can be ult determined, but the will of the majority; but it is also true that the majority may trespass on the rights of the minority.

2. Because if Religion be exempt from the authority of the Society at Large, still less can it be subject to that of the Legislative Body. The latter are but the creatu and vicegerents of the former. Their jurisdiction is both derivative and limited: it is limited with regard to the co-ordinate departments, more necessarily is it limited with regard to the constitu The preservation of a free Government requires not merely, that the metes and bounds which separate each department of power be invariably maintained; but more especially that neither of be suffered to overleap the great Barrier which defends the rights of the people. The Rulers who are guilty of such an encroachment, exceed the commission from which they derive their author and are Tyrants. The people who submit to it are governed by laws made neither by themselves nor by an authority derived from them, and are slaves.

3. Because it is proper to take alarm at the first experiment on our liberties. We hold this prudent jealousy to be the first duty of citizens, and one of the noblest characteristics of the late Revolution. The freemen of America did not wait till usurped power had strengthened itself by exercise, and entangled the question in precedents. They saw all consequences in the principle, and they avoided the consequences by denying the principle. We revere this lesson too much soon to forget it. Who does not see that the same authority which c establish Christianity, in exclusion of all other Religions, may establish with the same ease any particular sect of Christians, in exclusion of all other Sects? that the same authority which can force a citizen to contribute three pence only of his property for the support of any one establishment, may force him to conform to any other establishment in all cases whatsoever?

4. Because the Bill violates that equality which ought to be the basis of every law, and which is more indispensible, in proportion as the validity or expedien of any law is more liable to be impeached. "If all men are by nature equally free and independent," all men are to be considered as entering into Society on equal conditions; as relin -quishing no more, and therefore retaining no less, one than another, of their natural rights. Above all are they to be considered as retaining an "equal title to the free exercise of Relig according to the dictates of Conscience." Whilst we assert for ourselves a freedom to embrace, to profess and to observe the Religion which we believe to be of divine origin, we cannot deny an equa freedom to those whose minds have not yet yielded to the evidence which has convinced us. [illegible] an offence against God, not against man: To God, therefore, not to man, must an account it be rendered. As the Bill violates equality by subjecting some to peculiar burdens, so it violates the same principle, by granting to others peculiar exemptions. Are the Quakers and Menonists the only sects who think a compulsive support of their Religions unnecessary and unwarrantable? can their piety alone be entrusted with the care of public worship? Ought their Religions to be en -dowed above all others with extraordinary privileges by which proselytes may be enticed from all others? We think too favorably of the justice and good sense of these denominations to believe that th either covet pre-eminences over their fellow citizens, or that they will be seduced by them from the common opposition to the measure.

5. Because the Bill implies, either that the Civil Magistrate is a competent Judge of Religious truth; or that he may employ Religion as an engine of Civil policy. first is an arrogant pretension falsified by the contradictory opinions of Rulers in all ages, and throughout the world: the second an unhallowed perversion of the means of salvation.

6. Because the establishment proposed by the Bill is not requisite for the support of the Christian Religion. To say that it is, is a contradiction to the Christian R -gion itself; for every page of it disavows a dependence on the powers of this world: it is a contradiction to fact; for it is known that this Religion both existed and flourished, not only without the support of human laws, but in spite of every opposition from them; and not only during the period of miraculous aid, but long after it had been left to its own evidence and the ordinary of Providence: nay, it is a contradiction in terms; for a Religion not invented by human policy, must have pre-existed and been supported, before it was established by human policy. It is m -over to weaken in those who profess this Religion a pious confidence in its innate excellence and the patronage of its Author; and to foster in those who still reject it, a suspicion that i friends are too conscious of its fallacies, to trust it to its own merits.

7. Because experience witnesseth that ecclesiastical establishments, instead of maintaining the purity and efficacy of Religion, have had a contrary operation. almost fifteen centuries has the legal establishment of Christianity been on trial. What have been its fruits? more or less in all places, pride and indolence in the Clergy; ignorance and serv in the laity; in both, superstition, bigotry and persecution. Enquire of the Teachers of Christianity for the ages in which it appeared in its greatest lustre; those of every sect, point to the ages p to its incorporation with Civil policy. Propose a restoration of this primitive state, in which its Teachers depended on the voluntary rewards of their flocks, many of them predict its downfal. On side ought their testimony to have greatest weight, when for or when against their interest?

8. Because the establishment in question is not necessary for the support of Civil Government. If it be urged as necessary for the support of Civil Governme only as it is a means of supporting Religion, and it be not necessary for the latter purpose, it cannot be necessary for the former. If Religion be not within the cognizance of Civil Government, how its legal establishment be necessary to Civil Government? What influence in fact have ecclesiastical establishments had on Civil Society? In some instances they have been seen to erect a spiritual tyranny on the ruins of the Civil authority; in many instances they have been seen upholding the thrones of political tyranny: in no instance have they been seen the guardians of the liberties of the people. Rulers who wished to subvert the public liberty, may have found an established Clergy convenient auxiliaries. A just Government instituted to secure & perpetuate it needs them not. Such a Government will be best supported by protecting every citizen in the enjoyment of his Religion with the same equal hand which protects his person and his property, by neither invading the equal rights of any Sect, nor suffering any Sect to invade those of another.

9. Because the proposed establishment is a departure from that generous policy, which, offering an Asylum to the persecuted and oppressed of ever Nation and Religion, promised a lustre to our country, and an accession to the number of its citizens. What a melancholy mark is the Bill of sudden degeneracy? Instead of holding forth an asylum to the persecuted, it is itself a signal of persecution. It degrades from the equal rank of Citizens all those whose opinions in Religion do not bend to those of the Legislative auth Distant as it may be in its present form from the Inquisition, it differs from it only in degree. The one is the first step, the other the last in the career of intolerance. The magnanimous suffere under this cruel scourge in foreign Regions, must view the Bill as a Beacon on our coast, warning him to seek some other haven, where liberty and philanthropy in their due extent, may

James Madison's Memorial and Remonstrance (Library of Congress)

James Madison's Memorial and Remonstrance against Religious Assessments

1785

"It is proper to take alarm at the first experiment on our liberties."

Overview

During the American Revolution, Virginia made dramatic strides in the development of religious freedom. As a colony, Virginia had an established church—the Church of England—supported by establishment taxes; in the years leading up to the Revolution, the colony jailed scores of "dissenting" ministers who preached without a license, primarily Baptists. With the adoption of Article XVI of the Virginia Declaration of Rights (1776), Virginia promised a "free exercise of religion." By the end of 1776 taxes for the established church were suspended, and in 1779 they were repealed. Other reforms eliminated many regulations and limitations to which dissenting religionists had been subjected. This liberalization was threatened in 1784, however, when a majority of the Virginia House of Delegates, led by Patrick Henry, tentatively approved a proposal to impose a tax that would support the ministers or teachers of all Christian denominations. This was called the Bill Establishing a Provision for Teachers of the Christian Religion. After Henry was elevated to the governorship, removing him from the legislature, James Madison led a successful effort to delay the passage of the general assessment, or statewide tax, until the General Assembly could hear from citizens. In 1785 Madison's eloquent Memorial and Remonstrance against Religious Assessments was published anonymously as part of the successful petitioning campaign in opposition to the general assessment. Thousands of Virginia citizens endorsed copies of Madison's Memorial and Remonstrance and other petitions to the House of Delegates decrying a general assessment.

With almost eleven thousand names on petitions opposing the general assessment, the House of Delegates tabled the proposal in the October 1785 session. Seizing the opportunity created by the outpouring of citizen support for broadly defined religious liberty and separation of church and state, Madison successfully encouraged the General Assembly to adopt Thomas Jefferson's Act for Establishing Religious Freedom (1786). This created unparalleled protections for religious freedom in Virginia and marked a turning point for church/state relations in the United States. Both Madison's Memorial and Remonstrance and Jefferson's Act for Establishing Religious Freedom have since played a seminal role in the development and understanding of religious liberty in America and around the world. Madison's Memorial in particular has been seen as one of the most thorough and enduring statements in favor of religious freedom.

Context

During the early and mid-eighteenth century, most of the American colonies had an established state religion (Congregationalist in New England and Church of England in the South), but each practiced some degree of toleration of alternative, or dissenting, religions. These church establishments came under increasing pressure after a movement called the First Great Awakening (1730s and 1740s) led to an explosion in evangelical sects and division in many denominations. The result was an increase in denominational tension and, in some cases, intolerance. Moreover, in the years leading up to the American Revolution (1775–1783), colonists feared that Britain would establish bishops from the Church of England in America and provide them with political authority and tax-financed benefices such as they enjoyed in England. This led to considerable opposition to parliamentary authority. Similarly, the passage of the Quebec Act after conclusion of the French and Indian War (1754–1763), permitting the Catholic Church to continue its dominance in formerly French Canada, also generated opposition in the strongly Protestant colonies. While it would be inaccurate to see the American Revolution as caused primarily by religious strife, religious issues seethed below the surface in colonial America, sometimes erupting into major controversies. Some reform was inevitable. Virginia's development of religious freedom during the Revolution was to prove a bellwether for other new states.

In Virginia the established church was the Church of England, and dissenters from that church (primarily Presbyterians, Baptists, and Quakers) paid taxes to support its ministers, were subject to fines for failure to attend its services regularly, and were required to be married by its ministers. In addition, relief for the poor and some property dis-

Time Line

1768–1774

- More than sixty Virginia Baptist preachers are imprisoned for preaching without a license or disturbing the peace by preaching publicly.

1776

- **June 12**
The Virginia Declaration of Rights is adopted, recognizing in Article XVI a right of "free exercise of religion."

- **December 9**
Dissenters are exempted from establishment tax and religious penalties.

1779

- **December 18**
Virginia's establishment tax is repealed.

1780

- **December 18**
Marriage by dissenting ministers is permitted in Virginia.

1784

- **November 11**
The Virginia House of Delegates adopts a resolution in favor of a general assessment to support Christian ministers.

- **December 24**
Under Madison's leadership, the general assessment proposal is delayed while copies are printed and distributed for comment.

1785

- **June**
Madison drafts the Memorial and Remonstrance.

1786

- **January 19**
Jefferson's Act for Establishing Religious Freedom is adopted.

putes were controlled by vestries composed exclusively (in theory) of members of the Church of England. With religious tensions increasing upon the success of evangelicals after the First Great Awakening, Virginia jailed scores of dissenters from 1768 to 1774, primarily Baptist preachers. While no other colony so seriously persecuted dissenters before the war, neither did they provide full religious liberty by its conclusion. When the new federal Constitution was drafted in 1787, eleven of the thirteen new states had some form of religious requirement in their constitutions (limiting office to Protestant Christians, for example), with Virginia and Rhode Island being the exceptions. No other state had enacted protections of the breadth of Jefferson's Act for Establishing Religious Freedom.

During the war Virginia's political leaders were desperate to obtain strong support for mobilization from Virginia's dissenters, who accounted for as much as one-third of the populace. As a result, the Virginia establishment was forced to accept dissenter requests for religious liberty. Thus, when Virginia adopted its first constitution in June 1776, the statesman George Mason included in the proposed Declaration of Rights a provision for the broadest possible "toleration" of all religions. Recognizing that toleration was far from freedom, the young Madison, in his first session as a representative, led a successful effort to amend Article XVI of the declaration to provide for the "free exercise of religion." As the war proceeded and the necessity of maintaining unity among the populace increased, Virginia continued to liberalize its religious laws in response to a series of petitions from dissenters. The establishment tax initially was suspended and later was repealed. As the war approached its end, dissenting ministers were permitted to perform marriages (subject to limitations), and the legislature began the process of shifting the jurisdiction over poor relief from Church of England vestries to county officials.

With the end of the war, some Virginian political leaders expressed concern at the seeming decline in public virtue and religion that had accompanied the difficult and disruptive conflict. Leaders from the Church of England, reconstituted as the Protestant Episcopal Church, saw an opportunity to restore their struggling church to vigor. A concerted effort to restore state taxes to support ministers was launched; the proposals called for a "general assessment" to fund clergy from all Christian sects, with each taxpayer designating the denomination to receive his share. This proposal was championed by Henry, the most popular leader in the Virginia legislature. In November 1784 a resolution was adopted in favor of a general assessment. After Henry became governor later that month, however, Madison was successful in having the proposal delayed and, importantly, having copies of the general assessment bill printed and distributed throughout Virginia with a request for constituent comments. This set the scene for Madison's Memorial and Remonstrance.

In the spring of 1785 Mason and George Nicholas persuaded Madison to draft a remonstrance, or formal statement of opposition, against the general assessment. Once printed, the Memorial and Remonstrance was circulated broadly and signed by more than one thousand citizens, although Madison's authorship was not disclosed at the time. (One publisher listed Madison as author in a 1786 republication of the Memorial, although Madison did not formally acknowledge authorship until 1826.) The Memorial and Remonstrance joined a number of other petitions in opposition to the assessment. As a result, when the House of Delegates reconvened in October 1785, the general assessment was left to die on the table.

With the demise of the general assessment, Madison was successful in renewing legislative interest in the adoption of Jefferson's Act for Establishing Religious Freedom, which was steered through the legislature and signed into law on January 19, 1786. Several years later Madison championed the adoption of amendments to the Constitution by the first federal Congress; these eventually became the Bill of Rights, including the First Amendment's protection of religious freedom. The Supreme Court repeatedly has found the First Amendment grounded in the struggle that resulted in Madison's Memorial and Remonstrance and Jefferson's Act for Establishing Religious Freedom and has relied heavily on both documents in seeking to interpret the First Amendment.

About the Author

James Madison, the fourth U.S. president and widely known as the "father of the U.S. Constitution," held numerous important political positions in Virginia and the nation. His crucial role in the development of religious freedom in America, however, is sometimes forgotten.

Madison was born on March 16, 1751, in King George County, Virginia. He was raised on the plantation of James Madison, Sr., in Orange County, Virginia, later known as Montpelier. Madison's boyhood apparently passed relatively uneventfully, but he certainly enjoyed the privileges of being raised as the eldest son in a family of Virginia gentry.

Importantly, Madison's parents decided to send him to the College of New Jersey (later Princeton) in 1769 rather than sending him to the College of William and Mary in Williamsburg, the more common choice among Virginia gentry. In New Jersey, Madison studied under the new president of the college, the Reverend Jonathan Witherspoon, a Presbyterian minister and strong advocate of Scottish Enlightenment ideals. Later years would demonstrate that Madison's thinking was significantly influenced by his study under Witherspoon.

Madison was a revolutionary at a young age. In 1774 he was elected to the Orange County Committee of Safety, which his father chaired. In 1776, at the age of twenty-five, Madison was elected to the Virginia Convention (which adopted a resolution on independence) and to the first session of the Virginia House of Delegates. In 1779 he was elected to the Continental Congress. After returning to the Virginia House in 1784 and supporting the adoption of Jefferson's Act for Establishing Religious Freedom, Madison distinguished himself in 1787 as one of Virginia's representatives to the Constitutional Convention in Philadelphia. Madison played a key role in the development of the constitutional structure and, as a boon to future historians, kept careful notes on the proceedings. He also defended the Constitution from heated attacks by Henry in the Virginia convention and from Antifederalists across the new states in a series of essays now known as the Federalist Papers (coauthored with Alexander Hamilton and John Jay). Madison then was elected to the first federal Congress, where he played the leading role in the adoption of the proposed amendments to the Constitution that became the Bill of Rights.

When Jefferson became president in 1801, he appointed Madison secretary of state. After serving for eight years in that position, Madison was elected the fourth president of the United States in 1808; he served eight years as president, in particular presiding over the difficult War of 1812. In 1819 Madison took an extended retirement at his beloved Montpelier, from which he continued an extensive correspondence with Jefferson, James Monroe, and other early American luminaries. Madison died at home on June 28, 1836. He is remembered not only for his seminal role in the drafting of the Constitution and for his presidency but also as one of Jefferson's chief lieutenants in the so-called Revolution of 1800, referring to Jefferson's election as president, which brought an end to the power of Federalists in the new national government and began a long string of Democratic-Republican, also known as Jeffersonian Republican, presidencies.

Explanation and Analysis of the Document

Madison's Memorial and Remonstrance is structured around fifteen reasons to oppose a religious assessment; as a literary device, Madison begins each paragraph "Because." The document also includes a short preamble explaining that it is intended as a statement by citizens of reasons to oppose the Bill Establishing a Provision for Teachers of the Christian Religion; the intent was to encourage citizens to sign copies of the document or draft their own petitions against the general assessment. Substantively, the preamble warns that any religious assessment would be "a dangerous abuse of power." Madison concludes his introductory remarks by noting that the signatories are "bound as faithful members of a free State to remonstrate against" the proposed bill, thus justifying his own reluctant decision to take up the pen and encouraging others to do so.

◆ Paragraph 1

Madison begins by quoting the Virginia Declaration of Rights, in particular the admonition that "Religion or the duty which we owe to our Creator and the manner of discharging it, can be directed only by reason and conviction, not by force or violence." The declaration was a foundational document for Virginia's new state government and was very popular. Madison goes on to explain that "This duty [of religion] is precedent, both in order of time and in

www.milestonedocuments.com

James Madison in a drawing made during his presidency (Library of Congress)

degree of obligation, to the claims of Civil Society." For Madison and other Enlightenment thinkers, society is formed as a voluntary compact among citizens. It is therefore important that religion is antecedent to organized society and that religious obligations and rights cannot be ceded to society. As a result, the free exercise of religion becomes a "positive right"—a right for citizens to engage in an action, if necessary with government accommodation—rather than merely a "negative right"—a restriction on government action—against government interference.

◆ Paragraph 2

Madison takes the opportunity to make clear that a legislative body's authority is circumscribed both by the authority of coordinate branches and by limitations imposed by constituents, including, for example, written constitutions. Thus, as religion is not subject to the authority of government under the Virginia Constitution, so it cannot be subject to the authority of the legislature. The notions on limited government explained herein were to prove important both in the drafting of the Constitution and in the political success of Jeffersonian Republicans in the elections of 1800 and thereafter.

◆ Paragraph 3

Rights must be protected on principle, Madison notes. Thus, it is a "duty" of the citizens "to take alarm at the first experiment on our liberties," even if the encroachment seems otherwise relatively minor. Madison expressly draws an analogy to the actions of the founders in response to British usurpations before the Revolution (perhaps remembering the British decision to remove the Townshend duties on all imports other than tea). Once rights are impaired, Madison explains, it creates a precedent for further usurpation. Taking up again the question of governmental authority over religion, Madison warns that "the same authority which can establish Christianity, in exclusion of all other Religions, may establish with the same ease any particular sect of Christians."

◆ Paragraph 4

Madison calls for equal treatment of all persons in the area of belief and notes particularly that in claiming freedom of conscience, one cannot deny "an equal freedom" to others. Madison also reminds the General Assembly that any offense from those who do not believe "is an offence against God, not against man." Having discussed the impact of the proposal on nonbelievers, Madison comments that the bill provides ("unequal") benefits to Quakers and Mennonites by permitting them to allocate collected funds as they saw fit, not simply to ministers or teachers.

◆ Paragraph 5

The use of religion by civil magistrates to promote civil society is a perversion of religion, Madison explains. Nor are civil magistrates appropriate judges of "Religious Truth." This was an important point for Madison; in fact, in one of his rare legislative speeches, in December 1784, he had stressed that any assessment would inevitably put the legislators into the untenable position of settling questions of orthodoxy.

◆ Paragraph 6

During Virginia's debates over religious liberty, dissenters had argued vehemently that Christianity did not need state support; indeed, it had flourished in its earliest centuries when Christians were persecuted. Madison takes up this theme, noting that state support is inconsistent with Christianity by creating "a dependence on the powers of this world" and thereby weakening the faith of believers.

◆ Paragraph 7

For fifteen centuries, writes Madison, the establishment has created "pride and indolence in the Clergy, ignorance and servility in the laity, in both, superstition, bigotry and persecution." The theme in Paragraphs 6 and 7—the danger that state entanglement posed for churches—became a key element in opposition to the assessment from religious groups, particularly in the so-called Spirit of the Gospel petitions received primarily from Baptist churches. Fear of church entanglement with government became a cornerstone of the notion of separation of church and state in the early republic. (This contrasts with the notions of the English philosopher John Locke or Jefferson, who saw separation of church and state as necessary primarily to protect the independence of the government.)

◆ Paragraph 8

Madison explains that an established religion often has been used by a tyrannical government. Madison recognizes the value of religious citizens to a society but concludes that legitimate interests will best be protected by providing a nondiscriminatory right of free exercise of religion to all citizens.

◆ Paragraph 9

Religious liberty without an assessment provided "an Asylum to the persecuted and oppressed of every Nation and Religion," Madison argues, whereas a general assessment would discourage immigration and encourage potential citizens to travel elsewhere.

◆ Paragraph 10

Madison also concludes that passage of a general assessment would encourage emigration, already a problem in Virginia. The arguments in Paragraphs 9 and 10 were intended to appeal to Virginia's leaders as the state desired to encourage immigration, particularly among skilled tradesmen. This desire was heightened by the significant drain of human resources to the counties of Kentucky and the Northwest Territories.

◆ Paragraph 11

Harking back to the days in which sectarian battles pierced Virginia, Madison warns that a general assessment would result in a return to disputes such as those and the ones that drenched the old world in blood—an allusion to the Reformation and the Inquisition. Such violent strife over religion, according to Madison, is best relieved by liberalizing religious freedoms.

◆ Paragraph 12

Ingenuously, Madison explains that if a Christian state applies a general assessment or other religious test, it will actually discourage the dissemination of Christianity. After all, he reasons, more than half of the world is not Christian, and the proposed bill would discourage nonbelievers from coming into "the light of revelation" while at the same time countenancing by example non-Christian states' imposition of restrictions on Christianity.

◆ Paragraph 13

The adoption of laws that are in such general disrepute and difficult to enforce tends only to weaken support for law in general, Madison observes.

◆ Paragraph 14

Madison draws upon the need for democratic representation, not only insisting that such a major change should require the input from the citizens but also noting that the current system of representation in Virginia was unequal and therefore incapable of properly reflecting the people's views. This was a common problem in eighteenth- and nineteenth-century America: As new areas were settled, their populations often would grow much more quickly than their representation in the legislature. Mentioning the inequality of representation in the General Assembly would certainly tend to encourage support from the underrepresented western counties, which were also heavily populated by dissenters from the previously established Church of England. Madison's observation is interesting as the increase in representation of western counties in Virginia that had occurred since 1776 played a major role in the defeat of the general assessment proposal.

◆ Paragraph 15

Returning to the question of legislative authority, Madison warns that a legislature that exceeds its authority may quickly usurp the power of the executive and the judiciary or otherwise impose tyranny. Since the legislature lacks authority over religion and since religious freedom is a gift of nature, Madison concludes that either the legislature has no authority to adopt the proposed assessment bill or it can defeat any constraints on its power. The notion of an inherent inability of government to impair "natural rights" would play an important role in the formation of the Bill of Rights.

◆ Conclusion

In finalizing the appeal to the Virginia General Assembly, Madison calls upon "the Supreme Lawgiver of the Universe" to illuminate the minds of the legislators and guide their actions. Here, Madison joins his arguments to those of Virginia's religious dissenters that strong religious freedom and strict separation of church and state are needed to protect religion. This becomes a cornerstone of the willingness of many eighteenth-century religionists to support religious freedom so strongly.

Audience

While the Memorial and Remonstrance is nominally addressed to the General Assembly of Virginia, the audience for Madison was the Virginia populace. Madison hoped that citizens would take the opportunity provided by the delay in the general assessment to make their views known. Thus, the Memorial and Remonstrance is structured to permit interested citizens to circulate it for signatures and submit it to the General Assembly or to use some or all of the arguments in their own petitions.

The tone and content of the Memorial suggest that Madison was trying, in particular, to appeal to the Baptists and Presbyterians concentrated in the Virginia Piedmont and trans-Appalachian areas (including the Shenandoah Valley). These dissenters from the previously established Church of England had been instrumental in the fight for

www.milestonedocuments.com

Essential Quotes

"This duty [of religion] is precedent, both in order of time and in degree of obligation, to the claims of Civil Society."

(Paragraph 1)

"It is proper to take alarm at the first experiment on our liberties."

(Paragraph 3)

"The same authority which can establish Christianity, in exclusion of all other Religions, may establish with the same ease any particular sect of Christians."

(Paragraph 3)

"Whilst we assert for ourselves a freedom to embrace, to profess and to observe the Religion which we believe to be of divine origin, we cannot deny an equal freedom to those whose minds have not yet yielded to the evidence which has convinced us."

(Paragraph 4)

"The magnanimous sufferer … in foreign Regions, must view the Bill as a Beacon on our Coast, warning him to seek some other haven, where liberty and philanthrophy in their due extent, may offer a more certain repose from his Troubles."

(Paragraph 9)

an end to the established church, and Madison may have been interested in encouraging opposition, especially among the Presbyterian laity because of the Hanover Presbytery clergy's decision in 1784 to offer very cautious support for a general assessment. Madison considered the Hanover Presbytery's willingness to accept a general assessment a betrayal of the ideals for which he and the dissenting community had worked so long and hard. He complained to James Monroe, for example, that he did "not know of a more shameful contrast" than between prior Presbyterian statements against the establishment of the Church of England and their apparent support of a general assessment in 1784 (Rutland, p. 261). The opposition to the assessment that erupted from Presbyterian laity in 1785 played an important part in the proposal's defeat.

Impact

Madison's Memorial and Remonstrance played an important role in the defeat of the general assessment proposal and adoption of Jefferson's Act for Establishing Religious Freedom. It is worth remembering, however, that petitions opposed to the general assessment initiated by the Baptists and the Presbyterians gained more signatories than Madison's Memorial and Remonstrance. The House of Delegates received thirteen copies of Madison's Memorial with more than fifteen hundred signatures, but at the same time it received twenty-nine copies of the Baptist Spirit of the Gospel petitions with almost 4,900 signatories. A total of almost eleven thousand Virginians signed seventy-nine petitions opposing the assessment, compared with twenty petitions supporting an assessment with only about one-tenth the signatories. In fact, the reaction against the general assessment was broad and vehement across Virginia. Still, it is not too presumptive to imagine that Madison's particularly erudite arguments held particular sway with the members of the House of Delegates, of which he was still a member.

Historically, the Memorial and Remonstrance has cast a far longer shadow than most other early American documents concerning religious freedom. For example, in seeking to interpret First Amendment protections against the establishment of a religion and in favor of free exercise, the Supreme Court has characterized the Virginia fight against the general assessment and the resulting adoption of Jefferson's Act for Establishing Religious Freedom "as best reflecting the long and intensive struggle for religious freedom in America, and as particularly relevant in the search for First Amendment meaning" (*McGowan v. Maryland*, 366 U.S. 420, 437; 1961). The Court has explained that "Thomas Jefferson and James Madison led the fight against this tax. Madison wrote his great Memorial and Remonstrance against the law" (*Everson v. Board of Education*, 330 U.S. 1, 11–12; 1947). Madison's Memorial and Remonstrance, then, has become one of the central statements of the reasons for the protection of religious liberty in the U.S. Constitution and is still relied upon heavily by legislators, officials, students, and courts to understand the parameters of church/state and free-exercise issues.

Related Documents

"A Bill Establishing a Provision for Teachers of the Christian Religion." Library of Congress Web site. http://www.loc.gov/exhibits/religion/f0504s.jpg. Accessed on October 17, 2007. This 1784 bill, supported by Patrick Henry, Richard Henry Lee, Benjamin Harrison, and other leading Virginia politicians, was Madison's motivation for writing the Memorial and Remonstrance. The bill was tabled, never to be revived, in the October term, 1785. This copy includes the names of those members of the House of Delegates in support of and opposed to the delay to obtain input from the citizenry.

"Constitution of the United States: Bill of Rights." The Avalon Project at Yale Law School Web site. http://www.yale.edu/lawweb/avalon/rights1.htm. Accessed on October 17, 2007. The Supreme Court has repeatedly noted the seminal role of Madison's Memorial and Remonstrance, along with Jefferson's Act for Establishing Religious Freedom, in the development of religious freedom in the early republic and in understanding the First Amendment's protection of religious liberty.

Hutchinson, William T., and William M. E. Rachal, eds. *The Papers of James Madison*, vols. 1, 7, and 8. Chicago: University of Chicago Press, 1962, 1971, 1973. *The Papers of James Madison*, with the final volumes still being edited at the University of Virginia, provide the definitive resource on Madison's written contribution to the American Revolution and creation of the new republic. In particular, these three volumes provide detailed accounts of the drafting of Section 16 of the Virginia Declaration of Rights and Madison's Memorial and Remonstrance in opposition to the proposed general assessment.

"The Virginia Act for Establishing Religious Freedom." The Religious Freedoms Page Web site. http://religiousfreedom.lib.virginia.edu/sacred/vaact.html. Accessed on October 17, 2007. This statute was adopted after the general assessment bill was defeated, owing in part to Madison's Memorial and Remonstrance. Jefferson, the original author of the act, felt so strongly about its importance that he listed it as one of the three things for which he hoped to be remembered on his tombstone, the others being the Declaration of Independence and the founding of the University of Virginia.

"Virginia Declaration of Rights." The Avalon Project at Yale Law School Web site. http://www.yale.edu/lawweb/avalon/virginia.htm. Accessed on October 17, 2007. Madison's insistence that the Virginia Declaration of Rights of 1776 protect not just broad religious "toleration," as originally suggested by George Mason, but also the "free exercise of religion" played an important part in the development of religious freedom in Virginia and the rest of the nation. Madison's Memorial and Remonstrance quotes the Virginia Declaration several times, including the famous quotation from the declaration's drafting committee that "religion or the duty which we owe to our Creator and the manner of discharging it, can be directed only by reason and conviction, not by force or violence."

Bibliography

■ Books

Beneke, Chris. *Beyond Toleration: The Religious Origins of American Pluralism*. New York: Oxford University Press, 2006.

Bonomi, Patricia U. *Under the Cope of Heaven: Religion, Society, and Politics in Colonial America*. New York: Oxford University Press, 1986.

Brenner, Lenni, ed. *Jefferson and Madison on Separation of Church and State: Writings on Religion and Secularism*. Fort Lee, N.J.: Barricade Books, 2004.

Buckley, Thomas E. *Church and State in Revolutionary Virginia, 1776–1787*. Charlottesville: University of Virginia Press, 1977.

Butler, Jon. *Awash in a Sea of Faith: Christianizing the American People*. Cambridge, Mass.: Harvard University Press, 1990.

Curry, Thomas J. *The First Freedoms: Church and State in America to the Passage of the First Amendment*. New York: Oxford University Press, 1986.

Eckenrode, H. J. *Separation of Church and State in Virginia*. 1910. Reprint. New York: Da Capo Press, 1971.

Humphrey, Edward Frank. *Nationalism and Religion in America, 1774–1789*. New York: Russell & Russell, 1965.

www.milestonedocuments.com

Isaac, Rhys. *The Transformation of Virginia, 1740–1790* Chapel Hill: University of North Carolina Press, 1982.

James, Charles Fenton. *Documentary History of the Struggle for Religious Liberty in Virginia*. Lynchburg, Va.: J. P. Bell Co., 1900.

Ketcham, Ralph. *James Madison: A Biography*. Charlottesville: University of Virginia Press, 1990.

Peterson, Merrill D., and Robert C. Vaughan, eds. *The Virginia Statute for Religious Freedom: Its Evolution and Consequences in American History*. Cambridge, U.K.: Cambridge University Press, 1988.

Rutland, Robert A., et al., eds. *The Papers of James Madison*, vol. 8. Chicago: University of Chicago Press, 1973.

Stokes, Anson Phelps, and Leo Pfeffer. *Church and State in the United States*. New York: Harper & Row, 1964.

Van Schreeven, William J., and Robert L. Scribner. *Revolutionary Virginia: The Road to Independence*. 8 vols. Charlottesville: University of Virginia Press, 1973.

Web Sites

Constitution Society Web site.
http://www.constitution.org/. Accessed on November 24, 2007.

"Early Virginia Religious Petitions." Library of Congress "American Memory" Project Web site.
http://memory.loc.gov/ammem/collections/petitions/. Accessed on November 24, 2007.

"Religion and the Founding of the American Republic." Library of Congress Web site.
http://www.loc.gov/exhibits/religion/. Accessed on November 24, 2007.

"Religious Freedom Documents." First Freedom Center Web site.
http://www.firstfreedom.org/religiousfree/religfreedocs.html. Accessed on November 24, 2007.

"Roots of Religious Liberty." Bill of Rights Institute Web site (lesson plans).
http://www.billofrightsinstitute.org/instructional/resources/Lessons/Lessons_List.asp?action=showDetails&id=25&ref=showCatD&catId=4. Accessed on November 24, 2007.

—By John A. Ragosta

Questions for Further Study

1. What is the significance of Madison's assertion that the "duty" of religion "is precedent, both in order of time and in degree of obligation, to the claims of Civil Society"? Does this reflect current American thought? How would this idea influence the application of the First Amendment by the courts today?

2. Compare and contrast Patrick Henry's notions of religious liberty (strong protection of free exercise with nondiscriminatory state promotion of religion) with Madison's and Jefferson's (strong protection of free exercise while prohibiting state involvement in religion). What are the historic roots of each? Consider, for example, John Locke's work. How might Locke have influenced Madison's, Jefferson's, and Henry's views on religious liberty?

3. Is a guarantee of nondiscrimination against any particular sect or denomination adequate to protect minority rights in a pluralistic society? Which of Madison's arguments tend merely to nondiscriminatory treatment of religion and which insist upon government noninvolvement?

4. While Madison supported broad religious freedom in the eighteenth century, the twenty-first century presents a broad range of issues and problems that could not have been anticipated at that time. How might (or should) protection of religious freedom change in a society with far broader pluralism than Madison could have imagined and in a society faced with terrorism sometimes justified on religious grounds? In light of these developments, how should we (and the courts) treat Madison's Memorial and Remonstrance?

5. In Federalist Paper no. 10 Madison presents a compelling argument for the viability of a large republic by noting that different interests and factions will prevent any stable majority from developing and abusing the rights of a minority. Is the same true in the context of religion? Compare with Federalist Paper no. 51.

Glossary

Civil Society	a nation under a government, a polity
countenances	approves of, even if implicitly
enervate	weaken, sap the energy of
metes and bounds	limits; boundaries; in this context, limits of governmental power
prerogative	an exclusive right or authority
proselytes	believers, disciples
Providence	God's intervention in the world; God's grace or plan
redound	to lead to or reflect
remonstrance	document stating arguments in opposition to a proposal
salutary	beneficial
sect	a denomination or group of religious adherents
usurpation	seizing of power
vicegerents	subordinate rulers; in this context, being subject to the people

www.milestonedocuments.com

Document Text

James Madison's Memorial and Remonstrance against Religious Assessments

To the Honorable the General Assembly of the Commonwealth of Virginia

◆ A Memorial and Remonstrance

We the subscribers, citizens of the said Commonwealth, having taken into serious consideration, a Bill printed by order of the last Session of General Assembly, entitled "A Bill establishing a provision for Teachers of the Christian Religion," and conceiving that the same if finally armed with the sanctions of a law, will be a dangerous abuse of power, are bound as faithful members of a free State to remonstrate against it, and to declare the reasons by which we are determined. We remonstrate against the said Bill,

1. Because we hold it for a fundamental and undeniable truth, "that Religion or the duty which we owe to our Creator and the manner of discharging it, can be directed only by reason and conviction, not by force or violence." The Religion then of every man must be left to the conviction and conscience of every man; and it is the right of every man to exercise it as these may dictate. This right is in its nature an unalienable right. It is unalienable, because the opinions of men, depending only on the evidence contemplated by their own minds cannot follow the dictates of other men: It is unalienable also, because what is here a right towards men, is a duty towards the Creator. It is the duty of every man to render to the Creator such homage and such only as he believes to be acceptable to him. This duty is precedent, both in order of time and in degree of obligation, to the claims of Civil Society. Before any man can be considered as a member of Civil Society, he must be considered as a subject of the Governour of the Universe: And if a member of Civil Society, who enters into any subordinate Association, must always do it with a reservation of his duty to the General Authority; much more must every man who becomes a member of any particular Civil Society, do it with a saving of his allegiance to the Universal Sovereign. We maintain therefore that in matters of Religion, no mans right is abridged by the institution of Civil Society and that Religion is wholly exempt from its cognizance. True it is, that no other rule exists, by which any question which may divide a Society, can be ultimately determined, but the will of the majority; but it is also true that the majority may trespass on the rights of the minority.

2. Because if Religion be exempt from the authority of the Society at large, still less can it be subject to that of the Legislative Body. The latter are but the creatures and vicegerents of the former. Their jurisdiction is both derivative and limited: it is limited with regard to the co-ordinate departments, more necessarily is it limited with regard to the constituents. The preservation of a free Government requires not merely, that the metes and bounds which separate each department of power be invariably maintained; but more especially that neither of them be suffered to overleap the great Barrier which defends the rights of the people. The Rulers who are guilty of such an encroachment, exceed the commission from which they derive their authority, and are Tyrants. The People who submit to it are governed by laws made neither by themselves nor by an authority derived from them, and are slaves.

3. Because it is proper to take alarm at the first experiment on our liberties. We hold this prudent jealousy to be the first duty of Citizens, and one of the noblest characteristics of the late Revolution. The free men of America did not wait till usurped power had strengthened itself by exercise, and entangled the question in precedents. They saw all the consequences in the principle, and they avoided the consequences by denying the principle. We revere this lesson too much soon to forget it. Who does not see that the same authority which can establish Christianity, in exclusion of all other Religions, may establish with the same ease any particular sect of Christians, in exclusion of all other Sects? that the same authority

which can force a citizen to contribute three pence only of his property for the support of any one establishment, may force him to conform to any other establishment in all cases whatsoever?

4. Because the Bill violates that equality which ought to be the basis of every law, and which is more indispensible, in proportion as the validity or expediency of any law is more liable to be impeached. If "all men are by nature equally free and independent," all men are to be considered as entering into Society on equal conditions; as relinquishing no more, and therefore retaining no less, one than another, of their natural rights. Above all are they to be considered as retaining an "*equal* title to the free exercise of Religion according to the dictates of Conscience." Whilst we assert for ourselves a freedom to embrace, to profess and to observe the Religion which we believe to be of divine origin, we cannot deny an equal freedom to those whose minds have not yet yielded to the evidence which has convinced us. If this freedom be abused, it is an offence against God, not against man: To God, therefore, not to man, must an account of it be rendered. As the Bill violates equality by subjecting some to peculiar burdens, so it violates the same principle, by granting to others peculiar exemptions. Are the Quakers and Menonists the only sects who think a compulsive support of their Religions unnecessary and unwarrantable? Can their piety alone be entrusted with the care of public worship? Ought their Religions to be endowed above all others with extraordinary privileges by which proselytes may be enticed from all others? We think too favorably of the justice and good sense of these denominations to believe that they either covet preeminences over their fellow citizens or that they will be seduced by them from the common opposition to the measure.

5. Because the Bill implies either that the Civil Magistrate is a competent Judge of Religious Truth; or that he may employ Religion as an engine of Civil policy. The first is an arrogant pretension falsified by the contradictory opinions of Rulers in all ages, and throughout the world: the second an unhallowed perversion of the means of salvation.

6. Because the establishment proposed by the Bill is not requisite for the support of the Christian Religion. To say that it is, is a contradiction to the Christian Religion itself, for every page of it disavows a dependence on the powers of this world: it is a contradiction to fact; for it is known that this Religion both existed and flourished, not only without the support of human laws, but in spite of every opposition from them, and not only during the period of miraculous aid, but long after it had been left to its own evidence and the ordinary care of Providence. Nay, it is a contradiction in terms; for a Religion not invented by human policy, must have pre-existed and been supported, before it was established by human policy. It is moreover to weaken in those who profess this Religion a pious confidence in its innate excellence and the patronage of its Author; and to foster in those who still reject it, a suspicion that its friends are too conscious of its fallacies to trust it to its own merits.

7. Because experience witnesseth that ecclesiastical establishments, instead of maintaining the purity and efficacy of Religion, have had a contrary operation. During almost fifteen centuries has the legal establishment of Christianity been on trial. What have been its fruits? More or less in all places, pride and indolence in the Clergy, ignorance and servility in the laity, in both, superstition, bigotry and persecution. Enquire of the Teachers of Christianity for the ages in which it appeared in its greatest lustre; those of every sect, point to the ages prior to its incorporation with Civil policy. Propose a restoration of this primitive State in which its Teachers depended on the voluntary rewards of their flocks, many of them predict its downfall. On which Side ought their testimony to have greatest weight, when for or when against their interest?

8. Because the establishment in question is not necessary for the support of Civil Government. If it be urged as necessary for the support of Civil Government only as it is a means of supporting Religion, and it be not necessary for the latter purpose, it cannot be necessary for the former. If Religion be not within the cognizance of Civil Government how can its legal establishment be necessary to Civil Government? What influence in fact have ecclesiastical establishments had on Civil Society? In some instances they have been seen to erect a spiritual tyranny on the ruins of the Civil authority; in many instances they have been seen upholding the thrones of political tyranny: in no instance have they been seen the guardians of the liberties of the people. Rulers who wished to subvert the public liberty, may have found an established Clergy convenient auxiliaries. A just Government instituted to secure & perpetuate it needs them not. Such a Government will be best supported by protecting every Citizen in the enjoyment of his Religion with the same equal hand which protects his person and his property; by neither invading the equal rights of any Sect, nor suffering any Sect to invade those of another.

www.milestonedocuments.com

9. Because the proposed establishment is a departure from that generous policy, which, offering an Asylum to the persecuted and oppressed of every Nation and Religion, promised a lustre to our country, and an accession to the number of its citizens. What a melancholy mark is the Bill of sudden degeneracy? Instead of holding forth an Asylum to the persecuted, it is itself a signal of persecution. It degrades from the equal rank of Citizens all those whose opinions in Religion do not bend to those of the Legislative authority. Distant as it may be in its present form from the Inquisition, it differs from it only in degree. The one is the first step, the other the last in the career of intolerance. The magnanimous sufferer under this cruel scourge in foreign Regions, must view the Bill as a Beacon on our Coast, warning him to seek some other haven, where liberty and philanthrophy in their due extent, may offer a more certain repose from his Troubles.

10. Because it will have a like tendency to banish our Citizens. The allurements presented by other situations are every day thinning their number. To superadd a fresh motive to emigration by revoking the liberty which they now enjoy, would be the same species of folly which has dishonoured and depopulated flourishing kingdoms.

11. Because it will destroy that moderation and harmony which the forbearance of our laws to intermeddle with Religion has produced among its several sects. Torrents of blood have been spilt in the old world, by vain attempts of the secular arm, to extinguish Religious discord, by proscribing all difference in Religious opinion. Time has at length revealed the true remedy. Every relaxation of narrow and rigorous policy, wherever it has been tried, has been found to assuage the disease. The American Theatre has exhibited proofs that equal and compleat liberty, if it does not wholly eradicate it, sufficiently destroys its malignant influence on the health and prosperity of the State. If with the salutary effects of this system under our own eyes, we begin to contract the bounds of Religious freedom, we know no name that will too severely reproach our folly. At least let warning be taken at the first fruits of the threatened innovation. The very appearance of the Bill has transformed "that Christian forbearance, love and charity," which of late mutually prevailed, into animosities and jealousies, which may not soon be appeased. What mischiefs may not be dreaded, should this enemy to the public quiet be armed with the force of a law?

12. Because the policy of the Bill is adverse to the diffusion of the light of Christianity. The first wish of those who enjoy this precious gift ought to be that it may be imparted to the whole race of mankind. Compare the number of those who have as yet received it with the number still remaining under the dominion of false Religions; and how small is the former! Does the policy of the Bill tend to lessen the disproportion? No; it at once discourages those who are strangers to the light of revelation from coming into the Region of it; and countenances by example the nations who continue in darkness, in shutting out those who might convey it to them. Instead of Levelling as far as possible, every obstacle to the victorious progress of Truth, the Bill with an ignoble and unchristian timidity would circumscribe it with a wall of defence against the encroachments of error.

13. Because attempts to enforce by legal sanctions, acts obnoxious to so great a proportion of Citizens, tend to enervate the laws in general, and to slacken the bands of Society. If it be difficult to execute any law which is not generally deemed necessary or salutary, what must be the case, where it is deemed invalid and dangerous? And what may be the effect of so striking an example of impotency in the Government, on its general authority?

14. Because a measure of such singular magnitude and delicacy ought not to be imposed, without the clearest evidence that it is called for by a majority of citizens, and no satisfactory method is yet proposed by which the voice of the majority in this case may be determined, or its influence secured. "The people of the respective counties are indeed requested to signify their opinion respecting the adoption of the Bill to the next Session of Assembly." But the representation must be made equal, before the voice either of the Representatives or of the Counties will be that of the people. Our hope is that neither of the former will, after due consideration, espouse the dangerous principle of the Bill. Should the event disappoint us, it will still leave us in full confidence, that a fair appeal to the latter will reverse the sentence against our liberties.

15. Because finally, "the equal right of every citizen to the free exercise of his Religion according to the dictates of conscience" is held by the same tenure with all our other rights. If we recur to its origin, it is equally the gift of nature; if we weigh its importance, it cannot be less dear to us; if we consult the "Declaration of those rights which pertain to the good people of Virginia, as the basis and foundation of Government," it is enumerated with equal solemnity, or rather studied emphasis. Either then, we must say, that the Will of the Legislature is the

Document Text

only measure of their authority; and that in the plenitude of this authority, they may sweep away all our fundamental rights; or, that they are bound to leave this particular right untouched and sacred: Either we must say, that they may controul the freedom of the press, may abolish the Trial by Jury, may swallow up the Executive and Judiciary Powers of the State; nay that they may despoil us of our very right of suffrage, and erect themselves into an independent and hereditary Assembly or, we must say, that they have no authority to enact into law the Bill under consideration. We the Subscribers say, that the General Assembly of this Commonwealth have no such authority: And that no effort may be omitted on our part against so dangerous an usurpation, we oppose to it, this remonstrance; earnestly praying, as we are in duty bound, that the Supreme Lawgiver of the Universe, by illuminating those to whom it is addressed, may on the one hand, turn their Councils from every act which would affront his holy prerogative, or violate the trust committed to them: and on the other, guide them into every measure which may be worthy of his blessing, may redound to their own praise, and may establish more firmly the liberties, the prosperity and the happiness of the Commonwealth.

www.milestonedocuments.com

An ORDINANCE for the GOVERNMENT of the TERRITORY of the UNITED STATES, North-Weſt of the RIVER OHIO.

BE IT ORDAINED by the United States in Congreſs aſſembled, That the ſaid territory, for the purpoſes of temporary government, be one diſtrict; ſubject, however, to be divided into two diſtricts, as future circumſtances may, in the opinion of Congreſs, make it expedient.

Be it ordained by the authority aforeſaid, That the eſtates both of reſident and non-reſident proprietors in the ſaid territory, dying inteſtate, ſhall deſcend to, and be diſtributed among their children, and the deſcendants of a deceaſed child in equal parts; the deſcendants of a deceaſed child or grand-child, to take the ſhare of their deceaſed parent in equal parts among them: And where there ſhall be no children or deſcendants, then in equal parts to the next of kin, in equal degree; and among collaterals, the children of a deceaſed brother or ſiſter of the inteſtate, ſhall have in equal parts among them their deceaſed parents ſhare; and there ſhall in no caſe be a diſtinction between kindred of the whole and half blood; ſaving in all caſes to the widow of the inteſtate, her third part of the real eſtate for life, and one third part of the perſonal eſtate; and this law relative to deſcents and dower, ſhall remain in full force until altered by the legiſlature of the diſtrict. ——— And until the governor and judges ſhall adopt laws as herein after mentioned, eſtates in the ſaid territory may be deviſed or bequeathed by wills in writing, ſigned and ſealed by him or her, in whom the eſtate may be, (being of full age) and atteſted by three witneſſes; —— and real eſtates may be conveyed by leaſe and releaſe, or bargain and ſale, ſigned, ſealed, and delivered by the perſon being of full age, in whom the eſtate may be, and atteſted by two witneſſes, provided ſuch wills be duly proved, and ſuch conveyances be acknowledged, or the execution thereof duly proved, and be recorded within one year after proper magiſtrates, courts, and regiſters ſhall be appointed for that purpoſe; and perſonal property may be transferred by delivery, ſaving, however, to the French and Canadian inhabitants, and other ſettlers of the Kaſkaſkies, Saint Vincent's, and the neighbouring villages, who have heretofore profeſſed themſelves citizens of Virginia, their laws and cuſtoms now in force among them, relative to the deſcent and conveyance of property.

Be it ordained by the authority aforeſaid, That there ſhall be appointed from time to time, by Congreſs, a governor, whoſe commiſſion ſhall continue in force for the term of three years, unleſs ſooner revoked by Congreſs; he ſhall reſide in the diſtrict, and have a freehold eſtate therein, in one thouſand acres of land, while in the exerciſe of his office.

There ſhall be appointed from time to time, by Congreſs, a ſecretary, whoſe commiſſion ſhall continue in force for four years, unleſs ſooner revoked, he ſhall reſide in the diſtrict, and have a freehold eſtate therein, in five hundred acres of land, while in the exerciſe of his office; it ſhall be his duty to keep and preſerve the acts and laws paſſed by the legiſlature, and the public records of the diſtrict, and the proceedings of the governor in his executive department; and tranſmit authentic copies of ſuch acts and proceedings, every ſix months, to the ſecretary of Congreſs: There ſhall alſo be appointed a court to conſiſt of three judges, any two of whom to form a court, who ſhall have a common law juriſdiction, and reſide in the diſtrict, and have each therein a freehold eſtate in five hundred acres of land, while in the exerciſe of their offices; and their commiſſions ſhall continue in force during good behaviour.

The governor and judges, or a majority of them, ſhall adopt and publiſh in the diſtrict, ſuch laws of the original ſtates, criminal and civil, as may be neceſſary, and beſt ſuited to the circumſtances of the diſtrict, and report them to Congreſs, from time to time, which laws ſhall be in force in the diſtrict until the organization of the general aſſembly therein, unleſs diſapproved of by Congreſs; but afterwards the legiſlature ſhall have authority to alter them as they ſhall think fit.

The governor for the time being, ſhall be commander in chief of the militia, appoint and commiſſion all officers in the ſame, below the rank of general officers; all general officers ſhall be appointed and commiſſioned by Congreſs.

Previous to the organization of the general aſſembly, the governor ſhall appoint ſuch magiſtrates and other civil officers, in each county or townſhip, as he ſhall find neceſſary for the preſervation of the peace and good order in the ſame: After the general aſſembly ſhall be organized, the powers and duties of magiſtrates and other civil officers ſhall be regulated and defined by the ſaid aſſembly; but all magiſtrates and other civil officers, not herein otherwiſe directed, ſhall, during the continuance of this temporary government, be appointed by the governor.

For the prevention of crimes and injuries, the laws to be adopted or made ſhall have force in all parts of the diſtrict, and for the execution of proceſs, criminal and civil, the governor ſhall make proper diviſions thereof---and he ſhall proceed from time to time, as circumſtances may require, to lay out the parts of the diſtrict in which the Indian titles ſhall have been extinguiſhed, into counties and townſhips, ſubject, however, to ſuch alterations as may thereafter be made by the legiſlature.

So ſoon as there ſhall be five thouſand free male inhabitants, of full age, in the diſtrict, upon giving proof thereof to the governor, they ſhall receive authority, with time and place, to elect repreſentatives from their counties or townſhips, to repreſent them in the general aſſembly; provided that for every five hundred free male inhabitants there ſhall be one repreſentative, and ſo on progreſſively with the number of free male inhabitants, ſhall the right of repreſentation increaſe, until the number of repreſentatives ſhall amount to twenty-five, after which the number and proportion of repreſentatives ſhall be regulated by the legiſlature; provided that no perſon be eligible or qualified to act as a repreſentative, unleſs he ſhall have been a citizen of one of the United States three years and be a reſident in the diſtrict, or unleſs he ſhall have reſided in the diſtrict three years, and in either caſe ſhall likewiſe hold in his own right, in fee ſimple, two hundred acres of land within the ſame:---Provided alſo, that a freehold in fifty acres of land in the diſtrict, having been a citizen of one of the ſtates, and being reſident in the diſtrict; or the like freehold and two years reſidence in the diſtrict ſhall be neceſſary to qualify a man as an elector of a repreſentative.

The repreſentatives thus elected, ſhall ſerve for the term of two years, and in caſe of the death of a repreſentative, or removal from office, the governor ſhall iſſue a writ to the county or townſhip for which he was a member, to elect another in his ſtead, to ſerve for the reſidue of the term.

The general aſſembly, or legiſlature, ſhall conſiſt of the governor, legiſlative council, and a houſe of repreſentatives. The legiſlative council ſhall conſiſt of five members, to continue in office five years, unleſs ſooner removed by Congreſs, any three of whom to be a quorum, and the members of the council ſhall be nominated and appointed in the following manner, to wit: As ſoon as repreſentatives ſhall be elected, the governor ſhall appoint a time and place for them to

The Northwest Ordinance (National Archives and Records Administration)

Northwest Ordinance

1787

"Whenever any of the said States shall have sixty thousand free inhabitants therein, such State shall be admitted ... into the Congress of the United States, on an equal footing with the original States."

Overview

The Northwest Ordinance served as a bridge between the Declaration of Independence and the Articles of Confederation as well as between the Constitution and the Bill of Rights. It was the most significant legacy of the Confederation Congress. By providing a generous philosophical and practical structural framework for colonial territories to be governed and to evolve into full-fledged states, the Northwest Ordinance ensured that the United States would not encounter the same colonial problems as other empires. The cornerstone of the new imperial policy of the British Empire after 1763 was embodied in the Declaratory Act (1766), which proclaimed that Parliament could bind Americans "in all cases whatsoever" (http://www.constitution.org/bcp/decl_act.htm). The Northwest Ordinance did exactly the opposite, saying that once each of the American colonies reached a certain level of population, they could enter the Union as an equal member state. This policy, which was used for the five states that were carved out of the territory northwest of the Ohio River, served as the blueprint for most of the other territorial possessions of the United States that elected statehood.

At the time, some people (and later, some historians) condemned the Northwest Ordinance as antidemocratic because it abolished provisions of the Ordinance of 1784 that provided for immediate self-government in the territorial stage in preference for a system of colonial government in which Congress appointed the primary officers for an initial temporary territorial government. The Northwest Ordinance also withheld statehood until there was a population of sixty thousand, which is three times the size needed for permanent territorial government under the Ordinance of 1784. The Ordinance of 1784 then provided that the permanent territorial government could apply to Congress for statehood once the territory's population equaled the smallest population of the original thirteen states. According to Nathan Dane, the primary author of the Northwest Ordinance, "We wanted to abolish the old system [i.e., the Ordinance of 1784] and get a better one for the Government of the [Western] Country—and we finally found it necessary to adopt the best system we could get" (Nathan Dane to Rufus King, July 16, 1787; Smith, vol. 24, p. 358).

Context

The Treaty of Paris, which ended the American Revolution in 1783, gave the United States all land west to the Mississippi River, north to Canada, and south to Florida. Most of the land west of the Appalachian Mountains was unsettled except for a few scattered American, British, and French outposts. In essence, the thirteen original states had become the beneficiaries of a vast, unexplored empire thinly populated by American Indian tribes, most of which were hostile to the land-hungry white man. Thus, in winning its independence from colonial bondage, America ironically had itself become a colonial power. How would Americans administer their new empire? Would they make the same mistakes that Great Britain had made, or would new policies be formulated by the former colonists?

The first battle over the western lands occurred even before America had won its independence. America's first constitution, the Articles of Confederation, which Congress submitted to the states for their unanimous ratification on November 15, 1777, provided "that no state shall be deprived of territory for the benefit of the United States" (Article IX; Jensen et al., p. 90). This meant that those states that claimed western lands as a consequence of their colonial charters could not be forced to surrender that land to Congress.

Four states—Maryland, New Jersey, Delaware, and Rhode Island—had no claims to western lands. Maryland refused to ratify the Articles until the "landed states" ceded their western holdings to Congress. On October 10, 1780, Congress unsuccessfully tried to persuade the landed states to make cessions by promising that the western territory would be "formed into separate republican states, which shall become members of the federal union, and have the same rights and sovereignty, freedom and independence as the other states" (Ford et al., vol. 18, p. 915). Despite the states' refusal to cede their western lands to Congress, Maryland finally ratified the Articles on March, 1, 1781, because of the threat of a British invasion of the state.

Time Line

1777	■ **November 15** Congress submits the Articles of Confederation to the states for ratification.
1780	■ **October 10** Congress asks the states to cede their western lands.
1781	■ **January 2** Virginia cedes its lands northwest of the Ohio River to Congress; Congress does not accept it. ■ **March 1** Maryland's congressional delegates sign the Articles of Confederation, and the Articles are officially adopted.
1783	■ **October 15** Congress asks Virginia to make another cession of its western lands. ■ **December 20** Virginia makes its second cession of its western lands to Congress.
1784	■ **February 3** Congress appoints a committee to draft the Ordinance of 1784. ■ **March 1** Congress accepts Virginia's cession of western land. ■ **April 23** Congress adopts the Ordinance of 1784.
1785	■ **May 20** Congress approves the Ordinance of 1785 for the sale of western lands.
1786	■ **May 10** A committee of Congress reports that government should be established for the Northwest before the land is sold. ■ **September** Congress appoints a committee to draft the Northwest Ordinance.

Virginia had long been concerned about its extensive possessions, which included present-day Kentucky, West Virginia, Ohio, Indiana, Michigan, Illinois, Wisconsin, and part of Minnesota. While drafting its state constitution in 1776, several Virginians, citing a commonly held eighteenth-century theory that republics could survive only in small territories with homogeneous populations, stated that this vast Virginia empire threatened the state's republicanism. Thomas Jefferson, in particular, thought that Virginia, if it wanted to maintain any semblance of control, would be forced to rule over its western territory with despotic authority. This imperial despotism, it was feared, would lead to the loss of freedom and republicanism within the Old Dominion. Therefore, Jefferson and others argued that Virginia's western territory should be given independence and allowed to join other states as equals. Only in this way could the ideals of the Revolution be extended to the western lands and be preserved within those areas already settled.

Thus, Virginia delegates to Congress suggested a cession in 1777. The state formally ceded its western lands to Congress four years later but under restrictions that were unacceptable to a number of states. On October 15, 1783, Congress requested that Virginia make a new cession and resolved that government should be established "consistent with the principles of the Confederation" in the western territory as soon as possible (Jensen et al., p. 150). Two months later, on December 20, 1783, Virginia again offered Congress its territory northwest of the Ohio River.

On February 3, 1784, Congress appointed a committee, chaired by Jefferson, to draft provisions for the organization of the Northwest Territory. This committee was bound by the provisions of the resolutions of Congress of October 10, 1780, and October 15, 1783, and by the new Virginia cession, which required that the Northwest Territory be divided into states with borders not less than 100 miles nor more than 150 miles and that the new states be admitted into the Union on a basis of equality with the original states.

On March 1, 1784, Congress accepted Virginia's second cession, and on the same day it received the committee's report on the Northwest Territory. Congress debated the report and made several minor alterations and one major alteration before adopting the report on April 23, 1784. Congress deleted the committee's prohibition of slavery and indentured servitude. America's new colonial policy embodied in the Ordinance of 1784 would allow free, adult male settlers in a territory to create a temporary territorial government that would adopt a constitution and the laws of one of the original states. Once any territory attained a free population of twenty thousand it could call a convention, which would establish a permanent constitution and a republican form of government. Each new state had to agree to remain within the Confederation, to abide by the Articles of Confederation, to accept Congress's title to all land not already sold within its borders, and not to tax federal lands. When the new state attained a population equal to that of the smallest of the original thirteen states, it could petition Congress for admission to representation "on an equal footing" with the original states (Jensen et al., p. 152). Until then, each new state could be represented in Congress by a nonvoting delegate. Prior to the establishment of a temporary government, Congress would exercise control over the territory with "measures not inconsistent with the principles of the confederation, and necessary for the preservation of peace and good order among the settlers" (Jensen et al., p. 152).

It was thought that the entire western territory could be divided into fourteen new states, each approximating the size of New York. Jefferson's committee even suggested names for ten of the new states (Sylvania, Michigania, Assenisipia, Illinoia, Polypotamia, Cherronesus, Metropotamia, Saratoga, Pelisipia, and Washington), but the names were deleted from the final ordinance.

While Congress considered the Ordinance of 1784, it simultaneously considered provisions for the sale of the western territory. Public creditors, who saw the western lands as a source of revenue from which they could be paid, pressured Congress to devise a system for the sale of the public domain. Because of sectional disputes between the North and the South over how the land should be sold and settled, however, Congress did not agree to the Ordinance of 1785 until May 20, 1785.

By 1787 Congress faced a dilemma. Not all the states had ceded their western lands to the United States, and until that happened the Ordinance of 1784 would not be implemented. Furthermore, some of the northern states now had second thoughts about the creation of so many new states. Northerners feared that the new agricultural states of the West might be sympathetic with southern interests in Congress, thus shifting the balance of power against the North. In addition, America had just experienced a rash of violence in response to the economic depression of the mid-1780s. Farmers all over the country had tried to stop the operation of the civil courts in foreclosure proceedings. Sometimes this civil disobedience erupted in violence, most notably in Shays's Rebellion in Massachusetts and in the burning of two courthouses in backcountry Virginia. Could brash, unrestrained frontiersmen be expected to govern themselves responsibly when the "civilized" seacoast states found it difficult to control the more popular elements from electing majorities to the state legislatures and enacting radical social and economic policies? Rhode Island served as an example of what could happen if people led by demagogues seized power and used the machinery of government for their own interests. Perhaps the Ordinance of 1784, drafted during a time of euphoric prosperity, placed too much confidence in the people to govern themselves; perhaps a different colonial policy was needed.

At the same time that American politicians were questioning the advisability of the Ordinance of 1784, settlers were pouring into the western territories. The influx of these squatters heightened tensions with American Indians. Skirmishes occurred regularly on the frontier, and settlers demanded that the federal government protect them.

Time Line

1787

- **April**
  Congress begins debating the draft of the Northwest Ordinance.
- **May 25–September 17**
  The Constitutional Convention sits in Philadelphia.
- **July 13**
  Congress approves the Northwest Ordinance.
- **September 17**
  The Constitutional Convention proposes the Constitution.
- **October 27**
  Congress signs a contract with the Ohio Company for land purchase.

1788

- **June 21**
  New Hampshire is the ninth state to ratify the Constitution; thus, the Constitution is officially ratified.

1789

- **August 5**
  The first federal Congress adopts the Northwest Ordinance.
- **August 7**
  President Washington signs the act.

1803

- **February 10**
  Ohio is the first state from the Northwest Territory to enter the Union.

Easterners, however, could see only the huge expense of fighting American Indians in one war after another to satisfy the land-hungry appetites of westerners.

The West, however, did not merely pose problems for Congress. Beginning in late 1786, several land companies began to form with the intention of moving large groups of settlers to the western lands. These companies wanted to buy huge parcels of land from Congress, something Congress was eager to do because of its need to raise revenue to pay its wartime debt. Thus, the population of the West was about to soar from both this "legitimate" migration and from those many Americans who just picked up their belongings and moved to greener pastures. The increased population forced Congress to rethink its colonial policies.

In early 1786 Congress appointed a grand committee (one member from every state) to reconsider the Ordinance of 1784. Virginia delegate James Monroe had visited the

www.milestonedocuments.com

western territory and returned with an unfavorable opinion of the settlers. He stated that perhaps there would never be enough settlers to warrant their admittance into the Union as an equal state and, furthermore, that the settlers' interests might not coincide with those of the Confederation. On March 24, 1786, the grand committee reported that the expected ten states to be established in the Northwest Territory should be reduced to a smaller number. Another committee, which included Monroe, William Samuel Johnson of Connecticut, Rufus King of Massachusetts, and John Kean and Charles Pinckney of South Carolina and which was named on March 27, reported on May 10 that government over the territory should be established before any of the land was sold and that the officials of the territorial government ought to be appointed by Congress and not elected directly by inhabitants.

Congress debated the committee report of May 10 in July and September 1786, when a new committee was appointed consisting of chairman Nathan Dane of Massachusetts, Johnson, Pinckney, Melancton Smith of New York, and William Henry of Maryland. Congress considered the committee's report in April 1787, shortly before Congress officially received an offer to purchase western lands from the Ohio Company. Negotiations for the sale of the land and the debate over governmental policies for the territory proceeded simultaneously. On July 9, 1787, Congress appointed another committee to report a final ordinance. The committee consisted of Dane, Smith, Kean, and Edward Carrington and Richard Henry Lee of Virginia. On July 13 Congress approved the Northwest Ordinance by a unanimous vote of the attending eight states. Of the attending eighteen delegates, only Abraham Yates of New York voted against the ordinance; according to Nathan Dane, Yates "appeared in this Case, as in most other[s] not to understand the subject at all" (Nathan Dane to Rufus King, July 16, 1787; Smith, vol. 24, p. 358). Ten days later Congress authorized the Board of Treasury to negotiate a contract with the Ohio Company. A contract with the company's agents was signed on October 27, 1787.

Many of the provisions of the Northwest Ordinance were taken from the Ordinance of 1784, but there were some significant alterations. The Northwest Ordinance was composed of seven general provisions: (1) the organization of a territorial government; (2) a bill of rights; (3) the encouragement of schools and religion and the fair treatment of American Indians; (4) the obligations placed on inhabitants; (5) the creation of new states from the territory; (6) a prohibition of slavery and involuntary servitude; and (7) the repeal of the Ordinance of 1784. Because the new Constitution contained nothing in it guaranteeing that new states should be admitted into the Union on an equal basis with the original states, the first federal Congress on August 5, 1789, reaffirmed that promise by enacting the Northwest Ordinance into law. The law also gave the president, not Congress, the power to appoint territorial officers with the advice and consent of the Senate. President George Washington signed the bill two days later.

About the Author

Many people played a role in the various drafts of the 1784 and 1787 ordinances. Thomas Jefferson was the primary author of the Ordinance of 1784, and James Monroe was the congressional delegate who suggested that the liberal provisions of Jefferson's ordinance be replaced with greater congressional control over settlers in the territory. It is generally acknowledged, however, that Nathan Dane of Massachusetts was the primary author of the Northwest Ordinance. Three days after the passage of the ordinance, Dane wrote to a friend listing the members of the committee that submitted the final draft. Dane said, "We met several times and at last agreed on some principles, at least Lee, Smith & myself.... When I drew the ordinance which passed (in a few words excepted) as I originally formed it" (Nathan Dane to Rufus King, July 16, 1787; Smith, vol. 24, p. 357).

On March 26, 1830, Dane wrote a letter to Daniel Webster confirming that he was the author of the ordinance and that Thomas Hart Benton's attribution to Thomas Jefferson as the author was incorrect. Dane said that Benton ascribed the ordinance's

> formation, in substance to Mr. Jefferson; that is, that Mr. Jefferson formed an ordinance in 1784, & he seems to infer, from that the Ordinance of '87 was taken or copied. This inference of Benton's, has not the least foundation, as thus appears. Mr. Jefferson's resolve or plan, (not ordinance) of April 23d 1784, is contained in two pages & a half; is a mere incipient plan, in no manner matured for practice, as may be seen. The ordinance of July, 1787, contains eight pages, is in itself a complete system, & finished for practice; and what is very material, there cannot be found in it more than twenty lines taken from Jefferson's plan, & these worded differently. In fact, his plan & this ordinance, are totally different, in size, in style, in form, & in principle. Probably not one person in a thousand knows or suspects this essential difference. (Wiltse, vol. 3, pp. 43–44)

Nathan Dane, the son of a farmer, was born in Ipswich, Massachusetts, on December 29, 1752. After attending common schools, Dane studied on his own and was admitted to Harvard in 1774. He graduated in 1778 and studied law with William Wetmore in Salem. He married Mrs. Mary Brown in 1779 and moved to Beverly, Massachusetts. In 1782 he was admitted to the bar and was elected by Beverly to serve in the state House of Representatives. From 1785 to 1787 he served in the Confederation Congress. He was an ardent opponent of the new Constitution when it was debated in Congress in September 1787, and he was an unsuccessful candidate for the Massachusetts ratifying convention. In mid-1788 he helped persuade New York Antifederalist leaders to ratify the Constitution and work for amendments within Congress.

He retired from Congress in 1788 and resumed his law practice. In 1790 Essex County elected him to the state senate, where he served until 1798, when increasing deafness caused him to resign. In 1795 he became a commissioner to revise the state's laws—a task that took a decade to accomplish. In 1812 he was a presidential elector committed to De Witt Clinton of New York. His last public appearance was at the ill-fated Hartford Convention in 1814, where he attempted to restrain the more extreme Federalists. He died in Beverly on February 15, 1835.

Explanation and Analysis of the Document

According to the Northwest Ordinance, the land northwest of the Ohio River initially was to be governed as a single territory, subject to division later by Congress. During this territorial stage, Congress was to appoint the primary officeholders, who had to be residents of the territory and were required to take an oath of fidelity: a governor with a three-year term, a secretary with a five-year term, three judges to serve during good behavior, and all generals in the militia. The governor had to possess a freehold estate of one thousand acres, while the secretary and judges needed freeholds of at least five hundred acres. The governor would appoint all other officeholders and, with the judges, would adopt all civil and criminal laws subject only to the veto of Congress.

According to Section 9, when a territory reached a population of five thousand free adult males, it could establish a bicameral legislature. The territorial house of representatives would at first be proportioned at a ratio of one representative for every five hundred men. The number of representatives could increase to a maximum of twenty-five, after which the ratio would be adjusted to the increasing population. Each representative had to have been a citizen for three years and had to own two hundred acres of land. Only adult males who owned fifty acres of land and had been citizens for at least a year could vote.

A council of five would make up the second branch of the territorial legislature. The representatives would nominate ten men for the council, out of whom Congress would select five. Vacancies could be filled by the nomination of two names of qualified individuals, from whom Congress would select one person to serve the residue of the term. Laws could be passed only with the approval of both houses of the legislature and the concurrence of the governor. The legislature could elect a nonvoting delegate to Congress. The governor, representatives, and council made up the general assembly, which could pass all laws "not repugnant to the principles and articles in" the Northwest Ordinance (Section II). The governor could convene, prorogue, or dissolve the general assembly.

In Section 14, the ordinance contains an abbreviated bill of rights that guarantees the inhabitants of the territory freedom of religion, the writ of habeas corpus, the right to trial by jury, due process of law, reasonable bail and fines, no cruel or unusual punishments, and a proper proportionate representation in the legislature. Contracts could not be impaired, and government was required to make fair compensation when expropriating property under the right of eminent domain. The ordinance disallows primogeniture and entail. Religion and education, necessary ingredients to good government, are to be encouraged, while American Indians are to be treated fairly. Laws dealing with American Indians aimed at "preserving peace and friendship" had to be just and humane. Slavery and involuntary servitude were prohibited except as punishment for crimes of which the individual had been duly convicted.

Inhabitants of the territory were under certain obligations. They were committed to remain within the Confederation, to abide by the Articles of Confederation, and to pay their fair share of the country's governmental expenses. They had to acknowledge the Confederation's ownership of all land not yet sold and never tax federal property. Property of nonresidents could not be taxed at a higher rate than inhabitants' property; all navigable waters leading to the Mississippi and Saint Lawrence rivers, "and the carrying places between the same," were to be considered "common highways, and forever free" to all Americans.

Once any part of the territory attained a population of sixty thousand, it could apply to Congress for statehood "on an equal footing with the original States in all respects." The new state could then adopt a permanent constitution and state government, both of which had to be based on republican principles. A minimum of three and a maximum of five new states were to be created out of the Northwest Territory. The last provision of the ordinance repeals the Ordinance of 1784.

Audience

The Northwest Ordinance was primarily addressed to the people residing in the territory northwest of the Ohio River, who were told what rights they had and what obligations they were bound to observe. The rights and duties embodied in the ordinance were said to be a "compact between the original States and the people and States in the said territory and forever remain unalterable, unless by common consent." The ordinance was also addressed to future congresses and to peoples throughout the world, telling them that America would not keep another group of people in colonial status. Americans in the original states were also assured that territorial residents would be under restrictions to behave properly under limits set by Congress. They had to maintain a republican form of government, protect property, and abide by laws in conformity with the Articles of Confederation. By setting the blueprint for the evolution of territories into statehood, the ordinance extended its audience both in time and geography to include almost all the states that subsequently became part of the Union.

Impact

The Articles of Confederation, America's first constitution, is considered a failure by most historians. The thir-

www.milestonedocuments.com

Essential Quotes

"No person, demeaning himself in a peaceable and orderly manner, shall ever be molested on account of his mode of worship or religious sentiments, in the said territory."

(Section 14, Article 1)

"Religion, morality, and knowledge, being necessary to good government and the happiness of mankind, schools and the means of education shall forever be encouraged."

(Section 14, Article 3)

"The utmost good faith shall always be observed towards the Indians; their lands and property shall never be taken from them without their consent."

(Section 14, Article 3)

"The navigable waters leading into the Mississippi and St. Lawrence, and the carrying places between the same, shall be common highways and forever free, as well to the inhabitants of the said territory as to the citizens of the United States."

(Section 14, Article 4)

"Whenever any of the said States shall have sixty thousand free inhabitants therein, such State shall be admitted, by its delegates, into the Congress of the United States, on an equal footing with the original States in all respects whatever, and shall be at liberty to form a permanent constitution and State government: Provided, the constitution and government so to be formed, shall be republican, and in conformity to the principles contained in these articles."

(Section 14, Article 5)

"There shall be neither slavery nor involuntary servitude in the said territory, otherwise than in the punishment of crimes whereof the party shall have been duly convicted."

(Section 14, Article 6)

teen states, which successfully fought the mightiest nation in the world, now found that they were drifting apart during the eight short years of the Confederation. As dismal as the Confederation's record was, however, there were a number of significant successes. Perhaps the most important was the Confederation's land policy. This success is all the more remarkable because of the many obstacles that had to be overcome in formulating a policy that would remain intact for the complete continental expansion of the United States.

The initial problem faced by Congress was that it officially had no power to enact legislation dealing with the West. The Articles of Confederation were completely silent on these issues; consequently, Congress had no authorization to act. Despite this constitutional qualm, necessity demanded and obtained congressional action.

Difficulties also arose after 1786 because of the political and economic problems of the Confederation. Easterners, especially New Englanders, opposed the establishment of new states in the West because they feared the loss of their own population to the new states, which would translate into lower property values, reduced markets for goods, and higher prices for labor. These were serious matters during a time when the entire country was in the throes of a deep economic depression.

Northerners also feared that the new western states would ally with the South in congressional politics. Sectional politics, suppressed to a certain degree during the Revolution, continually operated in postwar America, reaching fever pitch in 1786, when it was disclosed that the northern states were willing to forgo America's right to navigate the Mississippi River for twenty-five or thirty years in exchange for a commercial treaty with Spain. Southerners and westerners adamantly protested this policy, which would have bottled the exports of the ever-increasing bulky agricultural produce of settlers in Kentucky and Tennessee.

Southerners feared that the expanding agricultural production of the Northwest Territory would compete with their staple crops. Prices for tobacco and indigo had already fallen precipitously. To forestall this competition, southerners, for the first time, joined northerners in agreeing to ban slavery from the Northwest Territory. Thus, in a fortunate coincidence, economics and egalitarianism combined to prohibit slavery. However, by overtly prohibiting slavery from the Northwest Territory, Congress was tacitly allowing the expansion of slavery into the Southwest Territory.

Easterners as a whole also realized that their own state's power in Congress would diminish with the admission of every new state. Since each state had but one vote in Congress, the admission of fourteen moderately sized new states in the West would have a greater effect than the addition of only three to five large states. Fourteen new western states could, in fact, outvote the thirteen original states. Therefore, the concept of forming small states that would be more likely to sustain republican forms of government gave way to a world of political realty in which sheer numbers of states, which would translate into numbers of congressional votes, became the dominant factor.

Easterners also worried about the danger of war emanating from the West. Great Britain had had similar fears and consequently proclaimed in 1763 that its American colonists could not migrate beyond the Appalachian Mountains. Now, with land-hungry Americans flooding into the West, conflicts with American Indians were inevitable. Western settlers could also provoke a war with the British in Canada and the Spanish in the Louisiana and West Florida territories. If war occurred, easterners knew that they would be taxed to pay for it. They also knew that in any war with Britain or Spain, the eastern seacoast and its commerce would be ravaged by the enemy's navy, especially since Congress had sold its last warship in 1786.

Because of these fears, many easterners wanted Congress to exercise control over westerners, especially during the territorial stage of development. Thus, the Northwest Ordinance provided that Congress would appoint the most important territorial officials, while the governor would appoint the lesser officials. Frontiersmen and settlers would not be given self-government immediately. They would have to earn their equal status with the other states. Some contemporaries and some later historians criticized this retreat from the more democratic principles of Jefferson's Ordinance of 1784.

At the same time, easterners remembered the events that led to the Declaration of Independence. They knew that a distant imperial government could easily become despotic. To guard the liberties of the territorial inhabitants, Congress incorporated an abbreviated bill of rights into the Northwest Ordinance. Some of the states had their own bills of rights at that time, but there was no federal bill of rights because the Articles of Confederation forbade Congress from acting directly on the people. Congress had to deal with the states; state governments dealt with the people. Now, Congress would be directly involved in the lives of people residing in the territories. Westerners thus needed a bill of rights to protect themselves from the potential oppression of a distant imperial government in which they had no representation.

Despite the easterners' fears, Americans always believed that the new western states should be admitted into the Union on an equal footing with the original states. Americans knew what it meant to be colonists. They had fought a long war to escape from colonial status and were not eager to reestablish a colonial relationship, even one in which they would be dominant. As they did not wish to be colonies, so they did not wish to be dominant over colonies. They knew such a position of dominance would affect the democratic ideals for which they had fought. They also knew that just as they had fought for their freedom, so too would their colonies fight for equality. Therefore, in an act of both generosity and great pragmatic omniscience, the Northwest Ordinance provided that future states should come into the Union as equals.

At the same time that Congress in New York City enacted the Northwest Ordinance, the Constitutional Convention sat in Philadelphia debating a new Constitution. The convention introduced two provisions from the Northwest

www.milestonedocuments.com

Ordinance into its debate on August 28 and agreed later that the fugitive slave clause and the prohibition on state governments from enacting any kind of impairment of contracts be included in the new Constitution. On August 29, on a motion of Gouverneur Morris of Pennsylvania, the convention agreed (nine states to two) to remove the clause guaranteeing that new states would be admitted to the Union on a basis of equality with the original states. Because the first federal Congress wanted the Northwest Ordinance to "continue to have full effect," a bill was enacted in August 1789 to adapt the ordinance to the new Constitution (Bickford and Veit, p. 1561). No longer would Congress make appointments and fill vacancies; the president, with the advice and consent of the U.S. Senate, would perform these duties.

Related Documents

Bickford, Charlene Bangs, and Helen E. Veit, eds. *Documentary History of the First Federal Congress of the United States of America*. Vol. 6: *Legislative Histories*. Baltimore, Md.: Johns Hopkins University Press, 1986. This volume contains the legislative history of Congress's passage of the Northwest Ordinance in 1789.

Farrand, Max, ed. *The Records of the Federal Convention of 1787*. 4 vols. New Haven, Conn.: Yale University Press, 1966. This collection of debates has the Constitutional Convention's consideration of three provisions from the Northwest Ordinance, enacted by Congress in New York City while the Convention continued to sit in Philadelphia.

Ford, Worthington C. et al., eds. *Journals of the Continental Congress, 1774–1789*. 34 vols. Washington, D.C.: U.S. Government Printing Office, 1904. All of Congress's committee assignments and resolutions with roll-call votes appear in this valuable collection.

Jensen, Merrill, John P. Kaminski, and Gaspare J. Saladino. *Constitutional Documents and Records, 1776–1787*. Vol. 1: *The Documentary History of the Ratification of the Constitution*. 20 vols. Madison: State Historical Society of Wisconsin, 1976. This volume contains the text of the land ordinances of 1784, 1785, and 1787, along with headnotes placing them in historical context.

Smith, Paul H., ed. *Letters of Delegates to Congress, 1774–1789*. 26 vols. Washington, D.C.: Library of Congress, 1976–2000. This collection has all of the letters written by delegates to Congress when the various land ordinances, including the Northwest Ordinance, were being considered.

Bibliography

■ Articles

Shriver, Philip R. "America's Other Bicentennial." *The Old Northwest* 9 (Fall 1983): 219–235.

■ Books

Cayton, Andrew R. L. *The Frontier Republic: Ideology and Politics in the Ohio Country, 1780–1825*. Kent, Ohio: Kent State University Press, 1986.

Eblen, Jack Ericson. *The First and Second United States Empires*. Pittsburgh, Pa.: University of Pittsburgh Press, 1968.

Jacobson, Daniel. *The Northwest Ordinance of 1787: A Special Teaching Unit*. East Lansing: Michigan State University Alumni Association, 1987.

Onuf, Peter S. *Statehood and Union: A History of the Northwest Ordinance*. Bloomington: Indiana University Press, 1987.

Patrick, John J. *Lessons on the Northwest Ordinance: A Teaching Unit of Six Lessons*. Bloomington: Social Studies Development Center of Indiana University, 1986.

Peckham, Howard, ed. *Liberty's Legacy: Our Celebration of the Northwest Ordinance and the United States Constitution*. Columbus: Ohio Historical Society, 1987.

Rakove, Jack N. *The Beginnings of National Politics: An Interpretive History of the Continental Congress*. New York: Alfred A. Knopf, 1979.

Skaggs, David Curtis, ed. *The Old Northwest in the American Revolution: An Anthology*. Madison: State Historical Society of Wisconsin, 1977.

Taylor, Robert M., Jr., ed. *The Northwest Ordinance, 1787: A Bicentennial Handbook*. Indianapolis: Indiana Historical Society, 1987.

Wiltse, Charles, ed. *The Papers of Daniel Webster*. 14 vols. Hanover, N.H.: University Press of New England, 1974–1989.

■ Web Sites

"The Declaratory Act, March 18, 1766." Constitution Society Web site.
http://www.constitution.org/bcp/decl_act.htm. Accessed on December 21, 2007.

"The Northwest Ordinance, 1787." Wisconsin Historical Society Web site.
http://www.wisconsinhistory.org/turningpoints/tp-009. Accessed on November 1, 2007.

—By John P. Kaminski

Questions for Further Study

1. Why was the Northwest Territory limited to become only three to five states?
2. Compare the Ordinance of 1784 and the Northwest Ordinance.
3. What future states did not use the provisions of the Northwest Ordinance in becoming states?
4. Were the policies of the Northwest Ordinance toward American Indians maintained?

www.milestonedocuments.com

Glossary

collaterals	collateral relatives as opposed to lineal ones
compact	an agreement between two or more parties
dower	the part of interest in the real estate of a deceased husband given to his widow during her life
freehold	land held free of obligation for life
intestate	having made no valid will
proprietors	owners
proportionate representation	an electoral system designed to represent in a legislative body each political group in proportion to its actual voting strength in the electorate
prorogue	to defer or postpone
quorum	the number of members of a body that when duly assembled is legally competent to do business
writ of habeas corpus	judicial order to bring a person before a court or judge

Document Text

Northwest Ordinance

An Ordinance for the government of the Territory of the United States northwest of the River Ohio.

◆ **Section 1.**

Be it ordained by the United States in Congress assembled, That the said territory, for the purposes of temporary government, be one district, subject, however, to be divided into two districts, as future circumstances may, in the opinion of Congress, make it expedient.

◆ **Sec 2.**

Be it ordained by the authority aforesaid, That the estates, both of resident and nonresident proprietors in the said territory, dying intestate, shall descent to, and be distributed among their children, and the descendants of a deceased child, in equal parts; the descendants of a deceased child or grandchild to take the share of their deceased parent in equal parts among them: And where there shall be no children or descendants, then in equal parts to the next of kin in equal degree; and among collaterals, the children of a deceased brother or sister of the intestate shall have, in equal parts among them, their deceased parents' share; and there shall in no case be a distinction between kindred of the whole and half blood; saving, in all cases, to the widow of the intestate her third part of the real estate for life, and one third part of the personal estate; and this law relative to descents and dower, shall remain in full force until altered by the legislature of the district. And until the governor and judges shall adopt laws as hereinafter mentioned, estates in the said territory may be devised or bequeathed by wills in writing, signed and sealed by him or her in whom the estate may be (being of full age), and attested by three witnesses; and real estates may be conveyed by lease and release, or bargain and sale, signed, sealed and delivered by the person being of full age, in whom the estate may be, and attested by two witnesses, provided such wills be duly proved, and such conveyances be acknowledged, or the execution thereof duly proved, and be recorded within one year after proper magistrates, courts, and registers shall be appointed for that purpose; and personal property may be transferred by delivery; saving, however to the French and Canadian inhabitants, and other settlers of the Kaskaskies, St. Vincents and the neighboring villages who have heretofore professed themselves citizens of Virginia, their laws and customs now in force among them, relative to the descent and conveyance, of property.

◆ **Sec. 3.**

Be it ordained by the authority aforesaid, That there shall be appointed from time to time by Congress, a governor, whose commission shall continue in force for the term of three years, unless sooner revoked by Congress; he shall reside in the district, and have a freehold estate therein in 1,000 acres of land, while in the exercise of his office.

◆ **Sec. 4.**

There shall be appointed from time to time by Congress, a secretary, whose commission shall continue in force for four years unless sooner revoked; he shall reside in the district, and have a freehold estate therein in 500 acres of land, while in the exercise of his office. It shall be his duty to keep and preserve the acts and laws passed by the legislature, and the public records of the district, and the proceedings of the governor in his executive department, and transmit authentic copies of such acts and proceedings, every six months, to the Secretary of Congress: There shall also be appointed a court to consist of three judges, any two of whom to form a court, who shall have a common law jurisdiction, and reside in the district, and have each therein a freehold estate in 500 acres of land while in the exercise of their offices; and their commissions shall continue in force during good behavior.

◆ **Sec. 5.**

The governor and judges, or a majority of them, shall adopt and publish in the district such laws of the original States, criminal and civil, as may be necessary and best suited to the circumstances of the district, and report them to Congress from time to time: which laws shall be in force in the district until the organization of the General Assembly therein, unless disapproved of by Congress; but afterwards the Legislature shall have authority to alter them as they shall think fit.

◆ **Sec. 6.**

The governor, for the time being, shall be commander in chief of the militia, appoint and commission all officers in the same below the rank of general officers; all general officers shall be appointed and commissioned by Congress.

◆ **Sec. 7.**

Previous to the organization of the general assembly, the governor shall appoint such magistrates and other civil officers in each county or township, as he shall find necessary for the preservation of the peace and good order in the same: After the general assembly shall be organized, the powers and duties of the magistrates and other civil officers shall be regulated and defined by the said assembly; but all magistrates and other civil officers not herein otherwise directed, shall during the continuance of this temporary government, be appointed by the governor.

◆ **Sec. 8.**

For the prevention of crimes and injuries, the laws to be adopted or made shall have force in all parts of the district, and for the execution of process, criminal and civil, the governor shall make proper divisions thereof; and he shall proceed from time to time as circumstances may require, to lay out the parts of the district in which the Indian titles shall have been extinguished, into counties and townships, subject, however, to such alterations as may thereafter be made by the legislature.

◆ **Sec. 9.**

So soon as there shall be five thousand free male inhabitants of full age in the district, upon giving proof thereof to the governor, they shall receive authority, with time and place, to elect a representative from their counties or townships to represent them in the general assembly: Provided, That, for every five hundred free male inhabitants, there shall be one representative, and so on progressively with the number of free male inhabitants shall the right of representation increase, until the number of representatives shall amount to twenty five; after which, the number and proportion of representatives shall be regulated by the legislature: Provided, That no person be eligible or qualified to act as a representative unless he shall have been a citizen of one of the United States three years, and be a resident in the district, or unless he shall have resided in the district three years; and, in either case, shall likewise hold in his own right, in fee simple, two hundred acres of land within the same; Provided, also, That a freehold in fifty acres of land in the district, having been a citizen of one of the states, and being resident in the district, or the like freehold and two years residence in the district, shall be necessary to qualify a man as an elector of a representative.

◆ **Sec. 10.**

The representatives thus elected, shall serve for the term of two years; and, in case of the death of a representative, or removal from office, the governor shall issue a writ to the county or township for which he was a member, to elect another in his stead, to serve for the residue of the term.

◆ **Sec. 11.**

The general assembly or legislature shall consist of the governor, legislative council, and a house of representatives. The Legislative Council shall consist of five members, to continue in office five years, unless sooner removed by Congress; any three of whom to be a quorum: and the members of the Council shall be nominated and appointed in the following manner, to wit: As soon as representatives shall be elected, the Governor shall appoint a time and place for them to meet together; and, when met, they shall nominate ten persons, residents in the district, and each possessed of a freehold in five hundred acres of land, and return their names to Congress; five of whom Congress shall appoint and commission to serve as aforesaid; and, whenever a vacancy shall happen in the council, by death or removal from office, the house of representatives shall nominate two persons, qualified as aforesaid, for each vacancy, and return their names to Congress; one of whom congress shall appoint and commission for the residue of the term. And every five years, four

www.milestonedocuments.com

months at least before the expiration of the time of service of the members of council, the said house shall nominate ten persons, qualified as aforesaid, and return their names to Congress; five of whom Congress shall appoint and commission to serve as members of the council five years, unless sooner removed. And the governor, legislative council, and house of representatives, shall have authority to make laws in all cases, for the good government of the district, not repugnant to the principles and articles in this ordinance established and declared. And all bills, having passed by a majority in the house, and by a majority in the council, shall be referred to the governor for his assent; but no bill, or legislative act whatever, shall be of any force without his assent. The governor shall have power to convene, prorogue, and dissolve the general assembly, when, in his opinion, it shall be expedient.

◆ Sec. 12.

The governor, judges, legislative council, secretary, and such other officers as Congress shall appoint in the district, shall take an oath or affirmation of fidelity and of office; the governor before the president of congress, and all other officers before the Governor. As soon as a legislature shall be formed in the district, the council and house assembled in one room, shall have authority, by joint ballot, to elect a delegate to Congress, who shall have a seat in Congress, with a right of debating but not voting during this temporary government.

◆ Sec. 13.

And, for extending the fundamental principles of civil and religious liberty, which form the basis whereon these republics, their laws and constitutions are erected; to fix and establish those principles as the basis of all laws, constitutions, and governments, which forever hereafter shall be formed in the said territory: to provide also for the establishment of States, and permanent government therein, and for their admission to a share in the federal councils on an equal footing with the original States, at as early periods as may be consistent with the general interest:

◆ Sec. 14.

It is hereby ordained and declared by the authority aforesaid, That the following articles shall be considered as articles of compact between the original States and the people and States in the said territory and forever remain unalterable, unless by common consent, to wit:

Art. 1. No person, demeaning himself in a peaceable and orderly manner, shall ever be molested on account of his mode of worship or religious sentiments, in the said territory.

Art. 2. The inhabitants of the said territory shall always be entitled to the benefits of the writ of habeas corpus, and of the trial by jury; of a proportionate representation of the people in the legislature; and of judicial proceedings according to the course of the common law. All persons shall be bailable, unless for capital offenses, where the proof shall be evident or the presumption great. All fines shall be moderate; and no cruel or unusual punishments shall be inflicted. No man shall be deprived of his liberty or property, but by the judgment of his peers or the law of the land; and, should the public exigencies make it necessary, for the common preservation, to take any person's property, or to demand his particular services, full compensation shall be made for the same. And, in the just preservation of rights and property, it is understood and declared, that no law ought ever to be made, or have force in the said territory, that shall, in any manner whatever, interfere with or affect private contracts or engagements, bona fide, and without fraud, previously formed.

Art. 3. Religion, morality, and knowledge, being necessary to good government and the happiness of mankind, schools and the means of education shall forever be encouraged. The utmost good faith shall always be observed towards the Indians; their lands and property shall never be taken from them without their consent; and, in their property, rights, and liberty, they shall never be invaded or disturbed, unless in just and lawful wars authorized by Congress; but laws founded in justice and humanity, shall from time to time be made for preventing wrongs being done to them, and for preserving peace and friendship with them.

Art. 4. The said territory, and the States which may be formed therein, shall forever remain a part of this Confederacy of the United States of America, subject to the Articles of Confederation, and to such alterations therein as shall be constitutionally made; and to all the acts and ordinances of the United States in Congress assembled, conformable thereto. The inhabitants and settlers in the said territory shall be subject to pay a part of the federal debts contracted or to be contracted, and a proportional part of the expenses of government, to be apportioned on them by Congress according to the same common rule and measure by which apportionments thereof shall be

Document Text

made on the other States; and the taxes for paying their proportion shall be laid and levied by the authority and direction of the legislatures of the district or districts, or new States, as in the original States, within the time agreed upon by the United States in Congress assembled. The legislatures of those districts or new States, shall never interfere with the primary disposal of the soil by the United States in Congress assembled, nor with any regulations Congress may find necessary for securing the title in such soil to the bona fide purchasers. No tax shall be imposed on lands the property of the United States; and, in no case, shall nonresident proprietors be taxed higher than residents. The navigable waters leading into the Mississippi and St. Lawrence, and the carrying places between the same, shall be common highways and forever free, as well to the inhabitants of the said territory as to the citizens of the United States, and those of any other States that may be admitted into the confederacy, without any tax, impost, or duty therefor.

Art. 5. There shall be formed in the said territory, not less than three nor more than five States; and the boundaries of the States, as soon as Virginia shall alter her act of cession, and consent to the same, shall become fixed and established as follows, to wit: The western State in the said territory, shall be bounded by the Mississippi, the Ohio, and Wabash Rivers; a direct line drawn from the Wabash and Post Vincents, due North, to the territorial line between the United States and Canada; and, by the said territorial line, to the Lake of the Woods and Mississippi. The middle State shall be bounded by the said direct line, the Wabash from Post Vincents to the Ohio, by the Ohio, by a direct line, drawn due north from the mouth of the Great Miami, to the said territorial line, and by the said territorial line. The eastern State shall be bounded by the last mentioned direct line, the Ohio, Pennsylvania, and the said territorial line: Provided, however, and it is further understood and declared, that the boundaries of these three States shall be subject so far to be altered, that, if Congress shall hereafter find it expedient, they shall have authority to form one or two States in that part of the said territory which lies north of an east and west line drawn through the southerly bend or extreme of Lake Michigan. And, whenever any of the said States shall have sixty thousand free inhabitants therein, such State shall be admitted, by its delegates, into the Congress of the United States, on an equal footing with the original States in all respects whatever, and shall be at liberty to form a permanent constitution and State government: Provided, the constitution and government so to be formed, shall be republican, and in conformity to the principles contained in these articles; and, so far as it can be consistent with the general interest of the confederacy, such admission shall be allowed at an earlier period, and when there may be a less number of free inhabitants in the State than sixty thousand.

Art. 6. There shall be neither slavery nor involuntary servitude in the said territory, otherwise than in the punishment of crimes whereof the party shall have been duly convicted: Provided, always, That any person escaping into the same, from whom labor or service is lawfully claimed in any one of the original States, such fugitive may be lawfully reclaimed and conveyed to the person claiming his or her labor or service as aforesaid.

• Be it ordained by the authority aforesaid, That the resolutions of the 23rd of April, 1784, relative to the subject of this ordinance, be, and the same are hereby repealed and declared null and void.

• Done by the United States, in Congress assembled, the 13th day of July, in the year of our Lord 1787, and of their soveriegnty and independence the twelfth.

www.milestonedocuments.com

We the People of the United States, in Order to form a more perfect Union, esta
nsure domestic Tranquility, provide for the common defence, promote the general Welfare, and secure the Blessings of Liber
nd our Posterity, do ordain and establish this Constitution for the United States of America.

Article. I.

Section. 1. All legislative Powers herein granted shall be vested in a Congress of the United States, which shall consist of a Sen
of Representatives.

Section. 2. The House of Representatives shall be composed of Members chosen every second Year by the People of the several Sta
n each State shall have the Qualifications requisite for Electors of the most numerous Branch of the State Legislature.

No Person shall be a Representative who shall not have attained to the Age of twenty five Years, and been seven Years a Citizen o
nd who shall not, when elected, be an Inhabitant of that State in which he shall be chosen.

Representatives and direct Taxes shall be apportioned among the several States which may be included within this Union, according to
Numbers, which shall be determined by adding to the whole Number of free Persons, including those bound to Service for a Term of Years, and
not taxed, three fifths of all other Persons. The actual Enumeration shall be made within three Years after the first Meeting of the Congress
nd within every subsequent Term of ten Years, in such Manner as they shall by Law direct. The Number of Representatives shall not e
irty Thousand, but each State shall have at Least one Representative; and until such enumeration shall be made, the State of New Ham
ntitled to chuse three, Massachusetts eight, Rhode Island and Providence Plantations one, Connecticut five, New York six, New Jersey f
ight, Delaware one, Maryland six, Virginia ten, North Carolina five, South Carolina five, and Georgia three.

When vacancies happen in the Representation from any State, the Executive Authority thereof shall issue Writs of Election to fill suc

The House of Representatives shall chuse their Speaker and other Officers; and shall have the sole Power of Impeachment.

Section. 3. The Senate of the United States shall be composed of two Senators from each State, chosen by the Legislature thereof, for six
Senator shall have one Vote.

Immediately after they shall be assembled in Consequence of the first Election, they shall be divided as equally as may be into thre
f the Senators of the first Class shall be vacated at the Expiration of the second Year, of the second Class at the Expiration of the fourth Year
lass at the Expiration of the sixth Year, so that one third may be chosen every second Year; and if Vacancies happen by Resignation, or other
Recess of the Legislature of any State, the Executive thereof may make temporary Appointments until the next Meeting of the Legislature, whic
uch Vacancies.

No Person shall be a Senator who shall not have attained to the Age of thirty Years, and been nine Years a Citizen of the United Sta
not, when elected, be an Inhabitant of that State for which he shall be chosen.

The Vice President of the United States shall be President of the Senate, but shall have no Vote, unless they be equally divided.

The Senate shall chuse their other Officers, and also a President pro tempore, in the Absence of the Vice President, or when he shall exer
President of the United States.

The Senate shall have the sole Power to try all Impeachments. When sitting for that Purpose, they shall be on Oath or Affirmatio
f the United States is tried, the Chief Justice shall preside: And no Person shall be convicted without the Concurrence of two thirds of the Members

Judgment in Cases of Impeachment shall not extend further than to removal from Office, and disqualification to hold and enjoy
Trust or Profit under the United States: but the Party convicted shall nevertheless be liable and subject to Indictment, Trial, Judgment an
ccording to Law.

Section. 4. The Times, Places and Manner of holding Elections for Senators and Representatives, shall be prescribed in each State
thereof; but the Congress may at any time by Law make or alter such Regulations, except as to the Places of chusing Senators.

The Congress shall assemble at least once in every Year, and such Meeting shall be on the first Monday in December, unless
ppoint a different Day.

Section. 5. Each House shall be the Judge of the Elections, Returns and Qualifications of its own Members, and a Majority of each sh
Quorum to do Business; but a smaller Number may adjourn from day to day, and may be authorized to compel the Attendance of abs
uch Manner, and under such Penalties as each House may provide.

Each House may determine the Rules of its Proceedings, punish its Members for disorderly Behaviour, and, with the Concurrence of
Member.

Each House shall keep a Journal of its Proceedings, and from time to time publish the same, excepting such Parts as may in their
Secrecy; and the Yeas and Nays of the Members of either House on any question shall, at the Desire of one fifth of those Present, be entered on th

Neither House, during the Session of Congress, shall, without the Consent of the other, adjourn for more than three days, nor to a
than that in which the two Houses shall be sitting.

Section. 6. The Senators and Representatives shall receive a Compensation for their Services, to be ascertained by Law, and paid ou
he United States. They shall in all Cases, except Treason, Felony and Breach of the Peace, be privileged from Arrest during their Atte
Session of their respective Houses, and in going to and returning from the same; and for any Speech or Debate in either House, they shall n
ny other Place.

No Senator or Representative shall, during the Time for which he was elected, be appointed to any civil Office under the Authority
which shall have been created, or the Emoluments whereof shall have been encreased during such time; and no Person holding any Office
States, shall be a Member of either House during his Continuance in Office.

tion. 7. All Bills for raising Revenue shall originate in the House of Representatives; but the Senate may propose or concur with Amend

Every Bill which shall have passed the House of Representatives and the Senate, shall, before it become a Law, be presented to the

The U.S. Constitution (National Archives and Records Administration)

Constitution of the United States

1787

"The United States shall guarantee to every State in this Union a Republican Form of Government."

Overview

After declaring independence from Great Britain, the thirteen American colonies adopted new constitutions for themselves and for the union that bound them together. The U.S. Constitution, which in 1787 proposed the federal government in the form known in the modern era, was in fact the second national constitution; the Articles of Confederation, enacted in 1781 as the first national constitution, provided for a weak central government that was little more than a league of friendship. A small group of nationalists had wanted a more powerful central government, but their efforts in the drafting of the articles had failed, as did their efforts to amend them and to give the Congress of the Confederation additional powers. When a postwar depression created political turmoil, social unrest, and violence, leading political figures throughout the country grew worried and agreed to amend the Articles of Confederation by means of a general convention of the states.

The Constitutional Convention convened in 1787 and deliberated in secret for four months. Controversy raged between delegates from the large and small states, between delegates from the northern and southern states, and between those who were nationalists and those who supported merely strengthening the existing confederation. Several compromises were eventually made, and a unique new form of government was presented to the states for ratification. After almost a year of public debate, the new U.S. Constitution was adopted, and Congress called for the first federal elections. Two years later the Bill of Rights was added to the Constitution, taking away one of the primary fears of the document's opponents—that it would reduce individual freedoms. Without the Constitution, the United States might have progressed much differently. The country could have developed a parliamentary system of government, adopted a monarchy, returned into the British Empire, or divided into multiple regional confederacies. Instead, the Constitution helped develop a large, powerful, and prosperous federal republic. However, since it failed to resolve the slavery issue, the Constitution aggravated the country's preexisting sectionalism and ultimately led to civil war.

Context

The presence of the common enemy inspired the thirteen states to cooperate during the American War of Independence. When the war ended, however, the states were less willing to abide by the dictates of Congress. Congress asked for revenue and the power to regulate commerce, but the states gave little money and surrendered no power to Congress. On the other hand, all of the states except Georgia ceded to Congress their rights to western lands; the sale of this public domain would potentially prove a huge source of revenue.

At the state level, despite universal support for the concept of separation of powers, assemblies were dominant. State constitutions placed few or no controls upon the actions of state assemblies, which were elected annually. Few problems surfaced until the inevitable postwar depression developed beginning in mid-1784. Farmers were still overproducing, but their markets, particularly in the West Indies, were restricted. Consequently, prices for American agricultural produce plunged. At the same time, taxes were raised, as Congress and the state legislatures had heavy war debts to pay, to both foreign and domestic creditors. Individuals and organizations who could not pay their taxes or their debts had their property confiscated by local authorities and sold at public auction. Debtors petitioned their assemblies for relief, and half of the states succumbed; in the other states, violence occurred. In western Virginia, courthouses were burned, destroying tax records. In Massachusetts, farmers in the western counties forcibly closed the civil courts in order to forestall future foreclosures on farms. Creditors, in the minority, worried that state assemblies would yield to vocal majorities—the debtors—and enact measures that would endanger their property rights. Anticreditor legislation, some modest, some radical, coupled with violence throughout the country frightened men like George Washington who believed that there were "combustibles" in every state ready to be ignited by a single spark.

All attempts to strengthen the Articles of Confederation failed. Finally, those who wished to preserve the Union decided to move outside of Congress and call a convention of the states to propose amendments to the articles. Nationalists, who had opposed the weak Articles of Con-

Time Line

1781

- **March 1**
Articles of Confederation adopted.

1785

- **March 28**
Commissioners from Virginia and Maryland meet at Mount Vernon to discuss commercial matters between their states.

1786

- **January 21**
Virginia calls for a commercial convention of all the states to meet in Annapolis, Maryland.

- **September 11–14**
Annapolis Convention meets and calls for a general convention of the states to meet in Philadelphia in May 1787 to consider amendments to the Articles of Confederation.

- **December 4**
Virginia authorizes the election of delegates to the Constitutional Convention.

1787

- **February 21**
Congress calls for Constitutional Convention to meet in Philadelphia in May 1787.

- **May 25**
Constitutional Convention attains a quorum and starts sessions.

- **July 13**
Northwest Ordinance passed by Congress.

- **September 17**
Constitution signed and convention adjourns.

- **September 20**
Congress receives and reads Constitution.

- **September 26–28**
Constitution debated in Congress.

- **September 28**
Congress sends Constitution to the states for ratification.

- **December 7**
Delaware becomes the first state to ratify the Constitution.

federation from the beginning, seized the opportunity not merely to amend the inherently defective articles but instead to create a new, more powerful and effective national government—one that would be able to act directly on the people and limit the actions of state assemblies. Many Americans viewed the Constitutional Convention as a last opportunity to peacefully adopt a viable federal constitution that would preserve the Union, promote justice and prosperity, and provide defense from both external aggression and domestic insurrection. The entire country waited anxiously while the Constitutional Convention deliberated in secrecy for four months. With George Washington and Benjamin Franklin present in the convention, a predilection swept over the country to accept whatever the convention proposed. Over the next year, Americans participated in a profound public debate over government and how best to preserve liberty.

About the Author

Fifty-five delegates attended the Constitutional Convention between May 25 and September 17, 1787. Averaging forty-four years old, the delegates were primarily lawyers, farmers, and merchants. The fifty-five-year-old George Washington was elected president of the convention. When the convention operated as a committee of the whole—that is, for the purpose of discussion under less official terms—Nathaniel Gorham, of Massachusetts, presided. Thirty-nine delegates signed the final document. Three delegates—Elbridge Gerry, from Massachusetts, and Edmund Randolph and George Mason, both from Virginia—were in attendance on the last day but refused to sign the Constitution.

All of the delegates were political leaders in their home states. Many had served in Congress and in their state governments. Only two—Randolph, of Virginia, and William Livingston, of New Jersey—were incumbent governors. All of the delegates and subsequent scholars acknowledged the leadership of the thirty-six-year-old James Madison, of Virginia. He was soon dubbed and is still often referred to as the "father of the Constitution"—an appellation he steadfastly rejected, as he believed that the Constitution was the product of many hands and many hearts. In essence, no one person was the "father of the Constitution"; instead, perhaps, a half dozen or so might be called "uncles."

Some delegates took the lead in making proposals and debating issues, while others only listened and voted. Some delegates arrived late, while others left early. Six delegates spoke most frequently—Gouverneur Morris, of Pennsylvania (173 times); Madison (168 times); Roger Sherman, of Connecticut (161 times); Mason (186 times); and Gerry (119 times). Six other delegates spoke between 61 and 78 times—Randolph, Hugh Williamson (N.C.), Rufus King (Mass.), Oliver Ellsworth (Conn.), Gorham, and Charles Pinckney (S.C.). Thirty delegates, or 54 percent of the attendees, either never spoke or were recorded as speaking fewer than a dozen times.

James Madison was the primary author of the Virginia Resolutions, presented on the first day of debates, which became the outline that the convention debated. Several key provisions of the Virginia proposal were rejected by the convention, leaving Madison despondent. Other proposals were presented by William Paterson (N.J.), Alexander Hamilton (N.Y.), and Pinckney. Other key delegates performed significant roles. The eighty-one-year-old Benjamin Franklin, though too frail to stand and speak himself, gave his Pennsylvania colleague James Wilson written speeches that Wilson then read. Franklin's speeches were often delivered when tempers flared, and his humor helped to reduce the tension. John Rutledge (S.C.) chaired the Committee of Detail; Gerry chaired the committee that proposed the Great Compromise, aimed at balancing representation from small and large states; and William Samuel Johnson (Conn.) chaired the Committee of Style. Morris wrote the preamble and the final version of the text of the entire Constitution. Jacob Shallus, the assistant clerk of the Pennsylvania Assembly, was the scribe who actually wrote the four-page engrossed copy of the Constitution.

Explanation and Analysis of the Document

In terms of governmental concepts, nothing in the Constitution is new; every part came from the Articles of Confederation, the state constitutions and bills of rights, or the Northwest Ordinance. The genius of the Founding Fathers lay in how they mixed together these disparate "old" provisions to create a federal republic different from any other previously formed state. The genesis of the Constitution came about through a series of compromises struck among delegates representing states with different interests. Delegates from large and small states first vied with each other over representation. Southern delegates differed with northern delegates on representation and a host of other issues. The southern delegates sought an agricultural society in which slavery would be protected from those who wished to abolish the South's peculiar institution, while northerners wanted to encourage commerce, fishing, and manufacturing. The country as a whole was divided between those who wanted a strong central government and those who merely wanted to give the Confederation Congress a few more necessary powers while keeping the primary political authority with the states. These competing forces were in fact essential to the shaping of the Constitution. By dividing power between the federal and state governments and by separating the different branches of the federal government through an intricate system of checks and balances, the convention created a uniquely strong and efficient federal government that could better protect the rights of its citizens.

The Constitution is introduced by a fifty-two-word preamble, written by Gouverneur Morris, that announces a major change in national philosophy. Opening with the famous words "We the People of the United States," the Constitution replaced the loose confederation of states with a contract forged among all of the nation's people. The new federal government would "form a more perfect Union, establish Justice, insure domestic Tranquility, provide for the common defence, promote the general Welfare, and secure the Blessings of Liberty to ourselves and our Posterity."

Seven articles follow the preamble. Article I—in length, half of the entire Constitution—gave all legislative power to a bicameral Congress. To be elected biennially by the people, the larger House of Representatives was apportioned among the states based upon population, including three-fifths of the slaves. Reapportionment in the House would occur every ten years after a federal census. For the smaller Senate, each state legislature would elect two federal senators to serve six-year terms. One-third of the Senate was to be elected every two years. Senators and representatives would vote individually, not as a state delegation. The vice president of the United States would serve as president of the Senate, casting votes only to break ties.

Time Line

1788

- **February 6**
  Massachusetts becomes the sixth state to ratify the Constitution but the first to propose recommendatory amendments; six of the remaining seven states will follow this precedent.
- **June 21**
  New Hampshire becomes the ninth state to adopt the Constitution, thus completing its official ratification.
- **June 25**
  Virginia ratifies Constitution.
- **July 26**
  New York ratifies Constitution.
- **September 13**
  Congress calls for first federal elections and the beginning of the new government.

1789

- **September 25**
  Congress proposes twelve amendments to the Constitution.

1790

- **May 29**
  Rhode Island becomes last of the thirteen states to ratify the Constitution.

1791

- **December 15**
  Adoption of first ten amendments, the Bill of Rights, to the Constitution.

www.milestonedocuments.com

Roger Sherman helped broker a key compromise during the drafting of the Constitution. (Library of Congress)

The states would set their own rules for electing members of Congress, but Congress could regulate elections that were not held. Congress would be required to sit at least once annually. Each house would elect its own officers, create its own rules, keep its own records, set qualifications for its own members, and determine the results of disputed elections. By law, Congress would set all governmental salaries, which would be paid out of the federal treasury. Mandatory rotation in office and the power of recall were eliminated. No member of Congress would be allowed to coincidentally hold another federal office.

Congress would be entitled to levy and collect taxes; regulate foreign and interstate commerce; declare war; raise and maintain an army and navy; provide rules for training state militias; establish post offices and post roads; borrow and coin money; punish counterfeiters; set uniform bankruptcy laws; pass laws for naturalization; fix standards for weights and measures; grant copyrights and patents; define and punish piracy and crimes at sea; create inferior federal courts; exercise exclusive jurisdiction over a federal capital and over federal forts, arsenals, and magazines; and "make all Laws which shall be necessary and proper, for carrying into Execution the foregoing Powers." Only the House could initiate money bills, but, unlike Great Britain's House of Lords, the Senate could amend money bills. The president could veto bills, but Congress could override the veto by a two-thirds vote in each house.

The last two sections of Article I placed limits on the actions of Congress and the states. Both were prohibited from passing bills of attainder, enacting ex post facto laws, and granting titles of nobility. Congress specifically could not levy export duties, close the foreign slave trade before 1808, or suspend the writ of habeas corpus except during rebellions and foreign invasion. The states were also prohibited from passing laws that would impair the obligation of contracts, coining money, issuing paper money, declaring anything but gold and silver legal tender, entering into treaties or alliances, or (without the consent of Congress) levying import or export duties.

Article II vested the executive power in a president to serve for four years and to be eligible for unlimited reelection. Special presidential electors, equal to the total number of each state's representatives and senators and chosen in a manner decided by the state legislatures, were to meet on the same day in their home states and cast two ballots—one of which could not be for a resident of their state. The person receiving the highest number of votes would be elected president; the person with the second highest number would become vice president. If two or more people tied—each with electoral votes that totaled a majority of the electors appointed—the House of Representatives would by ballot choose the winner. If no person had a vote that was a majority of the number of the electors, the House of Representatives would choose the president by ballot from among those with the five highest numbers of electoral votes. The Senate, voting per capita, would elect the vice president. The president—who had to be at least thirty-five years old, a natural-born citizen or a citizen at the time that the Constitution was adopted, and a resident of the United States for fourteen years—was to be commander in chief of the military and of the state militias whenever they were brought into federal service. He could grant pardons and reprieves—except in cases of impeachment—and, with the advice and consent of the Senate, make appointments (including diplomats and judges), enter into treaties (subject to the approval of a two-thirds vote of the Senate), and require in writing the opinions of the heads of the different executive departments. The president would receive a fixed salary that could not be raised or lowered during his term of office, and he would be required to take an oath to faithfully execute his duties and to defend the Constitution. From time to time the president was to make a "State of the Union" address to Congress containing "such Measures as he shall judge necessary and expedient." The president, vice president, and all other civil officers could be impeached by the House of Representatives for "Treason, Bribery, or other High Crimes and Misdemeanors." The Senate would try all impeachments, with conviction requiring a two-thirds vote. The chief justice would preside over impeachment trials of the president. Punishment was limited to removal from office, but those convicted were also subject to regular criminal prosecution.

Essential Quotes

"We the People of the United States, in Order to form a more perfect Union, establish Justice, insure domestic Tranquility, provide for the common defence, promote the general Welfare, and secure the Blessings of Liberty to ourselves and our Posterity, do ordain and establish this Constitution for the United States of America."

(Preamble)

"The Congress shall have the Power … to regulate Commerce with foreign Nations, and among the several States, and with the Indian Tribes."

(Article I, Section 8)

"The Congress shall have the Power … to make all Laws which shall be necessary and proper for carrying into Execution the foregoing Powers, and all other Powers vested by this Constitution in the Government of the United States, or in any Department or Officer thereof."

(Article I, Section 8)

"The United States shall guarantee to every State in this Union a Republican Form of Government."

(Article IV, Section 4)

"This Constitution, and the Laws of the United States which shall be made in Pursuance thereof; and all Treaties made, or which shall be made, under the Authority of the United States, shall be the supreme Law of the Land; and the Judges in every State shall be bound thereby, any Thing in the Constitution or Laws of any State to the Contrary notwithstanding."

(Article VI)

www.milestonedocuments.com

Article III provided for a federal judiciary to consist of one Supreme Court and such inferior courts as Congress deemed necessary. To be nominated by the president and confirmed by the Senate, federal judges were to serve during good behavior with salaries that could not be diminished. The judiciary's jurisdiction would extend to all cases of law and equity arising under the Constitution, federal laws, and treaties as well as to cases involving the United States, cases between citizens of different states, and cases involving foreigners. The original jurisdiction of the Supreme Court was delineated in the Constitution; in all other cases the Supreme Court would have appellate jurisdiction in law and fact, with such exceptions as provided by Congress. Unlike with the British House of Lords or in several state constitutions, no provision was made for legislative overview of Supreme Court decisions. By authority of the supremacy clause in Article VI, federal judges could declare state laws unconstitutional and thus null and void. As per the general principles of written constitutions, federal judges could also declare acts of Congress and of the president unconstitutional.

Jury trials were guaranteed in criminal cases within the state in which the crime had been committed. Treason was narrowly defined, and its punishment could not extend to the family of the traitor.

Article IV required that each state give "full Faith and Credit" to the public acts, records, and judicial proceedings of the other states. Citizens of each state would be entitled to the "Privileges and Immunities" of citizens in other states, while states would be required to extradite other states' fugitives from justice and runaway slaves. Congress could admit new states into the Union and could make rules and regulations for federal territories. The United States guaranteed each state a republican form of government, protection from foreign invasion, and assistance against domestic violence upon the application of the state legislature, or of the governor when the legislature was not in session.

Article V provided that amendments to the Constitution could be proposed either by a two-thirds vote in both houses of Congress or by a constitutional convention called on the application to Congress of two-thirds of the states. Proposed amendments could be ratified by three-quarters of the state legislatures or by state ratifying conventions, whichever method Congress directed.

Article VI provided that the new federal government assumed all the debts and engagements previously held by the Confederation government. It also specified that "This Constitution, and the Laws of the United States which shall be made in Pursuance thereof; and all Treaties made, or which shall be made, under the Authority of the United States, shall be the supreme Law of the Land; and the Judges in every State shall be bound thereby, any Thing in the Constitution or Laws of any State to the Contrary notwithstanding."

Article VII provided that the Constitution would be considered in each state by specially elected ratifying conventions and that whenever nine states ratified, the Constitution would go into effect among the ratifying states.

Audience

The Constitutional Convention had several audiences—the Confederation Congress, the state legislatures, the American people, and all of humankind. On the last day of the convention, delegates approved the text of a letter addressed to the president of Congress. The letter, signed by George Washington, was written in the tradition set by Congress of sending cover letters with various documents (including the Articles of Confederation) that it sent to the states. Meant for political purposes, the letter explained that the nation's central government needed many more powers but that granting additional powers to the unicameral Confederation Congress would be dangerous—"Hence results the necessity of a different organization." The difficulty lay in determining exactly how to distinguish and separate federal and state powers. Because the Union was thought to be essential, as stated in the letter, each state delegation had proved willing "to be less rigid on points of inferior magnitude, than might have been otherwise expected; and thus the Constitution, which we now present, is the result of a spirit of amity, and of that mutual deference and concession which the peculiarity of our political situation rendered indispensible" (Constitutional Convention to Congress, September 17, 1789; qtd. in Jensen, vol. 1, p. 305).

Wherever the Constitution was printed, this letter appeared above the signature of George Washington. Federalists asked opponents how they could doubt the benefits of the Constitution if it was being endorsed by Washington himself; the question was a hard one to answer.

The Constitutional Convention also passed two resolutions on its final day. The first asked Congress to send the Constitution to the states with a request that the state legislatures call specially elected conventions to ratify the new form of government. The second resolution suggested that once nine state conventions had ratified the Constitution, Congress should provide for its implementation.

Delegates to the convention collectively hoped that the American people would agree to call these special conventions and that they would seriously debate whether or not to ratify the Constitution. Alexander Hamilton addressed this issue in the first of a series of eighty-five newspaper essays—of which some were written by Hamilton, some by Madison, and a few by John Jay—that would later be compiled and published as *The Federalist*:

> It has been frequently remarked, that it seems to have been reserved to the people of this country, by their conduct and example, to decide the important question, whether societies of men are really capable or not, of establishing good government from reflection and choice, or whether they are forever destined to depend, for their political constitutions, on accident and force. If there be any truth in the remark, the crisis, at which we are arrived, may with propriety be regarded as the aera in which that decision is to be made; and a wrong election of the part we shall act, may, in this view, deserve to be considered as the general misfortune of mankind.

The delegates of the Constitutional Convention indeed hoped that people in other countries in the future would have the same opportunity to establish "good government from reflection and choice."

Impact

The introduction and implementation of the Constitution had a profound impact on the nation. At a time when the principles of the American Revolution were being questioned, it provided a necessary and revolutionary change in how the United States would be governed. If the Constitution had not been either proposed or adopted, the United

States might have stayed a loose confederation of states, evolved into a parliamentary system of government, become a monarchy, returned into the British Empire, become separate confederacies, or adopted a different form of government at a later time. All of the alternatives would have likely brought about dramatically different circumstances. As it is, the Constitution educated and continues to educate Americans about the nature of government and how best to preserve liberty, and it provided written historical assertions to help subsequent government officials, especially jurists such as John Marshall, interpret the Constitution. From the moment the Constitution was implemented, all sides endorsed it as an almost divinely inspired text. The debate then shifted from the topic of the quality of the Constitution to the question of how this veritably sacred text was to be interpreted.

Discussion over the nature of the new Constitution continued unabated from the time of its promulgation, through its ratification, and into and beyond the first decade of its implementation. During the first federal elections, Antifederalists continued their efforts to obtain amendments, while Federalists, many of whom had promised to support amendments after the Constitution had been ratified, opposed amendments and attacked those who campaigned for alterations. Ultimately, a set of additional rights was proposed by President Washington and Representative Madison. Sent to the states in October 1789, ten amendments were adopted in December 1791. Although unused throughout the nineteenth century, the Bill of Rights has become the most controversial part of the Constitution.

Throughout the 1790s a constitutional debate raged between Federalists and their opponents. The Federalists wanted an energetic federal government that would actively stimulate the economy and (in the late 1790s) suppress political opposition. The opponents of the Federalists (called Republicans, Democratic Republicans, or Jeffersonians) wanted a far more limited federal government with a laissez faire policy and with virtually no power to restrict the freedom of speech or the press. With the 1800 election of Thomas Jefferson as president and a Jeffersonian majority in both houses of Congress, a more laissez-faire interpretation of the Constitution took hold. Circumstances during the presidencies of Jefferson and Madison brought the constitutional interpretation of the Jeffersonians to a more centralist position, as Federalists became more extremist and isolated in New England. The presidency of James Monroe saw the demise of the Federalist Party and the emergence of what historians have called the Era of Good Feeling, during which a constitutional interpretation similar to what Federalists had advocated during the ratification debate of 1788 came to prominence—a view highlighted by several important constitutional decisions written by Chief Justice John Marshall.

Members of the old Federalist Party and many former Republicans now agreed on how to interpret the Constitution, but in the late 1820s a neo-Antifederalist party emerged that advocated states' rights with very limited powers for the federal government. A more democratic interpretation of the Constitution occurred under President Andrew Jackson and his successors. The role of the federal government with respect to slavery in federal territories created the greatest crisis in the interpretation of the Constitution—one that led nearly half of the states to secede from the Union in 1861 and adopt a written constitution providing for a far weaker central government. The catastrophic Civil War greatly strengthened the authority of the presidency. For the next three decades, the federal courts, citing the Constitution's commerce clause, broadly interpreted the Constitution in favor of private business interests. The progressive reformist movement beginning at the turn of the century, as bolstered by the enhanced roles of such dynamic leaders as Theodore Roosevelt, Woodrow Wilson, and Franklin D. Roosevelt—as well as by the crises of the two world wars and the Great Depression—called for an enlarged interpretation of the Constitution and a greatly expanded role for the federal government. Over the last half of the twentieth century, political leaders and social activists advocated various constitutional positions on civil rights for minorities and on the president's role as commander in chief.

Over the course of its 220-year history, the Constitution has provided each generation of Americans with a written form of government with enough elasticity to meet their needs. The assertions and laws presented in the Constitution continue to shape the policies of the federal and state governments and the lives of all Americans. This historic document will undoubtedly long remain the fulcrum of the most consequential national political debates.

Related Documents

Benton, Wilbourn E., ed. *1787: Drafting the U.S. Constitution*. 2 vols. College Station: Texas A&M University Press, 1986. For each clause of the Constitution, Benton presents its complete genesis during the debate in the Constitutional Convention, revealing how the individual clauses were introduced and then progressed to the final versions.

Farrand, Max, ed. *The Records of the Federal Convention of 1787*. 4 vols. New Haven: Yale University Press, 1966. The first two volumes of this work constitute the standard source regarding the day-by-day debates and proceedings of the Constitutional Convention. The third volume contains personal accounts of the Convention, largely in the form of private letters and diaries as well as profiles of the delegates; the fourth contains additional notes and letters and a voluminous index.

Jensen, Merrill, ed. *The Documentary History of the Ratification of the Constitution*. 21 vols. Madison: State Historical Society of Wisconsin, 1976–2005. This work, with volumes still forthcoming, presents a comprehensive and expansive record of the ratification of the Constitution, including various related historical documents, discussion of national debate, and an examination of each state's ratification.

www.milestonedocuments.com

Kaminski, John P., ed. *A Necessary Evil? Slavery and the Debate over the Constitution*. Madison, Wis.: Madison House, 1995. This collection of documents looks at slavery from 1774 to 1808, the debate over slavery in the Constitutional Convention, and the role of slavery in the ratification debates in New England, the Middle States, and the South.

Kaminski, John P., and Richard Leffler, eds. *Creating the Constitution*. Acton, Mass.: Copley Publishing Group, 1999. Taken from a newspaper series, this collection of documents, each with a narrative introduction, traces the drafting and ratification of the Constitution.

———, eds. *Federalists and Antifederalists: The Debate over the Ratification of the Constitution*. 2nd ed. Madison, Wis.: Madison House, 1998. This volume examines seven issues from the public ratification debate: the nature of republican government, the House of Representatives, the Senate, the presidency, the judiciary, the Bill of Rights, and the relationships among property, class, and government.

Taylor, Quentin P., ed. *The Essential Federalist: A New Reading of the Federalist Papers*. Madison, Wis.: Madison House, 1998. Taylor presents the biographies of the three authors of the Federalist Papers—Alexander Hamilton, James Madison, and John Jay—and an examination of how the essays were written, with select excerpts.

Bibliography

Books

Beard, Charles Austin. *An Economic Interpretation of the Constitution of the United States*. New York: Macmillan, 1913.

Bowen, Catherine Drinker. *Miracle at Philadelphia: The Story of the Constitutional Convention, May to September 1787*. Boston: Little, Brown, 1966.

Collier, Christopher, and James Lincoln Collier. *Decision in Philadelphia: The Constitutional Convention of 1787*. New York: Random House, Reader's Digest, 1986.

Conley, Patrick T., and John P. Kaminski, eds. *The Constitution and the States: The Role of the Original Thirteen in the Framing and Adoption of the Federal Constitution*. Madison, Wis.: Madison House, 1988.

Elkins, Stanley, and Eric McKitrick. *The Age of Federalism*. New York: Oxford University Press, 1993.

Farrand, Max. *The Framing of the Constitution of the United States*. New Haven: Yale University Press, 1913.

Gillespie, Michael Allen, and Michael Lienesch, eds. *Ratifying the Constitution*. Lawrence: University Press of Kansas, 1989.

Jensen, Merrill. *The Making of the American Constitution*. Princeton, N.J.: Van Nostrand, 1964.

Levy, Leonard W. *Original Intent and the Framers' Constitution*. New York: Macmillan, 1988.

Main, Jackson Turner. *The Antifederalists: Critics of the Constitution, 1781–1788*. Williamsburg, Va.: University of North Carolina Press, 1961.

McGuire, Robert A. *To Form a More Perfect Union: A New Economic Interpretation of the United States Constitution*. Oxford, U.K.: Oxford University Press, 2003.

Monk, Linda R. *The Words We Live By: Your Annotated Guide to the Constitution*. New York: Hyperion, 2003.

Rossiter, Clinton. *1787: The Grand Convention*. New York: Macmillan, 1966.

Rutland, Robert Allen. *The Ordeal of the Constitution: The Antifederalists and the Ratification Struggle of 1787–1788*. Norman: University of Oklahoma Press, 1966.

Van Doren, Carl. *The Great Rehearsal: The Story of the Making and Ratifying of the Constitution of the United States*. New York: Viking Press, 1948.

Web Sites

"Constitution of the United States." National Archives "Charters of Freedom" Web site.
http://www.archives.gov/national-archives-experience/charters/constitution.html. Accessed on October 5, 2007.

"Educational Resources." United States House of Representatives Web site.
http://www.house.gov/house/Educate.shtml. Accessed on October 5, 2007.

"The Federalist Papers." Founding Fathers.info Web site.
http://www.foundingfathers.info/federalistpapers/. Accessed on January 25, 2008.

"United States Constitution." Library of Congress "Primary Documents in American History" Web site.
http://www.loc.gov/rr/program/bib/ourdocs/Constitution.html. Accessed on October 5, 2007.

—By John P. Kaminski

www.milestonedocuments.com

Questions for Further Study

1. How did the opposing forces in the Constitutional Convention create a constitution of compromises?

2. How were the Founders able to create a stronger central government that would at the same time provide increased protection for the rights of its citizens?

3. How did the Constitution, which was designed to secure the rights of individuals, condone and even benefit those who owned slaves?

4. During the debate over ratification, James Madison argued that rights would be better secured from the structure of the Constitution than from a subsequently added bill of rights. What did he mean by this? Why did Madison only two years later champion a bill of rights?

Glossary

adjourn	to postpone to another time
Appropriation	money set aside from a budget to be used for a specific purpose
Arsenals	buildings used for manufacturing or storing weapons
Bill of Attainder	a legislative statement of guilt or conviction without a trial
certificates	formal documents attesting to the truthfulness of information
citizens	persons entitled to the rights and privileges of a freeman under a government
Compact	an agreement between two or more entities
Concurrence	agreement
counterfeiting	making an imitation of something else with intent to deceive, such as making a fake monetary note
Duties	governmental taxes placed on goods, typically exports or imports
Emoluments	compensations arising from office or employment
enumeration	a listing
equity	justice; a system of law developed to enlarge, supplement, or override a narrow, rigid system of law
Excises	taxes on the manufacture, sale, or use of goods within a country
expedient	suitable for achieving a particular end in a given circumstance
ex post facto	retroactively; applying to previous events
Forfeiture	the loss of property or money as a penalty for breaking a legal obligation
immunities	protections or exemptions from arrest
indictment	the process of charging someone with a crime

Glossary

Naturalization	admission to citizenship
piracies	robberies on the high seas
Posterity	descendants; future generations
Pursuance	carrying out or putting into effect
quorum	the minimum number of members needed to be present for a group to conduct valid business
Receipts	written acknowledgments of the receiving of goods or money
Recess	a period of time during which work is not done or business is not conducted
religious Test	oath acknowledging a deity
Reprieves	postponements in punishing
Republican	based upon representation
Securities	evidences of debt or of ownership
Tribunals	courts
Writ of Habeas Corpus	an order to bring a person before a court or judge, usually as a protection against illegal imprisonment

Constitution of the United States

We the People of the United States, in Order to form a more perfect Union, establish Justice, insure domestic Tranquility, provide for the common defense, promote the general Welfare, and secure the Blessings of Liberty to ourselves and our Posterity, do ordain and establish this Constitution for the United States of America.

Article I

◆ Section 1

All legislative Powers herein granted shall be vested in a Congress of the United States, which shall consist of a Senate and House of Representatives.

◆ Section 2

The House of Representatives shall be composed of Members chosen every second Year by the People of the several States, and the Electors in each State shall have the Qualifications requisite for Electors of the most numerous Branch of the State Legislature.

No Person shall be a Representative who shall not have attained to the Age of twenty five Years, and been seven Years a Citizen of the United States, and who shall not, when elected, be an Inhabitant of that State in which he shall be chosen.

Representatives and direct Taxes shall be apportioned among the several States which may be included within this Union, according to their respective Numbers, which shall be determined by adding to the whole Number of free Persons, including those bound to Service for a Term of Years, and excluding Indians not taxed, three fifths of all other Persons. The actual Enumeration shall be made within three Years after the first Meeting of the Congress of the United States, and within every subsequent Term of ten Years, in such Manner as they shall by Law direct. The Number of Representatives shall not exceed one for every thirty Thousand, but each State shall have at Least one Representative; and until such enumeration shall be made, the State of New Hampshire shall be entitled to chuse three, Massachusetts eight, Rhode-Island and Providence Plantations one, Connecticut five, New-York six, New Jersey four, Pennsylvania eight, Delaware one, Maryland six, Virginia ten, North Carolina five, South Carolina five, and Georgia three.

When vacancies happen in the Representation from any State, the Executive Authority thereof shall issue Writs of Election to fill such Vacancies.

The House of Representatives shall chuse their Speaker and other Officers; and shall have the sole Power of Impeachment.

◆ Section 3

The Senate of the United States shall be composed of two Senators from each State, chosen by the Legislature thereof for six Years; and each Senator shall have one Vote.

Immediately after they shall be assembled in Consequence of the first Election, they shall be divided as equally as may be into three Classes. The Seats of the Senators of the first Class shall be vacated at the Expiration of the second Year, of the second Class at the Expiration of the fourth Year, and of the third Class at the Expiration of the sixth Year, so that one third may be chosen every second Year; and if Vacancies happen by Resignation, or otherwise, during the Recess of the Legislature of any State, the Executive thereof may make temporary Appointments until the next Meeting of the Legislature, which shall then fill such Vacancies.

No Person shall be a Senator who shall not have attained to the Age of thirty Years, and been nine Years a Citizen of the United States, and who shall not, when elected, be an Inhabitant of that State for which he shall be chosen.

The Vice President of the United States shall be President of the Senate, but shall have no Vote, unless they be equally divided.

The Senate shall chuse their other Officers, and also a President pro tempore, in the Absence of the

www.milestonedocuments.com

Vice President, or when he shall exercise the Office of President of the United States.

The Senate shall have the sole Power to try all Impeachments. When sitting for that Purpose, they shall be on Oath or Affirmation. When the President of the United States is tried, the Chief Justice shall preside: And no Person shall be convicted without the Concurrence of two thirds of the Members present.

Judgment in Cases of Impeachment shall not extend further than to removal from Office, and disqualification to hold and enjoy any Office of honor, Trust or Profit under the United States: but the Party convicted shall nevertheless be liable and subject to Indictment, Trial, Judgment and Punishment, according to Law.

◆ Section 4

The Times, Places and Manner of holding Elections for Senators and Representatives, shall be prescribed in each State by the Legislature thereof; but the Congress may at any time by Law make or alter such Regulations, except as to the Places of chusing Senators.

The Congress shall assemble at least once in every Year, and such Meeting shall be on the first Monday in December, unless they shall by Law appoint a different Day.

◆ Section 5

Each House shall be the Judge of the Elections, Returns and Qualifications of its own Members, and a Majority of each shall constitute a Quorum to do Business; but a smaller Number may adjourn from day to day, and may be authorized to compel the Attendance of absent Members, in such Manner, and under such Penalties as each House may provide.

Each House may determine the Rules of its Proceedings, punish its Members for disorderly Behaviour, and, with the Concurrence of two thirds, expel a Member.

Each House shall keep a Journal of its Proceedings, and from time to time publish the same, excepting such Parts as may in their Judgment require Secrecy; and the Yeas and Nays of the Members of either House on any question shall, at the Desire of one fifth of those Present, be entered on the Journal.

Neither House, during the Session of Congress, shall, without the Consent of the other, adjourn for more than three days, nor to any other Place than that in which the two Houses shall be sitting.

◆ Section 6

The Senators and Representatives shall receive a Compensation for their Services, to be ascertained by Law, and paid out of the Treasury of the United States. They shall in all Cases, except Treason, Felony and Breach of the Peace, be privileged from Arrest during their Attendance at the Session of their respective Houses, and in going to and returning from the same; and for any Speech or Debate in either House, they shall not be questioned in any other Place.

No Senator or Representative shall, during the Time for which he was elected, be appointed to any civil Office under the Authority of the United States, which shall have been created, or the Emoluments whereof shall have been encreased during such time; and no Person holding any Office under the United States, shall be a Member of either House during his Continuance in Office.

◆ Section 7

All Bills for raising Revenue shall originate in the House of Representatives; but the Senate may propose or concur with Amendments as on other Bills.

Every Bill which shall have passed the House of Representatives and the Senate, shall, before it become a Law, be presented to the President of the United States: If he approve he shall sign it, but if not he shall return it, with his Objections to that House in which it shall have originated, who shall enter the Objections at large on their Journal, and proceed to reconsider it. If after such Reconsideration two thirds of that House shall agree to pass the Bill, it shall be sent, together with the Objections, to the other House, by which it shall likewise be reconsidered, and if approved by two thirds of that House, it shall become a Law. But in all such Cases the Votes of both Houses shall be determined by yeas and Nays, and the Names of the Persons voting for and against the Bill shall be entered on the Journal of each House respectively. If any Bill shall not be returned by the President within ten Days (Sundays excepted) after it shall have been presented to him, the Same shall be a Law, in like Manner as if he had signed it, unless the Congress by their Adjournment prevent its Return, in which Case it shall not be a Law.

Every Order, Resolution, or Vote to which the Concurrence of the Senate and House of Representatives may be necessary (except on a question of Adjournment) shall be presented to the President of the United States; and before the Same shall take Effect, shall be approved by him, or being disapproved by him, shall be repassed by two thirds of the Senate and

House of Representatives, according to the Rules and Limitations prescribed in the Case of a Bill.

◆ Section 8

The Congress shall have Power To lay and collect Taxes, Duties, Imposts and Excises, to pay the Debts and provide for the common Defence and general Welfare of the United States; but all Duties, Imposts and Excises shall be uniform throughout the United States;

To borrow Money on the credit of the United States;

To regulate Commerce with foreign Nations, and among the several States, and with the Indian Tribes;

To establish an uniform Rule of Naturalization, and uniform Laws on the subject of Bankruptcies throughout the United States;

To coin Money, regulate the Value thereof, and of foreign Coin, and fix the Standard of Weights and Measures;

To provide for the Punishment of counterfeiting the Securities and current Coin of the United States;

To establish Post Offices and post Roads;

To promote the Progress of Science and useful Arts, by securing for limited Times to Authors and Inventors the exclusive Right to their respective Writings and Discoveries;

To constitute Tribunals inferior to the supreme Court;

To define and punish Piracies and Felonies committed on the high Seas, and Offences against the Law of Nations;

To declare War, grant Letters of Marque and Reprisal, and make Rules concerning Captures on Land and Water;

To raise and support Armies, but no Appropriation of Money to that Use shall be for a longer Term than two Years;

To provide and maintain a Navy;

To make Rules for the Government and Regulation of the land and naval Forces;

To provide for calling forth the Militia to execute the Laws of the Union, suppress Insurrections and repel Invasions;

To provide for organizing, arming, and disciplining, the Militia, and for governing such Part of them as may be employed in the Service of the United States, reserving to the States respectively, the Appointment of the Officers, and the Authority of training the Militia according to the discipline prescribed by Congress;

To exercise exclusive Legislation in all Cases whatsoever, over such District (not exceeding ten Miles square) as may, by Cession of particular States, and the Acceptance of Congress, become the Seat of the Government of the United States, and to exercise like Authority over all Places purchased by the Consent of the Legislature of the State in which the Same shall be, for the Erection of Forts, Magazines, Arsenals, dock-Yards, and other needful Buildings;—And

To make all Laws which shall be necessary and proper for carrying into Execution the foregoing Powers, and all other Powers vested by this Constitution in the Government of the United States, or in any Department or Officer thereof.

◆ Section 9

The Migration or Importation of such Persons as any of the States now existing shall think proper to admit, shall not be prohibited by the Congress prior to the Year one thousand eight hundred and eight, but a Tax or duty may be imposed on such Importation, not exceeding ten dollars for each Person.

The Privilege of the Writ of Habeas Corpus shall not be suspended, unless when in Cases of Rebellion or Invasion the public Safety may require it.

No Bill of Attainder or ex post facto Law shall be passed.

No Capitation, or other direct, Tax shall be laid, unless in Proportion to the Census or enumeration herein before directed to be taken.

No Tax or Duty shall be laid on Articles exported from any State.

No Preference shall be given by any Regulation of Commerce or Revenue to the Ports of one State over those of another; nor shall Vessels bound to, or from, one State, be obliged to enter, clear, or pay Duties in another.

No Money shall be drawn from the Treasury, but in Consequence of Appropriations made by Law; and a regular Statement and Account of the Receipts and Expenditures of all public Money shall be published from time to time.

No Title of Nobility shall be granted by the United States: And no Person holding any Office of Profit or Trust under them, shall, without the Consent of the Congress, accept of any present, Emolument, Office, or Title, of any kind whatever, from any King, Prince, or foreign State.

◆ Section 10

No State shall enter into any Treaty, Alliance, or Confederation; grant Letters of Marque and Reprisal; coin Money; emit Bills of Credit; make any

www.milestonedocuments.com

Document Text

Thing but gold and silver Coin a Tender in Payment of Debts; pass any Bill of Attainder, ex post facto Law, or Law impairing the Obligation of Contracts, or grant any Title of Nobility.

No State shall, without the Consent of the Congress, lay any Imposts or Duties on Imports or Exports, except what may be absolutely necessary for executing its inspection Laws: and the net Produce of all Duties and Imposts, laid by any State on Imports or Exports, shall be for the Use of the Treasury of the United States; and all such Laws shall be subject to the Revision and Controul of the Congress.

No State shall, without the Consent of Congress, lay any Duty of Tonnage, keep Troops, or Ships of War in time of Peace, enter into any Agreement or Compact with another State, or with a foreign Power, or engage in War, unless actually invaded, or in such imminent Danger as will not admit of delay.

Article II

◆ Section 1

The executive Power shall be vested in a President of the United States of America. He shall hold his Office during the Term of four Years, and, together with the Vice President, chosen for the same Term, be elected, as follows:

Each State shall appoint, in such Manner as the Legislature thereof may direct, a Number of Electors, equal to the whole Number of Senators and Representatives to which the State may be entitled in the Congress: but no Senator or Representative, or Person holding an Office of Trust or Profit under the United States, shall be appointed an Elector.

The Electors shall meet in their respective States, and vote by Ballot for two Persons, of whom one at least shall not be an Inhabitant of the same State with themselves. And they shall make a List of all the Persons voted for, and of the Number of Votes for each; which List they shall sign and certify, and transmit sealed to the Seat of the Government of the United States, directed to the President of the Senate. The President of the Senate shall, in the Presence of the Senate and House of Representatives, open all the Certificates, and the Votes shall then be counted. The Person having the greatest Number of Votes shall be the President, if such Number be a Majority of the whole Number of Electors appointed; and if there be more than one who have such Majority, and have an equal Number of Votes, then the House of Representatives shall immediately chuse by Ballot one of them for President; and if no Person have a Majority, then from the five highest on the List the said House shall in like Manner chuse the President. But in chusing the President, the Votes shall be taken by States, the Representation from each State having one Vote; A quorum for this purpose shall consist of a Member or Members from two thirds of the States, and a Majority of all the States shall be necessary to a Choice. In every Case, after the Choice of the President, the Person having the greatest Number of Votes of the Electors shall be the Vice President. But if there should remain two or more who have equal Votes, the Senate shall chuse from them by Ballot the Vice President.

The Congress may determine the Time of chusing the Electors, and the Day on which they shall give their Votes; which Day shall be the same throughout the United States.

No Person except a natural born Citizen, or a Citizen of the United States, at the time of the Adoption of this Constitution, shall be eligible to the Office of President; neither shall any Person be eligible to that Office who shall not have attained to the Age of thirty five Years, and been fourteen Years a Resident within the United States.

In Case of the Removal of the President from Office, or of his Death, Resignation, or Inability to discharge the Powers and Duties of the said Office, the Same shall devolve on the Vice President, and the Congress may by Law provide for the Case of Removal, Death, Resignation or Inability, both of the President and Vice President, declaring what Officer shall then act as President, and such Officer shall act accordingly, until the Disability be removed, or a President shall be elected.

The President shall, at stated Times, receive for his Services, a Compensation, which shall neither be increased nor diminished during the Period for which he shall have been elected, and he shall not receive within that Period any other Emolument from the United States, or any of them.

Before he enter on the Execution of his Office, he shall take the following Oath or Affirmation:—"I do solemnly swear (or affirm) that I will faithfully execute the Office of President of the United States, and will to the best of my Ability, preserve, protect and defend the Constitution of the United States."

◆ Section 2

The President shall be Commander in Chief of the Army and Navy of the United States, and of the Militia of the several States, when called into the actual Service of the United States; he may require the Opinion, in writing, of the principal Officer in each of the executive Departments, upon any Subject relating to the Duties of their respective Offices, and he shall have Power to grant Reprieves and Pardons for Offences against the United States, except in Cases of Impeachment.

He shall have Power, by and with the Advice and Consent of the Senate, to make Treaties, provided two thirds of the Senators present concur; and he shall nominate, and by and with the Advice and Consent of the Senate, shall appoint Ambassadors, other public Ministers and Consuls, Judges of the supreme Court, and all other Officers of the United States, whose Appointments are not herein otherwise provided for, and which shall be established by Law: but the Congress may by Law vest the Appointment of such inferior Officers, as they think proper, in the President alone, in the Courts of Law, or in the Heads of Departments.

The President shall have Power to fill up all Vacancies that may happen during the Recess of the Senate, by granting Commissions which shall expire at the End of their next Session.

◆ Section 3

He shall from time to time give to the Congress Information of the State of the Union, and recommend to their Consideration such Measures as he shall judge necessary and expedient; he may, on extraordinary Occasions, convene both Houses, or either of them, and in Case of Disagreement between them, with Respect to the Time of Adjournment, he may adjourn them to such Time as he shall think proper; he shall receive Ambassadors and other public Ministers; he shall take Care that the Laws be faithfully executed, and shall Commission all the Officers of the United States.

◆ Section 4

The President, Vice President and all civil Officers of the United States, shall be removed from Office on Impeachment for, and Conviction of, Treason, Bribery, or other high Crimes and Misdemeanors.

Article III

◆ Section 1

The judicial Power of the United States shall be vested in one supreme Court, and in such inferior Courts as the Congress may from time to time ordain and establish. The Judges, both of the supreme and inferior Courts, shall hold their Offices during good Behaviour, and shall, at stated Times, receive for their Services a Compensation, which shall not be diminished during their Continuance in Office.

◆ Section 2

The judicial Power shall extend to all Cases, in Law and Equity, arising under this Constitution, the Laws of the United States, and Treaties made, or which shall be made, under their Authority;—to all Cases affecting Ambassadors, other public Ministers and Consuls;—to all Cases of admiralty and maritime Jurisdiction;—to Controversies to which the United States shall be a Party;—to Controversies between two or more States;— between a State and Citizens of another State;—between Citizens of different States;—between Citizens of the same State claiming Lands under Grants of different States, and between a State, or the Citizens thereof, and foreign States, Citizens or Subjects.

In all Cases affecting Ambassadors, other public Ministers and Consuls, and those in which a State shall be Party, the supreme Court shall have original Jurisdiction. In all the other Cases before mentioned, the supreme Court shall have appellate Jurisdiction, both as to Law and Fact, with such Exceptions, and under such Regulations as the Congress shall make.

The Trial of all Crimes, except in Cases of Impeachment, shall be by Jury; and such Trial shall be held in the State where the said Crimes shall have been committed; but when not committed within any State, the Trial shall be at such Place or Places as the Congress may by Law have directed.

◆ Section 3

Treason against the United States, shall consist only in levying War against them, or in adhering to their Enemies, giving them Aid and Comfort. No Person shall be convicted of Treason unless on the Testimony of two Witnesses to the same overt Act, or on Confession in open Court.

The Congress shall have Power to declare the Punishment of Treason, but no Attainder of Treason shall work Corruption of Blood, or Forfeiture except during the Life of the Person attainted.

Article IV

◆ Section 1

Full Faith and Credit shall be given in each State to the public Acts, Records, and judicial Proceedings

www.milestonedocuments.com

of every other State. And the Congress may by general Laws prescribe the Manner in which such Acts, Records and Proceedings shall be proved, and the Effect thereof.

◆ Section 2

The Citizens of each State shall be entitled to all Privileges and Immunities of Citizens in the several States.

A Person charged in any State with Treason, Felony, or other Crime, who shall flee from Justice, and be found in another State, shall on Demand of the executive Authority of the State from which he fled, be delivered up, to be removed to the State having Jurisdiction of the Crime.

No Person held to Service or Labour in one State, under the Laws thereof, escaping into another, shall, in Consequence of any Law or Regulation therein, be discharged from such Service or Labour, but shall be delivered up on Claim of the Party to whom such Service or Labour may be due.

◆ Section 3

New States may be admitted by the Congress into this Union; but no new State shall be formed or erected within the Jurisdiction of any other State; nor any State be formed by the Junction of two or more States, or Parts of States, without the Consent of the Legislatures of the States concerned as well as of the Congress.

The Congress shall have Power to dispose of and make all needful Rules and Regulations respecting the Territory or other Property belonging to the United States; and nothing in this Constitution shall be so construed as to Prejudice any Claims of the United States, or of any particular State.

◆ Section 4

The United States shall guarantee to every State in this Union a Republican Form of Government, and shall protect each of them against Invasion; and on Application of the Legislature, or of the Executive (when the Legislature cannot be convened), against domestic Violence.

Article V

The Congress, whenever two thirds of both Houses shall deem it necessary, shall propose Amendments to this Constitution, or, on the Application of the Legislatures of two thirds of the several States, shall call a Convention for proposing Amendments, which, in either Case, shall be valid to all Intents and Purposes, as Part of this Constitution, when ratified by the Legislatures of three fourths of the several States, or by Conventions in three fourths thereof, as the one or the other Mode of Ratification may be proposed by the Congress; Provided that no Amendment which may be made prior to the Year One thousand eight hundred and eight shall in any Manner affect the first and fourth Clauses in the Ninth Section of the first Article; and that no State, without its Consent, shall be deprived of its equal Suffrage in the Senate.

Article VI

All Debts contracted and Engagements entered into, before the Adoption of this Constitution, shall be as valid against the United States under this Constitution, as under the Confederation.

This Constitution, and the Laws of the United States which shall be made in Pursuance thereof; and all Treaties made, or which shall be made, under the Authority of the United States, shall be the supreme Law of the Land; and the Judges in every State shall be bound thereby, any Thing in the Constitution or Laws of any State to the Contrary notwithstanding.

The Senators and Representatives before mentioned, and the Members of the several State Legislatures, and all executive and judicial Officers, both of the United States and of the several States, shall be bound by Oath or Affirmation, to support this Constitution; but no religious Test shall ever be required as a Qualification to any Office or public Trust under the United States.

Article VII

The Ratification of the Conventions of nine States, shall be sufficient for the Establishment of this Constitution between the States so ratifying the Same.

The Word, "the," being interlined between the seventh and eighth Lines of the first Page, the Word "Thirty" being partly written on an Erazure in the fifteenth Line of the first Page, The Words "is tried" being interlined between the thirty second and thirty third Lines of the first Page and the Word "the" being interlined between the forty third and forty fourth Lines of the second Page.

Attest William Jackson Secretary

Done in Convention by the Unanimous Consent of the States present the Seventeenth Day of Septem-

Document Text

ber in the Year of our Lord one thousand seven hundred and Eighty seven and of the Independence of the United States of America the Twelfth In witness whereof We have hereunto subscribed our Names,

G". Washington
Presidt and deputy from Virginia

Delaware
Geo: Read
Gunning Bedford jun
John Dickinson
Richard Bassett
Jaco: Broom

Maryland
James McHenry
Dan of St Thos. Jenifer
Danl. Carroll

Virginia
John Blair
James Madison Jr.

North Carolina
Wm. Blount
Richd. Dobbs Spaight
Hu Williamson

South Carolina
J. Rutledge
Charles Cotesworth Pinckney
Charles Pinckney
Pierce Butler

Georgia
William Few
Abr Baldwin

New Hampshire
John Langdon
Nicholas Gilman

Massachusetts
Nathaniel Gorham
Rufus King

Connecticut
Wm. Saml. Johnson
Roger Sherman

New York
Alexander Hamilton

New Jersey
Wil: Livingston
David Brearley
Wm. Paterson
Jona: Dayton

Pennsylvania
B Franklin
Thomas Mifflin
Robt. Morris
Geo. Clymer
Thos. FitzSimons
Jared Ingersoll
James Wilson
Gouv Morris

www.milestonedocuments.com

Federalist 10 (National Archives and Records Administration)

Federalist Papers 10, 14, and 51

1787

"If men were angels, no government would be necessary."

Overview

The Articles of Confederation functioned as the first national government of the new republic from 1781 to 1788. The Confederation was a league of thirteen sovereign states with a one-house legislature and no executive. Congress had no independent income, had no authority to compel states to accept its rulings, and was unable to act directly on the states. It could not regulate either interstate or foreign trade, levy taxes or tariffs to raise revenue, or raise a military force for national defense. The Confederation was more an assembly of delegates from the states than a national government.

To correct the weaknesses of the Confederation, influential political figures met in Philadelphia to craft a constitution in the summer of 1787. When the convention adjourned, opponents of the proposed constitution mounted a furious campaign against its ratification. Termed Antifederalists, the opposition included Revolutionary heroes like Patrick Henry, Henry Lee, and Samuel Adams. To counter this effort, Alexander Hamilton, John Jay, and James Madison planned a series of modest essays to be published in New York City newspapers, explaining the theory and workings of the proposed constitution and arguing for its ratification. Eventually, the series numbered eighty-five essays, collectively termed *The Federalist* or simply Federalist Papers. Hamilton wrote about fifty of the essays; Jay, restricted by illness, wrote only five; and Madison contributed the balance. Madison wrote the three most influential essays: Federalist 10, 14, and 51.

Note: Seventy-seven essays were published serially in the various New York newspapers between October 1787 and August 1788. These essays and eight others were compiled in a collection called *The Federalist*, published in 1788 in two volumes. In the collected edition some material was changed, and the original numbers assigned to the essays shifted. The modern numbering of the Federalist Papers follows the number assignment of the collection.

Context

The Revolutionary War had forced the colonists to unite and view themselves as Americans. Having directly experienced their oppression as colonial subjects at the local level, the newly sovereign people saw themselves as citizens of the states where they lived. Having thrown off the yoke of imperial power, they were suspicious of centralized power, especially when it existed beyond their reach. How the separate states of the infant country would work together as a single national entity was perhaps the most vexing question before a newly sovereign people.

In May 1776, at the direction of Congress, the states drafted constitutions based on "natural rights" philosophy. With its assertion of the right of rebellion and of government based upon "the consent of the governed," the Declaration of Independence exemplified this theory. Given their experience with appointed colonial governors, the state constitutions had strong legislatures and weak executives. Typically, the new governors served for only one year and were elected by the legislature. The legislatures redrew electoral districts to correspond more closely to population, expanded the number of legislators, and lowered property requirements for voting. The states drafted "bills of rights" to protect citizens from abuses of power. In Pennsylvania a coalition of western farmers, artisans, and militiamen influenced by Revolutionary democrat Thomas Paine crafted a government with a single-house legislature and no governor at all.

When the war ended in 1783, Congress faced problems fulfilling the peace terms. England used the refusal of the states to repay its debts to British creditors as an excuse to continue occupying its forts on the Great Lakes. In 1784 Spain closed the Mississippi River to Americans. Unable to control commerce, levy taxes, conduct foreign relations, amend itself, enforce its own articles, or defend the Union, the Confederation was paralyzed. By the mid-1780s nationalists wanted to revise the Articles of Confederation.

In 1786 two events riveted the attention of influential citizens. Rhode Island passed a law requiring creditors to accept paper money in payment for debts. This law gave relief to indebted farmers at the expense of wealthier urban creditors. An agrarian rebellion against state collection of taxes and debts, led by a former captain in the Continental

Time Line

1776

- **July 4**
  Declaration of Independence is adopted in Philadelphia.
- **May**
  Second Continental Congress directs states to draft constitutions.

1781

- Articles of Confederation is ratified.
- States reject Congress's request for import tax; Continental currency collapses.

1783

- Treaty of Paris is signed, granting independence to the United States.
- Great Britain occupies Great Lakes forts after states refuse to honor Treaty of Paris terms concerning war debts and Loyalist compensation.

1784

- Spain closes Mississippi River to American navigation.

1786

- Annapolis Convention meets to discuss reforming government and issues call for a constitutional convention.

1786–1787

- Shays's Rebellion takes place in western Massachusetts; 1,500 farmers besiege Springfield Armory.

1787

- **May**
  The Constitutional Convention meets in Philadelphia.
- **September 19**
  The Constitution is published in a special issue of the *Pennsylvania Packet*; Antifederalists begin attacks on the Constitution, and Hamilton, Jay, and Madison counter with initial Federalist Papers in New York City newspapers under the name "Publius."

army, Daniel Shays, erupted in western Massachusetts. In the summer of 1786 armed rebels attacked the federal arsenal at Springfield, harassing merchants, creditors, and representatives of the state government. The state militia crushed the rebellion, several farmers were hanged, and Shays fled to Vermont. "Shays's Rebellion" hastened the movement to replace the Articles of Confederation. In May 1787 fifty-five delegates from every state save Rhode Island met in a convention in Philadelphia to reform the national government.

The first step toward general reform of the government came in September 1786 when five delegates, assembled to discuss interstate commerce, called for a convention to meet in Philadelphia in May 1787 to discuss measures to render a federal constitution "adequate to the exigencies of the Union." In May 1787 fifty-five delegates from every state except Rhode Island went to Philadelphia to meet in Independence Hall. The proposed constitution retained a federal governing structure in which power was shared between the states and the nation, but it decisively strengthened the power of the national government, granting to Congress the authority to "provide for the general welfare of the United States" as well as the power to make "all laws necessary and proper" for executing the powers vested "in the government of the United States." The Federalist framers left no doubt that the Constitution and "all laws passed under it" was to be the supreme law of the land (Article VI). After thirty-nine of the forty-two remaining delegates signed the document, the drafted constitution was forwarded to the states for ratification by special constitutional conventions.

With the debate moved to the states, proponents of the Constitution faced widespread and vocal opposition. The opposition coalesced in the Antifederalists, who viewed the proposed government as too centralized, too complex in structure, removed from direct control by the people, and lacking a bill of rights. The Antifederalist arguments enjoyed the sanction of the Revolutionary past. The common understanding held that republics could endure in only small areas, based on local governments ruled by men of virtue. The English revolution of the seventeenth century, which ended in the dictatorship of Oliver Cromwell, showed what happened to republics in larger states with heterogeneous populations. For many Americans governing themselves in the eleven years between 1776 and 1787, a central government with authority superceding that of the separate states seemed reminiscent of royal tyranny.

Aware of their opponents ideological advantage, Federalists moved quickly. The most important effort was the series of essays penned by Hamilton, Madison, and Jay, published in New York newspapers under the pseudonym of Publius. Collectively known as *The Federalist*, the papers argued that power, rather than the enemy of liberty, could be its greatest defender. The authors of *The Federalist* knew that the task before them was to revise the prevailing idea of republicanism and to craft a more complex understanding of republican government suited to the needs of a large and growing society.

About the Author

James Madison was born on March 16, 1751, into a wealthy Tidewater family. Raised on a Virginia plantation, he was a sickly child who suffered from unexplained seizures. After graduation from Princeton University, he returned home to pursue legal studies. In 1774 he took a seat on the local Committee of Safety, a pro-revolution group that oversaw the local militia. As a delegate to the Virginia Convention in 1776, Madison was embroiled in the independence debates. In 1778 he was appointed to the Virginia Council of State, which directed state affairs during the Revolution. There he cemented his relationship with Jefferson, who served as governor of Virginia during the war years.

Young Madison had a rare ability to understand and articulate issues. For three years he fought for legislation to strengthen the confederacy of former colonies, contending that military victory required vesting power in a central government. Returning to the House of Delegates in 1784, Madison feared that the Articles of Confederation left the infant republic open to foreign attack and domestic turmoil. He persuaded states rights advocate John Taylor to call a meeting in Annapolis, Maryland, to address problems of interstate commerce. The poorly attended assembly issued a call for a national convention. As leader of the Virginia delegation, Madison supported George Washington as chair.

Madison's Virginia Plan was the model for the eventual Constitution. His extensive notes detailing the proceedings of the convention are the best source of information available on the deliberations. By September 1787 Madison emerged as the most persuasive voice arguing for the new constitution, eventually earning him the sobriquet "Father of the Constitution."

When the Constitution was presented to the states for ratification, Madison, along with Hamilton and Jay, published *The Federalist*. This collection is considered the clearest explication of the theory and structure of the U.S. Constitution. Madison argued for a strong central government, subject to an extensive system of checks and balances. He participated in the debates of the Virginia ratification convention, where the Antifederalists were lead by Patrick Henry, Henry Lee, and James Monroe. His oratorical skill and reasoned arguments won Virginia for ratification.

Madison, elected to the House of Representatives in 1789, was Washington's chief supporter. When he guided the first ten amendments into law in 1791, Madison fulfilled his promise to Jefferson that the Constitution would have a bill of rights. He disagreed with Washington's support for Hamilton, who sought to create a stronger central government favoring commercial and financial over agrarian interests. He also disagreed with the administration's favoritism toward Britain and joined with Jefferson to form the Democratic-Republican Party. Ironically for Madison, an earlier proponent of centralism, the Democratic-Republicans identified localism, libertarianism, and agrarianism as the bedrock of true republicanism.

Time Line

1788

- **Spring** *The Federalist* first edition is published. On June 28 New Hampshire becomes ninth state to ratify the Constitution; Virginia and New York follow.
- **July 2** Congress announces that the Constitution is adopted, naming New York City as the temporary capital and setting dates for elections and for the meeting of the first Congress under the new Constitution.

1789

- **Fall** Madison guides the Bill of Rights into law as the first ten amendments.

During the Adams presidency, Madison led the fight against the Alien and Sedition Acts, designed to suppress opposition to the pro-British Federalist foreign policy. He authored the Virginia Resolution, which declared the laws an unconstitutional violation of civil liberties. In 1799 he campaigned for Jefferson as president. When Jefferson won, Madison became secretary of state, a position he retained until his own election to the presidency in 1808.

Although he was a weak executive, Madison's two terms are remarkable chiefly for the War of 1812. He allowed the expansionist "War Hawk" wing of the Republican Party, led by John Calhoun and Henry Clay, to drag him into declaring war over continued British violations of American maritime rights and support to the Indian insurgency in the Northwest. With an army of fewer than 8,000 men and no national bank, the war was a military disaster that accomplished nothing new for either side. In the wake of the war, Madison chartered the Second Bank of the United States over the opposition of his own party. Madison died in 1836 at the age of eighty-five, having devoted forty years of service to the fledgling American republic.

Explanation and Analysis of the Document

◆ Federalist 10: The Union as a Safeguard against Domestic Faction and Insurrection

Madison begins Federalist 10 by arguing that the most important advantage of a "well-constructed Union" is its tendency to "break and control the violence of faction." By "faction" Madison meant any combination of citizens united by a common interest "adverse to the rights of other citizens, or to the permanent and aggregate interests of the community." The political order was unstable because rival factions brought "superior force" and "overbearing majority" to pass laws favorable to themselves, thus violating the rights of minorities. Departing from the common under-

www.milestonedocuments.com

standing of factions as minorities, Madison saw the organized majority as the most common and dangerous faction. In paragraph 7 Madison attributes the root cause of faction to human nature, viewing humans as driven by passion rather than reason. Disputing the doctrine that liberty and equality produce a "natural aristocracy" based on wisdom, talent, and concern for the good of the whole, Madison countered, "It is in vain to say that enlightened statesmen will be able to adjust these clashing interests, and render them all subservient to the public good."

The factional disease can be cured by removing the cause or by controlling the effects. The cause can be removed either by "destroying the liberty which is essential to its existence" or by making all opinions and passions concur. The first cure is untenable since "liberty is to faction what air is to fire." Just as air is necessary for animal life, liberty is essential for political life. By seeing faction as both the product and the price of liberty, Madison dispenses with curing faction by limiting liberty. Making all opinions conform is no remedy either, since the fallibility of human reason dictates that "different opinions will be formed … concerning religion, concerning government."

In paragraph 6 Madison avers that "the first object of government" is the protection of the "rights of property" and of "the diversity in the faculties of men, from which the rights of property originate." For Madison the unequal capacity of people to acquire property gives rise to "a division of the society into different interests and parties." The inequality between the propertyless many and the propertied few has "divided mankind into parties, inflamed them with mutual animosity, and rendered them … disposed to vex and oppress each other (rather) than to co-operate for their common good." In the same passage (paragraph 7) Madison cites the different types of property arising in economically dynamic nations: "a landed interest, a manufacturing interest … a moneyed interest … [that] divide them into different classes, actuated by different sentiments and views." All of these "interfering interests" encourage the spirit of faction. The "principal task of modern legislation" is the regulation of these interests. The problem Madison raises is how competing claims may be decided: "Is a law proposed concerning private debts? It is a question to which the creditors are parties on one side and the debtors on the other. Justice ought to hold the balance between them." By the end of paragraph 8, Madison abandons the idea of a prudential solution: "The apportionment of taxes on the various descriptions of property … seems to require the most exact impartiality; yet there is, perhaps, no legislative act in which greater opportunity and temptation are given to a predominant party to trample on the rules of justice." Once again justice will go to the most numerous faction. So the causes of faction cannot be removed, and neither can the effects be eliminated. However, a government that restrains the majority while maintaining popular sovereignty can control the effects of faction. Madison argues (paragraph 12) that the impassioned majority "must be rendered, by their number and local situation, unable to concert and carry into effect schemes of oppression."

Madison asserts in the next paragraphs that democracy, "by which I mean a society consisting of a small number of citizens, who assemble and administer the government in person, can admit of no cure for the mischiefs of faction." He criticizes democracies as ever the "spectacles of turbulence and contention … found incompatible with personal security or the rights of property." He identifies direct democracy with mob rule, if not anarchy. He accuses democratic theorists of confusing equality of political rights, with equality in possessions, opinions, and passions—a view he has already denied as inconsistent with human nature. Republics, on the other hand, "by which I mean a government in which the scheme of representation takes place … refine and enlarge the public views, by passing them through the medium of a chosen body." The more indirect the representation is, the more majority opinion is filtered, until it becomes refined by the wisdom of the best men sitting in the upper legislative house.

But filtration alone is not enough. Factious men can scheme to get themselves elected. This is particularly true in small republics, where the ratio of representatives to constituents is low enough for constituents to exert direct influence. In a large republic, the greater ratio enables the representatives to "guard against the confusion of a multitude." In a large republic, where representatives will be chosen "by a greater number of citizens," it will be harder for "unworthy candidates" to maneuver to win elections. When constituents are spread over a greater area, they are freer to vote their consciences and to choose men of "merit … and established characters." Madison argues that the Constitution balances between the large republic's freedom from local pressure and the small republic's familiarity with constituent concerns: "The federal Constitution forms a happy combination in this respect; the great and aggregate interests being referred to the national, the local and particular to the State legislatures."

In paragraph 20 Madison argues that as the territory gets larger, it will be harder for members of the majority "to discover their own strength, and to act in unison with each other" because the greater numbers needed for concerted action will breed distrust among the whole. He argues that in a large republic the diversity of interest groups will work to prevent the formation of a single majority interest that will come together and "oppress the rest" (paragraph 20).

Madison ends Federalist 10 by repeating his concern for protecting private property. He argues that "a rage for paper money, for an abolition of debts, for an equal division of property" will be less likely to pervade the whole Union than any particular state. By ending on this note, Madison hoped to persuade wealthy merchants and creditors that their interests would be best served by the "proper structure of the Union" promised by the Constitution.

◆ Federalist 14: Objections to the Proposed Constitution from Extent of Territory Answered

In Federalist 14 Madison argues for a large republic on practical grounds. He accuses the Antifederalists of exploiting the prejudice against large republics by pointing to the small democracies of antiquity. He refutes this by referring to the actual territory of the proposed United States of America.

Madison formulates a geometrical axiom in paragraph 5: "The natural limit of a republic is that distance from the centre which will barely allow the representatives to meet as often as may be necessary for the administration of public affairs." Considering the longest side of the Union, the delegates from the most distant point on the Atlantic coast had no more difficulty assembling in Congress for the past thirteen years than those from states "in the neighborhood of Congress." In the next paragraph, computing the area ceded to the states by Britain, Madison concludes that the total area is "not a great deal larger than Germany," where supreme power resides in a federal diet.

In paragraph 8 Madison concedes that if the "general government" were the only legislative power and if the new Union abolished the states, its opponents would have "some ground for their objection." However, the federal government's jurisdiction will be limited to "enumerated objects, which concern all the members of the republic" and the "subordinate governments ... will retain their due authority and activity."

Madison next considers whether the expansion of the states into the Northwest Territory might make the republic too large. He responds by envisioning that the federal republic will have the capacity to build better roads, open the eastern waterways to navigation, multiply accommodations for travelers, and generally improve interaction throughout the Union. Constructing canals between the interior lakes and rivers will establish natural communication pathways between the "Western and Atlantic districts." Since the westernmost states will be on the frontier and in constant need of protection, they will be driven by necessity to pay the costs of the Union in order to receive the benefits of "its strength and resources."

Madison concludes Federalist 14 with an appeal to the American people to remember "the many cords of affection" knitting them together and to disregard the voice of the Antifederalists telling them they can no longer be fellow citizens or members of the same family. It is a voice that says the new government is a novel and rash attempt to accomplish the impossible and that the blood mingled in the revolution belonged to "aliens, rivals, enemies." Madison answers that the rashest novelty would be to "preserve our liberties and promote our happiness" by "rendering us in pieces." In rejecting the experiment because it is new, the opponents deny that "the glory of the people of America" has been to refuse to worship the gods of antiquity, tradition, or custom. For Madison reliance on "their own good sense, the knowledge of their own situation, and the lessons of their own experience" is the glory of Americans. Posterity's debt to America will be to the innovations "in favor of private rights and public happiness" and the willingness to act without precedent to accomplish a "revolution which has no parallel in the annals of human society."

Madison draws a straight line from revolution to Confederation, to the new Constitution. He ends by calling on Americans to deliberate and decide on this latest act of a continuing work in progress.

www.milestonedocuments.com

◆ Federalist 51: The Structure of the Government Must Furnish the Proper Checks and Balances between the Different Departments

In Federalist 51, Madison explains how the separation of powers between the branches of government will check the power of each branch. In paragraph 2 he argues that the branches must be absolutely separate for separation of powers to work. Each branch is like a person needing a "will of its own" to have its separate identity and to protect itself from the incursions of others. Since the members of each branch are absolutely separate, each branch should have nothing to do with the appointment of members of the other branches. This can best be attained when the members of all three branches are drawn "from the same fountain of authority, the people." Popular sovereignty, which locates power in the people as a whole, works to select members of the government from a source independent of the government or its branches. Madison exempts the judicial branch from the popular principle because of the "peculiar qualifications" essential for its members—a specialized knowledge of the law and lifetime tenure. With appointment for life, their deliberations will be independent of the president who appoints them. To avoid becoming dependent on the legislature for their salaries, both the executive and the judges must be totally independent. In paragraph 4 he insists that the greatest insurance against concentration of power in any one branch is reliance on "personal motives to resist encroachments." Human selfishness should work to make each branch jealous of the powers of the others; conversely, each branch will be wary of threats to its own powers. In this way, self-interest will drive each branch to defend its own powers. In short, "ambition must be made to counteract ambition."

Madison reminds the reader that government is only a reflection of human nature and that "if men were angels, no government would be necessary. If angels were to govern men, neither external nor internal controls on government would be necessary." Therefore, a government of men needs two things: It must first be able to control the governed and then be obliged to control itself.

Although the primary control on government ought to be the people, Madison contends that experience teaches that "auxiliary precautions" are necessary to ensure control. Since men cannot be trusted to act disinterestedly for either the private or the public good, a way must be found to use this moral defect in human nature so "that each may be a check on the other." This is what transpires at the local level, and "these inventions of prudence" must be made to operate "in the distribution of the supreme powers of the State." He then poses the problem of how this is to be accomplished.

Madison views the legislature as the dominant branch because proportional representation will ensure its greater weight. To remedy this "inconveniency," the Constitution

Federalist 51 (National Archives and Records Administration)

divides the legislature into two branches. This separates the Congress into lower and upper Houses. Madison asserts that the unelected nature of the Senate should act to render the two Houses "as little connected with each other as the nature of their common functions … will admit." If the president is weak, the power to veto acts of the legislature strengthens him. If the executive does not use the veto correctly, the unelected Senate can support the unelected president against the greater power of the directly elected House of Representatives.

In paragraph 9 Madison asserts that a federal republic has a "double security" that checks the "rights of the people." The popular power is first divided between the state and national governments. Power is further divided by apportionment between the separate departments at each level. The two different governments will control each other at the same time that "each will be controlled by itself" in a kind of balancing wheel within a balancing wheel mechanism.

Madison repeats in the following paragraph that in a republic not only must society be guarded "against the oppression of its rulers," but also any part of the society must be protected "against the injustice of the other part." Madison recalls the case of a majority faction violating the rights of the minority. Of the two methods of combating this, Madison rejects "creating a will in the community independent of the majority that is, of society itself." The creation of such a will would require a hereditary or some other "self-appointed authority" standing above the popular will. Madison rejects such an entity, since the security provided would be at best "precarious." It would not matter which interest was protected, because such a superior power could turn on either or both parties. The second method resides in the "federal republic of the United States," where, although the locus of authority resides in the society, the social body is "broken into so many parts, interests, and classes of citizens" that minority rights could not be threatened from "combinations of the majority." Madison envisions a society with such a complex division of labor, economic interests, and ideologies that an oppressive majority would be unlikely. The natural environment for such a diversity of interests could only be a large republic, extensive in area and population.

Madison links the federal Union with republican ideals more closely than previously. Whereas in Federalists 10 and 14 he had argued for a stronger "well-constructed Union" as a matter of necessity, in this passage he links the necessity for Union with the principles of liberty and justice: "In exact proportion as the territory of the Union may be formed into more circumscribed Confederacies, or States oppressive combinations of a majority will be facilitated." He implies that representative government is the only path between tyranny and anarchy. In societies where majorities can easily form to oppress minorities, "anarchy may as truly be said to reign as in a state of nature." The weaker are not secure against the force of the stronger and "even the stronger individuals are prompted, by the insecurity of their condition, to submit to a government which may protect the weak as well as themselves." Madison predicts that if left to itself as an independent state, Rhode Island, which boycotted the convention and had legislated that creditors accept paper money as payment for debts, would be so faction ridden and insecure that even the dominant majorities responsible for the anarchy would eventually call for a despotic power for protection.

In the "extended republic of the United States," the only majority that could form amidst such a diversity of interests, parties, and sects would be one united on the principles of justice and the common good. There are simply too many interest groups for a single one to seek its own interest at the expense of the others. Conversely, there cannot be a pretext for a despot to arise in order to protect some from the power of others.

Audience

The original aim of the Federalist Papers was to elect pro-Constitution delegates to the New York state ratification convention. The intended audience was the merchants of New York City, whose support was essential if

Essential Quotes

"Liberty is to faction what air is to fire, an ailment without which it instantly expires."

(Federalist 10, paragraph 5)

"But the most common and durable source of factions has been the various and unequal distribution of property. Those who hold and those who are without property have ever formed distinct interests in society."

(Federalist 10, paragraph 7)

"Ambition must be made to counteract ambition. The interest of the man must be connected with the constitutional rights of the place."

(Federalist 51, paragraph 4)

"If men were angels, no government would be necessary. If angels were to govern men, neither external nor internal controls on government would be necessary."

(Federalist 51, paragraph 4)

"In framing a government which is to be administered by men over men, the great difficulty lies in this: you must first enable the government to control the governed; and in the next place oblige it to control itself."

(Federalist 51, paragraph 4)

www.milestonedocuments.com

the upstate Antifederalists were to be defeated. This effort ultimately failed. Only nineteen Federalists were elected from New York City, while forty-six Antifederalists were elected from upstate, led by Governor George Clinton. The papers were printed in only a dozen papers outside of New York, and their influence on the overall vote was minimal.

Although Publius's abstract style was well received by urban merchants and lawyers, its complex argumentation was lost on most Antifederalists. The typical Antifederalist, steeped in the plain-speech discourse of Thomas Paine, was bewildered by the avalanche of words of the Federalist Papers. One perplexed Philadelphian spoke for most Antifederalists in complaining that Publius had "mistaken sound for argument … and endeavored to force conviction by a torrent of misplaced words" (Bailyn, 2003, p. 101).

Impact

Long before New York's delegates met, Antifederalists in the nine states needed for approval had been won over by an agreement to add a bill of rights to the Constitution. However, owing to the state's size and importance as a mercantile center, New York's support was crucial if the Constitution was to actually be put into effect. Hamilton eventually wore down the opposition, and New York became the eleventh state to ratify. Despite failing to influence many New York voters, the Federalist Papers had a major impact beyond New York. The essays had their greatest impact after they were published in a single volume as *The Federalist*. Madison mailed hundreds of copies to the Virginia delegation, including the future Supreme Court Justice John Marshall. Leading the debate for ratification, Madison made Virginia the tenth domino to fall, setting the stage for New York's ratification.

The Federalist Papers open a window to the thinking of the Constitution's framers. They have spawned libraries of scholarly commentary and assumed an aura of gravity never intended by the authors. By the year 2000 the papers had been cited a total of 291 times. The number of citations by the Supreme Court has increased with time, especially since 1980. Although the reason is unclear, the shift in the Supreme Court toward "originalists," who hold that ascertaining the original intent of the framers is paramount in rendering decisions, is a major factor. Perhaps the greatest impact of *The Federalist* lies in its unchallenged status as the uniquely American contribution to political science on a world scale.

Related Documents

Cooke, Jacob E., ed. *The Federalist*. Middletown, Conn.: Wesleyan University Press, 1982. This volume contains the original text without corrections; numbers 1 to 77 are from the newspapers in which they appeared, while numbers 78 to 85 are from McLean's first printing.

Farrand, Max, ed. *The Records of the Federal Convention of 1787*, rev ed. New Haven, Conn.: Yale University Press, 1966. The three volumes, the single best source on the Constitutional Convention, include Madison's notes, letters by other participants, and the various constitutional plans proposed during the Convention.

Hutchinson, William T., William M. E. Rachal, and Robert Allen Rutland, eds. *The Papers of James Madison*. 16 vols. Chicago: University of Chicago Press, 1962–1976.This set contains the complete papers of James Madison in exact chronological order, including both private and public papers.

Jensen, Merrill, John Kaminski, and Gaspare Saladino, eds. *The Documentary History of the Ratification of the Constitution*. Madison: Wisconsin Historical Society, 2005. This book contains documents of the ratification debate: legislative records, personal papers and records, newspapers, magazines, journals, notes taken by delegates and private reporters, and pamphlets and broadsides.

Storing, Herbert J. *The Complete Anti-Federalist*. Chicago: University of Chicago Press, 1981. This complete collection of pamphlets, newspaper articles, letters, essays, and speeches written in opposition to the Constitution during the ratification debate includes introduction and commentary to each entry.

Bibliography

■ Books

Bailyn, Bernard. *The Debate on the Constitution: Federalist and Antifederalist Speeches, Articles, and Letters during the Struggle over Ratification*. New York: Viking Press, 1993.

———. *To Begin the World Anew: The Genius and Ambiguities of the American Founders*. New York: Alfred E. Knopf, 2003.

Brant, Irving. *James Madison*. 6 vols. Indianapolis, Ind.: Bobbs-Merrill, 1941–1961.

Elkins, Stanley M., and Eric McKitrick. *The Age of Federalism: The Early American Republic, 1788–1800*. New York: Oxford University Press, 1993.

Main, Jackson Turner. *Political Parties before the Constitution*. Chapel Hill: University of North Carolina Press, 1973.

Matthews, Richard K. *If Men Were Angels: James Madison and the Heartless Empire of Reason*. Lawrence: University Press of Kansas, 1995.

McDonald, Forrest, ed. *Empire and Nation: Letters from a Farmer in Pennsylvania (John Dickinson). Letters from the Federal Farmer (Richard Henry Lee)*. Indianapolis, Ind.: Liberty Fund, 1999.

Middlekauff, Robert. *The Glorious Cause: The American Revolution, 1763–1789*. New York: Oxford University Press, 2005.

Wood, Gordon S. *The Creation of the American Republic, 1776–1787*. New York: W. W. Norton, 1972.

———. *The Radicalism of the American Revolution*. New York: Vintage Books, 1993.

———. *Revolutionary Characters: What Made the Founders Different*. New York: Penguin Press, 2006.

■ Web Sites

"Constitution of the United States." ushistory.org Historic Documents Web site.
http://www.ushistory.org/documents/constitution.htm. Accessed on July 22, 2007.

"The Federalist Papers." Founding Fathers.info Web site.
http://www.foundingfathers.info/federalistpapers/. Accessed on January 25, 2008.

"The James Madison Papers." The Library of Congress "American Memory" Web site.
http://memory.loc.gov/ammem/collections/madison_papers/. Accessed on July 14, 2007.

—By Robert Montgomery

Questions for Further Study

1. Some historians argue that the Constitution was a retreat from the Declaration of Independence. By allowing the continuation of slavery, creating a powerful central government with an unelected Senate and president, and limiting the options for structural change to the amending process, the Constitution is said to repudiate the Revolutionary, democratic, and equalitarian spirit of the Declaration. Others argue that the Constitution simply codified the Declaration by providing a legal framework for republican government. Discuss the relationship between the ideals of the two founding documents. Do they conflict with each other? Or are they in fundamental agreement? Refer to the Declaration of Independence and to Federalist 10, 14, and 51.

2. In your opinion, had the Constitution not been ratified by the required nine states, what would have happened to the United States? Would the states have collapsed into despotism, as Madison predicted? Would the Union have continued as a loose confederation of states? Would a new convention have fixed the defects of the Articles of Confederation, creating a national system of sovereign states? Would the states have formed into regional blocs and made treaties of alliance with different European powers?

3. The American presidency is often called "the imperial presidency," as the executive branch has progressively increased its powers over time. In the post-9/11 period the executive branch has added a Department of Homeland Security with new powers of its own and has utilized intelligence-gathering methods such as "warrantless wiretaps." In this light, how well has the constitutional system of separation of powers and checks and balances held up?

4. No president has yet left office as the result of impeachment. Antifederalists argued that impeachment is not an effective check on the president. Because the court would be the Senate, a group the president might easily dominate, and the presiding judge would be a chief justice, whom the president himself has nominated, the deck is stacked in the president's favor. Discuss whether impeachment is an effective check on the executive power. Refer to Federalist 51, to the Constitution (Article II, Section 4), and to the cases of Andrew Johnson, Richard Nixon, and Bill Clinton.

Glossary

agency	the means by which something is accomplished; instrumentality
aggregate	total or whole; collective
anarchy	the "war of all against all" in a state of nature where no rights are secure
artifice	trickery
cabals	conspiratorial groups of plotters or intriguers
commensurate	matching in size or degree; proportionate
concert	to act together as a unit
Confederacy	a league of states
consonant	being in agreement or accord
contiguous	sharing an edge or boundary; touching

www.milestonedocuments.com

Glossary

democracy	a small number of citizens who assemble and administer the government by majority vote
desideratum	something desired or considered essential
diet	a form of representative government in Europe
efficacy	power or capacity to produce a desired effect
emoluments	compensations
encroachments	acts of trespassing on the property or domain of another
enumerated	specified
equilibrium	a condition in which all acting influences are canceled by others, resulting in a stable or balanced system
expedient	something contrived or used to meet a need
faction	a group of citizens united by a common passion
faculties	the powers or capacities of the human mind
fallacy	a statement or an argument based on a false or unfounded supposition
fallible	capable of making an error
insuperable	insurmountable
intercourse	interaction between parts
interests	groups that each seek their own benefit or advantage
latent	potential but not evident or active
meliorated	improved
nominal	existing in name only and not in reality
obviated	rendered unnecessary
opprobrium	contempt
palliate	to make an offense or crime seem less serious
party	a group of persons interested in any act, affair, or transaction before a government
petulantly	peevishly or irritably
propensity	an innate inclination
prudence	good or cautious judgment
republic	a government where the citizens choose a small number of delegates to represent them
specious	having misleading allure
subservient	subordinate in capacity or function
unhallowed	lacking reverence; profane
usurpations	wrongful seizures or exercises of authority or privilege belonging to another
vex	to plague or afflict
vice	any immoral or evil habit or practice
virtue	moral excellence and righteousness; goodness

Federalist Papers 10, 14, and 51

www.milestonedocuments.com

Federalist 10

◆ The Same Subject Continued (The Union as a Safeguard Against Domestic Faction and Insurrection)

From the *New York Packet*, Friday, November 23, 1787

To the People of the State of New York:

AMONG the numerous advantages promised by a well-constructed Union, none deserves to be more accurately developed than its tendency to break and control the violence of faction. The friend of popular governments never finds himself so much alarmed for their character and fate, as when he contemplates their propensity to this dangerous vice. He will not fail, therefore, to set a due value on any plan which, without violating the principles to which he is attached, provides a proper cure for it. The instability, injustice, and confusion introduced into the public councils, have, in truth, been the mortal diseases under which popular governments have everywhere perished; as they continue to be the favorite and fruitful topics from which the adversaries to liberty derive their most specious declamations. The valuable improvements made by the American constitutions on the popular models, both ancient and modern, cannot certainly be too much admired; but it would be an unwarrantable partiality, to contend that they have as effectually obviated the danger on this side, as was wished and expected. Complaints are everywhere heard from our most considerate and virtuous citizens, equally the friends of public and private faith, and of public and personal liberty, that our governments are too unstable, that the public good is disregarded in the conflicts of rival parties, and that measures are too often decided, not according to the rules of justice and the rights of the minor party, but by the superior force of an interested and overbearing majority. However anxiously we may wish that these complaints had no foundation, the evidence, of known facts will not permit us to deny that they are in some degree true. It will be found, indeed, on a candid review of our situation, that some of the distresses under which we labor have been erroneously charged on the operation of our governments; but it will be found, at the same time, that other causes will not alone account for many of our heaviest misfortunes; and, particularly, for that prevailing and increasing distrust of public engagements, and alarm for private rights, which are echoed from one end of the continent to the other. These must be chiefly, if not wholly, effects of the unsteadiness and injustice with which a factious spirit has tainted our public administrations.

By a faction, I understand a number of citizens, whether amounting to a majority or a minority of the whole, who are united and actuated by some common impulse of passion, or of interest, adverse to the rights of other citizens, or to the permanent and aggregate interests of the community.

There are two methods of curing the mischiefs of faction: the one, by removing its causes; the other, by controlling its effects.

There are again two methods of removing the causes of faction: the one, by destroying the liberty which is essential to its existence; the other, by giving to every citizen the same opinions, the same passions, and the same interests.

It could never be more truly said than of the first remedy, that it was worse than the disease. Liberty is to faction what air is to fire, an aliment without which it instantly expires. But it could not be less folly to abolish liberty, which is essential to political life, because it nourishes faction, than it would be to wish the annihilation of air, which is essential to animal life, because it imparts to fire its destructive agency.

Document Text

The second expedient is as impracticable as the first would be unwise. As long as the reason of man continues fallible, and he is at liberty to exercise it, different opinions will be formed. As long as the connection subsists between his reason and his self-love, his opinions and his passions will have a reciprocal influence on each other; and the former will be objects to which the latter will attach themselves. The diversity in the faculties of men, from which the rights of property originate, is not less an insuperable obstacle to a uniformity of interests. The protection of these faculties is the first object of government. From the protection of different and unequal faculties of acquiring property, the possession of different degrees and kinds of property immediately results; and from the influence of these on the sentiments and views of the respective proprietors, ensues a division of the society into different interests and parties.

The latent causes of faction are thus sown in the nature of man; and we see them everywhere brought into different degrees of activity, according to the different circumstances of civil society. A zeal for different opinions concerning religion, concerning government, and many other points, as well of speculation as of practice; an attachment to different leaders ambitiously contending for pre-eminence and power; or to persons of other descriptions whose fortunes have been interesting to the human passions, have, in turn, divided mankind into parties, inflamed them with mutual animosity, and rendered them much more disposed to vex and oppress each other than to co-operate for their common good. So strong is this propensity of mankind to fall into mutual animosities, that where no substantial occasion presents itself, the most frivolous and fanciful distinctions have been sufficient to kindle their unfriendly passions and excite their most violent conflicts. But the most common and durable source of factions has been the various and unequal distribution of property. Those who hold and those who are without property have ever formed distinct interests in society. Those who are creditors, and those who are debtors, fall under a like discrimination. A landed interest, a manufacturing interest, a mercantile interest, a moneyed interest, with many lesser interests, grow up of necessity in civilized nations, and divide them into different classes, actuated by different sentiments and views. The regulation of these various and interfering interests forms the principal task of modern legislation, and involves the spirit of party and faction in the necessary and ordinary operations of the government.

No man is allowed to be a judge in his own cause, because his interest would certainly bias his judgment, and, not improbably, corrupt his integrity. With equal, nay with greater reason, a body of men are unfit to be both judges and parties at the same time; yet what are many of the most important acts of legislation, but so many judicial determinations, not indeed concerning the rights of single persons, but concerning the rights of large bodies of citizens? And what are the different classes of legislators but advocates and parties to the causes which they determine? Is a law proposed concerning private debts? It is a question to which the creditors are parties on one side and the debtors on the other. Justice ought to hold the balance between them. Yet the parties are, and must be, themselves the judges; and the most numerous party, or, in other words, the most powerful faction must be expected to prevail. Shall domestic manufactures be encouraged, and in what degree, by restrictions on foreign manufactures? are questions which would be differently decided by the landed and the manufacturing classes, and probably by neither with a sole regard to justice and the public good. The apportionment of taxes on the various descriptions of property is an act which seems to require the most exact impartiality; yet there is, perhaps, no legislative act in which greater opportunity and temptation are given to a predominant party to trample on the rules of justice. Every shilling with which they overburden the inferior number, is a shilling saved to their own pockets.

It is in vain to say that enlightened statesmen will be able to adjust these clashing interests, and render them all subservient to the public good. Enlightened statesmen will not always be at the helm. Nor, in many cases, can such an adjustment be made at all without taking into view indirect and remote considerations, which will rarely prevail over the immediate interest which one party may find in disregarding the rights of another or the good of the whole.

The inference to which we are brought is, that the *causes* of faction cannot be removed, and that relief is only to be sought in the means of controlling its *effects*.

If a faction consists of less than a majority, relief is supplied by the republican principle, which enables the majority to defeat its sinister views by regular vote. It may clog the administration, it may convulse the society; but it will be unable to execute and mask its violence under the forms of the Constitution. When a majority is included in a faction, the form of popular government, on the other hand, enables it to sacrifice to its ruling passion or interest both the public good and the rights of other citizens. To secure the public good and private rights against the danger of such a faction, and at the same time to preserve the spirit and the form of popular government, is then the great object to which our inquiries are directed. Let me add that it is the great desideratum by which this form of government can be rescued from the opprobrium under which it has so long labored, and be recommended to the esteem and adoption of mankind.

By what means is this object attainable? Evidently by one of two only. Either the existence of the same passion or interest in a majority at the same time must be prevented, or the majority, having such coexistent passion or interest, must be rendered, by their number and local situation, unable to concert and carry into effect schemes of oppression. If the impulse and the opportunity be suffered to coincide, we well know that neither moral nor religious motives can be relied on as an adequate control. They are not found to be such on the injustice and violence of individuals, and lose their efficacy in proportion to the number combined together, that is, in proportion as their efficacy becomes needful.

From this view of the subject it may be concluded that a pure democracy, by which I mean a society consisting of a small number of citizens, who assemble and administer the government in person, can admit of no cure for the mischiefs of faction. A common passion or interest will, in almost every case, be felt by a majority of the whole; a communication and concert result from the form of government itself; and there is nothing to check the inducements to sacrifice the weaker party or an obnoxious individual. Hence it is that such democracies have ever been spectacles of turbulence and contention; have ever been found incompatible with personal security or the rights of property; and have in general been as short in their lives as they have been violent in their deaths. Theoretic politicians, who have patronized this species of government, have erroneously supposed that by reducing mankind to a perfect equality in their political rights, they would, at the same time, be perfectly equalized and assimilated in their possessions, their opinions, and their passions.

A republic, by which I mean a government in which the scheme of representation takes place, opens a different prospect, and promises the cure for which we are seeking. Let us examine the points in which it varies from pure democracy, and we shall comprehend both the nature of the cure and the efficacy which it must derive from the Union.

The two great points of difference between a democracy and a republic are: first, the delegation of the government, in the latter, to a small number of citizens elected by the rest; secondly, the greater number of citizens, and greater sphere of country, over which the latter may be extended.

The effect of the first difference is, on the one hand, to refine and enlarge the public views, by passing them through the medium of a chosen body of citizens, whose wisdom may best discern the true interest of their country, and whose patriotism and love of justice will be least likely to sacrifice it to temporary or partial considerations. Under such a regulation, it may well happen that the public voice, pronounced by the representatives of the people, will be more consonant to the public good than if pronounced by the people themselves, convened for the purpose. On the other hand, the effect may be inverted. Men of factious tempers, of local prejudices, or of sinister designs, may, by intrigue, by corruption, or by other means, first obtain the suffrages, and then betray the interests, of the people. The question resulting is, whether small or extensive republics are more favorable to the election of proper guardians of the public weal; and it is clearly decided in favor of the latter by two obvious considerations:

In the first place, it is to be remarked that, however small the republic may be, the representatives must be raised to a certain number, in order to guard against the cabals of a few; and that, however large it may be, they must be limited to a certain number, in order to guard against the confusion of a multitude. Hence, the number of representatives in the two cases not being in proportion to that of the two constituents, and being proportionally greater in the small republic, it follows that, if the proportion of fit characters be not less in the large than in the small republic, the former will present a greater option, and consequently a greater probability of a fit choice.

In the next place, as each representative will be chosen by a greater number of citizens in the large than in the small republic, it will be more difficult for unworthy candidates to practice with success the vicious arts by which elections are too often carried; and the suffrages of the people being more free, will be more likely to centre in men who possess the most attractive merit and the most diffusive and established characters.

It must be confessed that in this, as in most other cases, there is a mean, on both sides of which incon-

www.milestonedocuments.com

veniences will be found to lie. By enlarging too much the number of electors, you render the representatives too little acquainted with all their local circumstances and lesser interests; as by reducing it too much, you render him unduly attached to these, and too little fit to comprehend and pursue great and national objects. The federal Constitution forms a happy combination in this respect; the great and aggregate interests being referred to the national, the local and particular to the State legislatures.

The other point of difference is, the greater number of citizens and extent of territory which may be brought within the compass of republican than of democratic government; and it is this circumstance principally which renders factious combinations less to be dreaded in the former than in the latter. The smaller the society, the fewer probably will be the distinct parties and interests composing it; the fewer the distinct parties and interests, the more frequently will a majority be found of the same party; and the smaller the number of individuals composing a majority, and the smaller the compass within which they are placed, the more easily will they concert and execute their plans of oppression. Extend the sphere, and you take in a greater variety of parties and interests; you make it less probable that a majority of the whole will have a common motive to invade the rights of other citizens; or if such a common motive exists, it will be more difficult for all who feel it to discover their own strength, and to act in unison with each other. Besides other impediments, it may be remarked that, where there is a consciousness of unjust or dishonorable purposes, communication is always checked by distrust in proportion to the number whose concurrence is necessary.

Hence, it clearly appears, that the same advantage which a republic has over a democracy, in controlling the effects of faction, is enjoyed by a large over a small republic,—is enjoyed by the Union over the States composing it. Does the advantage consist in the substitution of representatives whose enlightened views and virtuous sentiments render them superior to local prejudices and schemes of injustice? It will not be denied that the representation of the Union will be most likely to possess these requisite endowments. Does it consist in the greater security afforded by a greater variety of parties, against the event of any one party being able to outnumber and oppress the rest? In an equal degree does the increased variety of parties comprised within the Union, increase this security. Does it, in fine, consist in the greater obstacles opposed to the concert and accomplishment of the secret wishes of an unjust and interested majority? Here, again, the extent of the Union gives it the most palpable advantage.

The influence of factious leaders may kindle a flame within their particular States, but will be unable to spread a general conflagration through the other States. A religious sect may degenerate into a political faction in a part of the Confederacy; but the variety of sects dispersed over the entire face of it must secure the national councils against any danger from that source. A rage for paper money, for an abolition of debts, for an equal division of property, or for any other improper or wicked project, will be less apt to pervade the whole body of the Union than a particular member of it; in the same proportion as such a malady is more likely to taint a particular county or district, than an entire State.

In the extent and proper structure of the Union, therefore, we behold a republican remedy for the diseases most incident to republican government. And according to the degree of pleasure and pride we feel in being republicans, ought to be our zeal in cherishing the spirit and supporting the character of Federalists.

PUBLIUS.

Federalist 14

◆ Objections to the Proposed Constitution From Extent of Territory Answered

From the *New York Packet*, Friday, November 30, 1787

To the People of the State of New York:

WE have seen the necessity of the Union, as our bulwark against foreign danger, as the conservator of peace among ourselves, as the guardian of our commerce and other common interests, as the only substitute for those military establishments which have subverted the liberties of the Old World, and as the proper antidote for the diseases of faction, which have proved fatal to other popular governments, and of which alarming symptoms have been betrayed by our own. All that remains, within this branch of our inquiries, is to take notice of an objection that may be drawn from the great extent of country which the Union embraces. A few observations on this subject will be the more proper, as it is perceived that the adversaries of the new Constitution are availing themselves of the prevailing prejudice with regard to the practicable sphere of republican administration, in order to supply, by imaginary difficulties, the want of those solid objections which they endeavor in vain to find.

Document Text

The error which limits republican government to a narrow district has been unfolded and refuted in preceding papers. I remark here only that it seems to owe its rise and prevalence chiefly to the confounding of a republic with a democracy, applying to the former reasonings drawn from the nature of the latter. The true distinction between these forms was also adverted to on a former occasion. It is, that in a democracy, the people meet and exercise the government in person; in a republic, they assemble and administer it by their representatives and agents. A democracy, consequently, will be confined to a small spot. A republic may be extended over a large region.

To this accidental source of the error may be added the artifice of some celebrated authors, whose writings have had a great share in forming the modern standard of political opinions. Being subjects either of an absolute or limited monarchy, they have endeavored to heighten the advantages, or palliate the evils of those forms, by placing in comparison the vices and defects of the republican, and by citing as specimens of the latter the turbulent democracies of ancient Greece and modern Italy. Under the confusion of names, it has been an easy task to transfer to a republic observations applicable to a democracy only; and among others, the observation that it can never be established but among a small number of people, living within a small compass of territory.

Such a fallacy may have been the less perceived, as most of the popular governments of antiquity were of the democratic species; and even in modern Europe, to which we owe the great principle of representation, no example is seen of a government wholly popular, and founded, at the same time, wholly on that principle. If Europe has the merit of discovering this great mechanical power in government, by the simple agency of which the will of the largest political body may be concentrated, and its force directed to any object which the public good requires, America can claim the merit of making the discovery the basis of unmixed and extensive republics. It is only to be lamented that any of her citizens should wish to deprive her of the additional merit of displaying its full efficacy in the establishment of the comprehensive system now under her consideration.

As the natural limit of a democracy is that distance from the central point which will just permit the most remote citizens to assemble as often as their public functions demand, and will include no greater number than can join in those functions; so the natural limit of a republic is that distance from the centre which will barely allow the representatives to meet as often as may be necessary for the administration of public affairs. Can it be said that the limits of the United States exceed this distance? It will not be said by those who recollect that the Atlantic coast is the longest side of the Union, that during the term of thirteen years, the representatives of the States have been almost continually assembled, and that the members from the most distant States are not chargeable with greater intermissions of attendance than those from the States in the neighborhood of Congress.

That we may form a juster estimate with regard to this interesting subject, let us resort to the actual dimensions of the Union. The limits, as fixed by the treaty of peace, are: on the east the Atlantic, on the south the latitude of thirty-one degrees, on the west the Mississippi, and on the north an irregular line running in some instances beyond the forty-fifth degree, in others falling as low as the forty-second. The southern shore of Lake Erie lies below that latitude. Computing the distance between the thirty-first and forty-fifth degrees, it amounts to nine hundred and seventy-three common miles; computing it from thirty-one to forty-two degrees, to seven hundred and sixty-four miles and a half. Taking the mean for the distance, the amount will be eight hundred and sixty-eight miles and three-fourths. The mean distance from the Atlantic to the Mississippi does not probably exceed seven hundred and fifty miles. On a comparison of this extent with that of several countries in Europe, the practicability of rendering our system commensurate to it appears to be demonstrable. It is not a great deal larger than Germany, where a diet representing the whole empire is continually assembled; or than Poland before the late dismemberment, where another national diet was the depositary of the supreme power. Passing by France and Spain, we find that in Great Britain, inferior as it may be in size, the representatives of the northern extremity of the island have as far to travel to the national council as will be required of those of the most remote parts of the Union.

Favorable as this view of the subject may be, some observations remain which will place it in a light still more satisfactory.

In the first place it is to be remembered that the general government is not to be charged with the whole power of making and administering laws. Its jurisdiction is limited to certain enumerated objects, which concern all the members of the republic, but which are not to be attained by the separate provisions of any. The subordinate governments, which

www.milestonedocuments.com

Document Text

can extend their care to all those other subjects which can be separately provided for, will retain their due authority and activity. Were it proposed by the plan of the convention to abolish the governments of the particular States, its adversaries would have some ground for their objection; though it would not be difficult to show that if they were abolished the general government would be compelled, by the principle of self-preservation, to reinstate them in their proper jurisdiction.

A second observation to be made is that the immediate object of the federal Constitution is to secure the union of the thirteen primitive States, which we know to be practicable; and to add to them such other States as may arise in their own bosoms, or in their neighborhoods, which we cannot doubt to be equally practicable. The arrangements that may be necessary for those angles and fractions of our territory which lie on our northwestern frontier, must be left to those whom further discoveries and experience will render more equal to the task.

Let it be remarked, in the third place, that the intercourse throughout the Union will be facilitated by new improvements. Roads will everywhere be shortened, and kept in better order; accommodations for travelers will be multiplied and meliorated; an interior navigation on our eastern side will be opened throughout, or nearly throughout, the whole extent of the thirteen States. The communication between the Western and Atlantic districts, and between different parts of each, will be rendered more and more easy by those numerous canals with which the beneficence of nature has intersected our country, and which art finds it so little difficult to connect and complete.

A fourth and still more important consideration is, that as almost every State will, on one side or other, be a frontier, and will thus find, in regard to its safety, an inducement to make some sacrifices for the sake of the general protection; so the States which lie at the greatest distance from the heart of the Union, and which, of course, may partake least of the ordinary circulation of its benefits, will be at the same time immediately contiguous to foreign nations, and will consequently stand, on particular occasions, in greatest need of its strength and resources. It may be inconvenient for Georgia, or the States forming our western or northeastern borders, to send their representatives to the seat of government; but they would find it more so to struggle alone against an invading enemy, or even to support alone the whole expense of those precautions which may be dictated by the neighborhood of continual danger. If they should derive less benefit, therefore, from the Union in some respects than the less distant States, they will derive greater benefit from it in other respects, and thus the proper equilibrium will be maintained throughout.

I submit to you, my fellow-citizens, these considerations, in full confidence that the good sense which has so often marked your decisions will allow them their due weight and effect; and that you will never suffer difficulties, however formidable in appearance, or however fashionable the error on which they may be founded, to drive you into the gloomy and perilous scene into which the advocates for disunion would conduct you. Hearken not to the unnatural voice which tells you that the people of America, knit together as they are by so many cords of affection, can no longer live together as members of the same family; can no longer continue the mutual guardians of their mutual happiness; can no longer be fellow citizens of one great, respectable, and flourishing empire. Hearken not to the voice which petulantly tells you that the form of government recommended for your adoption is a novelty in the political world; that it has never yet had a place in the theories of the wildest projectors; that it rashly attempts what it is impossible to accomplish. No, my countrymen, shut your ears against this unhallowed language. Shut your hearts against the poison which it conveys; the kindred blood which flows in the veins of American citizens, the mingled blood which they have shed in defense of their sacred rights, consecrate their Union, and excite horror at the idea of their becoming aliens, rivals, enemies. And if novelties are to be shunned, believe me, the most alarming of all novelties, the most wild of all projects, the most rash of all attempts, is that of rendering us in pieces, in order to preserve our liberties and promote our happiness. But why is the experiment of an extended republic to be rejected, merely because it may comprise what is new? Is it not the glory of the people of America, that, whilst they have paid a decent regard to the opinions of former times and other nations, they have not suffered a blind veneration for antiquity, for custom, or for names, to overrule the suggestions of their own good sense, the knowledge of their own situation, and the lessons of their own experience? To this manly spirit, posterity will be indebted for the possession, and the world for the example, of the numerous innovations displayed on the American theatre, in favor of private rights and public happiness. Had no important step been taken by the leaders of the Revolution for which a precedent could not be discovered, no government established of which an exact model did not present itself, the people of the United States might, at this moment have been numbered among the melancholy victims of misguided councils, must at best have been laboring under the weight of some of those forms which have crushed the liberties of the rest of mankind. Happily for America, happily, we trust, for the whole human race, they pursued a new and more noble course. They accomplished a revolution which has no parallel in the annals of human society. They reared the fabrics of governments which have no model on the face of the globe. They formed the design of a great Confederacy, which it is incumbent on their successors to improve and perpetuate. If their works betray imperfections, we wonder at the fewness of them. If they erred most in the structure of the Union, this was the work most difficult to be executed; this is the work which has been new modelled by the act of your convention, and it is that act on which you are now to deliberate and to decide.

PUBLIUS.

Federalist 51

◆ The Structure of the Government Must Furnish the Proper Checks and Balances Between the Different Departments

From the *New York Packet*, Friday, February 8, 1788

To the People of the State of New York:

TO what expedient, then, shall we finally resort, for maintaining in practice the necessary partition of power among the several departments, as laid down in the Constitution? The only answer that can be given is, that as all these exterior provisions are found to be inadequate, the defect must be supplied, by so contriving the interior structure of the government as that its several constituent parts may, by their mutual relations, be the means of keeping each other in their proper places. Without presuming to undertake a full development of this important idea, I will hazard a few general observations, which may perhaps place it in a clearer light, and enable us to form a more correct judgment of the principles and structure of the government planned by the convention.

In order to lay a due foundation for that separate and distinct exercise of the different powers of government, which to a certain extent is admitted on all hands to be essential to the preservation of liberty, it is evident that each department should have a will of its own; and consequently should be so constituted that the members of each should have as little agency as possible in the appointment of the members of the others. Were this principle rigorously adhered to, it would require that all the appointments for the supreme executive, legislative, and judiciary magistracies should be drawn from the same fountain of authority, the people, through channels having no communication whatever with one another. Perhaps such a plan of constructing the several departments would be less difficult in practice than it may in contemplation appear. Some difficulties, however, and some additional expense would attend the execution of it. Some deviations, therefore, from the principle must be admitted. In the constitution of the judiciary department in particular, it might be inexpedient to insist rigorously on the principle: first, because peculiar qualifications being essential in the members, the primary consideration ought to be to select that mode of choice which best secures these qualifications; secondly, because the permanent tenure by which the appointments are held in that department, must soon destroy all sense of dependence on the authority conferring them.

It is equally evident, that the members of each department should be as little dependent as possible on those of the others, for the emoluments annexed to their offices. Were the executive magistrate, or the judges, not independent of the legislature in this particular, their independence in every other would be merely nominal.

But the great security against a gradual concentration of the several powers in the same department, consists in giving to those who administer each department the necessary constitutional means and personal motives to resist encroachments of the others. The provision for defense must in this, as in all other cases, be made commensurate to the danger of attack. Ambition must be made to counteract ambition. The interest of the man must be connected with the constitutional rights of the place. It may be a reflection on human nature, that such devices should be necessary to control the abuses of government. But what is government itself, but the greatest of all reflections on human nature? If men were angels, no government would be necessary. If angels were to govern men, neither external nor internal controls on government would be necessary. In framing a government which is to be administered by men over men, the great difficulty lies in this: you must first enable the government to control the governed; and in the

www.milestonedocuments.com

next place oblige it to control itself. A dependence on the people is, no doubt, the primary control on the government; but experience has taught mankind the necessity of auxiliary precautions.

This policy of supplying, by opposite and rival interests, the defect of better motives, might be traced through the whole system of human affairs, private as well as public. We see it particularly displayed in all the subordinate distributions of power, where the constant aim is to divide and arrange the several offices in such a manner as that each may be a check on the other that the private interest of every individual may be a sentinel over the public rights. These inventions of prudence cannot be less requisite in the distribution of the supreme powers of the State.

But it is not possible to give to each department an equal power of self-defense. In republican government, the legislative authority necessarily predominates. The remedy for this inconveniency is to divide the legislature into different branches; and to render them, by different modes of election and different principles of action, as little connected with each other as the nature of their common functions and their common dependence on the society will admit. It may even be necessary to guard against dangerous encroachments by still further precautions. As the weight of the legislative authority requires that it should be thus divided, the weakness of the executive may require, on the other hand, that it should be fortified. An absolute negative on the legislature appears, at first view, to be the natural defense with which the executive magistrate should be armed. But perhaps it would be neither altogether safe nor alone sufficient. On ordinary occasions it might not be exerted with the requisite firmness, and on extraordinary occasions it might be perfidiously abused. May not this defect of an absolute negative be supplied by some qualified connection between this weaker department and the weaker branch of the stronger department, by which the latter may be led to support the constitutional rights of the former, without being too much detached from the rights of its own department?

If the principles on which these observations are founded be just, as I persuade myself they are, and they be applied as a criterion to the several State constitutions, and to the federal Constitution it will be found that if the latter does not perfectly correspond with them, the former are infinitely less able to bear such a test.

There are, moreover, two considerations particularly applicable to the federal system of America, which place that system in a very interesting point of view.

First. In a single republic, all the power surrendered by the people is submitted to the administration of a single government; and the usurpations are guarded against by a division of the government into distinct and separate departments. In the compound republic of America, the power surrendered by the people is first divided between two distinct governments, and then the portion allotted to each subdivided among distinct and separate departments. Hence a double security arises to the rights of the people. The different governments will control each other, at the same time that each will be controlled by itself.

Second. It is of great importance in a republic not only to guard the society against the oppression of its rulers, but to guard one part of the society against the injustice of the other part. Different interests necessarily exist in different classes of citizens. If a majority be united by a common interest, the rights of the minority will be insecure. There are but two methods of providing against this evil: the one by creating a will in the community independent of the majority that is, of the society itself; the other, by comprehending in the society so many separate descriptions of citizens as will render an unjust combination of a majority of the whole very improbable, if not impracticable. The first method prevails in all governments possessing an hereditary or self-appointed authority. This, at best, is but a precarious security; because a power independent of the society may as well espouse the unjust views of the major, as the rightful interests of the minor party, and may possibly be turned against both parties. The second method will be exemplified in the federal republic of the United States. Whilst all authority in it will be derived from and dependent on the society, the society itself will be broken into so many parts, interests, and classes of citizens, that the rights of individuals, or of the minority, will be in little danger from interested combinations of the majority. In a free government the security for civil rights must be the same as that for religious rights. It consists in the one case in the multiplicity of interests, and in the other in the multiplicity of sects. The degree of security in both cases will depend on the number of interests and sects; and this may be presumed to depend on the extent of country and number of people comprehended under the same government. This view of the subject must particularly recommend a proper federal system to all the sincere and considerate friends of republican government, since it shows that in exact proportion as the territory of the Union may be formed into more circumscribed Confederacies, or States oppressive combinations of a majority will be facilitated: the best security, under the republican forms, for the rights of every class of citizens, will be diminished: and consequently the stability and independence of some member of the government, the only other security, must be proportionately increased. Justice is the end of government. It is the end of civil society. It ever has been and ever will be pursued until it be obtained, or until liberty be lost in the pursuit. In a society under the forms of which the stronger faction can readily unite and oppress the weaker, anarchy may as truly be said to reign as in a state of nature, where the weaker individual is not secured against the violence of the stronger; and as, in the latter state, even the stronger individuals are prompted, by the uncertainty of their condition, to submit to a government which may protect the weak as well as themselves; so, in the former state, will the more powerful factions or parties be gradually induced, by a like motive, to wish for a government which will protect all parties, the weaker as well as the more powerful. It can be little doubted that if the State of Rhode Island was separated from the Confederacy and left to itself, the insecurity of rights under the popular form of government within such narrow limits would be displayed by such reiterated oppressions of factious majorities that some power altogether independent of the people would soon be called for by the voice of the very factions whose misrule had proved the necessity of it. In the extended republic of the United States, and among the great variety of interests, parties, and sects which it embraces, a coalition of a majority of the whole society could seldom take place on any other principles than those of justice and the general good; whilst there being thus less danger to a minor from the will of a major party, there must be less pretext, also, to provide for the security of the former, by introducing into the government a will not dependent on the latter, or, in other words, a will independent of the society itself. It is no less certain than it is important, notwithstanding the contrary opinions which have been entertained, that the larger the society, provided it lie within a practical sphere, the more duly capable it will be of self-government. And happily for the *republican cause*, the practicable sphere may be carried to a very great extent, by a judicious modification and mixture of the *federal principle*.

PUBLIUS.

www.milestonedocuments.com

Fellow Citizens of the Senate
and
of the House of Representatives.

Among the vicissitudes
incident to life, no event could have
filled me with greater anxieties than
that of which the notification was
transmitted by your order, and received on the fourteenth day of the
present month: — On the one hand,
I was summoned by my Country, whose
voice I can never hear but with veneration and love, from a retreat which
I had chosen with the fondest predilection, and, in my flattering hopes,
with an immutable decision, as the
asylum of my declining years: a retreat which was rendered every day
more necessary as well as more dear
to me, by the addition of habit to inclination, and of frequent interruptions in my health to the gradual waste
committed on it by time. — On the
other hand, the magnitude and difficulty of the trust to which the voice
of my Country called me, being sufficient to awaken in the wisest and most
experienced of her citizens, a distrustful

George Washington's First Inaugural Address (National Archives and Records Administration)

George Washington's First Inaugural Address

1789

"The preservation of the sacred fire of liberty and the destiny of the republican model of government are … staked on the experiment entrusted to the hands of the American people."

Overview

Believing that he would be elected the first president under the Constitution of 1787, George Washington asked his close friend David Humphreys to draft an inaugural address. Washington discarded Humphreys's seventy-three-page draft, however, and asked James Madison to write a more appropriate address. Washington delivered his address on April 30, 1789, to a joint session of Congress in the Senate chambers in New York City's Federal Hall.

This simple, concise, well-polished address recognized the historical importance of the day and the trials to be faced in the future. Washington explained his reluctance to accept the presidency and highlighted his own deficiencies, among them occasional ill health, little experience in civil administration, and a lack of intellectual gifts. He left the matter of outlining a legislative agenda to Congress, except for one concern. He asked Congress to draft a bill of rights as an amendment to the Constitution. Such additional protection for liberty would satisfy most of those who had opposed the ratification of the Constitution. In closing, Washington recognized God's benevolence in watching over Americans during the war for independence and expressed his hope that God would continue to bless the new American nation.

Context

In mid-June 1783, after eight years as commander in chief of the American military forces fighting for independence from Great Britain, George Washington wrote his last circular letter to the states, in which he offered his advice to make America a great nation. The letter also contained Washington's promises to retire from the army at the end of the hostilities and refrain from serving again in public office. Six months later Washington surrendered his commission to Congress and retired to the life of "a private citizen on the banks of the Potomac … free from the bustle of a camp & the busy scenes of public life" (Washington to Lafayette, February 1, 1784; Abbot and Twohig, vol. 1, pp. 87–88).

Washington's countrymen did not follow his advice. When a severe economic depression enveloped America in 1784, political turmoil swept through the country. Demagogic state assemblies succumbed to the demands of desperate debtors in about half the states. Violence erupted throughout the country that included the burning of courthouses in western Virginia and the closing of the civil courts in western Massachusetts to halt foreclosures on debtors' farms. The Confederation Congress, with only limited "expressly delegated powers" from the Articles of Confederation, could do little to revive the economy or suppress the violence. Alarmed at what he saw, Washington wrote that there were combustibles in every state ready to be ignited by a single spark.

To address the country's problems, Congress called a general convention of the states to amend the Articles of Confederation and strengthen Congress. Setting an example for other states, the Virginia legislature quickly appointed a delegation to the convention, which was to be led by Washington. Washington, however, refused the appointment primarily because of his 1783 promise not to serve in public office again. Owing to the continuing pressure from prominent Virginians such as James Madison and Governor Edmund Randolph, Washington finally relented and accepted the appointment. To no one's surprise, Washington was elected president of the convention that sat from May 25 to September 17, 1787.

The convention proposed a new constitution that was ratified in June 1788. Washington was the only person Americans wanted to lead them. Although he preferred retirement, Washington realized that duty required him to accept the unanimous election as the country's first president.

Washington asked his close friend and adviser David Humphreys, of New Haven, Connecticut, to draft his inaugural address. Humphreys, an aide-de-camp to Washington during the war, had been residing at Mount Vernon for over a year while going through Washington's papers in preparation to write a biography. When Humphreys's lengthy draft of the inaugural address took two and a- half hours to read, however, Washington abandoned it and asked James Madison to write a second draft.

The draft in Humphreys's handwriting has not been located. Washington copied Humphreys's draft and sent it

Time Line

1775	■ **June 15** Washington becomes commander in chief of Continental military.
1783	■ **June 8–14** Washington sends his last circular to the states as commander in chief. ■ **December 23** Washington surrenders his commission to Congress.
1787	■ **May 25–September 17** Washington serves as president of the Constitutional Convention. ■ **September 17** Washington signs the Constitution and the convention's letter to the president of Congress.
1788	■ **June 21** The Constitution is officially ratified.
1789	■ **January** David Humphreys drafts Washington's First Inaugural Address, but Washington discards the draft and asks James Madison to craft a new one. ■ **February 22–March 1** Madison visits Washington at Mount Vernon to discuss the inaugural address. ■ **April 6** Washington is elected as the first president under the Constitution. ■ **April 14** Washington receives word that he has been elected president. ■ **April 16** Washington leaves Mount Vernon to be inaugurated in New York City. ■ **April 23** Washington arrives in New York City.

to Madison, who returned the copy to Washington at Mount Vernon in February 1789 when Madison was traveling north to attend Congress in New York City. Jared Sparks, the editor of Washington's papers in the 1830s, cut Washington's copy of Humphreys's draft into pieces and sent it to autograph seekers. Only a fraction of the snippets have been recovered.

Clad in a dark brown suit of Connecticut broadcloth with metal buttons displaying a spread-winged eagle, white silk stockings, and an ornate ceremonial sword, Washington took the oath of office about 1:00 PM on April 30, 1789, on the balcony of Federal Hall (Old City Hall), located where Wall Street meets Broad Street and Nassau Street in New York City. New York's chancellor, Robert R. Livingston, the highest-ranking judicial officer in the state, administered the oath. As the crowd shouted "God bless our Washington! Long live our beloved president" (Twohig, vol. 2, p. 155), Washington, Vice President John Adams, and the other attending dignitaries reentered the building and proceeded to the Senate chamber, where Washington delivered his four-page address in about twelve minutes to a joint session of Congress. Seated close to Washington, Massachusetts congressman Fisher Ames wrote,

> Time has made havoc upon his face. That, and many other circumstances not to be reasoned about, conspire to keep up the awe which I brought with me. He addressed the two Houses in the Senate chamber; it was a very touching scene, and quite of the solemn kind. His aspect grave, almost to sadness; his modesty, actually shaking; his voice deep, a little tremulous, and so low as to call for close attention … produced emotions of the most affecting kind upon the members. I sat entranced. It seemed to me an allegory in which virtue was personified. (Fisher Ames to George Richards Minot, May 3, 1789; Ames, vol. 1, p. 34.)

Following the address, the company walked about 700 yards to Saint Paul's Episcopal Chapel for services conducted by the Rev. Dr. Samuel Provost, the newly elected chaplain of the Senate. After the services, the president was escorted to his residence, where he dined with a small group of friends and advisers. The inaugural events ended that evening with a brilliant display of fireworks.

Each house, sitting separately, appointed committees to draft responses to the president. Madison chaired the House of Representatives' five-man committee and wrote that the speech was warmly received. The House joined with Washington in seeking the blessings of God for the country and in particular "on the most beloved of her citizens." The Senate rejoiced with all Americans "that, in Obedience to the Call of our common Country, you have returned once more to public life." They told Washington that "in you all Interests unite; and we have no doubt that your past Services, great as they have been, will be equaled by your future Exertions; and that your Prudence and Sagacity as a statesman will tend to avert the Dangers to which we were exposed, to give stability to the present Government, and Dignity and Splendor to that country, which your Skill and Valor as a Soldier, so eminently contributed to raise to independence and Empire." Members of the Senate assured Washington that they would work with him "in every Measure, which may strengthen the Union, conduce to the Happiness, or secure and perpetuate the Liberties of this great confederated Republic" (U.S. Senate to President Washington, May 16, 1789; Twohig, vol. 2, p. 311). Washington responded that he would "readily engage" with them "in the arduous, but pleasing, task, of attempting to make a Nation happy" (Washington to the U.S. Senate, May 18, 1789; Twohig, vol. 2, p. 324).

About the Author

George Washington was born into a middle-gentry family in Westmoreland County, Virginia, on February 22, 1732. When he was eleven years old, his father died and his older stepbrother Lawrence became a father figure to him. When Lawrence married into the wealthy Fairfax family, opportunities opened for the young Washington. Through this connection, Washington was appointed surveyor of Culpeper County on the fringe of the Virginia frontier. The seventeen-year-old surveyor adjusted to life in the wilderness and started to build his own estate by purchasing land.

Washington decided to make the military his career, and his ultimate goal was to receive a commission in the British army. Virginia governor Robert Dinwiddie sent Washington with orders to the French to leave what was thought by Virginians to be their territory (the present-day area around Pittsburgh). After several encounters with the French, Washington triggered the beginning of the French and Indian War, which then spread to Europe. In 1755 Washington served as a volunteer aide to the British general Edward Braddock. At the battle of the Monongahela, Washington escaped unscathed when most other officers were killed. He became commander in chief of the Virginia militia at the age of twenty-two. Despite Washington's military accomplishments, the British refused to give him a commission in the regular army.

Appreciative of his service on the frontier, the western district of Frederick County elected Washington to the colonial House of Burgesses for eight years. He served another ten years as a burgess from his Fairfax County home from 1766 to 1776. In January 1759 he married the wealthy widow Martha Dandridge Custis. Her inheritance consisted of land and slaves, which after their marriage were under Washington's guardianship.

Washington opposed the new British imperial policy instituted in 1763. Elected to the First and Second Continental Congresses, he arrived at the latter dressed in the uniform of a Virginia militia colonel—the only delegate so attired. On June 15, 1775, Congress elected him commander in chief, a position he held throughout the Revolutionary War.

Time Line

1789	■ **April 30** Washington is inaugurated as president and delivers his inaugural address to the Congress.
1792	■ **December 5** Washington is reelected president.
1793	■ **March 4** Washington is inaugurated a second time as president.
1796	■ **September 19** Washington's Farewell Address is published.
1797	■ **March 4** Washington serves his last day as president.
1799	■ **December 14** Washington dies at Mount Vernon.

In March 1783 Washington suppressed an uprising among the army officers, who were angry with Congress for not fulfilling their pension promises. Three months later Washington sent his last circular letter to the states, informing them that he would retire after the cessation of hostilities and would not serve again in public office. In this letter Washington included advice that he felt was necessary to make America great. Of paramount importance, the Union had to be preserved and Congress's powers had to be increased. The country's public credit and public justice had to be maintained by paying the wartime debt both to foreign and domestic public creditors, honoring promises made to the army and its officers, and providing pensions to invalid soldiers and widows and orphans of those who had died during the war. Congress also had to provide an adequate peacetime military establishment to replace the militia, which had been largely ineffective during the war. Last, Americans had to reestablish respect for government and develop a new sense of national identity. The old sectionalism and rampant animosities existing before and during the war had to give way to a new sense of American union and citizenry.

With the British evacuation of New York City on November 25, 1783, the war for independence ended. Washington left New York to perform his last duty as commander in chief. On December 23, 1783, he surrendered his commission to Congress in Annapolis, Maryland, and then retired to Mount Vernon after an absence of eight years.

www.milestonedocuments.com

A portrait of George Washington (Library of Congress)

After the war America prospered until a severe postwar economic depression swept across the country. Succumbing to the demands of desperate debtors, demagogic state assemblies enacted radical anticreditor legislation. In many states debtors resorted to violence. Two courthouses were burned in western Virginia, and the civil courts were forcibly closed in western Massachusetts to stop foreclosures on farms. The Confederation Congress, without coercive powers, was unable to pass relief measures or suppress violence. Calls were issued for a general convention of the states to amend the Articles of Confederation. The Virginia legislature quickly authorized and elected its convention delegation, which included Washington. After repeatedly rejecting the appointment, primarily because of his 1783 promise not to serve again in public office, Washington yielded to pressure from friends and advisers and accepted the appointment. The convention assembled in late May 1787 in Philadelphia, where Washington was elected president. On September 17, 1787, he signed both the Constitution and a letter from the convention to the president of Congress.

Because he felt that he might have to serve as the country's first president, Washington chose not to work openly for ratification of the Constitution. Much to the chagrin of Virginia Federalists, he even refused to be a delegate to the state ratifying convention. Once the Constitution was adopted, he reluctantly accepted the unanimous election as president and was inaugurated on April 30, 1789. Washington was ready to retire after one term, but his advisers convinced him that he must continue for a second term, because political turmoil at home and a raging war in Europe required his unifying leadership. With partisan politics ever increasing, Washington decided not to stand for a third term.

Washington retired to Mount Vernon in March 1797. Although he enjoyed his long-sought private life, he still maintained a vast correspondence and enjoyed almost daily visits from friends, old army compatriots, and curious Americans and Europeans who wanted to see the man universally recognized as the father of his country.

To prepare for a possible war with France in 1798, President John Adams appointed Washington commander in chief of a provisional army that was to be raised to defend the country against an expected invasion. Washington immediately dismissed others' attempts to abandon President Adams and persuade Washington to run for a third term. Adams's peace efforts eliminated the threat of war and thus the need for the army.

Healthy and vigorous at sixty-seven, Washington contracted a severe cold on December 10, 1799, after spending hours on horseback during a torrential storm on the plantation. His illness developed into a condition in which he was unable to breathe. His attending physicians further weakened him by bleeding him of thirty-two ounces of blood, a typical treatment for the era. He died on December 14, 1799, and was buried at Mount Vernon.

Explanation and Analysis of the Document

In the opening paragraph of the First Inaugural Address, Washington explains how his election as president changed his life. He had been happy with his "immutable decision" never again to assume public office after his retirement from the army in December 1783. He was content to spend his "declining years" on his plantation, which served as a private "asylum" from public responsibilities. The voice of his country, however, which he could "never hear but with veneration and love," reminded him of his duty.

His promise to refrain from further service in public office was not the only reason Washington was reluctant to become president. In his inaugural address, he explains his concern that he might be physically unable to do the job because of intermittent bad health and "the gradual waste committed on it by time." Although he had led the army for eight years, he realizes "his own deficiencies." He is inexperienced in "civil administration" and feels that he was not endowed with great natural intellect. He asks his fellow citizens to excuse any errors he might commit because of what he describes as "incapacity as well as disinclination for the weighty and untried cares before me."

In Washington's inaugural address, his "first official act" as president, he asks God to "consecrate" the new government to preserve the liberty and happiness of the American people. He further requests that each person employed in

Essential Quotes

"I was summoned by my Country, whose voice I can never hear but with veneration and love."

(Paragraph 1)

"It has been my faithful study to collect my duty from a just appreciation of every circumstance by which it might be affected."

(Paragraph 1)

"No people can be bound to acknowledge and adore the Invisible Hand which conducts the affairs of men more than those of the United States. Every step by which they have advanced to the character of an independent nation seems to have been distinguished by some token of providential agency."

(Paragraph 2)

"The foundation of our national policy will be laid in the pure and immutable principles of private morality, and the preeminence of free government be exemplified by all the attributes which can win the affections of its citizens and command the respect of the world."

(Paragraph 3)

"There exists in the economy and course of nature an indissoluble union between virtue and happiness; between duty and advantage; between the genuine maxims of an honest and magnanimous policy and the solid rewards of public prosperity and felicity."

(Paragraph 3)

"The preservation of the sacred fire of liberty and the destiny of the republican model of government are justly considered, perhaps, as deeply, as finally, staked on the experiment entrusted to the hands of the American people."

(Paragraph 3)

www.milestonedocuments.com

the new government be enabled to succeed in fulfilling "the functions allotted to his charge." Like the members of Congress and the American people, Washington pays homage to God. No other people could see so clearly the workings of the Almighty—"the Invisible Hand which conducts the affairs of men"—during the war for independence and "the important revolution just accomplished" in adopting a new efficient federal government. The peaceful, voluntary method of replacing the Articles of Confederation with the new Constitution during a time of "crisis" was unique in nation building. With "pious gratitude" for these past gifts, Washington anticipates "future blessings" for the "new and free government."

Among the powers of the president, the Constitution called upon him to recommend to Congress "such measures as he shall judge necessary and expedient." This, however, Washington says, was not the right time for him to present a list of things for Congress to consider. Instead, Washington pays tribute "to the talents, the rectitude, and the patriotism" of the members of Congress. By referring to the broad powers given to Congress by the Constitution, Washington tells the members of Congress to define "the objects to which your attention is to be given." Such a procedure is more congenial to Washington, who feels confident that "no local prejudices or attachments, no separate views nor party animosities, will misdirect the comprehensive and equal eye which ought to watch over" Congress. In so doing, Washington is confident "that the foundation of our national policy will be laid in the pure and immutable principles of private morality, and the preeminence of free government be exemplified by all the attributes which can win the affections of its citizens and command the respect of the world." Washington believes that if Congress fulfills its mission, America will thrive. He thinks that God will smile upon America if it follows "the eternal rules of order and right" ordained by "Heaven itself." "The preservation of the sacred fire of liberty and the destiny of the republican model of government" are perhaps completely dependent upon "the experiment entrusted to the hands of the American people."

Washington does make one specific recommendation for Congress to consider, however. Utilizing Article V of the Constitution, Washington asks Congress whether it is "expedient at the present juncture," to propose amendments in the form of a bill of rights. Because the lack of such a list of liberties had been the primary objection to the Constitution, the proposal and adoption of a bill of rights would quiet former Antifederalists. Rather than preparing a specific bill of rights to be proposed, Washington again assigns this duty to Congress, saying, "I shall again give way to my entire confidence in your discernment and pursuit of the public good." Washington feels confident that Congress will "carefully avoid every alteration which might endanger the benefits of an united and effective government, or which ought to await the future lessons of experience." Congress will assuredly determine the extent of "the characteristic rights of freemen" that will "advantageously" promote "the public harmony."

Washington has another specific provision primarily for the consideration of the House of Representatives. He reminds Congress that when he was appointed commander in chief in 1775, he refused to take a salary and charged Congress only for the expenses he incurred. Now he renounces compensation for his services as president, which he views as a duty he owes to his country.

In closing, Washington again appeals to God—"the benign Parent of the Human Race," who has blessed the American people with the opportunity to deliberate in "perfect tranquillity" and with the "dispositions for deciding with unparalleled unanimity on a [new] form of government for the security of their union and the advancement of their happiness." Washington says that he hopes the divine blessing will be bestowed on "the temperate consultations, and the wise measures on which the success of this Government must depend."

Audience

Washington delivered his First Inaugural Address to a joint session of Congress in New York City's Federal Hall, which forty-eight representatives, eleven senators, and Vice President John Adams attended. The president addressed them as "Fellow Citizens of the Senate, and the House of Representatives." As a tribute "to the talents, the rectitude, and the patriotism" of those elected to Congress, Washington decided not to present them with a legislative blueprint to follow because he felt that they were qualified to set their own agenda. He did, however, ask them to consider adding a bill of rights in the form of amendments to the Constitution. Again, he deferred to their "discernment and pursuit of the public good" in providing what would be included in the list of "the characteristic rights of freemen."

Washington also knew that he was addressing both his fellow citizens and the foreign diplomatic corps. The inaugural speech was quickly printed and reprinted in newspapers, broadsides, and pamphlets.

Impact

Washington's address was warmly received by Congress and by the American people. The president's willingness to defer to Congress in setting its legislative agenda augured well for a congenial arrangement between the legislative and executive branches of government. In not setting his own agenda, Washington alienated no one. His suggestion to members of the Federalist Congress that they propose a bill of rights gave confidence to Antifederalists that the new government would not be oppressive.

Washington unified the country at its birth unlike anyone else could have done. Perhaps Gouverneur Morris, the delegate in the Constitutional Convention who put the final wording to the Constitution, best captured the importance of Washington's presidency in a letter early in the ratification debate:

> Should the Idea prevail that you would not accept of the Presidency it would prove fatal in many Parts.... You are best fitted to fill that Office. Your cool steady Temper is indispensibly necessary to give a firm and manly Tone to the new Government. (Morris to Washington, October 30, 1787; Abbot and Twohig, vol. 5, p. 400.)

Washington realized the importance of his presidency in allowing the new federal republic time to establish itself. His voice, as expressed in his inaugural address, gave confidence to his countrymen that the new American experiment would succeed.

Related Documents

Ames, Seth, ed. *Works of Fisher Ames*. 2 vols. Boston: Little, Brown, 1854. Contains essays and letters to and from the young congressman from Massachusetts.

Abbot, W. W., and Dorothy Twohig, eds. *The Papers of George Washington*, Confederation Series, 6 vols. Charlottesville: University of Virginia Press, 1992–1997. This modern edition of the Washington papers has both sides of the correspondence, the text of his speeches, and the responses of the House and the Senate to the inaugural address.

Kaminski, John P., and Jill Adair McCaughan, eds. *A Great and Good Man: George Washington in the Eyes of His Contemporaries*. Madison, Wis.: Madison House, 1989. This collection of documents describes the public's attitude toward Washington before and after he became president.

Rhodehamel, John, ed. *George Washington: Writings*. New York: Library of America, 1997. This one-volume edition from the Library of America series contains an excellent sampling of Washington's letters (only outgoing and state documents).

Twohig, Dorothy, ed. *The Papers of George Washington*, Presidential Series, 12 vols. Charlottesville: University of Virginia Press, 1987–2007. This set of Washington's papers covers the first term of his presidency.

Bibliography

Books

Cunliffe, Marcus. *George Washington: Man and Monument*. Boston: Little, Brown, 1958.

Ferling, John E. *The First of Men: A Life of George Washington*. Knoxville: University of Tennessee Press, 1988.

Flexner, James Thomas. *Washington: The Indispensable Man*. Boston: Little, Brown, 1969.

Ford, Paul Leicester. *The True George Washington*. Philadelphia, Pa.: J. B. Lippincott, 1896.

Freeman, Douglas Southall. *George Washington: A Biography*. 7 vols. New York: Scribner, 1948–1957.

Grizzard, Frank E., Jr. *George Washington: A Biographical Companion*. Santa Barbara, Calif.: ABC-CLIO, 2002.

Higginbotham, Don. *George Washington: Uniting a Nation*. Lanham, Md.: Rowman & Littlefield, 2002.

Kaminski, John P. *George Washington: "The Man of the Age."* Madison, Wis.: Parallel Press, 2007.

Leibiger, Stuart. *Founding Friendship: George Washington, James Madison, and the Creation of the American Republic*. Charlottesville: University of Virginia Press, 1999.

Web Sites

"The Papers of George Washington Digital Edition." University of Virginia Press Web site.
rotunda.upress.virginia.edu/pgwde. Accessed on November 13, 2007.

"President George Washington's First Inaugural Speech (1789)." National Archives "Our Documents" Web site.
http://www.ourdocuments.gov/doc.php?flash=true&doc=11. Accessed on November 13, 2007.

"Washington's Inaugural Address of 1789." National Archives and Records Administration "American Originals" Web site.
http://www.archives.gov/exhibits/american_originals/inaugtxt.html. Accessed on November 13, 2007.

—By John P. Kaminski

www.milestonedocuments.com

Questions for Further Study

1. Compare Washington's attitude about the role America was to play in the preservation of the republican form of government in his farewell circular to the states in June 1783 and in his first inaugural address.

2. Compare Washington's inaugural address with the inaugural addresses of recent American presidents.

3. Why do you suppose Washington singled out the call for a bill of rights as the one specific act he wanted to see Congress propose?

4. Analyze Washington's five references to God in the inaugural address. How does he refer to God?

Glossary

actuate	to spur to action
animosities	feelings of ill will
ardent	impassioned; warm in feeling
arduous	requiring effort
asylum	sanctuary; place of refuge and protection
attachments	feelings of connection or affection
aver	to assert or declare
benediction	blessing
consecrate	to devote to a purpose, usually sacred
despondence	discouragement
discernment	good judgment
emoluments	payments or other forms of compensation
endowments	innate talents or abilities
expedient	serving to achieve an end or a purpose
felicity	feeling of well-being; happiness
homage	acknowledgment of respect
immutable	unchangeable
indissoluble	unable to be separated or dissolved
inquietude	worried state of mind
Invisible Hand	the workings of God
juncture	a specific point in time, especially one made important by a convergence of events
maxims	general principles

Glossary

magnanimous	kind or generous in spirit
palliated	mitigated; made less severe
pecuniary	monetary
predilection	predisposition in favor of something
providential agency	God's role
rectitude	integrity; uprightness
repaired	traveled; made one's way
supplications	humble appeals
transcendent	surpassing typical limits
veneration	deep respect
vicissitudes	unexpected or changeable circumstances

George Washington's First Inaugural Address

Fellow-Citizens of the Senate and of the House of Representatives:

Among the vicissitudes incident to life no event could have filled me with greater anxieties than that of which the notification was transmitted by your order, and received on the 14th day of the present month. On the one hand, I was summoned by my Country, whose voice I can never hear but with veneration and love, from a retreat which I had chosen with the fondest predilection, and, in my flattering hopes, with an immutable decision, as the asylum of my declining years—a retreat which was rendered every day more necessary as well as more dear to me by the addition of habit to inclination, and of frequent interruptions in my health to the gradual waste committed on it by time. On the other hand, the magnitude and difficulty of the trust to which the voice of my country called me, being sufficient to awaken in the wisest and most experienced of her citizens a distrustful scrutiny into his qualifications, could not but overwhelm with despondence one who (inheriting inferior endowments from nature and unpracticed in the duties of civil administration) ought to be peculiarly conscious of his own deficiencies. In this conflict of emotions all I dare aver is that it has been my faithful study to collect my duty from a just appreciation of every circumstance by which it might be affected. All I dare hope is that if, in executing this task, I have been too much swayed by a grateful remembrance of former instances, or by an affectionate sensibility to this transcendent proof of the confidence of my fellow-citizens, and have thence too little consulted my incapacity as well as disinclination for the weighty and untried cares before me, my error will be palliated by the motives which mislead me, and its consequences be judged by my country with some share of the partiality in which they originated.

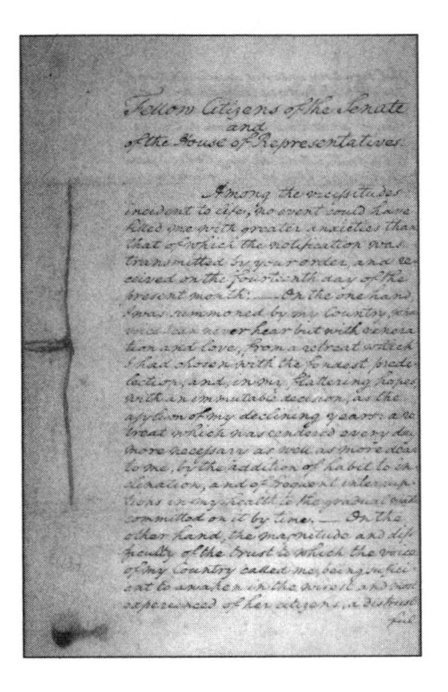
Fellow Citizens of the Senate
and
of the House of Representatives.

Among the vicissitudes
incident to life, no event could have
filled me with greater anxieties than
that of which the notification was
transmitted by your order, and received on the fourteenth day of the
present month: — On the one hand,
I was summoned by my Country, whose
voice I can never hear but with veneration and love, from a retreat which
I had chosen with the fondest predilection, and, in my flattering hopes,
with an immutable decision, as the
asylum of my declining years: a retreat which was rendered every day
more necessary as well as more dear
to me, by the addition of habit to inclination, and of frequent interruptions in my health to the gradual waste
committed on it by time. — On the
other hand, the magnitude and difficulty of the trust to which the voice
of my Country called me, being sufficient to awaken in the wisest and most
experienced of her citizens, a distrustful

Such being the impressions under which I have, in obedience to the public summons, repaired to the present station, it would be peculiarly improper to omit in this first official act my fervent supplications to that Almighty Being who rules over the universe, who presides in the councils of nations, and whose providential aids can supply every human defect, that His benediction may consecrate to the liberties and happiness of the people of the United States a Government instituted by themselves for these essential purposes, and may enable every instrument employed in its administration to execute with success the functions allotted to his charge. In tendering this homage to the Great Author of every public and private good, I assure myself that it expresses your sentiments not less than my own, nor those of my fellow-citizens at large less than either. No people can be bound to acknowledge and adore the Invisible Hand which conducts the affairs of men more than those of the United States. Every step by which they have advanced to the character of an independent nation seems to have been distinguished by some token of providential agency; and in the important revolution just accomplished in the system of their united government the tranquil deliberations and voluntary consent of so many distinct communities from which the event has resulted can not be compared with the means by which most governments have been established without some return of pious gratitude, along with an humble anticipation of the future blessings which the past seem to presage. These reflections, arising out of the present crisis, have forced themselves too strongly on my mind to be suppressed. You will join with me, I trust, in thinking that there are none under the influence of which the proceedings of a new and free government can more auspiciously commence.

By the article establishing the executive department it is made the duty of the President "to recommend to your consideration such measures as he shall judge necessary and expedient." The circumstances under which I now meet you will acquit me from entering into that subject further than to refer to the great constitutional charter under which you are assembled, and which, in defining your powers, designates the objects to which your attention is to be given. It will be more consistent with those circumstances, and far more congenial with the feelings which actuate me, to substitute, in place of a recommendation of particular measures, the tribute that is due to the talents, the rectitude, and the patriotism which adorn the characters selected to devise and adopt them. In these honorable qualifications I behold the surest pledges that as on one side no local prejudices or attachments, no separate views nor party animosities, will misdirect the comprehensive and equal eye which ought to watch over this great assemblage of communities and interests, so, on another, that the foundation of our national policy will be laid in the pure and immutable principles of private morality, and the preeminence of free government be exemplified by all the attributes which can win the affections of its citizens and command the respect of the world. I dwell on this prospect with every satisfaction which an ardent love for my country can inspire, since there is no truth more thoroughly established than that there exists in the economy and course of nature an indissoluble union between virtue and happiness; between duty and advantage; between the genuine maxims of an honest and magnanimous policy and the solid rewards of public prosperity and felicity; since we ought to be no less persuaded that the propitious smiles of Heaven can never be expected on a nation that disregards the eternal rules of order and right which Heaven itself has ordained; and since the preservation of the sacred fire of liberty and the destiny of the republican model of government are justly considered, perhaps, as deeply, as finally, staked on the experiment entrusted to the hands of the American people.

Besides the ordinary objects submitted to your care, it will remain with your judgment to decide how far an exercise of the occasional power delegated by the fifth article of the Constitution is rendered expedient at the present juncture by the nature of objections which have been urged against the system, or by the degree of inquietude which has given birth to them. Instead of undertaking particular recommendations on this subject, in which I could be guided by no lights derived from official opportunities, I shall again give way to my entire confidence in your discernment and pursuit of the public good; for I assure myself that whilst you carefully avoid every alteration which might endanger the benefits of an united and effective government, or which ought to await the future lessons of experience, a reverence for the characteristic rights of freemen and a regard for the public harmony will sufficiently influence your deliberations on the question how far the former can be impregnably fortified or the latter be safely and advantageously promoted.

To the foregoing observations I have one to add, which will be most properly addressed to the House of Representatives. It concerns myself, and will therefore be as brief as possible. When I was first honored with a call into the service of my country, then on the eve of an arduous struggle for its liberties, the light in which I contemplated my duty required that I should renounce every pecuniary compensation. From this resolution I have in no instance departed; and being still under the impressions which produced it, I must decline as inapplicable to myself any share in the personal emoluments which may be indispensably included in a permanent provision for the executive department, and must accordingly pray that the pecuniary estimates for the station in which I am placed may during my continuance in it be limited to such actual expenditures as the public good may be thought to require.

Having thus imparted to you my sentiments as they have been awakened by the occasion which brings us together, I shall take my present leave; but not without resorting once more to the benign Parent of the Human Race in humble supplication that, since He has been pleased to favor the American people with opportunities for deliberating in perfect tranquillity, and dispositions for deciding with unparalleled unanimity on a form of government for the security of their union and the advancement of their happiness, so His divine blessing may be equally conspicuous in the enlarged views, the temperate consultations, and the wise measures on which the success of this Government must depend.

www.milestonedocuments.com

3A

Speech
of the President of the United States to both
Houses of Congress—
January 8th 1790—

Fellow Citizens of the Senate and
House of Representatives

I embrace with great satisfaction
the opportunity, which now presents itself, of con:
:gratulating you upon the present favourable
prospects of our public affairs.— The recent ac:
:cession of the important State of North
Carolina to the Constitution of the United
States (of which official information has been
received)— the rising credit and respectability
of our Country— the general and increasing
good will towards the Government of the Union—
and the concord, peace and plenty, with which
we are blessed are circumstances auspicious in
an eminent degree, to our national prosperity.—

In resuming your consultations for
the general good, you can not but derive encou:
:ragement from the reflection that the measures
of the last Session have been as satisfactory to
your Constituents, as the novelty and difficulty
of the work allowed you to hope.— Still further
to

George Washington's First Annual Message to Congress (Library of Congress)

George Washington's First Annual Message to Congress

1790

"Knowledge is in every country the surest basis of publick happiness."

Overview

The Constitution requires that the president shall from time to time present to Congress an annual message (later to be called the State of the Union address) and recommend measures for its consideration. President Washington chose to present his First Annual Message at the beginning of the second session of Congress in early January 1790. In this address, Washington informs Congress, from his first-hand experience in touring the eastern states between October 15 and November 13, that great recovery has been made from the wartime destruction and dislocation. He also states that agriculture, commerce, and manufacturing are prosperous and that both the people and the officers of the states are very supportive of the federal government under the new Constitution. In his First Inaugural Address, delivered eight months earlier, Washington had asked Congress to consider only one item, a bill of rights. His First Annual Message, however, contains a list of more than six topics for Congress to consider. Washington lists tasks that the Constitution specifically delegates to Congress to do, such as to provide a uniform currency, set a standard of weights and measures, develop a system of patents for inventions, give copyrights in science and literature, ascertain a uniform rule of naturalization, and further develop the Post Office and Post Office roads to tie the country together. He also asks for Congress's cooperation in his executive duties, particularly in military and foreign affairs.

Context

In June 1783 Commander in Chief George Washington, in his last circular letter to the states, announced that he would retire from the army when hostilities ended and not serve again in public office. Shortly after the British evacuated New York City, Washington attended Congress in Annapolis, Maryland, and on December 23, 1783, surrendered his commission and returned to Mount Vernon, his home.

Washington greatly enjoyed the life of a Virginia planter. He spent his time restoring Mount Vernon from the dilapidated condition it had fallen into during his eight-year absence. Although he was retired, Washington was the most popular American in both the United States and Europe. He maintained a voluminous correspondence, read almost a dozen newspapers, worked to develop a system of canals and roads to tie the western farmers with eastern markets and seaports, and graciously hosted an avalanche of visitors at Mount Vernon.

Shortly after the end of the war America fell into a serious economic depression. Violence erupted throughout the country when angry debtors became increasingly frustrated. Some state legislatures enacted relief measures for desperate debtors. When Congress and the states were unable to amend the Articles of Confederation to empower Congress so that it could effectively deal with the depression and violence, a constitutional convention was called to amend the Articles of Confederation and strengthen Congress. The Virginia legislature readily endorsed the convention and elected a prestigious delegation led by Washington. Because he had promised in 1783 to refrain from serving again in public office, Washington refused the appointment. It was only after repeated overtures from James Madison, Virginia governor Edmund Randolph, and others that Washington agreed to serve. The Philadelphia convention sat from May 25 through September 17, 1787, with Washington serving as its president.

During and after the year-long ratification debate to adopt the new Constitution, everyone hoped that Washington would be the country's first president. He reluctantly accepted the unanimous election and was sworn into office on April 30, 1789, at which time he delivered his First Inaugural Address to a joint session of Congress. During the eight months between Washington's First Inaugural Address and his First Annual Message, Congress and the president worked hard to put the new federal government into motion. Also during this time, Americans anxiously watched the unfolding events in Europe as the French Revolution began, with the revolution at first favoring liberty but soon degenerating into an uncontrolled disaster.

As president, Washington hoped to visit every state in the Union. His tour of the eastern states that had ratified the Constitution began on October 15, 1789, while Congress recessed. The six-week trek through New York, Mass-

Time Line

1775

■ **June 15**
Washington becomes commander in chief of the Continental military.

1783

■ **June 8–14**
Washington sends his last circular to the states as commander in chief.

■ **December 23**
Washington surrenders his commission to Congress.

1787

■ **May 25–September 17**
Washington serves as president of the Constitutional Convention.

■ **September 17**
Washington signs the Constitution and the Constitutional Convention's letter to the president of Congress.

1788

■ **June 21**
Constitution is officially ratified.

1789

■ **April 6**
Washington is elected as the first president under the Constitution.

■ **April 30**
Washington is inaugurated as president.

■ **October 15–November 13**
Washington tours the eastern states.

1790

■ **January 8**
Washington delivers his First Annual Message to Congress.

■ **January 11**
The Senate approves its response to Washington.

■ **January 12**
The House of Representatives approves its response to Washington.

■ **May 29**
Rhode Island becomes the last state to ratify the Constitution.

achusetts, New Hampshire, and Connecticut gave him an opportunity to see firsthand the extensive recovery from wartime ravages and dislocations, the abundant harvests, the robust economic resurgence from the depression of the mid-1780s, and the enthusiastic support that the people and state leaders had for the new federal government under the Constitution. Washington made regular entries in his diary describing the events and impressions he gathered of the country and the people. The day after he returned to New York City, the *Gazette of the United States* (November 14, 1789) reported on the significance of the tour: "Independent of that personal respect which is paid to him as a Man, there is an invariable reference in all the addresses, to his political situation, and that Constitution over whose administration he presides. These national sentiments are universally reiterated—and plainly prove that the people are united in their hopes and expectations of public freedom, peace and happiness from the general government." The report went on to say that "The time to pull down, and destroy, is now past." Now it was the duty of every person "to build up, strengthen and support a Constitution, with which is inseparably connected all that is dear and valuable to us as citizens and freemen." Four days later the *Gazette* reported that the tour had convinced everyone "that the attachment of the people to the Constitution was solid and permanent." Washington's First Annual Message, delivered on January 8, 1790, was filled with the optimism he acquired while traveling through New England and New York.

Three days before Washington delivered the address, Abigail Adams, the wife of the vice president, captured the feeling most Americans had for their president: Washington, she said,

> has so happy a faculty of appearing to accommodate & yet carrying his point, that if he was not really one of the best intentioned men in the world he might be a very dangerous one. He is polite with dignity, affable without familiarity, distant without Haughtiness, Grave without Austerity, Modest, Wise & Good. These are traits in his Character which peculiarly fit him for the exalted station he holds, and God Grant that he may Hold it with the same applause & universal satisfaction for many many years, as it is my firm opinion that no other man could rule over this great people & consolidate them into one mighty Empire but He who is set over us. (Abigail Adams to Mary Cranch, January 5, 1790; Mitchell, p. 35.)

On Friday morning at eleven o'clock, January 8, 1790, Washington, dressed in a crow-colored suit, delivered his First Annual Message to a joint session of Congress in the Senate chamber in Federal Hall (the City Hall of New York City). Thirty-six representatives, eleven senators, and Vice President John Adams, the president of the Senate, attended.

Both houses adopted committee reports that responded to the president's speech. The Senate's response, adopted on January 11, was delivered to Washington three days later at his residence by Vice President Adams and the thirteen senators in attendance. After thanking Washington for his speech and agreeing with its provisions, members of the Senate told the president,

> Our cares and efforts shall be directed to the welfare of our Country; and we have the most perfect dependence upon your co-operating with us on all occasions in such measures as will insure to our fellow citizens, the blessings which they have a right to expect from a free, efficient, and equal government. (U.S. Senate to Washington, January 11, 1790; Twohig, vol. 4, p. 547).

Washington responded that, "relying on the continuance of your exertions for the public good, I anticipate for our Country the salutary effects of upright and prudent Counsels" (Washington to U.S. Senate, January 11, 1790; Twohig, vol. 4, p. 566). The House of Representatives approved its response to Washington's address on January 12. It ended with the following sentence:

> The prosperity of the United States is the primary object of all our deliberations; and we cherish the reflection, that every measure which we may adopt for its advancement, will not only receive your cheerful concurrence, but will at the same time derive from your co-operation, additional efficacy, in ensuring to our fellow-citizens the blessings of a free, efficient and equal government. (U.S. House of Representatives to Washington, January 12, 1790; Twohig, vol. 4, pp. 548–549).

Two days later, Washington responded: "I have full confidence that your deliberations will continue to be directed by an enlightened and virtuous zeal for the happiness of our Country" (Washington to U.S. House of Representatives, January 14, 1790; Twohig, vol. 4, p. 576). Congress and the president were ready to continue working together for the good of the new American nation.

Time Line

1790	■ **August 15–22** Washington visits Rhode Island.
1791	■ **March 21–July 6** Washington tours the southern states.
1792	■ **December 5** Washington is reelected president.
1793	■ **March 4** Washington is inaugurated as president a second time.
1796	■ **September 19** Washington's Farewell Address is published.
1797	■ **March 4** Washington serves his last day as president.
1799	■ **December 14** Washington dies at Mount Vernon.

About the Author

George Washington was born in Westmoreland County, Virginia, in 1732. His father, a middle-gentry planter, died when Washington was only eleven years old, and Washington's older stepbrother Lawrence became a father figure. When Lawrence married into the wealthy Fairfax family, it opened opportunities for the younger Washington. Through the influence of Lord Fairfax, Washington was appointed surveyor of Culpeper County on the Virginia frontier when he was only seventeen years old. The appointment served him well as he made many wealthy contacts and adapted to life in the wilderness among the Native Americans.

Washington chose a military career as opposed to the civilian life of a Virginia planter. As a special emissary from Lieutenant Governor Robert Dinwiddie to the French forces moving into territory claimed by Virginia, Washington helped instigate the French and Indian War. At the age of twenty-two he was appointed commander in chief of the Virginia militia, and he later emerged as one of only a few American heroes from that war. Unsuccessful at obtaining an officer's commission in the British army, Washington retired to Mount Vernon, which he had acquired after the deaths of his stepbrother Lawrence and Lawrence's widow. In 1759 Washington married Martha Dandridge Custis, a wealthy widow with two children. Martha's and the children's estates, now under the guardianship of Washington, made him one of the wealthiest planters in Virginia.

Washington joined the colonial opposition to Britain's new imperial policy instituted at the end of the French and Indian War in 1763. Serving in the Virginia House of Burgesses, elected first from Frederick County and then from his home of Fairfax County, Washington advocated protesting to Britain first by petition and then by economic boycotts. Only after these peaceful means failed did Washington consider military measures.

The House of Burgesses elected Washington to both the First and Second Continental Congresses. He arrived at the latter wearing the uniform of a Virginia militia colonel, the only delegate so attired. On June 15, 1775, Congress unan-

www.milestonedocuments.com

George Washington shown with his family (Library of Congress)

imously elected Washington commander in chief—a position he held for the remaining eight years of the Revolution.

Washington surrendered his commission to Congress on December 23, 1783. In his last circular letter to the states in June 1783, Washington had promised to retire from the army when the hostilities ended and not serve again in public office. He also offered advice that he believed would help make America a great nation.

Washington enjoyed the private life of a Virginia planter. When the country went into a severe economic depression in 1784, a convention was called to strengthen Congress along the lines that Washington had recommended in his June 1783 circular. The Virginia legislature appointed Washington to the convention, but he steadfastly refused the appointment. He eventually relented because of the persistent pleadings of several prominent Virginia leaders.

Washington was among the handful of delegates who wanted a radical change, not merely amendments to the Articles of Confederation. On March 31, 1787, two months before the convention assembled, Washington wrote to his fellow Virginia delegate James Madison, saying that it was his wish "that the Convention may adopt no temporising expedient, but probe the defects of the Constitution [i.e., the Articles of Confederation] to the bottom, and provide radical cures" (Washington to Madison, March 31, 1787; (Abbot and Twohig, vol. 5, p. 116). Washington was elected president of the convention and signed the new Constitution on September 17, 1787.

Everyone hoped that Washington would serve as the country's first president. He reluctantly accepted the unanimous election and was sworn in on April 30, 1789, delivering at that time his First Inaugural Address to a joint session of Congress. Congress and the president worked hard to implement the government under the new Constitution. When Congress recessed, Washington toured the eastern states (except for Rhode Island, which had not yet ratified the Constitution) and was delighted to see the recovery from wartime damages, the prosperity of agriculture and commerce, the expansion of manufacturing, and the American people's devotion to the new Constitution and its federal government.

Washington happily reported his findings in his First Annual Message to a joint session of Congress on January 8, 1790. He recommended congressional action on a number of matters and asked for Congress's cooperation in creating a peacetime military establishment and providing for America's foreign diplomatic corps. He also sought to cooperate with Congress in the treaty negotiations taking place with hostile Native American tribes in the South and West.

The First Annual Message probably marked the high point in congeniality between Congress and the president. Secretary of the Treasury Alexander Hamilton's economic policies, costly and deadly military expeditions against Native Americans primarily in the old Northwest Territory, and the divisiveness of foreign affairs—mainly the unfolding events of the French Revolution—caused friction throughout the country that was reflected in disagreements within the government.

Washington wanted to retire after only one term as president. His advisers convinced him, however, that he alone could keep the country unified and guide it through the difficult circumstances. Washington accepted a second term, during which partisanship increased significantly. In mid-September 1796 he announced his retirement in his Farewell Address. He left the presidency on March 4, 1797, and died almost two years later on December 14, 1799, at Mount Vernon.

Explanation and Analysis of the Document

At eleven o'clock on Friday morning on January 8, 1790, President Washington, accompanied by several aides and a secretary, entered the Senate chamber in New York City's Federal Hall to deliver his First Annual Message to a joint session of Congress. In his address, Washington forecasts "favourable prospects" for the country's public affairs "with great satisfaction." North Carolina had ratified the Constitution six weeks earlier, leaving only the tiny state of Rhode Island out of the Union. Public credit and respect for the country had been greatly restored. Throughout the country the people and state officials had shown goodwill and enthusiastic respect for the new central government. The president had toured the eastern states and saw firsthand that the country was blessed with "concord, peace and plenty," as he notes early on in his address. The economic depression and social unrest in the last years of the Confederation, he says, have given way to an auspicious "national prosperity."

Washington praises Congress for the previous year's legislative accomplishments. The novelty and difficulty of the issues made the successes of Congress that much more remarkable. Before securing all God's blessings, however, Washington believes Congress will have to meet new challenges with a "cool and deliberate exertion of your patriotism, firmness and wisdom."

Unlike in his First Inaugural Address, Washington here lists a number of specific matters for Congress to consider. Something had to be done about the country's defenses. In his June 1783 circular to the states, the outgoing commander in chief had recommended a permanent peacetime military establishment to replace the traditional, but often undependable, state militias. A month earlier, in May 1783, Washington, at the request of Congress, submitted his "Sentiments on a Peace Establishment," which called for a small permanent standing army and a small nationalized militia under the jurisdiction of Congress. In his address, Washington reminds Congress that "to be prepared for war is one of the most effectual means of preserving peace." A free people," Washington explains, "ought not only to be armed but disciplined; to which end a uniform and well digested plan is requisite." With the inherent danger of a necessary peacetime standing army of some sorts, Washington believes it is important that the officers and soldiers be appropriately compensated "with a due regard to economy" so that they will not be tempted to use their power against the civilian authorities. (Two weeks after the address, Washington delivered to Congress a plan that outlined his ideas about a national militia.)

But defense was not to be found only in an armed force. According to Washington, the country should "promote such manufactories, as tend to render them independent on others, for essential, particularly for military supplies." For all their histories, the colonies and now the states had largely exported natural resources and staple agricultural produce and imported manufactured goods. That, Washington intimates, had to change. America's economy had to become more well-rounded, integrated, and self-sufficient.

On a less optimistic note, Washington informs Congress that relations with hostile Native American tribes on the western and southern frontiers had not greatly improved. "We ought to be prepared," he states, "to afford protection to those parts of the Union; and, if necessary, to punish aggressors." At the end of the president's speech, he indicates that he will send Congress official documents on various subjects. Among these papers, delivered on January 11 and 12, were the terms that American commissioners were prepared to offer "the Creek Nation of Indians" and a statement from Americans on the southwestern frontier. Washington said when delivering those papers that he felt it was "proper" that Congress should be informed of the treaty negotiations "previous to its coming before you in your legislative capacity. Such a *confidential* communication of all the papers relative to the recent negociations with some of the southern tribes of Indians is indispensably requisite for the information of Congress" (Washington to U.S. Senate, January 11–12, 1790; Twohig, vol. 4, pp. 566, 568). Washington was confident that Congress would keep these documents secret. Three days after his speech, Washington received a letter from South Carolina governor Charles Pinckney. In it, Pinckney argued that "to have a permanent & solid peace—no State arrangement—no truce—no partial compromise will be suffi-

www.milestonedocuments.com

Essential Quotes

"To secure the blessings which a gracious Providence has placed within our reach, will in the course of the present important session, call for the cool and deliberate exertion of your patriotism, firmness and wisdom."

(Paragraph 2)

"To be prepared for war is one of the most effectual means of preserving peace."

(Paragraph 3)

"Knowledge is in every country the surest basis of publick happiness."

(Paragraph 11)

"The welfare of our country is the great object to which our cares and efforts ought to be directed."

(Paragraph 15)

"I shall derive great satisfaction from a cooperation with you, in the pleasing though arduous task of ensuring to our fellow citizens the blessings which they have a right to expect, from a free and equal government."

(Paragraph 15)

cient. They must be taught to revere the justice of the Union & look up to it as the sole means of giving them a lasting treaty & the secure possession of their real rights" (Pinckney to Washington, December 14, 1789; Twohig, vol. 4, p. 405). Washington responded by saying that his views were in agreement with Pinckney.

In his First Annual Message to Congress, Washington next turns to foreign affairs. Although the Constitution gave the president broad and exclusive powers to conduct foreign affairs, Washington asks for Congress's cooperation in enacting "such provisions as will enable me to fulfill my duty." To this end, Washington requests that provisions be made for a diplomatic corps and "a competent fund designated for defraying the expenses incident to the conduct of our foreign affairs." Vice President John Adams, Chief Justice John Jay, and Secretary of State Thomas Jefferson, all active diplomats during and after the war, could testify to the inadequate funding of foreign affairs under the Confederation. Washington hoped that Congress would correct this deficiency.

Conforming to the Constitution's list of the delegated powers of Congress, Washington asks Congress to ascertain "a uniform rule of naturalization," to provide for a uniform currency, to set a standard of weights and measures, to encourage inventions by establishing a system of patents, to promote science and literature by providing for copyrights, and to facilitate the connection between "distant parts of our country by a due attention to the Post Office and Post Roads." Within two months, Congress had passed bills for copyrights, patents, naturalization, and weights and measures.

Washington remarks that it is unnecessary to encourage Congress to consider the advancement of agriculture, commerce, and manufacturing. He believes that Congress is obviously as committed to these goals as he is.

Washington then addresses the importance of education. "Knowledge is in every country the surest basis of publick happiness." A free Constitution benefits from an enlightened people who value their own rights, who can tell when their rights are endangered, and who can distinguish between "the spirit of liberty" and licentiousness, "cherishing the first, avoiding the last, and uniting a speedy, but temperate vigilance against encroachments, with an inviolable respect to the laws." Washington is uncertain whether it is preferable to offer public support for existing institutions of higher education, to create a national university, or to provide some other alternative. He feels that Congress should deliberate on these matters.

Washington addresses the House of Representatives specifically by endorsing its resolutions from the last session to support the country's public credit. Knowing that the Senate will cooperate in such matters, Washington notes that it is unnecessary to make any specific suggestions to Congress in such matters that concern "the character and permanent interests of the United States."

In concluding, Washington comments that "the welfare of our country is the great object to which our cares and efforts ought to be directed." He will derive great pleasure from cooperating with Congress "in the pleasing though arduous task of ensuring to our fellow citizens the blessings which they have a right to expect, from a free and equal government."

Audience

In addressing his First Annual Message to his "Fellow Citizens of the Senate and House of Representatives," Washington fulfilled one of the constitutional obligations of his office. Thus, his primary audience was the Congress. However, Washington also realized that his speech would be read by Americans throughout the country and foreign diplomats stationed in America. He wanted to show these readers that the executive and legislative branches of the new government were working together amicably.

In a remarkable letter written the day after he delivered his address, Washington commented to Catherine Macaulay Graham, a prominent English historian and philanthropist, that all his actions would be viewed as precedents for his successors. Thus, his address was also aimed at future presidents who might follow his example. Washington also told Graham that he hoped the events of the American Revolution might serve as a pattern for the events emerging in France: "The renovation of the French Constitution is indeed one of the most wonderful events in the history of Mankind" (Washington to Graham, January 9, 1790; Twohig, vol. 4, p. 553). He hoped that the French leadership would be "sufficiently cool & moderate in making arrangements for the security of that liberty, of which it seems to be fully possessed" (Washington to Graham, January 9, 1790; Twohig, vol. 4, p. 553). Perhaps the president's address would encourage French moderates, like the Marquis de Lafayette, to keep the French Revolution on a balanced keel.

Impact

Washington's First Annual Message had an immediate impact on Congress and the nation. Within two months Congress submitted bills for Washington's signature dealing with naturalization, copyrights and patents, and weights and measures. Congress also began its consideration of Secretary of the Treasury Alexander Hamilton's economic plan one week after Washington's First Annual Message, although this matter would prove far more contentious.

In the areas of foreign affairs and in providing a peacetime military establishment, Washington indicated that he wanted to cooperate with Congress. In a letter to Sir Edward Newenham, a member of the Irish Parliament who had supported American interests, just one week after the address, Washington sensed that what America needed was "the sanction of time to give it that stability which can be expected from any human fabric" (Washington to Newenham, January 15, 1790; Twohig, vol. 4, p. 585). He hoped that his speech would clearly show the amicable relations already existing between Congress and him.

This attitude, however, soon changed, as many members of Congress feared any kind of a standing army, disliked the provisions of the Treaty of New York (August 7, 1790) with the Creek Indians, and abhorred the cavalier manner in which Washington sought the Senate's confirmation of that treaty. Divisions over Hamilton's economic plan and foreign affairs widened the breach between the administration and a significant minority of Congress. The First Annual Message was thus, perhaps, the high point in cooperation between Congress and the president.

Related Documents

Abbot, W. W., and Dorothy Twohig, eds. *The Papers of George Washington*, Confederation Series, 6 vols. Charlottesville: University of Virginia Press, 1992–1997. This modern edition of the Washington papers has both sides of the correspondence, the text of his speeches, and the responses of the House and the Senate to the inaugural address.

Kaminski, John P., and Jill Adair McCaughan, eds. *A Great and Good Man: George Washington in the Eyes of His Contemporaries*. Madison, Wis.: Madison House, 1989. This collection of documents describes the attitude of the public toward Washington before and after he became president. An interesting section deals with Washington's tours of the eastern states, Rhode Island, and the southern states.

Rhodehamel, John, ed. *George Washington: Writings*. New York: Library of America, 1997. This one-volume edition from the Library of America series contains an excellent sampling of Washington's letters (only outgoing and state documents).

Twohig, Dorothy, ed. *The Papers of George Washington*, Presidential Series, 12 vols. Charlottesville: University Press of Virginia,

www.milestonedocuments.com

1987–2007. This set of Washington's papers covers his first term as president.

Bibliography

■ Books

Cunliffe, Marcus. *George Washington: Man and Monument.* Boston: Little, Brown, 1958.

Ferling, John E. *The First of Men: A Life of George Washington.* Knoxville, Tenn.: University of Tennessee Press, 1988.

Flexner, James Thomas. *Washington: The Indispensable Man.* Boston: Little, Brown, 1969.

Ford, Paul Leicester. *The True George Washington.* Philadelphia, Pa.: J. B. Lippincott, 1896.

Freeman, Douglas Southall. *George Washington: A Biography.* 7 vols. New York: Scribner, 1948–1957.

Grizzard, Frank E., Jr. *George Washington: A Biographical Companion.* Santa Barbara, Calif.: ABC-CLIO, 2002.

Higginbotham, Don. *George Washington: Uniting a Nation.* Lanham, Md.: Rowman & Littlefield, 2002.

Kaminski, John P. *George Washington: "The Man of the Age."* Madison, Wis.: Parallel Press, 2007.

Leibiger, Stuart. *Founding Friendship: George Washington, James Madison, and the Creation of the American Republic.* Charlottesville: University of Virginia Press, 1999.

McDonald, Forrest. *The Presidency of George Washington.* Lawrence: University Press of Kansas, 1974.

Miller, John Chester. *The Federalist Era, 1789–1801.* New York: Harper, 1960.

Mitchell, Stewart, ed., *New Letters of Abigail Adams, 1788–1801.* Boston: Houghton Mifflin Company, 1947.

Smith, Thomas E. V. *The City of New York in the Year of Washington's Inauguration, 1789.* 1889. Reprint. Riverside, Conn: A.D.F. Randolph, 1972.

Warren, Jack D., Jr. *The Presidency of George Washington.* Mount Vernon, Va.: Mount Vernon Ladies' Association of the Union, 2000.

■ Web Sites

"George Washington Papers at the Library of Congress, 1741–1799." Library of Congress "American Memory" Web site.
http://memory.loc.gov/ammem/gwhtml/gwhome.html. Accessed on November 16, 2007.

"The Papers of George Washington Digital Edition." University of Virginia Press Web site.
http://rotunda.upress.virginia.edu/pgwde. Accessed on November 16, 2007.

—By John P. Kaminski

Questions for Further Study

1. How did Washington's tour of the eastern states influence his First Annual Message to Congress?

2. Compare Washington's attitude on a new peacetime military establishment in May and June 1783 with his position in the First Annual Message in January 1790.

4. How would you describe Washington's attitude toward Congress in his First Inaugural Address and in his First Annual Message?

Glossary

accession	addition
arduous	difficult or demanding
auspicious	favorable
conciliate	to reconcile
depredations	attacks
effectual	effective
encroachments	infringements; advances beyond accepted limits
exigencies	situations that make pressing demands
expedient	appropriate or useful in attaining a particular goal
facilitated	made less difficult
inducements	stimuli that lead one to action
inviolable	secure from being breached or attacked; unassailable
licentiousness	behavior lacking morality
naturalization	grant of citizenship
pacifick	pacifying
patronage	support
publick credit	financial trustworthiness of a government or country
requisite	necessary to a purpose
sanction	show of support
seminaries	institutions of higher education
superfluous	exceeding what is necessary
temperate	moderate

George Washington's First Annual Message to Congress

Fellow Citizens of the Senate, and House of Representatives,

I embrace with great satisfaction the opportunity, which now presents itself, of congratulating you on the present favourable prospects of our public affairs. The recent accession of the important state of North Carolina to the Constitution of the United States (of which official information has been received)—the ruling credit and respectability of our country—the general and increasing good will towards the government of the union, and the concord, peace and plenty, with which we are blessed, are circumstances auspicious, in an excellent degree, to our national prosperity.

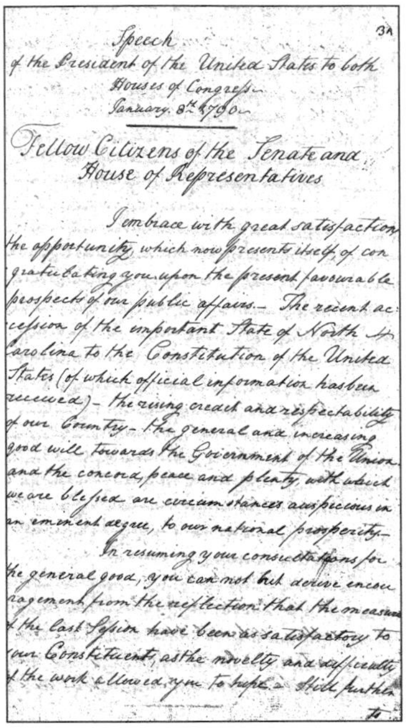

In reforming your consultations for the general good, you cannot but derive encouragement from the reflection, the measures of the last session have been as satisfactory to your constituents as the novelty and difficulty of the work allowed you to hope.— Still further to realize their expectations, and to secure the blessings which a gracious Providence has placed within our reach, will in the course of the present important session, call for the cool and deliberate exertion of your patriotism, firmness and wisdom.

Among the many interesting objects which will engage your attention, that of providing for the common defence will merit particular regard. To be prepared for war is one of the most effectual means of preserving peace.

A free people ought not only to be armed but disciplined; to which end a uniform and well digested plan is requisite: And their safety and interest require that they should promote such manufactories, as tend to render them independent on others, for essential, particularly for military supplies.

The proper establishment of the troops which may be deemed indispensable, will be entitled to mature consideration. In the arrangement which will be made respecting it, it will be of importance to conciliate the comfortable support of the officers and soldiers with a due regard to economy.

There was reason to hope, the pacifick measures adopted with regard to certain hostile tribes of Indians, would have relieved the inhabitants of our southern and western frontiers from their depredations. But you will perceive, from the information contained in the papers, which I shall direct to be laid before you, (comprehending a communication from the Commonwealth of Virginia) that we ought to be prepared to afford protection to those parts of the Union; and, if necessary, to punish aggressors.

The interests of the United States require, that our intercourse with other nations should be facilitated by such provisions as will enable me to fulfill my duty, in that respect, in the manner which circumstances may render most conducive to the publick good: And to this end, that the compensations to be made to the persons who may be employed, should, according to the nature of their appointments, be defined by law; and a competent fund designated for defraying the expenses incident to the conduct of our foreign affairs.

Various considerations also render it expedient, that the terms on which foreigners may be admitted to the rights of Citizens, should be speedily ascertained by a uniform rule of naturalization.

Uniformity in the currency, weights and measures of the United States, is an object of great importance, and will, I am persuaded, be duly attended to.

The advancement of agriculture, commerce and manufactures, by all proper means, will not, I trust, need recommendation. But I cannot forbear intimating to you the expediency of giving effectual encouragement as well to the introduction of new and useful inventions from abroad, as to the exertions of skill and genius in producing them at home; and of facilitating the intercourse between the distant parts of our country by a due attention to the Post Office and Post Roads.

Nor am I less persuaded, that you will agree with me in opinion, that there is nothing which can better deserve your patronage, than the promotion of Science and Literature. Knowledge is in every country the surest basis of publick happiness. In one, in which the measures of government receive their impression so immediately from the sense of the community, as in our's, it is proportionately essential. To the security of a free Constitution it contributes in various ways: By convincing those who are entrusted with the publick administration, that every valuable end of government is best answered by the enlightened confidence of the people: And by teaching the people themselves to know, and to value their own rights; to discern and provide against invasions of them; to distinguish between oppression and the necessary exercise of lawful authority; between burthens proceeding from a disregard to their convenience, and those resulting from the inevitable exigencies of society; to discriminate the spirit of liberty from that of licentiousness, cherishing the first, avoiding the last, and uniting a speedy, but temperate vigilance against encroachments, with an inviolable respect to the laws.

Whether this desirable object will be best promoted by affording aids to seminaries of learning already established, by the institution of a national university, or by any other expedients, will be well worthy of a place in the deliberations of the Legislature.

Gentlemen of the House of Representatives,

I saw with peculiar pleasure, at the close of the last session, the resolution entered into by you, expressive of your opinion, that an adequate provision for the support of the publick credit, is a matter of high importance to the national honour and prosperity.— In this sentiment, I entirely concur.— And to a perfect confidence in your best endeavors to devise such a provision as will be truly consistent with the end, I add an equal reliance on the cheerful cooperation of the other branch of the Legislature.— It would be superfluous to specify inducements to a measure in which the character and permanent interests of the United States so obviously and so deeply concerned; and which has received so explicit a sanction from your declaration.

Gentlemen of the Senate, and House of Representatives,

I have directed the proper officers to lay before you respectively such papers and estimates as regards the affairs particularly recommended to your consideration, and necessary to convey to you that information of the state of the union, which it is my duty to afford.

The welfare of our country is the great object to which our cares and efforts ought to be directed.— And I shall derive great satisfaction from a cooperation with you, in the pleasing though arduous task of ensuring to our fellow citizens the blessings which they have a right to expect, from a free and equal government.

www.milestonedocuments.com

The bill for establishing a National Bank undertakes, among other t

1. to form the subscribers into a Corporation.

2. to enable them, in their corporate capacities to receive grants of land;
so far is against the laws of Mortmain.*

3. to make alien-subscribers capable of holding lands, & so far is agai
the laws of Alienage.

4. to transmit these lands, on the death of a proprietor, to a certain line
successors: & so far changes the course of Descents.

5. to put the lands out of the reach of forfeiture or escheat: & so far is ag
the laws of Forfeiture & Escheat.

6 to transmit personal chattels to successors in a certain line: & so,
is against the laws of Distribution.

7 to give them the sole & exclusive right of banking under the nation
authority: & so far is against the laws of Monopoly.

8. to communicate to them a power to make laws paramount to
laws of the states: for so they must be construed, to protect the
-stitution from the control of the state legislatures; & so, prob
they will be construed.

I consider the foundation of the Constitution as laid on this gro
that "all powers not delegated to the U.S. by the Constitution, nor proh
by it to the states, are reserved to the states or to the people" [XIIth amend]
to take a single step beyond the boundaries thus specially drawn around the po
of Congress is to take possession of a boundless field of power, no longer susceptible of any definition.

*though the constitution controuls the laws of Mortmain so far as
[illegible] purposes, yet not so, far as to permit them to commu

Thomas Jefferson's Opinion on the Bank of the United States, noted in a letter to President George Washington on February 15, 1791. (Library of Congress)

Jefferson's and Hamilton's Opinions on the Constitutionality of the Bank of the United States

1791

"Can it be thought that the Constitution intended that ... Congress should be authorized to break down the most ancient and fundamental laws of the several States?"

Overview

The Bank of the United States was one of the keystones of Treasury Secretary Alexander Hamilton's plan for refinancing the Revolutionary War debt of the United States of America. After weeks of heated congressional debate that included questions about the proposed bank's constitutionality, President George Washington requested statements from Hamilton and from the secretary of state, Thomas Jefferson, who opposed the bank. Hamilton justified the bank by broadly construing the constitutional powers of Congress. Jefferson rejected Hamilton's argument by claiming that the ratified Constitution created a federal government that was strictly limited in its political and financial power.

The statements by these two respected political minds encapsulated the growing legal gulf that separated advocates of "loose construction" from those who supported a "strict construction" of the Constitution, a gulf manifested in the emerging American political party system between the Federalists and Republicans (often referred to as Democratic-Republicans), respectively. Additionally, the debate over the bank's constitutionality revealed an even more contentious disagreement over the role of the federal government in the economic life of the nation. In short, the debate over Hamilton's bank went far beyond finance to question the very meaning of federalism.

Context

The American Revolution was one of the longest-fought wars in American history, certainly the longest on North American soil, and one of the most costly. Immediately following the battles of Lexington and Concord, Massachusetts, in 1775, delegates to the Second Continental Congress made several fateful decisions regarding the future of the war, such as the choice to fight the British using conventional means, including a large standing army of regular troops. A national army, of course, would necessarily be armed, fed, clothed, and housed at the Continental Congress's expense.

Congress financed the Continental army by issuing a variety of debt instruments to be liquidated after the war by redemption and taxation. Congress also created a fiat currency of "continentals," which were declared legal tender by Congress without the backing of specie. As the war dragged on, Congress simply issued more currency and debt instruments, creating an inflationary spiral as leaders tried printing their way out of the financial crisis. The value of the currency and debt instruments both plummeted, leaving Americans the victors in war but nearing financial catastrophe.

By early 1786, a national solution appeared to be a lost cause, and debt holders increasingly turned to the state governments for assistance. In that year alone, interest on half of the total debt was paid by the states of Pennsylvania, New York, and Massachusetts. With the states now leading the way toward eliminating the Continental debt, nationalists feared for the worst, as they had planned to use that issue to grant more power and authority to the central government. Fortunately for the nationalists, the states failed to satisfy all creditors, to address British threats on the western frontier, or to squelch Shays's Rebellion in Massachusetts. Enough people were frightened by the circumstances to warrant the calling of a national convention in Philadelphia in 1787, where delegates boldly proposed a new federal government strong enough to gain economic controls over the states.

However, the framers did not want the new government's economic power to be absolute. On September 14, James Madison, of Virginia, moved to amend Article I, Section 8, "to grant charters of incorporation where the interest of the U.S. might require & the legislative provisions of individual States may be incompetent" (Madison, p. 638). In the ensuing discussion, at least one delegate stated that such wording could be construed to mean that Congress could charter a bank. Madison's motion was soundly defeated, with only the Pennsylvania and Georgia delegations voting in favor.

Following the ratification of the U.S. Constitution, Congress and President George Washington spent most of the first session, in 1789, creating the federal bureaucracy and tax structure. With those tasks completed, the newly minted secretary of the treasury, Alexander Hamilton, pressed for a major fiscal program for the new government.

Time Line

1775

■ **April**
American Revolution breaks out in Massachusetts.

■ **June**
Second Continental Congress commences financing paper money and issuing debt instruments.

1781

■ **March 1**
Articles of Confederation are ratified.

■ **May 14**
Robert Morris of Philadelphia becomes superintendent of finance and begins strengthening the economic policies of the national government.

■ **December**
The Bank of North America is chartered by Congress.

1783

■ Owing to Congress's monetary policies and the activities of the Bank of North America, the country enters a depression.

1786–1787

■ **August 1786–June 1787**
Shays's Rebellion is staged in Massachusetts.

■ **May–September 1787**
The Philadelphia Convention meets to revise the Articles of Confederation but ends up proposing the Constitution.

1789

■ **March 4**
In accord with the dictates of the Constitution, the First Congress of the United States convenes.

■ **April 15**
John Fenno first issues the pro-Federalist newspaper called the *Gazette of the United States.*

■ **September 11**
Alexander Hamilton becomes secretary of the treasury.

1790

■ **December**
Hamilton submits his "Report on a National Bank."

Commonly called "Hamiltonian finance," his plan was laid out in a series of reports issued between 1790 and 1791. The "Report on the Public Credit" (January 9, 1790) called on Congress to pay off all of the remaining Revolutionary War debt—including that of the states—at face value by issuing new federal debt certificates. Interest on and the principal of this new national debt would be paid by direct taxes (especially on distilled spirits like whiskey), a tariff, and land sales. The "Report on a National Bank" (December 13, 1790) defended the chartering of a federal bank that would issue a paper currency ostensibly based on its specie holdings, be a lender to the national government, and facilitate the collection of taxes. The "Report on the Subject of a Mint" (January 28, 1791) proposed the creation of a mint to coin gold and silver for national circulation. Finally, the "Report on the Subject of Manufacturers" (December 5, 1791) suggested that the government dispense direct subsidies to stimulate domestic industry, but Congress decided against the recommendation.

While Hamilton feared that too much political control could hamper economic progress, he did not favor free markets and unfettered capitalism. He viewed economic exchange as inherently unstable—indeed, chaotic—without the overarching hand of governing institutions, led by something like the Bank of England. Rather than simply trusting rural property holders like planters and yeoman farmers, Hamilton placed his faith in a commercial class of merchants like those who dominated British politics during the eighteenth century. Economic progress meant international trade and local commercial development, not the sprawling agrarian society envisioned by men like Thomas Jefferson. A national bank would encourage the creation of commercial banks, which would then lend funds to merchants and urban businessmen. In turn, the economy would prosper as these figures invested in foreign trade, manufacturing, and transportation improvements.

Opponents of the proposed national bank drew heavily on classical liberal political economy as well as on the history of the Bank of England to show that a national bank's inflationary policies, though perhaps funding an initial boom for the economy, would surely bring a financial crash. Defenders of the national bank wavered in the face of such attacks but eventually argued that regardless of the long-term consequences, the government would be more effective with a bank than without one. The dynamics of the debate shifted away from economic considerations to political ones, leading both sides to support their positions with constitutional claims.

Defenders relied on the "necessary and proper" clause of the Constitution (Article I, Section 8). They believed that anything allowing the federal government to more easily meet its delegated powers was constitutional; the preamble of the Constitution gave the government the power to promote the general welfare of the country, which is exactly what they expected the bank to do. A national bank would ease government functions by providing a national currency, making the collection of taxes easier, and providing the federal government with loans when needed. Thus, bank supporters resorted to an "efficiency" defense.

Opponents believed that the purpose of the U.S. Constitution was to carefully delineate those powers expressly granted to the federal government by the states and by the people. They rejected the arguments of bank supporters as mere semantics that could be used to justify virtually any prerogative. To opponents, "necessary" meant "absolutely indispensable," and efficiency was not as important as "limitation." Those against the bank relied upon the explicit wording of Article I as well as on the Ninth and Tenth Amendments.

Congressional debate on the bank's constitutionality stalled, giving way to a free-for-all, as fledgling party newspapers assaulted and mercilessly slandered their opponents. The coalition built by Hamilton began to fragment, and with it the bank bill's chances of being passed dwindled. It was in the midst of this crisis—the first genuine political deadlock faced by Congress—that President Washington requested written positions from three of his cabinet members: the attorney general Edmund Randolph, Hamilton, and Jefferson. Randolph opposed the national bank on constitutional grounds, but the low caliber of his treatise warranted scant attention, thus placing the focus on Jefferson and Hamilton. The treatises then written by these two men are among the first attempts to interpret the Constitution in light of a policy issue not directly addressed in the text.

About the Author

Few early American leaders were more different than Alexander Hamilton and Thomas Jefferson. Hamilton was born on the island of Nevis, in the West Indies, on January 11, 1757, grew up in a port town, and was forced to work in a countinghouse at an early age. Realizing the lack of opportunity on the island, Hamilton moved to New York City, where he quickly rose through the financial ranks. He served as General Washington's aide-de-camp and private secretary during the American Revolution, as a member of the Continental Congress, and as a delegate to the Philadelphia Convention before becoming secretary of the treasury. To Hamilton, the future of America lay in commerce, progress, and development. After his retirement from office in 1795, he practiced law in New York City. He died July 12, 1804, from wounds sustained in a duel with Vice President Aaron Burr.

Born April 13, 1743, into a planter family in the Tidewater region of Virginia, Thomas Jefferson received the best his world could offer. He studied at the College of William and Mary, married into a prominent family, and would have been content to spend the rest of his life as a tobacco planter. When hostilities broke out in 1775, however, Jefferson rose through the ranks of Virginia politics, serving as a delegate to the Second Continental Congress—where he drafted the Declaration of Independence—and as the state's governor. When conflict subsided, Jefferson traveled to France on behalf of the fledg-

Time Line

1791

■ **January 20**
The national bank bill passes the House of Representatives.

■ **February**
Attorney General Edmund Randolph, Secretary of State Thomas Jefferson, and Secretary of the Treasury Alexander Hamilton respond to President George Washington's request for written opinions on the national bank bill.

■ **February 8**
The bank bill passes the Senate.

■ **February 25**
President Washington signs the bank bill into law.

■ **July 4**
The first stock offering for the Bank of the United States takes place in Philadelphia.

■ **October 31**
Philip Freneau, a supporter of Thomas Jefferson, commences operation of the *National Gazette* as the opposition's newspaper.

■ **December 12**
Bank of the United States officially opens for business in Philadelphia.

1792

■ **March**
A financial panic starts in New York City and then spreads to neighboring cities during the year.

1793

■ **December 31**
Jefferson retires as secretary of state.

1795

■ Directors of the Bank of the United States institute a noninflationary monetary policy, thus stabilizing the economy.

■ **January 31**
Hamilton retires as secretary of the treasury.

1796

■ Jefferson becomes vice president of the United States after losing the presidential election to John Adams.

www.milestonedocuments.com

Time Line

1801	■ **February 11–17** After thirty-six ballots in the House of Representatives, Jefferson is elected president of the United States. ■ Secretary of the Treasury Albert Gallatin initiates sweeping financial reforms of the U.S. government, reversing many of Hamilton's initiatives.
1804	■ **July 11** Vice President Aaron Burr mortally wounds Alexander Hamilton in a duel in Weehawken, New Jersey.
1808	■ Congress begins the rechartering process for the Bank of the United States.
1811	■ **January–February** After several years of debate, the opposition, led by Henry Clay of Kentucky, prevents the rechartering of the Bank of the United States. ■ **March 3** The Bank of the United States closes.
1819	■ **March 6** Supreme Court delivers *McCulloch v. Maryland* opinion.

ling United States before returning home at the beginning of the Washington administration. He subsequently served as secretary of state, vice president, and, for two terms, president of the United States. He retired to Monticello, his family estate near Charlottesville, Virginia, where he also founded the University of Virginia. He died July 4, 1826. Jefferson believed that an agrarian society would best perpetuate American liberty, which he typically defined as independence and self-government rather than as financial success.

Explanation and Analysis of the Document

◆ Thomas Jefferson's "Opinion on the Constitutionality of a National Bank"

Jefferson's opinion was written prior to Hamilton's. In fact, Hamilton had the benefit of reading Jefferson's opinion before writing his own. It may seem odd that Jefferson began his opinion by listing eight legal dilemmas posed by the national bank legislation. However, any well-trained lawyer or anyone well-versed in land policy in the 1790s understood what was at stake, as these laws related to the ownership of land, its distribution upon the death of the owner, and how states regulated incorporated land companies. In effect, Jefferson argues that the national bank would be a privileged corporation beyond the scope of regulation because of its federal charter. Jefferson appears to be employing a standard states' rights argument, but he is actually attacking Hamilton. James Madison probably told Jefferson that Alexander Hamilton wrote Federalist no. 33 to help secure the ratification of the Constitution in New York. Therein, Hamilton bluntly states that the federal government would not have the power "to vary the law of descent" (one of Jefferson's stated legal dilemmas) and that the ability to do so would constitute a "tyrannical power" (Carey and McClellan, p. 160).

In Jefferson's view, the authority of the states and of the federal government rested on two different types of power. In that the states preceded the national government, they served as the primary basis of political authority in the United States of America. Thus, the states were the proper projections of the people's sovereignty, exercising all aspects of that sovereignty unless the people expressly reserved the exercise of a power for themselves. The federal government possessed no such inherent exercise of sovereignty, being limited to only those powers explicitly given by the people through the state ratifying conventions. Since the Constitution contains no mention of a national bank and, more important, no express delegation of the power to create federally chartered enterprises, the bank bill was unconstitutional. Such a power, Jefferson suggests, is further prohibited by the Tenth Amendment, which he calls the "Twelfth" because it was the twelfth submitted for ratification.

Jefferson offers some economic arguments against the bank, and he also alludes to the framers' voting down an attempt to give chartering power to Congress. He denies that a bank could be created simply to pay the debts of the country, to lend money to the federal government, or to help regulate interstate commerce. Indeed, Jefferson argues that a national bank would actually harm business interests by interfering in intrastate commerce, an area most believed to fall outside the jurisdiction of the federal government.

Jefferson's most stinging criticism, however, is aimed against the broad interpretation of powers employed by bank supporters to defend it. He fears that their arguments ultimately opposed the reason for having a constitution in the first place, which in his mind was to limit the power of the national government. Clearly, Jefferson was no ardent nationalist who believed that social order and happiness depended upon the exercise of strong political power by a central government. To his final days, Jefferson insisted that a massive, activist government was a burden for the citizenry. He understood that social order must flow from liberty, not vice versa.

He also believed that the federal government must be a government of limited powers. To Jefferson, this meant that it would be limited in its ends and in its means; the fact that Congress could levy taxes did not mean that it could levy taxes for anything it wanted. (It was still widely considered at the time that "general welfare," as mentioned in the Constitution, meant those things that fell *generally* throughout the nation, not those things confined to specific states or interest groups.) Like other bank detractors, Jefferson defines *necessary* as "essential" rather than as "convenient." A bank was not essential for any of the government's activities, and congressmen would be wrong to sacrifice constitutional prerogatives for the sake of convenience.

Jefferson concludes his opinion by returning to states' rights, which he believed best guarded against encroachments on liberty. He holds that the president must safeguard these rights, especially when confronted with a concerted effort in Congress to jeopardize popular liberties for the sake of pecuniary interests.

◆ Alexander Hamilton's "Opinion as to the Constitutionality of the Bank of the United States"

In his own treatise, Alexander Hamilton does little to alleviate Jefferson's suspicions. Jefferson portrays political power as the great corrupter: If congressmen thought a national bank was constitutional, then there could be no limit to what they might propose next. Hamilton is more restrained, offering a measured response to the situation at hand. The country's economy was in trouble, and a national bank would help rescue it.

Lacking the prosaic elegance typical of a refined Virginia planter, Hamilton delivers a point-by-point refutation that drowns his opponents in verbiage and rhetorical might. Essentially, his argument closely follows his belief that the national government must possess complete sovereignty and, as such, must possess all the means and powers requisite to the fulfillment of its purpose of securing "social order." These powers are supreme and cannot be undermined by any other institution, including the state governments. He agrees that the federal government possesses expressly delegated powers, but these are understood to be supplemented by "implied" powers and what Hamilton calls "resting powers." The power to erect or incorporate a national bank falls within the latter two spheres, not that of express delegations. For a policy to be constitutional to Hamilton, it merely needs "a natural relation to any of the acknowledged objects or lawful ends of the government."

Hamilton then attacks Jefferson's contention that the "necessary and proper" clause limits the federal government to engaging in matters deemed essential. Such was not the popular meaning of the term *necessary,* he claims, and would "beget endless uncertainty and embarrassment" in addition to making most policies inoperative. Anything deemed essential to the "advancement of the public good," he holds, should be "construed liberally." Hamilton insists that the national government is the bedrock of American society. While not admitting "that the national government is sovereign in all respects," Hamilton writes that "it is sovereign to a certain extent; that is, to the extent of the objects of its specified powers."

A portrait of Alexander Hamilton by John Trumbull
(Library of Congress)

With little patience for Jefferson's "originalist" doctrines, Hamilton insists that one could trust neither the memories of the delegates to the Philadelphia Convention nor the conflicting accounts of what the framers intended the new government to be. Instead, intention must "be sought for in the instrument [the Constitution] itself, according to the usual and established rules of construction." Hamilton honestly thinks that these rules allowed for the creation of a national bank. He asserts that these circumstances did not imply, as Jefferson and Randolph were contending, that federal government officials could simply do as they pleased.

After dismissing Jefferson's and Randolph's opinions, Hamilton spends considerable effort tracing the legality of a national bank outside the realm of constitutional jurisprudence. Equally impressive is his subsequent justification of banks in general and the important role that they could play in improving the economy and in funding future wars. He even goes so far as to claim that "the support of troops" depended on whether Congress could successfully create a national bank—an argument sure to move Washington, if he were to manage to read that far.

Hamilton clearly had the upper hand in the argument, not because of his rhetorical skill but because of the

www.milestonedocuments.com

Essential Quotes

"It would reduce the whole instrument to a single phrase, that of instituting a Congress with power to do whatever would be for the good of the United States; and, as they would be the sole judges of the good or evil, it would be also a power to do whatever evil they please."

(Jefferson's Opinion)

"Can it be thought that the Constitution intended that for a shade or two of convenience, *more or less, Congress should be authorized to break down the most ancient and fundamental laws of the several States; such as those against Mortmain, the laws of Alienage, the rules of descent, the acts of distribution, the laws of escheat and forfeiture, the laws of monopoly? Nothing but a necessity invincible by any other means, can justify such a prostitution of laws, which constitute the pillars of our whole system of jurisprudence."*

(Jefferson's Opinion)

"Will Congress be too strait-laced to carry the Constitution into honest effect, unless they may pass over the foundation-laws of the State government for the slightest convenience of theirs?"

(Jefferson's Opinion)

"This general and indisputable principle puts at once an end to the abstract question, whether the United States have power to erect a corporation; that is to say, to give a legal or artificial capacity to one or more persons, distinct from the natural. For it is unquestionably incident to sovereign power to erect corporations, and consequently to that of the United States, in relation to the objects intrusted to the management of the government. The difference is this: where the authority of the government is general, it can create corporations in all cases, where it is confined to certain branches of legislation, it can create corporations only in those cases."

(Hamilton's Opinion)

"To understand the word ['necessary'] as the Secretary of State does, would be to depart from its obvious and popular sense, and to give it a restrictive operation, an idea never before entertained. It would be to give it the same force as if the word absolutely or indispensably had been prefixed to it."

(Hamilton's Opinion)

nature of the subject. Jefferson accepted the terms of the debate when he echoed James Madison's reasoning on the floor of the House of Representatives, treating the bank bill as a matter of constitutionalism rather than sound economic policy. Jefferson's opinion, though perhaps more elegant, leaves open the question of whether a national bank would actually help the economy. Hamilton enjoys free reign in touting the economic virtues of the proposed bank, which makes his argument appear sounder than Jefferson's.

It is not clear who gained ground in the argument either in the president's cabinet or in Congress following the delivery of Jefferson's and Hamilton's opinions. The national bank bill did pass, but neither Hamilton nor Jefferson could be said to have claimed total victory or to have conceded defeat.

Audience

President Washington often solicited from his cabinet members their opinions on major policy matters. Many of his most famous public speeches were even written in this manner. Thus, Jefferson and Hamilton certainly viewed Washington as their principal audience. However, it is unlikely that either wished to keep his views private. Jefferson always circulated copies of his treatises, and Hamilton, by the very manner in which his opinion is written, indicates that he had a larger audience in mind. Both circulated their opinions among friends and political associates.

Impact

Historians have typically sided with Hamilton in regard to the national bank, either because they agree with his interpretation of the Constitution or owing to the perceived benefits of stabilizing the currency and funding the national debt. Hamilton's proposals were far from radical, as the British had a national bank, and a similar institution had been created under the Articles of Confederation. Nonetheless, many Americans considered these policies to be "un-American," and some politicians insisted that Hamilton was overly fascinated with British forms because he was an Anglophile.

The passage of the bank bill affected American politics in two ways. First, it provided a forum in which manners of constitutional interpretation were widely discussed. Neither Hamilton nor Jefferson conceded his argument, and their political descendants continued to defend their positions for decades to come. More significantly, the debate on the bank bill polarized national politics and proved instrumental to the creation of the first party system. Newspapers were formed, rallies were held, and myriad local movements—some of which were organized against the national bank—slowly coalesced into a formal structure of political activity.

Once under operation, the Bank of the United States further fueled the party system when its inflationary activity quickly brought about depression centered in New York City in 1792. Pamphleteers pilloried the bank as a sign of corruption, whereby "monied" interests used the federal government to enrich themselves at the public's expense. This characterization carried over to Republican rhetoric, which portrayed the Federalists as a commercial elite who had warped the Constitution to suit their purposes. Federalists responded by attacking the Republicans as inept farmers who would wreck the economy.

The elections of 1800 seemed to settle the matter, with the Republicans taking office. In fact, even though they changed the policies of the Bank of the United States to reflect their insistence on founding currency on hard money rather than allowing inflation, the Republicans did not suspend the bank's operation. In effect, the Republicans used Hamiltonian means to secure Jeffersonian ends. They kept a national bank but used it to extinguish the national debt as quickly as possible. The bank's charter expired in 1811.

Related Documents

Frisch, Morton J., ed. *The Pacificus-Helvidius Debates of 1793–1794: Toward the Completion of the American Founding*. Indianapolis Ind.: Liberty Fund, 2007. James Madison and Alexander Hamilton debate the meaning of federalism as it applies to executive power.

Gallatin, Albert. *A Sketch of the Finances of the United States*. New York: William A. Davis, 1796. Senator Albert Gallatin outlines his critique of Hamiltonian finance, arguing that it actually made the economy worse.

Hamilton, Alexander. *Writings*, ed. Joanne B. Freeman. New York: Literary Classics of the United States, 2001. This includes the best and most succinct summary of Hamilton's essential writings.

Jefferson, Thomas. *Writings*, ed. Merrill D. Peterson. New York: Literary Classics of the United States, 1984. This volume includes the best and most succinct summary of Jefferson's essential writings.

Taylor, John. *An Enquiry into the Principles and Tendency of Certain Public Measures*. Philadelphia: Thomas Dobson, 1794. The leading Jeffersonian political economist attacks Hamiltonian finance and inflationary banking practices.

Bibliography

■ Articles

Klubes, Benjamin. "The First Federal Congress and the First National Bank: A Case Study in Constitutional Interpretation." *Journal of the Early Republic* 10, no. 1 (1990): 19–41.

■ Books

Carey, George W., and James McClellan, eds. *The Federalist*. Indianapolis, Ind.: Liberty Fund, 2001.

www.milestonedocuments.com

Chernow, Ron. *Alexander Hamilton*. New York: Penguin Press, 2004.

Cowen, David J. *The Origins and Economic Impact of the First Bank of the United States, 1791–1797*. New York: Garland Publishing, 2000.

Cunningham, Noble E., Jr. *Jefferson vs. Hamilton: Confrontations That Shaped a Nation*. New York: Palgrave Macmillan, 2000.

Elkins, Stanley, and Eric McKitrick. *The Age of Federalism*. New York: Oxford University Press, 1993.

Hammond, Bray. *Banks and Politics in America, from the Revolution to the Civil War*. Princeton, N.J.: Princeton University Press, 1957.

Madison, James. *Notes of the Debates of the Federal Convention of 1787*. New York: W. W. Norton, 1966.

Perkins, Edwin. *American Public Finance and Financial Services, 1700–1815*. Columbus: Ohio State University Press, 1994.

■ Web Sites

The Online Library of Liberty Web site.
http://oll.libertyfund.org. Accessed on November 30, 2007.

—By Carey M. Roberts

Questions for Further Study

1. How did the constitutional arguments of Jefferson and Hamilton carry over to other policy debates in Congress?

2. How did “strict” and “loose” interpretations of the Constitution affect the emerging first party system?

3. How well did Jefferson adhere to a strict construction of the chief executive’s constitutional powers once he became president of the United States?

4. In what ways does the debate on the bank’s constitutionality reveal deep fissures within the country over the interpretation of the Constitution? What does this debate reveal about gauging the “original intent” of the framers?

Glossary

acts of distribution	rules allowing for the transfer of a person’s property if there is no will; typically, states allowed property to go to surviving blood relatives
bank circulation	banknotes being exchanged as money, typically as based on the amount of specie (money in coin) in holding
Bank of New York	formed in 1784 by Alexander Hamilton, the first commercial bank in New York City
bills of exchange	exchange instruments allowing a merchant to receive goods by providing a note promising full payment at a later date in a currency chosen by the seller; occasionally circulated as a money substitute
bounties	direct subsidies provided by a government to business operations in the form of payments of goods or services rendered
circulating medium	money or money substitute, such as banknotes, specie, or promissory notes of public debt, being used to facilitate economic exchange

Glossary

commercial balance	the amount owed to a seller or group of sellers
custom-house regulation	a statute or rule related to the collection of taxes imposed on imported goods
doctrine of implied powers	the belief that the U.S. Constitution allows Congress (or the executive) the authority to exercise any power to achieve another power explicitly granted
dollar out of the Nines	a mathematical formula for checking the addition of large numbers in a sequence, by which those digits adding up to nine are made equal to zero, thus "casting" the nine away
douceurs	tips or emoluments provided for a service
duties	taxes on imported goods
enumerated powers	those areas of authority specifically listed in a constitution
excises	taxes on imported goods
exportation of commodities	the selling of goods from a specific area, such as a state or nation, outside that area's territorial boundaries
Forfeiture and Escheat	the transfer of a person's property to the government if he or she dies intestate (without a will) or without legal heirs
imposts	taxes on imported goods
law of descents	the common law determination of how inheritance is transferred from the deceased to the heirs
laws of alienage	restrictions under English common law whereby foreigners could not own or inherit land because they were not under the jurisdiction of the king
laws of monopoly	rules regulating enterprises that do not have competition; early corporations were often granted monopoly status to encourage economic development
laws of *Mortmain*	regulations regarding property held by corporate entities, which by definition never die, or figuratively possess a *main mort*, French for "dead hand"
mercantile company	a business involved in the transfer of staple goods, usually overseas
paper (as a currency medium)	a fiat currency whereby a government may print currency notes irrespective of specie or other holdings to back it; the currency becomes legal tender owing to the "fiat" of the state
plenary and sovereign authority	complete power over a particular matter
regulation of pilots	statutes governing ship captains
rules of construction	the manner in which a law, statute, or constitution is interpreted
taxes in kind	payments made to the state with goods or services rather than with currency
treasury orders	promissory notes issued by treasury officials stipulating payment with interest at a future date

www.milestonedocuments.com

Document Text

Jefferson's and Hamilton's Opinions on the Constitutionality of the Bank of the United States

Thomas Jefferson's Opinion on the Constitutionality of a National Bank

The bill for establishing a National Bank undertakes among other things:

1. To form the subscribers into a corporation.

2. To enable them in their corporate capacities to receive grants of land; and so far is against the laws of *Mortmain*.

3. To make alien subscribers capable of holding lands, and so far is against the laws of *Alienage*.

4. To transmit these lands, on the death of a proprietor, to a certain line of successors; and so far changes the course of *Descents*.

5. To put the lands out of the reach of forfeiture or escheat, and so far is against the laws of *Forfeiture and Escheat*.

6. To transmit personal chattels to successors in a certain line and so far is against the laws of *Distribution*.

7. To give them the sole and exclusive right of banking under the national authority; and so far is against the laws of Monopoly.

8. To communicate to them a power to make laws paramount to the laws of the States; for so they must be construed, to protect the institution from the control of the State legislatures, and so, probably, they will be construed.

I consider the foundation of the Constitution as laid on this ground: That "all powers not delegated to the United States, by the Constitution, nor prohibited by it to the States, are reserved to the States or to the people." [XIIth amendment.] To take a single step beyond the boundaries thus specially drawn around the powers of Congress, is to take possession of a boundless field of power, no longer susceptible of any definition.

The incorporation of a bank, and the powers assumed by this bill, have not, in my opinion, been delegated to the United States, by the Constitution.

I. They are not among the powers specially enumerated: for these are: 1st A power to lay taxes for the purpose of paying the debts of the United States; but no debt is paid by this bill, nor any tax laid. Were it a bill to raise money, its origination in the Senate would condemn it by the Constitution.

2. "To borrow money." But this bill neither borrows money nor ensures the borrowing it. The proprietors of the bank will be just as free as any other money holders, to lend or not to lend their money to the public. The operation proposed in the bill first, to lend them two millions, and then to borrow them back again, cannot change the nature of the latter act, which will still be a payment, and not a loan, call it by what name you please.

3. To "regulate commerce with foreign nations, and among the States, and with the Indian tribes." To erect a bank, and to regulate commerce, are very different acts. He who erects a bank, creates a subject of commerce in its bills, so does he who makes a bushel of wheat, or digs a dollar out of the mines; yet neither of these persons regulates commerce thereby. To make a thing which may be bought and sold, is not to prescribe regulations for buying and selling. Besides, if this was an exercise of the power of regulating commerce, it would be void, as extending as much to the internal commerce of every State, as to its external. For the power given to Congress by the Constitution does not extend to the internal regulation of the commerce of a State, (that is to say of the commerce between citizen and citizen,) which remain exclusively with its own legislature; but to its external commerce only, that is to say, its commerce with another State, or with foreign nations, or with the Indian tribes. Accordingly the bill does not propose the measure as a regulation of trace, but as "productive of considerable advantages to trade." Still less are these powers covered by any other of the special enumerations.

Document Text

II. Nor are they within either of the general phrases, which are the two following:

1. To lay taxes to provide for the general welfare of the United States, that is to say, "to lay taxes for *the purpose of* providing for the general welfare." For the laying of taxes is the *power*, and the general welfare the *purpose* for which the power is to be exercised. They are not to lay taxes *ad libitum for any purpose they please*; but only *to pay the debts or provide for the welfare of the Union*. In like manner, they are not *to do anything they please* to provide for the general welfare, but only to *lay taxes* for that purpose. To consider the latter phrase, not as describing the purpose of the first, but as giving a distinct and independent power to do any act they please, which might be for the good of the Union, would render all the preceding and subsequent enumerations of power completely useless.

It would reduce the whole instrument to a single phrase, that of instituting a Congress with power to do whatever would be for the good of the United States; and, as they would be the sole judges of the good or evil, it would be also a power to do whatever evil they please.

It is an established rule of construction where a phrase will bear either of two meanings, to give it that which will allow some meaning to the other parts of the instrument, and not that which would render all the others useless. Certainly no such universal power was meant to be given them. It was intended to lace them up straitly within the enumerated powers, and those without which, as means, these powers could not be carried into effect. It is known that the very power now proposed *as a means* was rejected as *an end* by the Convention which formed the Constitution. A proposition was made to them to authorize Congress to open canals, and an amendatory one to empower them to incorporate. But the whole was rejected, and one of the reasons for rejection urged in debate was, that then they would have a power to erect a bank, which would render the great cities, where there were prejudices and jealousies on the subject, adverse to the reception of the Constitution.

2. The second general phrase is, "to make all laws *necessary* and proper for carrying into execution the enumerated powers." But they can all be carried into execution without a bank. A bank therefore is not *necessary*, and consequently not authorized by this phrase.

If has been urged that a bank will give great facility or convenience in the collection of taxes, Suppose this were true: yet the Constitution allows only the means which are "*necessary*," not those which are merely "convenient" for effecting the enumerated powers. If such a latitude of construction be allowed to this phrase as to give any non-enumerated power, it will go to everyone, for there is not one which ingenuity may not torture into a *convenience* in some instance *or other*, to *some one* of so long a list of enumerated powers. It would swallow up all the delegated powers, and reduce the whole to one power, as before observed. Therefore it was that the Constitution restrained them to the *necessary* means, that is to say, to those means without which the grant of power would be nugatory.

But let us examine this convenience and see what it is. The report on this subject, page 3, states the only *general* convenience to be, the preventing the transportation and re-transportation of money between the States and the treasury, (for I pass over the increase of circulating medium, ascribed to it as a want, and which, according to my ideas of paper money, is clearly a demerit.) Every State will have to pay a sum of tax money into the treasury; and the treasury will have to pay, in every State, a part of the interest on the public debt, and salaries to the officers of government resident in that State. In most of the States there will still be a surplus of tax money to come up to the seat of government for the officers residing there. The payments of interest and salary in each State may he made by treasury orders on the State collector. This will take up the greater part of the money he has collected in his State, and consequently prevent the great mass of it from being drawn out of the State. If there be a balance of commerce in favor of that State against the one in which the government resides, the surplus of taxes will be remitted by the bills of exchange drawn for that commercial balance. And so it must be if there was a bank. But if there be no balance of commerce, either direct or circuitous, all the banks in the world could not bring up the surplus of taxes, but in the form of money. Treasury orders then, and bills of exchange may prevent the displacement of the main mass of the money collected, without the aid of any bank; and where these fail, it cannot be prevented even with that aid.

Perhaps, indeed, bank bills may be a more *convenient* vehicle than treasury orders. But a little *difference* in the degree of *convenience* cannot constitute the necessity which the Constitution makes the ground for assuming any non-enumerated power.

Besides, the existing banks will, without a doubt, enter into arrangements for lending their agency, and the more favorable, as there will be a competition

www.milestonedocuments.com

among them for it; whereas the bill delivers us up bound to the national bank, who are free to refuse all arrangement, but on their own terms, and the public not free, on such refusal, to employ any other bank. That of Philadelphia I believe, now does this business, by their post-notes, which, by an arrangement with the treasury, are paid by any State collector to whom they are presented. This expedient alone suffices to prevent the existence of that *necessity* which may justify the assumption of a non-enumerated power as a means for carrying into effect an enumerated one. The thing may be done, and has been done, and well done, without this assumption, therefore it does not stand on that degree of *necessity* which can honestly justify it.

It may be said that a bank whose bills would have a currency all over the States, would be more convenient than one whose currency is limited to a single State. So it would be still more convenient that there should be a bank, whose bills should have a currency all over the world. But it does not follow from this superior conveniency, that there exists anywhere a power to establish such a bank; or that the world may not go on very well without it.

Can it be thought that the Constitution intended that for a shade or two of *convenience*, more or less, Congress should be authorized to break down the most ancient and fundamental laws of the several States; such as those against Mortmain, the laws of Alienage, the rules of descent, the acts of distribution, the laws of escheat and forfeiture, the laws of monopoly? Nothing but a necessity invincible by any other means, can justify such a prostitution of laws, which constitute the pillars of our whole system of jurisprudence. Will Congress be too strait-laced to carry the Constitution into honest effect, unless they may pass over the foundation-laws of the State government for the slightest convenience of theirs?

The negative of the President is the shield provided by the Constitution to protect against the invasions of the legislature: 1. The right of the Executive. 2. Of the Judiciary. 3. Of the States and State legislatures. The present is the case of a right remaining exclusively with the States, and consequently one of those intended by the Constitution to be placed under its protection,

It must be added, however, that unless the President's mind on a view of everything which is urged for and against this bill, is tolerably clear that it is unauthorized by the Constitution; if the pro and the con hang so even as to balance his judgment, a just respect for the wisdom of the legislature would naturally decide the balance in favor of their opinion. It is chiefly for cases where they are clearly misled by error, ambition, or interest, that the Constitution has placed a check in the negative of the President.

◆ Hamilton's Opinion as to the Constitutionality of the Bank of the United States, 1791

The Secretary of the Treasury having perused with attention the papers containing the opinions of the Secretary of State and Attorney General, concerning the constitutionality of the bill for establishing a National Bank, proceeds, according to the order of the President, to submit the reasons which have induced him to entertain a different opinion.

It will naturally have been anticipated, that in performing this task, he would feel uncommon solicitude. Personal considerations alone, arising from the reflection that the measure originated with him, would be sufficient to produce it. The sense which he has manifested of the great importance of such an institution to the successful administration of the department under his particular care, and an expectation of serious ill consequences to result from a failure of the measure, do not permit him to be without anxiety on public accounts. But the chief solicitude arises from a firm persuasion, that principles of construction like those espoused by the Secretary of State and Attorney General, would be fatal to the just and indispensable authority of the United States.

In entering upon the argument, it ought to be premised that the objections of the Secretary of State and Attorney General are founded on a general denial of the authority of the United States to erect corporations. The latter, indeed, expressly admits, that if there be anything in the bill which is not warranted by the Constitution, it is the clause of incorporation.

Now it appears to the Secretary of the Treasury that this general principle is inherent in the very definition of government, and essential to every step of progress to be made by that of the United States, namely: That every power vested in a government is in its nature sovereign, and includes, by force of the term, a right to employ all the means requisite and fairly applicable to the attainment of the ends of such power, and which are not precluded by restrictions and exceptions specified in the Constitution, or not immoral, or not contrary to the essential ends of political society.

This principle, in its application to government in general, would be admitted as an axiom; and it will be incumbent upon those who may incline to deny it, to prove a distinction, and to show that a rule which,

Document Text

in the general system of things, is essential to the preservation of the social order, is inapplicable to the United States.

The circumstance that the powers of sovereignty are in this country divided between the National and State governments, does not afford the distinction required. It does not follow from this, that each of the portion of powers delegated to the one or to the other, is not sovereign with regard to its proper objects. It will only follow from it, that each has sovereign power as to certain things, and not as to other things. To deny that the government of the United States has sovereign power, as to its declared purposes and trusts, because its power does not extend to all cases would be equally to deny that the State governments have sovereign power in any case, because their power does not extend to every case. The tenth section of the first article of the Constitution exhibits a long list of very important things which they may not do. And thus the United States would furnish the singular spectacle of a political society without sovereignty, or of a people governed, without government.

If it would be necessary to bring proof to a proposition so clear, as that which affirms that the powers of the federal government, as to its objects, were sovereign, there is a clause of its Constitution which would be decisive. It is that which declares that the Constitution, and the laws of the United States made in pursuance of it, and all treaties made, or which shall be made, under their authority, shall be the serene law of the land. The power which can create the supreme law of the land in any case, is doubtless sovereign as to such case.

This general and indisputable principle puts at once an end to the abstract question, whether the United States have power to erect a corporation; that is to say, to give a legal or artificial capacity to one or more persons, distinct from the natural. For it is unquestionably incident to sovereign power to erect corporations, and consequently to that of the United States, in relation to the objects intrusted to the management of the government. The difference is this: where the authority of the government is general, it can create corporations in all cases, where it is confined to certain branches of legislation, it can create corporations only in those cases.

Here then, as far as concerns the reasonings of the Secretary of State and the Attorney General, the affirmative of the constitutionality of the bill might be permitted to rest. It will occur to the President, that the principle here advanced has been untouched by either of them.

For a more complete elucidation of the point, nevertheless, the arguments which they had used against the power of the government to erect corporations, however foreign they are to the great and fundamental rule which has been stated, shall be particularly examined. And after showing that they do not tend to impair its force, it shall also be shown that the power of incorporation, incident to the government in certain cases, does fairly extend to the particular case which is the object of the bill.

The first of these arguments is, that the foundation of the Constitution is laid on this ground: "That all powers not delegated to the United States by the Constitution, nor prohibited to it by the States, are reserved for the States, or to the people." Whence it is meant to be inferred, that Congress can in no case exercise any power not included in those not enumerated in the Constitution. And it is affirmed, that the power of erecting a corporation is not included in any of the enumerated powers.

The main proposition here laid down, in its true signification is not to be questioned. It is nothing more than a consequence of this republican maxim, that all government is a delegation of power. But how much is delegated in each case, is a question of fact, to be made out by fair reasoning and construction, upon the particular provisions of the Constitution, taking as guides the general principles and general ends of governments.

It is not denied that there are implied well as express powers, and that the former are as effectually delegated as the tatter. And for the sake of accuracy it shall be mentioned, that there is another class of powers, which may be properly denominated resting powers. It will not be doubted, that if the United States should make a conquest of any of the territories of its neighbors, they would possess sovereign jurisdiction over the conquered territory. This would be rather a result, from the whole mass of the powers of the government, and from the nature of political society, than a consequence of either of the powers specially enumerated.

But be this as it may, it furnishes a striking illustration of the general doctrine contended for; it shows an extensive case in which a power of erecting corporations is either implied in or would result from, some or all of the powers vested in the national government. The jurisdiction acquired over such conquered country would certainly be competent to any species of legislation.

To return: It is conceded that implied powers are to be considered as delegated equally with express

www.milestonedocuments.com

ones. Then it follows, that as a power of erecting a corporation may as well be implied as any other thing, it may as well be employed as an instrument or mean of carrying into execution any of the specified powers, as any other instrument or mean whatever. The only question must be in this, as in every other case, whether the mean to be employed or in this instance, the corporation to be erected, has a natural relation to any of the acknowledged objects or lawful ends of the government. Thus a corporation may not be erected by Congress for superintending the police of the city of Philadelphia, because they are not authorized to regulate the police of that city. But one may be erected in relation to the collection of taxes, or to the trade with foreign countries, or to the trade between the States, or with the Indian tribes; because it is the province of the federal government to regulate those objects, and because it is incident to a general sovereign or legislative power to regulate a thing, to employ all the means which relate to its regulation to the best and greatest advantage.

A strange fallacy seems to have crept into the manner of thinking and reasoning upon the subject. Imagination appears to have been unusually busy concerning it. An incorporation seems to have been regarded as some great independent substantive thing; as a political end of peculiar magnitude and moment; whereas it is truly to be considered as a quality, capacity, or mean to an end. Thus a mercantile company is formed, with a certain capital, for the purpose of carrying on a particular branch of business. Here the business to be prosecuted is the end. The association, in order to form the requisite capital, is the primary mean. Suppose that an incorporation were added to this, it would only be to add a new quality to that association, to give it an artificial capacity, by which it would be enabled to prosecute the business with more safety and convenience.

That the importance of the power of incorporation has been exaggerated, leading to erroneous conclusions, will further appear from tracing it to its origin. The Roman law is the source of it, according to which a voluntary association of individuals, at any tome, or for any purpose, was capable of producing it. In England, whence our notions of it are immediately borrowed, it forms part of the executive authority, and the exercise of it has been often delegated by that authority. Whence, therefore, the ground of the supposition that it lies beyond the reach of all those very important portions of sovereign power, legislative as well as executive, which belongs to the government of the United States.

To this mode of reasoning respecting the right of employing all the means requisite to the execution of the specified powers of the government, it is objected, that none but necessary and proper means are to be employed; and the Secretary of State maintains, that no means are to be considered as necessary but those without which the grant of the power would be nugatory. Nay, so far does he go in his restrictive interpretation of the word, as even to make the case of necessity which shall warrant the constitutional exercise of the power to depend on casual and temporary circumstances; an idea which alone refutes the construction. The expediency of exercising a particular power, at a particular time, must, indeed depend on circumstances, but the constitutional right of exercising it must be uniform and invariable, the same to-day as to-morrow.

All the arguments, therefore, against the constitutionality of the bill derived from the accidental existence of certain State banks, institutions which happen to exist to-day, and, for aught that concerns the government of the United States, may disappear tomorrow, must not only be rejected as fallacious, but must be viewed as demonstrative that there is a radical source of error in the reasoning.

It is essential to the being of the national government, that so erroneous a conception of the meaning of the word necessary should be exploded.

It is certain that neither the grammatical nor popular sense of the term requires that construction. According to both, necessary often means no more than needful, requisite, incidental, useful, or conducive to. It is a common mode of expression to say, that it is necessary for a government or a person to do this or that thing, when nothing more is intended or understood, than that the interests of the government or person require, or will be promoted by, the doing of this or that thing. The imagination can be at no loss for exemplifications of the use of the word in this sense. And it is the true one in which it is to be understood as used in the Constitution. The whole turn of the clause containing it indicates, that it was the intent of the Convention, by that clause, to give a liberal latitude to the exercise of the specified powers. The expressions have peculiar comprehensiveness. They are, "to make all laws necessary and proper for carrying into execution the foregoing powers, and all other powers vested by the Constitution in the government of the United States, or in any department or officer thereof."

To understand the word as the Secretary of State does, would be to depart from its obvious and popu-

www.milestonedocuments.com

lar sense, and to give it a restrictive operation, an idea never before entertained. It would be to give it the same force as if the word absolutely or indispensably had been prefixed to it.

Such a construction would beget endless uncertainty and embarrassment. The cases must be palpable and extreme, in which it could be pronounced, with certainty, that a measure was absolutely necessary, or one, without which, the exercise of a given power would be nugatory. There are few measures of any government which would stand so severe a test. To insist upon it, would be to make the criterion of the exercise of any implied power, a case of extreme necessity; which is rather a rule to justify the overleaping of the bounds of constitutional authority, than to govern the ordinary exercise of it.

It may be truly said of every government, as well as of that of the United States, that it has only a right to pass such laws as are necessary and proper to accomplish the objects intrusted to it. For no government has a right to do merely what it pleases. Hence, by a process of reasoning similar to that of the Secretary of State, it might be proved that neither of the State governments has a right to incorporate a bank. It might be shown that all the public business of the state could be performed without a bank, and inferring thence that it was unnecessary, it might be argued that it could not be done, because it is against the rule which has been just mentioned. A like mode of reasoning would prove that there was no power to incorporate the inhabitants of a town, with a view to a more perfect police. For it is certain that an incorporation may be dispensed with, though it is better to have one. It is to be remembered that there is no express power in any State constitution to erect corporations.

The degree in which a measure is necessary, can never be a test of the legal right to adopt it; that must be a matter of opinion, and can only be a test of expediency. The relation between the measure and the end; between the nature of the mean employed toward the execution of a power, and the object of that power must be the criterion of constitutionality, not the more or less of necessity or utility.

The practice of the government is against the rule of construction advocated by the Secretary of State. Of this, the Act concerning lighthouses, beacons, buoys, and public piers, is a decisive example. This, doubtless, must be referred to the powers of regulating trade, and is fairly relative to it. But it cannot be affirmed that the exercise of that power in this instance was strictly necessity or that the power itself would be nugatory, with out that of regulating establishments of this nature.

This restrictive interpretation of the word necessary is also contrary to this sound maxim of construction, namely, that the powers contained in a constitution of government, especially those which concern the general administration of the affairs of a country, its finances, trade, defense, etc., ought to be construed liberally in advancement of the public good. This rule does not depend on the particular form of a government, or on the particular demarcation of the boundaries of its powers, but on the nature and object of government itself. The means by which national exigencies are to be provided for, national inconveniences obviated, national prosperity promoted, are of such infinite variety, extent, and complexity, that there must of necessity be great latitude of discretion in the selection and application of those means. Hence, consequently, the necessity and propriety of exercising the authorities intrusted to a government on principles of liberal construction.

The Attorney General admits the rule, but takes a distinction between a State and the Federal Constitution. The latter, he thinks, ought to be construed with greater strictness, because there is more danger of error in defining partial than General powers. But the reason of the rule forbids such a distinction. This reason is, the variety and extent of public exigencies, a far greater proportion of which, and of a far more critical kind, are objects of National than of State administration. The greater danger of error, as far as it is supposable, may be a prudential reason for caution in practice, but it cannot be a rule of restrictive interpretation.

In regard to the clause of the Constitution immediately under consideration, it is admitted by the Attorney General, that no restrictive effect can be ascribed to it. He defines the word necessary thus: "To be necessary is to be incidental, and may be denominated the natural means of executing a power."

But while on the one hand the construction of the Secretary of State is deemed inadmissible, it will not be contended, on the other, that the clause in question gives any new or independent power. But it gives an explicit sanction to the doctrine of implied powers, and is equivalent to an admission of the proposition that the government, as to its specified powers and objects, has plenary and sovereign authority, in some cases paramount to the States; in others, coordinate with it. For such is the plain import of the declaration, that it may pass all tams necessary and proper to carry into execution those powers.

Document Text

It is no valid objection to the doctrine to say, that it is calculated to extend the power of the government throughout the entire sphere of State legislation. The same thing has been said, and may be said, with regard to every exercise of power by implication or construction.

The moment the literal meaning is departed from, there is a chance of error and abuse. And yet an adherence to the letter of its powers would at once arrest the motions of government. It is not only agreed, on all hands, that the exercise of constructive powers is indispensable, but every act which has been passed, is more or less an exemplification of it. One has been already mentioned that relating to lighthouses, etc. that which declares the power of the President to remove officers at pleasure, acknowledges the same truth in another and a signal instance.

The truth is, that difficulties on this point are inherent in the nature of the Federal Constitution; they result inevitably from a division of the legislative power. The consequence of this division is, that there will be cases clearly within the power of the national government; others, clearly without its powers; and a third class, which will leave room for controversy and difference of opinion, and concerning which a reasonable latitude of judgment must be allowed.

But the doctrine which is contended for is not chargeable with the consequences imputed to it. It does not affirm that the national government is sovereign in all respects, but that it is sovereign to a certain extent; that is, to the extent of the objects of its specified powers.

It leaves, therefore, a criterion of what is constitutional, and of what is not so. This criterion is the end, to which the measure relates as a mean. If the end be clearly comprehended within any of the specified powers, and if the measure have an obvious relation to that end, and is not forbidden by any particular provision of the Constitution, it may safely be deemed to come within the compass of the national authority. There is also this further criterion, which may materially assist the decision: Does the proposed measure abridge a pre-existing right of any State or of any individual? If it does not, there is a strong presumption in favor of its constitutionality, and slighter relations to any declared object of the Constitution may be permitted to turn the scale.

The general objections, which are to be inferred from the reasonings of the Secretary of State and Attorney General, to the doctrine which has been advanced, have been stated, and it is hoped satisfactorily answered, Those of a more particular nature shall now be examined.

The Secretary of State introduces his opinion with an observation, that the proposed incorporation undertakes to create certain capacities, properties, or attributes, which are against the laws of alienage, descents, escheat and forfeiture, distribution and monopoly, and to confer a power to make laws paramount to those of the States. And nothing, says he, in another place, but necessity, invincible by other means, can justify such a prostration of laws, which constitute the pillars of our whole system of jurisprudence, and are the foundation laws of the State governments. If these are truly the foundation laws of the several States, then have most of them subverted their own foundations. For there is scarcely one of them which has not, since the establishment of its particular constitution, made material alterations in some of those branches of its jurisprudence, especially the law of descents. But it is not conceived how anything can be called the fundamental law of a State government which is not established in its constitution unalterable by the ordinary legislature. And, with regard to the question of necessity, it has been shown that this can only constitute a question of expediency, not of right.

To erect a corporation, is to substitute a legal or artificial for a natural person, and where a number are concerned, to give them individuality. To that legal or artificial person, once created, the common law of every State, of itself, annexes all those incidents and attributes which are represented as a prostration of the main pillars of their jurisprudence.

It is certainly not accurate to say, that the erection of a corporation is against those different head's of the State laws; because it is rather to create a kind of person or entity, to which they are inapplicable, and to which the general rule of those laws assign a different regimen. The laws of alienage cannot apply to an artificial person, because it can have no country; those of descent cannot apply to it, because it can have no heirs; those of escheat are foreign from it, for the same reason; those of forfeiture, because it cannot commit a crime; those of distribution, because, though it may be dissolved, it cannot die.

As truly might it be said, that the exercise of the power of prescribing the rule by which foreigners shall be naturalized, is against the law of alienage, while it is, in fact, only to put them in a situation to cease to be the subject of that law. To do a thing which is against a law, is to do something which it forbids, or which is a violation of it.

But if it were even to be admitted that the erection of a corporation is a direct alteration of the state laws, in the enumerated particulars, it would do nothing toward proving that the measure was unconstitutional. If the government of the United States can do no act which amounts to an alteration of a State law, all its powers are nugatory; for almost every new law is an alteration, in same way or other, of an old law, either common or statute.

There are laws concerning bankruptcy in some States. Some States have laws regulating the values of foreign coins. Congress are empowered to establish uniform laws concerning bankruptcy throughout the United States, and to regulate the values of foreign coins. The exercise of either of these powers by Congress, necessarily involves an alteration of the laws of those States.

Again. Every person, by the common law of each State, may export his property to foreign countries, at pleasure. But Congress, in pursuance of the power of regulating trade, may prohibit the exportation of commodities; in doing which, they would alter the common law of each State, in abridgment of individual right.

It can therefore never be good reasoning to say this or that act is unconstitutional, because it alters this or that law of a State. It must be shown that the act which makes the alteration is unconstitutional on other accounts, not because it makes the alteration.

There are two points in the suggestions of the Secretary of State, which have been noted, that are peculiarly incorrect. One is, that the proposed incorporation is against the laws of monopoly, because it stipulates an exclusive right of banking under the national authority; the other, that it gives power to the institution to make laws paramount to those of the States.

But, with regard to the first: The bill neither prohibits any State from erecting as many banks as they please, nor any number of individuals from associating to carry on the business, and consequently, is free from the charge of establishing a monopoly; for monopoly implies a legal impediment to the carrying on of the trade by others than those to whom it is granted.

And with regard to the second point, there is still less foundation. The by-laws of such an institution as a bank can operate only on its own members can only concern the disposition of its own property, and must essentially resemble the rules of a private mercantile partnership. They are expressly not to be contrary to law; and law must here mean the law of a State, as well as of the United States. There never can be a doubt, that a law of a corporation, if contrary to a law of a State, must be overruled as void unless the law of the State is contrary to that of the United States and then the question will not be between the law of the State and that of the corporation, but between the law of the State and that of the United States.

Another argument made use of by the Secretary of State is, the rejection of a proposition by the Convention to empower Congress to make corporations, either generally, or for some special purpose.

What was the precise nature or extent of this proposition, or what the reasons for refusing it, is not ascertained by any authentic document, or even by accurate recollection. As far as any such document exists, it specifies only canals. If this was the amount of it, it would, at most, only prove that it was thought inexpedient to give a power to incorporate for the purpose of opening canals, for which purpose a special power would have been necessary, except with regard to the western territory, there being nothing in any part of the Constitution respecting the regulation of canals. It must be confessed, however, that very different accounts are given of the import of the proposition, and of the motives for rejecting it. Some affirm, that it was confined to the opening of canals and obstructions in rivers, others, that it embraced banks; and others, that it extended to the power of incorporating generally. Some, again, allege, that it was disagreed to because it was thought improper to vest in Congress a power of erecting corporations. Others, because it was thought unnecessary to specify the power, and inexpedient to furnish an additional topic of objection to the Constitution. In this state of the matter, no inference whatever can be drawn from it.

But whatever may have been the nature of the proposition, or the reasons for rejecting it, nothing is included by it, that is the proposition, in respect to the real merits of the question. The Secretary of State will not deny, that, whatever may have been the intention of the framers of a constitution, or of a law, that intention is to be sought for in the instrument itself, according to the usual and established rules of construction. Nothing is more common than for laws to express and elect more or less than was intended. If, then, a power to erect a corporation in any case be deducible, by fair inference, from the whole or any part of the numerous provisions of the Constitution of the United States arguments drawn from extrinsic circumstances regarding the in tension of the Convention must be rejected.

Most of the arguments of the Secretary of State, which have not been considered in the foregoing

www.milestonedocuments.com

Document Text

remarks, are of a nature rather to apply to the expediency than to the constitutionality of the bill. They will, however, be noticed in the discussions which will be necessary in reference to the particular heads of the powers of the government which are involved in the question.

Those of the Attorney General will now properly come under view.

His first objection is, that the power of incorporation is not expressly given to Congress. This shall be conceded, but in this sense only, that it is not declared in express terms that Congress may erect a corporation. But this cannot mean, that there are not certain express powers which necessary include it. For instance Congress have express power to exercise exclusive legislation in all cases whatsoever, over such district (not exceeding ten miles square) as may, by cession of particular States and the acceptance of Congress, become the seat of the government of the United States; and to exercise like authority over all places purchased, by consent of the legislature of the State in which the same shall be for the erection of forts, arsenals, dock-yards, and other needful buildings. Here, then, is express power to exercise exclusive legislation, in all cases whatsoever, over certain Ices, that is to do, in respect to those places, all that any government whatsoever may do. For language does not afford a more complete designation of sovereign power than in those comprehensive terms. It is, in other words, a power to pass all laws whatsoever, and consequently, to pass laws for erecting corporations, as well as for any other purpose which is the proper object of law in a free govern meet.

Surely it can never be believed that Congress, with exclusive powers of legislation in all cases whatsoever, cannot erect a corporation within the district which shall become the seat of government, for the better regulation of its police. And yet there is an unqualified denial of the power to erect corporations in every case on the part both of the Secretary of State and of the Attorney General; the former, indeed, speaks of that power in these emphatical terms: That it is a right remaining exclusively with the States.

As far, then, as there is an express power to do any particular act of legislation, there is an express one to erect a corporation in the case above described. But, accurately speaking, no particular power is more than that implied in a, general one. Thus the power to lay a duty on a gallon of rum is only a particular implied in the general power to collect taxes, duties, imposts, and excises. This serves to explain in what sense it may be said that Congress have not an express power to make corporations.

This may not be an improper place to take notice of an argument which was used in debate in the House of Representatives. It was there argued, that if the Constitution intended to confer so important a power as that of erecting corporations, it would have been expressly mentioned. But the case which has been noticed is clearly one in which such a power exists, and yet without any specification of express grant of it, further than as every particular implied in a general power can be said to be so granted.

But the argument itself is founded upon an exaggerated and erroneous conception of the nature of the power. It has been shown that it is not of so transcendent a kind as the reasoning supposes, and that, viewed in a just light, it is a mean which ought to have been left to implication, rather than an end which ought to have been expressly granted.

Having observed that the power of erecting corporations is not expressly granted to Congress, the Attorney General proceeds thus:

"If it can be exercised by them, it must be

"1. Because the nature of the federal government implies it.

"2. Because it is involved in some of the specified powers of legislation.

"3. Because it is necessary and proper to carry into execution some of the specified powers."

To be implied in the nature of the federal government, says he, would beget a doctrine so indefinite as to grasp every power.

This proposition, it ought to be remarked, is not precisely, or even substantially, that which has been relied upon. The proposition relied upon is, that the specified powers of Congress are in their nature sovereign. That it is incident to sovereign power to erect corporations, and that therefore Congress have a right, within the sphere and in relation to the objects of their power, to erect corporations. It shall, however, be supposed that the Attorney General would consider the two propositions in the same light, and that the objection made to the one would be made to the other.

To this objection an answer has been already given. It is this, that the doctrine is stated with this express qualification, that the right to erect corporations does only extend to cases and objects within the sphere of the specified powers of the government. A general legislative authority implies a power to erect corporations in all cases. A particular legislative power implies authority to erect corporations in relation to cases arising under that power only.

Document Text

Hence the affirming that, as incident to sovereign power, Congress may erect a corporation in relation to the collection of their taxes, is no more to affirm that they may do whatever else they please, than the saying that they have a power to regulate trade, would be to affirm that they have a power to regulate religion; or than the maintaining that they have sovereign power as to taxation, would be to maintain that they have sovereign power as to everything else.

The Attorney General undertakes in the next place to show, that the power of erecting corporations is not involved in any of the specified powers of legislation confided to the national government. In order to this, he has attempted an enumeration of the particulars which he supposes to be comprehended under the several heads of the Covers to lay and collect taxes, &c.; to borrow money on the credit of the United States, to regulate commerce with sovereign nations; between the States, and with the Indian tribes, to dispose of and make all needful rules and regulations respecting the territory of other property belonging to the United States. The design of which enumeration is to show, what is included under those different heads of power, and negatively, that the power of erecting corporations is not included.

The truth of this inference or conclusion must depend on the accuracy of the enumeration. If it can be shown that the enumeration is defective, the inference is destroyed. To do this will be attended with no difficulty.

The heads of the power to lay and collect taxes are stated to be:

1. To stipulate the sum to be lent.

2. An interest or no interest to be paid.

3. The time and manner of repaying, unless the loan be placed on an irredeemable fund.

This enumeration is liable to a variety of objections. It omits in the first place, the pledging or mortgaging of a fund for the security of the money lent, an usual, and in most cases an essential ingredient.

The idea of a stipulation of an interest or no interest is too confined. It should rather have been said, to stipulate the consideration of the loan. Individuals often borrow on considerations other than the payment of interest, so may governments, and so they often find it necessary to do. Everyone recollects the lottery tickets and other douceurs often given in Great Britain as collateral inducements to the lending of money to the government. There are also frequently collateral conditions, which the enumeration does not contemplate. Every contract which has been made for moneys borrowed in Holland, induces stipulations that the sum due shall bedded from taxes, and from sequestration in time of war, and mortgages all the land and property of the United States for the reimbursement.

It is also known that a lottery is a common expedient for borrowing money, which certainly does not fall under either of the enumerated heads.

The heads of the power to regulate commerce with foreign nations, are stated to be:

1. To prohibit them or their commodities from our ports.

2. To impose duties on them, where none existed before, or to increase existing; duties on them.

3. To subject them to any species of customhouse regulation.

4. To grant them any exemptions or privileges which policy may suggest.

This enumeration is far more exceptionable than either of the former. It omits everything that relates to the citizens' vessels, or commodities of the United States.

The following palpable omissions occur at once:

1. Of the power to prohibit the exportation of commodities, which not only exists at all times, but which in time of war it would be necessary to exercise, particularly with relation to naval and warlike stores

2. Of the power to prescribe rules concerning the characteristics and privileges of an American bottom, how she shall be navigated, or whether by citizens or foreigners, or by a proportion of each

3. Of the power of regulating the manner of contracting with seamen; the police of ships on their voyages, &c., of which the Act for the government and regulation of seamen, in the merchants' service, is a specimen.

That the three preceding articles are omissions, will not be doubted there is a long list of items in addition, which admit of little, if any question, of which a few samples shall be given.

1. The granting of bounties to certain kinds of vessels, and certain species of merchandise; of this nature, is the allowance on dried and pickled fish and salted provisions

2. The prescribing of rules concerning the inspection of commodities to be exported. Though the States individually are competent to this regulation, yet there is no reason, in point of authority at least, why a general system might not be adopted by the United States.

3. The regulation of policies of insurance; of salvage upon goods found at sea, and the disposition of such goods.

4. The regulation of pilots.

www.milestonedocuments.com

Document Text

5. The regulation of bills of exchange drawn by a merchant of one State upon a merchant of another State. This last rather belongs to the regulation of trade between the States, but is equally omitted in the specifications under that head

The last enumeration relates to the power to dispose of, and make all needful rules and regulations respecting the territory or other property belonging to the United States.

The heads of this power are said to be:

1. To exert an ownership over the territory of the United States which may be properly called the property of the United States, as in the western territory, and to institute a government therein, or

2. To exert an ownership over the other property of the United States.

The idea of exerting an ownership over the territory or other property of the United States, is particularly indefinite and vague. It does not at all satisfy the conception of what must have been intended by a power to make all needful rules and regulations, nor would there have been any use for a special clause, which authorized nothing more. For the right of exerting an ownership is implied in the very definition of property. It is admitted, that in regard to the western territory, something more is intended; even the institution of a government, that is, the creation of a body politic, or corporation of the highest nature; one which, in its maturity, will be able itself to create other corporations. Why, then, does not the same clause authorize the erection of a corporation, in respect to the regulation or disposal of any other of the property of the United States.

This idea will be enlarged upon in another place.

Hence it appears, that the enumerations which have been attempted by the Attorney General, are so imperfect, as to authorize no conclusion whatever; they, therefore, have no tendency to disprove that each and every of the powers, to which they relate, includes that of erecting corporations, which they certainly do, as the subsequent illustrations will snore and more evince.

It is presumed to have been satisfactorily shown in the course of the preceding observations:

1. That the power of the government, as to the objects intrusted to its management, is, in its nature, sovereign.

2. That the right of erecting corporations is one inherent in, and inseparable from, the idea of sovereign power.

3. That the position, that the government of the United States can exercise no power, but such as is delegated to it by its Constitution, does not militate against this principle.

4. That the word necessary, in the general clause, can have no restrictive operation derogating from the force of this principle indeed' that the degree in which a measure is or is not necessary cannot be a test of constitutional right, but of expediency only.

5. That the power to erect corporations is not to be considered as an independent or substantive power, but as an incidental and auxiliary one, and was therefore more properly left to implication, than expressly granted.

6. That the principle in question does not extend the power of the government beyond the prescribed limits, because it only affirms a power to incorporate for purposes within the sphere of the specified powers.

And lastly, that the right to exercise such a power in certain cases is unequivocally granted in the most positive and comprehensive terms. To all which it only remains to be added, that such a power has actually been exercised in two very eminent instances; namely, in the erection of two governments, one northwest of the River Ohio, and the other southwest the last independent of any antecedent compact. And these result in a full and complete demonstration that the Secretary of State and the Attorney General are mistaken when they deny generally the power of the national government to erect corporations.

It shall now be endeavored to be shown that there is a power to erect one of the kind proposed by the bill. This will be done by tracing a natural and obvious relation between the institution of a bank and the objects of several of the enumerated powers of the government; and by showing that, politically speaking, it is necessary to the effectual execution of one or more of those powers.

In the course of this investigation, various instances will be stated, by way of illustration of a right to erect corporations under those powers.

Some preliminary observations may be proper.

The proposed bank is to consist of an association of persons, for the purpose of creating a joint capital, to be employed chiefly and essentially in loans. So far the object is not only lawful, but it is the mere exercise of a right which the law allows to every individual. The Bank of New York, which is not incorporated, is an example of such an association. The bill proposed ill addition that the government shall become a joint proprietor in this undertaking, and that it shall permit the bills of the company, payable on demand, to be receivable in its revenues; and stipulates that it shall not grant privileges, similar to those which are to be allowed to this company, to any others. All this is incontrovertibly within the compass of the discretion of the government. The only question is, whether it has a right to incorporate this company, in order to enable it the more effectually to accomplish ends which are in themselves lawful.

To establish such a right, it remains to show the relation of such an institution to one or more of the specified powers of the government. Accordingly it is affirmed that it has a relation, more or less direct, to the power of collecting taxes, to that of borrowing money, to that of regulating trade between the States, and to those of raising and maintaining fleets and armies. To the two former the relation Nay be said to be immediate; and in the last place it will be argued, that it is clearly within the provision which authorizes the making of all needful rules and regulations concerning the property of the United States, as the same has been practiced upon by the government.

A bank relates to the collection of taxes in two ways indirectly, by increasing the quantity of circulating medium and quickening circulation, which facilitates the means of paying directly, by creating a convenient! species of medium in which they are to be paid.

To designate or appoint the money or thing in which taxes are to be paid, is not only a proper, but a necessary exercise of the power of collecting them. Accordingly Congress, in the lava concerning the collection of the duties on imposts and tonnage, have provided that they shall be paid in gold and silver. But while it was an indispensable part of the work to say in what they should be paid, the choice of the specific thing was mere matter of discretion. The payment might have been required in the commodities themselves. Taxes in kind, however ill-judged, are not without precedents, even in the United States; or it Night have been in the paper money of the several States, or in the bills of the Bank of North America, New York and Massachusetts, all or either of them; or it might have been in bills issued under the authority of the United States.

No part of this can, it is presumed, be disputed. The appointment, then, of the money or thing in which the taxes are to be paid, is an incident to the power of collection. And among the expedients which may be adopted, is that of bills issued under the authority of the United States.

Now, the manner of issuing these bills is again matter of discretion. The government might doubtless proceed in the following manner:

It might provide that they should be issued under the direction of certain officers, payable on demand, and, in order to support their credit, and give them a ready circulation, it might, besides giving them a currency in its taxes, set apart, out of any moneys in its treasury, a given sum, and appropriate it, under the direction of those officers, as a fund for answering the bills, as presented for payment.

The constitutionality of all this would not admit of a question, and yet it would amount to the institution of a bank, with a view to the more convenient collection of taxes, For the simplest and most precise idea of a bank is, a deposit of coin, or other property, as a fund for circulating credit upon it, which is to answer the purpose of money. That such an arrangement would be equivalent to the establishment of a bank, would become obvious if the place where the fund to be set apart was kept should be made a receptacle of the moneys of all other persons who should incline to deposit them there for safe-keeping; and would become still more so, if the officers charged with the direction of the fund were authorized to make discounts at the usual rate of interest, upon good security. To deny the power of the government to add these ingredients to the plan, would be to refine away all government.

A further process will still more clearly illustrate the point. Suppose, when the species of bank which has been described was about to be instituted, it was to be urged that, in order to secure to it a due degree of confidence, the fund ought not only to be set apart and appropriated generally, but ought to be specifically vested in the officers who were to have the direction of it, and in their successors in office, to the end that it might acquire the character of private property, incapable of being resumed without a violation of the sanctions by which the rights of property are protected, and occasioning more serious and general alarm the apprehension of which might operate as a check upon the government. Such a proposition might be opposed by arguments against the expedience of it, or the solidity of the reason assigned for it, but it is not conceivable what could be urged against its constitutionality; and yet such a disposition of the thing would amount to the erection of a corporation; for the true definition of a corporation seems to be this: It is a legal person, or a person created by act of law, consisting of one or more natural persons authorized to hold property, or a franchise in succession, in a legal, as contradistinguished from natural, capacity.

Let the illustration proceed a step further. Suppose a bank of the mature which has been described, with

www.milestonedocuments.com

Document Text

or without incorporation, had been instituted, and that experience had evinced as it probably would, that, being wholly under a public direction, it possessed not the confidence requisite to the credit of the bills. Suppose, also, that, by some of those adverse conjunctures which occasionally attend nations, there had been a very great drain of the specie of the country, so as not only to cause general distress for want of an adequate medium of circulation, but to produce, in consequence of that circumstance, considerable defalcations in the public revenues. Suppose, also, that there was no bank instituted in any State; in such a posture of things, would it not be most manifest, that the incorporation of a bank like that proposed by the bill would be a measure immediately relative to the effectual collection of the taxes, and completely within the province of the sovereign power of providing, by all laws necessary and proper, for that collection? If it be said, that such a state of things would render that necessary, and therefore constitutional, which is not so now, the answer to this, and a solid one it doubtless is, must still be that which has been already stated circumstances may affect the expediency of the measure, but they can neither add to nor diminish its constitutionality.

A bank has a direct relation to the power of borrowing money, because it is an usual, and in sudden emergencies an essential, instrument in the obtaining of loans to government.

A nation is threatened with a war, large sums are wanted on a sudden to make the requisite preparations. Taxes are laid for the purpose, but it requires tine to obtain the benefit of them. Anticipation is indispensable. If there be a bank the supply can at once be had. If there be none, loans from individuals must be sought. The progress of these is often too slow for the exigency ill some situations they are not practicable at all. Frequently when they are, it is of great consequence to be able to anticipate the product of them by advance from a bank.

The essentiality of such an institution as an instrument of loans is exemplified at this very moment. An Indian expedition is to be prosecuted. The only fund, out of which the money can arise, consistently with the public engagements, is a tax, which only begins to be collected in July next. The preparations, however, are instantly to be made. The money must, therefore, be borrowed and of whom could it be borrowed if there were no public banks?

It happens that there are institutions of this kind, but if there were none, it would be indispensable to create one.

Let it then be supposed that the necessity existed, (as but for a casualty would be the case,) that proposals were made for obtaining a loan; that a number of individuals came forward and said, we are willing to accommodate the government with the money; with what we have in hand, and the credit we can raise upon it, we doubt not of being able to furnish the sum required; but in order to this, it is indispensable that we should be incorporated as a bank. This is essential toward putting it in our power to do what is desired, and we are obliged on that account to make it the consideration or condition of the loan.

Can it be believed that a compliance with this proposition would be unconstitutional? Does not this alone evince the contrary? It is a necessary part of a power to borrow, to be able to stipulate the consideration or conditions of a loan. It is efficient as has been remarked elsewhere, that this is not confined to the mere stipulation of a franchise. If it may, and it is not perceived why it may not, then the grant of a corporate capacity may be stipulated as a consideration of the loan. There seems to be nothing unfit or foreign from the nature of the thing in giving individuality, or a corporate capacity to a number of persons, who are willing to lend a sum of money to the government, the better to enable them to do it, and make them an ordinary instrument of loans in future emergencies of the state. But the more general view of the subject is still more satisfactory. The legislative power of borrowing money, and of making all laws necessary and proper for carrying into execution that power, seems obviously competent to the appointment of the organ, through which the abilities and wills of individuals may be roost efficaciously exerted for the accommodation of the government by loans.

The Attorney General opposes to this reasoning the following observation: "Borrowing money presupposes the accumulation of a fund to be lent, and is secondary to the creation of an ability to lend." This is plausible in theory, but is not true in fact. In a great number of cases, a previous accumulation of a fund equal to the whole sum required does not exist. And nothing more can be actually presupposed, than that there exist resources, which, put into activity to the greatest advantage by the nature of the operation with the government, will be equal to the effect desired to be produced. All the provisions and operations of government must be presumed to contemplate things as they really are.

The institution of a bank has also a natural relation to the regulation of trade between the States, in so far as it is conducive to the creation of a convenient medium of exchange between them, and to the keeping up a full circulation, by preventing the frequent displacement of the metals in reciprocal remittances. Money is the very hinge on which commerce turns. And this does not merely mean gold and silver; many other things have served the purpose, with different degrees of utility. Paper has been extensively employed.

It cannot, therefore, be admitted, with the Attorney General, that the regulation of trade between the States, as it concerns the medium of circulation and exchange, ought to be considered as confined to coin. It is even supposable that the whole or the greatest part, of the coin of the country might be carried out of it.

The Secretary of State objects to the relation here insisted upon by the following mode of reasoning: To erect a bank, says he, and to regulate commerce, are very different acts. He who creates a bank, creates a subject of commerce, so does he who snakes a bushel of wheat, or digs a dollar out of the Nines, yet neither of these persons regulates commerce thereby. To make a thing which may be bought and sold, is not to prescribe regulations for buying and selling.

This making the regulation of commerce to consist in prescribing rules for buying and selling this, indeed, is a species of regulation of trade, hut is one which falls more aptly within the province of the local jurisdictions than within that of the general government, whose care they must be presumed to have been intended to be directed to those general political arrangements concerning trade on which its aggregated interests depend, rather than to the details of buying and selling. Accordingly, such only are the regulations to be found in the laws of the United States whose objects are to give encouragement to the enterprise of our own merchants, and to advance our navigation and manufactures. And it is in reference to these general relations of commerce, that an establishment which furnishes facilities to circulation, and a convenient medium of exchange and alienation, is to be regarded as a regulation of trade.

The Secretary of State further argues, that if this was a regulation of commerce, it would be void, as extending as much to the internal commerce of every State as to its external. But what regulation of commerce does not extend to the internal commerce of every State? What are all the duties upon imported articles amounting to prohibitions, but so many bounties upon domestic manufactures, affecting the interests of different classes of citizens, in different ways? What are all the provisions in the Coasting Acts which relate to the trade between district and district of the same State? In short, what regulation of trade between the States but must affect the internal trade of each State? What can operate upon the whole, but must extend to every part?

The relation of a bank to the execution of the powers that concern the common defense has been anticipated. It has been noted, that, at this very moment, the aid of such an institution is essential to the measures to be pursued for the protection of our frontiers.

It now remains to show, that the incorporation of a bank is within the operation of the provision which authorizes Congress to make all needful rules and regulations concerning the property of the United States. But it is previously necessary to advert to a distinction which has been taken by the Attorney General.

He admits that the word property may signify personal property, however acquired, and yet asserts that it cannot signify money arising from the sources of revenue pointed out in the Constitution, "because," says he, "the disposal and regulation of money is the final cause for raising it by taxes."

But it would be more accurate to say that the object to which money is intended to be applied is thermal cause for raising it, than that the disposal and regulation of it is such.

The support of government—the support of troops for the common defense—the payment of the public debt, are the true final causes for raising money. The disposition and regulation of it, when raised, are the steps by which it is applied to tile ends for which it was raised, not the ends themselves. Hence, therefore, the money to be raised by taxes, as well as any other personal property, must be supposed to come within the meaning, as they certainly do within the letter, of authority to make all needful rules and regulations concerning the property of the United States.

A case will make this plainer. Suppose the public debt discharged, and the funds now pledged for it liberated. In some instances it would be found expedient to repeal tile taxes; in others, the repeal might injure our own industry, our agriculture and manufactures. In these cases they would, of course, be retained. Here, then, would be moneys arising from the authorized sources of revenue, which would not fall within the rule by which the Attorney General endeavors to except them from other personal property, and from the operation of the clause in question. The moneys being in the coffers of government, what is to hinder such a disposition to be made of

www.milestonedocuments.com

Document Text

them as is contemplated in the bill; or what an incorporation of the parties concerned, under the clause which has been cited?

It is admitted that with regard to the western territory they give a power to erect a corporation that is, to institute a government; and by what rule of construction can it be maintained, that the same words in a constitution of government will not have the same effect when applied to one species of property as to another as far as the subject is capable of it? Or that a legislative power to make all needful rules and regulations, or to pass all laws necessary and proper, concerning the public property, which is admitted to authorize an incorporation in one case, will not authorize it in another? will justify the institution of a government over the western territory, and will not justify the incorporation of a bank for the more useful management of the moneys of the United States? If it will do the last, as well as the first, then under this provision alone, the bill is constitutional, because it contemplates that the United States shall be joint proprietors of the stock of the bank.

There is an observation of the Secretary of State to this effect which may require notice in this place:—Congress, says he, are not to lay taxes ad libitum, for any purpose they please, but only to pay the debts or provide for the welfare of the Union. Certainly no inference can be drawn from this against the power of applying their money for the institution of a bank. It is true that they cannot without breach of trust lay taxes for any other purpose than the general welfare; but so neither can any other government. The welfare of the community is the only legitimate end for which money can be raised on the community. Congress can be considered as under only one restriction which does not apply to other governments, they cannot rightfully apply the money they raise to any purpose merely or purely local.

But, with this exception, they have as large a discretion in relation to the application of money as any legislature whatever. The constitutional test of a right application must always be, whether it be for a purpose of general or local nature. If the former, there can be no want of constitutional power. The quality of the object as how far it will really promote or not the welfare of the Union must be matter of conscientious discretion, and the arguments for or against a measure in this light must be arguments concerning expediency or inexpediency, not constitutional right. Whatever relates to the general order of the finances, to the general interests of trade, etc., being general objects, are constitutional ones for the Application of money.

A bank, then, whose bills are to circulate in all the revenues of the country, is evidently a general object, and, for that very reason, a constitutional one, as far as regards the appropriation of money to it. Whether it will really be a beneficial one or not, is worthy of careful examination, but is no more a constitutional point, in the particular referred to, than the question, whether the western lands shall be sold for twenty or thirty cents per acre.

A hope is entertained that it has, by this time, been made to appear, to the satisfaction of the President, that a bank has a natural relation to the power of collecting taxes—to that of regulating trade—to that of providing for the common defense and that, as the bill under consideration contemplates the government in the light of a joint proprietor of the stock of the bank, it brings the case within the provision of the clause of the Constitution which immediately respects the property of the United States.

Under a conviction that such a relation subsists, the Secretary of the Treasury, with all deference, conceives that it will result as a necessary consequence from the position that all the special powers of government are sovereign, as to the proper objects; and that the incorporation of a bank is a constitutional measure, and that the objections taken to the bill, in this respect, are ill-founded.

But, from an earnest desire to give the utmost possible satisfaction to the mind of the President, on so delicate and important a subject, the Secretary of the Treasury will ask his indulgence, while he gives some additional illustrations of cases in which a power of erecting corporations may be exercised, under some of those heads of the specified powers of the government, which are alleged to include the right of incorporating a bank.

1. It does not appear susceptible of a doubt, that if Congress had thought proper to provide, in the collection laws, that the bonds to be given for the duties should be given to the collector of the district, A or B. as the case might require, to inure to him and his successors in office, in trust for the United States, that it would have been consistent with the Constitution to make such an arrangement; and yet this, it is conceived, would amount to an incorporation.

2. It is not an unusual expedient of taxation to farm particular branches of revenue—that is, to mortgage or sell the product of them for certain definite sums, leaving the collection to the parties to whom they are mortgaged or sold. There are even

examples of this in the United States. Suppose that there was any particular branch of revenue which it was manifestly expedient to place on this footing, and there were a number of persons willing to engage with the government, upon condition that they should be incorporated, and the sums invested in them, as well for their greater safety, as for the more convenient recovery and management of the taxes. Is it supposable that there could be any constitutional obstacle to the measure? It is presumed that there could be none. It is certainly a mode of collection which it would be in the discretion of the government to adopt, though the circumstances must be very extraordinary that would induce the Secretary to think it expedient.

3. Suppose a new and unexplored branch of trade should present itself, with some foreign country. Suppose it was manifest that to undertake it with advantage required an union of the capitals of a number of individuals, and that those individuals would not be disposed to embark without an incorporation, as well to obviate that consequence of a private partnership which makes every individual liable in his whole estate for the debts of the company, to their utmost extent, as for the more convenient management of the business-what reason can there be to doubt that the national government would have a constitutional right to institute and incorporate such a company? None. They possess a general authority to regulate trade with foreign countries. This is a mean which has been practiced to that end, by all the principal commercial nations, who have trading companies to this day, which have subsisted for centuries. Why may not the United States, constitutionally, employ the means usual in other countries, for attaining the ends intrusted to them?

A power to make all needful rules and regulations concerning territory, has been construed to mean a power to erect a government. A power to regulate trade, is a power to make all needful rules and regulations concerning trade. Why may it not, then, include that of erecting a trading company, as well as, in other cases, to erect a government?

It is remarkable that the State conventions, who had proposed amendments in relation to this point, have most, if not all of them, expressed themselves nearly thus: Congress shall not grant monopolies, nor erect any company with exclusive advantages of commerce! Thus, at the same time, expressing their sense, that the power to erect trading companies or corporations was inherent in Congress, and objecting to it no further than as to the grant of exclusive privileges.

The Secretary entertains all the doubts which prevail concerning the utility of such companies, but he cannot fashion to his own mind a reason, to induce a doubt, that there is a constitutional authority in the United States to establish them. If such a reason were demanded, none could be given, unless it were this: That Congress cannot erect a corporation. Which would be no better than to say, they cannot do it, because they cannot do it—first presuming an inability, without reason, and then assigning that inability as the cause of itself. Illustrations of this kind might be multiplied without end. They shall, however, be pursued no further.

There is a sort of evidence on this point, arising from an aggregate view of the Constitution, which is of no inconsiderable weight: the very general power of laying and collecting taxes, and appropriating their proceeds—that of borrowing money indefinitely—that of coining money, and regulating foreign coins—that of making all needful rules and regulations respecting the property of the United States. These powers combined, as well as the reason and nature of the thing, speak strongly this language: that it is the manifest design and scope of the Constitution to vest in Congress all the powers requisite to the effectual administration of the finances of the United States. As far as concerns this object, there appears to be no parsimony of power.

To suppose, then, that the government is precluded from the employment of so usual and so important an instrument for the administration of its finances as that of a bank, is to suppose what does not coincide with the general tenor and complexion of the constitution, and what is not agreeable to impressions that any new spectator would entertain concerning it.

Little less than a prohibitory clause can destroy the strong presumptions which result from the general aspect of the government. Nothing but demonstration should exclude the idea that the power exists.

In all questions of this nature, the practice of mankind ought to have great weight against the theories of individuals.

The fact, for instance, that all the principal commercial nations have made use of trading corporations or companies, for the purpose of external commerce, is a satisfactory proof that the establishment of them is an incident to the regulation of the commerce.

This other fact, that banks are an usual engine in the administration of national finances, and an ordinary and the most effectual instrument of loan, and one which, in this country, has been found essential,

www.milestonedocuments.com

pleads strongly against the supposition that a government, clothed with most of the most important prerogatives of sovereignty in relation to its revenues, its debts, its credits, its defense, its trade, its intercourse with foreign nations, is forbidden to make use of that instrument as an appendage to its own authority.

It has been stated as an auxiliary test of constitutional authority to try whether it abridges any pre-existing right of any State, or any individual. The proposed investigation will stand the most severe examination on this point. Each State may still erect as many banks as it pleases. Every individual may still carry on the banking business to any extent he pleases.

Another criterion may be this. Whether the institution or thing has a more direct relation, as to its uses, to the objects of the reserved powers of the State governments than to those of the powers delegated by the United States. This, rule, indeed, is less precise than the former, but it may still serve as some guide. Surely a bank has more reference to the objects intrusted to the national government than to those left to the care of the State governments. The common defense is decisive in this comparison.

It is presumed that nothing of consequence in the observations of the Secretary of State, and Attorney General, has been left un-noticed.

There are, indeed, a variety of observations of the Secretary of State designed to show that the utilities ascribed to a bank, in relation to the collection of taxes, and to trade, could be obtained without it; to analyze which, would prolong the discussion beyond all bounds. It shall be forborne for two reasons. First, because the report concerning the bank, may speak for itself in this respect; and secondly, because all those observations are grounded on the erroneous idea that the quantum of necessity or utility is the test of a constitutional exercise of power.

One or two remarks only shall be made. One is, that he has taken no notice of a very essential advantage to trade in general which is mentioned in the report, as peculiar to the existence of a bank circulation, equal in the public estimation to gold and silver. It is this that renders it unnecessary to lock up the money of the country, to accumulate for months successively, in order to the periodical payment of interest. The other is this: that his arguments to show that treasury orders and bills of exchange, from the course of trade, will prevent any considerable displacement of the metals, are founded on a particular view of the subject. A case will prove this. The sums collected in a State may be small in comparison with the debt due to it; the balance of its trade direct and circuitous with the seat of government, may be even, or nearly so; here, then, without bank bills, which in that State answer the purpose of coin, there must be a displacement of the coin, in proportion to the difference between the sum collected in the State, and that to be paid in it. With bank bills, no such displacement would take place, or as far as it did, it would be gradual and insensible. In many other ways, also, would there be at least a temporary and inconvenient displacement of the coin, even where the course of trade would eventually return it to its proper channel.

The difference of the two situations in point of convenience to the treasury, can only be appreciated by one, who experiences the embarrassments of making provision for the payment of the interest on a stock, continually changing place in thirteen different places.

One thing which has been omitted, just occurs, although it is not very material to the main argument. The Secretary of State affirms that the bill only contemplates a repayment, not a loan, to the government. But here he is certainly mistaken. It is true the government invests in the stock of the bank a sum equal to that which it receives on loan. But let it be remembered, that it does not, therefore, cease to be a proprietor of the stock, which would be the case, if the money received back were in the nature of a payment. It remains a proprietor still, and will share in the profit or loss of the institution, according as the dividend is more or less than the interest it is to pay on the sum borrowed. Hence that sum is manifestly, and in the strictest sense, a loan.

Congress OF THE United States,
begun and held at the City of New-York, on
Wednesday the fourth of March, one thousand seven hundred and eightynine.

THE Conventions of a number of the States, having at the time of their adopting the Constitution, expressed a desire, in order
of its powers, that further declaratory and restrictive clauses should be added: And as extending the ground of public confidence in the Government, will best insure the beni
RESOLVED by the Senate and House of Representatives of the United States of America in Congress assembled,
ing, that the following Articles be proposed to the Legislatures of the several States, as amendments to the Constitution of the United States, all, or any of which Articles, when rati
Legislatures, to be valid to all intents and purposes, as part of the said Constitution; viz.

ARTICLES in addition to, and Amendment of the Constitution of the United States of America, proposed by Congress, an
veral States, pursuant to the fifth Article of the original Constitution.

st. ... After the first enumeration required by the first Article of the Constitution, there shall be one Representative for every thirty thousand, until the number shall amou
which, the proportion shall be so regulated by Congress, that there shall be not less than one hundred Representatives, nor less than one Representative f
until the number of Representatives shall amount to two hundred, after which the proportion shall be so regulated by Congress, that there shall not be less than t
nor more than one Representative for every fifty thousand persons.

cond ... No law, varying the compensation for the services of the Senators and Representatives, shall take effect, until an election of Representatives shall have intervened.

d ... Congress shall make no law respecting an establishment of religion, or prohibiting the free exercise thereof; or abridging the freedom of speech, or of the press, or the right
assemble, and to petition the Government for a redress of grievances.

rth ... A well regulated Militia, being necessary to the security of a free State, the right of the people to keep and bear Arms, shall not be infringed.

h ... No Soldier shall, in time of peace be quartered in any house, without the consent of the Owner, nor in time of war, but in a manner to be prescribed by law.

th ... The right of the people to be secure in their persons, houses, papers, and effects, against unreasonable searches and seizures, shall not be violated, and no Warra
probable cause, supported by Oath or affirmation, and particularly describing the place to be searched, and the persons or things to be seized.

enth ... No person shall be held to answer for a capital, or otherwise infamous crime, unless on a presentment or indictment of a Grand Jury, except in cases arising in the land
Militia, when in actual service in time of War or public danger; nor shall any person be subject for the same offence to be twice put in jeopardy of life or limb; nor
criminal case, to be a witness against himself, nor be deprived of life, liberty, or property, without due process of law; nor shall private property be taken for pu

hth ... In all criminal prosecutions, the accused shall enjoy the right to a speedy and public trial, by an impartial jury of the State and district wherein the crime shall
district shall have been previously ascertained by law, and to be informed of the nature and cause of the accusation; to be confronted with the witnesses against him
for obtaining Witnesses in his favor, and to have the Assistance of Counsel for his defence.

inth ... In suits at common law, where the value in controversy shall exceed twenty dollars, the right of trial by jury shall be preserved, and no fact tried by a jury, shall be
any Court of the United States, than according to the rules of the common law.

the ... Excessive bail shall not be required, nor excessive fines imposed, nor cruel and unusual punishments inflicted.

enth ... The enumeration in the Constitution, of certain rights, shall not be construed to deny or disparage others retained by the people.

lfth ... The powers not delegated to the United States by the Constitution, nor prohibited by it to the States, are reserved to the States respectively, or to the people.

TEST,

Frederick Augustus Muhlenberg Speaker of the House of Representatives.

John Adams, Vice-President of the United States, and Presid

The Bill of Rights (National Archives and Records Administration)

Bill of Rights

1791

"The enumeration in the Constitution, of certain rights, shall not be construed to deny or disparage others retained by the people."

Overview

The colonial revolt against British rule that began in North America in 1776 was fought not only for independence but also for the attainment of certain political ideas and ideals. The American Revolution was fought at a time when monarchies were being challenged, with democracy, the rule of law, and natural rights emerging as alternatives to hereditary government ruled by kings and queens. The Revolution came early in this historical transition, such that the framers of the new government had to make trailblazing efforts to translate democratic ideas into practical use.

After the Revolution, discussion over how to convert these ideas into governmental precepts proved contentious. The Constitution produced by the Founding Fathers in 1787 outlined the new government, but no guarantee of fundamental rights was included, a fact bemoaned by many. After all, the Revolution had been fought largely for such rights, and a government failing to account for these rights seemed liable to mimic the rule by monarchy that was just overthrown. As debates over the ratification of the new Constitution raged in the various states, some advocated adding a list of rights to the document. In the end, as a compromise, several of the most influential Founders agreed to subsequently add a list of rights as amendments to the Constitution. This effectively guaranteed that the new Constitution not only would be ratified by the states but also would have fairly widespread support across the nation. The first Congress debated and passed ten proposed amendments to the Constitution, and these amendments were approved by the states and incorporated as the first ten amendments to the Constitution, known as the Bill of Rights.

Context

The immigrants who came from Europe to the New World in the late 1600s and 1700s fled political and religious persecution, hoping to build new lives. Many were outcasts from a Europe still steeped in monarchies and hierarchical societies. Thus, many wanted to make their fortunes, while others hoped to build a new political community. At that time, the revolutionary ideas of John Locke and others were beginning to gain support and challenge the orthodoxy of the age. A new "contract theory" of political union was emerging, and questions regarding the legitimacy of hereditary government were becoming more pronounced. During this era, dubbed the Enlightenment, the subservience of the old era was being replaced by the Age of Reason. The average person was becoming bolder and demanding more rights and privileges, challenging the old order. The time was one of revolutionary fervor and political upheaval.

Many of the men and women who came to the American colonies were well versed in and amenable to accepting these new, radical ideas. Democracy, the rule of law, constitutionalism, common rights, and other revolutionary ideas were being discussed and embraced in the Americas. These ideas met with harsh resistance from the rulers of Great Britain, however, who still held sway over the colonies. This resistance, of course, led to revolt. The American Revolution was fought for political independence, but it was also fought for ideas: democracy, republicanism, rights, and constitutionalism. Translating these ideas into a workable government proved a great challenge.

The revolutionary fervor of the colonial fighters was in large part based on the radical ideas presented in Thomas Paine's pamphlet *Common Sense* and Thomas Jefferson's Declaration of Independence. These powerful and influential broadsides against the monarchy and in favor of democratic rule animated opposition to England and inspired the Revolution. Those who fought the British did so to gain rights and liberties that were denied under the oppressive hand of British domination. The liberation of the colonies was intended to guarantee those rights and liberties so resolutely denied by the British Crown.

Following the success of the Revolution, the first governing document of the new nation, the Articles of Confederation, proved weak and ineffective. Opposition to the articles grew and became fairly widespread, leading to a call for revision of the document. After initial attempts to call a new constitutional convention failed, the nation was finally able to gather together the states for the purpose of emending the articles. When the Founding Fathers gathered in Philadelphia during the hot summer of 1787, however, they

Time Line

1776

■ **July 4**
In the U.S. Declaration of Independence, Thomas Jefferson argues that the sole legitimate purpose of government is to protect individual rights.

1787

■ **September 17**
The U.S. Constitution establishes limited roles for the president and Congress but does not yet grant significant power to the Supreme Court.

1791

■ **December 15**
The Bill of Rights is added to the Constitution.

1795

■ **February 7**
The Eleventh Amendment to the U.S. Constitution is ratified by the needed number of states.

1833

■ **January**
The Supreme Court rules in *Barron v. Baltimore* that the Bill of Rights applies only to the U.S. government, not to the states.

1868

■ **July 28**
The unqualified certification of the Fourteenth Amendment makes it illegal for states to deny blacks their rights.

1896

■ **May 18**
In *Plessy v. Ferguson*, the Court says racial segregation does not violate the Fourteenth Amendment.

1919

■ **March 3**
In *Schenck v. United States*, the Court upholds the Espionage Act, saying free speech can be restricted during wartime.

1925

■ **June 8**
In *Gitlow v. New York*, the Court rules that the fourteenth amendment extends the rights of the first amendment from the federal government to state governments.

decided to scrap the Articles of Confederation and start afresh, writing a new constitution. This was a bold step, especially given that the deliberations were done in secret, and only when the new U.S. Constitution was finished did the Founders reveal its content to an anxious public.

For that Constitutional Convention, held in Philadelphia in 1787, seventy-four delegates were chosen by the states, although only fifty-five attended. The convention was held in the State House (now Independence Hall), in the room where just over a decade earlier many of the same men had met to sign the Declaration of Independence. Noticeable for their absence from the convention were some of the new nation's strongest advocates for democracy: Thomas Paine, Thomas Jefferson (who was in Paris), John Adams (who was in England), and Patrick Henry (who refused to go). Every state but Rhode Island sent delegates.

The delegates to the Constitutional Convention discussed the possibility of including a bill of rights in the original U.S. Constitution, but in the end they decided against one. This, of course, stirred fears in the Antifederalist camp and proved a significant impediment to ratification. "A bill of rights," Thomas Jefferson argued, "is what the people are entitled to"—a sentiment widely shared by his fellow citizens (Bowers, p. 330). When the delegates, having finally finished their work, exited the hall in Philadelphia, a woman in the crowd shouted to Benjamin Franklin, "What is it Dr. Franklin, a monarchy or a democracy?" Franklin responded, "A republic, if you can keep it" (McHenry, p. 618).

Ratification of the Constitution was by no means a foregone conclusion. As copies of the document were circulated, two major objections emerged: first, that the new president might too closely resemble the king of England, against whom the Revolution had recently been fought, and second—and more important at the time—that the document included no guarantee of the rights for which the Revolution was fought. These two objections, when joined together, raised a chill in many. Would this new Constitution bring a new king who could likewise trample on the people's rights and liberties?

The new Constitution had to be ratified by nine of the thirteen states, and many of the state-ratifying conventions proved contentious and difficult affairs. Several states ratified quickly, including Delaware, the first to ratify the Constitution, on December 7, 1787. Several weeks later, Pennsylvania, New Jersey, Georgia, and Connecticut followed. In February 1788, Massachusetts, too, ratified the Constitution, but only after supporters of the document agreed to amend it to include a bill of rights. On June 21, 1788, New Hampshire became the vital ninth state to agree to the Constitution. The test of ratification was over—but in the two most important and powerful states, Virginia and New York, strong opposition remained. Even though the new governing document had been ratified by the needed nine states, the Constitution would not survive unless Virginia and New York embraced it.

Debates raged, and at times all seemed lost. What indeed emerged from the critics of the Constitution, who were labeled Antifederalists, was an objection to the lack of rights therein. For them, this lack was the major stumbling block in the way of ratification, the deal breaker. Both New York and Virginia recommended the addition of a bill of rights to the Constitution.

In the end, a compromise between the Federalists, who supported the Constitution, and the Antifederalists was reached. James Madison and several other prominent framers agreed that upon the new Constitution's ratification, they would propose in the First Congress the addition of a set of amendments to the Constitution indeed listing and guaranteeing the rights of the citizens of the United States. This saved the day; both Virginia and New York embraced the new Constitution.

True to his word, Madison, in 1789, introduced a series of amendments to the Constitution, twelve of which were approved and sent to the states, ten of which were passed by the states—with Virginia, the last of the needed three-quarters of the states, effecting ratification on December 15, 1791. These amendments thus became the Bill of Rights. The two amendments that failed to gain the necessary votes from three-quarters of the states were intended to authorize the enlargement of the House of Representatives and to prevent members of the House of Representatives from raising their salaries.

Time Line

1943

- **June 14**
  In *West Virginia State Board of Education v. Barnette*, the Court rules that students can refuse to salute the flag under the First Amendment.

1954

- **May 17**
  In *Brown v. Board of Education*, the Court rules that the Fourteenth Amendment outlaws segregation.

1965

- **June 7**
  In *Griswold v. Connecticut*, the Court rules that state laws banning the use of birth control violate a constitutional right to privacy.

1972

- **June 19**
  The Court rules that wiretapping is a "search," as covered in the Fourth Amendment.

1973

- **January 22**
  In *Roe v. Wade*, the Court rules that the right to privacy protects a woman's right to an abortion.

1988

- **January 13**
  In *Hazelwood School District v. Kuhlmeier*, the Court rules that schools can censor student press and other activities.

About the Author

The Bill of Rights has no one author. The rights so listed are an accumulation and compilation of rights and liberties fought for in the Revolutionary War, as codified by the framers, presented by James Madison in the First Congress, and ultimately passed by the states. They represent the accumulated wisdom of the generation of radicals, rebels, and democrats who were animated by the desire to limit the government's powers, guarantee the rights of citizens, and confine the state under the rule of law.

Explanation and Analysis of the Document

The Bill of Rights opens with a preamble that describes why the Congress is passing these amendments ("in order to prevent misconstruction or abuse of its powers") and resolves that the amendments will become law when ratified by three fourths of the state legislatures.

◆ Amendment I

The establishment and free-exercise clauses of the First Amendment derive from the phrasing, "Congress shall make no law respecting an establishment of religion, or prohibiting the free exercise thereof." Under the establishment clause, Congress is restricted from establishing a national religion or giving preference to one religion over another or to irreligion over religion. Under the free exercise clause, Congress is prohibited from infringing upon religious practice. Taken together, the establishment and free-exercise clauses are generally referred to as the religion clauses of the First Amendment.

In an 1802 letter to a group of Connecticut Baptists, Thomas Jefferson wrote that the establishment and free-exercise clauses of the First Amendment built "a wall of separation between church and State" (Jefferson to Danbury Baptists, January 1, 1802). During colonial expansion, many religious sects sought settlement in America in order to escape religious persecution. As such, the right to free religious practice was of high importance to many early Americans.

Some have claimed that the free-exercise clause can, at times, come into conflict with the establishment clause of the First Amendment. Those who make this claim understand that the government's noninterference with religion may necessitate the government's accommodation of religion. However, as the more pronounced accommodation of one religion over another may indicate preference for one religion, a conflict between the religion clauses may emerge.

www.milestonedocuments.com

James Madison shown in an engraving from approximately 1828 (Library of Congress)

The speech-press clauses cover the right to freedom of expression. At the time of the document's drafting, Madison originally proposed that the speech-press clauses of the First Amendment should claim that citizens must not be deprived of their sentiments to speak, to write, or to publish. However, in the final draft of the First Amendment, Madison's emphasis on the right to *sentiment* was altered to a right to *expression* through speech, writing, and publication. What constitutes protected speech or publication has been a source of debate up to modern times. Particularly controversial Supreme Court decisions have been those protecting war protest, flag burning, and restricted forms of obscenity and pornography.

The last phrase of the First Amendment establishes a "right of the people peaceably to assemble, and to petition the Government for a redress of grievances." The right of assembly is the freedom to associate with and organize groups or clubs. The right to petition is the freedom to petition the government for correction of perceived injustices. The right to assemble may be said to be derivative of the right to petition, as the former is often considered to be for the purpose of the latter.

◆ Amendment II

Under the Second Amendment, citizens have the right to bear arms. Originally, this right was instituted for the purpose of maintaining armed state militias. The amendment was drafted largely in reaction to the oppression waged by British soldiers in pre-Revolutionary America. Beyond this context, the Founding Fathers actually perceived no use for a standing army in the early period of the United States. Rather, they decided that an armed citizenry would provide the best protection of American liberty. During the drafting of the Second Amendment, the citizen-soldier was the norm. In modern times, however, the development of the U.S. armed forces has made the citizen-soldier obsolete. As a result, the Second Amendment had taken on a new context by the turn of the twenty-first century.

Some theorists claim that the Second Amendment is generally to be understood as conveying a protection of ownership and the right to personal possession. Others, however, claim that the primary aim of this amendment was to provide for a militia, and therefore in the absence of a need for one, the amendment should be considered invalid. In practice, the Second Amendment holds the distinction of being the least enforced amendment contained in the Bill of Rights. The U.S. Supreme Court has never struck down a piece of legislation on the ground that it violated the Second Amendment.

◆ Amendment III

Like the Second Amendment, the Third Amendment derives from a pre-Revolutionary context. Prior to the American Revolution, colonial law required citizens to house British soldiers. This law, known as the Quartering Act, was a source of complaint among the American colonists and was even referenced in the Declaration of Independence as an indictment against King George III. Desiring not to allow this offense to be repeated, the Founders established the Third Amendment, which claims that no citizen shall be made to house soldiers. Although a common concern at the time of its drafting, with the advent of the modern military the Third Amendment has become mostly obsolete.

◆ Amendment IV

The Fourth Amendment requires that all searches and seizures by the government must be "reasonable." In those cases when a government official finds it necessary to issue a search or arrest warrant, the warrant must be supported by probable cause and be limited according to its purpose. Generally, through what is known as the exclusion rule, evidence obtained in violation of the Fourth Amendment may not be used in criminal trials. The exclusion rule is one way in which the government protects the Fourth Amendment.

The Fourth Amendment was written largely as a response to British writs of assistance, which were warrants issued by the British Crown that allowed British officials general search powers. The generality of the writs of assistance allowed for searches unconfined by specific location, person, or cause.

◆ Amendment V

Under the grand jury clause, criminals are to be tried by grand juries for infamous crimes. A grand jury is a jury of peers that decides upon criminal court cases in closed sessions. An infamous crime is a crime punishable by incarceration or death. However, in many cases, in crimes punishable by incarceration but not death, criminals may waive their Fifth Amendment rights and proceed with a trial without the indictment of a grand jury.

The double jeopardy clause protects defendants from being tried twice for a particular offence. Although the double jeopardy clause refers to "jeopardy of life or limb," the meaning of this clause has been interpreted to provide protection against double punishment by any means.

Under the self-incrimination clause, the Fifth Amendment protects witnesses of crimes from incriminating themselves. This protects against coercion by authorities, which could lead to false and involuntary confessions. From this clause comes the saying, often heard in television crime shows, "I plead the Fifth." To "plead the Fifth" means to refuse to testify under one's Fifth Amendment right against self-incrimination.

The due process clause restricts the government from extending punishment without "due process of law." Due process is generally interpreted as litigation that fully observes the legal rights of the accused in any case where the accused is punishable by the limitation of his or her rights to life, liberty, or property.

"Eminent domain" refers to the power of government to take private property for public use, following just compensation. Eminent domain has been commonly exercised in cases where private lands are needed in order to provide for transportation or other needs of the community. Under the eminent domain clause, individuals must be fairly compensated for the acquisition of their property by the government. In territory cases, this means that a fair market value must be offered to the property holder for the sale of his or her lands.

◆ Amendment VI

The speedy and public trial clause prevents undue and oppressive incarceration for those awaiting trial. This clause maintains what is called a "presumption of innocence," or the presumption that one is innocent until proved guilty.

The right to an impartial jury protects against the unjust persecution of defendants on the part of biased prosecutors and judges. Assuring the impartiality of jurors requires a rigorous screening process in many cases. The goal of assembling a jury is to arrive at a fair and representative cross section of the community.

The notice of accusation clause entitles defendants to the details of the offense with which they are being charged. Indictments must provide a full enumeration of all criminal charges pertinent to each arrest.

The confrontation clause gives defendants the right to be present at their own trials. Trials in absentia are rare and mostly occur only if a defendant fails to behave in court or if a compelling reason exists for keeping a defendant from facing accusers or other necessary parties. Furthermore, under this clause, a defendant may cross-examine witnesses and be a direct witness in his or her own case.

The compulsory process clause allows defendants to compel witnesses to appear and testify in their defense. Under the compulsory processes clause, the defendant also has the right to present his or her own defense.

Under the assistance of counsel clause, a defendant has the right to counsel from the first moment of police interrogation. In 1963, the Supreme Court case *Gideon v. Wainwright* expanded the assistance of counsel clause, making the assistance of counsel a fundamental right even for those without the financial means to hire a lawyer. In the modern American legal system, a court-appointed lawyer will assist indigent defendants who opt to be so represented, whenever there is a chance of incarceration.

◆ Amendment VII

The Seventh Amendment was established in order to ensure that every civil case be tried by a jury. The establishment of the Seventh Amendment was largely a reaction to the diversity of trial proceedings in early America. Prior to the Seventh Amendment, each state had it own codes for the conduct of court trials. The phrase in the Seventh Amendment prohibiting reexamination in federal court indicates that civil cases can be appealed only up to the level of the Supreme Court.

◆ Amendment VIII

Bail allows those involved in criminal trials access to their right to freedom. Under the Eighth Amendment, bail shall not be so excessively costly as to limit one's right to freedom. This being said, those involved in criminal cases do not always have a right to bail. Bail is commonly denied when there is evidence of the need for preventive detention.

The excessive fines clause protects those who cannot pay fines from being sent to jail simply on this ground. The excessive fines clause applies only to those fines to be accrued by the government; it does not apply to court fees and other litigation costs.

Foremost, the cruel and unusual punishment clause contains the order that a punishment be proportional to the crime in question. What constitutes "cruel and unusual punishments" has been a source of contention in criminal trials throughout the history of the United States. Perhaps most hotly debated has been the clause's application to capital punishment. Whereas some view the death penalty as cruel and disproportionate to any crime, others hold that the penalty of death can indeed be appropriate, given the nature of some crimes.

◆ Amendment IX

Like the Tenth Amendment, the Ninth Amendment is not truly substantive in terms of rights. Although some regard the Ninth Amendment as the foundation for a right to privacy, as written the Ninth Amendment simply states that the enumerated rights contained in the Bill of Rights are not an exhaustive list of all of the rights of U.S. citizens.

◆ Amendment X

The Tenth Amendment is best understood in its Antifederalist context. Antifederalists were those weary of the dangers of concentrated political power in the hands of a fed-

www.milestonedocuments.com

Essential Quotes

"Congress shall make no law respecting an establishment of religion, or prohibiting the free exercise thereof; or abridging the freedom of speech, or of the press; or the right of the people peaceably to assemble, and to petition the Government for a redress of grievances."

(First Amendment)

"A well regulated Militia, being necessary to the security of a free State, the right of the people to keep and bear Arms, shall not be infringed."

(Second Amendment)

"The enumeration in the Constitution, of certain rights, shall not be construed to deny or disparage others retained by the people."

(Ninth Amendment)

"The powers not delegated to the United States by the Constitution, nor prohibited by it to the States, are reserved to the States respectively, or to the people."

(Tenth Amendment)

eral government. In opposition to those championing federal power, Antifederalists wished state governments to be the primary sources of political power.

The Tenth Amendment provided assurance to Antifederalists that the federal government would not infringe upon the powers of the states. However, in the modern era, the situation has changed. When the Tenth Amendment was originally proposed, the Bill of Rights did not apply to states; it only applied to federal law. However, the Bill of Rights is now understood to apply equally to the states and to the federal branch. Thus, while still relevant, the Tenth Amendment holds much less power than it originally did.

Audience

The primary audience for the Bill of Rights is the government of the United States. The document is a set of guaranteed rights that limit the power of the federal government and grant to all persons in the United States a set of liberties that the government may not violate. It directs the government to respect legal boundaries beyond which it may not proceed.

In the era of the early Republic, the political considerations that led to the adoption of the Bill of Rights compelled the framers to make a compromise with one of the key audiences of the day—the Antifederalists. Largely against the adoption of the new Constitution, the Antifederalists were primarily made up of a loose coalition of detractors of the Constitution who joined together for various reasons in an effort to block ratification. Most of the Antifederalists were in favor of small government and states' rights and were concerned that the Constitution gave far too much power to the new federal government. While the Constitution was ratified by the requisite nine states without the support of the Antifederalists, to begin the government without the support of such a significant portion of the people might have jeopardized the stability and longevity of that government. Thus, the Antifederalist audience was key in the creation and sustaining of the Bill of Rights.

Impact

With the introduction and acceptance of the Bill of Rights as the first ten amendments to the U.S. Constitution, a new "rights regime" was created, in which the power and reach of the government would be limited by guaranteed rights that belonged to persons living in the United States. The facts that the government would be bound by the rule of law and that citizens and others had codified rights protecting them against the government constituted a bold experiment. Indeed, the Bill of Rights utterly transformed the style and scope of government in the United States and has had a profound impact throughout the world. Other nations followed the United States in enumerating such rights, and in modern times an international human rights movement has ensured that nascent international codes and laws, such as those of the European Union, have become rights based and limited in scope and authority. Thus, the Bill of Rights had a profound impact in its day and continues to have such an impact in the modern day.

Related Documents

European Union. "The Charter of Fundamental Rights of the European Union." European Parliament Web site. http://www.europarl.europa.eu/charter/default_en.htm. Accessed on December 21, 2007. The Charter of Fundamental Rights of the European Union is a proclamation of fundamental human rights as recognized by the European Union. The charter was signed by the presidents of the European Parliament in Nice, France, on December 7, 2000.

United Nations General Assembly. "Universal Declaration of Human Rights." United Nations Web site. http://www.un.org/Overview/rights.html. The Universal Declaration of Human Rights is a proclamation of fundamental human rights as recognized by the United Nations. The General Assembly of the United Nations accepted the declaration on December 10, 1948.

Bibliography

Articles

Jefferson, Thomas. "Jefferson's Letter to the Danbury Baptists." *Library of Congress Information Bulletin* 57, no. 6 (June 1998).

McHenry, James. "The Papers of Dr. James McHenry on the Federal Convention of 1787." *American Historical Review* 11, no. 3 (April 1906).

Books

Berkin, Carol. *A Brilliant Solution: Inventing the American Constitution*. New York: Harcourt, 2002.

Bowers, Claude G. *The Young Jefferson: 1743–1789*. Boston: Houghton Mifflin, 1945.

Farrand, Max. *The Framing of the Constitution of the United States*. New Haven, Conn.: Yale University Press, 1913.

Morgan, Edmund S. *The Birth of the Republic, 1763–89*, 3rd ed. Chicago: University of Chicago Press, 1992.

Rossiter, Clinton. *1787: The Grand Convention*. New York: Macmillan, 1966.

Wood, Gordon S. *The Creation of the American Republic, 1776–1787*. New York: W. W. Norton, 1972.

Web Sites

"Bill of Rights." National Archives "Charters of Freedom" Web site. http://www.archives.gov/national-archives-experience/charters/bill_of_rights.html. Accessed on August 8, 2007.

—By Michael A. Genovese and Kristina L. Rioux

Questions for Further Study

1. Is there a conflict between a rights-based political system and the power and authority of the government? That is, can the guarantee of rights so limit the reach of the government that governing becomes difficult, if not impossible? Or is a rights-based system more likely to strengthen popular support for the government, which is so vital in a democratic system?

2. In an age of terrorism, is a rights-based culture in conflict with the effective prosecution of a war against terrorism? Can a war against terrorism be effectively fought if the hands of the government are tied? Examine the series of conflicts that took place between the George W. Bush administration and rights activists and discuss which viewpoints seem to you to be more rationally grounded.

www.milestonedocuments.com

Glossary

amendment	an addition to a document or policy; a change to the original
capital crime	a serious crime where life or limb has been taken
construed	understood to mean; interpreted
Counsel	an attorney or lawyer
disparage	to not consider very important; to lessen the meaning of something
due process	a process of steps where everyone is treated equally and all have a chance to speak
enumeration	a listing of a number of things
Grand Jury	a group of people who listen to evidence and decide if enough evidence is present to charge someone with a crime prior to trial
infamous crime	crime or series of crimes by a person with an evil reputation
presentment	act of presenting a statement of action to an authority, as in a grand jury to a judge
probable cause	legal term referring to a police officer's reasonable belief that someone has committed a crime
redress	a remedy

Bill of Rights

www.milestonedocuments.com

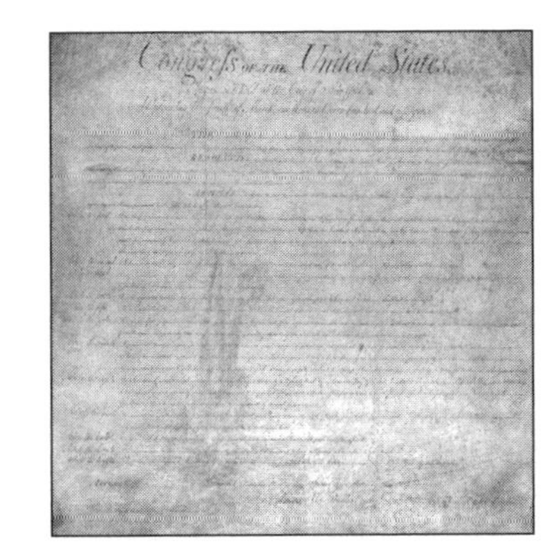

Amendment I

Congress shall make no law respecting an establishment of religion, or prohibiting the free exercise thereof; or abridging the freedom of speech, or of the press; or the right of the people peaceably to assemble, and to petition the Government for a redress of grievances.

Amendment II

A well regulated Militia, being necessary to the security of a free State, the right of the people to keep and bear Arms, shall not be infringed.

Amendment III

No Soldier shall, in time of peace be quartered in any house, without the consent of the Owner, nor in time of war, but in a manner to be prescribed by law.

Amendment IV

The right of the people to be secure in their persons, houses, papers, and effects, against unreasonable searches and seizures, shall not be violated, and no Warrants shall issue, but upon probable cause, supported by Oath or affirmation, and particularly describing the place to be searched, and the persons or things to be seized.

Amendment V

No person shall be held to answer for a capital, or otherwise infamous crime, unless on a presentment or indictment of a Grand Jury, except in cases arising in the land or naval forces, or in the Militia, when in actual service in time of War or public danger; nor shall any person be subject for the same offence to be twice put in jeopardy of life or limb; nor shall be compelled in any criminal case to be a witness against himself, nor be deprived of life, liberty, or property, without due process of law; nor shall private property be taken for public use, without just compensation.

Amendment VI

In all criminal prosecutions, the accused shall enjoy the right to a speedy and public trial, by an impartial jury of the State and district wherein the crime shall have been committed, which district shall have been previously ascertained by law, and to be informed of the nature and cause of the accusation; to be confronted with the witnesses against him; to have compulsory process for obtaining witnesses in his favor, and to have the Assistance of Counsel for his defence.

Amendment VII

In Suits at common law, where the value in controversy shall exceed twenty dollars, the right of trial by jury shall be preserved, and no fact tried by a jury, shall be otherwise re-examined in any Court of the United States, than according to the rules of the common law.

Amendment VIII

Excessive bail shall not be required, nor excessive fines imposed, nor cruel and unusual punishments inflicted.

Amendment IX

The enumeration in the Constitution, of certain rights, shall not be construed to deny or disparage others retained by the people.

Amendment X

The powers not delegated to the United States by the Constitution, nor prohibited by it to the States, are reserved to the States respectively, or to the people.

(1

Friends, & Fellow-Citizens.

The period for a new elec
tion of a Citizen, to Administer the Executi
Government of the United States, being not
far distant, and the time actually arri
ved, when your thoughts must be emplo
ed in designating the person, who is to be
cloathed with that important trust ~~for an~~
~~other term~~, it appears to me proper, especi
ally as it may conduce to a more distinct
expression of the public voice, that I shou
now apprise you of the resolution I have
formed, to decline being considered amon
the number of those, out of whom a choice is
to be made.—

I beg you, at the same time, to do
me the justice to be assured, that this resolu
tion has not been taken, without a strict
regard to all the considerations appertain
ing to the relation, which binds a dutiful
citizen to his country — and that, in with
drawing the tender of service which silen
in my situation might imply, I am influen
ced by no diminution of zeal for your futur
interest, no deficiency of grateful respect
for your past kindness; but am supported by a fu
convictio

George Washington's Farewell Address (National Archives and Records Administration)

George Washington's Farewell Address

1796

"It is our true policy to steer clear of permanent alliances with any portion of the foreign world."

Overview

A key element of George Washington's legacy to his country, his Farewell Address is one of the most memorable speeches in American history. In the first of two parts, Washington expresses his thanks for the opportunity to serve his country. In the second part, which is much longer, Washington stresses the importance of the Union in maintaining independence, peace, liberty, and prosperity. He fears that the Union may be threatened by the political turmoil and partisanship raging throughout the country because of a rise of political parties, attempts to undermine the Constitution's separation of powers, and the adherence to foreign powers at the expense of America's best interests. American foreign policy and commerce, Washington suggests, should be pragmatically developed on a country-by-country basis with America's interest always occupying center stage.

Context

After serving as commander in chief during the Revolution for eight years, Washington announced that he would retire from the army and not serve again in public office. In 1787 friends and advisers such as James Madison, Virginia governor Edmund Randolph, and Henry Knox (chief artillery officer of the Continental army and later the first U.S. Secretary of War) persuaded him to come out of retirement to serve as a delegate to a general convention of the states to amend the Articles of Confederation. When the new Constitution was ratified, Washington was unanimously elected as the country's first president. He reluctantly accepted the position and hoped to serve no longer than one full term. In May 1792, near the end of his first term, Washington asked Madison to assist in drafting a farewell address. (Madison had written Washington's presidential inaugural address in April 1789.) Domestic turmoil and European war coupled with the unified advice of the cabinet persuaded Washington to accept a second term, to which he was unanimously reelected. With partisanship raging in 1796, however, he refused to seek a third term.

Early in 1796, Washington decided to write a farewell address to announce his retirement, to thank his countrymen for the opportunity to serve, and to admonish Americans to preserve their Union. Washington had prepared farewell addresses on six previous occasions: to his fellow militia officers (January 1759), to the state executives (June 1783), to the army (November 1783), to the army officers at Fraunces Tavern in New York City (December 1783), to Congress in surrendering his commission (December 1783), and at the end of his first term as president when he asked Madison to prepare a draft address to the American people (May 1792). In February 1796, a year before the end of Washington's second term, he asked Alexander Hamilton for assistance in reworking the draft of his Farewell Address. Washington sent Hamilton the 1792 draft by Madison, his own revised copy of that draft, and some general sentiments that he wanted to express in the address. Hamilton returned all the documents to Washington with his revisions.

Washington and Hamilton exchanged ideas and copies of the address once more before Washington received Hamilton's final version, which Washington revised only slightly. Washington submitted his final version of the address to his cabinet on September 15, 1796, and all members endorsed it. Four days later, Washington publicly announced his decision to retire, and his Farewell Address was printed in the Philadelphia *American Daily Advertiser*. Reprinted in newspapers and as broadsides and pamphlets throughout the country, the address was immediately perceived as part of the partisan politics of the day—Federalists extolled it while Jeffersonians criticized it, especially Washington's harsh statements about political parties. Four years later, with Jefferson's victory in the election of 1800 and the gradual demise of the Federalist Party, the advice in Washington's Farewell Address was embraced by the Jeffersonians and came to be universally admired and perceived as Washington's legacy to his country.

About the Author

George Washington was born in Westmoreland County, Virginia, on February 22, 1732, into a middle-gentry family. His father died when he was only eleven years old. His

Time Line

1759	■ **January 10** Washington gives a letter to the officers of the Virginia Regiment.
1775	■ **June 15** Washington becomes commander in chief of Continental military.
1783	■ **March 15** Washington gives a speech to army officers at Newburgh, New York. ■ **June 8–14** Washington presents his last circular to the states as commander in chief. ■ **November 2** Washington gives farewell orders to the army. ■ **December 4** Washington bids farewell to his officers at Fraunces Tavern in New York City. ■ **December 23** Washington surrenders his commission to Congress.
1787	■ **May 25–September 17** Washington serves in the Constitutional Convention.
1788	■ **June 21** The Constitution is officially ratified.
1789	■ **April 6** Washington is elected first president under the Constitution. ■ **April 30** Washington is inaugurated as president.
1792	■ **June 20** James Madison sends Washington a draft of a farewell address. ■ **December 5** Washington is reelected president.

elder stepbrother Lawrence married into the prominent Fairfax family, and Washington often visited his brother at the Fairfax estate. It was through this connection that at age seventeen Washington was appointed surveyor of Culpeper County, which was on the fringe of the Virginia frontier. The young surveyor learned how to live in the wilderness and deal with Native Americans. He also made excellent personal and business connections and started to build his own estate by purchasing land.

Unlike most Virginia political leaders who rose to prominence through steady advancement in civilian offices, Washington's popularity came through the military. Governor Robert Dinwiddie sent Washington to order the French to leave an area Virginians considered their territory (the present-day area around Pittsburgh). Several encounters between Washington and the French led to the French and Indian War, which escalated into the Seven Years' War in Europe. In 1755 Washington escaped unscathed from the decimation of General Edward Braddock's British army. At twenty-two, Washington became commander in chief of the Virginia militia (1755–1758). Even though Washington emerged from the war as one of only a few American heroes, the British refused to give him a commission in the regular army.

Washington served in the Virginia House of Burgesses from the western district of Frederick County from 1758 to 1765 and from his home district of Fairfax County from 1766 to 1776. His marriage to the wealthy widow Martha Dandridge Custis in January 1759 brought him added land, slaves, and social prominence.

Washington joined those colonists who opposed the new imperial policy instituted after the end of the French and Indian War in 1763. He served in the First and Second Continental Congresses, arriving at the latter dressed in the uniform of a Virginia militia colonel—the only delegate dressed in a military uniform. On June 15, 1775, Congress elected him commander in chief, a position he held until the end of the war despite several early attempts to remove him.

In March 1783 Washington squelched an uprising among army officers who contemplated marching in on Congress to demand their back pay and pensions, which Congress had promised them in 1780 during the war. In early June 1783 Washington wrote his final circular letter to the chief executives of the states, informing them that he intended to retire to civilian life after the conflict ended and that he would not serve again in public office. The letter outlined what Washington thought was necessary for America to be great as a nation. First, the Union had to be preserved and Congress's powers had to be increased. Second, the country's public credit and public justice had to be maintained by paying the wartime debt both to foreign and domestic public creditors, honoring promises made to the army and its officers, and providing pensions to invalid soldiers and widows and orphans of those who had died during the war. Third, Congress had to provide an appropriate peacetime military establishment. The old militia system had been largely ineffective, thus demonstrating that some kind of standing army was essential. Last, Washington suggested that Americans develop a new respect for government. After eight years attempting to overthrow imperial authorities, Americans had to erect and maintain a new government and foster a sense of nationhood. The sectionalism of states and their animosities toward each other both before and during the war had to give way to a new sense of American unity and citizenry.

When the British army evacuated New York City on November 25, 1783, Washington and Governor George Clinton rode into the city, which had been occupied by the British for seven years. After ten days of peaceful celebrations, Washington met with his officers at Fraunces Tavern to bid them farewell. He hoped that their latter years would be as happy and prosperous as their former ones had been honorable and glorious. He left New York City to perform his last mission as commander in chief. On December 23, 1783, Washington surrendered his commission to Congress, which had assembled in Annapolis, Maryland. He then retired to Mount Vernon, the plantation he had seen only once during the previous eight years.

Washington enjoyed his retirement. He continued to maintain a voluminous correspondence with both Americans and Europeans, and, as a hospitable southern gentleman, he entertained visitors at his home almost daily. He kept busy by improving the five farms that constituted Mount Vernon and developing canal-building enterprises to connect the new western settlements with the Atlantic states via the James and Potomac Rivers.

Unfortunately, Washington's countrymen did not follow his advice. After a short period of prosperity, the country fell into a severe postwar economic depression. State assemblies enacted radical legislation to ease the plight of desperate debtors, while insufficient efforts to relieve the distressed in other states resulted in violence. Congress, under the largely deficient Articles of Confederation, was unable to pass relief measures or suppress violence. In late 1786 and early 1787, calls were issued for a general convention of the states to amend the articles. The Virginia legislature unanimously elected Washington as one of its convention delegates. After repeatedly rejecting the appointment, primarily because of his 1783 promise not to serve in public office again, Washington succumbed to pressure and accepted. He was elected president of the convention and on September 17, 1787, formally signed both the Constitution and a letter from the convention to the president of Congress.

Washington actively worked for ratification of the Constitution behind the scenes from Mount Vernon. He did not, however, become personally involved in the campaign and refused to be a delegate to the Virginia ratifying convention. The entire country knew that if the Constitution were ratified, Washington would be the only person Americans would want as the country's first president. He reluctantly accepted the unanimous election as president and was inaugurated on April 30, 1789. He was ready to retire after one term, but his advisers convinced him that he must continue for a second term, because domestic unrest and war in Europe required his unifying leadership. As the end of his second term neared, Washington decided not to stand for a third term. He made this decision public with his Farewell Address, which was printed first in the Philadelphia *American Daily Advertiser* on September 19, 1796. Widely reprinted, the address was viewed as Washington's legacy to his country.

Washington happily retired to Mount Vernon in March 1797. He actively worked on the plantation and continued his vast correspondence. In 1798 President John Adams appointed Washington commander in chief of the provisional army that was to be raised to defend the country against an expected invasion by France. Some talk arose among Hamilton's supporters that Washington should be brought out of retirement to serve a third term as president, but Washington scuttled such a movement in its infancy. Adams's efforts to maintain peace succeeded and eliminated the threat of war and thus the need for the army.

Healthy and vigorous at sixty-seven, Washington contracted a severe cold on December 10, 1799, after spending hours outdoors exposed to a harsh storm on the plantation. His illness developed into a condition in which he was unable to breathe. Further weakened by attending physicians who bled him of thirty-two ounces of blood, a typical treatment for the times, Washington died on December 14, 1799. He was buried at Mount Vernon.

Time Line

1793

- **March 4**
  Washington is inaugurated as president a second time.
- **April 22**
  Washington issues the Proclamation of Neutrality.

1796

- **February**
  Washington asks Alexander Hamilton to revise the draft of his Farewell Address.
- **September 19**
  The Farewell Address is first printed in Philadelphia.

1797

- **March 4**
  Washington serves his last day as president.

1799

- **December 14**
  Washington dies at Mount Vernon.

Explanation and Analysis of the Document

In the first paragraphs of the Farewell Address, Washington announces that he will not seek a third term as presi-

www.milestonedocuments.com

dent. He feels that he has fulfilled his duty and is inclined to live a private life. He believes that such a desire neither indicates a "diminution of zeal" for America's future nor any "deficiency of grateful respect for your past kindness." He is happy that retirement does not conflict with his sense of duty or propriety. He explains that he had entered the presidency knowing his fallibilities, and the "weight of years" had only increased his desire for "the shade of retirement." He believes "that, while choice and prudence invite me to quit the political scene, patriotism does not forbid it."

In looking forward to retirement, Washington thanks his beloved country for the many honors it has conferred upon him and the "steadfast confidence" with which he has been supported. He thanks his countrymen for the opportunities he "enjoyed of manifesting my inviolable attachment, by services faithful and persevering." He acknowledges that there have been difficult times, but "the constancy of your support was the essential prop of the efforts, and a guarantee of the plans by which they were effected."

Washington hopes that God will continue to smile on America and that the Union of "brotherly affection" will be perpetual under "the free Constitution, which is the work of your hands." He hopes that every department of the government will "be stamped with wisdom and virtue" and that the people's liberty and happiness will be preserved.

At the beginning of paragraph 7, he wonders aloud if he should end the address here. However, he notes that the desire he has for the welfare of his country, "which cannot end but with my life," and the apprehensions he has for the dangers surrounding America force him to recommend "some sentiments" that are "the result of much reflection" on "the permanency of your felicity as a people." He offers these sentiments as "the disinterested warnings of a parting friend, who can possibly have no personal motive to bias his counsel."

Washington's persistent theme throughout the address is the importance of the "national union to your collective and individual happiness," as he notes in paragraph 9. Union, according to Washington "is a main pillar in the edifice of your real independence, the support of your tranquility at home; your peace abroad; of your safety; of your prosperity; of that very liberty which you so highly prize." Many "internal and external enemies," Washington warns, will "covertly and insidiously" attempt to weaken the importance of Union "in your minds." But Americans must "cherish a cordial, habitual, and immovable attachment" to the Union. It must be thought of as

> the palladium of your political safety and prosperity; watching for its preservation with jealous anxiety; discountenancing whatever may suggest even a suspicion that it can in any event be abandoned; and indignantly frowning upon the first dawning of every attempt to alienate any portion of our country from the rest, or to enfeeble the sacred ties which now link together the various parts.

In paragraph 10, Washington stresses the far greater significance of American citizenship rather than allegiance to one's home state. He feels that Americans have but slight variations among them. They share "the same religion, manners, habits, and political principles." They fought a common enemy to preserve their rights and "triumphed together; the independence and liberty you possess are the work of joint counsels, and joint efforts of common dangers, sufferings, and successes."

Even beyond these fraternal bonds, Washington feels that Americans from "every portion of our country" should stay united because it is in their best interest. The maritime and manufacturing interests of the North complement the agricultural South. The economies of the East and the West will steadily become more interconnected as "the interior communications by land and water" improve. United, the individual parts will enjoy greater strength, greater resources, less frequent involvement in war, and "an exemption from those broils and wars between themselves, which so frequently afflict neighboring countries not tied together by the same governments." Likewise, a united America will "avoid the necessity of those overgrown military establishments [i.e., standing armies], which, under any form of government, are inauspicious to liberty."

In paragraph 16, Washington says that he believes that a permanent Union by a single strong government is "indispensable." No alliance could be as unifying. Americans have "improved" their "first essay" (i.e., the Articles of Confederation) by adopting a new constitution. Washington concedes that "the basis of our political systems is the right of the people to make and to alter their constitutions of government. But the Constitution which at any time exists, till changed by an explicit and authentic act of the whole people, is sacredly obligatory upon all." The Revolution, Washington says, is now over.

Washington then alludes to the dangers facing the Union. All obstructions to laws, all combinations and associations and political parties aimed at controlling or counteracting the established government, are inherently dangerous. Led by "cunning, ambitious, and unprincipled men," these groups want to "subvert the power of the people" and "usurp for themselves the reins of government." Attempts will be made to use the amendment provision of the Constitution to "impair the energy of the system, and thus to undermine what cannot be directly overthrown." The Constitution should be given a fair chance to show its effectiveness. "Time and habit," Washington insists, are as necessary "to fix the true character of governments as of other human institutions."

Party spirit has "baneful effects" rooted in human nature. "The alternate domination of one faction over another, sharpened by the spirit of revenge, natural to party dissension … is itself a frightful despotism." It distracts the public councils, enfeebles the administration, agitates the community "with ill-founded jealousies and false alarms; kindles the animosity of one part against another," and foments riot and insurrection.

In paragraph 26, Washington worries that attempts are being made to "to consolidate the powers of all the departments in one, and thus to create, whatever the form of government, a real despotism." The separation of powers and the checks and balances built into the Constitution act as "the guardian of the public weal against invasions by the others." The individual departments must maintain their integrity. Specifically, Washington fears that Congress is attempting to impinge upon the powers and prerogatives of the presidency.

"Religion and morality," Washington states, are "indispensable supports" to good government and political prosperity. They are the "great pillars of human happiness," the "firmest props of the duties of men and citizens," and the connection between "private and public felicity." Coupled with religion and morality, education is of "primary importance," especially in republics where it is "essential that public opinion should be enlightened."

Washington stresses the importance of public credit. Government spending should be kept to a minimum, but it should always be remembered "that timely disbursements to prepare for danger frequently prevent much greater disbursements to repel it." "Vigorous exertion" should be made in peace to discharge debts incurred during unavoidable wars. Revenues are necessary to pay debts, but revenues require taxes, which are always "inconvenient and unpleasant."

The most memorable part of the address deals with foreign affairs. In paragraph 31, Washington counsels his countrymen to "observe good faith and justice towards all nations; cultivate peace and harmony with all. Religion and morality enjoin this conduct; and can it be, that good policy does not equally enjoin it?" No nation, especially America, should harbor "a habitual hatred, or a habitual fondness" toward another country. To do so is to be slavish in some degree. America should always steer clear of European conflicts. Neutrality, as proclaimed by Washington on April 22, 1793, is surely the proper stance to avoid expensive and bloody conflicts. "It is our true policy to steer clear of permanent alliances with any portion of the foreign world," he says. "Justice and humanity" require that every nation seek "to maintain inviolate the relations of peace and amity towards other nations."

Washington hopes that "these counsels of an old and affectionate friend" will have a "strong and lasting impression" on his countrymen. He hopes that in his retirement he will feel "the benign influence of good laws under a free government, the ever-favorite object of my heart, and the happy reward, as I trust, of our mutual cares, labors, and dangers."

Audience

Washington's Farewell Address had two primary audiences: his immediate constituency and all American posterity. In May 1792, Madison (who served unofficially as Washington's protocol secretary) suggested to Washington that the presidential Farewell Address should originally be published in newspapers—unlike Washington's June 1783 farewell as commander in chief, which was sent as a handwritten circular letter to the state governors, who then sub-

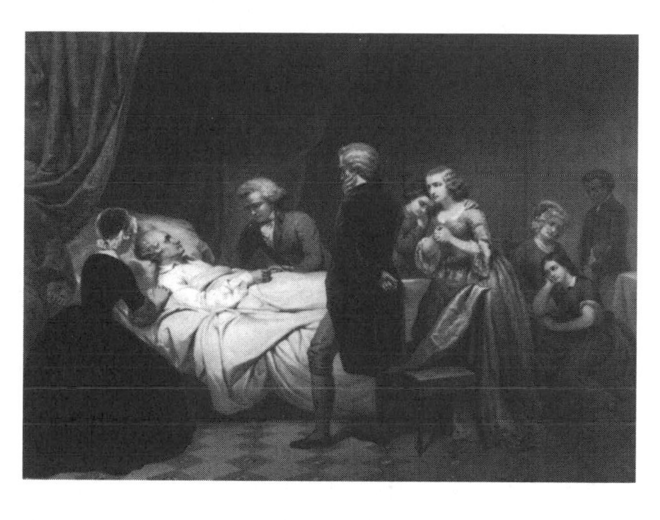

George Washington on his deathbed, as portrayed by Junius B. Stearns (Library of Congress)

mitted it to the state legislatures. The situation had changed. The president's constituency was the people, and newspapers were the best medium in which to address them. Washington agreed, and the address was first printed in the Philadelphia *American Daily Advertiser* addressed to "Friends and Fellow Citizens." Washington hoped to diffuse the political turmoil and partisanship raging in American politics, which he saw as an imminent danger to the continuance of the Union.

Washington also intended that the ideas, warnings, and admonitions in his farewell be addressed to the American posterity in the hope that in the future Americans would be instructed on how best to preserve the Union. Washington had little success in defusing the current political animosity, but after the election of 1800 the American public and public officials accepted Washington's advice and avoided military alliances. In fact, it was not until 1949 that the United States entered into a permanent military alliance with European powers via the North Atlantic Treaty Organization (NATO).

Impact

Washington's birthday has been celebrated ever since his presidency. The Farewell Address became part of that celebration, and for years into the 1970s it was read in the U.S. Senate on February 22 as an expression of the American national credo, only to be supplanted by Abraham Lincoln's First Inaugural Address and more succinctly by Lincoln's Gettysburg Address. Washington's advice was revisited whenever treaties were considered. The country continued to abide by Washington's sage advice on avoiding permanent military alliances until 1949, when the United States joined NATO. Despite Washington's fear of political parties, these parties persisted after his retirement. At times, the bitter partisanship that Washington spoke of greatly endangered the Union. The geographical sectional-

www.milestonedocuments.com

Essential Quotes

"Citizens, by birth or choice, of a common country, that country has a right to concentrate your affections. The name of American, which belongs to you in your national capacity, must always exalt the just pride of patriotism more than any appellation derived from local discrimination."

(Paragraph 10)

"This government, the offspring of our own choice, uninfluenced and unawed, adopted upon full investigation and mature deliberation, completely free in its principles, in the distribution of its powers, uniting security with energy, and containing within itself a provision for its own amendment, has a just claim to your confidence and your support."

(Paragraph 16)

"The basis of our political systems is the right of the people to make and to alter their constitutions of government. But the Constitution which at any time exists, till changed by an explicit and authentic act of the whole people, is sacredly obligatory upon all."

(Paragraph 16)

"Time and habit are at least as necessary to fix the true character of governments as of other human institutions."

(Paragraph 19)

"Experience is the surest standard."

(Paragraph 19)

"A government of as much vigor as is consistent with the perfect security of liberty is indispensable. Liberty itself will find in such a government, with powers properly distributed and adjusted, its surest guardian."

(Paragraph 19)

"Of all the dispositions and habits which lead to political prosperity, religion and morality are indispensable supports."

(Paragraph 27)

ism that ideologically divided the United States in the 1850s actually dismembered the Union, which was reassembled after the American Civil War.

Two hundred years after Washington's Farewell Address, party politics have become so bitter that the national government has been much less effective than Washington would have hoped. The politics of compromise seems to be a thing of the past. Pleas are continually made to revert to the "brotherly affection" advocated by Washington, but American politicians of the twenty-first century seem to have little interest in doing what Washington advised.

Related Documents

Fitzpatrick, John C., ed. *The Writings of George Washington from the Original Manuscript Sources, 1745–1799.* 39 vols. Washington, D.C.: U.S. Government Printing Office, 1931–1944. This collection contains almost all of Washington's outgoing correspondence, some of it dealing with the attempts to get Madison to draft a farewell address in 1792 and to enlist Hamilton's assistance in writing such an address in 1796.

Crackel, Theodore J., ed. *The Papers of George Washington.* Charlottesville: University of Virginia Press, 1976–. This modern edition of the Washington papers has both sides of the correspondence to and from Congress.

Kaminski, John P., and Jill Adair McCaughan, eds. *A Great and Good Man: George Washington in the Eyes of His Contemporaries.* Madison, Wis.: Madison House, 1989. This collection of documents describes the attitude of the public toward Washington before and after he wrote some of his farewell addresses.

Paltsits, Victor Hugo. *Washington's Farewell Address.* New York: New York Public Library, 1935. This volume brings together a facsimile of the address with transliterations of all drafts of Washington, Madison, and Hamilton, along with their correspondence and other supporting documents; the volume includes a history of the address's origin, reception by the nation, rise of the controversy respecting its authorship, and a bibliography.

Syrett, Harold C., ed. *The Papers of Alexander Hamilton.* 27 vols. New York: Columbia University Press, 1961–1987. This completed collection of both incoming and outgoing letters has the full correspondence between Hamilton and Washington on the writing of the Farewell Address.

Bibliography

■ Articles

De Conde, Alexander. "Washington's Farewell, the French Alliance, and the Election of 1796." *Mississippi Valley Historical Review* 43 (1957): 641–658.

Hoetetler, Michael. "Washington's Farewell Address: Distance as Bane and Blessing." *Rhetoric & Public Affairs* 5 (2002): 393–407.

Ryan, Halford. "The Rhetoric of George Washington's Farewell Address." *Speaker and Gavel* 38 (2001): 1–15.

■ Books

Cunliffe, Marcus. *George Washington: Man and Monument.* Boston, Mass.: Little, Brown, 1958.

De Conde, Alexander. *Entangling Alliance: Politics and Diplomacy under George Washington.* Durham, N.C.: Duke University Press, 1969.

Ferling, John E. *The First of Men: A Life of George Washington.* Knoxville: University of Tennessee Press, 1988.

Flexner, James Thomas. *Washington: The Indispensable Man.* Boston, Mass.: Little, Brown, 1969.

Ford, Paul Leicester. *The True George Washington.* Philadelphia, Pa.: J. B. Lippincott Company, 1896.

Freeman, Douglas Southall. *George Washington: A Biography.* 7 vols. New York: Scribner, 1948–1957.

Gilbert, Felix. *To the Farewell Address: Ideas of Early American Foreign Policy.* Princeton, N.J.: Princeton University Press, 1961.

Grizzard, Frank E., Jr. *George Washington: A Biographical Companion.* Santa Barbara, Calif.: ABC-CLIO, 2002.

Higginbotham, Don. *George Washington: Uniting a Nation.* Lan ham, Md.: Rowman & Littlefield, 2002.

Kaminski, John P. *George Washington: "The Man of the Age."* Madison, Wis.: Parallel Press, 2007.

Kaufman, Burton I., ed. *Washington's Farewell Address: The View from the 20th Century.* Chicago: Quadrangle Books, 1969.

Leibiger, Stuart. *Founding Friendship: George Washington, James Madison, and the Creation of the American Republic.* Charlottesville: University of Virginia Press, 1999.

Lucas, Stephen E., and Susan Zaeske. "George Washington." In *U.S. Presidents as Orators,* ed. Halford Ryan. Westport, Conn.: 1995.

Smith, Richard Norton. *Patriarch: George Washington and the New American Nation.* Boston, Mass.: Houghton Mifflin, 1993.

Spaulding, Matthew, and Patrick J. Garrity. *A Sacred Union of Citizens: George Washington's Farewell Address and the American Character.* Lanham, Md.: Rowman & Littlefield, 1996.

■ Web Sites

"Washington's Farewell Address 1796." The Avalon Project at Yale Law School Web site.
http://www.yale.edu/lawweb/avalon/washing.htm. Accessed on January 28, 2008.

www.milestonedocuments.com

"The Papers of George Washington Digital Edition." University of Virginia Press Web site.
http://rotunda.upress.virginia.edu/pgwde. Accessed on November 29, 2007.

"President George Washington's Farewell Address (1796)." 100 Milestone Documents Web site.
http://www.ourdocuments.gov/doc.php?flash=true&doc=15. Accessed on November 29, 2007.

—By John P. Kaminski

Questions for Further Study

1. How might alliances with foreign powers detract from the best interests of America?

2. Compare and contrast Washington's advice in the Farewell Address with Thomas Paine's advice in *Common Sense* in 1776, Washington's circular letter to the states in June 1783, and Abraham Lincoln's First Inaugural Address in 1861.

3. How do you explain Alexander Hamilton's writing the portions of the Farewell Address in which political parties are attacked when, at the time, Hamilton was the partisan leader of the Federalist Party?

4. The Soviet Union dissolved in the late 1980s into several individual nations. Do you think that it would be beneficial for the United States to divide into five or six separate confederations held together by a limited federal government? Why or why not?

5. Have recent American administrations followed Washington's advice?

Glossary

actuate	to stir to action
amicable	friendly
amity	friendliness
baneful	harmful
caprice	whim; impulse
diffidence	reserve; hesitancy
envenomed	poisonous
expedients	opportunistic ways of working
felicity	happiness
incongruous	inappropriate in a particular context
inestimable	immeasurable

Glossary

intractable	resistant to influence or persuasion
inviolate	pure; not violated
maxims	general truths
neutrality	nonalignment with one or the other side in a dispute
odious	deserving contempt or strong dislike
palladium	a defense or protection
progenitors	ancestors
recompense	compensation; payment
requisite	necessary; required
salutary	beneficial
scrupulously	painstakingly or conscientiously
solicitude	conscientious care
specious	deceptively alluring or attractive
umbrage	offense; affront
usurp	to seize and hold without entitlement or justification
vicissitudes	changeable affairs
weal	welfare

George Washington's Farewell Address

Friends and Fellow Citizens:

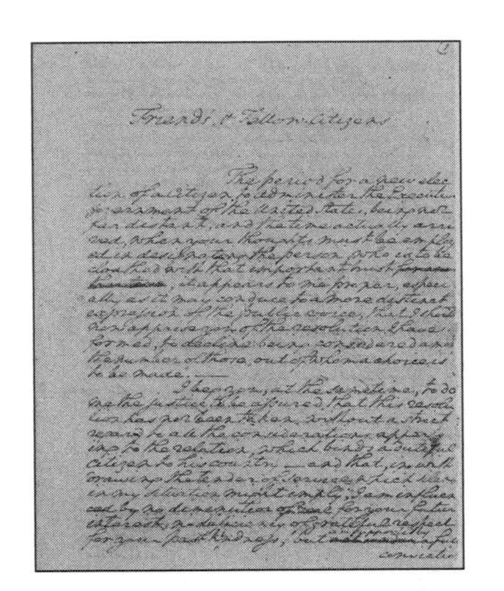

The period for a new election of a citizen to administer the executive government of the United States being not far distant, and the time actually arrived when your thoughts must be employed in designating the person who is to be clothed with that important trust, it appears to me proper, especially as it may conduce to a more distinct expression of the public voice, that I should now apprise you of the resolution I have formed, to decline being considered among the number of those out of whom a choice is to be made.

I beg you, at the same time, to do me the justice to be assured that this resolution has not been taken without a strict regard to all the considerations appertaining to the relation which binds a dutiful citizen to his country; and that in withdrawing the tender of service, which silence in my situation might imply, I am influenced by no diminution of zeal for your future interest, no deficiency of grateful respect for your past kindness, but am supported by a full conviction that the step is compatible with both.

The acceptance of, and continuance hitherto in, the office to which your suffrages have twice called me have been a uniform sacrifice of inclination to the opinion of duty and to a deference for what appeared to be your desire. I constantly hoped that it would have been much earlier in my power, consistently with motives which I was not at liberty to disregard, to return to that retirement from which I had been reluctantly drawn. The strength of my inclination to do this, previous to the last election, had even led to the preparation of an address to declare it to you; but mature reflection on the then perplexed and critical posture of our affairs with foreign nations, and the unanimous advice of persons entitled to my confidence, impelled me to abandon the idea.

I rejoice that the state of your concerns, external as well as internal, no longer renders the pursuit of inclination incompatible with the sentiment of duty or propriety, and am persuaded, whatever partiality may be retained for my services, that, in the present circumstances of our country, you will not disapprove my determination to retire.

The impressions with which I first undertook the arduous trust were explained on the proper occasion. In the discharge of this trust, I will only say that I have, with good intentions, contributed towards the organization and administration of the government the best exertions of which a very fallible judgment was capable. Not unconscious in the outset of the inferiority of my qualifications, experience in my own eyes, perhaps still more in the eyes of others, has strengthened the motives to diffidence of myself; and every day the increasing weight of years admonishes me more and more that the shade of retirement is as necessary to me as it will be welcome. Satisfied that if any circumstances have given peculiar value to my services, they were temporary, I have the consolation to believe that, while choice and prudence invite me to quit the political scene, patriotism does not forbid it.

In looking forward to the moment which is intended to terminate the career of my public life, my feelings do not permit me to suspend the deep acknowledgment of that debt of gratitude which I owe to my beloved country for the many honors it has conferred upon me; still more for the steadfast confidence with which it has supported me; and for the opportunities I have thence enjoyed of manifesting my inviolable attachment, by services faithful and persevering, though in usefulness unequal to my zeal. If benefits have resulted to our country from these services, let it always be remembered to your praise, and as an instructive example in our annals, that under circumstances in which the passions, agitated in every direction, were liable to mislead, amidst appearances sometimes dubious, vicissitudes of fortune often discouraging, in situations in which not unfrequently want of success has countenanced the spirit of criticism, the constancy of your support was the essential prop of the efforts, and a guarantee of the plans by which they were effected. Profoundly penetrated with this idea, I shall carry it with me to my grave, as a strong incitement to unceasing vows that heaven may continue to you the choicest tokens of its beneficence; that your union and brotherly affection may be perpetual; that the free Constitution, which is the work of your hands, may be sacredly maintained; that its administration in every department may be stamped with wisdom and virtue; that, in fine, the happiness of the people of these States, under the auspices of liberty, may be made complete by so careful a preservation and so prudent a use of this blessing as will acquire to them the glory of recommending it to the applause, the affection, and adoption of every nation which is yet a stranger to it.

Here, perhaps, I ought to stop. But a solicitude for your welfare, which cannot end but with my life, and the apprehension of danger, natural to that solicitude, urge me, on an occasion like the present, to offer to your solemn contemplation, and to recommend to your frequent review, some sentiments which are the result of much reflection, of no inconsiderable observation, and which appear to me all-important to the permanency of your felicity as a people. These will be offered to you with the more freedom, as you can only see in them the disinterested warnings of a parting friend, who can possibly have no personal motive to bias his counsel. Nor can I forget, as an encouragement to it, your indulgent reception of my sentiments on a former and not dissimilar occasion.

Interwoven as is the love of liberty with every ligament of your hearts, no recommendation of mine is necessary to fortify or confirm the attachment.

The unity of government which constitutes you one people is also now dear to you. It is justly so, for it is a main pillar in the edifice of your real independence, the support of your tranquility at home, your peace abroad; of your safety; of your prosperity; of that very liberty which you so highly prize. But as it is easy to foresee that, from different causes and from different quarters, much pains will be taken, many artifices employed to weaken in your minds the conviction of this truth; as this is the point in your political fortress against which the batteries of internal and external enemies will be most constantly and actively (though often covertly and insidiously) directed, it is of infinite moment that you should properly estimate the immense value of your national union to your collective and individual happiness; that you should cherish a cordial, habitual, and immovable attachment to it; accustoming yourselves to think and speak of it as of the palladium of your political safety and prosperity; watching for its preservation with jealous anxiety; discountenancing whatever may suggest even a suspicion that it can in any event be abandoned; and indignantly frowning upon the first dawning of every attempt to alienate any portion of our country from the rest, or to enfeeble the sacred ties which now link together the various parts.

For this you have every inducement of sympathy and interest. Citizens, by birth or choice, of a common country, that country has a right to concentrate your affections. The name of American, which belongs to you in your national capacity, must always exalt the just pride of patriotism more than any appellation derived from local discriminations. With slight shades of difference, you have the same religion, manners, habits, and political principles. You have in a common cause fought and triumphed together; the independence and liberty you possess are the work of joint counsels, and joint efforts of common dangers, sufferings, and successes.

But these considerations, however powerfully they address themselves to your sensibility, are greatly outweighed by those which apply more immediately to your interest. Here every portion of our country finds the most commanding motives for carefully guarding and preserving the union of the whole.

The North, in an unrestrained intercourse with the South, protected by the equal laws of a common government, finds in the productions of the latter great additional resources of maritime and commercial enterprise and precious materials of manufacturing industry. The South, in the same intercourse, benefiting by the agency of the North, sees its agriculture grow and its commerce expand. Turning partly into its own channels the seamen of the North, it finds its particular navigation invigorated; and, while it contributes, in different ways, to nourish and increase the general mass of the national navigation, it looks forward to the protection of a maritime strength, to which itself is unequally adapted. The East, in a like intercourse with the West, already finds, and in the progressive improvement of interior communications by land and water, will more and more find a valuable vent for the commodities which it brings from abroad, or manufactures at home. The West derives from the East supplies requisite to its growth and comfort, and, what is perhaps of still greater consequence, it must of necessity owe the secure enjoyment of indispensable outlets for its own productions to the weight, influence, and the

www.milestonedocuments.com

future maritime strength of the Atlantic side of the Union, directed by an indissoluble community of interest as one nation. Any other tenure by which the West can hold this essential advantage, whether derived from its own separate strength, or from an apostate and unnatural connection with any foreign power, must be intrinsically precarious.

While, then, every part of our country thus feels an immediate and particular interest in union, all the parts combined cannot fail to find in the united mass of means and efforts greater strength, greater resource, proportionably greater security from external danger, a less frequent interruption of their peace by foreign nations; and, what is of inestimable value, they must derive from union an exemption from those broils and wars between themselves, which so frequently afflict neighboring countries not tied together by the same governments, which their own rival ships alone would be sufficient to produce, but which opposite foreign alliances, attachments, and intrigues would stimulate and embitter. Hence, likewise, they will avoid the necessity of those overgrown military establishments which, under any form of government, are inauspicious to liberty, and which are to be regarded as particularly hostile to republican liberty. In this sense it is that your union ought to be considered as a main prop of your liberty, and that the love of the one ought to endear to you the preservation of the other.

These considerations speak a persuasive language to every reflecting and virtuous mind, and exhibit the continuance of the Union as a primary object of patriotic desire. Is there a doubt whether a common government can embrace so large a sphere? Let experience solve it. To listen to mere speculation in such a case were criminal. We are authorized to hope that a proper organization of the whole with the auxiliary agency of governments for the respective subdivisions, will afford a happy issue to the experiment. It is well worth a fair and full experiment. With such powerful and obvious motives to union, affecting all parts of our country, while experience shall not have demonstrated its impracticability, there will always be reason to distrust the patriotism of those who in any quarter may endeavor to weaken its bands.

In contemplating the causes which may disturb our Union, it occurs as matter of serious concern that any ground should have been furnished for characterizing parties by geographical discriminations, Northern and Southern, Atlantic and Western; whence designing men may endeavor to excite a belief that there is a real difference of local interests and views. One of the expedients of party to acquire influence within particular districts is to misrepresent the opinions and aims of other districts. You cannot shield yourselves too much against the jealousies and heartburnings which spring from these misrepresentations; they tend to render alien to each other those who ought to be bound together by fraternal affection. The inhabitants of our Western country have lately had a useful lesson on this head; they have seen, in the negotiation by the Executive, and in the unanimous ratification by the Senate, of the treaty with Spain, and in the universal satisfaction at that event, throughout the United States, a decisive proof how unfounded were the suspicions propagated among them of a policy in the General Government and in the Atlantic States unfriendly to their interests in regard to the Mississippi; they have been witnesses to the formation of two treaties, that with Great Britain, and that with Spain, which secure to them everything they could desire, in respect to our foreign relations, towards confirming their prosperity. Will it not be their wisdom to rely for the preservation of these advantages on the Union by which they were procured ? Will they not henceforth be deaf to those advisers, if such there are, who would sever them from their brethren and connect them with aliens?

To the efficacy and permanency of your Union, a government for the whole is indispensable. No alliance, however strict, between the parts can be an adequate substitute; they must inevitably experience the infractions and interruptions which all alliances in all times have experienced. Sensible of this momentous truth, you have improved upon your first essay, by the adoption of a constitution of government better calculated than your former for an intimate union, and for the efficacious management of your common concerns. This government, the offspring of our own choice, uninfluenced and unawed, adopted upon full investigation and mature deliberation, completely free in its principles, in the distribution of its powers, uniting security with energy, and containing within itself a provision for its own amendment, has a just claim to your confidence and your support. Respect for its authority, compliance with its laws, acquiescence in its measures, are duties enjoined by the fundamental maxims of true liberty. The basis of our political systems is the right of the people to make and to alter their constitutions of government. But the Constitution which at any time exists, till changed by an explicit and authentic act of the whole people, is sacredly obligatory upon all. The very idea of the power and the right of the people to establish government presupposes the duty of every individual to obey the established government.

All obstructions to the execution of the laws, all combinations and associations, under whatever plausible character, with the real design to direct, control, counteract, or awe the regular deliberation and action of the constituted authorities, are destructive of this fundamental principle, and of fatal tendency. They serve to organize faction, to give it an artificial and extraordinary force; to put, in the place of the delegated will of the nation the will of a party, often a small but artful and enterprising minority of the community; and, according to the alternate triumphs of different parties, to make the public administration the mirror of the ill-concerted and incongruous projects of faction, rather than the organ of consistent and wholesome plans digested by common counsels and modified by mutual interests.

However combinations or associations of the above description may now and then answer popular ends, they are likely, in the course of time and things, to become potent engines, by which cunning, ambitious, and unprincipled men will be enabled to subvert the power of the people and to usurp for themselves the reins of government, destroying afterwards the very engines which have lifted them to unjust dominion.

Towards the preservation of your government, and the permanency of your present happy state, it is requisite, not only that you steadily discountenance irregular oppositions to its acknowledged authority, but also that you resist with care the spirit of innovation upon its principles, however specious the pretexts. One method of assault may be to effect, in the forms of the Constitution, alterations which will impair the energy of the system, and thus to undermine what cannot be directly overthrown. In all the changes to which you may be invited, remember that time and habit are at least as necessary to fix the true character of governments as of other human institutions; that experience is the surest standard by which to test the real tendency of the existing constitution of a country; that facility in changes, upon the credit of mere hypothesis and opinion, exposes to perpetual change, from the endless variety of hypothesis and opinion; and remember, especially, that for the efficient management of your common interests, in a country so extensive as ours, a government of as much vigor as is consistent with the perfect security of liberty is indispensable. Liberty itself will find in such a government, with powers properly distributed and adjusted, its surest guardian. It is, indeed, little else than a name, where the government is too feeble to withstand the enterprises of faction, to confine each member of the society within the limits prescribed by the laws, and to maintain all in the secure and tranquil enjoyment of the rights of person and property.

I have already intimated to you the danger of parties in the State, with particular reference to the founding of them on geographical discriminations. Let me now take a more comprehensive view, and warn you in the most solemn manner against the baneful effects of the spirit of party generally.

This spirit, unfortunately, is inseparable from our nature, having its root in the strongest passions of the human mind. It exists under different shapes in all governments, more or less stifled, controlled, or repressed; but, in those of the popular form, it is seen in its greatest rankness, and is truly their worst enemy.

The alternate domination of one faction over another, sharpened by the spirit of revenge, natural to party dissension, which in different ages and countries has perpetrated the most horrid enormities, is itself a frightful despotism. But this leads at length to a more formal and permanent despotism. The disorders and miseries which result gradually incline the minds of men to seek security and repose in the absolute power of an individual; and sooner or later the chief of some prevailing faction, more able or more fortunate than his competitors, turns this disposition to the purposes of his own elevation, on the ruins of public liberty.

Without looking forward to an extremity of this kind (which nevertheless ought not to be entirely out of sight), the common and continual mischiefs of the spirit of party are sufficient to make it the interest and duty of a wise people to discourage and restrain it.

It serves always to distract the public councils and enfeeble the public administration. It agitates the community with ill-founded jealousies and false alarms, kindles the animosity of one part against another, foments occasionally riot and insurrection. It opens the door to foreign influence and corruption, which finds a facilitated access to the government itself through the channels of party passions. Thus the policy and the will of one country are subjected to the policy and will of another.

There is an opinion that parties in free countries are useful checks upon the administration of the government and serve to keep alive the spirit of liberty. This within certain limits is probably true; and in governments of a monarchical cast, patriotism

www.milestonedocuments.com

Document Text

may look with indulgence, if not with favor, upon the spirit of party. But in those of the popular character, in governments purely elective, it is a spirit not to be encouraged. From their natural tendency, it is certain there will always be enough of that spirit for every salutary purpose. And there being constant danger of excess, the effort ought to be by force of public opinion, to mitigate and assuage it. A fire not to be quenched, it demands a uniform vigilance to prevent its bursting into a flame, lest, instead of warming, it should consume.

It is important, likewise, that the habits of thinking in a free country should inspire caution in those entrusted with its administration, to confine themselves within their respective constitutional spheres, avoiding in the exercise of the powers of one department to encroach upon another. The spirit of encroachment tends to consolidate the powers of all the departments in one, and thus to create, whatever the form of government, a real despotism. A just estimate of that love of power, and proneness to abuse it, which predominates in the human heart, is sufficient to satisfy us of the truth of this position. The necessity of reciprocal checks in the exercise of political power, by dividing and distributing it into different depositaries, and constituting each the guardian of the public weal against invasions by the others, has been evinced by experiments ancient and modern; some of them in our country and under our own eyes. To preserve them must be as necessary as to institute them. If, in the opinion of the people, the distribution or modification of the constitutional powers be in any particular wrong, let it be corrected by an amendment in the way which the Constitution designates. But let there be no change by usurpation; for though this, in one instance, may be the instrument of good, it is the customary weapon by which free governments are destroyed. The precedent must always greatly overbalance in permanent evil any partial or transient benefit, which the use can at any time yield.

Of all the dispositions and habits which lead to political prosperity, religion and morality are indispensable supports. In vain would that man claim the tribute of patriotism, who should labor to subvert these great pillars of human happiness, these firmest props of the duties of men and citizens. The mere politician, equally with the pious man, ought to respect and to cherish them. A volume could not trace all their connections with private and public felicity. Let it simply be asked: Where is the security for property, for reputation, for life, if the sense of religious obligation desert the oaths which are the instruments of investigation in courts of justice? And let us with caution indulge the supposition that morality can be maintained without religion. Whatever may be conceded to the influence of refined education on minds of peculiar structure, reason and experience both forbid us to expect that national morality can prevail in exclusion of religious principle.

It is substantially true that virtue or morality is a necessary spring of popular government. The rule, indeed, extends with more or less force to every species of free government. Who that is a sincere friend to it can look with indifference upon attempts to shake the foundation of the fabric?

Promote then, as an object of primary importance, institutions for the general diffusion of knowledge. In proportion as the structure of a government gives force to public opinion, it is essential that public opinion should be enlightened.

As a very important source of strength and security, cherish public credit. One method of preserving it is to use it as sparingly as possible, avoiding occasions of expense by cultivating peace, but remembering also that timely disbursements to prepare for danger frequently prevent much greater disbursements to repel it, avoiding likewise the accumulation of debt, not only by shunning occasions of expense, but by vigorous exertion in time of peace to discharge the debts which unavoidable wars may have occasioned, not ungenerously throwing upon posterity the burden which we ourselves ought to bear. The execution of these maxims belongs to your representatives, but it is necessary that public opinion should co-operate. To facilitate to them the performance of their duty, it is essential that you should practically bear in mind that towards the payment of debts there must be revenue; that to have revenue there must be taxes; that no taxes can be devised which are not more or less inconvenient and unpleasant; that the intrinsic embarrassment, inseparable from the selection of the proper objects (which is always a choice of difficulties), ought to be a decisive motive for a candid construction of the conduct of the government in making it, and for a spirit of acquiescence in the measures for obtaining revenue, which the public exigencies may at any time dictate.

Observe good faith and justice towards all nations; cultivate peace and harmony with all. Religion and morality enjoin this conduct; and can it be, that good policy does not equally enjoin it? It will be worthy of a free, enlightened, and at no distant period, a great nation, to give to mankind the magnanimous and too novel example of a people always guided by an exalted justice and benevolence. Who can doubt that, in the course of time and things, the fruits of such a plan would richly repay any temporary advantages which might be lost by a steady adherence to it? Can it be that Providence has not connected the permanent felicity of a nation with its virtue? The experiment, at least, is recommended by every sentiment which ennobles human nature. Alas! is it rendered impossible by its vices?

In the execution of such a plan, nothing is more essential than that permanent, inveterate antipathies against particular nations, and passionate attachments for others, should be excluded; and that, in place of them, just and amicable feelings towards all should be cultivated. The nation which indulges towards another a habitual hatred or a habitual fondness is in some degree a slave. It is a slave to its animosity or to its affection, either of which is sufficient to lead it astray from its duty and its interest. Antipathy in one nation against another disposes each more readily to offer insult and injury, to lay hold of slight causes of umbrage, and to be haughty and intractable, when accidental or trifling occasions of dispute occur. Hence, frequent collisions, obstinate, envenomed, and bloody contests. The nation, prompted by ill-will and resentment, sometimes impels to war the government, contrary to the best calculations of policy. The government sometimes participates in the national propensity, and adopts through passion what reason would reject; at other times it makes the animosity of the nation subservient to projects of hostility instigated by pride, ambition, and other sinister and pernicious motives. The peace often, sometimes perhaps the liberty, of nations, has been the victim.

So likewise, a passionate attachment of one nation for another produces a variety of evils. Sympathy for the favorite nation, facilitating the illusion of an imaginary common interest in cases where no real common interest exists, and infusing into one the enmities of the other, betrays the former into a participation in the quarrels and wars of the latter without adequate inducement or justification. It leads also to concessions to the favorite nation of privileges denied to others which is apt doubly to injure the nation making the concessions; by unnecessarily parting with what ought to have been retained, and by exciting jealousy, ill-will, and a disposition to retaliate, in the parties from whom equal privileges are withheld. And it gives to ambitious, corrupted, or deluded citizens (who devote themselves to the favorite nation), facility to betray or sacrifice the interests of their own country, without odium, sometimes even with popularity; gilding, with the appearances of a virtuous sense of obligation, a commendable deference for public opinion, or a laudable zeal for public good, the base or foolish compliances of ambition, corruption, or infatuation.

As avenues to foreign influence in innumerable ways, such attachments are particularly alarming to the truly enlightened and independent patriot. How many opportunities do they afford to tamper with domestic factions, to practice the arts of seduction, to mislead public opinion, to influence or awe the public councils? Such an attachment of a small or weak towards a great and powerful nation dooms the former to be the satellite of the latter.

Against the insidious wiles of foreign influence (I conjure you to believe me, fellow-citizens) the jealousy of a free people ought to be constantly awake, since history and experience prove that foreign influence is one of the most baneful foes of republican government. But that jealousy to be useful must be impartial; else it becomes the instrument of the very influence to be avoided, instead of a defense against it. Excessive partiality for one foreign nation and excessive dislike of another cause those whom they actuate to see danger only on one side, and serve to veil and even second the arts of influence on the other. Real patriots who may resist the intrigues of the favorite are liable to become suspected and odious, while its tools and dupes usurp the applause and confidence of the people, to surrender their interests.

The great rule of conduct for us in regard to foreign nations is in extending our commercial relations, to have with them as little political connection as possible. So far as we have already formed engagements, let them be fulfilled with perfect good faith. Here let us stop. Europe has a set of primary interests which to us have none; or a very remote relation. Hence she must be engaged in frequent controversies, the causes of which are essentially foreign to our concerns. Hence, therefore, it must be unwise in us to implicate ourselves by artificial ties in the ordinary vicissitudes of her politics, or the ordinary combinations and collisions of her friendships or enmities.

Our detached and distant situation invites and enables us to pursue a different course. If we remain one people under an efficient government. the period is not far off when we may defy material injury from external annoyance; when we may take such an attitude as will cause the neutrality we may at any time

www.milestonedocuments.com

Document Text

resolve upon to be scrupulously respected; when belligerent nations, under the impossibility of making acquisitions upon us, will not lightly hazard the giving us provocation; when we may choose peace or war, as our interest, guided by justice, shall counsel.

Why forego the advantages of so peculiar a situation? Why quit our own to stand upon foreign ground? Why, by interweaving our destiny with that of any part of Europe, entangle our peace and prosperity in the toils of European ambition, rivalship, interest, humor or caprice?

It is our true policy to steer clear of permanent alliances with any portion of the foreign world; so far, I mean, as we are now at liberty to do it; for let me not be understood as capable of patronizing infidelity to existing engagements. I hold the maxim no less applicable to public than to private affairs, that honesty is always the best policy. I repeat it, therefore, let those engagements be observed in their genuine sense. But, in my opinion, it is unnecessary and would be unwise to extend them.

Taking care always to keep ourselves by suitable establishments on a respectable defensive posture, we may safely trust to temporary alliances for extraordinary emergencies.

Harmony, liberal intercourse with all nations, are recommended by policy, humanity, and interest. But even our commercial policy should hold an equal and impartial hand; neither seeking nor granting exclusive favors or preferences; consulting the natural course of things; diffusing and diversifying by gentle means the streams of commerce, but forcing nothing; establishing (with powers so disposed, in order to give trade a stable course, to define the rights of our merchants, and to enable the government to support them) conventional rules of intercourse, the best that present circumstances and mutual opinion will permit, but temporary, and liable to be from time to time abandoned or varied, as experience and circumstances shall dictate; constantly keeping in view that it is folly in one nation to look for disinterested favors from another; that it must pay with a portion of its independence for whatever it may accept under that character; that, by such acceptance, it may place itself in the condition of having given equivalents for nominal favors, and yet of being reproached with ingratitude for not giving more. There can be no greater error than to expect or calculate upon real favors from nation to nation. It is an illusion, which experience must cure, which a just pride ought to discard.

In offering to you, my countrymen, these counsels of an old and affectionate friend, I dare not hope they will make the strong and lasting impression I could wish; that they will control the usual current of the passions, or prevent our nation from running the course which has hitherto marked the destiny of nations. But, if I may even flatter myself that they may be productive of some partial benefit, some occasional good; that they may now and then recur to moderate the fury of party spirit, to warn against the mischiefs of foreign intrigue, to guard against the impostures of pretended patriotism; this hope will be a full recompense for the solicitude for your welfare, by which they have been dictated.

How far in the discharge of my official duties I have been guided by the principles which have been delineated, the public records and other evidences of my conduct must witness to you and to the world. To myself, the assurance of my own conscience is, that I have at least believed myself to be guided by them.

In relation to the still subsisting war in Europe, my proclamation of the twenty-second of April, 1793, is the index of my plan. Sanctioned by your approving voice, and by that of your representatives in both houses of Congress, the spirit of that measure has continually governed me, uninfluenced by any attempts to deter or divert me from it.

After deliberate examination, with the aid of the best lights I could obtain, I was well satisfied that our country, under all the circumstances of the case, had a right to take, and was bound in duty and interest to take, a neutral position. Having taken it, I determined, as far as should depend upon me, to maintain it, with moderation, perseverance, and firmness.

The considerations which respect the right to hold this conduct, it is not necessary on this occasion to detail. I will only observe that, according to my understanding of the matter, that right, so far from being denied by any of the belligerent powers, has been virtually admitted by all.

The duty of holding a neutral conduct may be inferred, without anything more, from the obligation which justice and humanity impose on every nation, in cases in which it is free to act, to maintain inviolate the relations of peace and amity towards other nations.

The inducements of interest for observing that conduct will best be referred to your own reflections and experience. With me a predominant motive has been to endeavor to gain time to our country to settle and mature its yet recent institutions, and to progress without interruption to that degree of strength and consistency which is necessary to give it, humanly speaking, the command of its own fortunes.

Document Text

Though, in reviewing the incidents of my administration, I am unconscious of intentional error, I am nevertheless too sensible of my defects not to think it probable that I may have committed many errors. Whatever they may be, I fervently beseech the Almighty to avert or mitigate the evils to which they may tend. I shall also carry with me the hope that my country will never cease to view them with indulgence; and that, after forty five years of my life dedicated to its service with an upright zeal, the faults of incompetent abilities will be consigned to oblivion, as myself must soon be to the mansions of rest.

Relying on its kindness in this as in other things, and actuated by that fervent love towards it, which is so natural to a man who views in it the native soil of himself and his progenitors for several generations, I anticipate with pleasing expectation that retreat in which I promise myself to realize, without alloy, the sweet enjoyment of partaking, in the midst of my fellow-citizens, the benign influence of good laws under a free government, the ever-favorite object of my heart, and the happy reward, as I trust, of our mutual cares, labors, and dangers.

United States
19th September, 1796
Geo. Washington

www.milestonedocuments.com

FIFTH *CONGRESS* OF THE UNITED STATES:

At the Second Session,

Begun and held at the city of *Philadelphia*, in the ſtate of PENNSYLVANIA, on *Monday*, the thirteenth of *November*, one thouſand ſeven hundred and ninety-ſeven.

An ACT *concerning aliens.*

BE it enacted by the Senate and House of Representatives of the United States of America, in Congreſs aſſembled, That it shall be
for the President of the United States at any time during the continuance of this act, to order all such aliens as he shall judge dangerous to the peace and safety
United States, or shall have reasonable grounds to suspect are concerned in any treasonable or secret machinations against the government thereof, to depart
the territory of the United States, within such time as shall be expressed in such order. Which order shall be served on such alien by delivering him a copy
or leaving the same at his usual abode, and returned to the office of the Secretary of State, by the Marshal or other person to whom the same shall be
d. And in case any alien so ordered to depart, shall be found at large within the United States after the time limited in such order for his departure,
not having obtained a licence from the President to reside therein, or having obtained such licence shall not have conformed thereto, every such alien
on conviction thereof, be imprisoned for a term not exceeding three years and shall never after be admitted to become a citizen of the United States.
vided always, and be it further enacted, That if any alien so ordered to depart shall prove to the satisfaction of the President, by evidence to
ken before such person or persons as the President shall direct, who are for that purpose hereby authorized to administer oaths, that no injury or danger
e United States will arise from suffering such alien to reside therein, the President may grant a licence to such alien to remain within the United State
ch time as he shall judge proper, and at such place as he may designate. And the President may also require of such alien to enter into a bond to the
ted States, in such penal sum as he may direct, with one or more sufficient sureties to the satisfaction of the person authorized by the President to take th
e, conditioned for the good behaviour of such alien during his residence in the United States, and not violating his licence. which licence the President may revok
never he shall think proper.

Sect. 2. And be it further enacted, That it shall be lawful for the President of the United States, whenever he may deem it necessary for the public
ty, to order to be removed out of the territory thereof, any alien who may or shall be in prison in pursuance of this act; and to cause to be arrested and sent ou
e United States such of those aliens as shall have been ordered to depart therefrom and shall not have obtained a licence as aforesaid, in all cases where
the opinion of the President the public safety requires a speedy removal. And if any alien so removed or sent out of the United States by the President sha
ntarily return thereto, unless by permission of the President of the United States, such alien on conviction thereof, shall be imprisoned so long as in the opinion of the
sident, the public safety may require.

Sect. 3. And be it further enacted, That every master or commander of any ship or vessel which shall come into any port of the United States after the
t day of July next, shall immediately on his arrival make report in writing to the collector or other chief officer of the customs of such port, of all aliens, if any, on
rd his vessel, specifying their names, age, the place of nativity, the country from which they shall have come, the nation to which they belong and owe allegianc
ir occupation and a description of their persons, as far as he shall be informed thereof, and on failure every such master and commander shall forfeit and pa
ree hundred dollars, for the payment whereof on default of such master or commander, such vessel shall also be holden, and may by such collector or other
ficer of the customs be detained. And it shall be the duty of such collector or other officer of the customs, forthwith to transmit to the office of the department of Sta
e copies of all such returns.

Sect. 4. And be it further enacted, That the circuit and district courts of the United States, shall respectively have cognizance of all crimes and offences
ainst this act. And all marshals and other officers of the United States are required to execute all precepts and orders of the President of the United States issued in
rsuance or by virtue of this act.

Sect. 5. And be it further enacted, That it shall be lawful for any alien who may be ordered to be removed from the United States, by virtue of this Act, to take
ith him such part of his goods, chattels, or other property, as he may find convenient; and all property left in the United States, by any alien, who may be removed
foresaid, shall be, and remain subject to his order and disposal, in the same manner, as if this act had not been passed.

Sect. 6. And be it further enacted, That this act shall continue and be in force for and during the term of two years from the passing thereof.

Jonathan Dayton Speaker of the House of Representatives.

Th: Jefferson Vice President of the United States and President of the Senate.

Approved June 25. 1798
John Adams
President of the United States

I certify that this act did originate in the Sen
Attest
Samuel A. Otis Secretary

The Act Concerning Aliens (National Archives and Records Administration)

Alien and Sedition Acts

1798

"It shall be lawful for the President ... to order all such aliens as he shall judge dangerous ... to depart out of the territory of the United States."

Overview

The Alien and Sedition Acts of 1798 actually involved three distinct acts: the Act Concerning Aliens, the Act Respecting Alien Enemies, and the Act for the Punishment of Certain Crimes against the United States (or the Sedition Act). Although they were passed in the same year and reflected common concerns, the acts raised distinct legal and constitutional questions. The acts were all passed by a Federalist Congress and signed by the Federalist president John Adams at a time of international crisis and looming threats of war between the United States and the revolutionary French government. The legislation reflected Federalist fears of domestic subversion and revolution and the widespread Federalist view that their political opponents were disloyal. In fact, both the Act Concerning Aliens and the Sedition Act were partisan Federalist measures designed to promote Federalist political dominance over Thomas Jefferson's Republican Party. The acts raised important and distinct issues of civil liberty in times of crisis.

The two Alien Acts addressed national policy regarding aliens, citizens of foreign countries residing in the United States. The Act Respecting Alien Enemies dealt with citizens or residents of a nation with which "there shall be a declared war" or a nation that has invaded or has threatened to invade the territory of the United States. In the final version, that act was not controversial. The Act Concerning Aliens dealt with all other aliens present in the United States. To distinguish it from the Alien Enemies Act, it is referred to as the Alien Friends Act. The Alien Acts raised basic questions about the constitutional rights of aliens, issues that continue to be of significance in the modern era.

In contrast to the Alien Acts, the Sedition Act dealt with citizens as well as anyone else in the United States. The controversial second section of the Sedition Act made it a crime for any person to write, utter, or publish any false, scandalous, and malicious words against the government of the United States, either house of Congress, or the president with the intent to defame them, bring them into contempt or disrepute, or excite against them the hatred of the people of the United States. The John Adams administration (1797–1801) used the act to prosecute supporters of Jefferson, including pro-Jefferson newspaper editors and a Jeffersonian Republican congressman.

The Sedition Act was of great significance, because it curtailed the First Amendment right to criticize the president and Congress and suppressed legitimate criticism of government policy and government officials. Indeed, the act was specifically intended to prevent public criticism of the Federalist Congress and the Federalist president John Adams by supporters of Thomas Jefferson and of the Republican Party.

Context

The Alien and Sedition Acts were passed in 1798, only seven years after the 1791 ratification of the first ten amendments to the Constitution, the Bill of Rights. The First Amendment provides that Congress will not pass any law that curtails the freedom of speech or of the press. The due process clause of the Fifth Amendment provides that no person shall be deprived of life, liberty, or property without the due process of law. The Bill of Rights also includes guarantees for those accused of crimes, including a jury trial, a grand jury indictment, a copy of the charge against them, and the right to confront witnesses against them.

The end of the eighteenth century was a time of crisis. The French Revolution occurred in 1789, and soon the French king and queen became virtual prisoners of the revolutionary government. In 1791 the Austrian and Prussian kings demanded that the revolutionary French government liberate the French monarchs and warned of intervention by other European powers if the monarchs were harmed. Faced with these threats, the revolutionary French government beheaded the king and queen and launched a preventive war that engulfed the Continent in conflict. Eventually, the revolutionary French armies managed to dominate much of Europe.

During the American Revolution, the French monarch had signed a treaty of alliance with the United States. Although the French had beheaded the king and queen in their own revolution, French leaders continued to believe that the United States was bound to France by the treaty.

Time Line

1775

■ **April 19**
Battle of Lexington signals the beginning of the American Revolution.

1776

■ **July 4**
Second Continental Congress approves the Declaration of Independence, which asserts that government derives its just powers from the consent of the governed.

1787

■ **September 17**
Thirty-nine of the delegates at the Constitutional Convention endorse the proposed Constitution, which the Continental Congress subsequently submits to the states. A major objection to the Constitution is the lack of a bill of rights; the Constitution is ratified in 1788.

1789

■ **July 14**
French citizens storm the Bastille prison, effectively commencing the French Revolution.

■ **September 25**
Congress submits amendments to the Constitution.

1791

■ **December 15**
The required number of states ratify the first ten amendments, known as the Bill of Rights. Among these amendments' provisions are freedom of speech and of the press and due process of law for those accused of crimes.

1796

■ **February 29**
President Washington declares the Jay Treaty in effect, establishing commercial relations with Great Britain.

■ **July 2**
France announces that it will capture and search all ships of neutral nations bound for Great Britain. An undeclared naval war between the United States and France follows.

The United States, however, attempted to remain neutral when international hostilities broke out and to trade with all the warring parties, including the British; the United States even signed a commercial treaty with Great Britain. The French responded by attacking American ships bound for England, ostensibly to deny England supplies during the war. An undeclared naval war thus broke out between the United States and France.

When the Alien and Sedition Acts were passed, two contending American political parties were emerging. One, the Federalist Party, controlled Congress and the presidency in the person of John Adams. The Republican Party coalesced around Vice President Thomas Jefferson and James Madison. Jefferson, who was not protected by the Sedition Act, was widely expected to be Adams's opponent in the presidential election of 1800. Indeed, Jefferson ran against Adams that year.

Although the Constitution, which had been adopted after spirited debate, was widely accepted, many Federalists believed that an opposition political party was not legitimate. Federalists favored rule by an elite of the wealthy and talented, and they distrusted appeals to the masses. Federalists generally opposed Republican efforts to expand the right to vote to more male citizens. John Adams and Alexander Hamilton, two Federalist leaders, had initially feared that the American form of government established by the Constitution was excessively democratic. While both said that they were willing to give the experiment a chance, each had favored a more "balanced" constitution with fewer democratic elements. During the Constitutional Convention, Hamilton had favored a president and a senate elected for life, and by 1790 Adams thought that a hereditary president and senate would eventually be required.

On the other hand, at least some Jeffersonians found the new government insufficiently democratic. In addition, the Jeffersonians had generally supported the French Revolution after the Federalists turned against it. Leading Federalists asserted that Republicans and their allies—whom they often labeled "Jacobins," after a French Revolutionary group—were subversive enemies of the American government. The Federalists feared or said they feared that Republicans and aliens were planning to rebel against the government of the United States. Republicans, in turn, labeled Federalists as monarchists who were too willing to change the government in an aristocratic direction.

Although Republican support for the French Revolution largely disappeared after the commencement of the naval war, Republicans strongly wished to avoid all-out war with France. They also feared, with justification, that troops being raised would be used for domestic political purposes. George Washington, who was placed in charge of the new U.S. Army, had cautioned subordinates against commissioning any "professed democrats" as officers (Curtis, pp. 62–63).

At the time, many of the nation's new immigrants, including the Irish and some of the French, were anti-British and favored greater democracy. They tended to support the Jeffersonian Republican Party. Thus, the Federalists had, in addition to their expressed broader fears of subversion and revolution, partisan reasons to target immigrants. Earlier in 1798, the Federalist-controlled Congress had passed a law extending the time to become a U.S. citizen from five to fourteen years. The ensuing Alien Acts directly addressed Federalist concerns about immigrants' potential roles in American political matters. Some of the more extreme Federalists favored denying naturalized citizens the right to hold office or to vote.

The Sedition Act, in turn, was designed to protect the Federalist Congress and president from "false" and "malicious" utterances designed to bring them into contempt or disrepute. Notably, it did not protect Vice President Thomas Jefferson or individual Republican congressmen from similar "false" and "malicious" utterances. The Federalist Party used the act to prosecute supporters of Jefferson, Republican journalists, a Republican congressman, and others for criticisms of President Adams.

The Republicans criticized the Sedition Act as abridging the freedoms of speech and press guaranteed by the First Amendment. In addition, they charged that it went beyond the power delegated to the national government. Republicans insisted that the act was a politically motivated measure designed to hobble the Republican Party and to keep the Federalists in power. The Federalists defended the constitutionality of the act, insisting that the federal government had the right and power to protect itself against revolution; it therefore also needed to have the power to suppress speech or press that would tend to bring the government into disrepute and therefore encourage revolt.

Scholars have debated whether the freedoms of speech and press protected by the First Amendment were originally designed to give broad protection—against the federal government—to the discussion of public affairs. Whatever the legal understanding, the American press had often exercised a freedom of speech far broader than what would be allowed under the law punishing seditious libel. This was so both before and after the American Revolution, although during the war, Patriots supported the suppression of Tory speech.

Before the American Revolution, some British writers, such as James Burgh and the authors of *Cato's Letters*, had made arguments for broadly protecting speech and press about governmental affairs. Others had said and done things inconsistent with that view. In the 1735 trial of the printer John Peter Zenger, Zenger's lawyer had argued that "freeborn Englishmen" had a right to criticize public officials if the charges were true. The jury, ignoring a hanging charge from the judge, acquitted. Zenger's case was widely discussed both in the colonies and in England.

About the Author

Since the Alien and Sedition Acts were acts of Congress (which require the signature of the president to be effective), Congress was technically the author of the acts. In fact, the acts were passed by a closely divided Congress, with the nearly unanimous support of Federalist congress-

Time Line

1796

- **December 7**
John Adams defeats Thomas Jefferson by a 71–68 electoral vote, becoming the second president of the United States.

1798

- **June 18**
The Federalist Congress passes the Naturalization Act, extending the time required for immigrants to become citizens from five to fourteen years.

- **June 25**
Congress passes the Act Concerning Aliens.

- **July 6**
Congress passes the Act Respecting Alien Enemies.

- **July 14**
A closely divided Congress passes the Act for the Punishment of Certain Crimes against the United States, known as the Sedition Act, banning "false" and "malicious" criticisms of the president or Congress. Prosecutions of leading Republican editors and of some Republican politicians follow, with federal judges upholding the convictions.

1800

- Jefferson is elected president, defeating Adams. The Sedition Act expires, and Jefferson pardons all convicted under the act.

1868

- **July 28**
Secretary of State William Seward issues a proclamation recognizing the ratification of the Fourteenth Amendment to the Constitution. The Supreme Court later holds that the amendment requires states to observe the rights and immunities set out in the First Amendment.

1964

- **March 9**
In the case of *New York Times Co. v. Sullivan*, the Supreme Court establishes a rule broadly protecting critics of government and of government officials, with the opinion holding that the Sedition Act of 1798 was unconstitutional.

www.milestonedocuments.com

men and senators and despite the solid opposition of supporters of Jefferson. As such, the Federalists in Congress can reasonably be viewed as the authors of the acts. Some leading proponents of the need for alien and sedition laws were Representatives Harrison Gray Otis of Massachusetts, Robert Goodloe Harper of South Carolina, and John Allen of Connecticut. Allen specifically favored a bill to suppress Jeffersonian newspapers and was one of the earliest advocates of a bill targeting aliens who were not citizens of a foreign power. Harper described Republicans as pro-French traitors, and Otis accused Republicans of sedition.

Explanation and Analysis of the Document

◆ An Act Concerning Aliens

This act, also known as the Alien Friends Act, dealt with all aliens resident in the United States. Most had come to the nation hoping to make it their home. The act had a sunset provision: It would continue in force for only two years after June 25, 1798, the date it was passed.

The text of the Alien Friends Act gives the president broad power over aliens. He is enabled to order the removal of such aliens "as he shall judge dangerous to the peace and safety of the United States, or shall have reasonable grounds to suspect are concerned in any treasonable or secret machinations against the government." Aliens who fail to depart from the nation when ordered or who fail to abide by the terms of a license by which the president allows them to remain could be imprisoned for three years and could never thereafter become citizens. The act allows aliens who are ordered to depart to appear before persons selected by the president to prove that no danger would arise if they were permitted to remain. If the alien is able to prove harmlessness, he could be granted a license to remain for such time and under such terms as the president thinks proper. The alien who proves his harmlessness could also be required to post a bond to guarantee good behavior and against violation of the license. He could also be required to provide sureties, or persons who would guarantee his bond and his good behavior.

The act is sensitive to the property rights of aliens required to leave the country. They could take with them that part of their "goods" and "chattels"—their personal property—as they "may find convenient." The property they are unable to take with them remains "subject to [their] order and disposal."

Republicans attacked the Alien Friends Act as unconstitutional and unwise. In the congressional debates on the act, they denied that the plots to which the Federalists referred existed and demanded proof of the plots. Federalists, however, did not provide proof. The Republican representative Edward Livingston of New York complained that the act departed from basic rules for a free government. In a free government, he insisted, "Legislative power prescribes the rule of action; the Judiciary applies that general rule to particular cases, and it is the province of the Executive to see that laws are carried into full effect" (U.S. Congress, vol. 8, p. 2008). By the terms of the Alien Friends Act, however, the president would set the rule, would see that it was carried out, and would judge its application to particular cases.

Livingston treated the act as establishing a new and extremely vague crime. "The crime is 'exciting the suspicions of the President,' but no man can tell what conduct will avoid that suspicion—a careless word, perhaps misrepresented, or never spoken may be sufficient evidence; a look may destroy; and idle gesture may insure punishment; no innocence … can protect [him]" (U.S. Congress, vol. 8, p. 2008). Meanwhile, all the safeguards of the Bill of Rights were removed: "The grand inquest is removed; the trial by jury is abolished; the 'public trial' required by the Constitution is changed into a secret … tribunal; instead of being 'confronted with his accusers,' [the targeted alien] is kept alike ignorant of their names and their existence" (U.S. Congress, vol. 8, p. 2010).

Finally, Livingston savaged the provision allowing the alien to prove that he was not properly suspected. It was, he noted, a

> miserable mockery of justice. Appoint an arbitrary Judge armed with Legislative and Executive powers.… Let him condemn the unheard, unaccused object of his suspicion; then to cover the injustice of the scene, gravely tell him, you ought not to complain—you need only disprove facts that you have never heard—remove suspicions that have never been communicated to you. (U.S. Congress, vol. 8, p. 2008)

Representative Otis, a Federalist, answered Livingston. He asserted that Livingston's mistake was his "very erroneous hypothesis" that "aliens are parties to our Constitution, that it was made for their benefit as well as our own, and that they may claim equal rights and privileges with our own citizens" (U.S. Congress, vol. 8, p. 2018). Otis asserted that jury trial, due process, and other guarantees constitutionally protected those only who were concerned in making that compact—the people of the United States. These protections were extended to aliens in criminal cases as a matter of grace and humanity but not as a matter of constitutional right. Otis and other Federalists maintained that under international law, aliens had no right to remain in the country. As a result, they could be expelled without the procedural safeguards ordinarily required to protect liberty or property. In any case, guarantees of basic rights did not extend to the decision to expel foreigners from the nation. Proceedings under the Alien Acts were not criminal prosecutions; all nations, Otis said, retained broad powers over aliens, including the power to exclude and expel.

Federalist Representative Harper, of South Carolina, also supported the measure. He said that it was needed because "there existed a domestic … conspiracy, a faction leagued with a foreign Power to effect a revolution or a subjugation of this country, by the arms of that foreign Power" (U.S. Congress, vol. 8, p. 2024). He said it was true that citizens "might be more dangerous to the peace and safety of the country than aliens, because they cannot so easily be restricted" (U.S. Congress, vol. 8, p. 2025). His answer to that problem was to pass a sedition act.

◆ An Act Respecting Alien Enemies

The Alien Enemies Act is held to apply in states of "declared war between the United States and any foreign nation or government, or [when] any invasion or predatory incursion" is perpetrated or threatened. When the president proclaims such an event, all male citizens or residents of the hostile power who are fourteen years of age or older would be liable to be "apprehended, restrained, secured and removed." The president is given broad power to determine the "manner and degree of the restraint" to be used in apprehension and the security required for those allowed to remain, as well as to "provide for the removal of those, who, not being permitted to reside within the United States, shall" refuse to depart voluntarily. The act makes it the duty of the federal and state courts to enforce the act against aliens who resided in their jurisdictions and who remained "at large" contrary to regulations set by the president.

◆ An Act for the Punishment of Certain Crimes against the United States

Violators of the Sedition Act of 1798 could be given a maximum prison sentence of two years and a one-thousand-dollar fine. The act has three sections. The first section punishes forcible resistance to the laws of the United States or conspiracies to resist the law. This section was not controversial. The second section makes it a crime for any person to write, utter, or publish any false, scandalous, and malicious writing against the government of the United States, either house of Congress, or the president of the United States with the intent (among others) to defame them, bring them into contempt or disrepute, or excite against them the hatred of the people of the United States. The third section makes truth a defense and allows the jury hearing a case to decide if all the elements of the crime were proved.

In making truth a defense and allowing the jury to decide if all elements of the crime were met, the Sedition Act seemed to be a substantial improvement over the English common law of seditious libel. By common law in England, seditious libel was the crime of criticizing the government or government officials. Truth was no defense in seditious libel cases. The greater the truth, as one judge explained, the greater the libel—a rule that essentially limited the jury to deciding whether the defendant had indeed published the alleged libel. The judge, who had been appointed by the Crown, would decide if the publication was in fact seditious libel. In the American colonies before the Revolution, judges held office at the pleasure of the king, another reason they would likely favor the prosecution in trials for seditious libel.

Under the new U.S. Constitution, judges served during "good behavior"—basically life tenure. All of the federal judges in the young nation had been appointed by the Federalist presidents Washington and Adams. Prosecuting U.S. attorneys, in turn, were all appointed or retained by Adams. Federalist prosecutors brought actions against Republican newspaper editors and politicians, juries convicted, and the Federalist judges upheld the convictions.

John Adams (Library of Congress)

While the Sedition Act on its face seemed only to cover "false" criticisms of the president or the Federalist Congress, as applied it extended to "false" opinions as well as to false facts. As one critic noted, "false" praise of the president or of Congress was not a crime. More significantly, "false" and malicious criticism of Thomas Jefferson—Adams's likely opponent in the presidential election of 1800—was not prohibited. Nor was it a crime to engage in false and malicious criticism of the Republican minority in Congress. Finally, the act had a sunset provision: It would expire at the end of John Adams's term of office.

Audience

The audience for the Alien Acts was the people of the United States. By passing the acts and making the arguments for them, the Federalists reinforced their claim that dangerous revolutionary conspiracies threatened the United States. The audience also included aliens, many of whom were supporters of the Jeffersonian Republicans. The message to such noncitizens was that they stayed in the United States at the sufferance of the Federalist president, should avoid pro-Jefferson political activity, and, in any case, were liable to be expelled.

The audience for the Sedition Act was also the people of the United States. The prosecutions launched under the

www.milestonedocuments.com

Essential Quotes

"It shall be lawful for the President of the United States at any time during the continuance of this act, to order all such aliens as he shall judge dangerous to the peace and safety of the United States, or shall have reasonable grounds to suspect are concerned in any treasonable or secret machinations against the government thereof, to depart out of the territory of the United States."

(Act Concerning Aliens, Section 1)

"Whenever there shall be a declared war between the United States and any foreign nation or government, or any invasion or predatory incursion shall be perpetrated, attempted, or threatened against the territory of the United States, by any foreign nation or government, and the President of the United States shall make public proclamation of the event, all natives, citizens, denizens, or subjects of the hostile nation or government, being males of the age of fourteen years and upwards, who shall be within the United States, and not actually naturalized, shall be liable to be apprehended, restrained, secured and removed, as alien enemies."

(Act Respecting Alien Enemies, Section 1)

"If any person shall write, print, utter or publish … any false, scandalous and malicious writing or writings against the government of the United States, or either house of the Congress of the United States, or the President of the United States, with intent to defame the said government, or either house of the said Congress, or the said President, … then such person, being thereof convicted before any court of the United States having jurisdiction thereof, shall be punished by a fine not exceeding two thousand dollars, and by imprisonment not exceeding two years."

(An Act for the Punishment of Certain Crimes against the United States, Section 2)

act were designed to punish Republicans and others for their criticisms of the Federalist president and of the Federalist-controlled Congress and to deter further "false" criticisms. Moreover, the act served to brand much of the opposition as illegitimate in the eyes of the people. As such, it was aimed to persuade politically active citizens of the nefarious nature of the administration's critics. The intended audience also specifically included Republican newspaper editors and politicians who were being warned in no uncertain terms that "false" and "malicious" criticisms of the president and the Federalist Congress would no longer be tolerated. Finally, committed Federalists were also part of the audience for the act; it served to energize them in their efforts to combat Republicans.

Impact

The historian James Morton Smith reports that the Adams administration did not deport a single person under the Aliens Friends Act, an act that had originally been justified as an essential defense against dangerous aliens. According to Smith, John Adams gave the law a stricter interpretation than that demanded by extreme Federalists. Adams did approve the use of the act against several targets, but for various reasons enforcement was not successful. For example, an Irish pro-Jefferson newspaper editor agreed to leave the country to avoid expulsion under the act, but the editor went into hiding and evaded authorities until the act expired. A second reason for the lack of expulsions was that a number of French aliens actually fled the United States before the act went into effect.

The Supreme Court has since held that aliens within the territory of the United States are entitled to the protections of the Bill of Rights before they can be convicted of a crime. Aliens are also covered by the Fourteenth Amendment's guarantee that no person within the jurisdiction of a state may be deprived of the equal protection of the laws. Still, as the professor Gerald L. Newman has written, "Deportation remains an anomalous qualification to the general recognition of aliens' constitutional rights within United States territory" (p. 62).

The Sedition Act of 1798 had an immense impact. It sparked the first comprehensive debate in American history on the meaning of the First Amendment and of free speech and press. Opponents of the act charged that it violated the Constitution because it contravened the First Amendment: Congress shall make no law abridging freedom of speech and press. They also argued that it violated the Constitution because that document—even before the addition of the First Amendment—gives the federal government no delegated power over the press. According to the critics, to the extent that such power existed, it was held by the states. States were not required to respect the rights of free speech and press set out in the Bill of Rights for some time—not until the Supreme Court belatedly held in the 1930s that the Fourteenth Amendment, ratified in 1868, indeed required the states to obey the commands of the First Amendment. Once states were required to respect the national liberties of speech and press, the debate over the Sedition Act became more important in shaping the law. At that point, the national right of free speech affected laws in every state.

Supporters of the Sedition Act denied that it violated the rights of free speech and press set out in the First Amendment. In fact, some of the act's supporters argued that it was more protective of freedom of speech and press than the Constitution required, because it made truth a defense. Federalist defenders of the act argued that since the act punished only malicious falsehood, it did not abridge the freedom of the press. They insisted that freedom of the press had a technical meaning based on English law. According to this technical understanding, a newspaper could not be required to get approval from a government censor before publishing an article, but the writer and editor could be punished afterward if the article was seditious.

Federalists further insisted that freedom of the press was not intended to protect lying. Finally, Federalist supporters argued that false criticisms of the president and of Congress would have the tendency in the long run to cause disaffection, lawlessness, and revolt. Since the federal government had the power to put down lawlessness and revolution, it must also have the power to prevent speech that would tend to cause that result.

Republicans rejected the Federalist claims. They noted that the act covered not only false facts but also "false" opinions. Republicans considered the Sedition Act a partisan measure that violated the Constitution and undermined government by the people. How, the Republican congressman Albert Gallatin asked, could one prove the truth of the opinion that the act was despotic? The judgment on this question, he said, would depend on the political predilections of prosecutors, judges, and juries.

As the Republicans saw it, the American government was ultimately to be controlled by the "people." The Sedition Act's threat of fine and imprisonment would have the effect of silencing or muting opposition. The result would be that the people of the nation would hear only one side of the political debate and would be deprived of the information that they needed to make electoral choices. The speech and debate clause of the Constitution gave members of Congress absolute immunity from criminal prosecution for things said in debate in Congress. Similarly, some argued, representative government required that a similar immunity be given to the people when they discussed public affairs. At any rate, critics of the Sedition Act insisted on the right of U.S. citizens to have broad freedom to discuss public measures and the conduct of public persons as it related to government.

Republicans repudiated the claim that English law was the model to be followed. James Madison wrote that in Britain, sovereignty (ultimate political authority) resided in the king in Parliament, a body composed of a House of Commons and a hereditary House of Lords. In America, sovereignty resided in the people, who exercised it through their elective franchise. Free speech and press were essential so that U.S. citizens could intelligently exercise their right to vote. Several Republicans also rejected the notion that the bad tendency claim—the claim that speech or press causing people to be disaffected from the government might therefore cause them to rebel—justified the suppression of free speech. Critics of the Sedition Act insisted on distinguishing between speech critical of government, which was protected, and lawless acts, which were not.

In their attacks on the Sedition Act, a number of critics made broad democratic arguments for free speech and press that logically applied to both the states and the federal government. On at least one occasion, these arguments were used against a state prosecution: The state of Massachusetts prosecuted two brothers who ran a Republican newspaper and who were charged with violating the Massachusetts common law of seditious libel. The lawyer for the brother who was tried (and convicted) made many of the democratic free speech and press arguments that critics of the Sedition Act had made. However, since at the

www.milestonedocuments.com

time the guarantees of the First Amendment did not limit state prosecutions, he based his arguments on protections he claimed under the laws and constitution of Massachusetts. James Madison also seems to have assumed that democratic principles and ideas of free speech and press should limit state power as well as federal power.

Some Republicans held that the problem with the Sedition Act's ban on malicious "falsehood" aimed at government officials was a Federalism problem, not a free speech problem. According to Thomas Jefferson, the problem with the act was that it had been passed by the federal government, which lacked any delegated power over the press. In addition, according to Jefferson, the act flouted the prohibitions contained in the First Amendment. Jefferson believed, however, that states could still bring seditious libel prosecutions. In fact, when Jefferson later served as president, he wrote to the governor of Pennsylvania to urge a few state prosecutions of his critics, but the suggestion seems to have gone nowhere.

After the election of 1800, the Sedition Act expired. President Jefferson pardoned those convicted under the act. Gradually, seditious libel prosecutions—prosecutions aimed at critics of actions of the government and of the way public officials did their job—tended to die out.

In the twentieth century, in the case of *New York Times Co. v. Sullivan* (1964), the Supreme Court ruled that public officials can collect damages for false statements about their conduct of governmental affairs only if the statements were either intentionally false or reckless. In the *Sullivan* case, the Court treated the Sedition Act as an unconstitutional violation of the First Amendment. As the Court saw it, the act was a negative precedent: it was an example of an abuse to be avoided. In support of its conclusions, the Court cited arguments about the nature of free speech and press in a representative government that had been made by James Madison and other Republican critics of the Sedition Act.

According to the Supreme Court's current interpretation of the First Amendment, an act outlawing even false criticisms of one political group or its members but allowing false criticisms of that group's opponents would be a flagrant violation of the First Amendment. The law would be seen as "viewpoint discrimination," meaning that it punishes one viewpoint while allowing the opposing one to go unpunished.

Related Documents

Blackstone, William. *Commentaries on the Laws of England*, 3rd ed. 4 vols. Dublin: John Exshaw, et al., 1769. Herein, Sir William Blackstone sets out the restrictive English view of freedom of the press, a view cited and embraced by leading Federalists.

Burgh, James. *Political Disquisitions*. 3 vols. New York: Da Capo Press, 1971. Burgh defends broad protections for speech and press critical of government and its officials. His view was contrary to that followed by the British courts but, like *Cato's Letters*, shows a dissenting tradition supporting broad protection for critical speech and press.

"Declaration of Independence." National Archives "Charters of Freedom" Web site. http://www.archives.gov/national-archives-experi ence /charters/declaration_transcript.html. Accessed on December 14, 2007. This founding document of the American nation strongly supports the idea that "the people" are the ultimate source of political authority, famously declaring that "all Men are created equal, that they are endowed by their Creator with certain unalienable Rights, that among these are Life, Liberty, and the pursuit of Happiness." Interpretations of the idea of popular sovereignty were at the heart of the debate over the Sedition Act.

Iredell, James. "A Charge Delivered to the Grand Jury of the U. States." *Aurora General Advertiser*, May 23, 28, and 30, 1799. This charge to a grand jury delivered by the Supreme Court justice James Iredell contains a defense of the Sedition Act, as reprinted in the *Aurora*, the Jeffersonian paper.

Madison, James. *Writings*, ed. Jack N. Rakove. New York: Library of America, 1999. Madison's *Virginia Report of 1799–1800*, on the Alien and Sedition Acts, contains his arguments against the Sedition Act.

New York Times Co. v. Sullivan, 376 U.S. 254 (1964). The *New York Times* case sets out the modern constitutional law related to seditious libel and libel of public officials.

Trenchard, John, and Thomas Gordon. *Cato's Letters: Essays on Liberty, Civil and Religious, and Other Important Subjects*. 1755. Reprint. New York: Da Capo Press, 1971. These letters contain early praise for freedom of speech and of the press as needed for citizens to keep a watchful eye on government; they are in considerable tension with the concept of seditious libel. The essays were widely reprinted in the American colonies before the Revolution.

United States v. Cooper, 25 Fed.Cas. 631 (C.C.D.Pa. 1800). This case reports the trial of Thomas Cooper, an attorney and Republican writer, for his criticisms of President Adams.

United States v. Lyon, 15 Fed.Cas. 1183 (C.C.D.Vt. 1798). This case reports the trial of Matthew Lyon, a Republican congressman who was convicted of violating the Sedition Act because of his criticisms of President Adams.

U.S. Congress. *Annals of the Congress of the United States, 1798–1824*. 42 vols. Washington, D.C.: Gales and Seaton, 1834–1856. The records from 1798 and 1799 include the debates over the Sedition Act and the effort to repeal it in the House of Representatives; Senate debates were not reported at the time. The *Annals of Congress* for 1800 contain House debates on reenacting the Sedition Act.

Wortman, Tunis. *A Treatise Concerning Political Enquiry and the Liberty of the Press*. New York: George Forman, 1800. Wortman argues that since the people have the ultimate right even to dissolve their constitution and replace it with another, they and each individual must have the right of freedom to discuss political matters and public or political transactions.

Bibliography

■ Articles

Berns, Walter. "Freedom of the Press and the Alien and Sedition Laws: A Reappraisal." *Supreme Court Review* 1970 (1970): 109–159.

Chesney, Robert. "Democratic-Republican Societies, Subversion, and the Limits of Legitimate Political Dissent in the Early Republic." *North Carolina Law Review* 82 (2004): 1525–1579.

Herbeck, Dale A. "Justice Brennan's Beautiful Lie: *New York Times v. Sullivan.*" *Free Speech Yearbook* 28 (1990): 37–57.

Kalven, Harry, Jr. "The New York Times Case: A Note on 'The Central Meaning of the First Amendment.'" *Supreme Court Review* 1964 (1964): 191–221.

Rabban, David. "The Ahistorical Historian: Leonard Levy on Freedom of Expression in Early American History." *Stanford Law Review* 37, no. 3 (February 1985): 795–856.

Smith, Stephen. "The Origins of the Free Speech Clause." *Free Speech Yearbook* 29 (1991): 48–82.

■ Books

Curtis, Michael Kent. *Free Speech, "The People's Darling Privilege": Struggles for Freedom of Expression in American History*. Durham, N.C.: Duke University Press, 2000.

Levy, Leonard W. *Emergence of a Free Press*. New York: Oxford University Press, 1985.

Newman, Gerald L. *Strangers to the Constitution: Immigrants, Borders, and Fundamental Law*. Princeton, N.J.: Princeton University Press, 1996.

Rosenberg, Norman L. *Protecting the Best Men: An Interpretative History of the Law of Libel*. Chapel Hill: University of North Carolina Press, 1986.

Rosenfeld, Richard N. *American Aurora—A Democratic-Republican Returns: The Suppressed History of Our Nation's Beginnings and the Heroic Newspaper That Tried to Report It*. New York: St. Martin's Press, 1997.

Smith, James Morton. *Freedom's Fetters: The Alien and Sedition Laws and American Civil Liberties*. Ithaca, N.Y.: Cornell University Press, 1956.

■ Web Sites

"An Act in Addition to the Act, Entitled 'An Act for the Punishment of Certain Crimes against the United States.'" The Avalon Project at Yale Law School Web site.
http://www.yale.edu/lawweb/avalon/statutes/sedact.htm. Accessed on November 23, 2007.

"Annals of Congress." Library of Congress Web site.
http://memory.loc.gov/ammem/amlaw/lwac.html. Accessed on November 23, 2007.

"Cato's Letters No. 15: Of Freedom of Speech." University of Arkansas Web site.
http://www.uark.edu/depts/comminfo/cambridge/cato15.html. Accessed on November 23, 2007.

—By Michael Kent Curtis

www.milestonedocuments.com

Questions for Further Study

1. Should Congress have passed the Alien Friends Act? Why or why not?

2. Should aliens lawfully present in the United States be entitled to constitutional protections, such as those in the Bill of Rights? Why or why not?

3. Which side do you think had the better argument about the Alien Friends Act? Explain the basis for your opinion.

4. Compare and contrast the Sedition Act with the First Amendment to the U.S. Constitution.

5. Are references to "freedom of speech or of the press" in the First Amendment meant to protect all speech and press, no matter what is said or written? If not, how should a court or a citizen decide what speech or press is protected by the "freedom of speech and of the press" and what is unprotected?

6. Should false speech about the government or government officials be protected speech? Should it be protected always, sometimes, or never? What should the criteria be for deciding when it should be protected?

7. Does the idea that the government of the United States is based on the sovereignty of the people (that the people are the ultimate boss) contribute to an understanding of how broad the protection should be for freedom of speech and press? Why or why not?

8. If the Sedition Act was unconstitutional, why did courts at the time not hold it to be unconstitutional?

9. Should Congress have passed the Sedition Act? Why or why not?

Glossary

alien	a resident or citizen of a foreign nation
goods and chattels	personal property as distinguished from land and typically from the buildings on the land
sedition	the causing of resistance to or revolt against the government

Document Text

Alien and Sedition Acts

FIFTH CONGRESS OF THE UNITED STATES:

At the Second Session,

Begun and held at the city of Philadelphia, in the state of Pennsylvania, on Monday, the thirteenth of November, one thousand seven hundred and ninety-seven.

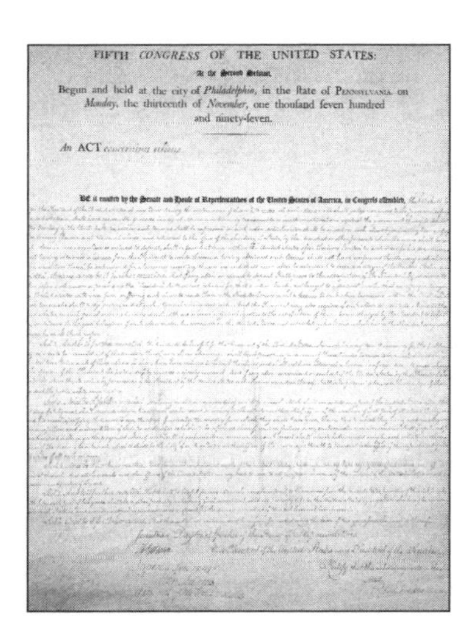

FIFTH CONGRESS OF THE UNITED STATES:

Begun and held at the city of Philadelphia, in the state of Pennsylvania, on Monday, the thirteenth of November, one thousand seven hundred and ninety-seven.

An ACT concerning aliens.

An Act Concerning Aliens

SECTION 1. Be it enacted by the Senate and the House of Representatives of the United States of America in Congress assembled, That it shall be lawful for the President of the United States at any time during the continuance of this act, to order all such aliens as he shall judge dangerous to the peace and safety of the United States, or shall have reasonable grounds to suspect are concerned in any treasonable or secret machinations against the government thereof, to depart out of the territory of the United Slates, within such time as shall be expressed in such order, which order shall be served on such alien by delivering him a copy thereof, or leaving the same at his usual abode, and returned to the office of the Secretary of State, by the marshal or other person to whom the same shall be directed. And in case any alien, so ordered to depart, shall be found at large within the United States after the time limited in such order for his departure, and not having obtained a license from the President to reside therein, or having obtained such license shall not have conformed thereto, every such alien shall, on conviction thereof, be imprisoned for a term not exceeding three years, and shall never after be admitted to become a citizen of the United States. Provided always, and be it further enacted, that if any alien so ordered to depart shall prove to the satisfaction of the President, by evidence to be taken before such person or persons as the President shall direct, who are for that purpose hereby authorized to administer oaths, that no injury or danger to the United Slates will arise from suffering such alien to reside therein, the President may grant a license to such alien to remain within the United States for such time as he shall judge proper, and at such place as he may designate. And the President may also require of such alien to enter into a bond to the United States, in such penal sum as he may direct, with one or more sufficient sureties to the satisfaction of the person authorized by the President to take the same, conditioned for the good behavior of such alien during his residence in the United States, and not violating his license, which license the President may revoke, whenever he shall think proper.

SEC. 2. And be it further enacted, That it shall be lawful for the President of the United States, whenever he may deem it necessary for the public safety, to order to be removed out of the territory thereof, any alien who mayor shall be in prison in pursuance of this act; and to cause to be arrested and sent out of the United States such of those aliens as shall have been ordered to depart therefrom and shall not have obtained a license as aforesaid, in all cases where, in the opinion of the President, the public safety requires a speedy removal. And if any alien so removed or sent out of the United Slates by the President shall voluntarily return thereto, unless by permission of the President of the United States, such alien on conviction thereof, shall be imprisoned so long as, in the opinion of the President, the public safety may require.

SEC. 3. And be it further enacted, That every master or commander of any ship or vessel which shall come into any port of the United States after the first day of July next, shall immediately on his arrival make report in writing to the collector or other chief officer of the customs of such port, of all aliens, if any, on board his vessel, specifying their names, age, the place of nativity, the country from which they shall have come, the nation to which they belong and owe allegiance, their occupation and a description of their persons, as far as he shall be

www.milestonedocuments.com

informed thereof, and on failure, every such master and commander shall forfeit and pay three hundred dollars, for the payment whereof on default of such master or commander, such vessel shall also be holden, and may by such collector or other officer of the customs be detained. And it shall be the duty of such collector or other officer of the customs, forthwith to transmit to the office of the department of state true copies of all such returns.

SEC. 4. And be it further enacted, That the circuit and district courts of the United States, shall respectively have cognizance of all crimes and offences against this act. And all marshals and other officers of the United States are required to execute all precepts and orders of the President of the United States issued in pursuance or by virtue of this act.

SEC. 5. And be it further enacted, That it shall be lawful for any alien who may be ordered to be removed from the United States, by virtue of this act, to take with him such part of his goods, chattels, or other property, as he may find convenient; and all property left in the United States by any alien, who may be removed, as aforesaid, shall be, and remain subject to his order and disposal, in the same manner as if this act had not been passed.

SEC. 6. And be it further enacted, That this act shall continue and be in force for and during the term of two years from the passing thereof.

Jonathan Dayton, Speaker of the House of Representatives.

TH. Jefferson, Vice President of the United States and President of the Senate.

I Certify that this Act did originate in the Senate.

Attest, Sam. A. Otis, Secretary

APPROVED, June 25, 1798.

John Adams

President of the United States.

An Act Respecting Alien Enemies

SECTION 1. Be it enacted by the Senate and House of Representatives of the United States of America in Congress assembled, That whenever there shall be a declared war between the United States and any foreign nation or government, or any invasion or predatory incursion shall be perpetrated, attempted, or threatened against the territory of the United States, by any foreign nation or government, and the President of the United States shall make public proclamation of the event, all natives, citizens, denizens, or subjects of the hostile nation or government, being males of the age of fourteen years and upwards, who shall be within the United States, and not actually naturalized, shall be liable to be apprehended, restrained, secured and removed, as alien enemies. And the President of the United States shall be, and he is hereby authorized, in any event, as aforesaid, by his proclamation thereof, or other public act, to direct the conduct to be observed, on the part of the United States, towards the aliens who shall become liable, as aforesaid; the manner and degree of the restraint to which they shall be subject, and in what cases, and upon what security their residence shall be permitted, and to provide for the removal of those, who, not being permitted to reside within the United States, shall refuse or neglect to depart therefrom; and to establish any other regulations which shall be found necessary in the premises and for the public safety: Provided, that aliens resident within the United States, who shall become liable as enemies, in the manner aforesaid, and who shall not be chargeable with actual hostility, or other crime against the public safety, shall be allowed, for the recovery, disposal, and removal of their goods and effects, and for their departure, the full time which is, or shall be stipulated by any treaty, where any shall have been between the United States, and the hostile nation or government, of which they shall be natives, citizens, denizens or subjects: and where no such treaty shall have existed, the President of the United States may ascertain and declare such reasonable time as may be consistent with the public safety, and according to the dictates of humanity and national hospitality.

SEC. 2. And be it further enacted, That after any proclamation shall be made as aforesaid, it shall be the duty of the several courts of the United States, and of each state, having criminal jurisdiction, and of the several judges and justices of the courts of the United States, and they shall be, and are hereby respectively, authorized upon complaint, against any alien or alien enemies, as aforesaid, who shall be resident and at large within such jurisdiction or district, to the danger of the public peace or safety, and contrary to the tenor or intent of such proclamation, or other regulations which the President of the United States shall and may establish in the premises, to cause such alien or aliens to be duly apprehended and convened before such court, judge or justice; and after a full examination and hearing on such complaint, and sufficient cause therefor appearing, shall and may order such alien or aliens to be removed out of the territory of the United States, or to give sureties of their good behaviour, or to be otherwise restrained, conformably to the proclamation or regulations which shall and may be established as aforesaid, and may imprison, or otherwise secure such alien or aliens, until the order which shall and may be made, as aforesaid, shall be performed.

SEC. 3. And be it further enacted, That it shall be the duty of the marshal of the district in which any alien enemy shall be apprehended, who by the President of the United States, or by order of any court, judge or justice, as aforesaid, shall be required to depart, and to be removed, as aforesaid, to provide therefor, and to execute such order, by himself or his deputy, or other discreet person or persons to be employed by him, by causing a removal of such alien out of the territory of the United States; and for such removal the marshal shall have the warrant of the President of the United States, or of the court, judge or justice ordering the same, as the case may be.

APPROVED, July 6, 1798.

FIFTH CONGRESS OF THE UNITED STATES:

At the Second Session,

Begun and held at the city of Philadelphia, in the state of Pennsylvania, on Monday, the thirteenth of November, one thousand seven hundred and ninety-seven.

An Act in Addition to the Act, Entitled "An Act for the Punishment of Certain Crimes Against the United States"

SECTION 1. Be it enacted by the Senate and House of Representatives of the United States of America, in Congress assembled, That if any persons shall unlawfully combine or conspire together, with intent to oppose any measure or measures of the government of the United States, which are or shall be directed by proper authority, or to impede the operation of any law of the United States, or to intimidate or prevent any person holding a place or office in or under the government of the United States, from undertaking, performing or executing his trust or duty, and if any person or persons, with intent as aforesaid, shall counsel, advise or attempt to procure any insurrection, riot, unlawful assembly, or combination, whether such conspiracy, threatening, counsel, advice, or attempt shall have the proposed effect or not, he or they shall be deemed guilty of a high misdemeanor, and on conviction, before any court of the United States having jurisdiction thereof, shall be punished by a fine not exceeding five thousand dollars, and by imprisonment during a term not less than six months nor exceeding five years; and further, at the discretion of the court may be holden to find sureties for his good behaviour in such sum, and for such time, as the said court may direct.

SEC. 2. And be it farther enacted, That if any person shall write, print, utter or publish, or shall cause or procure to be written, printed, uttered or published, or shall knowingly and willingly assist or aid in writing, printing, uttering or publishing any false, scandalous and malicious writing or writings against the government of the United States, or either house of the Congress of the United States, or the President of the United States, with intent to defame the said government, or either house of the said Congress, or the said President, or to bring them, or either of them, into contempt or disrepute; or to excite against them, or either or any of them, the hatred of the good people of the United States, or to stir up sedition within the United States, or to excite any unlawful combinations therein, for opposing or resisting any law of the United States, or any act of the President of the United States, done in pursuance of any such law, or of the powers in him vested by the constitution of the United States, or to resist, oppose, or defeat any such law or act, or to aid, encourage or abet any hostile designs of any foreign nation against United States, their people or government, then such person, being thereof convicted before any court of the United States having jurisdiction thereof, shall be punished by a fine not exceeding two thousand dollars, and by imprisonment not exceeding two years.

SEC. 3. And be it further enacted and declared, That if any person shall be prosecuted under this act, for the writing or publishing any libel aforesaid, it shall be lawful for the defendant, upon the trial of the cause, to give in evidence in his defence, the truth of the matter contained in publication charged as a libel. And the jury who shall try the cause, shall have a right to determine the law and the fact, under the direction of the court, as in other cases.

SEC. 4. And be it further enacted, That this act shall continue and be in force until the third day of March, one thousand eight hundred and one, and no longer: Provided, that the expiration of the act shall not prevent or defeat a prosecution and punishment of any offence against the law, during the time it shall be in force.

Jonathan Dayton, Speaker of the House of Representatives.

www.milestonedocuments.com

Document Text

Theodore Sedgwick, President of the Senate pro tempore.

I Certify that this Act did originate in the Senate.

Attest, Sam. A. Otis, Secretary

APPROVED, July 14, 1798

John Adams

President of the United States.

Friends & fellow citizens

Called upon to undertake the duties of the first Executive office of

I avail myself of the presence of that portion of my fellow citizens which is
-bled to express my grateful thanks for the favor with which they have been pleased to look
to declare a sincere consciousness that the task is above my talents, & that I approach it
& awful presentiments which the greatness of the charge & the weakness of my powers so just
a rising nation, spread over a wide & fruitful land, traversing all the seas with the
-ductions of their industry, engaged in commerce with nations who feel power & f
advancing rapidly to destinies beyond the reach of mortal eye; when I contemplate
-cendent objects, & see the honour, the happiness, & the hopes of this beloved country, co
to the issue & the auspices of this day, I shrink from the contemplation, & humble
before the magnitude of the undertaking. utterly indeed should I despair, did n
-sence of many, whom I here see, remind me, that, in the other high authorities pro
our constitution, I shall find resources of wisdom, of virtue, & of zeal, on which to rely u
difficulties. to you then, gentlemen, who are charged with the sovereign function
-lation, & to those associated with you, I look with encouragement for that guidance
which may enable us to steer with safety the vessel in which we are all embarked,
the conflicting elements of a troubled world.

During the contest of opinion through which we have past, the
of discussions & of exertions has sometimes worn an aspect which might impose o
unused to think freely, & to speak & to write what they think. but this being now
by the voice of the nation, enounced according to the rules of the constitution
of course arrange themselves under the will of the law, & unite in common efforts
all too will bear in mind this sacred principle that the will of the majority is in all c
common good.
that will, to be rightful, must be reasonable; that the minority poss
equal rights, which equal laws must protect, & to violate would be oppression. let
fellow citizens, unite with one heart & one mind, let us restore to social intercourse th
& affection without which liberty, & even life itself, are but dreary things. and let us refle
having banished from our land that religious intolerance under which mankind so long bled
we have yet gained little if we countenance a political intolerance, as despotic, as wicked, &

Thomas Jefferson's draft of his First Inaugural Address (Library of Congress)

Thomas Jefferson's First Inaugural Address

1801

"We are all Republicans, we are all Federalists."

Overview

Thomas Jefferson's First Inaugural Address, given on March 4, 1801, is one of the great documents of democratic government and oratorical rhetoric. After the bitter election campaign of 1800, Vice President Jefferson defeated the Federalist incumbent, President John Adams. Adams peacefully surrendered his authority to his opponent, and Jefferson assumed power pledging there would be no retaliation against his opponents, whether they held political office or not. "We are all Republicans, we are all Federalists," Jefferson asserted. The new administration, unlike the old, would allow dissent. The Sedition Act of 1798, which elevated criticism of the government to a high crime and targeted Jeffersonian Republicans, would be allowed to die, and those still imprisoned under it were released. Those who now opposed the government would be left "undisturbed as monuments of the safety with which error of opinion may be tolerated where reason is left free to combat it." Jefferson then laid out his "general principle" of government, predicated upon the maxim of "equal and exact justice to all men, of whatever state or persuasion, religious or political."

Knowing that he lacked the universal confidence held by George Washington when he became president, Jefferson asked for the people's indulgence when he erred and support from them against the errors of others. He hoped the "Infinite Power which rules the destinies of the universe" would "lead our councils to what is best," and provide "peace and prosperity" for America.

Context

The new federal Constitution was adopted in 1788, and the federal government was implemented in 1789. President George Washington selected Jefferson as the secretary of state and Alexander Hamilton as the secretary of the treasury. Although the public debate over ratifying the Constitution had been bitter, by 1790 the Constitution was thought to be almost a sacred document. Debate now shifted to how the Constitution would be interpreted. Jefferson and Hamilton staunchly disagreed: The former espoused a laissez-faire government; the latter preferred government intervention that primarily assisted the wealthy, which would ultimately benefit the entire economy. Jefferson, who supported the French Revolution, wanted to maintain the treaties that connected France and the United States, while Hamilton favored a closer connection with the British and feared that the French Revolution's radicalism might be transferred to America.

Throughout the 1790s partisan politics heated to a fever pitch, especially over foreign affairs. Great Britain and France were at war during most of this decade. Jefferson retired as the secretary of state in December 1793, after which President Washington generally followed Hamilton's policies. As relations with Britain worsened, Washington sent Chief Justice John Jay to London to negotiate a treaty. The British agreed to abide by their 1783 commitment to evacuate the forts along the Great Lakes on U.S. territory but made no other concessions. Jefferson and James Madison formed the Republican Party (later the Democratic-Republican Party, the forerunner of the modern Democratic Party), bent on opposing Hamilton's economic policies and the adoption of the Jay Treaty of 1794 (also known as the Treaty of London). The Republicans failed at both.

When President Washington announced his plans to retire after his second term, the Republicans supported Jefferson in opposition to Vice President Adams. In 1796 Adams was narrowly elected as the president, while Jefferson, with the second-highest number of electoral votes, became the vice president. Adams and Jefferson made initial gestures to work together, but soon Adams backed away from reconciliation, and partisan politics continued unabated. Hamilton, who had retired from the Treasury in early 1795, retained his influence with the members of Adams's cabinet, who were all carryovers from Washington's administration.

When the French realized the benefits the British derived from the Jay Treaty, they started to assail American merchantmen on the high seas. By 1798 the United States and France were involved in an undeclared naval war. Beginning in the early 1790s, many Frenchmen immigrated to America, and most of them became Jeffersonians. Opposition to Adams's policies rose steadily, and Congress,

Time Line

1743	■ **April 13** Birth of Jefferson at Shadwell, Goochland (later Albemarle) County, Virginia.
1760–1762	■ Jefferson studies at the College of William and Mary.
1769–1774	■ Jefferson serves in Virginia House of Burgesses.
1774	■ Jefferson writes *A Summary View of the Rights of British America.*
1775–1776	■ Jefferson serves in Second Continental Congress.
1776	■ **June to July** Jefferson drafts Declaration of Independence.
1776–1779	■ Jefferson serves in Virginia House of Delegates.
1779–1781	■ Jefferson serves as the governor of Virginia.
1783–1784	■ Jefferson serves in Confederation Congress.
1784–1785	■ Jefferson serves in Europe as one of the three U.S. commissioners to draft commercial treaties.
1785–1789	■ Jefferson serves as the U.S. minister to France.
1790–1793	■ Jefferson serves as the U.S. secretary of state.
1797–1801	■ Jefferson serves as the U.S. vice president.
1801	■ **February 17** U.S. House of Representatives elects Jefferson as the president.

dominated by Federalists, enacted the Alien and Sedition Acts (a set of four separate laws) in 1798. No one was prosecuted under the alien laws, but many Democratic-Republican newspaper editors and one congressman were indicted, convicted, and sentenced to the full extent under the sedition law. Jefferson and Madison drafted resolutions for the legislatures of Kentucky and Virginia, respectively, denouncing the Sedition Act (known formally as An Act for the Punishment of Certain Crimes against the United States) and advocating that the states work together to have the law repealed.

With war fever at its height, President Adams's popularity soared. In a special session Congress voted to expand the navy and raise a provisional army of 25,000 to defend against a possible French invasion. Democratic-Republicans denounced the war measures and the taxes needed to pay for them. They feared that the army, with Hamilton named second in command to Washington, would be used to suppress Democratic-Republican opposition. Adams's popularity suffered only when war was averted after he repeatedly sent peace envoys to France (most of whom were rebuffed) and the French were convinced that peace was in both countries' best interests.

While some southerners advocated a division of the Union, Jefferson pleaded for "a little patience, and we shall see the reign of witches pass over, their spells dissolve, and the people recovering their true sight, restore their government to its true principles" (Jefferson to John Tyler, June 4, 1798; Peterson, p. 1050). The election of 1800—both congressional and presidential—was one of the most bitterly fought elections in American history. Jefferson and Aaron Burr ran as the Democratic-Republican presidential candidates, while Adams ran for reelection with Charles Cotesworth Pinckney of South Carolina on the Federalist ticket. Hamilton secretly worked to have Pinckney elected as the president. Jefferson and Burr each received 73 electoral votes, Adams 65 votes, and Pinckney 64. The Democratic-Republicans won majorities in both houses of Congress. On February 17, 1801, after thirty-six ballots, the lame-duck, Federalist-controlled House of Representatives elected Jefferson as the president, with Burr as the vice president.

On March 4, 1801, the fifty-seven-year-old Jefferson, without a ceremonial sword and indistinguishable from other Washingtonians except that he was escorted by a small company of Washington artillery and Alexandria riflemen and militia officers, walked from his residence at Conrad and McMunn's boardinghouse on New Jersey Avenue to the unfinished Capitol to take the oath of office. President Adams, an embittered man, had left Washington at five o'clock that morning. Jefferson sat in the overcrowded Senate chamber (now the old Supreme Court chambers) with Burr, the new vice president, on his right, and John Marshall, the new chief justice, on his left. The three men profoundly disliked and distrusted each other. Jefferson had asked Marshall, a distant cousin, if he would administer the oath of office—perhaps a gesture of conciliation in line with the tone of the entire address that followed. Jefferson then delivered his

First Inaugural Address in almost an inaudible voice to a joint session of Congress and a crowded audience of more than 1,100 guests. A copy of the speech was given in advance to Samuel Harrison Smith, the editor of the *National Intelligencer*, who had a broadside printing available by the time the ceremony had ended. Newspaper, broadside, and pamphlet editions of the address were published throughout the country and abroad. Both Federalists and Democratic-Republicans praised the speech for its conciliatory tone, while a small group of Jefferson's supporters felt it was too mild.

Time Line

1801	■ **March 4** Jefferson is inaugurated as the third U.S. president and gives his First Inaugural Address.
1809	■ **March 4** Jefferson serves last day as the U.S. president.
1826	■ **July 4** Jefferson dies at Monticello, near Charlottesville, Virginia.

www.milestonedocuments.com

About the Author

Jefferson was born on Shadwell, the family plantation, in Goochland (later Albemarle) County, Virginia, on April 13, 1743, the eldest of seven children. His father, Peter, a self-made planter and surveyor, had married well into the prominent Randolph family. Peter Jefferson, who raised his family in the tradition of the Enlightenment, died when Thomas was only fourteen.

Jefferson studied at local schools until his father's death, when he studied for two years under James Maury, the local Anglican minister. At the age of seventeen, Jefferson left Shadwell and studied at the College of William and Mary under the tutelage of Dr. William Small and George Wythe. When Small returned to Scotland in 1762, Jefferson returned to Shadwell, where he continued his own studies, assisted in the law long-distance by Wythe.

Jefferson was admitted to the bar in 1767, at which time he decided to build his own house—Monticello ("little mountain"), near Charlottesville, Virginia. In 1770 Shadwell burned, and Jefferson moved into a one-room brick cottage at Monticello. In the summer of 1771, while trying cases near Williamsburg, Jefferson met Martha Wayles Skelton, a twenty-three-year-old widow who lived on her father's plantation. The couple was married on January 1, 1772, and moved to Monticello. In May 1773 Martha's father died, bringing Jefferson 5,000 acres of land, fifty slaves, and debts that would haunt him for the rest of his life.

Jefferson was active in the Revolutionary movement in Virginia. While serving in the House of Burgesses he wrote *A Summary View of the Rights of British America* (1774), which gave him prominence in the Patriot cause and established his reputation as a great writer. When serving in the Second Continental Congress, he was appointed to a five-man committee to draft a declaration of independence. The committee selected him to draft the document.

Jefferson left Congress and served for two years in the Virginia House of Delegates, where he chaired a committee to recodify the state laws. Only a few of these revisions were actually adopted while Jefferson served in the legislature. Elected as the governor of Virginia in 1779, he served two one-year terms. He was charged with cowardice and dereliction of duty when the British raided Williamsburg and Charlottesville, where the Patriot government had fled. Although the House of Delegates exonerated him, a disconcerted Jefferson retired from public service. His wife died shortly after childbirth in 1782, and a seriously depressed (almost suicidal) Jefferson was encouraged by friends to return to government service.

Jefferson was appointed to the peace commission in Paris, but before he left for Europe word arrived that the preliminary treaty had been signed. Jefferson then became a very active delegate in Congress. Among his many committee assignments, he wrote the Ordinance of 1784, which provided for the territorial government of the land north and west of the Ohio River. In 1784 Jefferson was appointed as one of three commissioners (with Adams and Benjamin Franklin) authorized to negotiate commercial treaties with European and North African countries. When Franklin returned to America in 1785, Congress appointed Jefferson to be his successor as the minister plenipotentiary to France. While serving in France, Jefferson's draft Bill for Religious Freedom was shepherded through the Virginia legislature by James Madison in January 1786.

When Jefferson temporarily returned to Virginia in late 1789, he discovered that he had been appointed as the secretary of state. Jefferson reluctantly accepted the position. After serving in President Washington's cabinet for four years, where he regularly opposed the policies of Secretary of the Treasury Hamilton, Jefferson retired again from public service.

Jefferson and Madison spearheaded the movement to create the Democratic-Republican Party, which opposed Hamilton's economic policies and the adoption of the Jay Treaty. When in 1796 Washington announced his retirement, Jefferson challenged Vice President Adams for the presidency. Adams won a narrow victory, and Jefferson became the vice president.

Democratic-Republican opposition to the Adams administration heightened when the United States and France became involved in the Quasi-War of 1798 to 1800. Jefferson and Burr defeated Adams and Pinckney in the presidential election of 1800. With Jefferson and Burr tied with seventy-three electoral votes, it took thirty-six ballots for the lame-duck, Federalist-dominated House of Representatives to elect Jefferson on February 17, 1801.

Thomas Jefferson (Library of Congress)

Jefferson's first administration was one of the best of any president's; his second was disastrous, leaving a divided country foundering toward war with Great Britain. Early in his second term, Jefferson decided to retire even though he would have been overwhelmingly reelected to a third term. He lived the remaining seventeen years of his life at Monticello, where he took the lead in founding the University of Virginia. He died on July 4, 1826, the fiftieth anniversary of the adoption of the Declaration of Independence.

Explanation and Analysis of the Document

Jefferson's First Inaugural Address was written with the same felicity with which he wrote the Declaration of Independence. In the first part, the address sets a highly idealistic spirit for democratic government, but elsewhere it lists the practical stance that would become Jefferson's political credo as president. In 1,716 words, forty-one sentences, and six paragraphs, Jefferson captures the political aspirations of the Enlightenment.

In the first paragraph Jefferson thanks the American people for the trust they showed in electing him as the president. As was customary at the time, the newly elected executive officer declares his limited talents to face the daunting tasks ahead. Looking at the huge expanse of American territory with its tremendous bounty and fruitfulness, the industry of its people, and the fear with which European nations look upon it, he believes that America's destiny is far beyond the ability of "mortal eye" to comprehend. He is humbled to think that "the honor, the happiness, and the hopes of this beloved country" are entrusted to his care. He knows by looking over the faces in the audience that he will "find resources of wisdom, of virtue, and of zeal on which to rely under all difficulties." He tells Congress that he will look to them "for that guidance and support which may enable us to steer with safety the vessel in which we are all embarked amidst the conflicting elements of a troubled world."

In the second paragraph Jefferson looks at the bitter election just completed. People elsewhere would have been shocked at the vehemence of the campaign. But the campaign and election are now over and "the voice of the nation, announced according to the rules of the Constitution," has been heard and will be put into effect "for the common good." All must agree that in a republic "the will of the majority is in all cases to prevail." But the majority "to be rightful must be reasonable" and must respect the rights of the minority, "which equal law must protect, and to violate would be oppression."

Americans should now "unite with one heart and one mind" and "restore to social intercourse that harmony and affection without which liberty and even life itself are but dreary things." Religious oppression had long since been banished from America; it was now time to ban "political intolerance as despotic, as wicked, and capable of as bitter and bloody persecutions." Some feared political differences more than others, "but every difference of opinion is not a difference of principle.... We are all Republicans, we are all Federalists." Those who might wish to dissolve the Union or change the American system of republican government should be left free "as monuments of the safety with which error of opinion may be tolerated where reason is left free to combat it."

Jefferson acknowledges that some men fear that republican governments in general and the American government specifically are not strong enough to survive. He, however, believes that the government that obtained independence and "has so far kept us free and firm" is "the world's best hope" and should not be exchanged for "the theoretic and visionary fear" of a few. (Here Jefferson turns the table on his opponents who had long accused him of being visionary.) America, according to Jefferson, possesses the strongest government in the world—one in which the people would rally to defeat any aggressor. Some might question whether man is capable of governing himself. If such were the case, how, Jefferson asks, could we expect man to govern others?

In the third paragraph Jefferson lists the blessings that allow Americans to pursue federal and republican principles and maintain the Union and representative government "with courage and confidence." Being separated from Europe by a vast ocean has kept and will keep Americans out of the "havoc" of European politics. Living in "a chosen country" with land enough for generation after generation is a wonderful blessing. Americans also possess "a due sense of our equal right to the use of our own faculties," to

Essential Quotes

"All … will bear in mind this sacred principle, that though the will of the majority is in all cases to prevail, that will to be rightful must be reasonable; that the minority possess their equal rights, which equal law must protect, and to violate would be oppression."

(Paragraph 2)

"Let us restore to social intercourse that harmony and affection without which liberty and even life itself are but dreary things."

(Paragraph 2)

"Every difference of opinion is not a difference of principle. We have called by different names brethren of the same principle. We are all Republicans, we are all Federalists. If there be any among us who would wish to dissolve this Union or to change its republican form, let them stand undisturbed as monuments of the safety with which error of opinion may be tolerated where reason is left free to combat it."

(Paragraph 2)

"Sometimes it is said that man can not be trusted with the government of himself. Can he, then, be trusted with the government of others? … Let history answer this question."

(Paragraph 2)

"Let us, then, with courage and confidence pursue our own Federal and Republican principles, our attachment to union and representative government."

(Paragraph 3)

"With all these blessings, what more is necessary to make us a happy and a prosperous people? Still one thing more, fellow-citizens—a wise and frugal Government, which shall restrain men from injuring one another, shall leave them otherwise free to regulate their own pursuits of industry and improvement, and shall not take from the mouth of labor the bread it has earned. This is the sum of good government, and this is necessary to close the circle of our felicities."

(Paragraph 3)

www.milestonedocuments.com

benefit from our own industry, to rise in society from our own abilities not as a result of our birth. We enjoy a benign religion in a variety of sects that all inculcate "honesty, truth, temperance, gratitude, and the love of man; acknowledging and adoring an overruling Providence, which by all its dispensations proves that it delights in the happiness of man here and his greater happiness hereafter." What more, Jefferson asks, "is necessary to make us a happy and a prosperous people?" He answers his own question: "Still one thing more, fellow-citizens—a wise and frugal Government, which shall restrain men from injuring one another, shall leave them otherwise free to regulate their own pursuits of industry and improvement, and shall not take from the mouth of labor the bread it has earned. This is the sum of good government, and this is necessary to close the circle of our felicities."

In the fourth paragraph Jefferson identifies "the essential principles of our Government and consequently those which ought to shape its Administration." He compresses them by merely "stating the general principle" and omitting the detail: "Equal and exact justice to all men" no matter their political or religious beliefs; peace, commerce, and friendly relations with all countries but "entangling alliances with none"; the support of the state governments as the most competent authorities to administer domestic affairs, with the general government serving as the "sheet anchor of our peace at home and safety abroad"; free elections with mild corrections for those who try to obtain redress of grievances by the sword when unsuccessful by peaceable means; acquiescence to the rule of the majority, which is "the vital principle of republics"; a viable militia system that is the first line of defense in peace and war until relieved by a national army in time of war; the subservience of the military to the civilian authority; limited expenditure of funds with low taxes and the steady and complete payment of the national debt; the preservation of public faith; "the encouragement of agriculture, and of commerce as its handmaid"; and the freedom of the press, freedom of religion, the privilege of the writ of habeas corpus, and the impartiality of jury trials. These, Jefferson asserted, are the basic principles that have guided both our ancestors and those who fought for independence and a reformation of the American government. The wisdom of sages and the blood of heroes had sought these goals. "They should be the creed of our political faith, the text of civic instruction, the touchstone by which to try the services of those we trust." If we wander from these goals "in moments of error or of alarm," we should return to them as soon as possible as the only pathway that "leads to peace, liberty, and safety."

In his penultimate paragraph Jefferson says that subordinate positions he held allow him to appreciate the difficulties inherent in the presidency. He understands "that it will rarely fall to the lot of imperfect man to retire from this station with the reputation and the favor which bring him into it." He knows that he does not enjoy the degree of confidence that people had in Washington when he first became president. Still, he asks for the people's indulgence when he errs, "which will never be intentional," and their "support against the errors of others." He again thanks the American people for their confidence. He will continue to seek their "good opinion" as he works "to be instrumental to the happiness and freedom of all."

In his closing paragraph Jefferson expresses his reliance upon the "good will" of the American people. He will gladly retire when they have found a better choice to fill the presidency. Until then, he hopes "that Infinite Power which rules the destinies of the universe [will] lead our councils to what is best, and give them a favorable issue for your peace and prosperity."

Audience

Jefferson's First Inaugural Address was delivered to a joint session of Congress in the Senate chambers (now the old Supreme Court chambers) in the unfinished Capitol in Washington, D.C. The gallery was filled to capacity; because of Jefferson's poor abilities as a public speaker, only a fraction of the 1,200 people in attendance actually heard what the president said. The address was meant to alert both Democratic-Republicans and Federalists in and out of Congress that the new president was not planning a vindictive campaign against his opponents.

In a broader sense, the address emulates Jefferson's Declaration of Independence in spirit and tone. In sweeping general statements as well as in specific details, the address announces to the world, to the American public, and to posterity the basic tenets of the American representative government. Instead of listing a bill of indictment as the Declaration did, the address lists Jefferson's political creed. In this sense, Jefferson was setting forth the contractual relationship between the American people and their government.

Impact

Jefferson's First Inaugural Address completed the peaceful transfer of power from one hostile administration to another, setting a tradition in American politics. In this sense it marked one of the great moments in the history of democratic government. It signaled to Federalists that they had nothing to fear from a vindictive new president and to Democratic-Republicans that they should be just and conciliatory toward their political opponents.

To a great extent, the policies advocated in the inaugural address were those that Jefferson attempted to implement during his administration. Often elements in Jefferson's own political party made it difficult for him to fulfill the pledges in the address. However, by the end of his two terms, Jefferson had followed his own general principles and achieved widespread support from the American public. The Federalist Party was in complete disarray and on the verge of annihilation.

Related Documents

Oberg, Barbara B., ed. *The Papers of Thomas Jefferson*. Princeton, N.J.: Princeton University Press, 1950–. These volumes contain all of Jefferson's correspondence and public papers throughout his presidency. Volume 33 contains a scholarly headnote and the final text of the inaugural address and two drafts.

Peterson, Merrill D., ed. *Jefferson: Writings*. New York: Library of America, 1984. This one-volume collection contains a sampling of Jefferson's private correspondence, both of his inaugural addresses, and some of his annual messages to Congress.

Bibliography

■ Articles

Browne, Stephen Howard. "'The Circle of Our Felicities': Thomas Jefferson's First Inaugural Address and the Rhetoric of Nationhood." *Rhetoric and Public Affairs* 5, no. 3 (2002): 409–438.

■ Books

Appleby, Joyce. *Thomas Jefferson*. New York: Times Books, 2003.

Cunningham, Noble E., Jr. *The Inaugural Addresses of President Thomas Jefferson, 1801 and 1805*. Columbia: University of Missouri Press, 2001.

Golden, James L., and Alan L. Golden. *Thomas Jefferson and the Rhetoric of Virtue*. Lanham, Md.: Rowman & Littlefield, 2002.

Kaminski, John P. *Thomas Jefferson: Philosopher and Politician*. Madison, Wis.: Parallel Press, 2005.

Malone, Dumas. *Jefferson and His Time*. 6 vols. Boston: Little, Brown, 1948–1981.

Mayer, David N. *The Constitutional Thought of Thomas Jefferson*. Charlottesville: University of Virginia Press, 1994.

Risjord, Norman K. *Thomas Jefferson*. Madison, Wis.: Madison House, 1994.

■ Web Sites

"First Inaugural Address." The Papers of Thomas Jefferson, Princeton University Web site.
http://www.princeton.edu/~tjpapers/inaugural/inednote.html. Accessed on November 5, 2007.

—By John P. Kaminski

Questions for Further Study

1. Compare Jefferson's First Inaugural Address with George Washington's First Inaugural Address, especially their references to God.

2. Compare Jefferson's First Inaugural Address with the inaugural addresses of recent American presidents.

3. Jefferson once said that in any country there are two political parties: One fears the people, the other the government. Which political party does Jefferson seem to favor in his First Inaugural Address?

4. In what ways did Jefferson try to make his First Inaugural Address conciliatory to his opponents?

www.milestonedocuments.com

Glossary

animation	the state or act of showing vigor or zest
arraignment	formal charge or accusation of wrongdoing
auspices	favorable signs
billows	waves or surges
bulwarks	solid wall-like structures built for defense
constellation	assemblage or collection
creed	a set of fundamental beliefs
despotism	a government of absolute power
dispensations	general arrangements or orders of things; provisions
felicities	instances of great happiness
handmaid	assistant or aid
indulgence	leniency or generosity; tolerance
Infinite Power	God
presentiments	feelings that something is about to happen; premonitions
repair	travel; proceed
sheet anchor	something that constitutes a main support or dependence
solicitude	attentive care and protectiveness
sovereign	supreme
throes	painful effects of a struggle
touchstone	a standard or criterion by which to judge
transcendent	superior; beyond ordinary limits or categories

Thomas Jefferson's First Inaugural Address

Friends and fellow-citizens,

Called upon to undertake the duties of the first executive office of our country, I avail myself of the presence of that portion of my fellow-citizens which is here assembled to express my grateful thanks for the favor with which they have been pleased to look toward me, to declare a sincere consciousness that the task is above my talents, and that I approach it with those anxious and awful presentiments which the greatness of the charge and the weakness of my powers so justly inspire. A rising nation, spread over a wide and fruitful land, traversing all the seas with the rich productions of their industry, engaged in commerce with nations who feel power and forget right, advancing rapidly to destinies beyond the reach of mortal eye—when I contemplate these transcendent objects, and see the honor, the happiness, and the hopes of this beloved country committed to the issue and the auspices of this day, I shrink from the contemplation, and humble myself before the magnitude of the undertaking. Utterly, indeed, should I despair did not the presence of many whom I here see remind me that in the other high authorities provided by our Constitution I shall find resources of wisdom, of virtue, and of zeal on which to rely under all difficulties. To you, then, gentlemen, who are charged with the sovereign functions of legislation, and to those associated with you, I look with encouragement for that guidance and support which may enable us to steer with safety the vessel in which we are all embarked amidst the conflicting elements of a troubled world.

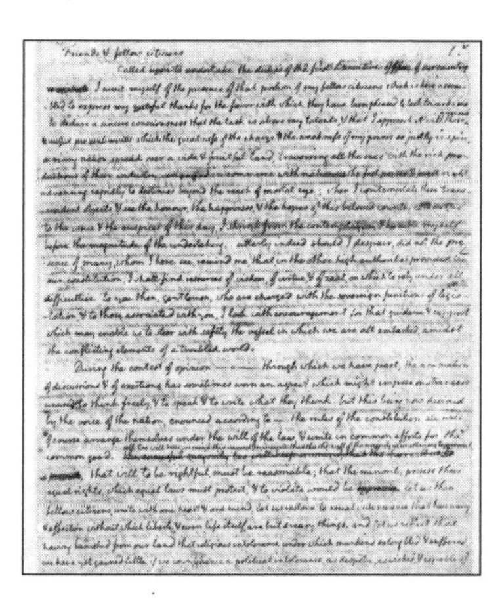

During the contest of opinion through which we have passed the animation of discussions and of exertions has sometimes worn an aspect which might impose on strangers unused to think freely and to speak and to write what they think; but this being now decided by the voice of the nation, announced according to the rules of the Constitution, all will, of course, arrange themselves under the will of the law, and unite in common efforts for the common good. All, too, will bear in mind this sacred principle, that though the will of the majority is in all cases to prevail, that will to be rightful must be reasonable; that the minority possess their equal rights, which equal law must protect, and to violate would be oppression. Let us, then, fellow-citizens, unite with one heart and one mind. Let us restore to social intercourse that harmony and affection without which liberty and even life itself are but dreary things. And let us reflect that, having banished from our land that religious intolerance under which mankind so long bled and suffered, we have yet gained little if we countenance a political intolerance as despotic, as wicked, and capable of as bitter and bloody persecutions. During the throes and convulsions of the ancient world, during the agonizing spasms of infuriated man, seeking through blood and slaughter his long-lost liberty, it was not wonderful that the agitation of the billows should reach even this distant and peaceful shore; that this should be more felt and feared by some and less by others, and should divide opinions as to measures of safety. But every difference of opinion is not a difference of principle. We have called by different names brethren of the same principle. We are all Republicans, we are all Federalists. If there be any among us who would wish to dissolve this Union or to change its republican form, let them stand undisturbed as monuments of the safety with which error of opinion may be tolerated where reason is left free to combat it. I know, indeed, that some honest men fear that a republican government can not be strong, that this Government is not strong enough; but would the honest patriot, in the full tide of successful experiment, abandon a government which has so far kept us free and firm on the theoretic and visionary fear that this Government, the world's best hope, may by possibility want energy to preserve itself? I trust not. I believe this, on the contrary, the strongest Government on earth. I believe it the only one where every man, at the call of the law, would fly to the standard

www.milestonedocuments.com

Document Text

of the law, and would meet invasions of the public order as his own personal concern. Sometimes it is said that man can not be trusted with the government of himself. Can he, then, be trusted with the government of others? Or have we found angels in the forms of kings to govern him? Let history answer this question.

Let us, then, with courage and confidence pursue our own Federal and Republican principles, our attachment to union and representative government. Kindly separated by nature and a wide ocean from the exterminating havoc of one quarter of the globe; too high-minded to endure the degradations of the others; possessing a chosen country, with room enough for our descendants to the thousandth and thousandth generation; entertaining a due sense of our equal right to the use of our own faculties, to the acquisitions of our own industry, to honor and confidence from our fellow-citizens, resulting not from birth, but from our actions and their sense of them; enlightened by a benign religion, professed, indeed, and practiced in various forms, yet all of them inculcating honesty, truth, temperance, gratitude, and the love of man; acknowledging and adoring an overruling Providence, which by all its dispensations proves that it delights in the happiness of man here and his greater happiness hereafter—with all these blessings, what more is necessary to make us a happy and a prosperous people? Still one thing more, fellow-citizens—a wise and frugal Government, which shall restrain men from injuring one another, shall leave them otherwise free to regulate their own pursuits of industry and improvement, and shall not take from the mouth of labor the bread it has earned. This is the sum of good government, and this is necessary to close the circle of our felicities.

About to enter, fellow-citizens, on the exercise of duties which comprehend everything dear and valuable to you, it is proper you should understand what I deem the essential principles of our Government, and consequently those which ought to shape its Administration. I will compress them within the narrowest compass they will bear, stating the general principle, but not all its limitations. Equal and exact justice to all men, of whatever state or persuasion, religious or political; peace, commerce, and honest friendship with all nations, entangling alliances with none; the support of the State governments in all their rights, as the most competent administrations for our domestic concerns and the surest bulwarks against antirepublican tendencies; the preservation of the General Government in its whole constitutional vigor, as the sheet anchor of our peace at home and safety abroad; a jealous care of the right of election by the people—a mild and safe corrective of abuses which are lopped by the sword of revolution where peaceable remedies are unprovided; absolute acquiescence in the decisions of the majority, the vital principle of republics, from which is no appeal but to force, the vital principle and immediate parent of despotism; a well-disciplined militia, our best reliance in peace and for the first moments of war till regulars may relieve them; the supremacy of the civil over the military authority; economy in the public expense, that labor may be lightly burthened; the honest payment of our debts and sacred preservation of the public faith; encouragement of agriculture, and of commerce as its handmaid; the diffusion of information and arraignment of all abuses at the bar of the public reason; freedom of religion; freedom of the press, and freedom of person under the protection of the habeas corpus, and trial by juries impartially selected. These principles form the bright constellation which has gone before us and guided our steps through an age of revolution and reformation. The wisdom of our sages and blood of our heroes have been devoted to their attainment. They should be the creed of our political faith, the text of civic instruction, the touchstone by which to try the services of those we trust; and should we wander from them in moments of error or of alarm, let us hasten to retrace our steps and to regain the road which alone leads to peace, liberty, and safety.

I repair, then, fellow-citizens, to the post you have assigned me. With experience enough in subordinate offices to have seen the difficulties of this the greatest of all, I have learnt to expect that it will rarely fall to the lot of imperfect man to retire from this station with the reputation and the favor which bring him into it. Without pretensions to that high confidence you reposed in our first and greatest revolutionary character, whose preeminent services had entitled him to the first place in his country's love and destined for him the fairest page in the volume of faithful history, I ask so much confidence only as may give firmness and effect to the legal administration of your affairs. I shall often go wrong through defect of judgment. When right, I shall often be thought wrong by those whose positions will not command a view of the whole ground. I ask your indulgence for my own errors, which will never be intentional, and your support against the errors of others, who may condemn what they would not if seen in all its parts. The approbation implied by your suffrage is a great consolation

Document Text

to me for the past, and my future solicitude will be to retain the good opinion of those who have bestowed it in advance, to conciliate that of others by doing them all the good in my power, and to be instrumental to the happiness and freedom of all.

Relying, then, on the patronage of your good will, I advance with obedience to the work, ready to retire from it whenever you become sensible how much better choice it is in your power to make. And may that Infinite Power which rules the destinies of the universe lead our councils to what is best, and give them a favorable issue for your peace and prosperity.

www.milestonedocuments.com

Confidential.

Gentlemen of the Senate and of the House of Representatives.
As the continuance of the Act for establishing trading
Indian tribes will be under the consideration of the legislature
session, I think it my duty to communicate the views which
in the execution of that act; in order that you may decide or
continuing it, in the present or any other form, or disconti
if that shall, on the whole, seem most for the public good.
The Indian tribes residing within the limits of the U
-siderable time, been growing more & more uneasy at the const
of the territory they occupy, altho' effected by their own volunta
policy has long been gaining strength with them of refusing abs
sale on any conditions. insomuch that, at this time, it hazar
and excites dangerous jealousies & perturbations in their min
overture for the purchase of the smallest portions of their land.
only are not yet obstinately in these dispositions. In orde
counteract this policy of theirs, and to provide an extension of t
rapid increase of our numbers will call for, two measures are
-ent. First, to encourage them to abandon hunting, to a
-ing stock, to agriculture and domestic manufacture, and t
themselves that less land & labour will maintain them in th
their former mode of living. the extensive forests necessary in t
will then become useless, & they will see advantage in exchang
means of improving their farms, & of increasing their domes
Secondly to multiply trading houses among them, & place
those things which will contribute more to their domestic comfort
extensive but uncultivated wilds. experience & refl

Thomas Jefferson's Message to Congress about the Lewis and Clark Expedition (National Archives and Records Administration)

Thomas Jefferson's Message to Congress about the Lewis and Clark Expedition

1803

"I trust and believe we are acting for their greatest good."

Overview

Twenty-five years after the Declaration of Independence was first signed, the foreign territory beyond the Mississippi River remained vast, largely undiscovered terrain to the U.S. government. The land was sparsely populated by various Native American tribes as well as by occasional explorers and trappers from Spain, France, Britain, and the United States. In 1803, President Thomas Jefferson proposed sending an exploratory team to investigate the territory. In making his request for a small, specialized group of military personnel, dubbed the Corps of Discovery, to be used for exploration, Jefferson marked a new era in U.S. history: While governmental sponsorship of exploration had been used in other nations, Jefferson's request was the first made by a president of the United States. His message specifically proposed the use of federal funds and personnel to explore the west, as he believed that accessing and recording information about the continent and its opportunities would be critically important to the growth and development of the nation. With his strong commitment to pursuing western discovery, Jefferson set a precedent for the application of federal funds to the mapping of western North America.

President Jefferson shared a draft of his first annual congressional message with members of his cabinet in December 1802. Within this preliminary version was a request for legislative support in funding a western expedition to explore from the Mississippi River to the Pacific Ocean. Since the request included travel through western lands that were beyond U.S. territory, the secretary of the treasury, Albert Gallatin, quietly recommended that Jefferson not include it in his first annual address but instead make a separate, confidential appeal to Congress. Jefferson indeed agreed with this recommendation, in part because he knew to expect opposition from his political rivals; he was not yet ready to divulge his full intentions to the public, specifically to his opponents in Spain, France, and Britain as well as to his own political challengers. On January 18, 1803, in a secret message to Congress, President Jefferson petitioned the legislators for support in his goal to send explorers west.

Context

In 1801, as Jefferson assumed the first term of his presidency, the new administration learned that during the previous year, Spain had given France legal control of Louisiana, which at the time included the majority of the Mississippi River basin. Charles IV of Spain had agreed to cede this land obtained in 1763, at the end of the Seven Years' War. This return of Louisiana to France, later known as the retrocession, led the president to worry that Pinckney's Treaty—an agreement with Spain also known as the Treaty of San Lorenzo—would be canceled, effectively eliminating U.S. citizens' rights to navigate the Mississippi River and to use New Orleans as a transport station. Jefferson and several other federal officials believed that western settlers critically needed New Orleans in order to access the seafaring market; the port was seen as vital to the area's economic development and therefore could not be ignored. Further, they considered control of the Mississippi River to be essential to the United States. Before long, Spain indeed announced the closure of the port of New Orleans. The land transfer from Spain also caused Jefferson's administration anxiety regarding a likely buildup of the French Empire on the continent, with associated concerns regarding American safety. Jefferson and his allies saw France as a stronger and more dangerous neighbor than Spain. Jefferson and James Madison, then the secretary of state, ultimately agreed that it would be wise to campaign for the purchase of New Orleans and also of East and West Florida.

Spain immediately opposed the U.S. government's land purchase proposal, but circumstances in France led to a more positive response from Napoléon Bonaparte. Clear evidence of England's superior sea power, in conjunction with illness, upheaval, and slave revolt in the most prosperous French colony, Saint Domingue (later called Haiti), on the western portion of the island of Hispaniola, led Napoléon to conclude that the French Empire was unlikely to flourish in North America. The American diplomats Robert R. Livingston, the U.S. minister to France, and James Monroe, a special envoy, were dispatched to Paris to negotiate the purchase of the New Orleans district and the Floridas. Around that same time, Jefferson asked Meriwether Lewis, his private secretary and a fellow Virginian and U.S. Army captain,

Time Line

1763	■ **February 10** Treaty of Paris of 1763 is signed, ending Seven Years' War; France loses North American possessions.
1776	■ **July 4** American independence is declared.
1783	■ **September 3** Treaty of Paris of 1783 is signed, establishing the Mississippi River as the western boundary of the United States.
1787	■ **July 13** Northwest Ordinance, officially known as an Ordinance for the Government of the Territory of the United States, North-West of the River Ohio, allows for the admission of new states east of the Mississippi and north of the Ohio once enough residents are present. ■ **September 17** U.S. Constitution is signed in Pennsylvania.
1795	■ **October 27** Pinckney's Treaty, also known as the Treaty of San Lorenzo, allows Americans to use New Orleans for commerce.
1800	■ **October 1** Third Treaty of San Ildefonso transfers ownership of New Orleans and lands west of the Mississippi River from Spain back to France.
1801	■ **March 4** Thomas Jefferson is inaugurated as president of the United States.
1802	■ **October** Spanish consider Pinckney's Treaty to be suspended.

to project the costs of an expedition west. In the spring of 1803 the negotiations between the United States and France were settled, with the Louisiana Purchase including, to the Americans' delight, all of the lands in the retrocession in exchange for $15 million in cash and debt reductions. The grand purchase eased the U.S. government's concerns regarding navigation of the Mississippi River, removed the threat posed by a potential neighboring empire, nearly doubled the expanse of American territory, and provided opportunities to search for new trade routes. Although the purchase did not include the Floridas, which remained under Spanish control, the acquisition was a major event and changed the course of American expansion westward. Official plans to explore and discover the western lands, including the territory within the Louisiana Purchase, started with Jefferson's secret message to Congress.

Thomas Jefferson had long been interested in science and exploration. Much of his early correspondence provides clear evidence that he was captivated by nature and intrigued by the potential opportunities available west of the Mississippi River. He was interested in charting the lay of the land and particularly in seeking a new water route to the ocean. He was mesmerized by flora and fauna and had a genuine interest in the sciences, including geology, geography, astronomy, botany, and zoology. While science was definitely of key importance in Jefferson's desire for an expedition, he assigned research secondary importance in his message to Congress. He understood that trade was a subject that would be more likely to gain legislative support, and he needed congressional backing to move forward with his plan. Indeed, while he only alluded to scientific interests in his message to Congress, a letter to Meriwether Lewis dated June 20, 1803, indicated that scientific study was an important part of the journey.

In the instructions to Lewis included in that letter, Jefferson explains that he requires detailed geographical charting and mapping of the territory, and he also requests soil samples, comprehensive information on animals and minerals discovered, and particulars about climatic conditions. His declared interests further include ethnographic and cultural information regarding Native Americans. Jefferson's desire for detailed knowledge of the West accorded with exploration practices from the Enlightenment era; beginning in the late 1760s, explorers such as James Cook, George Vancouver, Joseph Banks, and Alexander Mackenzie had begun observing and documenting all aspects of their journeys. Jefferson wanted his corps, as had these travelers, to discover as much as possible and subsequently share all facets of their findings. His orders to Lewis task the expedition with finding a western route for commerce, making friends with the western Native Americans, and meticulously documenting all relevant scientific data. Jefferson wanted to assure that the mission would succeed and worked to guarantee that Lewis, William Clark—the fellow Virginian who was second in command—and their men would be well prepared for the expedition. They were well stocked with essential supplies and resources, given pleasurable luxury items, and trained by scientists to be knowledgeable in their endeavors. Jefferson's secret message to Congress was the first step in assuring that the exploration of the American West would be successful.

About the Author

Thomas Jefferson, the third child of Peter and Jane Randolph Jefferson, was born on the plantation of Shadwell, Virginia, on April 13, 1743. In March 1760, just before his seventeenth birthday, Jefferson entered the College of William and Mary, and he later studied law; his interests also included science, history, philosophy, and literature. In 1767 he was admitted to the bar and became a country lawyer, carefully documenting information about each of his legal cases. Two years later Jefferson began service as a representative in the Virginia House of Burgesses.

While practicing law and also serving as a local surveyor, Jefferson read architecture books and began designing his home at Monticello. He married the young widow Martha Wayles Skelton on January 1, 1772, and two years later he ended his law practice in order to dedicate his attention to Monticello and his plantation. As with his law practice, Jefferson maintained meticulous records of his home, property, and slaves. In 1775 and 1776, though not always able to be present, he served in the Continental Congress and also wrote the initial draft of the Declaration of Independence. Jefferson next served in the Virginia House of Delegates for three years and as governor of Virginia from 1779 to 1781. Sadly, in September 1782, he lost his wife, Martha, who during their ten years of marriage had borne him six children, two of whom would live until adulthood. In 1783 Jefferson drafted his second proposal for a Virginia state constitution, and in 1784 he produced a proposal for overseeing western territories, which three years later became the basis of the Northwest Ordinance. In 1785 Jefferson published *Notes on the State of Virginia*, a book that not only detailed the flora, fauna, and landscape of the state but also covered laws, government, education, and religion.

Also in 1785, Jefferson succeeded Benjamin Franklin as the U.S. minister to France. During his four years in Paris, Jefferson absorbed Enlightenment ideas, considered different perspectives on religion, and learned architectural designs that he would apply upon returning to his home country. From 1789 to 1793 Jefferson served as George Washington's secretary of state. After a four-year break at Monticello, Jefferson became vice president under John Adams, serving for one term. On March 4, 1801, Thomas Jefferson was sworn in as the third president of the United States, which office he would hold until 1809. As president, Jefferson was instrumental in reducing the militia, improving freedom of the press, and expanding the country westward. He himself never traversed the land that he sought for the nation, but his efforts were invaluable in the acquisition of the West. As a scholar and statesman, he provided future generations with an important body of writings that still remain critical references in the functioning of the government. Late in his life, Jefferson funded and helped design the University of Virginia, the first public state university. One of the most important Founding Fathers of the United States of America, Thomas Jefferson died on Independence Day, July 4, 1826, at his home of Monticello, in Virginia.

Time Line

1803	**January 12** A congressional committee authorizes negotiations with France and with Spain for the purchases of New Orleans and of East and West Florida, respectively.
	January 18 In a secret message, Jefferson asks Congress for an appropriation of $2,500 for a westward exploratory team.
	February 28 Congress approves funds for exploration of the West.
	April 30 Louisiana Purchase is completed in Paris, with the United States acquiring approximately 828,000 square miles for $15 million.
	June 20 Jefferson sends Meriwether Lewis instructions for the exploration.
	October 20 Senate ratifies the Louisiana Purchase.
1804	**May 14** Lewis and Clark set out on their expedition.
1805	**November 15** Lewis and Clark reach the Pacific Ocean.
1806	**September 23** Having returned east, Lewis and Clark reach St. Louis and conclude their expedition.

Explanation and Analysis of the Document

◆ Greeting

The salutation of President Thomas Jefferson's Message to Congress about the Lewis and Clark Expedition is marked "confidential," indicating that it is a secret or private letter. He addresses the letter to each of the houses of the U.S. Congress.

www.milestonedocuments.com

Meriwether Lewis (Library of Congress)

◆ Introduction

In the opening paragraph, Jefferson begins with a lengthy sentence that introduces his purpose for communicating with Congress. He declares that since he knows Congress will soon be discussing the issue of "establishing trading houses" with Native Americans, it is his responsibility to inform the legislators of his reasons for supporting and encouraging their further development. He asserts that the knowledge he is sharing will assist Congress in making a well-informed decision regarding this issue.

◆ The Indian Tribes

Jefferson begins the main body of his letter with an extremely lengthy paragraph discussing unrest among Native Americans in regard to the reductions in the size of their lands. He justifies the decreases in Indian lands as resulting from voluntary sales but goes on to note a growing Native American resistance to additional land deals. Observing that not all tribes have come to stubbornly resist sales, he argues that two important steps need to be considered in order to preserve peace and provide for additional U.S. territorial expansion. First, he suggests that Native Americans should be strongly encouraged to adapt to a new lifestyle. Specifically, he proposes that they be encouraged to abandon their hunter-gatherer existences and adopt lives based around agriculture and also manufacturing. He surmises that after accomplishing agricultural subsistence, Native Americans would then naturally want modern farming conveniences and would be willing to trade their now-unneeded lands for these benefits.

Jefferson continues his lengthy paragraph with his second point, advocating an increase in the number of trading posts on Native American lands and the use of them to entice the Indians to willingly follow his plan of assimilation. With firsthand exposure to materials at the government-run trading centers, the Native Americans would quickly learn the benefits of trading for these materials. Jefferson contends that this dependency on U.S. posts would be in everyone's best interest because the Native Americans would naturally align themselves with the settlers and their political powers. Over time, he asserts, the Indians would adopt new ways and no longer need vast quantities of hunting land. Jefferson concludes that once these tracts of land ceased to be critical to the lives of the Native Americans, they would be more willing to trade land for other goods that they now wanted or needed.

Jefferson goes on to urge Congress to act to achieve his goal. He requests that Congress make every effort to ensure that the trading centers are well stocked and that the merchandise within them is offered at markdown prices. These discount public trading centers, Jefferson contends, will attract commerce from Native Americans, drive out competition, and drastically reduce the potential for anarchy as a result of the presence of unwanted challengers. Jefferson notes that he is particularly eager to establish this trading plan in the land surrounding the Mississippi River; he posits that current events indicate that Congress would be wise to hold land in this area. He explains that the United States has rights to access certain parts of the region and can most likely acquire rights to other nearby parts, but the nation could not presently expect to acquire the part between the Ohio and Yazoo rivers constituting the land of the Chickasaw. Jefferson argues that Congress must strongly support the gaining of rights to this area by encouraging the Chickasaw to adopt his agricultural plan. Jefferson claims that he is obligated to notify both branches of Congress of his plans but that confidentiality and discretion are paramount at this point in time.

◆ Extension of Public Commerce

In the third paragraph of the message Jefferson continues to argue for the discounting of merchandise at trading centers selling to Native Americans. He acknowledges that the traders operating the posts would not gain great profits, but he reiterates that the public would reap other benefits through the reduced prices. In the next section of this paragraph, Jefferson finally begins to address his main purpose in writing the letter. He explains that while the Native Americans, the Missouri River basin, and the Missouri's link to the Mississippi River were basically unfamiliar to the U.S. government, another nation—Great Britain—was earning revenue from the resources in the area. In particular, furs and other goods from the area were being transported over a cumbersome trade route. Jefferson surmises that commerce could be improved for the United States with the discovery of a better passage, perhaps along the rivers.

Jefferson next proposes that "an intelligent officer"—the person in question would be Meriwether Lewis—along with a select group of about a dozen enthusiastic soldiers should be sent to explore the West, perhaps as far as the Pacific Ocean. Their tasks would include communicating with Native Americans in regard to commerce and discussing potential trading posts. They would be given two years for their sojourn. Jefferson justifies this request by explaining that since the selected explorers would be officers already commissioned by the government, little additional compensation would be necessary for the exploration. Jefferson enumerates a small list of necessary supplies, including weapons and tools for the explorers and gifts for the Native Americans. He also mentions that as was their right, the explorers would, upon their return, be entitled to a small parcel of land.

Toward the end of his message, Jefferson discreetly inserts his other hope for the adventure. He notes that other countries have spent large amounts of money undertaking trips to explore new areas and that the U.S. government had the right and responsibility to do likewise. Since some of the lands proposed for exploration were territories claimed by other nations—France, Spain, and Great Britain—Jefferson recommends that the anticipated journey be portrayed as a "literary pursuit." A trip undertaken for the sake of knowledge and science, he urges, would be viewed most favorably by these other nations.

Jefferson subsequently reiterates that the legislature would be well advised to approve spending for this proposed journey. He emphasizes the recommendation that during their journey, the explorers seek a convenient trade passageway across the country. Defining the principal objective of the mission as the search for this route, he declares, would rightfully place the requested funds within the jurisdiction of Congress. That is, the trip would be conducted to locate trade routes in the name of national commerce; if other scientific and geographic knowledge could be gleaned from the journey, then it would be even more productive. The acquisition of further understanding and awareness of the land and people would be added benefits of the exploration.

Overall, within his message to Congress, Jefferson presents commerce as the main purpose for his request for the support of western exploration. He provides a lengthy discussion on the importance of commerce and only briefly mentions the relevance of scientific discoveries. He partly reveals his interest in science when he refers to a need for "instruments of observation" and the desire to "advance the geographical knowledge of our own continent."

Jefferson concludes his secret message to Congress with a request for $2,500. He recommends that these funds be approved under a general line item "for the Purpose of extending the external commerce of the United States." This blanket line item would provide administrative powers while avoiding the argumentation that would inevitably develop if the request were put forth in a more detailed manner. The letter is signed "TH. Jefferson" and dated January 18, 1803.

William Clark (Library of Congress)

Audience

President Thomas Jefferson wrote his message regarding the Lewis and Clark expedition in 1803 to members of the Seventh Congress, consisting of the House of Representatives and the Senate. When the two houses met between March 4, 1801, and March 3, 1803, the majority of the congressmen were from the Democratic-Republican Party, founded by Jefferson and James Madison, who believed in states' rights and the importance of yeomen farmers. The minority members from the Federalist Party, founded by Alexander Hamilton, who believed in a strong national government, were an important presence in Congress; while Jefferson and Hamilton were both intelligent men who had served in George Washington's administration, they had opposing political ideologies. Jefferson believed that a strong federal government would reduce personal liberties, while Hamilton thought that a strong government would work in the best interests of the people. These differing views of ideal governance were relevant to Jefferson's decision to issue a confidential message to request funding for a small expedition to explore the lands west of the Mississippi River. This request, coming from a president who had won office campaigning for limited federal spending and a reduced national debt, could have been

www.milestonedocuments.com

Essential Quotes

"Secondly: to multiply trading houses among them, and place within their reach those things which will contribute more to their domestic comfort, than the possession of extensive, but uncultivated wilds."

(Paragraph 2)

"In leading [the Native Americans] to agriculture, to manufactures, and civilization; in bringing together their and our settlements, and in preparing them ultimately to participate in the benefits for our governments, I trust and believe we are acting for their greatest good."

(Paragraph 2)

"While other civilized nations have encountered great expense to enlarge the boundaries of knowledge by undertaking voyages of discovery, and for other literary purposes, in various parts and directions, our nation seems to owe to the same object, as well as to its own interests, to explore this, the only line of easy communication across the continent, and so directly traversing our own part of it."

(Paragraph 3)

"The appropriation of two thousand five hundred dollars, 'for the purpose of extending the external commerce of the United States,' while understood and considered by the Executive as giving the legislative sanction, would cover the undertaking from notice, and prevent the obstructions which interested individuals might otherwise previously prepare in its way."

(Paragraph 3)

seen as opposing his own cause and could thus have ruptured his political base.

Impact

On February 28, 1803, Congress approved Jefferson's request and appropriated funding for the expedition. Over the next few months, Jefferson and Meriwether Lewis meticulously detailed the potential requirements for the journey, trying to consider all of the various prospects the travelers might encounter. Lewis received scientific training, learning principles of botany, mapmaking, medicine, and mathematics, and he chose William Clark as his partner in leading the expedition. The insightfulness of Jefferson and Lewis would prove rather remarkable, as the Corps of Discovery would have all of its essential needs met for the entire twenty-eight-month trek.

The 8,800-mile expedition that was initiated by President Jefferson's message to Congress gave the administration firsthand knowledge of the immense western lands that lay beyond the Mississippi River. Jefferson's subsequent strict instructions to Lewis accorded with the Enlightenment aims of discovering and documenting new lands and their inhabitants. Indeed, in this age of discovery, explorers not only ventured into new territory but also named and mapped the land, studied the soil, examined the plants and animals, and observed the inhabitants. The Louisiana Purchase had nearly doubled the size of U.S. territory, assuring access to the Mississippi River and providing the country with rich farmland. The Lewis and Clark expedition provided valuable knowledge about the land that was included in this purchase.

Jefferson's secret message to Congress, while carefully devised, was not without its problems. Congressional approval of the funding appropriation led to controversy concerning the constitutionality of the purchases in question. Many politicians, especially Federalists, argued that the Constitution did not provide for such purchases. Others debated the fairness of uprooting Native American tribes and potentially extending slavery into Missouri, Texas, Arkansas, and Louisiana. The document also caused difficulties because the vague agreement presented questions regarding the actual boundaries of the territory.

The Lewis and Clark expedition, which took nearly two and a half years, did not uncover a water route to the Pacific. However, its scientific discoveries, research, and affirmation of vast rich farmlands to the west confirmed the enormous benefits obtained through the Louisiana Purchase. Perhaps Jefferson's most noteworthy presidential accomplishment was his strong commitment to national expansion westward. The final cost of the Lewis and Clark expedition actually exceeded the initial request by nearly $36,500. During the mission, one explorer succumbed to illness.

Related Documents

A Compilation of the Messages and Papers of the Presidents: Prepared under the Direction of the Joint Committee on Printing, of the House and Senate, Pursuant to an Act of the Fifty-second Congress of the United States. 20 vols. New York: Bureau of National Literature, 1917. This compilation provides transcripts of various public documents issued by U.S. presidents.

Lewis, Meriwether. *History of the Expedition under the Command of Captains Lewis and Clarke to the Sources of the Missouri, Thence across the Rocky Mountains and down the River Columbia to the Pacific Ocean: Performed during the Years 1804–5–6 by Order of the Government of the United States*. 3 vols. New York: Allerton Book Co., 1922. As the lengthy title indicates, this work is Lewis's firsthand account of the expedition he co-led with William Clark from 1804 to 1806.

Oberg, Barbara B., ed. *The Papers of Thomas Jefferson*. 33 vols. Princeton, N.J.: Princeton University Press, 1950–. This magnum opus containing Jefferson's papers and letters as well as the correspondence he received from others comprised 33 volumes as of 2006 and was projected to include 60 volumes by its completion.

Osgood, Ernest Staples, ed. *The Field Notes of Captain William Clark, 1803–1805*. New Haven, Conn.: Yale University Press, 1964. This work includes transcripts and facsimiles of documents penned by William Clark on his expedition with Meriwether Lewis.

Smith, James Morton, ed. *The Republic of Letters: The Correspondence between Thomas Jefferson and James Madison, 1776–1826*. 3 vols. New York: W. W. Norton, 1995. These volumes show that Jefferson and Madison were friends who shared a great deal of correspondence regarding the early development of the United States.

"Louisiana Purchase Treaty; April 30, 1803: Treaty between the United States of America and the French Republic." The Avalon Project at Yale Law School Web site. http://www.yale.edu.lawweb/avalon/diplomacy/france/louis1.htm. Accessed on January 29, 2008. This is the treaty that formed the primary part of the Louisiana Purchase, conducted by France and the United States.

Bibliography

■ Articles

Lamm, Kimberly. "Reinventing Empire, Celebrating Commerce: Two Lewis and Clark Bicentennial Exhibitions." *American Quarterly* 58, no. 1 (2006): 181–203.

Nash, Robert. "Jefferson, Thomas." In *The New Encyclopedia of the American West*, ed. Howard R. Lamar. New Haven, Conn.: Yale University Press, 1998.

Ronda, James P. "'A Knowledge of Distant Parts': The Shaping of the Lewis and Clark Exedition." *Montana: The Magazine of Western History* 41, no. 4 (1991): 4–19.

———. "Jefferson and the Imperial West." *Journal of the West* 31 (July 1992): 13–19.

Sheehan, Bernard W. "Jefferson's 'Empire for Liberty.'" *Indiana Magazine of History* 100 (December 2004): 346–363.

Tobin-Schlesinger, Kathleen. "Jefferson to Lewis: The Study of Nature in the West." *Journal of the West* 29, no. 1 (1990): 54–61.

Worsham, James. "Jefferson Looks Westward: President Secretly Sought Funds from Congress to Explore Louisiana Territory, Develop Trade." *Prologue* 34, no. 4 (2002): 254–259.

■ Books

Ambrose, Stephen E. *Undaunted Courage: Meriwether Lewis, Thomas Jefferson, and the Opening of the American West*. New York: Simon & Schuster, 1996.

Foley, William E. *Wilderness Journey: The Life of William Clark*. Columbia: University of Missouri Press, 2004.

Fresonke, Kris, and Mark Spence, eds. *Lewis and Clark: Legacies, Memories, and New Perspectives*. Berkeley: University of California Press, 2004.

Jackson, Donald, ed. *Letters of the Lewis and Clark Expedition, with Related Documents, 1783–1854*. Urbana: University of Illinois Press, 1962.

www.milestonedocuments.com

Jones, Landon Y. *William Clark and the Shaping of the West*. New York: Hill and Wang, 2004.

Kastor, Peter J., ed. *The Louisiana Purchase: Emergence of an American Nation*. Washington, D.C.: CQ Press, 2002.

Lavender, David. *The Way to the Western Sea: Lewis and Clark across the Continent*. New York: Harper & Row, 1988.

Tucker, Robert W., and David C. Hendrickson. *Empire of Liberty: The Statecraft of Thomas Jefferson*. New York: Oxford University Press, 1990.

■ Web Sites

"Rivers, Edens, Empires: Lewis and Clark and the Revealing of America," Library of Congress Web site. http://www.loc.gov/exhibits/lewisandclark/lewis-landc.html. Accessed on June 11, 2007.

Thomas Jefferson's Monticello Web site. http://www.monticello.org/index.html. Accessed on January 29, 2008.

—By Cynthia J. W. Svoboda

Questions for Further Study

1. Jefferson's instructions to Meriwether Lewis of June 20, 1803, provide details regarding the requirements for the expedition. Compare and contrast Jefferson's letter to Lewis with his secret message to Congress, noting similarities and differences between the two.

2. Compare and contrast the opinions of the Democratic-Republicans and the Federalists with respect to the Louisiana Purchase. How did their reactions differ?

3. In 1800 Jefferson's Democratic-Republican Party defeated the Federalist Party on a platform supporting limited government, the reduction of the federal debt, and decreased administrative spending. How could Jefferson justify requesting expensive journeys and land purchases after winning with a position in support of less government?

4. In his secret message to Congress, Jefferson expresses his views on assimilating Native Americans into agricultural society. Review the document and consider the issue from a Native American viewpoint. What might someone from a Native American tribe say about this letter today?

Glossary

accoutrements	equipment other than weapons
connexion	connection
continuance	act of continuing; sequel
diminution	act of diminishing; lessening
dispositions	mood, temperament, habits, or inclinations
expedient	a means to an end
intercourse	exchange, communication
obstinately	with a stubborn attitude
peltry	undressed pelts
perturbations	acts of being perturbed or thrown into confusion
portage	the carrying of supplies overland
traversing	moving or passing across

www.milestonedocuments.com

Document Text

Thomas Jefferson's Message to Congress about the Lewis and Clark Expedition

Confidential

Gentlemen of the Senate and of the House of Representatives:

As the continuance of the act for establishing trading houses with the Indian tribes will be under the consideration of the Legislature at its present session, I think it my duty to communicate the views which have guided me in the execution of that act, in order that you may decide on the policy of continuing it, in the present or any other form, or discontinue it altogether, if that shall, on the whole, seem most for the public good.

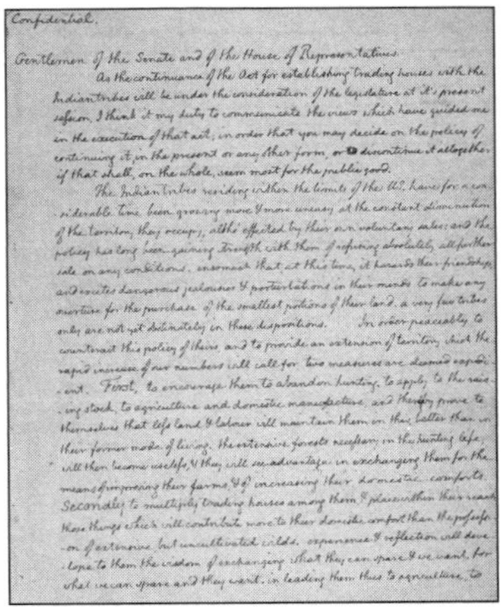

Confidential.

Gentlemen of the Senate and of the House of Representatives

As the continuance of the Act for establishing trading houses with the Indian tribes will be under the consideration of the legislature at it's present session, I think it my duty to communicate the views which have guided me in the execution of that act; in order that you may decide on the policy of continuing it, in the present or any other form, or discontinue it altogether if that shall, on the whole, seem most for the public good.

The Indian tribes residing within the limits of the U.S. have for a considerable time been growing more & more uneasy at the constant diminution of the territory they occupy, altho' effected by their own voluntary sales: and the policy has long been gaining strength with them of refusing absolutely all further sale on any conditions, insomuch that, at this time, it hazards their friendship, and excites dangerous jealousies & perturbations in their minds to make any overture for the purchase of the smallest portions of their land. a very few tribes only are not yet obstinately in these dispositions. In order peaceably to counteract this policy of theirs, and to provide an extension of territory which the rapid increase of our numbers will call for, two measures are deemed expedient. First, to encourage them to abandon hunting, to apply to the raising stock, to agriculture and domestic manufacture, and thereby prove to themselves that less land & labour will maintain them in this better than in their former mode of living. the extensive forests necessary in the hunting life, will then become useless, & they will see advantage in exchanging them for the means of improving their farms, & of increasing their domestic comforts. Secondly to multiply trading houses among them, & place within their reach those things which will contribute more to their domestic comfort than the possession of extensive, but uncultivated wilds. experience & reflection will develope to them the wisdom of exchanging what they can spare & we want, for what we can spare and they want. in leading them thus to agriculture, to

The Indian tribes residing within the limits of the United States, have, for a considerable time, been growing more and more uneasy at the constant diminution of the territory they occupy, although effected by their own voluntary sales: and the policy has long been gaining strength with them, of refusing absolutely all further sale, on any conditions; insomuch that, at this time, it hazards their friendship, and excites dangerous jealousies and perturbations in their minds to make any overture for the purchase of the smallest portions of their land. A very few tribes only are not yet obstinately in these dispositions. In order peaceably to counteract this policy of theirs, and to provide an extension of territory which the rapid increase of our numbers will call for, two measures are deemed expedient. First: to encourage them to abandon hunting, to apply to the raising stock, to agriculture and domestic manufacture, and thereby prove to themselves that less land and labor will maintain them in this, better than in their former mode of living. The extensive forests necessary in the hunting life, will then become useless, and they will see advantage in exchanging them for the means of improving their farms, and of increasing their domestic comforts. Secondly: to multiply trading houses among them, and place within their reach those things which will contribute more to their domestic comfort, than the possession of extensive, but uncultivated wilds. Experience and reflection will develop to them the wisdom of exchanging what they can spare and we want, for what we can spare and they want. In leading them to agriculture, to manufactures, and civilization; in bringing together their and our settlements, and in preparing them ultimately to participate in the benefits of our governments, I trust and believe we are acting for their greatest good. At these trading houses we have pursued the principles of the act of Congress, which directs that the commerce shall be carried on liberally, and requires only that the capital stock shall not be diminished. We consequently undersell private traders, foreign and domestic, drive them from the competition; and thus, with the good will of the Indians, rid ourselves of a description of men who are constantly endeavoring to excite in the Indian mind suspicions, fears, and irritations towards us. A letter now enclosed, shows the effect of our competition on the operations of the traders, while the Indians, perceiving the advantage of purchasing from us, are soliciting generally, our establishment of trading houses among them. In one quarter this is particularly interesting. The Legislature, reflecting on the late occurrences on the Mississippi, must be sensible how desirable it is to possess a respectable breadth of country on that river, from our Southern limit to the Illinois at least; so that we may present as firm a front on that as on our Eastern border. We possess what is below the Yazoo, and can probably acquire a certain breadth from the Illinois and Wabash to the Ohio; but between the Ohio and Yazoo, the country all belongs to the Chickasaws, the most friendly tribe within our limits, but the most decided against the alienation of lands. The portion of their country most important for us is exactly that which they do not inhabit. Their settlements are not on the Mississippi, but in the interior country. They have lately shown a desire to become agricultural; and this leads to the desire of buying implements and comforts. In the strengthening and gratifying of these wants, I see the only prospect of planting on the Mississippi itself, the means of its own safety. Duty has required me to submit these views to the judgment of the Legislature; but as their disclosure might embarrass and defeat their effect, they are committed to the special confidence of the two Houses.

While the extension of the public commerce among the Indian tribes, may deprive of that source of profit such of our citizens as are engaged in it, it might be worthy the attention of Congress, in their care of individual as well as of the general interest, to point, in another direction, the enterprise of these citizens, as profitably for themselves, and more usefully for the public. The river Missouri, and the Indians inhabiting it, are not as well known as is rendered desirable by their connexion with the Mississippi, and consequently with us. It is, however, understood, that the country on that river is inhabited by numerous tribes, who furnish great supplies of furs and peltry to the trade of another nation, carried on in a high latitude, through an infinite number of portages and lakes, shut up by ice through a long season. The commerce on that line could bear no competition with that of the Missouri, traversing a moderate climate, offering according to the best accounts, a continued navigation from its source, and possibly with a single portage, from the Western Ocean, and finding to the Atlantic a choice of channels through the Illinois or Wabash, the lakes and Hudson, through the Ohio and Susquehanna, or Potomac or James rivers, and through the Tennessee and Savannah, rivers. An intelligent officer, with ten or twelve chosen men, fit for the enterprise, and willing to undertake it, taken from our posts, where they may be spared without inconvenience, might explore the whole line, even to the Western Ocean, have conferences with the natives on the subject of commercial intercourse, get admission among them for our traders, as others are admitted, agree on convenient deposits for an interchange of articles, and return with the information acquired, in the course of two summers. Their arms and accoutrements, some instruments of observation, and light and cheap presents for the Indians, would be all the apparatus they could carry, and with an expectation of a soldier's portion of land on their return, would constitute the whole expense. Their pay would be going on, whether here or there. While other civilized nations have encountered great expense to enlarge the boundaries of knowledge by undertaking voyages of discovery, and for other literary purposes, in various parts and directions, our nation seems to owe to the same object, as well as to its own interests, to explore this, the only line of easy communication across the continent, and so directly traversing our own part of it. The interests of commerce place the principal object within the constitutional powers and care of Congress, and that it should incidentally advance the geographical knowledge of our own continent, cannot be but an additional gratification. The nation claiming the territory, regarding this as a literary pursuit, which is in the habit of permitting within its dominions, would not be disposed to view it with jealousy, even if the expiring state of its interests there did not render it a matter of indifference. The appropriation of two thousand five hundred dollars, "for the purpose of extending the external commerce of the United States," while understood and considered by the Executive as giving the legislative sanction, would cover the undertaking from notice, and prevent the obstructions which interested individuals might otherwise previously prepare in its way.

TH. Jefferson
Jan. 18. 1803.

www.milestonedocuments.com

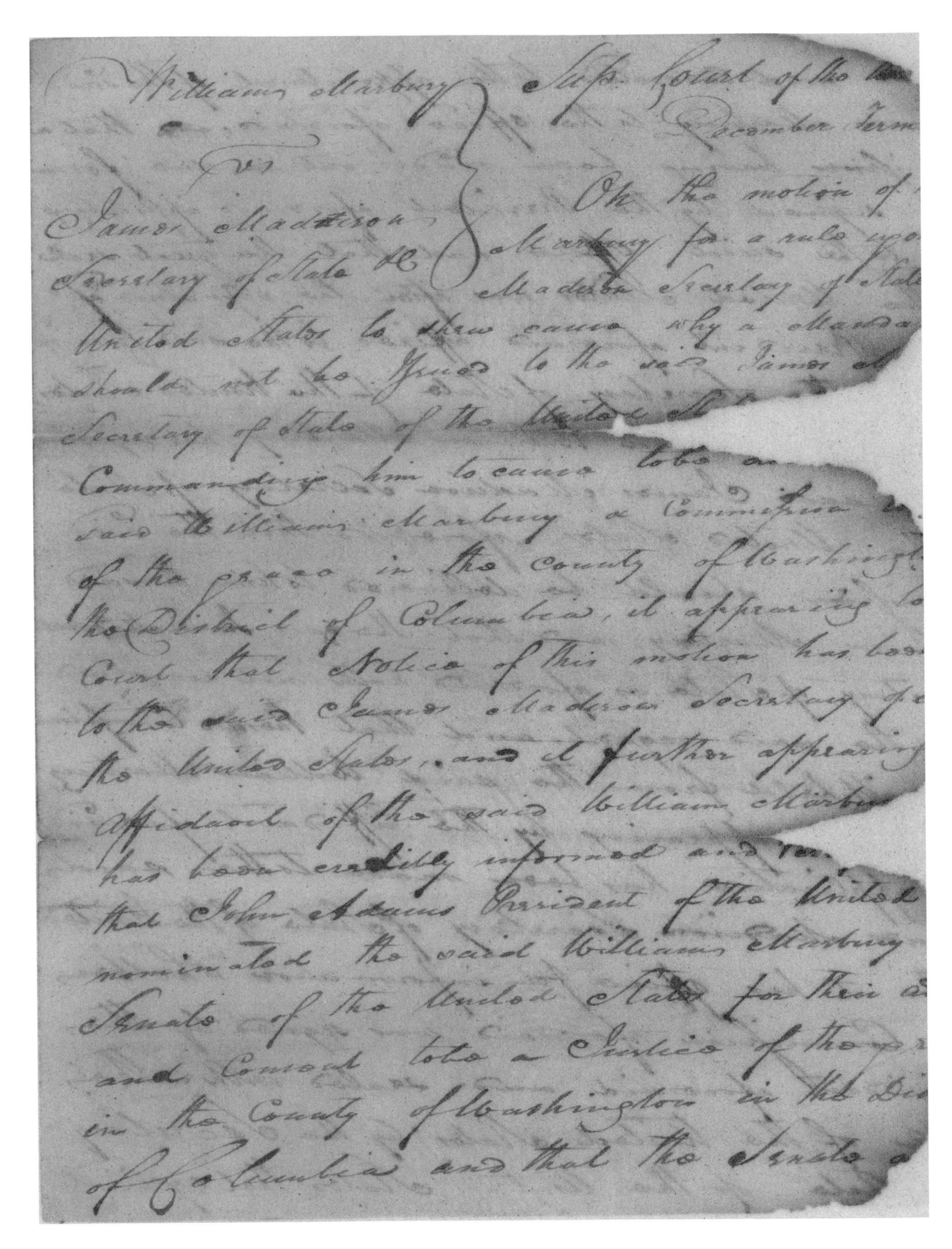
William Marbury } Sup. Court of the
December Term
vs
James Madison } On the motion of
Secretary of State &c } Marbury for a rule upon
Madison Secretary of State
United States to shew cause why a Manda
should not be issued to the said James M
Secretary of State of the United St
Commanding him to cause to be a
said William Marbury a Commission
of the peace in the county of Washingt
the District of Columbia, it appearing to
Court that Notice of this motion has been
to the said James Madison Secretary of
the United States, and it further appearing
Affidavit of the said William Marbu
has been credibly informed and be
that John Adams President of the United
nominated the said William Marbury
Senate of the United States for their a
and Consent to be a Justice of the pe
in the County of Washington in the Di
of Columbia and that the Senate a

Marbury v. Madison (National Archives and Records Administration)

Marbury v. Madison

1803

"It is emphatically the province and duty of the judicial department to say what the law is."

Overview

Marbury v. Madison was the first significant decision handed down by the U.S. Supreme Court after John Marshall was sworn in as its chief justice in 1801. In *Marbury*, for the first time, the Supreme Court declared an act of Congress unconstitutional; it would not do so again until *Scott v. Sandford* outlawed slavery in 1857. *Marbury* was not the Court's first exercise of judicial review—the power to determine the constitutionality of legislative and administrative acts—but by declaring the Court the final arbiter of constitutional questions, this seminal decision fully empowered the third branch of government, making the concept of federal checks and balances a reality.

Chief Justice William Rehnquist once described *Marbury* as "the most famous case ever decided by the United States Supreme Court" (Rehnquist, http://www.supremecourtus.gov/publicinfo/speeches/sp_05-08-01.html). It is not surprising that the late chief justice, who headed one of the most activist Courts in the nation's history—one that overturned a notably high number of federal statutes—should hold *Marbury* in such high regard. But Rehnquist is hardly alone in his admiration for this decision, which governments around the world consider a blueprint for drafting constitutions and formatting the role of judicial systems. With *Marbury*, the judiciary became something more than an institution—it became political.

Context

The significance of *Marbury*—like that of its author, Marshall—is bound up with that of Marshall's second cousin and primary rival, Thomas Jefferson. By the time of the fourth presidential election in 1800, the previously dominant Federalist Party, of which Marshall was a leading member, was in disarray. The High Federalists, a party faction dominated by Alexander Hamilton, actively undermined the reelection of John Adams, their party's nominee. The Republicans nominated Thomas Jefferson and Aaron Burr, and they won the election handily, garnering seventy-three electoral votes to the Federalists' sixty-five.

Naming the next president, however, proved far more difficult. Electoral rules of the day dictated that the runner-up be declared vice president, irrespective of party affiliation. Republican solidarity resulted in a tie between Jefferson and Burr, and by constitutional fiat the election was thrown into the House of Representatives. The House—dominated by Federalists—supported Burr, believing him to be more malleable than Jefferson, an impression that Burr encouraged. Nonetheless, Jefferson was declared the winner after the thirty-sixth ballot and took the presidential oath of office one month after Marshall was sworn in as chief justice.

In the final days of the Adams administration, the Federalists, attempting to pack the federal judiciary with party loyalists, passed two laws: the 1801 Judiciary Act, which the Republicans later repealed, and a law creating a number of justice of the peace positions in the District of Columbia. Adams made his appointments to these positions on March 2, 1801, two days before Jefferson's inauguration, and the appointees were confirmed the following day. Some of the appointees' commissions, however, were not delivered before midnight of March 3, when the Jefferson administration took over, and Jefferson ordered these commissions held back. One of the affected appointees was William Marbury, who then petitioned the Supreme Court for a writ of mandamus requiring the secretary of state, James Madison, to surrender his commission.

About the Author

Born on the northwestern frontier of Virginia, John Marshall was the eldest of fifteen children. Marshall's formal education lasted only two years. His education came mainly from his father, who not only schooled his son in *Blackstone's Commentaries on the Laws of England* but also introduced him to politics. The senior Marshall, who served in the Virginia House of Burgesses, also acted as George Washington's assistant surveyor. Father and son enlisted together after war broke out between England and its American colonies in 1776. Serving first with the Culpepper Minute Men and then in the Continental Army, John Marshall was with George Washington at Valley Forge during

Time Line

1788

■ **June 14**
The Federalist 78, written by Alexander Hamilton and exploring the power of the judicial branch, is published.

1789

■ **September 24**
The First Congress establishes the federal judiciary with the Judiciary Act of 1789.

1790

■ **February 1**
The United States Supreme Court convenes its first session.

1801

■ **February 4**
John Marshall takes the oath of office as the fourth chief justice of the Supreme Court.

■ **February 13**
The Federalist Congress passes the 1801 Judiciary Act.

■ **February 17**
Thomas Jefferson is voted president by the House of Representatives on the thirty-sixth ballot.

■ **March 2**
Pursuant to the 1801 Judiciary Act, President John Adams appoints forty-two new Federalist justices of the peace, including William Marbury.

■ **March 4**
Jefferson is inaugurated as president.

1802

■ **March 8**
The Republican Congress repeals the 1801 Judiciary Act.

1803

■ **February 24**
The Supreme Court decides *Marbury v. Madison*.

1805

■ **March 1**
Republican attempts to remove Justice Samuel Chase from the Court following impeachment fail in the Senate.

1807

■ **September 1**
Aaron Burr is acquitted of charges of treason at a circuit court trial presided over by Chief Justice Marshall.

the long, cold winter of 1777 to 1778. This experience of watching his fellow soldiers freeze owing to congressional impotence and inaction ostensibly fostered Marshall's lifelong commitment to a strong central government.

After the war, Marshall attended law lectures at the College of William and Mary in Williamsburg before being admitted to the bar. He set up his law practice in Richmond, where he devoted his time to defending Virginia debtors attempting to avoid prewar obligations to British debtors, eventually arguing one such case—*Ware v. Hylton* (1796)—before the U.S. Supreme Court. This was his only appearance before the Court as an attorney. Marshall became involved in state and local politics, serving several terms in the Virginia House of Delegates. Marshall's passionate advocacy for a federal constitution at the Virginia ratifying conventional led Washington to offer him a commission as the first United States attorney for the District of Columbia. Marshall declined this offer, as he did offers to serve as minister to France and associate justice of the U.S. Supreme Court.

Marshall's reasons for refusing such honors seem to have been primarily financial. Marshall, who was married and had ten children to support, was deeply in debt owing to land speculation. Financial considerations also weighed heavily in his decision to accept a commission to write the five volumes of *The Life of George Washington*, which appeared between 1805 and 1807. In the interim he did accept a government appointment as special envoy to France, a job that promised significant financial rewards. His mission was aborted by the infamous XYZ Affair, during which the French demanded a bribe as a condition to negotiating an end to naval hostilities with the United States. But Marshall's services, including a published response to the blackmailers, earned him $20,000 and public acclaim. Shortly afterward, at Washington's urging Marshall ran for and won a seat in the U.S. House of Representatives, where he successfully defended the Adams administration from Republican attacks. In 1800 the grateful president made Marshall his secretary of state. During the final days of the Adams administration, Marshall served both in this capacity and as chief justice of the Supreme Court.

Thus Marshall began his tenure on the Court under a cloud—one that darkened a month later when his arch antagonist Jefferson took office, making Marshall the first justice to serve under a president from the opposing political party. For Jefferson and his followers, the chief justice was himself one of the spurious "midnight judges." It was not long, however, before Marshall established his authority—as well as the Court's authority—by writing the majority opinion in *Marbury*. Any justice in Marshall's position today would be obliged to recuse him- or herself because of a potential conflict of interest, but Marshall, exercising his considerable powers of logic and diplomacy, managed to craft a decision that at once made the Supreme Court the ultimate arbiter of the constitutionality of legislation and launched his career as the "Great Chief Justice."

Marshall dominated the Court as no other chief justice has. His forceful but engaging personality helped him unite his brother justices, and his enormous capacity for work consolidated his power by allowing him to write the majority of his Court's opinions. Later, as Republicans came to outnumber Federalists on the high bench, Marshall still managed to make most Court decisions unanimous. In *McCulloch v. Maryland* (1819), the case that best illustrates the power of judicial review, the Court unanimously upheld Congress's right to charter a national bank, despite the Republican claim that the Constitution did not grant Congress this right and that the Tenth Amendment reserved all unenumerated powers for the states. Ever the Federalist, Marshall famously countered this argument by saying, "We must never forget that it is a *constitution* we are expounding … intended to endure for ages to come, and consequently, to be adapted to the various *crises* of human affairs" (McCulloch v. Maryland, http://www.landmarkcases.org/mcculloch/home.html).

During the final decade of Marshall's tenure, the Court—like the nation as a whole—confronted the steadily increasing power of the states' rights movement. The movement, long championed by Jeffersonian Republicans, reached a kind of apogee under the newly formed Democratic-Republican Party and its standard-bearer Andrew Jackson. Marshall suffered his first significant defeat when the seventh president of the United States refused to honor the chief justice's opinion for the Court in *Worcester v. Georgia* (1832), upholding the sovereignty of the Cherokee Nation: Jackson is reported to have greeted news of *Worcester* by saying, "Well, John Marshall has made his decision; now let him enforce it" (Breyer, http://www.supremecourtus.gov/publicinfo/speeches/sp_05-23-03.html). Having spent three decades enhancing the power of the Court, Marshall seems to have met his match. He hoped to outlast Jackson, believing that Jackson's successor might return some balance to the Court, but Marshall did not succeed. On July 6, 1835, grieving his wife's death and suffering from a liver ailment, he succumbed to injuries incurred in a stage coach accident and became the first chief justice to die while still on the bench.

Explanation and Analysis of the Document

Marshall's opinion for the Court opens with a brief recital of the legal history of the case. During its previous term, the Court had handed down a ruling requiring Secretary of State James Madison to "show cause" or offer evidence as to why the Court should not issue a writ of mandamus compelling him to deliver the commission making William Marbury a justice of the peace for the District of Columbia. Because Madison had failed to produce such evidence, Marbury made a motion for the Court to issue a writ forcing Madison's hand. Because of what Marshall calls "the peculiar delicacy" and "novelty" of the facts surrounding Marbury's case as well as the "real difficulty" of the legal issues they present, the Court is obliged to consider the following issues:

Does Marbury have a right to the commission he demands to receive?

Marbury v. Madison ***was the first important decision of Chief Justice John Marshall's term.*** (Library of Congress)

If Marbury is entitled to his commission, and if his right to receive it has been violated, do the laws of the United States provide him with a legal remedy?

If such a remedy exists in law, is the correct method of achieving its execution a writ of mandamus issued by the Supreme Court?

Marshall then considers each issue in turn. First, he declares that once the president has signed a federal commission, an appointment has been made, and the commission becomes "complete" when the secretary of state fixes the paper memorializing the commission with the seal of the United States. Because both these preconditions have been met, withholding the commission from its intended recipient (Marbury) constitutes a violation of a right legally conferred upon him. Marshall next considers the second issue, declaring that the "very essence of civil liberty" is the right of everyone to be protected from harm by the laws of the land. Marshall then cites as support for this proposition a truism that dates from the foundation of the republic—the United States is a government of laws, not men. That is, the law applies equally to every citizen of this country, regardless of who he or she is and regardless of his or her station in life. A republic, unlike a monarchy, exists only because its inhabitants have consented to be governed by

www.milestonedocuments.com

representatives they themselves select. By such reasoning, Marshall underscores the significance of Marbury's case, making his right to his commission representative of the rights of all Americans to be treated equally under the law.

Marshall next parses the law as it applies to the facts of Marbury's case. Marbury's commission as a justice of the peace is a product of the constitutional grant of certain discretionary powers to the president, who is permitted to appoint individuals to help him perform his constitutionally mandated duties. These officers, who act on his order and who carry the weight of his authority, are of his own choosing; in selecting them the president is answerable to the people only in political terms (for example, during elections) and to his own conscience. Offices such as the one Marbury claims as his own are decidedly political appointments, and those who occupy them do so at the behest of the president. They are not elected and therefore are accountable to the people only indirectly through the leader they have chosen.

Marshall's next rhetorical tack is almost a sleight of hand: He compares political appointees chosen by the president and acting as the president's surrogates ("their acts are his acts") with government officials acting at the behest of the legislature. We are meant to understand that the first is William Marbury, while the second is the other party to this case, James Madison. The problem with this analysis is that, as secretary of state, Madison arguably occupies the same space Marbury occupies as a presidential political appointee. Marshall does not let such niceties stand in his way. When a government officer is charged with carrying out acts that the rights of others depend on, such an officer is acting under cover of law and, Marshall claims, is, therefore, answerable to the law, not just to the president. This logic extends, the chief justice says, even to "political or confidential agents of the executive" when they are charged—by law—with fulfilling responsibilities that the rights of others depend on. Because Marbury was legally entitled to his commission, he was deprived of his rights when Madison refused to deliver it. Therefore, Marshall asserts, William Marbury has a legal right to receive something that properly belongs to him.

So far, his decision is good. Marshall, however, has painted himself into a corner. If Marbury, the plaintiff in this case, has a legal right to his commission, then the implication is that the defendant, Madison, can be legally obligated to deliver it. We are now swimming in murky waters, for Madison unquestionably is himself a political appointee acting on behalf of the president. How can the judiciary constitutionally force the administrative branch to carry out what is at bottom a political act? To answer this unstated question, Marshall next considers two things: (1) the power of the Supreme Court and (2) the nature of the writ for which Marbury has applied.

Marshall handily dismisses the question of Marbury's chosen instrument: The case for a writ of mandamus is "plain." The other question, however, goes to the heart of the matter and is far more complex. Marshall proceeds cautiously. The judiciary is granted original jurisdiction in cases involving federal officials by law—specifically, by section 13 of the Judiciary Act of 1789—and is given the right to issue writs of mandamus against such officials. Because a writ of mandamus is the appropriate vehicle for carrying out the law in this case, if the Court cannot issue such a writ under the present circumstances, the only logical conclusion is that the empowering legislation is unconstitutional. But Marshall says wait: The Constitution vests the whole judicial power in one Supreme Court and in lower courts created by Congress. Because this power carries with it the responsibility to adjudicate all cases arising under the laws of the United States, the Court clearly has jurisdiction over the current case. The Constitution also grants the Court original jurisdiction "in all cases affecting ambassadors, other public ministers and consuls, and those in which a state shall be a party. In all other cases, the supreme court shall have appellate jurisdiction." But in directly accepting Marbury's case rather than referring it to a lower court, the Supreme Court is exercising original jurisdiction.

Madison's attorneys argued that the constitutional grant of original jurisdiction is too general and unspecific to be taken literally. They argued that the framers of the Constitution intended Congress to be responsible for assigning original jurisdiction in cases involving parties others than those spelled out in Article III. Marshall counters that this argument is a tautology; if the framers intended for Congress to assign original jurisdiction to one federal court or another, most of the language creating the Court is unnecessary. Looked at this way, the constitutional distribution of jurisdiction is "form without substance." Next, Marshall plays his trump card: "It cannot be presumed that any clause in the constitution is intended to be without effect; and therefore such construction is inadmissible, unless the words require it." If Madison's argument carries the day, it renders parts of the nation's foundation document meaningless. Plainly, such a proposition is untenable—and besides, this interpretation goes against the plain meaning of the words in the document.

Article III of the Constitution organizes the judiciary into one Supreme Court and as many lower courts as the legislature deems necessary. It goes on to enumerate the respective powers of these two types of courts, specifying which types of cases can come before the Supreme Court directly and stating that in all other cases the Court will have appellate jurisdiction or the power to review decisions of lower courts. If the Supreme Court were to issue a writ of mandamus, either it would be exercising its original jurisdiction, or such an action would be necessary to the exercise of its appellate jurisdiction. A mandamus can be issued to a lower court, but if the Supreme Court did so in this instance, ordering Madison, a political officer, to deliver Marbury's commission, it would be exercising original jurisdiction. Because section 13 the Judiciary Act of 1789 authorizes the Court to perform this act, Marshall is obliged to conclude that at least this aspect of the legislation establishing the U.S. court system is unconstitutional.

The Court is left with the question of whether it can actually exercise jurisdiction in the case before it, given that the grant of such jurisdiction is constitutionally suspect. Marshall rather blithely dismisses this issue: "The question, whether an act, repugnant to the constitution, can become the law of the land, is a question deeply interesting to the United States; but, happily, not of an intricacy proportioned to its interest." Arguably, he is within his rights in doing so. Marbury brought his case under section 13 of the 1789 Judiciary Act, invoking the Court's original jurisdiction. If the Court is unable, in this case, to exercise original jurisdiction, it need not decide Marbury's case on its merits. Instead, as the chief justice asserts, "It seems only necessary to recognise certain principles, supposed to have been long and well established, to decide it."

Citing the right of a people to formulate rules it proposes to live by, Marshall endorses the supremacy of the Constitution, which, he says, should be a singular endeavor. In the United States the foundation document both sets up discrete branches of government and spells out limitations on each of them. Restrictions the framers of the Constitution placed on the legislature, for example, were not intended to be flexible. If they were, the very idea that informs our country would be negated: "The distinction between a government with limited and unlimited powers is abolished, if those limits do not confine the persons on whom they are imposed, and if acts prohibited and acts allowed are of equal obligation." Marshall follows this observation with a statement that goes to the heart of the larger issues at stake in *Marbury*: "It is a proposition too plain to be contested, that the constitution controls any legislative act repugnant to it; or, that the legislature may alter the constitution by an ordinary act." Either the Constitution is paramount, superior law inhospitable to amendment, or it is on a par with ordinary legislation and changeable at will. Governments with written constitutions must assume the former and, as a result, must also declare laws at odds with their constitutions null and void.

But is a court bound to follow a law even if it is unconstitutional? This question provokes Marshall to issue one of the most resonant statements in Supreme Court history: "It is emphatically the province and duty of the judicial department to say what the law is." Thus the concept of judicial review was elevated to the status of law. The Supreme Court, since its earliest days, had been working toward this idea, which is rooted in English common law but only implicit in the U.S. Constitution. For Marshall, judicial review was a matter of first principles as well as common sense. If a rule is applied to a given case, it is the judiciary's job to interpret that rule. If two laws conflict, it is up to the judiciary to decide the proper operation of each. And if a law appears to be at odds with the Constitution, as in the present case, only a court can decide which law governs. "This is of the very essence of judicial duty."

Marshall states that those who argue that ordinary legislation trumps the Constitution undermine the very foundation of all written constitutions. With rising Federalist feeling, he declares that to do so gives the legislature license to do what is expressly forbidden by the Constitution and lends it the kind of power and omnipotence the Constitution was

Alexander Hamilton (Library of Congress)

designed to proscribe. Because in America written constitutions are so revered, bowing to the changeable dictates of legislation would not be brooked. But while Marshall takes away from the legislative branch with one hand, he gives to the judiciary with the other. The Constitution extends the right to decide all cases arising under it to the judicial branch. He asks rhetorically whether it was the intention of the framers that, in deciding such cases, the judiciary should interpret the Constitution—the very document that grants this branch its power. He flatly answers, "This is too extravagant to be maintained," and then he provides a number of examples to illustrate the absurdity of rulings made in the absence of judicial examination of constitutional precepts. As evidence of the judiciary's significance to the constitutional scheme of governance, Marshall also cites a number of passages seemingly addressed specifically to the courts such as "No person … shall be convicted of treason unless on the testimony of two witnesses to the same overt act, or on confession in open court." Evidence like this, he says, proves that the framers intended the Constitution to be as binding on the judicial branch as it is upon the legislature and other "departments."

Marshall concludes the opinion of the Court with what seems almost an afterthought: "The rule must be discharged." In the end, William Marbury's petition was rejected, but not on the ground that the judiciary had no power over the executive branch, which had occasioned the case by refusing to deliver Marbury's commission. Instead

www.milestonedocuments.com

Essential Quotes

"The very essence of civil liberty certainly consists in the right of every individual to claim the protection of the laws, whenever he receives an injury. One of the first duties of government is to afford that protection.... The government of the United States has been emphatically termed a government of laws, and not of men."

"It is a proposition too plain to be contested, that the constitution controls any legislative act repugnant to it; or, that the legislature may alter the constitution by an ordinary act."

"Certainly all those who have framed written constitutions contemplate them as forming the fundamental and paramount law of the nation, and consequently the theory of every such government must be, that an act of the legislature repugnant to the constitution is void."

"It is emphatically the province and duty of the judicial department to say what the law is."

"So if a law be in opposition to the constitution: if both the law and the constitution apply to a particular case, so that the court must either decide that case conformably to the law, disregarding the constitution; or conformably to the constitution, disregarding the law; the court must determine which of these conflicting rules governs the case. This is of the very essence of judicial duty."

of ceding power to the presidency by simply dismissing Marbury's application, or trampling on the executive branch by demanding that Madison deliver the plaintiff's commission, Marshall skillfully expanded the authority of the judiciary, making it a truly coequal branch of the governing structure. The federal government may be based on a system of checks and balances, but after *Marbury*, the Court would always control the scales of justice.

Audience

In the largest sense, John Marshall's opinion for the Court in *Marbury* was intended for the American people as a whole, who now could rest assured that theirs was a government of laws rather than of men. According to the Court historian Charles Warren, however, "To the public of 1803 the case represented the determination of Marshall and his Associates to interfere with the authority of the Executive, and it derived its chief importance from that aspect" (p. 232). The animosity between Marshall and Jefferson was well known at the time, and many assumed—with some reason—that although Marshall devoted a good deal of his opinion to cutting the legislative branch down to size, the president was his real target.

Because the Court ruled against Marbury, however, the Jefferson administration had little to say about the decision. Republicans in Congress also had few grounds for complaint, as *Marbury* succeeded in expanding the Court's power by disowning a legislative grant of jurisdiction. On its face, *Marbury* seemed to decrease the importance of the judiciary. Marshall's opinion, in short, was a stroke of genius. As the lynchpin of American constitutional function, it remains so today.

Impact

Although the doctrine of judicial review was always a part of the American legal tradition, *Marbury* placed it squarely at the heart of U.S. governance. Had Marshall not challenged the authority of the legislative branch with such skill, another fifty years might have passed before the Court disputed the constitutionality of a federal statute. After such a long period of judicial inaction, this attempt to overturn legally sanctioned slavery might not have succeeded. In addition to reinforcing judicial independence, Marshall's opinion shored up the principle of separation of powers, which helps maintain America's identity as a nation of laws, not men. There is some indication that Marshall played a role in directing William Marbury's actions in filing his petition with the Supreme Court rather than with a lower court, where his chances of success were clearly better, but Marbury did not lose his suit because of who he was—or even because of his political affiliation.

Chief Justice Marshall never again ruled against the constitutionality of a piece of legislation, and *Marbury* itself was not cited as legal precedent for judicial review until 1887. Another eight years would pass before the case would be employed as a tool for striking down an act of Congress. In the present day, however, judicial review has come into its own as activist Courts overturn laws on a regular basis. On the other hand, the precedent Marshall set in *Marbury* of protecting the Court by avoiding a confrontation with Jefferson has been revisited on numerous occasions, with the Court deferring to executive authority, especially in time of war or other national emergency. Lacking either an army or the power to impose taxes, the Court is left with a mere concept as a means of enforcing its decisions—but without *Marbury v. Madison*, it would not have even that much.

Related Documents

"Constitution of the United States." The National Archives "Charters of Freedom" Web site. http://www.archives.gov/national-archives-experience/charters/constitution_ transcript.html. Accessed on September 1, 2007. Article III of the Constitution sets up the judicial branch of the federal government. Special attention should be paid to section 2, which contains the language parsed in *Marbury*.

"The Federalist No. 78: The Judiciary Department." The Constitution Society Web site. http://www.constitution.org/fed/federa78.htm. Accessed on September 1, 2007. This installment of the Federalist Papers was written by Alexander Hamilton, although like other installments, it was signed pseudonymously "Publius." Hamilton used no. 78 to argue the case for a federal judiciary, in the process arguing for the necessity of judicial review.

"Transcript of Federal Judiciary Act (1789)." National Archives "Our Documents" Web site. http://www.ourdocuments.gov/doc.php?flash=true&doc=12&page=transcript. Accessed on September 1, 2007. William Marbury brought his case to the Supreme Court under this law. Special attention should be paid to section 13, which the *Marbury* declared an unconstitutional expansion of the Supreme Court's jurisdiction.

Bibliography

■ Books

Kahn, Paul W. *The Reign of Law: Marbury v. Madison and the Construction of America*, new ed. New Haven: Yale University Press, 2002.

Nelson, William E. *Marbury v. Madison: The Origins and Legacy of Judicial Review*. Lawrence: Kansas University Press, 2000.

Paddock, Lisa. *Facts about the Supreme Court of the United States*. New York: H. W. Wilson, 1996.

Schwartz, Bernard. *A History of the Supreme Court*. New York: Oxford University Press, 1993.

Tushnet, Mark, ed. *Arguing Marbury v. Madison*. Palo Alto, Calif.: Stanford University Press, 2005.

Warren, Charles. *The Supreme Court in United States History*. 3 vols. Boston: Little, Brown, 1924.

■ Web Sites

Breyer, Stephen. "Boston College Law School Commencement Remarks, May 23, 2003." Supreme Court of the United States Web site.
http://www.supremecourtus.gov/publicinfo/speeches/sp_05-23-03.html. Accessed on December 20, 2007.

"*Marbury v. Madison* (1803)." Landmark Supreme Court Cases Web site.
http://www.landmarkcases.org/marbury/home.html. Accessed on September 1, 2007.

"*McCulloch v. Maryland* (1819)." Landmark Supreme Court Cases Web site.
http://www.landmarkcases.org/mcculloch/home.html. Accessed on December 20, 2007.

Rehnquist, William H. "Remarks of the Chief Justice William H. Renquist: Federal Judges Association, May 8, 2001." Supreme Court of the United States Web site.
http://www.supremecourtus.gov/publicinfo/speeches/sp_05-08-01.html. Accessed on December 20, 2007.

—By Lisa Paddock

www.milestonedocuments.com

Questions for Further Study

1. Given that judicial review grants the right to say what the law is to unelected judges, can this principle ever be reconciled with democratic ideals?

2. How can judicial review be considered central to constitutional interpretation when our founding document does not even acknowledge the concept?

3. Why do you think the Supreme Court has resorted to judicial review so frequently in modern times?

Glossary

jurisdiction	the power to hear and decide cases
writ	a court order mandating performance of a specified act
writ of mandamus	a court order compelling a government official to perform some necessary duty

Marbury v. Madison

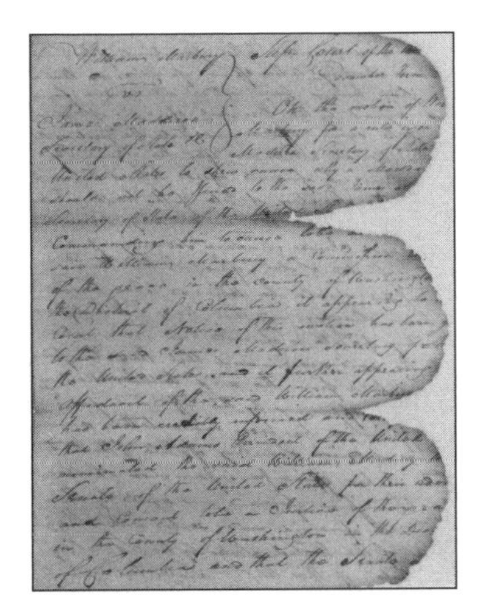

AT the December term 1801, William Marbury, Dennis Ramsay, Robert Townsend Hooe, and William Harper, by their counsel severally moved the court for a rule to James Madison, secretary of state of the United States, to show cause why a mandamus should not issue commanding him to cause to be delivered to them respectively their several commissions as justices of the peace in the district of Columbia.

This motion was supported by affidavits of the following facts: that notice of this motion had been given to Mr. Madison; that Mr. Adams, the late president of the United States, nominated the applicants to the senate for their advice and consent to be appointed justices of the peace of the district of Columbia; that the senate advised and consented to the appointments; that commissions in due form were signed by the said president appointing them justices, &c. and that the seal of the United States was in due form affixed to the said commissions by the secretary of state; that the applicants have requested Mr. Madison to deliver them their said commissions, who has not complied with that request; and that their said commissions are withheld from them; that the applicants have made application to Mr. Madison as secretary of state of the United States at his office, for information whether the commissions were signed and sealed as aforesaid; that explicit and satisfactory information has not been given in answer to that inquiry, either by the secretary of state, or any officer in the department of state; that application has been made to the secretary of the senate for a certificate of the nomination of the applicants, and of the advice and consent of the senate, who has declined giving such a certificate; whereupon a rule was made to show cause on the fourth day of this term. This rule having been duly served—Mr. Jacob Wagner and Mr. Daniel Brent, who had been summoned to attend the court, and were required to give evidence, objected to be sworn, alleging that they were clerks in the department of state, and not bound to disclose any facts relating to the business or transactions of the office.

The court ordered the witnesses to be sworn, and their answers taken in writing; but informed them that when the questions were asked they might state their objections to answering each particular question, if they had any.

Mr. Lincoln, who had been the acting secretary of state, when the circumstances stated in the affidavits occurred, was called upon to give testimony. He objected to answering. The questions were put in writing.

The court said there was nothing confidential required to be disclosed. If there had been, he was not obliged to answer it, and if he thought any thing was communicated to him confidentially he was not bound to disclose, nor was he obliged to state any thing which would criminate himself.

The questions argued by the counsel for the relators were, 1. Whether the supreme court can award the writ of mandamus in any case. 2. Whether it will lie to a secretary of state, in any case whatever. 3. Whether in the present case the court may award a mandamus to James Madison, secretary of state.

Mr. Chief Justice MARSHALL delivered the opinion of the court.

At the last term, on the affidavits then read and filed with the clerk, a rule was granted in this case, requiring the secretary of state to show cause why a mandamus should not issue, directing him to deliver to William Marbury his commission as a justice of the peace for the county of Washington, in the district of Columbia.

No cause has been shown, and the present motion is for a mandamus. The peculiar delicacy of this case, the novelty of some of its circumstances, and the real difficulty attending the points which occur in it, require a complete exposition of the principles on which the opinion to be given by the court is founded.

www.milestonedocuments.com

Document Text

These principles have been, on the side of the applicant, very ably argued at the bar. In rendering the opinion of the court, there will be some departure in form, though not in substance, from the points stated in that argument.

In the order in which the court has viewed this subject, the following questions have been considered and decided.

1. Has the applicant a right to the commission he demands?

2. If he has a right, and that right has been violated, do the laws of his country afford him a remedy?

3. If they do afford him a remedy, is it a mandamus issuing from this court?

The first object of inquiry is,

1. Has the applicant a right to the commission he demands?

His right originates in an act of congress passed in February 1801, concerning the district of Columbia.

After dividing the district into two counties, the eleventh section of this law enacts, "that there shall be appointed in and for each of the said counties, such number of discreet persons to be justices of the peace as the president of the United States shall, from time to time, think expedient, to continue in office for five years." It appears from the affidavits, that in compliance with this law, a commission for William Marbury as a justice of peace for the county of Washington was signed by John Adams, then president of the United States; after which the seal of the United States was affixed to it; but the commission has never reached the person for whom it was made out.

In order to determine whether he is entitled to this commission, it becomes necessary to inquire whether he has been appointed to the office. For if he has been appointed, the law continues him in office for five years, and he is entitled to the possession of those evidences of office, which, being completed, became his property.

The second section of the second article of the constitution declares, "the president shall nominate, and, by and with the advice and consent of the senate, shall appoint ambassadors, other public ministers and consuls, and all other officers of the United States, whose appointments are not otherwise provided for."

The third section declares, that "he shall commission all the officers of the United States."

An act of congress directs the secretary of state to keep the seal of the United States, "to make out and record, and affix the said seal to all civil commissions to officers of the United States to be appointed by the president, by and with the consent of the senate, or by the president alone; provided that the said seal shall not be affixed to any commission before the same shall have been signed by the president of the United States."

These are the clauses of the constitution and laws of the United States, which affect this part of the case. They seem to contemplate three distinct operations:

1. The nomination. This is the sole act of the president, and is completely voluntary.

2. The appointment. This is also the act of the president, and is also a voluntary act, though it can only be performed by and with the advice and consent of the senate.

3. The commission. To grant a commission to a person appointed, might perhaps be deemed a duty enjoined by the constitution. "He shall," says that instrument, "commission all the officers of the United States."

The acts of appointing to office, and commissioning the person appointed, can scarcely be considered as one and the same; since the power to perform them is given in two separate and distinct sections of the constitution. The distinction between the appointment and the commission will be rendered more apparent by adverting to that provision in the second section of the second article of the constitution, which authorises congress "to vest by law the appointment of such inferior officers as they think proper, in the president alone, in the courts of law, or in the heads of departments;" thus contemplating cases where the law may direct the president to commission an officer appointed by the courts or by the heads of departments. In such a case, to issue a commission would be apparently a duty distinct from the appointment, the performance of which perhaps, could not legally be refused.

Although that clause of the constitution which requires the president to commission all the officers of the United States, may never have been applied to officers appointed otherwise than by himself, yet it would be difficult to deny the legislative power to apply it to such cases. Of consequence the constitutional distinction between the appointment to an office and the commission of an officer who has been appointed, remains the same as if in practice the president had commissioned officers appointed by an authority other than his own.

It follows too, from the existence of this distinction, that, if an appointment was to be evidenced by any public act other than the commission, the per-

www.milestonedocuments.com

formance of such public act would create the officer; and if he was not removable at the will of the president, would either give him a right to his commission, or enable him to perform the duties without it.

These observations are premised solely for the purpose of rendering more intelligible those which apply more directly to the particular case under consideration. This is an appointment made by the president, by and with the advice and consent of the senate, and is evidenced by no act but the commission itself. In such a case therefore the commission and the appointment seem inseparable; it being almost impossible to show an appointment otherwise than by proving the existence of a commission: still the commission is not necessarily the appointment; though conclusive evidence of it.

But at what stage does it amount to this conclusive evidence?

The answer to this question seems an obvious one. The appointment being the sole act of the president, must be completely evidenced, when it is shown that he has done every thing to be performed by him.

Should the commission, instead of being evidence of an appointment, even be considered as constituting the appointment itself; still it would be made when the last act to be done by the president was performed, or, at furthest, when the commission was complete.

The last act to be done by the president, is the signature of the commission. He has then acted on the advice and consent of the senate to his own nomination. The time for deliberation has then passed. He has decided. His judgment, on the advice and consent of the senate concurring with his nomination, has been made, and the officer is appointed. This appointment is evidenced by an open, unequivocal act; and being the last act required from the person making it, necessarily excludes the idea of its being, so far as it respects the appointment, an inchoate and incomplete transaction.

Some point of time must be taken when the power of the executive over an officer, not removable at his will, must cease. That point of time must be when the constitutional power of appointment has been exercised. And this power has been exercised when the last act, required from the person possessing the power, has been performed. This last act is the signature of the commission. This idea seems to have prevailed with the legislature, when the act passed converting the department of foreign affairs into the department of state. By that act it is enacted, that the secretary of state shall keep the seal of the United States, "and shall make out and record, and shall affix the said seal to all civil commissions to officers of the United States, to be appointed by the president:" "provided that the said seal shall not be affixed to any commission, before the same shall have been signed by the president of the United States; nor to any other instrument or act, without the special warrant of the president therefor."

The signature is a warrant for affixing the great seal to the commission; and the great seal is only to be affixed to an instrument which is complete. It attests, by an act supposed to be of public notoriety, the verity of the presidential signature.

It is never to be affixed till the commission is signed, because the signature, which gives force and effect to the commission, is conclusive evidence that the appointment is made.

The commission being signed, the subsequent duty of the secretary of state is prescribed by law, and not to be guided by the will of the president. He is to affix the seal of the United States to the commission, and is to record it.

This is not a proceeding which may be varied, if the judgment of the executive shall suggest one more eligible, but is a precise course accurately marked out by law, and is to be strictly pursued. It is the duty of the secretary of state to conform to the law, and in this he is an officer of the United States, bound to obey the laws. He acts, in this respect, as has been very properly stated at the bar, under the authority of law, and not by the instructions of the president. It is a ministerial act which the law enjoins on a particular officer for a particular purpose.

If it should be supposed, that the solemnity of affixing the seal, is necessary not only to the validity of the commission, but even to the completion of an appointment, still when the seal is affixed the appointment is made, and the commission is valid. No other solemnity is required by law; no other act is to be performed on the part of government. All that the executive can do to invest the person with his office, is done; and unless the appointment be then made, the executive cannot make one without the co-operation of others.

After searching anxiously for the principles on which a contrary opinion may be supported, none have been found which appear of sufficient force to maintain the opposite doctrine.

Such as the imagination of the court could suggest, have been very deliberately examined, and after allowing them all the weight which it appears possi-

Document Text

ble to give them, they do not shake the opinion which has been formed.

In considering this question, it has been conjectured that the commission may have been assimilated to a deed, to the validity of which, delivery is essential.

This idea is founded on the supposition that the commission is not merely evidence of an appointment, but is itself the actual appointment; a supposition by no means unquestionable. But for the purpose of examining this objection fairly, let it be conceded, that the principle, claimed for its support, is established.

The appointment being, under the constitution, to be made by the president personally, the delivery of the deed of appointment, if necessary to its completion, must be made by the president also. It is not necessary that the livery should be made personally to the grantee of the office: it never is so made. The law would seem to contemplate that it should be made to the secretary of state, since it directs the secretary to affix the seal to the commission after it shall have been signed by the president. If then the act of livery be necessary to give validity to the commission, it has been delivered when executed and given to the secretary for the purpose of being sealed, recorded, and transmitted to the party.

But in all cases of letters patent, certain solemnities are required by law, which solemnities are the evidences of the validity of the instrument. A formal delivery to the person is not among them. In cases of commissions, the sign manual of the president, and the seal of the United States, are those solemnities. This objection therefore does not touch the case.

It has also occurred as possible, and barely possible, that the transmission of the commission, and the acceptance thereof, might be deemed necessary to complete the right of the plaintiff.

The transmission of the commission is a practice directed by convenience, but not by law. It cannot therefore be necessary to constitute the appointment which must precede it, and which is the mere act of the president. If the executive required that every person appointed to an office, should himself take means to procure his commission, the appointment would not be the less valid on that account. The appointment is the sole act of the president; the transmission of the commission is the sole act of the officer to whom that duty is assigned, and may be accelerated or retarded by circumstances which can have no influence on the appointment. A commission is transmitted to a person already appointed; not to a person to be appointed or not, as the letter enclosing the commission should happen to get into the post-office and reach him in safety, or to miscarry.

It may have some tendency to elucidate this point, to inquire, whether the possession of the original commission be indispensably necessary to authorize a person, appointed to any office, to perform the duties of that office. If it was necessary, then a loss of the commission would lose the office. Not only negligence, but accident or fraud, fire or theft, might deprive an individual of his office. In such a case, I presume it could not be doubted, but that a copy from the record of the office of the secretary of state, would be, to every intent and purpose, equal to the original. The act of congress has expressly made it so. To give that copy validity, it would not be necessary to prove that the original had been transmitted and afterwards lost. The copy would be complete evidence that the original had existed, and that the appointment had been made, but not that the original had been transmitted. If indeed it should appear that the original had been mislaid in the office of state, that circumstance would not affect the operation of the copy. When all the requisites have been performed which authorize a recording officer to record any instrument whatever, and the order for that purpose has been given, the instrument is in law considered as recorded, although the manual labour of inserting it in a book kept for that purpose may not have been performed.

In the case of commissions, the law orders the secretary of state to record them. When therefore they are signed and sealed, the order for their being recorded is given; and whether inserted in the book or not, they are in law recorded.

A copy of this record is declared equal to the original, and the fees to be paid by a person requiring a copy are ascertained by law. Can a keeper of a public record erase therefrom a commission which has been recorded? Or can he refuse a copy thereof to a person demanding it on the terms prescribed by law?

Such a copy would, equally with the original, authorize the justice of peace to proceed in the performance of his duty, because it would, equally with the original, attest his appointment.

If the transmission of a commission be not considered as necessary to give validity to an appointment; still less is its acceptance. The appointment is the sole act of the president; the acceptance is the sole act of the officer, and is, in plain common sense, posterior to the appointment. As he may resign, so may

www.milestonedocuments.com

he refuse to accept: but neither the one nor the other is capable of rendering the appointment a nonentity.

That this is the understanding of the government, is apparent from the whole tenor of its conduct.

A commission bears date, and the salary of the officer commences from his appointment; not from the transmission or acceptance of his commission. When a person, appointed to any office, refuses to accept that office, the successor is nominated in the place of the person who has declined to accept, and not in the place of the person who had been previously in office and had created the original vacancy.

It is therefore decidedly the opinion of the court, that when a commission has been signed by the president, the appointment is made; and that the commission is complete when the seal of the United States has been affixed to it by the secretary of state.

Where an officer is removable at the will of the executive, the circumstance which completes his appointment is of no concern; because the act is at any time revocable; and the commission may be arrested, if still in the office. But when the officer is not removable at the will of the executive, the appointment is not revocable and cannot be annulled. It has conferred legal rights which cannot be resumed.

The discretion of the executive is to be exercised until the appointment has been made. But having once made the appointment, his power over the office is terminated in all cases, where by law the officer is not removable by him. The right to the office is then in the person appointed, and he has the absolute, unconditional power of accepting or rejecting it.

Mr. Marbury, then, since his commission was signed by the president and sealed by the secretary of state, was appointed; and as the law creating the office gave the officer a right to hold for five years independent of the executive, the appointment was not revocable; but vested in the officer legal rights which are protected by the laws of his country.

To withhold the commission, therefore, is an act deemed by the court not warranted by law, but violative of a vested legal right.

This brings us to the second inquiry; which is,

2. If he has a right, and that right has been violated, do the laws of his country afford him a remedy? The very essence of civil liberty certainly consists in the right of every individual to claim the protection of the laws, whenever he receives an injury. One of the first duties of government is to afford that protection. In Great Britain the king himself is sued in the respectful form of a petition, and he never fails to comply with the judgment of his court.

In the third volume of his Commentaries, page 23, Blackstone states two cases in which a remedy is afforded by mere operation of law.

"In all other cases," he says, "it is a general and indisputable rule, that where there is a legal right, there is also a legal remedy by suit or action at law whenever that right is invaded."

And afterwards, page 109 of the same volume, he says, "I am next to consider such injuries as are cognizable by the courts of common law. And herein I shall for the present only remark, that all possible injuries whatsoever, that did not fall within the exclusive cognizance of either the ecclesiastical, military, or maritime tribunals, are, for that very reason, within the cognizance of the common law courts of justice; for it is a settled and invariable principle in the laws of England, that every right, when withheld, must have a remedy, and every injury its proper redress."

The government of the United States has been emphatically termed a government of laws, and not of men. It will certainly cease to deserve this high appellation, if the laws furnish no remedy for the violation of a vested legal right.

If this obloquy is to be cast on the jurisprudence of our country, it must arise from the peculiar character of the case.

It behoves us then to inquire whether there be in its composition any ingredient which shall exempt from legal investigation, or exclude the injured party from legal redress. In pursuing this inquiry the first question which presents itself, is, whether this can be arranged with that class of cases which come under the description of damnum absque injuria—a loss without an injury.

This description of cases never has been considered, and it is believed never can be considered as comprehending offices of trust, of honour or of profit. The office of justice of peace in the district of Columbia is such an office; it is therefore worthy of the attention and guardianship of the laws. It has received that attention and guardianship. It has been created by special act of congress, and has been secured, so far as the laws can give security to the person appointed to fill it, for five years. It is not then on account of the worthlessness of the thing pursued, that the injured party can be alleged to be without remedy.

Is it in the nature of the transaction? Is the act of delivering or withholding a commission to be considered as a mere political act belonging to the execu-

Document Text

tive department alone, for the performance of which entire confidence is placed by our constitution in the supreme executive; and for any misconduct respecting which, the injured individual has no remedy.

That there may be such cases is not to be questioned; but that every act of duty to be performed in any of the great departments of government constitutes such a case, is not to be admitted.

By the act concerning invalids, passed in June 1794, the secretary at war is ordered to place on the pension list all persons whose names are contained in a report previously made by him to congress. If he should refuse to do so, would the wounded veteran be without remedy? Is it to be contended that where the law in precise terms directs the performance of an act in which an individual is interested, the law is incapable of securing obedience to its mandate? Is it on account of the character of the person against whom the complaint is made? Is it to be contended that the heads of departments are not amenable to the laws of their country?

Whatever the practice on particular occasions may be, the theory of this principle will certainly never be maintained. No act of the legislature confers so extraordinary a privilege, nor can it derive countenance from the doctrines of the common law. After stating that personal injury from the king to a subject is presumed to be impossible, Blackstone, Vol. III. p. 255, says, "but injuries to the rights of property can scarcely be committed by the crown without the intervention of its officers: for whom, the law, in matters of right, entertains no respect or delicacy; but furnishes various methods of detecting the errors and misconduct of those agents by whom the king has been deceived and induced to do a temporary injustice."

By the act passed in 1796, authorizing the sale of the lands above the mouth of Kentucky river, the purchaser, on paying his purchase money, becomes completely entitled to the property purchased; and on producing to the secretary of state the receipt of the treasurer upon a certificate required by the law, the president of the United States is authorized to grant him a patent. It is further enacted that all patents shall be countersigned by the secretary of state, and recorded in his office. If the secretary of state should choose to withhold this patent; or the patent being lost, should refuse a copy of it; can it be imagined that the law furnishes to the injured person no remedy?

It is not believed that any person whatever would attempt to maintain such a proposition.

It follows then that the question, whether the legality of an act of the head of a department be examinable in a court of justice or not, must always depend on the nature of that act.

If some acts be examinable, and others not, there must be some rule of law to guide the court in the exercise of its jurisdiction.

In some instances there may be difficulty in applying the rule to particular cases; but there cannot, it is believed, be much difficulty in laying down the rule.

By the constitution of the United States, the president is invested with certain important political powers, in the exercise of which he is to use his own discretion, and is accountable only to his country in his political character, and to his own conscience. To aid him in the performance of these duties, he is authorized to appoint certain officers, who act by his authority and in conformity with his orders.

In such cases, their acts are his acts; and whatever opinion may be entertained of the manner in which executive discretion may be used, still there exists, and can exist, no power to control that discretion. The subjects are political. They respect the nation, not individual rights, and being entrusted to the executive, the decision of the executive is conclusive. The application of this remark will be perceived by adverting to the act of congress for establishing the department of foreign affairs. This officer, as his duties were prescribed by that act, is to conform precisely to the will of the president. He is the mere organ by whom that will is communicated. The acts of such an officer, as an officer, can never be examinable by the courts.

But when the legislature proceeds to impose on that officer other duties; when he is directed peremptorily to perform certain acts; when the rights of individuals are dependent on the performance of those acts; he is so far the officer of the law; is amenable to the laws for his conduct; and cannot at his discretion sport away the vested rights of others.

The conclusion from this reasoning is, that where the heads of departments are the political or confidential agents of the executive, merely to execute the will of the president, or rather to act in cases in which the executive possesses a constitutional or legal discretion, nothing can be more perfectly clear than that their acts are only politically examinable. But where a specific duty is assigned by law, and individual rights depend upon the performance of that duty, it seems equally clear that the individual who considers himself injured has a right to resort to the laws of his country for a remedy.

Document Text

If this be the rule, let us inquire how it applies to the case under the consideration of the court. The power of nominating to the senate, and the power of appointing the person nominated, are political powers, to be exercised by the president according to his own discretion. When he has made an appointment, he has exercised his whole power, and his discretion has been completely applied to the case. If, by law, the officer be removable at the will of the president, then a new appointment may be immediately made, and the rights of the officer are terminated. But as a fact which has existed cannot be made never to have existed, the appointment cannot be annihilated; and consequently if the officer is by law not removable at the will of the president, the rights he has acquired are protected by the law, and are not resumable by the president. They cannot be extinguished by executive authority, and he has the privilege of asserting them in like manner as if they had been derived from any other source.

The question whether a right has vested or not, is, in its nature, judicial, and must be tried by the judicial authority, If, for example, Mr. Marbury had taken the oaths of a magistrate, and proceeded to act as one; in consequence of which a suit had been instituted against him, in which his defence had depended on his being a magistrate; the validity of his appointment must have been determined by judicial authority.

So, if he conceives that by virtue of his appointment he has a legal right either to the commission which has been made out for him or to a copy of that commission, it is equally a question examinable in a court, and the decision of the court upon it must depend on the opinion entertained of his appointment.

That question has been discussed, and the opinion is, that the latest point of time which can be taken as that at which the appointment was complete, and evidenced, was when, after the signature of the president, the seal of the United States was affixed to the commission.

It is then the opinion of the court,

1. That by signing the commission of Mr. Marbury, the president of the United States appointed him a justice of peace for the county of Washington in the district of Columbia; and that the seal of the United States, affixed thereto by the secretary of state, is conclusive testimony of the verity of the signature, and of the completion of the appointment; and that the appointment conferred on him a legal right to the office for the space of five years.

2. That, having this legal title to the office, he has a consequent right to the commission; a refusal to deliver which is a plain violation of that right, for which the laws of his country afford him a remedy.

It remains to be inquired whether,

3. He is entitled to the remedy for which he applies. This depends on,

1. The nature of the writ applied for. And,

2. The power of this court.

1. The nature of the writ.

Blackstone, in the third volume of his Commentaries, page 110, defines a mandamus to be, "a command issuing in the king"s name from the court of king"s bench, and directed to any person, corporation, or inferior court of judicature within the king"s dominions, requiring them to do some particular thing therein specified which appertains to their office and duty, and which the court of king"s bench has previously determined, or at least supposes, to be consonant to right and justice."

Lord Mansfield, in 3 Burrows, 1266, in the case of The King v. Baker et al. states with much precision and explicitness the cases in which this writ may be used.

"Whenever," says that very able judge, "there is a right to execute an office, perform a service, or exercise a franchise (more especially if it be in a matter of public concern or attended with profit), and a person is kept out of possession, or dispossessed of such right, and has no other specific legal remedy, this court ought to assist by mandamus, upon reasons of justice, as the writ expresses, and upon reasons of public policy, to preserve peace, order and good government." In the same case he says, "this writ ought to be used upon all occasions where the law has established no specific remedy, and where in justice and good government there ought to be one."

In addition to the authorities now particularly cited, many others were relied on at the bar, which show how far the practice has conformed to the general doctrines that have been just quoted.

This writ, if awarded, would be directed to an officer of government, and its mandate to him would be, to use the words of Blackstone, "to do a particular thing therein specified, which appertains to his office and duty, and which the court has previously determined or at least supposes to be consonant to right and justice." Or, in the words of Lord Mansfield, the applicant, in this case, has a right to execute an office of public concern, and is kept out of possession of that right.

These circumstances certainly concur in this case.

Still, to render the mandamus a proper remedy, the officer to whom it is to be directed, must be one

www.milestonedocuments.com

to whom, on legal principles, such writ may be directed; and the person applying for it must be without any other specific and legal remedy.

1. With respect to the officer to whom it would be directed. The intimate political relation, subsisting between the president of the United States and the heads of departments, necessarily renders any legal investigation of the acts of one of those high officers peculiarly irksome, as well as delicate; and excites some hesitation with respect to the propriety of entering into such investigation. Impressions are often received without much reflection or examination; and it is not wonderful that in such a case as this, the assertion, by an individual, of his legal claims in a court of justice, to which claims it is the duty of that court to attend, should at first view be considered by some, as an attempt to intrude into the cabinet, and to intermeddle with the prerogatives of the executive.

It is scarcely necessary for the court to disclaim all pretensions to such a jurisdiction. An extravagance, so absurd and excessive, could not have been entertained for a moment. The province of the court is, solely, to decide on the rights of individuals, not to inquire how the executive, or executive officers, perform duties in which they have a discretion. Questions, in their nature political, or which are, by the constitution and laws, submitted to the executive, can never be made in this court.

But, if this be not such a question; if so far from being an intrusion into the secrets of the cabinet, it respects a paper, which, according to law, is upon record, and to a copy of which the law gives a right, on the payment of ten cents; if it be no intermeddling with a subject, over which the executive can be considered as having exercised any control; what is there in the exalted station of the officer, which shall bar a citizen from asserting, in a court of justice, his legal rights, or shall forbid a court to listen to the claim; or to issue a mandamus, directing the performance of a duty, not depending on executive discretion, but on particular acts of congress and the general principles of law?

If one of the heads of departments commits any illegal act, under colour of his office, by which an individual sustains an injury, it cannot be pretended that his office alone exempts him from being sued in the ordinary mode of proceeding, and being compelled to obey the judgment of the law. How then can his office exempt him from this particular mode of deciding on the legality of his conduct, if the case be such a case as would, were any other individual the party complained of, authorize the process?

It is not by the office of the person to whom the writ is directed, but the nature of the thing to be done, that the propriety or impropriety of issuing a mandamus is to be determined. Where the head of a department acts in a case in which executive discretion is to be exercised; in which he is the mere organ of executive will; it is again repeated, that any application to a court to control, in any respect, his conduct, would be rejected without hesitation.

But where he is directed by law to do a certain act affecting the absolute rights of individuals, in the performance of which he is not placed under the particular direction of the president, and the performance of which the president cannot lawfully forbid, and therefore is never presumed to have forbidden; as for example, to record a commission, or a patent for land, which has received all the legal solemnities; or to give a copy of such record; in such cases, it is not perceived on what ground the courts of the country are further excused from the duty of giving judgment, that right to be done to an injured individual, than if the same services were to be performed by a person not the head of a department.

This opinion seems not now for the first time to be taken up in this country.

It must be well recollected that in 1792 an act passed, directing the secretary at war to place on the pension list such disabled officers and soldiers as should be reported to him by the circuit courts, which act, so far as the duty was imposed on the courts, was deemed unconstitutional; but some of the judges, thinking that the law might be executed by them in the character of commissioners, proceeded to act and to report in that character.

This law being deemed unconstitutional at the circuits, was repealed, and a different system was established; but the question whether those persons, who had been reported by the judges, as commissioners, were entitled, in consequence of that report, to be placed on the pension list, was a legal question, properly determinable in the courts, although the act of placing such persons on the list was to be performed by the head of a department.

That this question might be properly settled, congress passed an act in February 1793, making it the duty of the secretary of war, in conjunction with the attorney general, to take such measures as might be necessary to obtain an adjudication of the supreme court of the United States on the validity of any such rights, claimed under the act aforesaid.

After the passage of this act, a mandamus was moved for, to be directed to the secretary at war, commanding him to place on the pension list a person stating himself to be on the report of the judges.

There is, therefore, much reason to believe, that this mode of trying the legal right of the complainant, was deemed by the head of a department, and by the highest law officer of the United States, the most proper which could be selected for the purpose.

When the subject was brought before the court the decision was, not, that a mandamus would not lie to the head of a department, directing him to perform an act, enjoined by law, in the performance of which an individual had a vested interest; but that a mandamus ought not to issue in that case—the decision necessarily to be made if the report of the commissioners did not confer on the applicant a legal right.

The judgment in that case is understood to have decided the merits of all claims of that description; and the persons, on the report of the commissioners, found it necessary to pursue the mode prescribed by the law subsequent to that which had been deemed unconstitutional, in order to place themselves on the pension list.

The doctrine, therefore, now advanced is by no means a novel one.

It is true that the mandamus, now moved for, is not for the performance of an act expressly enjoined by statute.

It is to deliver a commission; on which subjects the acts of congress are silent. This difference is not considered as affecting the case. It has already been stated that the applicant has, to that commission, a vested legal right, of which the executive cannot deprive him. He has been appointed to an office, from which he is not removable at the will of the executive; and being so appointed, he has a right to the commission which the secretary has received from the president for his use. The act of congress does not indeed order the secretary of state to send it to him, but it is placed in his hands for the person entitled to it; and cannot be more lawfully withheld by him, than by another person.

It was at first doubted whether the action of detinue was not a specific legal remedy for the commission which has been withheld from Mr. Marbury; in which case a mandamus would be improper. But this doubt has yielded to the consideration that the judgment in detinue is for the thing itself, or its value. The value of a public office not to be sold, is incapable of being ascertained; and the applicant has a right to the office itself, or to nothing. He will obtain the office by obtaining the commission, or a copy of it from the record.

This, then, is a plain case of a mandamus, either to deliver the commission, or a copy of it from the record; and it only remains to be inquired,

Whether it can issue from this court.

The act to establish the judicial courts of the United States authorizes the supreme court "to issue writs of mandamus, in cases warranted by the principles and usages of law, to any courts appointed, or persons holding office, under the authority of the United States."

The secretary of state, being a person, holding an office under the authority of the United States, is precisely within the letter of the description; and if this court is not authorized to issue a writ of mandamus to such an officer, it must be because the law is unconstitutional, and therefore absolutely incapable of conferring the authority, and assigning the duties which its words purport to confer and assign.

The constitution vests the whole judicial power of the United States in one supreme court, and such inferior courts as congress shall, from time to time, ordain and establish. This power is expressly extended to all cases arising under the laws of the United States; and consequently, in some form, may be exercised over the present case; because the right claimed is given by a law of the United States.

In the distribution of this power it is declared that "the supreme court shall have original jurisdiction in all cases affecting ambassadors, other public ministers and consuls, and those in which a state shall be a party. In all other cases, the supreme court shall have appellate jurisdiction."

It has been insisted at the bar, that as the original grant of jurisdiction to the supreme and inferior courts is general, and the clause, assigning original jurisdiction to the supreme court, contains no negative or restrictive words; the power remains to the legislature to assign original jurisdiction to that court in other cases than those specified in the article which has been recited; provided those cases belong to the judicial power of the United States.

If it had been intended to leave it in the discretion of the legislature to apportion the judicial power between the supreme and inferior courts according to the will of that body, it would certainly have been useless to have proceeded further than to have defined the judicial power, and the tribunals in which it should be vested. The subsequent part of the section is mere surplusage, is entirely without meaning, if such is to be the construction. If congress remains at liberty to give this court appellate jurisdiction, where the constitution has declared

www.milestonedocuments.com

their jurisdiction shall be original; and original jurisdiction where the constitution has declared it shall be appellate; the distribution of jurisdiction made in the constitution, is form without substance.

Affirmative words are often, in their operation, negative of other objects than those affirmed; and in this case, a negative or exclusive sense must be given to them or they have no operation at all.

It cannot be presumed that any clause in the constitution is intended to be without effect; and therefore such construction is inadmissible, unless the words require it. If the solicitude of the convention, respecting our peace with foreign powers, induced a provision that the supreme court should take original jurisdiction in cases which might be supposed to affect them; yet the clause would have proceeded no further than to provide for such cases, if no further restriction on the powers of congress had been intended. That they should have appellate jurisdiction in all other cases, with such exceptions as congress might make, is no restriction; unless the words be deemed exclusive of original jurisdiction.

When an instrument organizing fundamentally a judicial system, divides it into one supreme, and so many inferior courts as the legislature may ordain and establish; then enumerates its powers, and proceeds so far to distribute them, as to define the jurisdiction of the supreme court by declaring the cases in which it shall take original jurisdiction, and that in others it shall take appellate jurisdiction, the plain import of the words seems to be, that in one class of cases its jurisdiction is original, and not appellate; in the other it is appellate, and not original. If any other construction would render the clause inoperative, that is an additional reason for rejecting such other construction, and for adhering to the obvious meaning.

To enable this court then to issue a mandamus, it must be shown to be an exercise of appellate jurisdiction, or to be necessary to enable them to exercise appellate jurisdiction.

It has been stated at the bar that the appellate jurisdiction may be exercised in a variety of forms, and that if it be the will of the legislature that a mandamus should be used for that purpose, that will must be obeyed. This is true; yet the jurisdiction must be appellate, not original.

It is the essential criterion of appellate jurisdiction, that it revises and corrects the proceedings in a cause already instituted, and does not create that case. Although, therefore, a mandamus may be directed to courts, yet to issue such a writ to an officer for the delivery of a paper, is in effect the same as to sustain an original action for that paper, and therefore seems not to belong to appellate, but to original jurisdiction. Neither is it necessary in such a case as this, to enable the court to exercise its appellate jurisdiction.

The authority, therefore, given to the supreme court, by the act establishing the judicial courts of the United States, to issue writs of mandamus to public officers, appears not to be warranted by the constitution; and it becomes necessary to inquire whether a jurisdiction, so conferred, can be exercised.

The question, whether an act, repugnant to the constitution, can become the law of the land, is a question deeply interesting to the United States; but, happily, not of an intricacy proportioned to its interest. It seems only necessary to recognise certain principles, supposed to have been long and well established, to decide it.

That the people have an original right to establish, for their future government, such principles as, in their opinion, shall most conduce to their own happiness, is the basis on which the whole American fabric has been erected. The exercise of this original right is a very great exertion; nor can it nor ought it to be frequently repeated. The principles, therefore, so established are deemed fundamental. And as the authority, from which they proceed, is supreme, and can seldom act, they are designed to be permanent.

This original and supreme will organizes the government, and assigns to different departments their respective powers. It may either stop here; or establish certain limits not to be transcended by those departments.

The government of the United States is of the latter description. The powers of the legislature are defined and limited; and that those limits may not be mistaken or forgotten, the constitution is written. To what purpose are powers limited, and to what purpose is that limitation committed to writing; if these limits may, at any time, be passed by those intended to be restrained? The distinction between a government with limited and unlimited powers is abolished, if those limits do not confine the persons on whom they are imposed, and if acts prohibited and acts allowed are of equal obligation. It is a proposition too plain to be contested, that the constitution controls any legislative act repugnant to it; or, that the legislature may alter the constitution by an ordinary act.

Between these alternatives there is no middle ground. The constitution is either a superior, paramount law, unchangeable by ordinary means, or it is on a level with ordinary legislative acts, and like other acts, is alterable when the legislature shall please to alter it.

If the former part of the alternative be true, then a legislative act contrary to the constitution is not law: if the latter part be true, then written constitutions are absurd attempts, on the part of the people, to limit a power in its own nature illimitable.

Certainly all those who have framed written constitutions contemplate them as forming the fundamental and paramount law of the nation, and consequently the theory of every such government must be, that an act of the legislature repugnant to the constitution is void.

This theory is essentially attached to a written constitution, and is consequently to be considered by this court as one of the fundamental principles of our society. It is not therefore to be lost sight of in the further consideration of this subject.

If an act of the legislature, repugnant to the constitution, is void, does it, notwithstanding its invalidity, bind the courts and oblige them to give it effect? Or, in other words, though it be not law, does it constitute a rule as operative as if it was a law? This would be to overthrow in fact what was established in theory; and would seem, at first view, an absurdity too gross to be insisted on. It shall, however, receive a more attentive consideration.

It is emphatically the province and duty of the judicial department to say what the law is. Those who apply the rule to particular cases, must of necessity expound and interpret that rule. If two laws conflict with each other, the courts must decide on the operation of each. So if a law be in opposition to the constitution: if both the law and the constitution apply to a particular case, so that the court must either decide that case conformably to the law, disregarding the constitution; or conformably to the constitution, disregarding the law: the court must determine which of these conflicting rules governs the case. This is of the very essence of judicial duty.

If then the courts are to regard the constitution; and he constitution is superior to any ordinary act of the legislature; the constitution, and not such ordinary act, must govern the case to which they both apply.

Those then who controvert the principle that the constitution is to be considered, in court, as a paramount law, are reduced to the necessity of maintaining that courts must close their eyes on the constitution, and see only the law.

This doctrine would subvert the very foundation of all written constitutions. It would declare that an act, which, according to the principles and theory of our government, is entirely void, is yet, in practice, completely obligatory. It would declare, that if the legislature shall do what is expressly forbidden, such act, notwithstanding the express prohibition, is in reality effectual. It would be giving to the legislature a practical and real omnipotence with the same breath which professes to restrict their powers within narrow limits. It is prescribing limits, and declaring that those limits may be passed at pleasure.

That it thus reduces to nothing what we have deemed the greatest improvement on political institutions—a written constitution, would of itself be sufficient, in America where written constitutions have been viewed with so much reverence, for rejecting the construction. But the peculiar expressions of the constitution of the United States furnish additional arguments in favour of its rejection.

The judicial power of the United States is extended to all cases arising under the constitution. Could it be the intention of those who gave this power, to say that, in using it, the constitution should not be looked into? That a case arising under the constitution should be decided without examining the instrument under which it arises?

This is too extravagant to be maintained.

In some cases then, the constitution must be looked into by the judges. And if they can open it at all, what part of it are they forbidden to read, or to obey?

There are many other parts of the constitution which serve to illustrate this subject.

It is declared that "no tax or duty shall be laid on articles exported from any state." Suppose a duty on the export of cotton, of tobacco, or of flour; and a suit instituted to recover it. Ought judgment to be rendered in such a case? ought the judges to close their eyes on the constitution, and only see the law.

The constitution declares that "no bill of attainder or ex post facto law shall be passed."

If, however, such a bill should be passed and a person should be prosecuted under it, must the court condemn to death those victims whom the constitution endeavours to preserve?

"No person," says the constitution, "shall be convicted of treason unless on the testimony of two witnesses to the same overt act, or on confession in open court."

Here the language of the constitution is addressed especially to the courts. It prescribes, directly for them, a rule of evidence not to be departed from. If the legislature should change that rule, and declare one witness, or a confession out of court,

www.milestonedocuments.com

Document Text

sufficient for conviction, must the constitutional principle yield to the legislative act?

From these and many other selections which might be made, it is apparent, that the framers of the constitution contemplated that instrument as a rule for the government of courts, as well as of the legislature.

Why otherwise does it direct the judges to take an oath to support it? This oath certainly applies, in an especial manner, to their conduct in their official character. How immoral to impose it on them, if they were to be used as the instruments, and the knowing instruments, for violating what they swear to support!

The oath of office, too, imposed by the legislature, is completely demonstrative of the legislative opinion on this subject. It is in these words: "I do solemnly swear that I will administer justice without respect to persons, and do equal right to the poor and to the rich; and that I will faithfully and impartially discharge all the duties incumbent on me as according to the best of my abilities and understanding, agreeably to the constitution and laws of the United States."

Why does a judge swear to discharge his duties agreeably to the constitution of the United States, if that constitution forms no rule for his government? if it is closed upon him and cannot be inspected by him.

If such be the real state of things, this is worse than solemn mockery. To prescribe, or to take this oath, becomes equally a crime.

It is also not entirely unworthy of observation, that in declaring what shall be the supreme law of the land, the constitution itself is first mentioned; and not the laws of the United States generally, but those only which shall be made in pursuance of the constitution, have that rank.

Thus, the particular phraseology of the constitution of the United States confirms and strengthens the principle, supposed to be essential to all written constitutions, that a law repugnant to the constitution is void, and that courts, as well as other departments, are bound by that instrument.

The rule must be discharged.

ships and three sections, shall be appropriated and vested, for the purposes aforesaid, only on condition that the legislature of the state of Ohio shall, within one year after the passing of this act, pass a law accepting the said eighteen quarter townships and three sections, for the purposes aforesaid, in lieu of the thirty-sixth part of the tract commonly called "the Virginia military reservation," heretofore appropriated and vested by law for the use of schools within the same; and releasing to the United States, all their claim, right, title, and interest, and all the right, title and interest of the inhabitants of the tract of land last mentioned, to the thirty-sixth part of the said tract heretofore appropriated and vested by law for the use of schools within the same. And if the legislature of the said state shall not pass a law as aforesaid, within one year after the passing of this act, the said eighteen quarter townships and three sections shall not be considered and held as appropriated and vested for the purposes aforesaid, but shall be disposed of in the same manner as is or may be provided, by law, for the disposal of other public lands in the same tract.

Legislature of Ohio to accept this grant in lieu of the part of the Virginia military reservation.

1803, ch. 21.

APPROVED, March 2, 1807.

STATUTE II.

March 2, 1807.

CHAP. XXII.—*An Act to prohibit the importation of Slaves into any port or place within the jurisdiction of the United States, from and after the first day of January, in the year of our Lord one thousand eight hundred and eight.*(a)

Act of March 22, 1794, ch. 11.
Act of May 10, 1800, ch. 51.
Act of Feb. 28, 1803, ch. 10.
Act of April 20, 1818, ch. 83.
Act of May 15, 1820, ch. 112, sec. 4, 5.

Be it enacted by the Senate and House of Representatives of the United States of America in Congress assembled, That from and after the first day of January, one thousand eight hundred and eight, it shall not be lawful to import or bring into the United States or the territories thereof from any foreign kingdom, place, or country, any negro, mulatto, or person of colour, with intent to hold, sell, or dispose of such negro, mulatto, or person of colour, as a slave, or to be held to service or labour.

Importation of slaves into the U. S. forbidden after Jan. 1, 1808.

SEC. 2. *And be it further enacted*, That no citizen or citizens of the United States, or any other person, shall, from and after the first day of January, in the year of our Lord one thousand eight hundred and eight, for himself, or themselves, or any other person whatsoever, either as master, factor, or owner, build, fit, equip, load or otherwise prepare any ship or vessel, in any port or place within the jurisdiction of the United States, nor shall cause any ship or vessel to sail from any port or place within the same, for the purpose of procuring any negro, mulatto, or person of colour, from any foreign kingdom, place, or country, to be transported to any port or place whatsoever, within the jurisdiction of the United States, to be held, sold, or disposed of as slaves, or to be held to service or labour: and if any ship or vessel shall be so fitted out for the purpose aforesaid, or shall be caused to sail so as aforesaid, every such ship or vessel, her tackle, apparel, and furniture, shall be forfeited to the United States, and shall be liable to be seized, prosecuted, and condemned in any of the circuit courts or district courts, for the district where the said ship or vessel may be found or seized.

Forfeiture of vessels fitted out for the slave trade after Jan. 1, 1808.

SEC. 3. *And be it further enacted*, That all and every person so building, fitting out, equipping, loading, or otherwise preparing or sending away, any ship or vessel, knowing or intending that the same shall be employed in such trade or business, from and after the first day of January, one thousand eight hundred and eight, contrary to the true intent and meaning of this act, or any ways aiding or abetting therein, shall

Penalties for being engaged in such expeditions.

An Act to Prohibit the Importation of Slaves (Library of Congress)

Act to Prohibit the Importation of Slaves

1807

"I congratulate you … [on withdrawing] the citizens of the United States from all further participation in those violations of human rights which have been so long continued on the unoffending inhabitants of Africa."

Overview

In 1807 Congress passed a law banning the importation of slaves to the United States. The law went into effect on January 1, 1808. This act ended large-scale importations of slaves into the United States. In the eight years before the law made the trade illegal, the United States imported about forty thousand new slaves from Africa. From 1808 until the Civil War broke out in 1861, less than a fifth of that number of slaves would be illegally smuggled into the nation. The law thus ended American participation in one of the most immoral violations of human rights in world history. The law did not, of course, end slavery itself in the United States. That would not take place until the Civil War and the adoption of the Thirteenth Amendment in 1865 ended all slavery in the nation.

Context

Before the American Revolution, both the colonies and Great Britain regulated the African slave trade to what became the United States. The British government protected the Royal African Company, which brought more slaves to the American colonies than any other single entity. The Royal African Company attracted investors from the most important segments of English society, including members of the royal family. The slave trade was an important part of Britain's economic policy. Britain collected taxes on imported slaves while British merchants made fortunes buying and selling human beings.

Most of the colonial governments both taxed slaves and occasionally sought to limit importations. After the Stono Rebellion (1739), South Carolina imposed a prohibitive tax on imported slaved for three years because the colony's leaders believed large numbers of freshly imported Africans would undermine the safety of the colony. Later, in 1751, the colony imposed a special tax on imported slaves to slow down the trade. In 1760 South Carolina once again banned the trade because the colonists feared the growing number of African-born slaves, but royal authorities disallowed the law. The trade was too important to the British economy to let colonists regulate it. In 1764 South Carolina levied new taxes on imported slaves because, as the legislature noted, the growing number of African-born slaves "may prove of the most dangerous consequence" (qtd. in Du Bois, p. 7).

Shortly before the Revolution, Virginia also tried to ban the trade, not for prudential reasons but for economic reasons. Too much money was leaving Virginia, ending up in the bank accounts of British merchants. Thus, the Virginia legislature attempted to use prohibitive taxes to discourage the trade. Once again the British government overruled this law because the trade was vital to the British economy and because the Royal African Company had powerful patrons in the government. In *A Summary View of the Rights of British America* (1774), Thomas Jefferson asserted that Virginians favored the "abolition of domestic slavery" and that as the first step toward this end "it is necessary to exclude all further importations from Africa." He complained, however, that "our repeated attempts to effect this … by imposing duties which might amount to a prohibition, have been hitherto defeated by his majesty's negative" (Ford, p. 440). Jefferson's language was self-serving and disingenuous, if not dishonest. Few white Virginians had in fact taken a stand against slavery, and there is no evidence that anyone but a few Quakers and other religious dissenters in the colony favored the "abolition of domestic slavery." The young Jefferson was himself on the way to becoming a fabulously rich master, ultimately owning more than two hundred slaves in addition to the nearly one hundred slaves he sold in the 1780s and 1790s.

In his first draft of the Declaration of Independence, Jefferson condemned the Crown in more forceful language. He asserted that the king had "waged cruel war against human nature itself, violating its most sacred rights of life and liberty" by perpetuating the African slave trade. Calling the African trade "piratical warfare," Jefferson asserted that "the CHRISTIAN king of Great Britain" was so "determined to keep open a market where MEN" were bought and sold that he used his "negative" to suppress "every legislative attempt to prohibit or to restrain this execrable commerce" (http://www.pbs.org/jefferson/archives/documents/frame_ih198172.htm).

Time Line

1607	■ Jamestown is settled.
1619	■ **August** Blacks arrive in Virginia as indentured servants.
1688	■ Germantown Quakers issue first protest against slavery and the slave trade in the New World.
1739	■ **September 9** Beginning of the Stono Rebellion in South Carolina.
1740	■ **April 5** South Carolina imposes a prohibitive duty on imported slaves for three years in response to Stono Rebellion.
1764	■ **August 25** South Carolina places new taxes on the slave trade to discourage importations for fear of too many blacks in the state.
1774	■ In his *Summary View of the Rights of British America* (1774), Thomas Jefferson asserts that Virginians favor the "abolition of domestic slavery" and that as the first step toward this end "it is necessary to exclude all further importations from Africa."
1775	■ In his first draft of the Declaration of Independence, Jefferson condemns the king for forcing the slave trade on to the colonists; the Continental Congress removes this paragraph.
1780	■ **March 1** Pennsylvania passes a gradual abolition act that permanently ends the slave trade to that state.

The Continental Congress removed Jefferson's tirade from the draft of the Declaration because it did not ring true. The colonists, for the most part, had been willing and eager purchasers of slaves. Nor is there any evidence that even during the Revolution either Jefferson or any other Virginia leaders had any interest in actually ending slavery. Virginia's attempt to ban the trade was purely economic, not based on any moral opposition to slavery. Similarly, the Crown's refusal to allow the state to limit or end the trade was economic.

During the Revolution all the new states banned or suspended the trade. Most slaves came on English ships, and even those on American ships were often purchased from the Royal African Company. Thus, a ban on the trade was part of the general revolutionary boycott of British commerce.

In some of the new northern states abolition of the trade also had a moral basis. During or immediately after the Revolution, five states would either end slavery outright (Massachusetts and New Hampshire) or pass gradual abolition acts (Pennsylvania, Rhode Island, and Connecticut) that would lead to a relatively speedy end to slavery. In those states a ban on the trade was consistent with growing opposition to slavery itself. In the remaining new states, opposition to the trade was economic and political but not essentially moral. After the Revolution, South Carolina, Georgia, and North Carolina reopened the trade but then suspended it or levied a prohibitive tax on new slaves. In 1787, when the Constitutional Convention met in Philadelphia, only Georgia was importing slaves. Nevertheless, with the expectation of reopening the trade, the delegates from the Deep South jealously guarded their right to import slaves.

At the convention, delegates from the Deep South demanded that Congress be prohibited from closing the African slave trade. They wanted a specific exception written into the Constitution to prevent Congress from using its power to regulate commerce to end the African trade. Many of the northern delegates opposed this because they found slavery deeply immoral as well as a fundamental violation of the principles of the Revolution. Some Americans (in the North and the South) who were comfortable with, or at least resigned to, the continuation of slavery nevertheless believed that the African trade was particularly immoral and pernicious. It might be possible to justify holding people in bondage who were born to that condition, but they saw no good reason for bringing more slaves to the nation. Many Americans who had no strong moral feelings about the trade, or even slavery, nevertheless believed that slavery was inherently dangerous to society and that the further importation of African slaves would only worsen an already dangerous situation. Having just fought a revolution for their own liberty, many Americans worried that slaves might soon follow the model of their masters. Finally, many slave owners in Virginia and Maryland opposed the African trade for narrowly economic reasons. They had more slaves than they needed and knew that if the trade ended, their surplus slaves would be more valuable.

At the convention the delegates from South Carolina, supported by other southerners, insisted on explicit protection of the African trade in the Constitution. The debates over this issue were among the most intense at the convention. These debates were not part of the debate over slave representation that led to the three-fifths clause, but they were influenced by that clause. Once the convention agreed to count slaves for purposes of representation in Congress, the status of the trade became more important. A continuation of the trade not only would lead to an increase of slaves and human misery in the new nation but also would strengthen the South in Congress, giving more political power to the supporters of bondage. This prospect led Gouverneur Morris, who represented Pennsylvania at the convention, to denounce the immorality of political compromises over slavery, which, he said,

> when fairly explained comes to this: that the inhabitant of Georgia and South Carolina who goes to the Coast of Africa, and in defiance of the most sacred laws of humanity tears away his fellow creatures from their dearest connections and damns them to the most cruel bondages, shall have more votes in a Government instituted for protection of the rights of mankind, than the Citizen of Pennsylvania or New Jersey who views with a laudable horror, so nefarious a practice. (Finkelman, 2001, chap. 1)

Despite the attempts of Morris and a few others to raise the question of the morality of slavery, most of the delegates focused on compromise and economic necessity. In August the convention debated the commerce clause, which could have given Congress the power to regulate international and interstate commerce by a simple majority. Before that debate could take place, the South Carolina delegation insisted on protection for the African slave trade and a ban on export taxes. Southerners believed that export taxes could be used to tax the commodities produced by slave labor, such as tobacco and rice, and thus indirectly harm slavery. South Carolina's John Rutledge noted that he would vote for the commerce clause as it stood, but only "on condition that the subsequent part relating to negroes should also be agreed to" (Finkelman, 2001, chap. 1). Delegates from Connecticut and Massachusetts indicated some support for Rutledge's position. What should be called the "dirty compromise" of the Convention was taking shape. The South Carolina delegation would support the commerce clause if New England would support a prohibition on export taxes and a clause protecting the slave trade. This understanding soon solidified.

In late August the convention debated how the Constitution would deal with the African slave trade. The first issue was whether to allow an import tax on slaves. Rutledge opposed this with a two-pronged attack. He first told the convention that the "true question at present is whether the Southern States shall or shall not be parties to the Union." The implied threat of secession was clear. He then told the northern delegates that, if they would "consult their interest," they would "not oppose the increase of slaves which will increase the commodities of which they

Time Line

1790

- Benjamin Franklin petitions Congress to end the slave trade. In response to a vitriolic attack by Congressman James Jackson of Georgia, Franklin publishes his final essay, a sarcastic parody on the slave trade in which a fictitious character defends enslaving Christians in exactly the same language that Jackson and others defended enslaving blacks.

1792

- South Carolina once again bans the importation of slaves from Africa into the state. The state will continue to ban the trade until 1803.

1794

- **March 22**
Congress passes legislation prohibiting American ships from participating in the African slave trade.

1800

- **May 10**
Congress amends 1794 law with harsher penalties for Americans participating in the trade.

1803

- U.S. purchases Louisiana, providing new markets for slaves.

- **February 28**
U.S. Congress passes a new law to further prevent American ships from participating in the African trade and to prevent American citizens or resident aliens from serving on slave ships.

1806

- **December 2**
In his annual message in December, Jefferson urges Congress to pass a law to ban the slave trade, effective January 1, 1808.

1807

- **March 2**
Congress passes a slave trade ban, effective January 1, 1808.

- **March 25**
Great Britain bans British participation in the slave trade, effective May 1, 1807.

www.milestonedocuments.com

Time Line

1808	■ **January 1** Act to Prohibit the Importation of Slaves goes into effect.
1818	■ **April 10** Congress passes new legislation to further enforce the ban on the trade.
1819	■ **March 3** Congress passes another act to enforce the slave trade ban.
1820	■ **May 15** In a statute meant to last only two years Congress makes slave trading piracy punishable by death.
1823	■ **January 30** Congress makes the 1820 law permanent.

will become the carriers" (Finkelman, 2001, chap. 1). Oliver Ellsworth of Connecticut agreed, refusing to debate the "morality or wisdom of slavery" and simply asserting that "what enriches a part enriches the whole" (Finkelman, 2001, chap. 1) The alliance for profit between the Deep South and New England was now fully developed. Charles Pinckney then reaffirmed that South Carolina would "never receive the plan if it prohibits the slave trade" (Finkelman, 2001, chap. 1). Shrewdly, Pinckney equated a tax on imported slaves with a prohibition on the trade itself.

Like Ellsworth, Connecticut's Roger Sherman declared his personal disapproval of slavery but refused to condemn it in other parts of the nation. He then argued against a prohibition of the slave trade. First, he asserted that "the public good did not require" an end to the trade. Noting that the states already had the right to import slaves, Sherman saw no point in taking a right away from the states unnecessarily because "it was expedient to have as few objections as possible" to the new Constitution (Finkelman, 2001, chap. 1). Here Sherman assumed it was necessary to defuse southern opposition to the Constitution, which might result from a ban on the slave trade, but he did not think it necessary to placate those who might oppose the Constitution if it allowed the slave trade to continue. Sherman was prepared to appease those who supported the slave trade, but he apparently was unconcerned about the strong opposition to the slave trade in his own region.

Next, Sherman observed that "the abolition of slavery seemed to be going on in the U.S." If left alone, the "good sense of the several States" would soon put an end to all slavery in the country (Finkelman, 2001, chap. 1). In making this argument Sherman either confused the abolition of the slave trade with the abolition of slavery itself, or he foolishly believed that because New England and Pennsylvania had begun to abolish slavery, the rest of the nation would soon follow. Finally, revealing his priorities, Sherman urged the delegates to hurry and finish their business, noting, no doubt, that they had been in session for almost three months.

George Mason of Virginia responded to Sherman with a fierce attack on the "infernal traffic" in slaves, which he blamed on "the avarice of British Merchants." Reflecting the sectional hostilities at the convention, as well as trying to lay blame on anyone but Virginians for the problem of slavery, Mason then "lamented" that his "Eastern brethren had from a lust of gain embarked in this nefarious traffic." Mason declared slavery an "evil" system that produced "the most pernicious effect on manners But in fact this owner of more than two hundred slaves did not oppose slavery itself, just the slave trade. Despite his apparent attack on the whole institution, Mason ended his speech by demanding only that the national government "have power to prevent the increase of slavery" by prohibiting the African trade (Finkelman, 2001, chap. 1).

Mason failed to say in this speech that Virginia, like Maryland, had a surplus of slaves and did not need the African slave trade any longer. But James McHenry of Maryland candidly wrote in his private notes "that the population or increase of slaves in Virginia exceeded their calls for their services," and thus a prohibition of the slave trade "would be a monopoly" in Virginia's "favor" (Finkelman, 2001, chap. 1).

Ellsworth of Connecticut, adopting the same pose as Sherman, answered Mason. Because "he had never owned a slave," Ellsworth declared he "could not judge of the effects of slavery on character." However, if slavery were as wrong, as Mason had suggested, merely ending the trade was insufficient. Ellsworth, of course, knew that the Virginians opposed allowing the national government to abolish slavery. Therefore, since there were many slaves in Virginia and Maryland and fewer in the Deep South, Ellsworth argued that any prohibition on the trade would be "unjust towards S. Carolina and Georgia" (Finkelman, 2001, chap. 1). Ellsworth urged the Convention not to "intermeddle" in the affairs of other states. The convention had now witnessed the unusual phenomenon of a New Englander defending the slave trade against the attacks of a Virginian.

The Carolinians were, of course, quite capable of defending their own institution. Charles Pinckney, citing ancient Rome and Greece, declared that slavery was "justified by the example of all the world." He warned that any prohibition of the slave trade would "produce serious objections to the Constitution which he wished to see adopted" (Finkelman, 2001, chap. 1). His cousin, General Charles Cotesworth Pinckney, also declared his support for the Constitution, but noted that his "personal influence … would be of no avail towards obtaining the assent" of his home state. He believed Virginia's opposition to the trade was more pecuniary than moral. Virginia would "gain by stopping the importations" because "her slaves will rise in value, and she has more than she wants." Prohibiting the trade would force South Carolina and Georgia "to confederate" on "unequal terms." While Virginia might gain, the nation as a whole would not. More slaves would produce more goods, and that result would help not only the South but also states involved in "the carrying trade." Furthermore, he declared, "the more consumption also, and the more of this, the more of revenue for the common treasury." Seeing the slave trade solely as an economic issue, Pinckney thought it "reasonable" that imported slaves be taxed. But a prohibition of the slave trade would be "an exclusion of S. Carolina from the Union." As he had made clear at the beginning of his speech, "S. Carolina and Georgia cannot do without slaves" (Finkelman, 2001, chap. 1).

Supporting South Carolina, Sherman of Connecticut declared that "it was better to let the S. States import slaves than to part with them, if they made that a sine qua non." However, in what may have been an attempt to give his remarks an antislavery tone, he argued that taxing imported slaves was morally wrong because that "implied they were property" (Finkelman, 2001, chap. 1). This position undoubtedly pleased Sherman's southern allies, who did not want to pay taxes on any slaves they imported. Sherman's speech also underscored the profound support that the Carolinians and Georgians found among some New Englanders.

On the other side of the issue, John Dickinson of Delaware, reflecting his Quaker heritage, vigorously opposed allowing the slave trade to continue, arguing that the trade was "inadmissible on every principle of honor and safety" (Finkelman, 2001, chap. 1). Furthermore, he was prepared to call the Carolinians' bluff on the question of union, doubting that the Deep South would reject the Constitution if the trade were prohibited. James Wilson of Pennsylvania was also skeptical of southern threats, but he did not offer any strong rebuttal. Nor did Rufus King of Massachusetts, who only pointed out that prohibiting a tax on imported Africans was an "inequality that could not fail to strike the commercial sagacity of the Northern and middle States" (Finkelman, 2001, chap. 1).

The convention then considered a proposal that Congress be barred from prohibiting the African slave trade until 1800 but that in the meantime a reasonable tax could be levied on imported slaves. South Carolina's General Pinckney immediately urged that the date be changed to 1808, which would be twenty years after the Constitution was ratified. Nathaniel Gorham of Massachusetts seconded this motion. Virginia's James Madison, a future president, complained that this provision was "dishonorable to the National character" and to the Constitution and that the "twenty years will produce all the mischief that can be apprehended from the liberty to import slaves" (Finkelman, 2001, chap. 1). Nevertheless, the delegates accepted Pinckney's change by a seven-to-four vote. Three New England states, Maryland, and the three Deep South states supported Pinckney's motion.

The final text of the slave trade provision was designed to obscure what the convention had done. The clause read:

Thomas Jefferson signed the Act to Prohibit the Importation of Slaves in March 1807. (Library of Congress)

"The Migration or Importation of such Persons as any of the State now existing shall think proper to admit shall not be prohibited by the Congress prior to the Year one thousand eight hundred and eight, but a Tax or duty may be imposed on such Importation, not exceeding ten dollars for each Person" (Finkelman, 2001, chap. 1).

It is important to understand that the clause did not require an end to the trade in 1808. Moreover, the clause reflected the assumption, held by almost everyone at the convention, that the Deep South would grow faster than the rest of the nation and that by 1808 the states that most wanted to continue the trade would have enough political power, and enough allies, to prevent an end to the trade. Ending the trade would require that a bill pass both houses of Congress and be signed by the president. That process would give the supporters of the trade three opportunities to stop a bill and keep the trade open.

The slave trade provision was a significant factor in the debates over ratification, but its impact was complicated. Opponents of the Constitution, in both the North and the South, roundly condemned the clause. On the other hand, supporters of the Constitution—even those who were ambivalent or hostile to slavery—praised the clause.

Antifederalists in the North and the Upper South hammered home, again and again, the fundamental immorality of the clause. On the last day of the convention Virginia's George Mason, to no one's surprise, declared he would not sign the Constitution, citing the slave trade provisions as

www.milestonedocuments.com

one of his major objections and asserting that "such importations render the United States weaker, more vulnerable, and less capable of defense" (Finkelman, 2001, chap. 1). He did not add, but could have if he had been totally honest, that the slave trade would also diminish the value of the many slaves he already owned.

Many in the North, and some in the South, took a more principled stand against the Constitution because of the slave trade provision. A New Yorker complained that the Constitution condoned "drenching the bowels of Africa in gore, for the sake of enslaving its free-born innocent inhabitants" (Finkelman, 2001, chap. 1) In New Hampshire, Joshua Atherton opposed ratification because it would make all Americans "consenters to, and partakers in, the sin and guilt of this abominable traffic" (Finkelman, 2001, chap. 1). A Virginian thought the slave trade provision was an "excellent clause" for "an Algerian constitution: but not so well calculated (I hope) for the latitude of America" (Finkelman, 2001, chap. 1).

Northern supporters of the Constitution were at a rhetorical disadvantage in this debate, but they nevertheless had to engage the issue. James Wilson of Pennsylvania offered an argument that was intellectually dishonest but politically shrewd. He argued that the slave trade clause would, in fact, allow for the end of slavery itself. Speaking to the Pennsylvania ratifying convention, he made the subtle shift from the "trade" to slavery, and since most of his listeners were not as legally sophisticated as Wilson, he was able to fudge the issue. Thus, Wilson told the Pennsylvania ratifying convention that after "the lapse of a few years … Congress will have power to exterminate slavery from within our borders" (Finkelman, 2001, chap. 1). Since Wilson attended all the debates over this clause, it is impossible to accept this statement as his understanding of the slave trade clause. More likely, he simply made this argument to win support for the Constitution.

Supporters in Massachusetts and New Hampshire made similar arguments. In New Hampshire a supporter of the Constitution also argued that the slave trade clause gave Congress the power to end slavery. He was quickly disabused of this notion by Joshua Atherton. A more sophisticated response to the trade was to note that without the Constitution the states could keep the trade open indefinitely because the Congress under the Articles of Confederation had no power to regulate commerce, but under the Constitution it would be possible, in *just* twenty years, to end the trade.

Upper South supporters of the Constitution, like Madison, also made the argument that a ban on the trade was impossible under the Articles of Confederation, and thus the Constitution, even if imperfect, was still a good bargain. Deep South supporters of the Constitution, like Charles Cotesworth Pinckney, simply bragged that they had won a great victory—as indeed they had—in protecting the trade for *at least* twenty years. In summing up the entire Constitution, General Pinckney, who had been one of the ablest defenders of slavery at the Convention, proudly told the South Carolina House of Representatives: "In short, considering all circumstances, we have made the best terms for the security of this species of property it was in our power to make. We would have made better if we could; but on the whole, I do not think them bad" (Finkelman, 2001, chap. 1).

While Congress did not have the power to end the trade, it did have the power to regulate the trade, and starting in 1794 Congress did just that. In March, Congress prohibited the use of any U.S. port or shipyard for the purpose of fitting out or building any ship to be used in the trade. The law (An Act to Prohibit the Carrying on the Slave Trade from the United States to Any Foreign Place or Country) also prohibited ships sailing from U.S. ports from trafficking in slaves to foreign countries. Ships sailing from the United States to Africa, even if of foreign registry, were required to "give bond with sufficient sureties, to the treasurer of the United States, that none of the natives of Africa, or any other foreign country or place, shall be taken on board … to be transported, or sold as slaves, in any other foreign port or place, within nine months thereafter" (p. 349). Penalties under the law included fines ranging from $2,000 for outfitting a ship to $200 for an individual working on such a ship. The act provided that the actual ships involved in the trade could be confiscated. The law gave half of all fines to any informants, thus providing an incentive for ship captains and mariners to monitor the activities of anyone they suspected of being involved in the illegal trade.

In 1800 Congress amended the 1794 act by dramatically increasing fines for illegal American participation in the trade and giving informants a right to the entire value of any ship condemned under the law. In addition to not allowing American ships to participate in the trade, the new law (An Act in Addition to the Act Intitled [sic], "An Act to Prohibit the Carrying on the Slave Trade from the United States to Any Foreign Place or Country") prohibited any American from having any interest in a ship involved in the trade. Thus, Americans could no longer invest in the trade, even if it was carried on legally by non-U.S. ships. If convicted of having an interest in the trade, an American was subject to a fine that was double the value of his investment in the vessel and also double the value of any slaves in which he had an interest. The 1800 amendment explicitly prohibited any American citizen or resident alien from voluntarily serving "on board of any foreign ship or vessel … employed in the slave trade" (p. 71). It no longer mattered if the ship was U.S. bottom or even if the ship left an American port. American sailors found on slavers were now subject to a $2,000 fine. The law authorized all "commissioned vessels of the United States, to seize and take any vessels employed" (p. 71) in the trade contrary to the law, with the crew receiving half the value of the ship when it was sold. This provided an enormous incentive for American ships to police the trade.

In 1803 Congress provided new fines for people who brought slaves into states that banned the importation of slaves (An Act to Prevent the Importation of Certain Persons into Certain States Where, by the Laws Thereof, Their Admission Is Prohibited). The law applied to a "negro, mulatto, or other person of color" (p. 205) imported from Africa or the Caribbean. This language was apparently used to prevent people who might bring in Africans by claiming they were not slaves but servants or indentured servants.

All three of these laws had been designed to limit American participation in the trade but could not be used to stop the trade itself. Significantly, all the laws passed before 1807 focused on ships, sailors, and investors. None of the laws had any provision for what should happen to slaves illegally imported into the United States. Indeed, while the 1794 law provided for the sale of a ship and its "tackle, furniture, apparel and other appurtenances" (p. 349) of a slaver, it did not mention what should happen to any slaves or other cargo on the ship. Presumably, they, too, would be sold for the benefit of the United States, the informant, or any other claimant under the three laws.

In his annual message to Congress in December 1806, Jefferson, who had long opposed the trade (but not slavery itself), reminded the nation that on January 1, 1808, the constitutional suspension of congressional power on this issue would finally expire. He took a moment in his address to "congratulate" his "fellow-citizens, on the approach of the period at which you may interpose your authority constitutionally to withdraw the citizens of the United States from all further participation in those violations of human rights which have been so long continued on the unoffending inhabitants of Africa, and which the morality, the reputation, and the best interests of our country have long been eager to proscribe." He noted that any law passed by Congress could not take effect until January 1, 1808, but he urged Congress to act quickly "to prevent by timely notice expeditions which can not be completed before that day" (Jefferson, 1897, p. 396). Congress readily complied with legislation to absolutely ban all importations of slavery after January 1, 1808. The 1807 act was a comprehensive attempt to close the African trade. By passing the law in March, Congress gave all slave traders nine months to close down their operations in the United States.

About the Author

Senator Stephen R. Bradley of Vermont introduced the bill in the Senate in December 1806. Bradley was born in Connecticut. During the Revolution he served in the Connecticut militia, rising to the rank of major, but then left the military to study at Yale. In 1779 he moved to Vermont, where he was named a brigadier general in the militia of what was then the Republic of Vermont—a region trying to break away from both New York and New Hampshire. During this period he became a lawyer and served as a prosecutor and in the Vermont legislature. In 1791 he became one of Vermont's first two U.S. senators. Defeated for reelection, be was appointed to the state supreme court. In 1801 he went back to the Senate, were he remained until 1813.

Recognized as a skilled constitutional expert, Bradley was the primary author of the Twelfth Amendment to the U.S. Constitution. In December 1805 he announced that he would introduce legislation to ban the slave trade. Congress tabled the issue until December 1806, when Bradley's bill was introduced, sent to committee, and finally passed. Bradley had hoped to make slave trading a capital offence, but the House of Representatives would not accept this, and ultimately the death penalty provision was deleted from the bill.

Explanation and Analysis of the Document

The ten sections of the 1807 act were designed to eliminate all American participation in the slave trade. Section 1 of the new law set the tone of the legislation. After January 1, 1808, it would "not be lawful to import or bring into the United States or the territories thereof from any foreign kingdom, place, or country, any negro, mulatto, or person of colour, with intent to hold, sell, or dispose of such [person] ... as a slave, or to be held to service or labour." The act provided an enormous penalty—up to $20,000—for anyone building a ship for the slave trade or fitting out an existing ship to be used in the trade.

Penalties for participating in the slave trade varied. American citizens participating in the trade were subject to fines of up to $10,000 and jail terms of no less than five years or more than ten years. Ships of any nation found in American ports or hovering off the American coast with slaves on them could be seized and forfeited, with the captain facing a $10,000 fine and up to four years in prison. Any American who purchased an illegally imported slave would lose that slave and be fined $800 for every slave purchased. The law allowed the U.S. Navy to interdict ships involved in the illegal trade. The law required ships transporting slaves legally in the United States from one part of the nation to another to register their cargo with port authorities before commencing their voyage. This provision was designed to further prevent the illegal importation of slaves.

The law had teeth to it. Fines under the statute were enormous, and the potential jail time was enough to discourage most slave smugglers. Moreover, for the Jefferson administration, which never much liked federal power, this act constituted a huge granting of power to the national government. Had Congress provided sufficient funding to enforce the law, it would have surely eliminated almost all slave imports. Funding the suppression of the trade, would, however, be problematic until the Civil War.

The 1808 law had one other problem: the disposition of illegally imported slaves. Logically, illegally imported slaves should have been either freed in the United States or sent back to Africa. After all, one of the goals of the law was to end the importation of new slaves from Africa. Given the views of President Jefferson and many of the leaders of his

www.milestonedocuments.com

Essential Quotes

"From and after the first day of January, one thousand eight hundred and eight, it shall not be lawful to import or bring into the United States or the territories thereof from any foreign kingdom, place, or country, any negro, mulatto, or person of colour, with intent to hold, sell, or dispose of such negro, mulatto, or person of colour, as a slave, or to be held to service or labour."

(Section 1)

"I congratulate you, fellow-citizens, on the approach of the period at which you may interpose your authority constitutionally to withdraw the citizens of the United States from all further participation in those violations of human rights which have been so long continued on the unoffending inhabitants of Africa, and which the morality, the reputation, and the best interests of our country have long been eager to proscribe. Although no law you pass can take prohibitory effect till the first day of the year 1808, yet the intervening period is not too long to prevent by timely notice expeditions which can not be completed before that day."

(Thomas Jefferson, Sixth Annual Message to Congress, 1806)

party, either option was impossible. Jefferson was deeply hostile to the presence of free blacks in the United States. In a letter to Edward Coles, written shortly after he left office, Jefferson referred to them as "pests" on society (qtd. in Finkelman, 2001, chap. 6). Thus, his administration had no interest in freeing Africans who were illegally imported into the nation. Nor was the deeply parsimonious Jefferson likely to support spending any money on returning the Africans to their homeland. They may have been illegally seized as slaves and illegally brought to America, but that did not mean they should be free.

So what would the nation do with slaves illegally brought to its shores? Reflecting Jefferson's states' rights ideology, his hatred of free blacks and his refusal to spend money unless absolutely necessary, the law provided that any slaves illegally found in the United States would be treated according to the law of the state in which they were found—or brought to. In practice this meant the Africans would become slaves in the United States and that the states would profit from the illegal trade by selling the Africans.

Under the law, the United States would gain money from the sale of confiscated ships and the large fines imposed on anyone involved in the slave trade. People informing on those who violated the law, as well as the crews of naval ships that seized traders, would also share in the proceeds from the sale of ships that were seized. Southern states would have the proceeds from the sale of illegally imported slaves, and southern slave owners would have access to a few more slaves. The law anticipated the logic of Chief Justice Roger Taney's decision in *Dred Scott v. Sandford* (1857) because the Africans themselves would "have no rights" and remain slaves. In sum, the 1897 act provided heavy penalties—great disincentives—for slave traders but ignored the slaves themselves. They were treated like merchandise to be transferred from the smuggler to some owner who could get a clear title to them. The 1807 act sought to end the trade but did nothing to undermine the legitimacy of holding men and women in bondage. In that respect it represented the ideology of the president who signed it into law.

Between 1818 and 1823 Congress passed four acts that fixed some of the problems with the statute. The end result was that the U.S. government would not return illegally imported blacks to Africa and slave trading was declared piracy, punishable by death. The 1819 act ("An Act in Addition to the Acts Prohibiting the Slave Trade") authorized the president to send "armed vessels of the

United States, to be employed to cruise on any of the coasts of the United States … or of the coast of Africa" (p. 532) to interdict slave traders. This was the beginning of what became known as the African Squadron, which patrolled the waters off the coast of Africa in an attempt to stop the slave trade at its source.

The final statute to regulate the trade was passed in 1820, with the unlikely title "An Act to Continue in Force 'An Act to Protect the Commerce of the United States, and to Punish the Crime of Piracy,' and Also to Make Further Provisions for Punishing the Crime of Piracy." The key elements of the law were two sections declaring that any American citizen engaging in the African slave trade "shall be adjudged a pirate; and, on conviction thereof before the circuit court of the United States for the district wherein he may be brought or found, shall suffer death" (p. 601). The same language was applied to non-Americans found on board slavers owned or commissioned by Americans.

This law was to be in force for only two years, but on January 3, 1823, Congress made it a permanent statute. Some slaves were smuggled into the United States after 1820. But the risks were high, and the numbers were relatively few. After 1820 it is unlikely that more than eight thousand illegal Africans were successfully landed in the United States, and the number may have been much lower than that. American-born slaves would be shipped south in large numbers, as the internal slave trade replaced the African trade and hundreds of thousands of African-American slaves were uprooted and moved farther south and west. The cost of ending that trade would be much higher than ending the African trade. But the moral issue was set in 1819 and 1820 when the United States finally stated unequivocally that enslaving people was a "wrong" and those who engaged in the African trade were no better than common pirates. And, like common pirates, they deserved to be hanged.

Audience

The main audience for this law was the people of the United States and anyone in any country involved in the maritime industry. The law put the entire world on notice that it was no longer legal to import slaves into the United States.

Impact

The 1807 law was moderately successful in ending the slave trade. Almost immediately large-scale importations stopped. In the five years before the law went into effect, imports into Charleston, South Carolina, averaged about eight thousand a year. After 1808 this was reduced to a trickle of illegally imported Africans. Smuggling of slaves continued after 1808, but the numbers were always small. In 1818, 1819, and 1820 Congress passed new laws to close loopholes in the 1807 law and to increase punishments, ultimately making slave trading a capital offence. Before the Civil War no presidential administration pushed for a death penalty, but in 1862 the Lincoln administration executed Nathaniel Gordon, who had been convicted in November 1861.

www.milestonedocuments.com

Related Documents

Jefferson, Thomas. "Sixth Annual Message." In *A Compilation of the Messages and Papers of the Presidents*, ed. James D. Richardson. Vol. 1. New York: Bureau of National Literature, 1897. In this annual message—what today is called the State of the Union Address—Jefferson asked Congress to ban the African slave trade.

Parliament of Great Britain. "An Act for the Abolition of the Slave Trade." In *The Statutes at Large from Magna Charta to the End of the Eleventh Parliament of Great Britain*, ed. Danby Pickering. Cambridge, U.K.: J. Bentham, 1762–1807. Passed shortly after the American law but taking effect immediately, this law made it illegal for any Englishman to trade in slaves and abolished the trade to the British colonies.

U.S. Congress. "An Act in Addition to the Act Intitled, 'An Act to Prohibit the Carrying on the Slave Trade from the United States to Any Foreign Place or Country.'" In *Annals of the Congress of the United States, 1789–1824*. Washington, D.C.: Gales and Seaton, 1834–1856. An amendment to the 1794 law, this law strengthened the government's hand in prosecuting Americans who were involved in slave trading.

———. "An Act in Addition to 'An Act to Prohibit the Introduction (Importation) of Slaves….'" In *Annals of the Congress of the United States, 1789–1824*. Washington, D.C.: Gales and Seaton, 1834–1856. A supplemental law to the 1807 act, this law required that any ship captain "prove" that any African on his ship was not an illegally imported slave.

———. "An Act in Addition to the Acts Prohibiting the Slave Trade." In *Annals of the Congress of the United States, 1789–1824*. Washington, D.C.: Gales and Seaton, 1834–1856. This law provided that illegally imported Africans would be returned to Africa at the expense of the U.S. government.

———. "An Act to Continue in Force 'An Act to Protect the Commerce of the United States, and to Punish the Crime of Piracy,' and Also to Make Further Provisions for Punishing the Crime of Piracy." In *Annals of the Congress of the United States, 1789–1824*. Washington, D.C.: Gales and Seaton, 1834–1856. This law made it a capital offence, punishable by hanging, to engage in the slave trade.

———. "An Act to Prevent the Importation of Certain Persons into Certain States Where, by the Laws Thereof, Their Admission Is Prohibited." In *Annals of the Congress of the United States, 1789–1824*. Washington, D.C.: Gales and Seaton, 1834–1856. This act made it a crime for an American ship to bring anyone of African ancestry into the United States.

———. "An Act to Prohibit the Carrying on the Slave Trade from the United States to Any Foreign Place or Country." In *Annals of the Congress of the United States, 1789–1824*. Washington, D.C.:

Gales and Seaton, 1834–1856. This law made it illegal for Americans to participate in the African slave trade.

Bibliography

■ Articles

Shugerman, Jed H. "The Louisiana Purchase and South Carolina's Reopening of the Slave Trade in 1803." *Journal of the Early Republic* 22 (Summer 2002): 263–290.

Wallenstein, Peter. "Flawed Keepers of the Flame: The Interpreters of George Mason." *Virginia Magazine of History and Biography* 102 (April 1994): 229–260.

■ Books

Davis, David Brion. *The Problem of Slavery in the Age of Revolution, 1770–1823*. Ithaca, N.Y.: Cornell University Press, 1975.

Du Bois, W. E. B. *The Suppression of the African Slave-Trade to the United States of America, 1683–1870*. 1896. Reprint. New York: Oxford University Press, 2007.

Fehrenbacher, Don E. *The Slaveholding Republic*. New York: Oxford University Press, 2001.

Finkelman, Paul. *Slavery in the Courtroom: An Annotated Bibliography of American Cases*. Washington, D.C.: Government Printing Office, 1985.

———. *Slavery and the Founders: Race and Liberty in the Age of Jefferson*, 2nd ed. Armonk, N.Y.: M. E. Sharpe, 2001.

Ford, Paul Leicester, ed. *The Writings of Thomas Jefferson*. Vol. 1: *1760–1775*. New York: G.P. Putnam Sons, 1892.

Robinson, Donald L. *Slavery in the Structure of American Politics, 1765–1820*. New York: Harcourt, Brace, Jovanovich, 1971.

■ Web Sites

"Declaration of Independence: Earliest Known Draft, June 1776." PBS Thomas Jefferson Online Web site.
http.www.pbs.org/jefferson/archives/documents/frame_ih198172.htm. Accessed on January 30, 2008.

—By Paul Finkelman

Questions for Further Study

1. What were the weaknesses of this law?
2. What happened to illegally imported slaves under the law?
3. If you had to change the law in any significant way, what would you add or subtract?

Glossary

burthen	burden
moiety	a part of whole
mulatto	a person of mixed-race heritage

Document Text

Act to Prohibit the Importation of Slaves

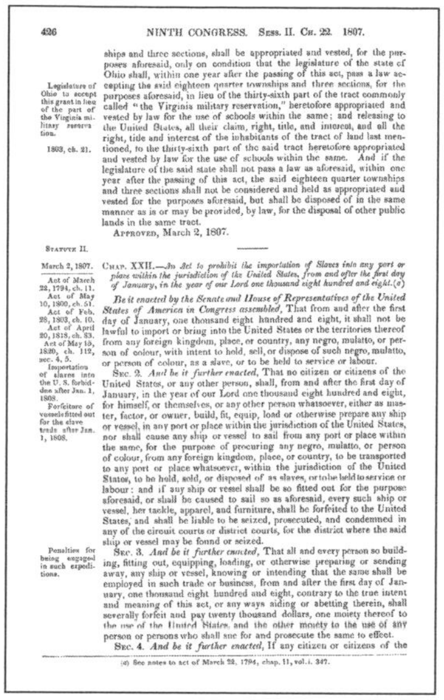

An Act to Prohibit the Importation of Slaves into any Port or Place Within the Jurisdiction of the United States, From and After the First Day of January, in the Year of our Lord One Thousand Eight Hundred and Eight.

Be it enacted by the Senate and House of Representatives of the United States of America in Congress assembled, That from and after the first day of January, one thousand eight hundred and eight, it shall not be lawful to import or bring into the United States or the territories thereof from any foreign kingdom, place, or country, any negro, mulatto, or person of colour, with intent to hold, sell, or dispose of such negro, mulatto, or person of colour, as a slave, or to be held to service or labour.

SECTION 2. And be it further enacted, That no citizen or citizens of the United States, or any other person, shall, from arid after the first day of January, in the year of our Lord one thousand eight hundred and eight, for himself, or themselves, or any other person whatsoever, either as master, factor, or owner, build, fit, equip, load or otherwise prepare any ship or vessel, in any port or place within the jurisdiction of the United States, nor shall cause any ship or vessel to sail from any port or place within the same, for the purpose of procuring any negro, mulatto, or person of colour, from any foreign kingdom, place, or country, to be transported to any port or place whatsoever, within the jurisdiction of the United States, to be held, sold, or disposed of as slaves, or to be held to service or labour: and if any ship or vessel shall be so fitted out for the purpose aforesaid, or shall be caused to sail so as aforesaid, every such ship or vessel, her tackle, apparel, and furniture, shall be forfeited to the United States, and shall be liable to be seized, prosecuted, and condemned in any of the circuit courts or district courts, for the district where the said ship or vessel may be found or seized.

SECTION 3. And be it further enacted, That all and every person so building, fitting out, equipping, loading, or otherwise preparing or sending away, any ship or vessel, knowing or intending that the same shall be employed in such trade or business, from and after the first day of January, one thousand eight hundred and eight, contrary to the true intent and meaning of this act, or any ways aiding or abetting therein, shall severally forfeit and pay twenty thousand dollars, one moiety thereof to the use of the United States, and the other moiety to the use of any person or persons who shall sue for and prosecute the same to effect.

SECTION 4. And be it further enacted, If any citizen or citizens of the United States, or any person resident within the jurisdiction of the same, shall, from and after the first day of January, one thousand eight hundred and eight, take on board, receive or transport from any of the coasts or kingdoms of Africa, or from any other foreign kingdom, place, or country, any negro, mulatto, or person of colour, in any ship or vessel, for the purpose of selling them in any port or place within the jurisdiction of the United States as slaves, or to be held to service or labour, or shall be in any ways aiding or abetting therein, such citizen or citizens, or person, shall severally forfeit and pay five thousand dollars, one moiety thereof to the use of any person or persons who shall sue for and prosecute the same to effect; and every such ship or vessel in which such negro, mulatto, or person of colour, shall have been taken on board, received, or transported as aforesaid, her tackle, apparel, and furniture, and the goods and effects which shall be found on board the same, shall be forfeited to the United States, and shall be liable to be seized, prosecuted, and condemned in any of the circuit courts or district courts in the district where the said ship or vessel may be found or seized. And neither the importer, nor any person or persons claiming from or under him, shall hold any right or title whatsoever to any negro, mulatto, or person of colour, nor to the service or labour thereof, who may

www.milestonedocuments.com

Document Text

be imported or brought within the United States, or territories thereof, in violation of this law, but the same shall remain subject to any regulations not contravening the provisions of this act, which the legislatures of the several states or territories at any time hereafter may make, for disposing of any such negro, mulatto, or person of colour.

SECTION 5. And be it further enacted, That if any citizen or citizens of the United States, or any other person resident within the jurisdiction of the same, shall, from and after the first day of January, one thousand eight hundred and eight, contrary to the true intent and meaning of this act, take on board any ship or vessel from any of the coasts or kingdoms of Africa, or from any other foreign kingdom, place, or country, any negro, mulatto, or person of colour, with intent to sell him, her, or them, for a slave, or slaves, or to be held to service or labour, and shall transport the same to any port or place within the jurisdiction of the United States, and there sell such negro, mulatto, or person of colour, so transported as aforesaid, for a slave, or to be held to service or labour, every such offender shall be deemed guilty of a high misdemeanor, and being thereof convicted before any court having competent jurisdiction, shall suffer imprisonment for not more than ten years nor less than five years, and be fined not exceeding ten thousand dollars, nor less than one thousand dollars.

SECTION 6. And be it further enacted, That if any person or persons whatsoever, shall, from and after the first day of January, one thousand eight hundred and eight, purchase or sell any negro, mulatto, or person of colour, for a slave, or to be held to service or labour, who shall have been imported, or brought from any foreign kingdom, place, or country, or from the dominions of any foreign state, immediately adjoining to the United States, into any port or place within the jurisdiction of the United States, after the last day of December, one thousand eight hundred and seven, knowing at the time of such purchase or sale, such negro, mulatto or person of colour, was so brought within the jurisdiction of the Unified States, as aforesaid, such purchaser and seller shall severally forfeit and pay for every negro, mulatto, or person of colour, so purchased or sold as aforesaid, eight hundred dollars; one moiety thereof to the United States, and the other moiety to the use of any person or persons who shall sue for and prosecute the same to effect: Provided, that the aforesaid forfeiture shall not extend to the seller or purchaser of any negro, mulatto, or person of colour, who may be sold or disposed of in virtue of any regulation which may hereafter be made by any of the legislatures of the several states in that respect, in pursuance of this act, and the constitution of the United States.

SECTION 7. And be it further enacted, That if any ship or vessel shall be found, from and after the first day of January, one thousand eight hundred and eight, in any river, port, bay, or harbor, or on the high seas, within the jurisdictional limits of the United States, or hovering on the coast thereof, having on board any negro, mulatto, or person of colour, for the purpose of selling them as slaves, or with intent to land the same, in any port or place within the jurisdiction of the United States, contrary to the prohibition of this act, every such ship or vessel, together with her tackle, apparel, and furniture, and the goods or effects which shall be found on board the same, shall be forfeited to the use of the United States, and may be seized, prosecuted, and condemned, in any court of the United States, having jurisdiction thereof. And it shall be lawful for the President of the United States, and he is hereby authorized, should he deem it expedient, to cause any of the armed vessels of the United States to be manned and employed to cruise on any part of the coast of the United States, or territories thereof, where he may judge attempts will be made to violate the provisions of this act, and to instruct and direct the commanders of armed vessels of the United States, to seize, take, and bring into any port of the United States all such ships or vessels, and moreover to seize, take, and bring into any port of the United States all ships or vessels of the United States, wheresoever found on the high seas, contravening the provisions of this act, to be proceeded against according to law, and the captain, master, or commander of every such ship or vessel, so found and seized as aforesaid, shall be deemed guilty of a high misdemeanor, and shall be liable to be prosecuted before any court of the United States, having jurisdiction thereof; and being thereof convicted, shall be fined not exceeding ten thousand dollars, and be imprisoned not less than two years, and not exceeding four years. And the proceeds of all ships and vessels, their tackle, apparel, and furniture, and the goods and effects on board of them, which shall be so seized, prosecuted and condemned, shall be divided equally between the United States and the officers and men who shall make such seizure, take, or bring the same into port for condemnation, whether such seizure be made by an armed vessel of the United States, or revenue cutters hereof, and the same shall be distributed in like manner, as is provided by law, for the distribution of prizes taken from an enemy: Provided, that the officers and men, to be entitled to one half of the proceeds aforesaid, shall safe keep every negro, mulatto, or person of colour, found on board of any ship or vessel so by them seized, taken, or brought into port for condemnation, and shall deliver every such negro, mulatto, or person of colour, to such person or persons as shall be appointed by the respective states, to receive the same, and if no such person or persons shall be appointed by the respective states, they shall deliver every such negro, mulatto, or person of colour, to the overseers of the poor of the port or place where such ship or vessel may be brought or found, and shall immediately transmit to the governor or chief magistrate of the state, an account of their proceedings, together with the number of such Negroes, mulattoes, or persons of colour, and a descriptive list of the same, that he may give directions respecting such Negroes, mulattoes, or persons of colour.

SECTION 8. And be it further enacted, That no captain, master or commander of any ship or vessel, of less burthen than forty tons, shall, from and after the first day of January, one thousand eight hundred and eight, take on board and transport any negro, mulatto, or person of colour, to any port or place whatsoever, for the purpose of selling or disposing of the same as a slave, or with intent that the same may be sold or disposed of to be held to service or labour, on penalty of forfeiting for every such negro, mulatto, or person of colour, so taken on board and transported, as aforesaid, the sum of eight hundred dollars; one moiety thereof to the use of the United States, and the other moiety to any person or persons who shall sue for, and prosecute the same to effect: Provided however, That nothing in this section shall extend to prohibit the taking on board or transporting on any river, or inland bay of the sea, within the jurisdiction of the United States, any negro, mulatto, or person of colour, (not imported contrary to the provisions of this act) in any vessel or species of craft whatever.

SECTION 9. And be it further enacted, That the captain, master, or commander of any ship or vessel of the burthen of forty tons or more, from and after the first day of January, one thousand eight hundred and eight, sailing coastwise, from any port in the United States, to any port or place within the jurisdiction of the same, having on board any negro, mulatto, or person of colour, for the purpose of transporting them to be sold or disposed of as slaves, or to be held to service or labour, shall, previous to the departure of such ship or vessel, make out and subscribe duplicate manifests of every such negro, mulatto, or person of colour, on board such ship or vessel, therein specifying the name and sex of each person, their age and stature, as near as may be, and the class to which they respectively belong, whether negro, mulatto, or person of colour, with the name and place of residence of every owner or shipper of the same, and shall deliver such manifests to the collector of the port, if there be one, otherwise to the surveyor, before whom the captain, master, or commander, together with the owner or shipper, shall severally swear or affirm to the best of their knowledge and belief, that the persons therein specified were not imported or brought into the United States, from and after the first day of January, one thousand eight hundred and eight, and that under the laws of the state, they are held to service or labour; whereupon the said collector or surveyor shall certify the same on the said manifests, one of which he shall return to the said captain, master, or commander, with a permit, specifying thereon the number, names, and general description of such persons, and authorizing him to proceed to the port of his destination. And if any ship or vessel, being laden and destined as aforesaid, shall depart from the port where she may then be, without the captain, master, or commander having first made out and subscribed duplicate manifests, of every negro, mulatto, and person of colour, on board such ship or vessel, as aforesaid, and without having previously delivered the same to the said collector or surveyor, and obtained a permit, in manner as herein required, or shall, previous to her arrival at the port of her destination, take on board any negro, mulatto, or person of colour, other than those specified in the manifests, as aforesaid, every such ship or vessel, together with her tackle, apparel and furniture, shall be forfeited to the use of the United States, and may be seized, prosecuted and condemned in any court of the United States having jurisdiction thereof; and the captain, master, or commander of every such ship or vessel, shall moreover forfeit, for every such negro, mulatto, or person of colour, so transported, or taken on board, contrary to the provisions of this act, the sum of one thousand dollars, one moiety thereof to the United States, and the other moiety to the use of any person or persons who shall sue for and prosecute the same to effect.

SECTION 10. And be it further enacted, That the captain, master, or commander of every ship or ves-

www.milestonedocuments.com

Document Text

sel, of the burthen of forty tons or more, from and after the first day of January, one thousand eight hundred and eight, sailing coastwise, and having on board any negro, mulatto, or person of colour, to sell or dispose of as slaves, or to be held to service or labour, and arriving in any port within the jurisdiction of the United States, from any other port within the same, shall, previous to the unlading or putting on shore any of the persons aforesaid, or suffering them to go on shore, deliver to the collector, if there be one, or if not, to the surveyor residing at the port of her arrival, the manifest certified by the collector or surveyor of the port from whence she sailed, as is herein before directed, to the truth of which, before such officer, he shall swear or affirm, and if the collector or surveyor shall be satisfied therewith, he shall thereupon grant a permit for unlading or suffering such negro, mulatto, or person of colour, to be put on shore, and if the captain, master, or commander of any such ship or vessel being laden as aforesaid, shall neglect or refuse to deliver the manifest at the time and in the manner herein directed, or shall land or put on shore any negro, mulatto, or person of colour, for the purpose aforesaid, before he shall have delivered his manifest as aforesaid, and obtained a permit for that purpose, every such captain, master, or commander, shall forfeit and pay ten thousand dollars, one moiety thereof to the United States, the other moiety to the use of any person or persons who shall sue for and prosecute the same to effect.

***Joseph Story wrote the opinion in* Martin v. Hunter's Lessee.** (Library of Congress)

Martin v. Hunter's Lessee

1816

"The Constitution unavoidably deals in general language."

Overview

Martin v. Hunter's Lessee (1816), a landmark U.S. Supreme Court decision in the development of federal-state relations, asserted for the first time the Supreme Court's authority under Section 25 of the federal Judiciary Act of 1789 to hear appellate state supreme court cases involving the constitutionality of federal laws or treaties. *Martin*'s origins lay in 300,000 acres of land in Virginia's "Northern Neck" region, which Charles II of England had granted to the Fairfax family in 1649. In 1776, when the American colonies declared independence from Britain, many colonists—including Thomas Fairfax, the sixth Lord Fairfax—remained loyal to Britain. From 1779 to 1785, however, Virginia's legislature passed several acts confiscating Loyalist-owned lands. When Fairfax died in 1781, he willed his property to his nephew, Denny Martin. The following year, however, Virginia legislators passed an act arguing that Martin, a foreign national, could not inherit property in the Old Dominion. Virginia took formal possession of the Fairfax estate and granted it to private citizens, such as David Hunter, who received 788 acres. To complicate matters, John Marshall, who would become chief justice of the United States, successfully represented Martin's land claims in *Hite v. Fairfax* (1786). The Fairfax litigation may have led Martin to sell 160,000 acres to a Virginia land speculators cartel that included John and James Marshall.

In 1800 Martin died and willed his land to his brother, Thomas Martin. When Thomas Martin attempted to take the property, Hunter sued him in Virginia court in *Hunter v. Fairfax's Devisee* (1810). When the Court of Appeals of Virginia upheld Hunter's claim, Martin appealed the decision on a writ of error to the U.S. Supreme Court. As chief justice, Marshall recused himself owing to his financial interests in the Fairfax lands. In *Fairfax's Devisee v. Hunter's Lessee* (1813), Justice Joseph Story ruled that English common law, international precedents, the Treaty of Paris (1783), and the Jay Treaty (1794) gave Martin title to the land. Story remanded the case to the Virginia courts, ordering them to recognize Martin's claims. In *Hunter v. Martin* (1815), however, the Court of Appeals of Virginia chief justice Spencer Roane declared that Section 25 of the Judiciary Act of 1789 unconstitutionally violated state sovereignty. Martin repealed the case to the Supreme Court, and in *Martin v. Hunter's Lessee* (1816), Story argued that the American people, not the states, created the Constitution, Congress, and federal judiciary and that only impartial federal courts could hear cases involving international law. Under the Judiciary Act of 1789, the Supreme Court had the authority to hear state cases involving international treaties. The Constitution's supremacy clause likewise compelled state judges to abide by federal rulings. Martin, therefore, remained the land's owner. Although it was a defining moment in Story's judicial career, *Martin v. Hunter's Lessee* was an unpopular decision and a victory for noncitizens' property rights. Land speculators, such as Martin and Marshall, secured fortunes of the expansive estates, while Roane decried the decision as an example of a "consolidationist" Supreme Court increasing the federal government's power at the expense of the states.

Context

In the seventeenth century, English monarchs such as James I and Charles I granted large North American land tracts to loyal political supporters like the Fairfax family. Well-established social patterns of paternalism and deference allowed large, landholding families to wield considerable power over the landless masses in colonial Virginia. But increasing tensions over taxation between the British government and the American colonies led to the 1775 outbreak of the American Revolution, with many of the colonies divided between Patriot and Loyalist camps. Many Loyalists like Lord Fairfax escaped the conflict to Canada or Britain. In 1779 Thomas Jefferson, a leading advocate of independence, became Virginia's wartime governor. Under his administration, the state legislature passed a series of acts confiscating abandoned Loyalist land. These confiscation acts were often upheld by state courts that were eager to pay down Virginia's war debts and strike a blow against the unpopular Tories.

In 1781, at the end of the Revolutionary War, Loyalist land claims remained unresolved. In the Treaty of Paris, American delegates pledged to honor prewar debts owed to

Time Line

1649

■ **September 18**
Charles II grants Thomas Fairfax, the third Lord Fairfax of Cameron, and other English nobles 5.2 million acres of land in the "Northern Neck" portion of Virginia.

1735–1737

■ Thomas Fairfax, the sixth Lord Fairfax, permanently moves to Virginia.

1759

■ **July 20**
George Washington arrives in northern Virginia to survey the Fairfax land grant.

1775

■ **April 19**
The American Revolution begins with the battles of Lexington and Concord.

1776

■ **July 4**
The United States declares its independence from Great Britain.

1779

■ **May**
The Virginia legislature passes the Confiscation Act, authorizing the seizure of all Loyalist land within state borders.

1781

■ **December 9**
Thomas Fairfax dies in Virginia and wills his lands to his nephew, Denny Martin.

1783

■ **September 3**
American and British delegates sign the Treaty of Paris, ending the American Revolution and establishing the independence of the United States; American delegates pledge to urge the states to recognize British property rights.

1786

■ **May**
The Virginia Supreme Court rules in *Hite v. Fairfax* that Martin retains control of his family lands in northern Virginia; John Marshall serves as Martin's attorney in the case.

British creditors, encourage state legislatures to honor British and Loyalist land claims, and prevent future confiscation of Loyalist property. The government created by the Articles of Confederation attempted to enforce these treaty provisions but met stubborn resistance from the states. In the 1780s Federalists such as Alexander Hamilton and James Madison promoted a stronger central government to protect property rights and international treaty obligations. Following the creation and partial ratification of the U.S. Constitution in 1787, the Federalist administrations of George Washington and John Adams cultivated stronger diplomatic and economic ties with Britain. When Britain declared war on France after the French Revolution, President Washington dispatched Chief Justice John Jay to Britain to negotiate a secret treaty declaring American neutrality in the conflict. When Congress ratified the unpopular Jay Treaty in 1796, it agreed to recognize the property rights of British subjects on American soil.

When Jefferson assumed office in March 1801, he immediately announced a new direction in federal power, lowering taxes, slashing federal spending, and reducing the U.S. military. Jefferson heavily criticized the "midnight appointments" of his predecessor and experimented with impeaching federal judicial appointees. When Republicans failed to impeach U.S. Supreme Court Justice Samuel Chase, Jefferson appointed the Republicans Joseph Story and William Johnson to the Court. Ironically, Story became Marshall's closest friend and collaborator, and Johnson frequently made more nationalistic decisions than Marshall did. Anti-British sentiment remained high during the Jeffersonian period. In 1807 the HMS *Leopard*, a British warship, fired on the USS *Chesapeake* off the Virginia coast, prompting Jefferson to issue embargo acts against Britain and France. Frequent British impressment of American sailors worsened diplomatic relations between the two nations. Under these circumstances, many Americans felt lingering hostility toward those who had remained loyal to the British government during the Revolutionary War and considered the forfeiture of their lands as a fair prize of war.

Anti-British sentiment was particularly high in Virginia, where Roane and Thomas Ritchie, editor of the *Richmond Enquirer*, formed a political machine called the "Richmond Junto," which controlled Republican politics in the Old Dominion. Roane, Ritchie, and Jefferson watched with concern as the federal government and the Marshall Court became more powerful after the War of 1812. Roane decided to use the issue of Loyalist lands to express his views on federal-state relations in *Fairfax's Devisee v. Hunter's Lessee* (1813). The public anticipated the U.S. Supreme Court's decision in *Martin v. Hunter's Lessee* in the spring of 1816 with great interest.

About the Author

Joseph Story was born on September 18, 1779, in Marblehead, Massachusetts. His parents were ardent Unitarians and Patriots during the Revolutionary War. His father was a leading member of the Sons of Liberty, participated in the Boston Tea Party, and was a Continental army physician. Story excelled academically at Marblehead Academy and Harvard University and graduated in 1798, second in his class. The prominent Massachusetts attorneys Samuel Sewall and Samuel Putnam trained Story as a legal specialist in maritime and admiralty cases.

During his private law career in Salem, Massachusetts, Story became a Jeffersonian Republican. He was elected to the Massachusetts House of Representatives in 1805. Four years later the Massachusetts governor appointed Story to complete a congressional term left vacant by the death of Jacob Crowinshield. Story broke party ranks to speak against Jefferson's embargo acts, earning him the president's lifelong dislike. Story resumed his law practice in 1809 and successfully argued *Fletcher v. Peck* before the U.S. Supreme Court in 1810. Story became speaker of the Massachusetts House of Representatives the following year. In November 1811 President James Madison nominated Story as a U.S. Supreme Court justice. On February 3, 1812, Story became the High Court's youngest justice at age thirty-two, and he served for thirty-two years. For much of his early career, he worked closely with the chief justice, John Marshall, to uphold a broad interpretation of the Constitution and a strong federal government that could keep state powers in check. Story tried unsuccessfully to promote a national common law system that would have provided uniform precedents and punishments for federal criminal and civil cases.

Story received a major opportunity to expound his nationalistic theories in 1813 in *Fairfax's Devisee v. Hunter's Lessee*. The case ultimately dealt with the U.S. Supreme Court's appellate jurisdiction for cases involving federal law or treaties under Section 25 of the Judiciary Act of 1789. Story reversed the decision of the Court of Appeals of Virginia and ordered Hunter to return the land to Martin. When the Virginia court refused to comply with the decision, Martin again appealed the case to the Supreme Court. Story's subsequent decision in *Martin v. Hunter's Lessee* provided an endorsement of federalism that would become a landmark constitutional decision.

Story often clashed over Federalist issues with Johnson, his Jefferson-appointed colleague. Johnson, born in South Carolina in 1771, sprang from working-class roots. He attended Princeton, became an attorney, and served three terms as a Republican congressman, serving briefly as Speaker of the House of Representatives. In 1802 Jefferson appointed Johnson to the Supreme Court, primarily to counterbalance Marshall's nationalist tendencies. Johnson, however, proved to be an independent figure, defying his nationalist-minded colleagues, such as Marshall and Story, as well as Jefferson on several occasions. In *Martin v. Hunter's Lessee*, Johnson concurred with Story's validation of Section 25 of the Judiciary Act of 1789, but he did so from different constitutional grounds.

Time Line

1787

■ **September 17**
The framers at the Philadelphia Convention complete the U.S. Constitution.

1788

■ **July 26**
New York becomes the eleventh state to ratify the U.S. Constitution, prompting the formation of the fledgling federal government.

1789

■ **September 24**
Congress passes the Judiciary Act of 1789; Section 25 of the act grants the U.S. Supreme Court jurisdiction over state supreme court cases involving the constitutionality of federal laws.

■ **April 30**
Virginia government grants 788 acres, part of the former Fairfax estate, to the land speculator David Hunter.

1793

■ **May 17**
Martin agrees to sell 160,000 acres of his Virginia land to a cartel of land speculators including Marshall.

1794

■ **November 19**
John Jay and British authorities secretly negotiate the Jay Treaty, in which America pledges neutrality in British-French conflicts and agrees to respect Loyalist property rights. Congress ratifies the treaty in 1796.

1800

■ **April 15**
Martin dies, willing his Virginia property to his brother, Thomas Martin.

1801

■ **January 2**
President John Adams appoints Marshall as the chief justice of the United States.

■ **March 4**
Thomas Jefferson becomes the third U.S. president.

www.milestonedocuments.com

Time Line

1810

■ **April 23**
Chief Justice Spencer Roane of the Court of Appeals of Virginia upholds Hunter's claims to Fairfax estate lands in *Hunter v. Fairfax's Devisee.*

1811

■ **November 18**
President James Madison appoints Joseph Story as a U.S. Supreme Court justice.

1812

■ **March 15**
Story upholds Thomas Martin's Virginia land claims in the U.S. Supreme Court case *Fairfax's Devisee v. Hunter's Lessee.*

1815

■ **December 16**
Roane declares Section 25 of the federal Judiciary Act of 1789 unconstitutional in the Virginia Court of Appeals case *Hunter v. Martin.*

1816

■ **March 20**
In *Martin v. Hunter's Lessee,* Story reaffirms both Thomas Martin's Virginia land claims and the rights of the U.S. Supreme Court to hear state court cases under Section 25 of the federal Judiciary Act of 1789; Johnson gives a concurring opinion upholding the decision.

Explanation and Analysis of the Document

◆ Syllabus

The case includes a syllabus of the facts and background events of *Martin v. Hunter's Lessee*. The syllabus discusses the writ of error that brings the case before the Court, and it quotes Roane's *Hunter v. Martin* decision that "so much of the 25th section of the act of Congress to establish the judicial courts of the United States, as extends the appellate jurisdiction of the Supreme Court to this Court, is not in pursuance of the Constitution of the United States." The syllabus chronicles the original state court case launched in April 1791 by Hunter against Martin and lists the facts of the case.

◆ Story's Opinion of the Court

In Story's *Martin v. Hunter's Lessee* decision, he cites Roane's *Hunter v. Martin* decision and acknowledges the current case's complexity. He notes that the "people of the United States," not the states, created the Constitution. The American people have the right to regulate and limit state powers under the Constitution. The Tenth Amendment to the Constitution reveals that states remain sovereign except in those areas where the framers granted power to the federal government. Story then argues that although the federal government can claim only powers granted under the Constitution, such powers should be reasonably, not strictly, construed. The framers created a Constitution "to endure through a long lapse of ages," with Congress creating laws to carry out constitutional goals during changing social circumstances. Article III of the Constitution created the Supreme Court, empowered Congress to create lower federal courts, and set jurisdictional boundaries for all federal courts. The American people empower these courts through the Constitution to act on individuals and states.

Article III obligates Congress to establish federal courts and staff them with tenured judges. Without a federal court system, the federal government cannot carry out its powers expressly granted under the Constitution, such as punishing crimes committed against the United States or hearing court cases that involved two states. In order to create such a federal court system, Congress must be allowed to vest the entire judicial power of the federal government in the federal court system. Story admits that what types of inferior courts Congress is obligated to create is a difficult question. He maintains that under Article III, Congress must create some inferior federal courts, which could serve as courts of original jurisdiction for cases involving constitutional issues, federal laws, treaties, and so on. The Constitution does not specify what courts to create, however, so Congress has discretion to organize such tribunals.

Story makes these general points before turning to a more specific discussion of which cases the Supreme Court wields jurisdiction over. He insists that under Article III, Section 2, the Supreme Court wields appellate jurisdiction over "all cases" involving the Constitution, federal laws, and treaties. Story also admits, however, that the Constitution grants the Supreme Court jurisdiction over "controversies to which the United States shall be a party." Thus the Constitution gives the Supreme Court automatic jurisdiction over national security issues, such as federal laws and treaties, but leaves it to Congress to grant the Supreme Court the power to hear other types of cases that might become more important to national interests over time. Story, making this distinction, nevertheless remarks that, regardless of whether federal court jurisdiction is granted by the Constitution or Congress, such authority can be wielded only by federal, not state, courts. Furthermore, it could be fully exercised where such federal jurisdiction existed.

Story argues that as the Constitution does not specifically limit the ability of Congress to grant the Supreme Court appellate jurisdiction, Congress could give the Court appellate jurisdiction over types of cases not specifically mentioned by the Constitution, including cases originating in state courts. Ultimately, "it is the case, then, and not the court, that gives the jurisdiction." Congress has merely to show that the Supreme Court deserves such power through clear and necessary implication. Story reasons that if federal appellate power applied only to federal but not to state courts, then the federal courts could not carry out their enumerated jurisdiction over cases specifically mentioned in the Constitution. If Congress creates no lower federal courts, then, of course, the Supreme Court would have appellate powers over state courts—in those areas in which the Constitution grants the Supreme Court such power.

Story states that the framers had foreseen that cases involving national issues might arise in state courts. They accordingly created Article VI of the Constitution, which made the Constitution, federal laws, and treaties "the supreme law of the land" and which bound state court judges to obey these precedents. Without the supremacy clause, state courts could rule on matters such as issuing paper money or ex post facto laws, which are powers the Constitution grants to Congress. For these reasons, federal appellate power must obviously extend to state court cases.

Story dismisses criticisms that federal appellate jurisdiction over state cases goes against the spirit of the Constitution and impairs states' rights. He points to the fact that the Constitution limits state power in a number of areas, such as senatorial and presidential elections. State judges are likewise bound by their oaths and the supremacy clause to uphold the Constitution and federal law. In response to the charge that federal courts might abuse their power to revise federal or state law, Story responds, "From the very nature of things, the absolute right of decision, in the last resort, must rest somewhere—wherever it may be vested, it is susceptible of abuse." It is simply a matter of common and legal sense that appellate courts, rather than courts of original jurisdiction, should be given the right to make final determinations in such cases.

Story likewise argues that giving the federal courts appellate powers was perfectly in keeping with American constitutional traditions. Under the Articles of Confederation, Congress had been granted the power to establish courts to rule on state prizes cases. Far from being a threat to states' rights, such a measure had been seen as important to public safety and national security. The fact that the Constitution, which called for a much stronger central government, gives jurisdiction of prizes cases to the federal courts reveals that federal appellate jurisdiction is in no way an aberration in American jurisprudence.

In addition to arguments that federal appellate powers are unconstitutional, Story contends with charges that such a system is impractical as well. After all, state judges would obey their oaths and uphold federal laws in all state cases, regardless of federal jurisdiction. In a similar fashion, Congress could remove all cases from state to federal court before they were decided at the local level. Story admits that state and federal judges are quite similar in "learning, integrity, and wisdom." The American people, however, have created the Constitution to remove important cases involving national security from local concerns and temptations, so that they might be resolved by an impartial tribunal that spoke for the entire country. Federal appellate jurisdiction would likewise help regulate and harmonize state court cases into a manageable whole. A federal appeals process would also protect the rights of defendants who have lost cases in state court and who would otherwise have no rights to appeal.

Story admits that the Constitution does not grant any branch of the federal government the express power to remove cases from state to federal court. Yet such a power is a necessary one for the federal courts to have. Since the Constitution does not prohibit Congress from exercising such power, it could allow federal courts to take charge of state court cases at any time in their deliberations. Under these circumstances, it is perfectly appropriate for a federal court to review a state court case on a writ of error. Furthermore, if state courts could refuse to obey such writs, the resulting legal chaos would undermine private rights and public safety. Under these circumstances, Section 25 of the federal Judiciary Act of 1789 is "supported by the letter and spirit of the Constitution."

Although Story grounds his defense of federal appellate power on the Constitution, he shows how his decision also makes sense within a historical context. He points out as a matter of historical fact that both Federalists and Antifederalists had widely accepted the fact that if the Constitution were adopted, it would grant appellate jurisdiction over state courts. In a similar fashion, many of these same Federalists had gone on to serve in the first Congress and had helped to create the Judiciary Act of 1789. Until the current controversy, Story notes, state courts had frequently acquiesced when the Supreme Court reviewed their cases. Such compliance places federal appellate power "upon a foundation of authority which cannot be shaken without delivering over the subject to perpetual and irremediable doubts."

Having defended the rights of federal courts to hear state court cases on appeal, Story examines whether the current controversy is admissible in federal court under Section 25 of the Judiciary Act of 1789. Stripped of jargon, Section 25 states that state supreme court decisions involving federal law, constitutional issues, or federal treaties could be appealed to the U.S. Supreme Court on a writ of error. As the Court of Appeals of Virginia declares the Supreme Court's decision in *Fairfax's Devisee v. Hunter's Lessee* null and void, the matter pertains perfectly to the guidelines for a writ of error under Section 25, in which state supreme court cases that conflict with federal law could be appealed to the U.S. Supreme Court.

Despite this reasoning, Story argues that without the Virginia court's unwillingness to support a Supreme Court decision, Martin still has a right to have his case heard in federal court. Story admits that the case is centered on private land claims contested by two Virginia citizens under state law. Martin's inheritance of Virginia land hinges upon the validity of Denny Martin's land claims under the provisions of the Treaty of Paris and the Jay Treaty. The Court of Appeals of Virginia has considered Martin's land claims in relation to these treaties and rejects them to rule in favor

www.milestonedocuments.com

of Hunter. Thus the Supreme Court could examine the same legal matters and rule in favor of Martin.

Story addresses the question of whether the Supreme Court could rule only on the matter of federal treaties and not state land titles. He responds that Congress grants the Supreme Court the latitude to consider all legal points in a case when determining its outcome. The Supreme Court could also consider the Jay Treaty, which upholds Loyalist property rights, even though the treaty was created only after the Hunter-Fairfax controversy had begun. Story asserts that when Congress had ratified the Jay Treaty, it became the supreme law of the land and attached itself to the case.

Story rejects the remaining arguments against Martin's land claims as merely procedural rather than substantive in nature. The writ of error has been properly submitted from the Virginia Court of Errors and is therefore eligible for review by the Supreme Court. Even though the judge issuing the writ of error had not followed procedure and taken a bond, the writ had still been issued in good faith and was therefore valid. Story also declines to discuss whether the Supreme Court could legally issue a writ of mandamus to the Court of Appeals of Virginia, as the matter is not necessary to solve the case before the Court. He thus concludes his opinion by stating that it is "the opinion of the whole Court that the judgment of the Court of Appeals of Virginia, rendered on the mandate in this cause, be reversed, and the judgment of the District Court, held at Winchester, be, and the same is hereby, affirmed."

◆ Johnson's Separate Opinion

In his concurring opinion, commenting on Story's decision not to determine whether federal courts could issue writs of mandamus to state courts, Johnson states that the Supreme Court is correspondingly supreme in its jurisdiction but not willing to force the state courts to comply with its decisions. Against such a backdrop, Johnson stresses his agreement with Story's decision, "but not altogether in the reasoning or opinion of my brother who delivered it." Given the natural tendency for people to disagree, Johnson feels a need to defend his concurring opinion on his own terms.

Johnson states that he wishes to express his opinion because he views "this question as one of the most momentous importance; as one which may affect, in its consequences, the permanence of the American Union." The important case represents a collision between federal law and the laws of one of the most powerful states in the Union. Johnson warns that the federal government must carry out its constitutionally mandated powers or cease to exist. On the other hand, to subordinate states' rights to federal interests would destroy democratic government in the United States. Although Johnson admires the Old Dominion's pluck for standing up for its rights, he criticizes the Court of Appeals of Virginia for taking such an extreme position. The legal issue at hand is whether the Virginia court was bound to obey the Supreme Court's orders in *Fairfax's Devisee v. Hunter's Lessee*. Instead, Roane and his colleagues had provoked a larger confrontation over whether the Supreme Court has jurisdiction over state courts at all.

Johnson maintains that Virginia's stance is an alarming one. If Virginia could challenge Supreme Court decisions, then what could prevent other states from doing likewise? Although the Supreme Court is no more infallible than the state courts, it has a tradition of respect and comity with the state courts. Furthermore, the Supreme Court represents every state in the Union, and thus one can count on it to be more magnanimous, especially when the public interest is at stake.

To further promote the Supreme Court's virtue, Johnson places the blame for the current conflict squarely on the shoulders of the Virginia courts. He points out that Roane had acquiesced to the Supreme Court's writ of error in the original case of *Fairfax's Devisee v. Hunter's Lessee*. The Supreme Court, therefore, believes that the Court of Appeals of Virginia would abide by its decision, regardless of how the Court rules. Had Roane refused to comply with the initial writ and raised jurisdictional issues at that point, at least the Supreme Court would have been aware of the crisis. In such a case, the Supreme Court would not have issued an order demanding that the Court of Appeals of Virginia comply with the *Fairfax* decision, and the matter could have been amicably disposed of in Circuit Court. The Founders anticipated that state courts might refuse to obey federal court decisions and thus gave the federal courts the power to compel them to obey. But federal courts could use their discretion in exercising such powers with the hope that comity might prevent crises between the states and federal government. By its rash actions, writes Johnson, Virginia forces the Supreme Court to take an adversarial position; the current situation is Virginia's own making.

Johnson begins his opinion by stating that, even though the Treaty of Paris and the Jay Treaty were not central to the land issues in *Fairfax's Devisee v. Hunter's Lessee*, any part of the case that calls into question the validity of these treaties makes it applicable for review by the Supreme Court. To declare that the Supreme Court could rule on the constitutionality of federal treaties but on not state land laws would mean that the Court could render a hypothetical decision in favor of Martin but have no means of actually enforcing it. Rather than view the case as a matter of federal courts invading the state legal system, Johnson argues that the more proper question is "whether the State tribunals can constitutionally exercise jurisdiction in any of the cases to which the judicial power of the United States extends." Johnson admits that the Constitution is vague as to whether state courts could act in federal matters if Congress or the federal courts refused to do so. Johnson sees the Constitution as a "tripartite" contract between the people, states, and federal government. Under the terms of this agreement, each party surrenders part of its powers for the greater good, particularly the right to mete out justice. In addition, the framers wrote the Constitution in plain, obvious language that empowers the federal government to fully exercise the powers it was given in the areas assigned

Essential Quotes

"The Constitution of the United States was ordained and established not by the States in their sovereign capacities, but emphatically, as the preamble of the Constitution declares, by 'the people of the United States.' There can be no doubt that it was competent to the people to invest the general government with all the powers which they might deem proper and necessary, to extend or restrain these powers according to their own good pleasure, and to give them a paramount and supreme authority."

(Chief Justice Joseph Story, paragraph 4)

"This instrument, like every other grant, is to have a reasonable construction, according to the import of its terms, and where a power is expressly given in general terms, it is not to be restrained to particular cases unless that construction grow out of the context expressly or by necessary implication. The words are to be taken in their natural and obvious sense, and not in a sense unreasonably restricted or enlarged."

(Chief Justice Joseph Story, paragraph 6)

"The Constitution unavoidably deals in general language. It did not suit the purposes of the people, in framing this great charter of our liberties, to provide for minute specifications of its powers or to declare the means by which those powers should be carried into execution. It was foreseen that this would be a perilous and difficult, if not an impracticable, task."

(Chief Justice Joseph Story, paragraph 7)

"On the other hand, so firmly am I persuaded that the American people can no longer enjoy the blessings of a free government whenever the State sovereignties shall be prostrated at the feet of the General Government, nor the proud consciousness of equality and security any longer than the independence of judicial power shall be maintained consecrated and intangible, that I could borrow the language of a celebrated orator and exclaim, 'I rejoice that Virginia has resisted.'"

(Justice William Johnson, paragraph 4)

www.milestonedocuments.com

to it by the Constitution, such as the power to extend federal appellate power over certain controversies or cases. Just as individuals could renounce rights created for their benefit, so too state courts could act in areas in which Congress declines to rule. The federal government could curtail such state power at any time.

The central issue remains whether federal courts have appellate power over state courts, and Johnson admits that he is undecided. He merely maintains that Congress at no point makes a systematic attempt to turn the state courts into inferior courts. Certainly, instances in which states could arrest, imprison, and sentence to death foreign ministers or federal agents exist. Under such circumstances, federal appellate power is necessary to preserve both justice and the Union. If ever the federal courts should attempt to force state courts to adopt federal law, then the Supreme Court would have to deal with the matter as it arose. For the moment, however, it is merely enough to show that Congress has the authority to grant the Supreme Court the right to hear state supreme court cases in civil matters. Congress, in passing the Judiciary Act of 1789, had allowed states to retain a great deal of their sovereignty. Congress gave plaintiffs and defendants the ability to appeal their cases in both state and federal court. State court justices can issue or decline to issue writs of error to the Supreme Court. Cases under review require that both parties appear and explain their legal arguments to a new court. In any event, the Supreme Court seeks to hear cases based on their merits and not on whether they come from a state or federal court in particular.

Johnson reasons that Congress gave federal courts appellate power over state cases for two specific reasons. First, a federal appeals process gives defendants full rights to appeal their state cases, a right they would not enjoy under state law. Second, even if Congress grants federal courts original jurisdiction over all cases involving the Constitution and federal laws, there would still be entire classes of cases beyond the reach of federal jurisdiction. This could lead to endless confusion throughout the nation as different courts handed down conflicting decisions, with no means of regulation.

Johnson concludes that he believes his opinions are not merely constitutional but also practical and that they jeopardize neither the survival of the Union nor the dignity of the states. State courts should not fear federal power simply because the federal courts provide another forum to hear their cases. With a common commitment to justice and comity, the federal and state courts could work together, without the need for compulsion, which neither Congress nor the Supreme Court attempts nor plans to attempt.

Audience

As a landmark U.S. Supreme Court decision, *Martin v. Hunter's Lessee* aimed to convince a national audience as to the importance of the federal government and its court system. Throughout his opinion, Story depicted the framers as "men of learning and integrity" who had banded together to create a constitution that would "endure through a long lapse of ages." He framed his constitutional arguments in patriotic language, which was in vogue during the outburst of patriotism following the War of 1812. Like his mentor, Marshall, Story realized the importance of writing a decision that would appeal to a broad number of Americans and thus help solidify support for the federal courts.

More specifically, Story's decision sought to reassure American businessmen and foreign investors that the United States was a nation that respected property rights, the rule of law, and the obligation of contracts. This aided Story's and Marshall's goals to promote an effective legal system that would enhance a national market economy and a sense of cultural nationalism. Story had initially sought to achieve these purposes through the creation of a federal common law that would bring uniformity and oversight to the federal courts. Having failed in these efforts, Story now sought to use the federal judiciary to regulate state courts, particularly in commercially sensitive areas like land speculation. Story aimed specific parts of the decision at Roane and at the Richmond Junto. He sought to remind those who advocated for states' rights that their sentiments risked not only bringing chaos to the American constitutional order but also national security, in much the same way that the delegates to the Hartford Convention had undermined American resolve in the recent conflict with Great Britain.

In his concurring opinion, Johnson claimed that he agreed with Story's basic arguments but for different reasons. Nevertheless, Johnson invoked the Constitution as a "tripartite" agreement between the people, states, and the Constitution and described the Supreme Court as an impartial, reasonable body seeking to bring order to a chaotic system of state courts. He also brazenly took Roane and the Virginia courts to task for not merely challenging the authority of the Supreme Court but for cynically widening the controversy to provoke a showdown between federal and state powers.

Impact

Martin v. Hunter's Lessee received mixed reviews from the American public. Northern newspapers generally supported it but gave the case clinical summaries rather than ringing endorsements. On the other hand, southern papers voiced concerns about an increase in federal power over the states. The Richmond Junto's official party organ, the *Richmond Enquirer*, printed a verbatim copy of Johnson's opinion but not that of Story. Many contemporaries believed that even though Marshall had recused himself from the case, he and Story had informally colluded to craft a nationalistic decision that upheld both the right of the Supreme Court to review state court cases and Marshall's Virginia land claims.

Story's success in defending federal power in Martin inspired the Marshall Court to further expand its authority over state courts in areas like banking, contracts, lottery tickets, and interstate commerce. Yet following the election of Andrew Jackson as president in 1828, the Supreme Court began to moderate its nationalistic approach. The Civil War sparked a revolution in federal-state relations. Union victory solidified federal control over the states and led to the creation of the Fourteenth Amendment, which made the Bill of Rights binding on the states. Following the Great Depression in 1929 and the New Deal of the 1930s, the Supreme Court gradually began to allow the federal government direct control over traditionally state-granted affairs.

Related Documents

Ford, Paul Leicester, ed. *The Works of Thomas Jefferson*. 19 vols. New York: G. P. Putnam's Sons and Knickerbocker Press, 1904. Although Jefferson had retired from public life long before the Supreme Court's decision in *Martin v. Hunter's Lessee*, he remained an important figure in the case. His letters reveal his motives in appointing Story and Johnson to the U.S. Supreme Court. He also avidly corresponded with Spencer Roane about federal state relations and states' rights in the young republic.

Marshall, John. *The Papers of John Marshall*, ed. Herbert A. Johnson. 12 vols. Chapel Hill: University of North Carolina Press, 1974–2006. Although Marshall recused himself from *Martin v. Hunter's Lessee*, he remained personally and professionally connected to the Fairfax estate of northern Virginia. His papers, therefore, contain important information on land speculation and attempts by the Fairfax family to regain control over their Virginia lands.

Story, William Wetmore, ed. *Life and Letters of Joseph Story*. 2 vols. Boston: C. C. Little and J. Brown, 1851. This selective collection of Joseph Story's letters and documents, edited by his son, reveals Story's opinions on federal-state relations that lay at the heart of his *Martin* decision.

Bibliography

■ Books

Beeman, Richard. *The Old Dominion and the New Nation, 1788–1801*. Lexington: University Press of Kentucky, 1972.

Currie, David P. *The Constitution in the Supreme Court: The First Hundred Years, 1789–1888*. Chicago: University of Chicago Press, 1985.

Henkin, Louis. *Foreign Affairs and the United States Constitution*. New York: Oxford University Press, 1996.

Horwitz, Morton J. *The Transformation of American Law, 1780–1860*. Cambridge, Mass.: Harvard University Press, 1977.

Johnson, Herbert A. *The Chief Justiceship of John Marshall, 1801–1835*. Columbia: University of South Carolina Press, 1997.

Marcus, Maeva, ed. *Origins of the Federal Judiciary: Essays on the Judiciary Act of 1789*. New York: Oxford University Press, 1992.

Middlekauff, Robert. *The Glorious Cause: The American Revolution, 1763–1789*. New York: Oxford University Press, 1985.

Newmeyer, R. Kent. *Supreme Court Justice Joseph Story: Statesman of the Old Republic*. Chapel Hill: University of North Carolina Press, 1985.

Robarge, David S. *A Chief Justice's Progress: John Marshall From Revolutionary Virginia to the Supreme Court*. Westport, Conn.: Greenwood Press, 2000.

Roeber, A. G. *Faithful Magistrates and Republican Lawyers: Creators of Virginia Legal Culture, 1680–1810*. Chapel Hill: University of North Carolina Press, 1981.

White, G. Edward. *The Marshall Court and Cultural Change, 1815–1835*. New York: Oxford University Press, 1991.

■ Web Sites

"*Martin v. Hunter's Lessee*." Cornell University Law School Web site. http://www.law.cornell.edu/supct/html/historics/USSC_CR_0014_0304_ZS.html. Accessed on October 23, 2007.

"*Martin v. Hunter's Lessee*." U.S. Supreme Court Media Oyez Web site. http://www.oyez.org/cases/1792-1850/1816/1816_0/. Accessed on October 23, 2007.

"The Thomas Jefferson Papers." The Library of Congress "American Memory" Web site. http://memory.loc.gov/ammem/collections/jefferson_papers/index.html. Accessed on October 23, 2007.

—By Thomas H. Cox

www.milestonedocuments.com

Questions for Further Study

1. Given the sheer size of the Fairfax estates, why did neither David Hunter nor Thomas Martin seek an out-of-court resolution? Why did both men fight so hard to win title over a relatively meager 788 acres of land when America enjoyed a booming frontier?

2. Why did Spencer Roane wait until relatively late in the judicial proceedings to declare a U.S. Supreme Court decision unconstitutional? Why not simply refuse to allow the Supreme Court the ability to review the case in the first place?

3. Why did the Virginia Court of Appeals attempt to turn a matter involving land claims into a wider dispute over the right of federal courts to hear state cases?

4. In contrast, why did the Supreme Court decline to issue a writ of mandamus to force the Virginia court to appeal with its initial decision in 1813?

Glossary

appellate jurisdiction	the right of a court to hear cases previously heard by other, lower courts
comity	legal reciprocity shown between different governments or jurisdictions
coram non judice	a legal term used to describe a legal proceeding without proper venue or jurisdiction
devisee	a person who inherits land through a will
ejectment	a common law term to describe the recovery of land ("real property")
escheat	the right of a state to take property that has no legal heirs or claimants
ex industria	by industry or labor
ex post facto	operating retroactively
General Government	the federal government of the United States
in pais	performed out of court
non constat	a legal term meaning "it is not certain"; refers to information that is hard to argue in court
original jurisdiction	the right of a court to hear a case for the first time
quo minus	a writ sworn out by a debtor, claiming that he has been injured by his or her creditor and is thus unable to pay his or her debt
right of removal	the right to transfer a case from one court to another
vested	granted or endowed; said of a right that, when granted, cannot be taken away
vide	see
viz	namely
writ of error	a writ from an appellate court to a court of original jurisdiction for a record of the case in question, so that the case may be reviewed for possible legal errors

Martin v. Hunter's Lessee

◆ **STORY, J., delivered the opinion of the Court.**

This is a writ of error from the Court of Appeals of Virginia founded upon the refusal of that Court to obey the mandate of this Court requiring the judgment rendered in this very cause, at February Term, 1813, to be carried into due execution. The following is the judgment of the Court of Appeals rendered on the mandate:

> The Court is unanimously of opinion, that the appellate power of the Supreme Court of the United States does not extend to this Court, under a sound construction of the Constitution of the United States; that so much of the 25th section of the act of Congress to establish the judicial courts of the United States, as extends the appellate jurisdiction of the Supreme Court to this Court, is not in pursuance of the Constitution of the United States; that the writ of error in this cause was improvidently allowed under the authority of that act; that the proceedings thereon in the Supreme Court were *coram non judice* in relation to this Court, and that obedience to its mandate be declined by the Court.

The questions involved in this judgment are of great importance and delicacy. Perhaps it is not too much to affirm that, upon their right decision rest some of the most solid principles which have hitherto been supposed to sustain and protect the Constitution itself. The great respectability, too, of the Court whose decisions we are called upon to review, and the entire deference which we entertain for the learning and ability of that Court, add much to the difficulty of the task which has so unwelcomely fallen upon us. It is, however, a source of consolation, that we have had the assistance of most able and learned arguments to aid our inquiries; and that the opinion which is now to be pronounced has been weighed with every solicitude to come to a correct result, and matured after solemn deliberation.

Before proceeding to the principal questions, it may not be unfit to dispose of some preliminary considerations which have grown out of the arguments at the bar.

The Constitution of the United States was ordained and established not by the States in their sovereign capacities, but emphatically, as the preamble of the Constitution declares, by "the people of the United States." There can be no doubt that it was competent to the people to invest the general government with all the powers which they might deem proper and necessary, to extend or restrain these powers according to their own good pleasure, and to give them a paramount and supreme authority. As little doubt can there be that the people had a right to prohibit to the States the exercise of any powers which were, in their judgment, incompatible with the objects of the general compact, to make the powers of the State governments, in given cases, subordinate to those of the nation, or to reserve to themselves those sovereign authorities which they might not choose to delegate to either. The Constitution was not, therefore, necessarily carved out of existing State sovereignties, nor a surrender of powers already existing in State institutions, for the powers of the States depend upon their own Constitutions, and the people of every State had the right to modify and restrain them according to their own views of the policy or principle. On the other hand, it is perfectly clear that the sovereign powers vested in the State governments by their respective Constitutions remained unaltered and unimpaired except so far as they were granted to the Government of the United States.

These deductions do not rest upon general reasoning, plain and obvious as they seem to be. They have been positively recognised by one of the articles in amendment of the Constitution, which declares that

www.milestonedocuments.com

> The powers not delegated to the United States by the Constitution, nor prohibited by it to the States, are reserved to the States respectively, or to the people.

The government, then, of the United States can claim no powers which are not granted to it by the Constitution, and the powers actually granted, must be such as are expressly given, or given by necessary implication. On the other hand, this instrument, like every other grant, is to have a reasonable construction, according to the import of its terms, and where a power is expressly given in general terms, it is not to be restrained to particular cases unless that construction grow out of the context expressly or by necessary implication. The words are to be taken in their natural and obvious sense, and not in a sense unreasonably restricted or enlarged.

The Constitution unavoidably deals in general language. It did not suit the purposes of the people, in framing this great charter of our liberties, to provide for minute specifications of its powers or to declare the means by which those powers should be carried into execution. It was foreseen that this would be a perilous and difficult, if not an impracticable, task. The instrument was not intended to provide merely for the exigencies of a few years, but was to endure through a long lapse of ages, the events of which were locked up in the inscrutable purposes of Providence. It could not be foreseen what new changes and modifications of power might be indispensable to effectuate the general objects of the charter, and restrictions and specifications which at the present might seem salutary might in the end prove the overthrow of the system itself. Hence its powers are expressed in general terms, leaving to the legislature from time to time to adopt its own means to effectuate legitimate objects and to mould and model the exercise of its powers as its own wisdom and the public interests, should require.

With these principles in view, principles in respect to which no difference of opinion ought to be indulged, let us now proceed to the interpretation of the Constitution so far as regards the great points in controversy.

The third article of the Constitution is that which must principally attract our attention. The 1st. section declares,

> The judicial power of the United States shall be vested in one Supreme Court, and in such other inferior Courts as the Congress may, from time to time, ordain and establish.

The 2d section declares, that

> The judicial power shall extend to all cases in law or equity, arising under this Constitution, the laws of the United States, and the treaties made, or which shall be made, under their authority; to all cases affecting ambassadors, other public ministers and consuls; to all cases of admiralty and maritime jurisdiction; to controversies to which the United States shall be a party; to controversies between two or more States; between a State and citizens of another State; between citizens of different States; between citizens of the same State, claiming lands under the grants of different States; and between a State or the citizens thereof, and foreign States, citizens, or subjects.

It then proceeds to declare, that

> in all cases affecting ambassadors, other public ministers and consuls, and those in which a State shall be a party, the Supreme Court shall have original jurisdiction. In all the other cases before mentioned, the Supreme Court shall have appellate jurisdiction both as to law and fact, with such exceptions and under such regulations, as the Congress shall make.

Such is the language of the article creating and defining the judicial power of the United States. It is the voice of the whole American people solemnly declared, in establishing one great department of that Government which was, in many respects, national, and in all, supreme. It is a part of the very same instrument which was to act not merely upon individuals, but upon States, and to deprive them altogether of the exercise of some powers of sovereignty and to restrain and regulate them in the exercise of others.

Let this article be carefully weighed and considered. The language of the article throughout is manifestly designed to be mandatory upon the Legislature. Its obligatory force is so imperative, that Congress could not, without a violation of its duty, have refused to carry it into operation. The judicial power of the United States shall be vested (not may be vested) in one Supreme Court, and in such inferior Courts as Congress may, from time to time, ordain

www.milestonedocuments.com

and establish. Could Congress have lawfully refused to create a Supreme Court, or to vest in it the constitutional jurisdiction?

> The judges, both of the supreme and inferior courts, shall hold their offices during good behaviour, and shall, at stated times, receive, for their services, a compensation which shall not be diminished during their continuance in office.

Could Congress create or limit any other tenure of the judicial office? Could they refuse to pay at stated times the stipulated salary, or diminish it during the continuance in office? But one answer can be given to these questions: it must be in the negative. The object of the Constitution was to establish three great departments of Government—the legislative, the executive, and the judicial departments. The first was to pass laws, the second to approve and execute them, and the third to expound and enforce them. Without the latter, it would be impossible to carry into effect some of the express provisions of the Constitution. How, otherwise, could crimes against the United States be tried and punished? How could causes between two States be heard and determined? The judicial power must, therefore, be vested in some court by Congress; and to suppose that it was not an obligation binding on them, but might, at their pleasure, be omitted or declined, is to suppose that, under the sanction of the Constitution, they might defeat the Constitution itself, a construction which would lead to such a result cannot be sound.

The same expression, "shall be vested," occurs in other parts of the Constitution in defining the powers of the other coordinate branches of the Government. The first article declares that "all legislative powers herein granted shall be vested in a Congress of the United States." Will it be contended that the legislative power is not absolutely vested? that the words merely refer to some future act, and mean only that the legislative power may hereafter be vested? The second article declares that "the executive power shall be vested in a President of the United States of America." Could Congress vest it in any other person, or is it to await their good pleasure whether it is to vest at all? It is apparent that such a construction, in either case, would be utterly inadmissible. Why, then, is it entitled to a better support in reference to the judicial department?

If, then, it is a duty of Congress to vest the judicial power of the United States, it is a duty to vest the whole judicial power. The language, if imperative as to one part, is imperative as to all. If it were otherwise, this anomaly would exist, that Congress might successively refuse to vest the jurisdiction in any one class of cases enumerated in the Constitution, and thereby defeat the jurisdiction as to all, for the Constitution has not singled out any class on which Congress are bound to act in preference to others.

The next consideration is as to the Courts in which the judicial power shall be vested. It is manifest that a Supreme Court must be established; but whether it be equally obligatory to establish inferior Courts is a question of some difficulty. If Congress may lawfully omit to establish inferior Courts, it might follow that, in some of the enumerated cases, the judicial power could nowhere exist. The Supreme Court can have original jurisdiction in two classes of cases only, *viz.*, in cases affecting ambassadors, other public ministers and consuls, and in cases in which a State is a party. Congress cannot vest any portion of the judicial power of the United States except in Courts ordained and established by itself, and if, in any of the cases enumerated in the Constitution, the State courts did not then possess jurisdiction, the appellate jurisdiction of the Supreme Court (admitting that it could act on State courts) could not reach those cases, and, consequently, the injunction of the Constitution that the judicial power "shall be vested," would be disobeyed. It would seem therefore to follow that Congress are bound to create some inferior Courts in which to vest all that jurisdiction which, under the Constitution, is exclusively vested in the United States, and of which the Supreme Court cannot take original cognizance. They might establish one or more inferior Courts; they might parcel out the jurisdiction among such Courts, from time to time, at their own pleasure. But the whole judicial power of the United States should be at all times vested, either in an original or appellate form, in some Courts created under its authority.

This construction will be fortified by an attentive examination of the second section of the third article. The words are "the judicial power shall extend," &c. Much minute and elaborate criticism has been employed upon these words. It has been argued that they are equivalent to the words "may extend," and that "extend" means to widen to new cases not before within the scope of the power. For the reason which have been already stated, we are of opinion that the words are used in an imperative sense. They import an absolute grant of judicial power. They cannot have a relative signification applicable to powers already granted, for the American people had not made any previous grant. The Constitution was for a new Government, organized with new substantive powers, and not a mere supplementary charter to a Government already existing. The Confederation was a compact between States, and its structure and powers were wholly unlike those of the National Government. The Constitution was an act of the people of the United States to supersede the Confederation, and not to be ingrafted on it, as a stock through which it was to receive life and nourishment.

If, indeed, the relative signification could be fixed upon the term "extend," it could not (as we shall hereafter see) subserve the purposes of the argument in support of which it has been adduced. This imperative sense of the words "shall extend" is strengthened by the context. It is declared that, "in all cases affecting ambassadors, &c., that the Supreme Court shall have original jurisdiction." Could Congress withhold original jurisdiction in these cases from the Supreme Court? The clause proceeds—

> in all the other cases before mentioned, the Supreme Court shall have appellate jurisdiction, both as to law and fact, with such exceptions, and under such regulations, as the Congress shall make.

The very exception here shows that the framers of the Constitution used the words in an imperative sense. What necessity could there exist for this exception if the preceding words were not used in that sense? Without such exception, Congress would, by the preceding words, have possessed a complete power to regulate the appellate jurisdiction, if the language were only equivalent to the words "may have" appellate jurisdiction. It is apparent, then, that the exception was intended as a limitation upon the preceding words, to enable Congress to regulate and restrain the appellate power, as the public interests might, from time to time, require.

Other clauses in the Constitution might be brought in aid of this construction, but a minute examination of them cannot be necessary, and would occupy too much time. It will be found that whenever a particular object is to be effected, the language of the Constitution is always imperative, and cannot be disregarded without violating the first principles of public duty. On the other hand, the legislative powers are given in language which implies discretion, as, from the nature of legislative power, such a discretion must ever be exercised.

It being, then, established that the language of this clause is imperative, the next question is as to the cases to which it shall apply. The answer is found in the Constitution itself. The judicial power shall extend to all the cases enumerated in the Constitution. As the mode is not limited, it may extend to all such cases, in any form, in which judicial power may be exercised. It may therefore extend to them in the shape of original or appellate jurisdiction, or both, for there is nothing in the nature of the cases which binds to the exercise of the one in preference to the other.

In what cases (if any) is this judicial power exclusive, or exclusive at the election of Congress? It will be observed that there are two classes of cases enumerated in the Constitution between which a distinction seems to be drawn. The first class includes cases arising under the Constitution, laws, and treaties of the United States, cases affecting ambassadors, other public ministers and consuls, and cases of admiralty and maritime jurisdiction. In this class, the expression is, and that the judicial power shall extend to all cases; but in the subsequent part of the clause which embraces all the other cases of national cognizance, and forms the second class, the word "all" is dropped, seemingly *ex industria*. Here the judicial authority is to extend to controversies (not to all controversies) to which the United States shall be a party, &c. From this difference of phraseology, perhaps, a difference of constitutional intention may, with propriety, be inferred. It is hardly to be presumed that the variation in the language could have been accidental. It must have been the result of some determinate reason, and it is not very difficult to find a reason sufficient to support the apparent change of intention. In respect to the first class, it may well have been the intention of the framers of the Constitution imperatively to extend the judicial power either in an original or appellate form to all cases, and in the latter class to leave it to Congress to qualify the jurisdiction, original or appellate, in such manner as public policy might dictate.

The vital importance of all the cases enumerated in the first class to the national sovereignty might warrant such a distinction. In the first place, as to cases arriving under the Constitution, laws, and treaties of the United States. Here the State courts could not ordinarily possess a direct jurisdiction. The jurisdiction over such cases could not exist in the State courts previous to the adoption of the Constitution, and it could not afterwards be directly conferred on them, for the Constitution expressly requires the judicial power to be vested in courts ordained and established by the United States. This class of cases would embrace civil as well as criminal jurisdiction, and affect not only our internal policy, but our foreign relations. It would therefore be perilous to restrain it in any manner whatsoever, inasmuch as it might hazard the national safety. The same remarks may be urged as to cases affecting ambassadors, other public ministers, and consuls, who are emphatically placed under the guardianship of the law of nations, and as to cases of admiralty and maritime jurisdiction, the admiralty jurisdiction embraces all questions of prize and salvage, in the correct adjudication of which foreign nations are deeply interested; it embraces also maritime torts, contracts, and offences, in which the principles of the law and comity of nations often form an essential inquiry. All these cases, then, enter into the national policy, affect the national rights, and may compromit the national sovereignty. The original or appellate jurisdiction ought not therefore to be restrained, but should be commensurate with the mischiefs intended to be remedied, and, of course, should extend to all cases whatsoever.

A different policy might well be adopted in reference to the second class of cases, for although it might be fit that the judicial power should extend to all controversies to which the United States should be a party, yet this power night not have been imperatively given, least it should imply a right to take cognizance of original suits brought against the United States as defendants in their own Courts. It might not have been deemed proper to submit the sovereignty of the United States, against their own will to judicial cognizance, either to enforce rights or to prevent wrongs; and as to the other cases of the second class, they might well be left to be exercised under the exceptions and regulations which Congress might, in their wisdom, choose to apply. It is also worthy of remark that Congress seem, in a good degree, in the establishment of the present judicial system, to have adopted this distinction. In the first class of cases, the jurisdiction is not limited except by the subject matter; in the second, it is made materially to depend upon the value in controversy.

We do not, however, profess to place any implicit reliance upon the distinction which has here been stated and endeavoured to be illustrated. It has the rather been brought into view in deference to the legislative opinion, which has so long acted upon, and enforced this distinction. But there is, certainly, vast weight in the argument which has been urged that the Constitution is imperative upon Congress to vest all the judicial power of the United States, in the shape of original jurisdiction, in the Supreme and inferior courts created under its own authority. At all events, whether the one construction or the other prevail, it is manifest that the judicial power of the United States is unavoidably, in some cases, exclusive of all State authority, and in all others, may be made so at the election of Congress. No part of the criminal jurisdiction of the United States can, consistently with the Constitution, be delegated to State tribunals. The admiralty and maritime jurisdiction is of the same exclusive cognizance, and it can only be in those cases where, previous to the Constitution, State tribunals possessed jurisdiction independent of national authority that they can now constitutionally exercise a concurrent jurisdiction. Congress, throughout the Judicial Act, and particularly in the 9th, 11th, and 13th sections, have legislated upon the supposition that, in all the cases to which the judicial powers of the United States extended, they might rightfully vest exclusive jurisdiction in their own Courts.

But even admitting that the language of the Constitution is not mandatory, and that Congress may constitutionally omit to vest the judicial power in Courts of the United States, it cannot be denied that, when it is vested, it may be exercised to the utmost constitutional extent.

This leads us to the consideration of the great question as to the nature and extent of the appellate jurisdiction of the United States. We have already seen that appellate jurisdiction is given by the Constitution to the Supreme Court in all cases where it has not original jurisdiction, subject, however, to such exceptions and regulations as Congress may prescribe. It is therefore capable of embracing every case enumerated in the Constitution which is not exclusively to be decided by way of original jurisdiction. But the exercise of appellate jurisdiction is far from being limited by the terms of the Constitution to the Supreme Court. There can be no doubt that Congress may create a succession of inferior tribunals, in each of which it may vest appellate as well as original jurisdiction. The judicial power is delegated by the Constitution in the most general terms, and may therefore be exercised by Congress under every variety of form of appellate or original jurisdiction. And as there is nothing in the Constitution which restrains or limits this power, it must therefore, in all other cases, subsist in the utmost latitude of which, in its own nature, it is susceptible.

As, then, by the terms of the Constitution, the appellate jurisdiction is not limited as to the

www.milestonedocuments.com

Supreme Court, and as to this Court it may be exercised in all other cases than those of which it has original cognizance, what is there to restrain its exercise over State tribunals in the enumerated cases? The appellate power is not limited by the terms of the third article to any particular Courts. The words are, "the judicial power (which includes appellate power) shall extend to all cases," &c., and "in all other cases before mentioned, the Supreme Court shall have appellate jurisdiction." It is the case, then, and not the court, that gives the jurisdiction. If the judicial power extends to the case, it will be in vain to search in the letter of the Constitution for any qualification as to the tribunal where it depends. It is incumbent, then, upon those who assert such a qualification to show its existence by necessary implication. If the text be clear and distinct, no restriction upon its plain and obvious import ought to be admitted, unless the inference be irresistible.

If the Constitution meant to limit the appellate jurisdiction to cases pending in the Courts of the United States, it would necessarily follow that the jurisdiction of these Courts would, in all the cases enumerated in the Constitution, be exclusive of State tribunals. How otherwise could the jurisdiction extend to all cases arising under the Constitution, laws, and treaties of the United States, or to all cases of admiralty and maritime jurisdiction? If some of these cases might be entertained by State tribunals, and no appellate jurisdiction as to them should exist, then the appellate power would not extend to all, but to some, cases. If State tribunals might exercise concurrent jurisdiction over all or some of the other classes of cases in the Constitution without control, then the appellate jurisdiction of the United States might, as to such cases, have no real existence, contrary to the manifest intent of the Constitution. Under such circumstances, to give effect to the judicial power, it must be construed to be exclusive, and this not only when the *casus foederis* should arise directly, but when it should arise incidentally in cases pending in State courts. This construction would abridge the jurisdiction of such Court far more than has been ever contemplated in any act of Congress.

On the other hand, if, as has been contended, a discretion be vested in Congress to establish or not to establish inferior Courts, at their own pleasure, and Congress should not establish such Courts, the appellate jurisdiction of the Supreme Court would have nothing to act upon unless it could act upon cases pending in the State courts. Under such circumstances it must be held that the appellate power would extend to State courts, for the Constitution is peremptory that it shall extend to certain enumerated cases, which cases could exist in no other Courts. Any other construction, upon this supposition, would involve this strange contradiction that a discretionary power vested in Congress, and which they might rightfully omit to exercise, would defeat the absolute injunctions of the Constitution in relation to the whole appellate power.

But it is plain that the framers of the Constitution did contemplate that cases within the judicial cognizance of the United States not only might, but would, arise in the State courts in the exercise of their ordinary jurisdiction. With this view, the sixth article declares, that

> This Constitution, and the laws of the United States which shall be made in pursuance thereof, and all treaties made, or which shall be made, under the authority of the United States, shall be the supreme law of the land, and the judges in every State shall be bound thereby, anything in the Constitution or laws of any State to the contrary notwithstanding.

It is obvious that this obligation is imperative upon the State judges in their official, and not merely in their private, capacities. From the very nature of their judicial duties, they would be called upon to pronounce the law applicable to the case in judgment. They were not to decide merely according to the laws or Constitution of the State, but according to the Constitution, laws and treaties of the United States—"the supreme law of the land."

A moment's consideration will show us the necessity and propriety of this provision in cases where the jurisdiction of the State courts is unquestionable. Suppose a contract for the payment of money is made between citizens of the same State, and performance thereof is sought in the courts of that State; no person can doubt that the jurisdiction completely and exclusively attaches, in the first instance, to such courts. Suppose at the trial the defendant sets up in his defence a tender under a State law making paper money a good tender, or a State law impairing the obligation of such contract, which law, if binding, would defeat the suit. The Constitution of the United States has declared that no State shall make any thing but gold or silver coin a tender in payment of debts, or pass a law impairing the obligation of contracts. If Congress shall not have passed a law providing for the removal of such a suit to the courts of the United States, must not the State court proceed to hear and determine it? Can a mere plea in defence be, of itself, a bar to further proceedings, so as to prohibit an inquiry into its truth or legal propriety when no other tribunal exists to whom judicial cognizance of such cases is confided? Suppose an indictment for a crime in a State court, and the defendant should allege in his defence that the crime was created by an *ex post facto* act of the State, must not the State court, in the exercise of a jurisdiction which has already rightfully attached, have a right to pronounce on the validity and sufficiency of the defence? It would be extremely difficult, upon any legal principles, to give a negative answer to these inquiries. Innumerable instances of the same sort might be stated in illustration of the position, and unless the State courts could sustain jurisdiction in such cases, this clause of the sixth article would be without meaning or effect, and public mischiefs of a most enormous magnitude would inevitably ensue.

It must therefore be conceded that the Constitution not only contemplated, but meant to provide for, cases within the scope of the judicial power of the United States which might yet depend before State tribunals. It was foreseen that, in the exercise of their ordinary jurisdiction, State courts would incidentally take cognizance of cases arising under the Constitution, the laws, and treaties of the United States. Yet to all these cases the judicial power, by the very terms of the Constitution, is to extend. It cannot extend by original jurisdiction if that was already rightfully and exclusively attached in the State courts, which (as has been already shown) may occur; it must therefore extend by appellate jurisdiction, or not at all. It would seem to follow that the appellate power of the United States must, in such cases, extend to State tribunals; and if in such cases, there is no reason why it should not equally attach upon all others within the purview of the Constitution.

It has been argued that such an appellate jurisdiction over State courts is inconsistent with the genius of our Governments, and the spirit of the Constitution. That the latter was never designed to act upon State sovereignties, but only upon the people, and that, if the power exists, it will materially impair the sovereignty of the States, and the independence of their courts. We cannot yield to the force of this reasoning; it assumes principles which we cannot admit, and draws conclusions to which we do not yield our assent.

It is a mistake that the Constitution was not designed to operate upon States in their corporate capacities. It is crowded with provisions which restrain or annul the sovereignty of the States in some of the highest branches of their prerogatives. The tenth section of the first article contains a long list of disabilities and prohibitions imposed upon the States. Surely, when such essential portions of State sovereignty are taken away or prohibited to be exercised, it cannot be correctly asserted that the Constitution does not act upon the States. The language of the Constitution is also imperative upon the States as to the performance of many duties. It is imperative upon the State legislatures to make laws prescribing the time, places, and manner of holding elections for senators and representatives, and for electors of President and Vice-President. And in these as well as some other cases, Congress have a right to revise, amend, or supersede the laws which may be passed by State legislatures. When therefore the States are stripped of some of the highest attributes of sovereignty, and the same are given to the United States; when the legislatures of the States are, in some respects, under the control of Congress, and in every case are, under the Constitution, bound by the paramount authority of the United States, it is certainly difficult to support the argument that the appellate power over the decisions of State courts is contrary to the genius of our institutions. The courts of the United States can, without question, revise the proceedings of the executive and legislative authorities of the States, and if they are found to be contrary to the Constitution, may declare them to be of no legal validity. Surely the exercise of the same right over judicial tribunals is not a higher or more dangerous act of sovereign power.

Nor can such a right be deemed to impair the independence of State judges. It is assuming the very ground in controversy to assert that they possess an absolute independence of the United States. In respect to the powers granted to the United States, they are not independent; they are expressly bound to obedience by the letter of the Constitution, and if they should unintentionally transcend their authority or misconstrue the Constitution, there is no more reason for giving their judgments an absolute and irresistible force than for giving it to the acts of the other coordinate departments of State sovereignty.

The argument urged from the possibility of the abuse of the revising power is equally unsatisfactory. It is always a doubtful course to argue against the use or existence of a power from the possibility of its abuse. It is still more difficult by such an argument to ingraft upon a general power a restriction which is

www.milestonedocuments.com

not to be found in the terms in which it is given. From the very nature of things, the absolute right of decision, in the last resort, must rest somewhere—wherever it may be vested, it is susceptible of abuse. In all questions of jurisdiction, the inferior or appellate court must pronounce the final judgment; and common sense, as well as legal reasoning, has conferred it upon the latter.

It has been further argued against the existence of this appellate power that it would form a novelty in our judicial institutions. This is certainly a mistake. In the Articles of Confederation, an instrument framed with infinitely more deference to State rights and State jealousies, a power was given to Congress to establish "courts for revising and determining, finally, appeals in all cases of captures." It is remarkable that no power was given to entertain original jurisdiction in such cases, and consequently the appellate power (although not so expressed in terms) was altogether to be exercised in revising the decisions of State tribunals. This was, undoubtedly, so far a surrender of State sovereignty, but it never was supposed to be a power fraught with public danger or destructive of the independence of State judges. On the contrary, it was supposed to be a power indispensable to the public safety, inasmuch as our national rights might otherwise be compromitted and our national peace been dangered. Under the present Constitution, the prize jurisdiction is confined to the courts of the United States, and a power to revise the decisions of State courts, if they should assert jurisdiction over prize causes, cannot be less important or less useful than it was under the Confederation.

In this connexion, we are led again to the construction of the words of the Constitution, "the judicial power shall extend," &c. If, as has been contended at the bar, the term "extend" have a relative signification, and mean to widen an existing power, it will then follow, that, as the confederation gave an appellate power over State tribunals, the Constitution enlarged or widened that appellate power to all the other cases in which jurisdiction is given to the Courts of the United States. It is not presumed that the learned counsel would choose to adopt such a conclusion.

It is further argued that no great public mischief can result from a construction which shall limit the appellate power of the United States to cases in their own Courts, first because State judges are bound by an oath to support the Constitution of the United States, and must be presumed to be men of learning and integrity, and secondly because Congress must have an unquestionable right to remove all cases within the scope of the judicial power from the State courts to the courts of the United States at any time before final judgment, though not after final judgment. As to the first reason—admitting that the judges of the State courts are, and always will be, of as much learning, integrity, and wisdom as those of the courts of the United States (which we very cheerfully admit), it does not aid the argument. It is manifest that the Constitution has proceeded upon a theory of its own, and given or withheld powers according to the judgment of the American people, by whom it was adopted. We can only construe its powers, and cannot inquire into the policy or principles which induced the grant of them. The Constitution has presumed (whether rightly or wrongly we do not inquire) that State attachments, State prejudices, State jealousies, and State interests might sometimes obstruct or control, or be supposed to obstruct or control, the regular administration of justice. Hence, in controversies between States, between citizens of different States, between citizens claiming grants under different States, between a State and its citizens, or foreigners, and between citizens and foreigners, it enables the parties, under the authority of Congress, to have the controversies heard, tried, and determined before the national tribunals. No other reason than that which has been stated can be assigned why some, at least, of those cases should not have been left to the cognizance of the State courts. In respect to the other enumerated cases—the cases arising under the Constitution, laws, and treaties of the United States, cases affecting ambassadors and other public ministers, and cases of admiralty and maritime jurisdiction—reasons of a higher and more extensive nature, touching the safety, peace, and sovereignty of the nation, might well justify a grant of exclusive jurisdiction.

This is not all. A motive of another kind, perfectly compatible with the most sincere respect for State tribunals, might induce the grant of appellate power over their decisions. That motive is the importance, and even necessity, of uniformity of decisions throughout the whole United States upon all subjects within the purview of the Constitution. Judges of equal learning and integrity in different States might differently interpret a statute or a treaty of the United States, or even the Constitution itself; if there were no revising authority to control these jarring and discordant judgments and harmonize them into uniformity, the laws, the treaties, and the Constitution of the United States would be different in

www.milestonedocuments.com

different States, and might perhaps never have precisely the same construction, obligation, or efficacy in any two States. The public mischiefs that would attend such a State of things would be truly deplorable, and it cannot be believed that they could have escaped the enlightened convention which formed the Constitution. What, indeed, might then have been only prophecy has now become fact, and the appellate jurisdiction must continue to be the only adequate remedy for such evils.

There is an additional consideration, which is entitled to great weight. The Constitution of the United States was designed for the common and equal benefit of all the people of the United States. The judicial power was granted for the same benign and salutary purposes. It was not to be exercised exclusively for the benefit of parties who might be plaintiffs, and would elect the national forum, but also for the protection of defendants who might be entitled to try their rights, or assert their privileges, before the same forum. Yet, if the construction contended for be correct, it will follow that, as the plaintiff may always elect the State court, the defendant may be deprived of all the security which the Constitution intended in aid of his rights. Such a State of things can in no respect be considered as giving equal rights. To obviate this difficulty, we are referred to the power which it is admitted Congress possess to remove suits from State courts to the national Courts, and this forms the second ground upon which the argument we are considering has been attempted to be sustained.

This power of removal is not to be found in express terms in any part of the Constitution; if it be given, it is only given by implication, as a power necessary and proper to carry into effect some express power. The power of removal is certainly not, in strictness of language; it presupposes an exercise of original jurisdiction to have attached elsewhere. The existence of this power of removal is familiar in courts acting according to the course of the common law in criminal as well as civil cases, and it is exercised before as well as after judgment. But this is always deemed in both cases an exercise of appellate, and not of original, jurisdiction. If, then, the right of removal be included in the appellate jurisdiction, it is only because it is one mode of exercising that power, and as Congress is not limited by the Constitution to any particular mode or time of exercising it, it may authorize a removal either before or after judgment. The time, the process, and the manner must be subject to its absolute legislative control. A writ of error is indeed but a process which removes the record of one court to the possession of another court, and enables the latter to inspect the proceedings, and give such judgment as its own opinion of the law and justice of the case may warrant. There is nothing in the nature of the process which forbids it from being applied by the legislature to interlocutory as well as final judgments. And if the right of removal from State courts exist before judgment, because it is included in the appellate power, it must for the same reason exist after judgment. And if the appellate power by the Constitution does not include cases pending in State courts, the right of removal, which is but a mode of exercising that power, cannot be applied to them. Precisely the same objections therefore exist as to the right of removal before judgment as after, and both must stand or fall together. Nor, indeed, would the force of the arguments on either side materially vary if the right of removal were an exercise of original jurisdiction. It would equally trench upon the jurisdiction and independence of State tribunals.

The remedy, too, of removal of suits would be utterly inadequate to the purposes of the Constitution if it could act only on the parties, and not upon the State courts. In respect to criminal prosecutions, the difficulty seems admitted to be insurmountable; and in respect to civil suits, there would, in many cases, be rights without corresponding remedies. If State courts should deny the constitutionality of the authority to remove suits from their cognizance, in what manner could they be compelled to relinquish the jurisdiction? In respect to criminal cases, there would at once be an end of all control, and the state decisions would be paramount to the Constitution; and though, in civil suits, the courts of the United States might act upon the parties, yet the State courts might act in the same way, and this conflict of jurisdictions would not only jeopardise private rights, but bring into imminent peril the public interests.

On the whole, the Court are of opinion that the appellate power of the United States does extend to cases pending in the State courts, and that the 25th section of the judiciary act, which authorizes the exercise of this jurisdiction in the specified cases by a writ of error, is supported by the letter and spirit of the Constitution. We find no clause in that instrument which limits this power, and we dare not interpose a limitation where the people have not been disposed to create one.

Strong as this conclusion stands upon the general language of the Constitution, it may still derive

Document Text

support from other sources. It is an historical fact that this exposition of the Constitution, extending its appellate power to State courts, was, previous to its adoption, uniformly and publicly avowed by its friends and admitted by its enemies as the basis of their respective reasonings, both in and out of the State conventions. It is an historical fact that, at the time when the Judiciary Act was submitted to the deliberations of the first Congress, composed, as it was, not only of men of great learning and ability but of men who had acted a principal part in framing, supporting, or opposing that Constitution, the same exposition was explicitly declared and admitted by the friends and by the opponents of that system. It is an historical fact that the Supreme Court of the United States have, from time to time, sustained this appellate jurisdiction in a great variety of cases brought from the tribunals of many of the most important States in the Union, and that no State tribunal has ever breathed a judicial doubt on the subject, or declined to obey the mandate of the Supreme Court until the present occasion. This weight of contemporaneous exposition by all parties, this acquiescence of enlightened State courts, and these judicial decisions of the Supreme Court through so long a period do, as we think, place the doctrine upon a foundation of authority which cannot be shaken without delivering over the subject to perpetual and irremediable doubts.

The next question which has been argued is whether the case at bar be within the purview of the 25th section of the Judiciary Act, so that this Court may rightfully sustain the present writ of error. This section, stripped of passages unimportant in this inquiry, enacts, in substance, that a final judgment or decree in any suit in the highest court of law or equity of a State, where is drawn in question the validity of a treaty or statute of, or an authority excised under, the United States, and the decision is against their validity, or where is drawn in question the validity of a statute of, or an authority exercised under, any State, on the ground of their being repugnant to the Constitution, treaties, or laws, of the United States, and the decision is in favour of such their validity, or of the Constitution, or of a treaty or statute of, or commission held under, the United States, and the decision is against the title, right, privilege, or exemption specially set up or claimed by either party under such clause of the said Constitution, treaty, statute, or commission, may be reexamined and reversed or affirmed in the Supreme Court of the United States upon a writ of error in the same manner, and under the same regulations, and the writ shall have the same effect, as if the judgment or decree complained of had been rendered or passed in a Circuit Court, and the proceeding upon the reversal shall also be the same, except that the Supreme Court, instead of remanding the cause for a final decision, as before provided, may, at their discretion, if the cause shall have been once remanded before, proceed to a final decision of the same and award execution. But no other error shall be assigned or regarded as a ground of reversal in any such case as aforesaid, than such as appears upon the face of the record, and immediately respects the before-mentioned question of validity or construction of the said Constitution, treaties, statutes, commissions, or authorities in dispute.

That the present writ of error is founded upon a judgment of the Court below which drew in question and denied the validity of a statute of the United States is incontrovertible, for it is apparent upon the face of the record. That this judgment is final upon the rights of the parties is equally true, for if well founded, the former judgment of that court was of conclusive authority, and the former judgment of this Court utterly void. The decision was therefore equivalent to a perpetual stay of proceedings upon the mandate, and a perpetual denial of all the rights acquired under it. The case, then, falls directly within the terms of the Act. It is a final judgment in a suit in a State court denying the validity of a statute of the United States, and unless a distinction can be made between proceedings under a mandate and proceedings in an original suit, a writ of error is the proper remedy to revise that judgment. In our opinion, no legal distinction exists between the cases.

In causes remanded to the Circuit Courts, if the mandate be not correctly executed, a writ of error or appeal has always been supposed to be a proper remedy, and has been recognized as such in the former decisions of this Court. The statute gives the same effect to writs of error from the judgments of State courts as of the Circuit Courts, and in its terms provides for proceedings where the same cause may be a second time brought up on writ of error before the Supreme Court. There is no limitation or description of the cases to which the second writ of error may be applied, and it ought therefore to be coextensive with the cases which fall within the mischiefs of the statute. It will hardly be denied that this cause stands in that predicament; and if so, then the appellate jurisdiction of this Court has rightfully attached.

Document Text

But it is contended, that the former judgment of this Court was rendered upon a case not within the purview of this section of the Judicial Act, and that, as it was pronounced by an incompetent jurisdiction, it was utterly void, and cannot be a sufficient foundation to sustain any subsequent proceedings. To this argument several answers may be given. In the first place, it is not admitted that, upon this writ of error, the former record is before us. The error now assigned is not in the former proceedings, but in the judgment rendered upon the mandate issued after the former judgment. The question now litigated is not upon the construction of a treaty, but upon the constitutionality of a statute of the United States, which is clearly within our jurisdiction. In the next place, in ordinary cases a second writ of error has never been supposed to draw in question the propriety of the first judgment, and it is difficult to perceive how such a proceeding could be sustained upon principle. A final judgment of this Court is supposed to be conclusive upon the rights which it decides, and no statute has provided any process by which this Court can revise its own judgments. In several cases which have been formerly adjudged in this Court, the same point was argued by counsel, and expressly overruled. It was solemnly held that a final judgment of this Court was conclusive upon the parties, and could not be reexamined.

In this case, however, from motives of a public nature, we are entirely willing to wave all objections and to go back and reexamine the question of jurisdiction as it stood upon the record formerly in judgment. We have great confidence that our jurisdiction will, on a careful examination, stand confirmed as well upon principle as authority. It will be recollected that the action was an ejectment for a parcel of land in the Northern Neck, formerly belonging to Lord Fairfax. The original plaintiff claimed the land under a patent granted to him by the State of Virginia in 1789, under a title supposed to be vested in that State by escheat or forfeiture. The original defendant claimed the land as devisee under the will of Lord Fairfax. The parties agreed to a special statement of facts in the nature of a special verdict, upon which the District Court of Winchester, in 1793, gave a general judgment for the defendant, which judgment was afterwards reversed in 1810 by the Court of Appeals, and a general judgment was rendered for the plaintiff; and from this last judgment a writ of error was brought to the Supreme Court. The statement of facts contained a regular deduction of the title of Lord Fairfax until his death, in 1781, and also the title of his devisee. It also contained a regular deduction of the title of the plaintiff, under the State of Virginia, and further referred to the treaty of peace of 1783, and to the acts of Virginia respecting the lands of Lord Fairfax, and the supposed escheat or forfeiture thereof, as component parts of the case. No facts disconnected with the titles thus set up by the parties were alleged on either side. It is apparent from this summary explanation that the title thus set up by the plaintiff might be open to other objections; but the title of the defendant was perfect and complete if it was protected by the treaty of 1783. If therefore this Court had authority to examine into the whole record, and to decide upon the legal validity of the title of the defendant, as well as its application to the treaty of peace, it would be a case within the express purview of the 25th section of the Act, for there was nothing in the record upon which the Court below could have decided but upon the title as connected with the treaty; and if the title was otherwise good, its sufficiency must have depended altogether upon its protection under the treaty. Under such circumstances it was strictly a suit where was drawn in question the construction of a treaty, and the decision was against the title specially set up or claimed by the defendant. It would fall, then, within the very terms of the Act.

The objection urged at the bar is that this Court cannot inquire into the title, but simply into the correctness of the construction put upon the treaty by the Court of Appeals, and that their judgment is not reexaminable here unless it appear on the face of the record that some construction was put upon the treaty. If therefore that court might have decided the case upon the invalidity of the title (and, *non constat*, that they did not) independent of the treaty, there is an end of the appellate jurisdiction of this Court. In support of this objection, much stress is laid upon the last clause of the section, which declares that no other cause shall be regarded as a ground of reversal than such as appears on the face of the record and immediately respects the construction of the treaty, &c., in dispute.

If this be the true construction of the section, it will be wholly inadequate for the purposes which it professes to have in view, and may be evaded at pleasure. But we see no reason for adopting this narrow construction; and there are the strongest reasons against it founded upon the words as well as the intent of the legislature. What is the case for which the body of the section provides a remedy by writ of error? The answer must be in the words of the section, a suit

www.milestonedocuments.com

Document Text

where is drawn in question the construction of a treaty, and the decision is against the title set up by the party. It is therefore the decision against the title set up with reference to the treaty, and not the mere abstract construction of the treaty itself, upon which the statute intends to found the appellate jurisdiction. How, indeed, can it be possible to decide whether a title be within the protection of a treaty until it is ascertained what that title is, and whether it have a legal validity? From the very necessity of the case, there must be a preliminary inquiry into the existence and structure of the title before the Court can construe the treaty in reference to that title. If the Court below should decide, that the title was bad, and therefore not protected by the treaty, must not this Court have a power to decide the title to be good, and therefore protected by the treaty? Is not the treaty, in both instances, equally construed, and the title of the party, in reference to the treaty, equally ascertained and decided? Nor does the clause relied on in the objection impugn this construction. It requires that the error upon which the Appellate Court is to decide shall appear on the face of the record, and immediately respect the questions before mentioned in the section. One of the questions is as to the construction of a treaty upon a title specially set up by a party, and every error that immediately respects that question must, of course, be within the cognizance, of the Court. The title set up in this case is apparent upon the face of the record, and immediately respects the decision of that question; any error therefore in respect to that title must be reexaminable, or the case could never be presented to the Court.

The restraining clause was manifestly intended for a very different purpose. It was foreseen that the parties might claim under various titles, and might assert various defences altogether independent of each other. The Court might admit or reject evidence applicable to one particular title, and not to all, and, in such cases, it was the intention of Congress to limit what would otherwise have unquestionably attached to the Court, the right of revising all the points involved in the cause. It therefore restrains this right to such errors as respect the questions specified in the section; and, in this view, it has an appropriate sense, consistent with the preceding clauses. We are therefore satisfied that, upon principle, the case was rightfully before us, and if the point were perfectly new, we should not hesitate to assert the jurisdiction.

But the point has been already decided by this Court upon solemn argument. In *Smith v. The State of Maryland*, 6 Cranch 286, precisely the same objection was taken by counsel, and overruled by the unanimous opinion of the Court. That case was, in some respects, stronger than the present; for the court below decided expressly that the party had no title, and therefore the treaty could not operate upon it. This Court entered into an examination of that question, and, being of the same opinion, affirmed the judgment. There cannot, then, be an authority which could more completely govern the present question.

It has been asserted at the bar that, in point of fact, the Court of Appeals did not decide either upon the treaty or the title apparent upon the record, but upon a compromise made under an act of the legislature of Virginia. If it be true (as we are informed) that this was a private act, to take effect only upon a certain condition, *viz.*, the execution of a deed of release of certain lands, which was matter *in pais*, it is somewhat difficult to understand how the Court could take judicial cognizance of the act or of the performance of the condition, unless spread upon the record. At all events, we are bound to consider that the Court did decide upon the facts actually before them. The treaty of peace was not necessary to have been stated, for it was the supreme law of the land, of which all Courts must take notice. And at the time of the decision in the Court of Appeals and in this Court, another treaty had intervened, which attached itself to the title in controversy and, of course, must have been the supreme law to govern the decision if it should be found applicable to the case. It was in this view that this Court did not deem it necessary to rest its former decision upon the treaty of peace, believing that the title of the defendant was, at all events, perfect under the treaty of 1794.

The remaining questions respect more the practice than the principles of this Court. The forms of process and the modes of proceeding in the exercise of jurisdiction are, with few exceptions, left by the Legislature to be regulated and changed as this Court may, in its discretion, deem expedient. By a rule of this Court, the return of a copy of a record of the proper court, under the seal of that court, annexed to the writ of error, is declared to be "a sufficient compliance with the mandate of the writ." The record in this case is duly certified by the clerk of the Court of Appeals and annexed to the writ of error. The objection therefore which has been urged to the sufficiency of the return cannot prevail.

Another objection is that it does not appear that the judge who granted the writ of error did, upon issuing the citation, take the bond required by the 22d section of the Judiciary Act.

We consider that provision as merely directory to the judge; and that an omission does not avoid the writ of error. If any party be prejudiced by the omission, this Court can grant him summary relief by imposing such terms on the other party as, under all the circumstances, may be legal and proper. But there is nothing in the record by which we can judicially know whether a bond has been taken or not, for the statute does not require the bond to be returned to this Court, and it might with equal propriety be lodged in the Court below, who would ordinarily execute the judgment to be rendered on the writ. And the presumption of law is, until the contrary appears, that every judge who signs a citation has obeyed the injunctions of the Act.

We have thus gone over all the principal questions in the cause, and we deliver our judgment with entire confidence that it is consistent with the Constitution and laws of the land.

We have not thought it incumbent on us to give any opinion upon the question, whether this Court have authority to issue a writ of mandamus to the Court of Appeals to enforce the former judgments, as we do not think it necessarily involved in the decision of this cause.

It is the opinion of the whole Court that the judgment of the Court of Appeals of Virginia, rendered on the mandate in this cause, be reversed, and the judgment of the District Court, held at Winchester, be, and the same is hereby, affirmed.

◆ J. Johnson

It will be observed in this case that the Court disavows all intention to decide on the right to issue compulsory process to the State courts, thus leaving us, in my opinion, where the Constitution and laws place us—supreme over persons and cases as far as our judicial powers extend, but not asserting any compulsory control over the State tribunals.

In this view I acquiesce in their opinion, but not altogether in the reasoning or opinion of my brother who delivered it. Few minds are accustomed to the same habit of thinking, and our conclusions are most satisfactory to ourselves when arrived at in our own way.

I have another reason for expressing my opinion on this occasion. I view this question as one of the most momentous importance; as one which may affect, in its consequences, the permanence of the American Union. It presents an instance of collision between the judicial powers of the Union, and one of the greatest States in the Union, on a point the most delicate and difficult to be adjusted. On the one hand, the General Government must cease to exist whenever it loses the power of protecting itself in the exercise of its constitutional powers. Force, which acts upon the physical powers of man, or judicial process, which addresses itself to his moral principles or his fears, are the only means to which governments can resort in the exercise of their authority. The former is happily unknown to the genius of our Constitution except as far as it shall be sanctioned by the latter, but let the latter be obstructed in its progress by an opposition which it cannot overcome or put by, and the resort must be to the former, or government is no more.

On the other hand, so firmly am I persuaded that the American people can no longer enjoy the blessings of a free government whenever the State sovereignties shall be prostrated at the feet of the General Government, nor the proud consciousness of equality and security any longer than the independence of judicial power shall be maintained consecrated and intangible, that I could borrow the language of a celebrated orator and exclaim, "I rejoice that Virginia has resisted."

Yet here I must claim the privilege of expressing my regret, that the opposition of the high and truly respected tribunal of that State had not been marked with a little more moderation. The only point necessary to be decided in the case then before them was "whether they were bound to obey the mandate emanating from this Court?" But, in the judgment entered on their minutes, they have affirmed that the case was, in this Court, *coram non judice*, or, in other words, that this Court had not jurisdiction over it.

This is assuming a truly alarming latitude of judicial power. Where is it to end? It is an acknowledged principle of, I believe, every Court in the world that not only the decisions, but everything done under the judicial process of courts not having jurisdiction are, *ipso facto*, void. Are, then, the judgments of this Court to be reviewed in every court of the Union? and is every recovery of money, every change of property, that has taken place under our process to be considered as null, void, and tortious?

We pretend not to more infallibility than other courts composed of the same frail materials which compose this. It would be the height of affectation to close our minds upon the recollection that we have been extracted from the same seminaries in which originated the learned men who preside over the State tribunals. But there is one claim which we can

www.milestonedocuments.com

Document Text

with confidence assert in our own name upon those tribunals—the profound, uniform, and unaffected respect which this Court has always exhibited for State decisions give us strong pretensions to judicial comity. And another claim I may assert, in the name of the American people; in this Court, every State in the Union is represented; we are constituted by the voice of the Union, and when decisions take place which nothing but a spirit to give ground and harmonize can reconcile, ours is the superior claim upon the comity of the State tribunals. It is the nature of the human mind to press a favourite hypothesis too far, but magnanimity will always be ready to sacrifice the pride of opinion to public welfare.

In the case before us, the collision has been, on our part, wholly unsolicited. The exercise of this appellate jurisdiction over the State decisions has long been acquiesced in, and when the writ of error in this case was allowed by the President of the Court of Appeals of Virginia, we were sanctioned in supposing that we were to meet with the same acquiescence there. Had that Court refused to grant the writ in the first instance, or had the question of jurisdiction, or on the mode of exercising jurisdiction, been made here originally, we should have been put on our guard, and might have so modelled the process of the Court as to strip it of the offensive form of a mandate. In this case it might have been brought down to what probably the 25th section of the Judiciary Act meant it should be, to-wit, an alternative judgment either that the State court may finally proceed at its option to carry into effect the judgment of this Court or, if it declined doing so, that then this Court would proceed itself to execute it. The language, sense, and operation of the 25th section on this subject merit particular attention. In the preceding section, which has relation to causes brought up by writ of error from the Circuit Courts of the United States, this Court is instructed not to issue executions, but to send a special mandate to the Circuit Court to award execution thereupon. In case of the Circuit Court's refusal to obey such mandate, there could be no doubt as to the ulterior measures; compulsory process might, unquestionably, be resorted to. Nor, indeed, was there any reason to suppose that they ever would refuse, and therefore there is no provision made for authorizing this Court to execute its own judgment in cases of that description. But not so in cases brought up from the State courts; the framers of that law plainly foresaw that the State courts might refuse, and not being willing to leave ground for the implication that compulsory process must be resorted to, because no specific provision was made, they have provided the means, by authorizing this Court, in case of reversal of the State decision, to execute its own judgment. In case of reversal, only was this necessary, for, in case of affirmance, this collision could not arise. It is true that the words of this section are that this Court may, in their discretion, proceed to execute its own judgment. But these words were very properly put in, that it might not be made imperative upon this Court to proceed indiscriminately in this way, as it could only be necessary in case of the refusal of the State courts, and this idea is fully confirmed by the words of the 13th section, which restrict this Court in issuing the writ of mandamus, so as to confine it expressly to those Courts which are constituted by the United States.

In this point of view, the Legislature is completely vindicated from all intention to violate the independence of the State judiciaries. Nor can this Court, with any more correctness, have imputed to it similar intentions. The form of the mandate issued in this case is that known to appellate tribunals, and used in the ordinary cases of writs of error from the courts of the United States. It will, perhaps, not be too much, in such cases, to expect of those who are conversant in the forms, fictions, and technicality of the law not to give the process of courts too literal a construction. They should be considered with a view to the ends they are intended to answer and the law and practice in which they originate. In this view, the mandate was no more than a mode of submitting to that court the option which the 25th section holds out to them.

Had the decision of the Court of Virginia been confined to the point of their legal obligation to carry the judgment of this Court into effect, I should have thought it unnecessary to make any further observations in this cause. But we are called upon to vindicate our general revising power, and its due exercise in this particular case.

Here, that I may not be charged with arguing upon a hypothetical case, it is necessary to ascertain what the real question is which this Court is now called to decide on.

In doing this, it is necessary to do what, although, in the abstract, of very questionable propriety, appears to be generally acquiesced in, to-wit, to review the case as it originally came up to this Court on the former writ of error. The cause, then, came up upon a case stated between the parties, and under the practice of that State, having the effect of a special verdict. The case stated brings into view the

www.milestonedocuments.com

treaty of peace with Great Britain, and then proceeds to present the various laws of Virginia and the facts upon which the parties found their respective titles. It then presents no particular question, but refers generally to the law arising out of the case. The original decision was obtained prior to the Treaty of 1794, but before the case was adjudicated in this Court, the Treaty of 1794 had been concluded.

The difficulties of the case arise under the construction of the 25th section above alluded to, which, as far as it relates to this case, is in these words:

> A final judgment or decree in any suit, in the highest Court of law or equity of a State in which a decision in the suit could be had, … where is drawn in question the construction of any clause of the Constitution or of a treaty, … and the decision is against the title set up or claimed by either party under such clause, may be reexamined and reversed, or affirmed.… But no other error shall be assigned or regarded as a ground of reversal in any such case as aforesaid than such as appears on the face of the record and immediately respects the before-mentioned questions of validity or construction of the said treaties,

&c.

The first point decided under this state of the case was that, the judgment being a part of the record, if that judgment was not such as, upon that case, it ought to have been, it was an error apparent on the face of the record. But it was contended that the case there stated presented a number of points upon which the decision below may have been founded, and that it did not therefore necessarily appear to have been an error immediately respecting a question on the construction of a treaty. But the Court held that, as the reference was general to the law arising out of the case, if one question arose which called for the construction of a treaty, and the decision negatived the right set up under it, this Court will reverse that decision, and that it is the duty of the party who would avoid the inconvenience of this principle so to mould the case as to obviate the ambiguity. And under this point arises the question whether this Court can inquire into the title of the party, or whether they are so restricted in their judicial powers as to be confined to decide on the operation of a treaty upon a title previously ascertained to exist.

If there is any one point in the case on which an opinion may be given with confidence, it is this, whether we consider the letter of the statute, or the spirit, intent, or meaning, of the Constitution and of the legislature, as expressed in the 27th section, it is equally clear that the title is the primary object to which the attention of the Court is called in every such case. The words are, "and the decision be against the title," so set up, not against the construction of the treaty contended for by the party setting up the title. And how could it be otherwise? The title may exist notwithstanding the decision of the State courts to the contrary, and, in that case, the party is entitled to the benefits intended to be secured by the treaty. The decision to his prejudice may have been the result of those very errors, partialities, or defects in State jurisprudence against which the Constitution intended to protect the individual. And if the contrary doctrine be assumed, what is the consequence? This Court may then be called upon to decide on a mere hypothetical case—to give a construction to a treaty without first deciding whether there was any interest on which that treaty, whatever be its proper construction, would operate. This difficulty was felt and weighed in the case of *Smith and the State of Maryland*, and that decision was founded upon the idea that this Court was not thus restricted.

But another difficulty presented itself: the Treaty of 1794 had become the supreme law of the land since the judgment rendered in the Court below. The defendant, who was at that time an alien, had now become confirmed in his rights under that treaty. This would have been no objection to the correctness of the original judgment. Were we, then, at liberty to notice that treaty in rendering the judgment of this Court?

Having dissented from the opinion of this Court in the original case on the question of title, this difficulty did not present itself in my way in the view I then took of the case. But the majority of this Court determined that, as a public law, the treaty was a part of the law of every case depending in this Court; that, as such, it was not necessary that it should be spread upon the record, and that it was obligatory upon this Court, in rendering judgment upon this writ of error, notwithstanding the original judgment may have been otherwise unimpeachable. And to this opinion I yielded my hearty consent, for it cannot be maintained that this Court is bound to give a judgment unlawful at the time of rendering it, in consideration that the same judgment would have been lawful at any prior time. What judgment can now be lawfully rendered between the parties is the question to which the attention of the Court is called. And if the law which sanctioned the original judgment expire pending an appeal, this Court has repeatedly reversed the judgment below, although rendered whilst the law existed. So, too, if the plaintiff in error die pending suit, and his land descend on an alien, it cannot be contended that this Court will maintain the suit in right of the judgment in favour of his ancestor, notwithstanding his present disability.

It must here be recollected that this is an action of ejectment. If the term formally declared upon expires pending the action, the Court will permit the plaintiff to amend by extending the term—why? Because, although the right may have been in him at the commencement of the suit, it has ceased before judgment, and, without this amendment, he could not have judgment. But suppose the suit were really instituted to obtain possession of a leasehold, and the lease expire before judgment, would the Court permit the party to amend in opposition to the right of the case? On the contrary, if the term formally declared on were more extensive than the lease in which the legal title was founded, could they give judgment for more than costs? It must be recollected that, under this judgment, a writ of restitution is the fruit of the law. This, in its very nature, has relation to, and must be founded upon, a present existing right at the time of judgment. And whatever be the cause which takes this right away, the remedy must, in the reason and nature of things, fall with it.

When all these incidental points are disposed of, we find the question finally reduced to this—does the judicial power of the United States extend to the revision of decisions of State courts in cases arising under treaties? But in order to generalize the question and present it in the true form in which it presents itself in this case, we will inquire whether the Constitution sanctions the exercise of a revising power over the decisions of State tribunals in those cases to which the judicial power of the United States extends?

And here it appears to me that the great difficulty is on the other side. That the real doubt is whether the State tribunals can constitutionally exercise jurisdiction in any of the cases to which the judicial power of the United States extends.

Some cession of judicial power is contemplated by the third article of the Constitution; that which is ceded can no longer be retained. In one of the Circuit Courts of the United States, it has been decided (with what correctness I will not say) that the cession of a power to pass an uniform act of bankruptcy, although not acted on by the United States, deprives the States of the power of passing laws to that effect. With regard to the admiralty and maritime jurisdiction, it would be difficult to prove that the States could resume it if the United States should abolish the Courts vested with that jurisdiction; yet it is blended with the other cases of jurisdiction in the second section of the third article, and ceded in the same words. But it is contended that the second section of the third article contains no express cession of jurisdiction; that it only vests a power in Congress to assume jurisdiction to the extent therein expressed. And under this head arose the discussion on the construction proper to be given to that article.

On this part of the case, I shall not pause long. The rules of construction, where the nature of the instrument is ascertained, are familiar to every one. To me, the Constitution appears, in every line of it, to be a contract which, in legal language, may be denominated tripartite. The parties are the people, the States, and the United States. It is returning in a circle to contend that it professes to be the exclusive act of the people, for what have the people done but to form this compact? That the States are recognised as parties to it is evident from various passages, and particularly that in which the United States guaranty to each State a republican form of Government.

The security and happiness of the whole was the object, and, to prevent dissention and collision, each surrendered those powers which might make them dangerous to each other. Well aware of the sensitive irritability of sovereign States, where their wills or interests clash, they placed themselves, with regard to each other, on the footing of sovereigns upon the ocean, where power is mutually conceded to act upon the individual, but the national vessel must remain unviolated. And to remove all ground for jealousy and complaint, they relinquish the privilege of being any longer the exclusive arbiters of their own justice where the rights of others come in question or the great interests of the whole may be affected by those feelings, partialities, or prejudices, which they meant to put down forever.

Nor shall I enter into a minute discussion on the meaning of the language of this section. I have seldom found much good result from hypercritical severity in examining the distinct force of words. Language is essentially defective in precision, more so than those are aware of who are not in the habit of subjecting it to philological analysis. In the case before us, for instance, a rigid construction might be made which would annihilate the powers intended to be ceded. The words are, "shall extend to;" now that which extends to does not necessarily include in, so that the circle may enlarge until it reaches the objects that limit it, and yet not take them in. But the plain and obvious sense and meaning of the word "shall," in this sentence, is in the future sense, and has nothing imperative in it. The language of the framers of the Constitution is "We are about forming a General Government—when that Government is formed, its powers shall extend," &c. I therefore see nothing imperative in this clause, and certainly it would have been very unnecessary to use the word in that sense; for, as there was no controlling power constituted, it would only, if used in an imperative sense, have imposed a moral obligation to act. But the same result arises from using it in a future sense, and the Constitution everywhere assumes as a postulate that wherever power is given, it will be used, or at least used as far as the interests of the American people require it, if not from the natural proneness of man to the exercise of power, at least from a sense of duty and the obligation of an oath.

Nor can I see any difference in the effect of the words used in this section, as to the scope of the jurisdiction of the United States' courts over the cases of the first and second description comprised in that section. "Shall extend to controversies," appears to me as comprehensive in effect as "shall extend to all cases." For if the judicial power extend "to controversies between citizen and alien," &c., to what controversies of that description does it not extend? If no case can be pointed out which is excepted, it then extends to all controversies.

But I will assume the construction as a sound one that the cession of power to the General Government means no more than that they may assume the exercise of it whenever they think it advisable. It is clear that Congress have hitherto acted under that impression, and my own opinion is in favour of its correctness. But does it not then follow that the jurisdiction of the State court, within the range ceded to the General Government, is permitted, and may be withdrawn whenever Congress think proper to do so? As it is a principle that everyone may renounce a right introduced for his benefit, we will admit that, as Congress have not assumed such jurisdiction, the State courts may constitutionally exercise jurisdiction in such cases. Yet surely the general power to withdraw the exercise of it includes in it the right to modify, limit, and restrain that exercise.

> This is my domain, put not your foot upon it; if you do, you are subject to my laws; I have a right to exclude you altogether; I have, then, a right to prescribe the terms of your admission to a participation. As long as you conform to my laws, participate in peace, but I reserve to myself the right of judging how far your acts are conformable to my laws.

Analogy, then, to the ordinary exercise of sovereign authority would sustain the exercise of this controlling or revising power.

But it is argued that a power to assume jurisdiction to the constitutional extent does not necessarily carry with it a right to exercise appellate power over the State tribunals.

This is a momentous questions, and one on which I shall reserve myself uncommitted for each particular case as it shall occur. It is enough, at present, to have shown that Congress has not asserted, and this Court has not attempted, to exercise that kind of authority *in personam* over the State courts which would place them in the relation of an inferior responsible body without their own acquiescence. And I have too much confidence in the State tribunals to believe that a case ever will occur in which it will be necessary for the General Government to assume a controlling power over these tribunals. But is it difficult to suppose a case which will call loudly for some remedy or restraint? Suppose a foreign minister or an officer acting regularly under authority from the United States, seized today, tried tomorrow, and hurried the next day to execution. Such cases may occur, and have occurred, in other countries. The angry vindictive passions of men have too often made their way into judicial tribunals, and we cannot hope forever to escape their baleful influence. In the case supposed, there ought to be a power somewhere to restrain or punish, or the Union must be dissolved. At present, the uncontrollable exercise of criminal jurisdiction is most securely confided to the State tribunals. The Courts of the United States are vested with no power to scrutinize into the proceedings of the State courts in criminal cases; on the contrary, the General Government has, in more than one instance, exhibited their confidence by a wish to vest them with the execution of their own penal law. And extreme, indeed, I flatter myself, must be the case in which the General Government could ever be induced to assert this right. If ever such a case should occur, it will be time enough to decide upon their constitutional power to do so.

But we know that, by the 3d article of the Constitution, judicial power, to a certain extent, is vested in the General Government, and that, by the same

www.milestonedocuments.com

instrument, power is given to pass all laws necessary to carry into effect the provisions of the Constitution. At present, it is only necessary to vindicate the laws which they have passed affecting civil cases pending in State tribunals.

In legislating on this subject, Congress, in the true spirit of the Constitution, have proposed to secure to everyone the full benefit of the Constitution without forcing any one necessarily into the courts of the United States. With this view, in one class of cases, they have not taken away absolutely from the State courts all the cases to which their judicial power extends, but left it to the plaintiff to bring his action there originally if he choose, or to the defendant to force the plaintiff into the courts of the United States where they have jurisdiction, and the former has instituted his suit in the State courts. In this case, they have not made it legal for the defendant to plead to the jurisdiction, the effect of which would be to put an end to the plaintiff's suit and oblige him, probably at great risk or expense, to institute a new action; but the Act has given him a right to obtain an order for a removal, on a petition to the State court, upon which the cause, with all its existing advantages, is transferred to the Circuit Court of the United States. This, I presume, can be subject to no objection, as the Legislature has an unquestionable right to make the ground of removal a ground of plea to the jurisdiction, and the Court must then do no more than it is now called upon to do, to-wit, give an order or a judgment, or call it what we will, in favour of that defendant. And so far from asserting the inferiority of the State tribunal, this act is rather that of a superior, inasmuch as the Circuit Court of the United States becomes bound, by that order, to take jurisdiction of the case. This method, so much more unlikely to affect official delicacy than that which is resorted to in the other class of cases, might perhaps have been more happily applied to all the cases which the Legislature thought it advisable to remove from the State courts. But the other class of cases, in which the present is included, was proposed to be provided for in a different manner. And here, again, the Legislature of the Union evince their confidence in the State tribunals, for they do not attempt to give original cognizance to their own Circuit Courts of such cases, or to remove them by petition and order; but still believing that their decisions will be generally satisfactory, a writ of error is not given immediately as a question within the jurisdiction of the United States shall occur, but only in case the decision shall finally, in the Court of the last resort, be against the title set up under the Constitution, treaty, &c.

In this act I can see nothing which amounts to an assertion of the inferiority or dependence of the State tribunals. The presiding judge of the State court is himself authorized to issue the writ of error, if he will, and thus give jurisdiction to the Supreme Court; and if he thinks proper to decline it, no compulsory process is provided by law to oblige him. The party who imagines himself aggrieved is then at liberty to apply to a judge of the United States, who issues the writ of error, which (whatever the form) is, in substance, no more than a mode of compelling the opposite party to appear before this Court and maintain the legality of his judgment obtained before the state tribunal. An exemplification of a record is the common property of every one who chooses to apply and pay for it, and thus the case and the parties are brought before us; and so far is the court itself from being brought under the revising power of this Court that nothing but the case, as presented by the record and pleadings of the parties, is considered, and the opinions of the court are never resorted to unless for the purpose of assisting this Court in forming their own opinions.

The absolute necessity that there was for Congress to exercise something of a revising power over cases and parties in the State courts will appear from this consideration.

Suppose the whole extent of the judicial power of the United States vested in their own courts, yet such a provision would not answer all the ends of the Constitution, for two reasons:

1st. Although the plaintiff may, in such case, have the full benefit of the Constitution extended to him, yet the defendant would not, as the plaintiff might force him into the court of the State at his election.

2dly. Supposing it possible so to legislate as to give the courts of the United States original jurisdiction in all cases arising under the Constitution, laws, &c., in the words of the 2d section of the 3d article (a point on which I have some doubt, and which in time might perhaps, under some *quo minus* fiction or a willing construction, greatly accumulate the jurisdiction of those Courts), yet a very large class of cases would remain unprovided for. Incidental questions would often arise, and as a Court of competent jurisdiction in the principal case must decide all such questions, whatever laws they arise under, endless might be the diversity of decisions throughout the Union upon the Constitution, treaties, and laws of the United States, a subject on which the tranquillity of the Union, internally and externally, may materially depend.

Document Text

I should feel the more hesitation in adopting the opinions which I express in this case were I not firmly convinced that they are practical, and may be acted upon without compromitting the harmony of the Union or bringing humility upon the State tribunals. God forbid that the judicial power in these States should ever for a moment, even in its humblest departments, feel a doubt of its own independence. Whilst adjudicating on a subject which the laws of the country assign finally to the revising power of another tribunal, it can feel no such doubt. An anxiety to do justice is ever relieved by the knowledge that what we do is not final between the parties. And no sense of dependence can be felt from the knowledge that the parties, not the Court, may be summoned before another tribunal. With this view, by means of laws, avoiding judgments obtained in the State courts in cases over which Congress has constitutionally assumed jurisdiction, and inflicting penalties on parties who shall contumaciously persist in infringing the constitutional rights of others—under a liberal extension of the writ of injunction and the habeas corpus *ad subjiciendum*, I flatter myself that the full extent of the constitutional revising power may be secured to the United States, and the benefits of it to the individual, without ever resorting to compulsory or restrictive process upon the State tribunals; a right which, I repeat again, Congress has not asserted, nor has this Court asserted, nor does there appear any necessity for asserting.

The remaining points in the case being mere questions of practice, I shall make no remarks upon them.

Judgment affirmed.

www.milestonedocuments.com

84) February Term 1819- (Judgments

Henry Aston
53-
vs
Bazaleel Wells & the heirs and Representatives of Arnold H. Dohrman dec'd.

This cause came on to be heard on the Transcript of the Record and was argued by Counsel on considera-tion whereof- It is Decreed and ordered, that the Decree of the Circuit Court for the District of Ohio in this case be and the same is hereby affirmed with Costs. March 6th

James W. McCulloch
66-
vs
The State of Maryland & John James, as well for the State as for himself

This cause came on to be heard on the Transcript of the Record of the Court of Appeals of the State of Maryland, and was argued by Counsel, on consideration whereof, It is the opinion of this Court, that the act of the Legislature of Maryland entitled "An act to impose a tax on all Banks or Branches thereof in the State of Maryland not chartered by the Legislature" is contrary to the Constitution of the United States and void, and therefore that the said Court of Appeals of the State of Maryland erred in affirming the Judgment of the Baltimore County Court- in which Judgment was rendered against James W. McCulloch but that the said Court of Appeals of Maryland ought to have reversed the said Judgment of the said Baltimore County Court and to have given Judgment for the said appellant McCulloch - It is therefore adjudged and ordered, that the said Judgment of the said Court of Appeals of the state of Maryland in this case be and the same is hereby reversed and annulled - and this Court proceeding to render such Judgment as the said Court of Appeals should have rendered; It is further adjudged and ordered, that the judgment of the said Baltimore County Court be reversed and annulled, and that Judgment be entered in the said Bal-

McCulloch v. Maryland (National Archives and Records Administration)

McCulloch v. Maryland

1819

"We must never forget that it is a constitution we are expounding."

Overview

Federalism, the division of sovereign power between national and state governments, creates perpetual tension over the degree of power possessed by each level of government. Innovating such a division in 1787, the framers of the U.S. Constitution could offer only an impressionistic blueprint. Granting the new national government power with regard to several broadly worded subjects, the framers left the details—and thus the precise division of power—to future development. How much power did those grants actually bestow on the national government of the United States? Chief Justice John Marshall's 1819 opinion in *McCulloch v. Maryland* was the foundational Supreme Court decision that initiated the process of answering that question, which very much remains relevant in modern times.

Context

The scope of the national government's power became one of the most controversial political issues in the years following the ratification of the Constitution. On one side, such members of the founding generation as Thomas Jefferson and James Madison pressed for constitutional interpretations that would seriously constrain the power of the national government and, as a result, enhance the power of the states. Against them, arguing for interpretations that would enhance national power at the expense of the states, were such figures as Alexander Hamilton, John Adams, and, though trying to remain above the fray, George Washington himself. Although slavery and race would later define debates about "states' rights" and have too often been ignored as a subtext of this early controversy, the disagreement was about far more. Broader matters of individual liberty, self-government, unity, and even national security were thought to be at stake. The competing conceptions of federalism became a major impetus behind the rise of political parties in this era, with Jeffersonian Republicans favoring a weaker national government and Hamiltonian Federalists a stronger one.

In this clash over federalism, the national government's incorporation of a bank became an early flashpoint. Hamilton, as Washington's secretary of the treasury, proposed a national bank in 1790 as a way to spur economic investment, support national debt management, facilitate federal tax collection, and, less officially, give monied interests a stake in the success of the national government. Congress approved the bank bill and sent it to Washington for his signature. Jefferson, then Washington's secretary of state, vigorously opposed the incorporation of a bank as exceeding the constitutional powers of the national government. Washington, however, agreed with Hamilton's defense of the bank's constitutionality and signed the bill, creating the First Bank of the United States.

After the electoral revolution of 1800, when Jefferson and his Republicans ousted Federalists from Congress and the presidency, political polarization over federalism diminished. As president, Jefferson exercised broader powers than he previously would have conceded to the national government, such as with his conclusion of the Louisiana Purchase, while Federalists, no longer in control, became less vigorous advocates for broad national power once it was wielded by their opponents. When the expiration of the First Bank in 1811 contributed to financial woes, which the War of 1812 only exacerbated, Madison, having succeeded Jefferson as president, signed a bill to incorporate the Second Bank of the United States on April 10, 1816. Even though as a House member Madison had strenuously opposed Hamilton's original bill as unconstitutional, he waived those earlier objections based on the general acceptance of the First Bank's constitutionality during the ensuing years. By then, nationalism was ascendant in the United States, as it coincidentally was in Europe as well.

Within three years, however, the Second Bank was publicly reviled, though not principally because of objections related to federalism. The bank's loose lending practices during an economic boom gave way in the depression that followed to policies of strict recapture. Maryland and other states then moved against the bank by taxing its operation; two states even banned its operation altogether. At the same time, word was emerging that James McCulloch, the chief agent of the Baltimore branch, and some unscrupulous conspirators had bilked the bank out of $1 million. Opposition

Time Line

1790

■ **December**
Hamilton recommends the incorporation of a national bank.

1791

■ **February 8**
Congress approves the bill for the first national bank.

■ **February 25**
Washington signs the first bank bill into law.

■ **December 12**
The First Bank of the United States begins operations.

1800

■ **November**
Jefferson is elected president, and the Federalists lose control of Congress.

1801

■ **February 4**
Marshall takes the oath as Chief Justice of the United States at the end of the administration of John Adams.

1811

■ **March 3**
The First Bank's charter expires.

1812

■ **June 18**
War of 1812 begins when the United States declares war on Great Britain.

1815

■ **February 17**
War of 1812 ends with the U.S. ratification of the Treaty of Ghent.

1816

■ **April 10**
Madison signs the second national bank bill into law.

1817

■ **January 7**
The Second Bank of the United States begins operations.

to national power had diminished, but opposition to the Second Bank itself was great, and Congress seriously debated abolishing it. It was in this atmosphere that the Supreme Court decided the *McCulloch* case, in which the Court affirmed Congress's power to incorporate a national bank and struck down Maryland's attempt to tax it.

About the Author

Despite cultural similarities to Jefferson and Madison, John Marshall was a consummate Federalist and a strong supporter of national power. Born in 1755 in Virginia to a successful and locally prominent family, Marshall became a lawyer and served as state politician, diplomat, and secretary of state before becoming chief justice of the United States on February 4, 1801. Appointed by President Adams, a Federalist, in the waning days of his administration, Marshall and other judicial appointees would remain the only source of Federalist power after the imminent Jeffersonian takeover of the presidency and Congress. Marshall did not disappoint. By the time he died in 1835 after serving as the Supreme Court's chief justice for nearly thirty-five years, Marshall had greatly expanded the reputation and influence of the Court and had penned landmark legal opinions that laid the foundations for dramatic expansions in the scope of the national government that would occur over the ensuing two centuries. Jeffersonians may have won the elections of 1800, but owing to Marshall's commanding Federalist presence on the Court, they ultimately lost the struggle to give federalism a strongly decentralized bent.

At least two factors that distinguished Marshall from his Virginia contemporaries may help to explain his regionally dissident opinion in favor of national power. First, Marshall saw extensive action as a first lieutenant during the Revolutionary War, including enduring the harsh winter at Valley Forge. He witnessed the problems of supply and support that plagued the Continental army owing to the weak national government and selfish recalcitrance among the states in the era before the Constitution. Second, neither Marshall nor his family ever engaged in large-scale agricultural production, although they held significant land. As a result, Marshall, who never owned more than a handful of slaves, was less invested in the slavery-dependent plantation economy of the South. Indeed, his writings, particularly in later years, disclose a disdain for slavery. From his position on the Court, he ruled that slaves were people, not property, and his will bestowed freedom upon his longtime personal servant.

Explanation and Analysis of the Document

Paragraphs 1–10 are background materials that precede Marshall's actual opinion, which begins at paragraph 11. Paragraph 1 indicates that the Supreme Court took the case by issuing a writ of error to Maryland's highest court. Paragraph 2 is a "statement of the case," a summary of proceedings to date. On behalf of Maryland, John James, a state treasurer, sued James McCulloch, the chief agent of the Second Bank's Baltimore branch, to recover unpaid taxes that the bank allegedly owed the state. A county court ruled for Maryland based on an agreed-upon "statement of facts," a procedure that avoided a trial. On appeal, Maryland's highest court upheld the county court's judgment.

Paragraphs 3–5 reproduce the statement of facts, as confirmed by both parties to the case. Paragraph 3 cites the federal statute that established the Second Bank and the Maryland statute that taxed the bank. The Second Bank was organized in Philadelphia and, without Maryland's authorization, established a Baltimore branch. The branch engaged in certain transactions with George Williams, a shady business partner of McCulloch. The bank did not pay the Maryland tax even though the state did nothing to obstruct payment. Paragraph 4 identifies the case's primary question—whether Maryland's tax is constitutional—and specifies the remedies sought by each side. Paragraph 5 notes that the parties preserve their appeals and agree to be bound by the statement of facts.

Paragraphs 6–10 reproduce the Maryland tax statute. As paragraph 8 discloses, the statute taxed the transactions of any bank lacking a state charter. As paragraph 9 discloses, the statute imposed penalties on bank employees.

◆ Chief Justice John Marshall's Opinion for the Court

Paragraph 11 marks the start of Marshall's opinion, which was unanimously joined by the associate justices. In paragraph 12 Marshall explains that Maryland ("the defendant") challenges the constitutionality of the federal law incorporating the Second Bank and that McCulloch ("the plaintiff") challenges the constitutionality of Maryland's tax. The Supreme Court, Marshall observes, bears the "awful responsibility" of adjudicating this dispute, which may have significant ramifications for federalism.

◆ Power of Congress to Charter a Bank

In paragraph 13 Marshall turns to the first main issue: the power of Congress to charter a bank. In paragraphs 14–17 Marshall explains why judicial review should be restrained. In paragraph 14 he cites long-standing congressional and judicial acquiescence as a reason to presume the Second Bank constitutional. He concedes in paragraph 15 that the Court could halt an obvious constitutional violation ("a bold and daring usurpation") but also that the historical acquiescence cautions against it. The acquiescence is held to particularly matter when only federalism, not civil liberties, is at stake.

In paragraph 16 Marshall adverts to the extensive political debate over the bank's constitutionality. He makes tacit reference to James Madison's opposition to the original bill in Congress, Thomas Jefferson's opposition to it inside George Washington's cabinet, Washington's decision to approve the original bill, and Madison's subsequent change of opinion after the original act lapsed. Given this background, a court would be hard pressed to view the bank as obviously unconstitutional, although Marshall adds in paragraph 17 that the constitutionality of the Second Bank does not necessarily depend on this background.

In paragraphs 18–22 Marshall rejects a compact theory of federalism, which would view the Constitution as emanating from the states, not the people. He acknowledges in paragraph 19 that state legislatures chose the delegates to the Constitutional Convention of 1787 and that the Constitution was ratified on a state-by-state basis. He reasons,

Time Line

1818

- **May 18**
  Maryland sues the Second Bank agent James McCulloch over the bank's failure to pay the state tax.
- **May**
  Baltimore county court rules for Maryland in the Second Bank case.
- **June**
  Maryland's highest court upholds the county court's judgment.
- **September 18**
  The U.S. Supreme Court takes the case *McCulloch v. Maryland.*

1819

- **February 22**
  Oral arguments in *McCulloch v. Maryland* begin.
- **March 3**
  Oral arguments in the case end.
- **March 6**
  Marshall announces the judgment of the Supreme Court in favor of McCulloch.

1832

- **July 10**
  President Andrew Jackson vetoes a bill to extend the Second Bank's charter.

1833

- **September 18**
  Jackson announces the removal of federal funds from the bank.

1835

- **July 6**
  Chief Justice Marshall dies.

1836

- **March 4**
  The Second Bank's charter expires.

www.milestonedocuments.com

however, that the document was ratified not by state legislatures but by the people in representative conventions, the closet mechanism to statewide direct democracy in the eighteenth century. In paragraph 20 Marshall quotes from the Constitution's preamble and identifies the people, not the states, as the foundational source of the Constitution's authority. Implicitly referencing the Declaration of Independence, Marshall reasons in paragraph 21 that even though the people had already delegated their sovereign power to state governments, they could reclaim it and re-delegate it to a new system of government. In paragraph 22 Marshall emphasizes the federal government's popular basis, anticipating Abraham Lincoln's Gettysburg Address.

In paragraph 23 Marshall acknowledges that Congress possesses only limited powers as enumerated in the Constitution (principally in Article I, Section 8). He calls the point so obvious that the Constitution's "enlightened friends"—the authors of the Federalist Papers—devoted more time than necessary to establishing the proposition. But the difficult question, Marshall says, is identifying the scope of those powers.

In paragraphs 24–26 Marshall establishes that federal laws take precedence over state laws. In paragraph 25 he offers a functional justification: In a collective, the whole must bind the parts. In paragraphs 25 and 26 he adds a textual justification—the "supremacy" clause of the Constitution (Article VI, Clause 2), which expressly declares federal law supreme.

In paragraph 27—a critical passage—Marshall introduces the doctrine of "implied powers." Even though the chartering of a bank or other corporation is not an enumerated power, this doctrine establishes how Congress might nevertheless have that power as adjunct to its enumerated powers. Marshall offers a comparative textual justification for this doctrine. While the Articles of Confederation, the forerunner of the Constitution, reserved to the states all powers that were not "expressly delegated" to the Confederation Congress (Article II), the parallel provision of the Constitution itself (Amendment X) omits the word "expressly," thus allowing the inference that Congress possesses some powers that are not specifically enumerated. Marshall then reinforces his view by considering the very nature of a constitution, which he characterizes as a concise document that contains only "great outlines," not implementation details. Marshall alludes to this conception when he famously announces here that "it is a constitution we are expounding."

In paragraph 28 Marshall introduces a critical distinction between means and ends. He holds that Congress does not have the power to charter a bank merely because that power is lesser than the great enumerated powers. Rather, Congress has power to charter a bank because, in Marshall's view, that power is not an end in itself but merely a means to an end. The enumerated powers, he reasons, address ends, not means, so one would not expect to find the power to charter a bank—a mere means—among the enumerated powers. Further, the framers of the Constitution could not have intended to grant Congress "ample powers" without "ample means" for executing them. Surely, Marshall says, the power of Congress to raise and spend revenue (Article I, Section 8, Clause 1) includes as an implied power the means of transporting revenue from the place it was raised to the place it will be spent.

In paragraphs 29–31 Marshall requires Maryland to explain how the power to charter a bank is different from any other means that Congress might use in executing its enumerated powers. Although Maryland holds that the power is a sovereign one, Marshall states that the same is true of other means, such as physically transporting federal revenue. In paragraph 32 Marshall notes that the question is not whether chartering a bank is a sovereign power but, rather, which sovereign possesses the power in a system where sovereignty is split. Marshall then rejects Maryland's argument that the chartering of banks is a state power because states had that power first. The argument is untenable because it would not apply to any state admitted to the Union after the ratification of the Constitution. Marshall then reiterates that the chartering of a bank is an apt means to a legitimate federal end and is thus an implicit adjunct to Congress's enumerated powers.

In paragraph 33 Marshall turns from implied powers to the Constitution's "necessary and proper" clause (Article I, Section 8, Clause 18), which explicitly empowers Congress to enact all laws that are "necessary and proper" for executing its enumerated powers. In paragraph 34 Marshall accuses Maryland of arguing that the clause is not, as written, a grant of power but a restriction on Congress's choice of means. In paragraphs 35–36 Marshall digresses to reject Maryland's argument that the clause merely ensures that Congress can enact laws. Marshall notes that that power is already obvious from other provisions.

In paragraph 37 Marshall introduces Maryland's principal argument: that the word *necessary* means "indispensably necessary," such that the clause in question empowers Congress to make only those laws that are indispensable to the execution of its enumerated powers, limiting Congress to only those means that are the "most direct and simple." In paragraph 38 Marshall reasons that *necessary* need not be interpreted as "indispensable," as it can have less strong senses. The Constitution itself elsewhere uses a related phrase with a qualifying word, "absolutely necessary" (Article I, Section 10), to convey the sense of "indispensable." Marshall reasons that such ambiguous words as *necessary* should thus be interpreted in light of "the subject, the context, [and] the intention of the person using them." Marshall then considers each of those three matters in turn.

In paragraph 39 Marshall first discusses the "necessary and proper" clause's subject, which he describes as facilitation of the execution of Congress's "great powers." Interpreting the word *necessary* to limit Congress's choice of means would contradict that function. Marshall again invokes the nature of a constitution, which is "to endure for ages to come" and be "adapted to the various *crises* of human affairs." Limiting Congress's choice of means in achieving its designated ends would unduly tie the hands of future generations. This limitation would make the Constitution function more like a legal code, as if the framers had intended to preemptively micromanage "exigencies which, if foreseen at all, must have been seen dimly, and which can be best provided for as they occur." Marshall then cites statutory oaths of office as being not indispensably necessary to the execution of Congress's powers while still being something that Congress surely can require.

In paragraphs 40–43 Marshall analogizes the incorporation of a bank to the enactment of criminal restrictions. He observes in paragraph 40 that the power to punish people is not an enumerated power and that Congress could execute its enumerated powers without creating any criminal restrictions. Although Congress could set up a postal system and federal courts without criminalizing interference with their operations, Marshall states in paragraph 41 that such criminal restrictions are nevertheless useful. The power to punish, Marshall reasons in paragraph 42, is a means for executing Congress's enumerated powers and is within Congress's power even if merely conducive, but not actually indispensable, to its execution of enumerated powers. If *necessary* should not be interpreted to mean "indispensable" with respect to the creation of criminal restrictions, Marshall asks in paragraph 43, why should it be read that way with respect to the incorporation of a bank?

In paragraph 44 Marshall considers the specific context in which the word *necessary* appears in the clause in question. He explains that qualifying the word by pairing it with the phrase *and proper* would not make sense if *necessary* already meant "indispensable."

In paragraphs 45–47 Marshall further considers the intentions of the framers. He rejects Maryland's restrictive interpretation of "necessary" in paragraph 45 because it would effectively function as a limitation on Congress's power, given that broader power could be inferred even without the "necessary and proper" clause. The restriction of Congress's power could not have been the intent because, as Marshall observes in paragraph 46, the clause is placed among the grants of power to Congress (Article I, Section 8), not among the restrictions on the power of Congress (Article I, Section 9). Moreover, he argues in paragraph 47 that the clause indeed reads like a grant of power, yet if the framers had had any incentive to conceal a provision's true purpose, the incentive would have been to conceal grants of power, not to conceal restrictions on power.

In paragraph 48 Marshall concludes that the "necessary and proper" clause does not restrict the discretion of Congress to choose the appropriate means for executing its enumerated powers. If nothing else, he holds, the clause removes any doubt about the power of Congress to legislate.

In paragraph 49 Marshall articulates the enduring standard for determining whether a law is within Congress's power: "Let the end be legitimate, let it be within the scope of the constitution, and all means which are appropriate, which are plainly adapted to that end, which are not prohibited, but consist with the letter and spirit of the constitution, are constitutional."

In paragraphs 50–52 Marshall reasons that chartering a bank is an appropriate means for achieving congressional ends. In paragraph 50 he reiterates that the creation of a corporation is not an end in itself but is merely a means for achieving other ends. As such, there is no reason to suppose that it would be enumerated in the Constitution as a distinct power of Congress. In paragraph 51 Marshall analogizes a corporation to a territorial government, which he says is universally regarded as an appropriate, corporate means for exercising Congress's power to regulate federal territory. In paragraph 52 Marshall reasons that if Congress may create one kind of corporate entity, a territorial legislature, it may create other kinds, including banks, where doing so is an appropriate adjunct to the execution of its enumerated powers. Experts agree, he adds, that a bank is a useful took. Even James Madison (among the era's "statesmen of the first class"), who initially opposed the bank, eventually approved of it. Marshall points out that the erstwhile Confederation Congress also felt a need to create a bank, even though doing so might well have exceeded its powers under the Articles of Confederation.

In paragraph 53 Marshall explains that the extent to which a federal law is necessary is a matter for Congress, not the judiciary, to determine. In paragraph 54 he rejects the argument that the existence of banks chartered by the states deprives Congress of the power to charter banks. In paragraphs 55–57, Marshall at last concludes that the Second Bank of the United States is constitutional.

◆ Maryland's Power to Tax the Bank

In paragraph 58 Marshall turns to the second main issue: the power of the state of Maryland to tax the Second Bank. In paragraphs 59–65 Marshall explains that the supremacy of federal law implicitly restricts the power of states to tax whenever an exercise of that power is incompatible with federal law, echoing his opinion in *Marbury v. Madison* (1803) at the end of paragraph 59. In paragraphs 60–61 he alludes to the Constitution's "supremacy" clause (Article VI, Clause 2), reasoning that the power to destroy something is incompatible with the power to create and preserve it. After complimenting the attorneys in paragraph 62, Marshall turns Maryland's key argument back onto the state in paragraphs 63–64. Referring to the Constitution's explicit restriction on state import and export taxes (Article I, Section 10), he rejects the negative inference that all other state taxes must be permissible. Instead, Marshall views the provision as textual confirmation that the power of states to tax must sometimes yield to the supremacy of federal law. The question, then, is whether a particular state tax would "defeat the legitimate operations" of the federal government.

Before addressing that issue, Marshall digresses in paragraphs 66–72 in order to offer an alternative line of reasoning based on democratic theory and state sovereignty. His overall point here is that states might not have the power to tax any federal entity at all. Reminiscent of the "no taxation without representation" credo of the American Revolution, Marshall observes in paragraphs 66–67 that a legislator's interest in reelection is the "only security" against "erroneous and oppressive taxation." But this security is

www.milestonedocuments.com

Essential Quotes

"We must never forget that it is a constitution we are expounding."

(Paragraph 27)

"Let the end be legitimate, let it be within the scope of the constitution, and all means which are appropriate, which are plainly adapted to that end, which are not prohibited, but consist with the letter and spirit of the constitution, are constitutional."

(Paragraph 49)

"The power to tax involves the power to destroy."

(Paragraph 74)

lacking, he reasons, when a state taxes a federal entity. The people of other states, who have an equal financial interest in the federal entity, have no democratic check on the legislators of the taxing state. Marshall concedes in paragraph 68–69 that a state may tax foreign goods when present in the state, despite the similar absence of a democratic check. That concession prompts him to refocus the inquiry on the scope of state sovereignty in paragraphs 70–71. Although a state may tax things over which it has sovereignty, including foreign goods when present in the state, a state has no sovereignty over federal entities because those entities owe their existence to the people of the entire nation, not to the state. Marshall concludes in paragraph 72 that, in this view, there is no need to ask whether the Constitution deprives states of any power to tax federal entities because that power was never part of their sovereign powers anyway.

In paragraphs 73–75 Marshall rejects Maryland's appeal to self-restraint. Noting famously in paragraph 74 that "the power to tax involves the power to destroy," Marshall specifically rejects Maryland's argument that the security of federal operations must rest solely on confidence that states will voluntarily refrain from using their taxing power to destroy those operations. In paragraph 75 Marshall relies again on democratic theory. Only Congress, he reasons, can be trusted to control federal operations because only Congress represents all of the people. In contrast, the people of other states have no electoral check on the Maryland legislature if it decides to tax federal operations.

In paragraphs 76–78 Marshall extrapolates from Maryland's argument to show that, taken to its logical conclusion, the argument would effectively subordinate the federal government to the individual states. If states may tax a federally chartered bank, Marshall reasons in paragraph 77, they may also tax any other federal operation, such as federal courts. In paragraph 78 Marshall dismisses as inconsequential Maryland's disavowal of any present intention to tax anything other than federal property within its borders. If states could tax federal operations, he adds, they could even regulate federal operations using state powers other than taxation. At its core, Marshall concludes, Maryland's view would subvert the principle of federal supremacy that is expressly established in the supremacy clause.

In paragraphs 79–80 Marshall rejects Maryland's appeal to the Federalist Papers. Maryland cited Federalist Paper no. 33, in which Alexander Hamilton argues that the "necessary and proper" clause does not empower Congress to prohibit state taxes. Quoting Federalist no. 31, Marshall responds by limiting Hamilton's argument to the context in which he made it: a discussion over whether Congress could directly outlaw state taxes in general. Marshall explains in paragraph 80 that Hamilton was not considering the possibility that states might try to tax federal operations.

In paragraphs 81–83 Marshall returns to democratic theory to reject Maryland's argument that if Congress can tax a state-chartered bank, then states must be able to tax a federally chartered bank. In paragraph 82 Marshall denies this asserted reflexivity with another tacit appeal to the Revolutionary-era credo of "no taxation without representation." If Congress taxes state-chartered banks, people of the states are represented in Congress and are taxing themselves. On the other hand, if one state taxes a federally chartered bank, affecting the interests of everyone in the nation, people in other states have no representation in the

www.milestonedocuments.com

taxing state's legislature and thus no electoral check on its taxing decision. In paragraph 83 Marshall suggests, in the alternative, that even if Maryland's equation of the two situations were accurate, he would deny either government the power to tax the other; he still would not grant Maryland the power to tax a federal operation.

Marshall finally announces in paragraphs 84–86 the conclusion that Maryland's tax is an unconstitutional interference with a federal operation. Significantly, however, he qualifies the Court's opinion in paragraph 86. He leaves open the possibility that Maryland might be able to tax the bank's real estate and shareholders, as long as such taxes apply on a nondiscriminatory basis to all real estate and shareholders, not just to the Second Bank of the United States.

In paragraph 87 Marshall renders judgment. Holding the Maryland courts to have erred, Marshall orders the county court to rule for McCulloch.

Audience

Marshall's opinion in *McCulloch* was written for a variety of audiences. As a judicial decision, it was obviously written most immediately for the litigants and their attorneys. The opinion was also written for attorneys and judges more generally, those in Marshall's time as well as subsequent generations. The famous sentence beginning with the phrase "Let the end be legitimate," for example, articulates a legal "standard" that lawyers and judges can borrow for evaluating the constitutionality of other congressional enactments in other cases. The public in general was also an audience. Although the inclusion of some legal jargon was unavoidable and some of the reasoning is quite intricate, the opinion includes examples and analogies designed to illustrate its points as well as a few compelling phrases that have the accessibility of a modern bumper sticker, such as Marshall's characterization of the taxing power as involving the power to destroy.

The legal reasoning itself is classic Marshall rhetoric. Where other judges might base conclusions on simple references to textual provisions of the Constitution, Marshall repeatedly uses the constitutional text merely to confirm conclusions that he has already reached through what he himself calls "general reasoning" in paragraph 33. He initially endeavors to convince the reader of a point through reasoning based on the structure or function of the American system of government, only later invoking a textual provision that arguably articulates the same point. Arguably, Marshall's rhetorical tactics are ingenius, as here, he fully affirms his conclusions despite the fact that the literal text of the Constitution neither authorizes Congress to incorporate a bank nor prohibits states from taxing one.

Impact

In the present as in the past, Supreme Court decisions are apt to be immediately judged by the public based not on the legal principles established but on the specific outcomes in the cases at hand. The particular issue of state taxation of the Second Bank was in fact short lived, becoming wholly moot when the bank's charter expired in 1836.

Despite the diminished polarization concerning federalism and the prevailing acceptance that the bank was constitutional, Marshall's opinion nevertheless generated some intense reactions on federalism grounds. Spencer Roane, a judge of the Virginia Court of Appeals, published a series of popular essays attacking the decision for adopting a broadly nationalistic conception of federalism that, in his view, threatened the continued viability of the states. Criticism of *McCulloch* on that basis was sufficiently serious, in fact, to induce Marshall himself to take the highly unusual step of defending his own opinion in his own series of popular essays, which he published under a pseudonym. Still, polarization over federalism had diminished enough by 1819 that *McCulloch* survived the contemporaneous attacks.

In the modern era, no one reads *McCulloch* in order to figure out whether Congress has the power to incorporate a bank. Rather, *McCulloch* remains one of the most significant Supreme Court decisions of all time because of its embrace of a broad view of national power. While relatively unexploited during the remainder of the nineteenth century, that view allowed for a breathtaking expansion of the federal government in the twentieth century, particularly during and after the Great Depression of the 1930s. *McCulloch* underlay famous Court decisions upholding the power of Congress to tell a lone farmer in Ohio how much wheat he could grow for his own personal use, to prohibit a local restaurant from maintaining a "whites only" policy, and to criminalize one person's simple possession of marijuana.

Some two centuries of experience have largely confirmed the fears of *McCulloch*'s critics. Indeed, national power has expanded beyond anything Marshall himself could have imagined. At the same time, however, into the twenty-first century the United States not only remained intact and resisted tyranny but also developed into one of the world's wealthiest, most advanced, and most powerful countries. A different *McCulloch*, one adopting a stingier view of national power, would have produced a United States that would be unrecognizable today, if still united at all.

Related Documents

"Articles of Confederation (1777)." National Archives "Our Documents" Web site. http://www.ourdocuments.gov/doc.php?doc=3. Accessed on December 20, 2007. Before the Constitution, the national government of the United States was a loose confederation of states established by the Articles of Confederation, which were adopted through ratification in 1781.

"Constitution of the United States (1787)." National Archives "Our Documents" Web site. http://www.ourdocuments.gov/doc.php?doc=9. Accessed on December 20, 2007. Marshall's opinion in *McCulloch* draws upon numerous provisions of the U.S. Constitution as well as on its overall structure.

Cooke, Jacob E., ed. *The Federalist*. Middletown, Conn.: Wesleyan University Press, 1961. James Madison, Alexander Hamilton, and John Jay published a series of essays explaining and defending the U.S. Constitution while New Yorkers were considering whether to ratify it. Their essays, known collectively as the Federalist Papers, are collected in this volume.

Gunther, Gerald, ed. *John Marshall's Defense of* McCulloch v. Maryland. Stanford, Calif.: Stanford University Press, 1969. Marshall engaged in an anonymous public debate over the *McCulloch* decision with the states' rights defender Spencer Roane, judge of the Virginia Court of Appeals, after the decision was rendered. Their competing essays are collected in this volume.

Marbury v. Madison, 5 U.S. (1 Cranch) 137 (1803). Marshall delivered the opinion of the Supreme Court in this earlier decision, which affirmed the Court's power to strike down unconstitutional legislation.

Rubin, Edward, and Malcolm Feeley. "Federalism: Some Notes on a National Neurosis." *UCLA Law Review* 41 (April 1994): 903–952.

Wechsler, Herbert. "The Political Safeguards of Federalism: The Role of the States in the Composition and Selection of the National Government." *Columbia Law Review* 54 (1954): 543–560.

Bibliography

■ Articles

Amar, Akhil Reed. "Intratextualism." *Harvard Law Review* 112, no. 4 (February 1999): 747–827.

Barnett, Randy E. "The Original Meaning of the Necessary and Proper Clause." *University of Pennsylvania Journal of Constitutional Law* 6 (2003): 183–221.

Beck, J. Randy. "The New Jurisprudence of the Necessary and Proper Clause." *University of Illinois Law Review* 2002 (2002): 581–649.

Clark, Stephen. "Progressive Federalism? A Gay Liberationist Perspective." *Albany Law Review* 66 (2003): 719–757.

Currie, David P. "The Constitution in the Supreme Court: State and Congressional Powers, 1801–1835." *University of Chicago Law Review* 49, no. 4 (1982): 887–975.

Finkelman, Paul. "The Constitution and the Intentions of the Framers: The Limits of Historical Analysis." *University of Pittsburgh Law Review* 50 (1989): 349–398.

Frankfurter, Felix. "John Marshall and the Judicial Function." *Harvard Law Review* 69, no. 2 (December 1955): 217–238.

Kurland, Philip B. "Curia Regis: Some Comments on the Divine Right of Kings and Courts 'To Say What the Law Is.'" *Arizona Law Review* 23 (1981): 581–597.

Lawson, Gary, and Patricia B. Granger. "The 'Proper' Scope of Federal Power: A Jurisdictional Interpretation of the Sweeping Clause." *Duke Law Journal* 43, no. 2 (November 1993): 267–336.

■ Books

Black, Charles L., Jr. *Structure and Relationship in Constitutional Law*. Woodbridge, Conn.: Ox Bow Press, 1985.

Dangerfield, George. *The Awakening of American Nationalism, 1815–1828*. New York: Harper & Row, 1965.

Ellis, Richard E. *Aggressive Nationalism:* McCulloch v. Maryland *and the Foundation of Federal Authority in the Young Republic*. Oxford, U.K.: Oxford University Press, 2007.

Ely, John Hart. *Democracy and Distrust: A Theory of Judicial Review*. Cambridge, Mass.: Harvard University Press, 1980.

Killenbeck, Mark R. M'Culloch v. Maryland: *Securing a Nation*. Lawrence: University Press of Kansas, 2006.

Shapiro, David L. *Federalism: A Dialogue*. Evanston, Ill.: Northwestern University Press, 1995.

Simon, James F. *What Kind of Nation: Thomas Jefferson, John Marshall, and the Epic Struggle to Create a United States*. New York: Simon & Schuster, 2002.

Smith, Jean Edward. *John Marshall: Definer of a Nation*. New York: H. Holt, 1996.

White, G. Edward. *The Marshall Court and Cultural Change, 1815–35*. New York: Macmillan, 1988.

■ Web Sites

"*McCulloch* v. *Maryland* (1819)." Landmark Supreme Court Cases Web site.
http://www.landmarkcases.org/mcculloch/home.html. Accessed on November 26, 2007.

"McCulloch v. Maryland (1819)." National Archives "Our Documents" Web site.
http://www.ourdocuments.gov/doc.php?flash=true&doc=21. Accessed on November 26, 2007.

"McCulloch v. Maryland (1977)." Internet Archive Web site.
http://www.archive.org/details/gov.ntis.AVA02154VNB1. Accessed on November 26, 2007.

—By Stephen Clark

Questions for Further Study

1. A traditional ideal holds that judges should set aside their own political preferences and interpret the Constitution as neutrally as humanly possible. Is Marshall's opinion in *McCulloch* persuasive as a neutral interpretation of the Constitution, or does it seem driven by his own Federalist preferences for a strong national government?

2. Marshall reasons in paragraph 28 that a government given "ample powers" must also have "ample means" for executing those powers, and he repeatedly stresses that the choice of means should be left to the discretion of Congress. A fundamental principle in the law of the European Union, however, is "subsidiarity." This principle postulates that a governmental function should be performed by the lowest level of government that can effectively and efficiently perform it. Compare and contrast the rationale under subsidiarity for transferring a power to a higher level of government and Marshall's rationale for recognizing an implied power in the national government. Would subsidiarity accord with Marshall's rejection of the argument, in paragraph 54, that Congress lacks the power to incorporate a bank because state-incorporated banks are more than adequate to serve Congress's needs? If not, which rationale is superior? Why?

3. The framers of the Constitution were influenced by the eighteenth-century French philosopher Montesquieu, who advocated a form of federalism in Volume 1, Book IX of his work *The Spirit of Laws*. What would Montesquieu have thought of the result in *McCulloch* and of Marshall's justifications for his conclusions?

4. Unlike the U.S. Constitution, the Constitution Act of Canada grants enumerated powers not only to the Parliament of Canada (section 91) but also to the provincial legislatures (section 92). If, as in *McCulloch*, it was unclear whether a particular power could be exercised by Parliament or by a provincial legislature, how would the Supreme Court of Canada resolve the dispute under the Constitution Act? Compare and contrast its probable approach with Marshall's approach in *McCulloch*.

5. In paragraph 86 of the *McCulloch* opinion, Marshall leaves open the question of whether Maryland could subject the Second Bank of the United States to the same property taxes that it imposes on all other property in Maryland. In light of the rationales that Marshall offers in striking down the tax at issue in *McCulloch*, how should this open question have been answered if Maryland had subsequently tried to subject the bank to its ordinary property tax laws? How would you resolve any contradictions that might arise among the rationales that Marshall offers if applied to such a situation?

www.milestonedocuments.com

Glossary

action of debt	a type of lawsuit seeking to obtain something owed
defendant in error	a litigant who has won in the lower court and is opposing an appeal
enumerated powers	governmental powers that are explicitly listed in the text of the Constitution as having been bestowed upon Congress
implied powers	governmental powers that are not explicitly listed in the text of the Constitution as having been bestowed upon Congress but that can be inferred as adjuncts to Congress's enumerated powers
judgment of *non pros*	short for "judgment of *non prosequitur*," a judgment rendered against a plaintiff who has failed to litigate his or her case
legal code	a systematic consolidation of all the enacted laws of a jurisdiction
plaintiff in error	a litigant who has lost in the lower court and has appealed
prolixity	state of being excessively detailed or tedious
writ of error	a written court order requiring a lower court to send a case up to an appellate court for a review of the lower court's ruling

McCulloch v. State of Maryland et al.

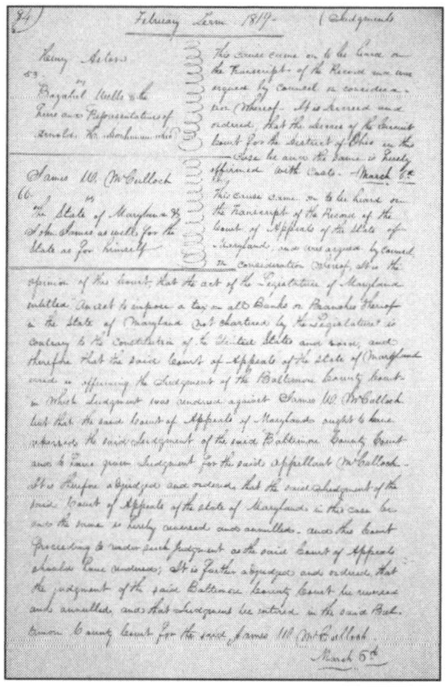

This was an action of debt, brought by the defendant in error, John James, who sued as well for himself as for the State of Maryland, in the County Court of Baltimore County, in the said State, against the plaintiff in error, McCulloch, to recover certain penalties, under the act of the legislature of Maryland, hereafter mentioned. Judgment being rendered against the plaintiff in error, upon the following statement of facts, agreed and submitted to the Court by the parties, was affirmed by the Court of Appeals of the State of Maryland, the highest Court of law of said State, and the cause was brought, by writ of error, to this Court.

It is admitted by the parties in this cause, by their counsel, that there was passed, on the 10th day of April 1816, by the Congress of the United States, an act, entitled, "an act to incorporate the subscribers to the Bank of the United States;" and that there was passed on the 11th day of February 1818, by the general assembly of Maryland, an act, entitled, "an act to impose a tax on all Banks, or branches thereof, in the State of Maryland, *not chartered by the legislature*," which said acts are made part of this statement, and it is agreed, may be read from the statute books in which they are respectively printed. It is further admitted, that the President, Directors and Company of the Bank of the United States, incorporated by the act of Congress aforesaid, did organize themselves, and go into full operation, in the city of Philadelphia, in the State of Pennsylvania, in pursuance of the said act, and that they did on the ___ day of _____ 1817, establish a branch of the said Bank, or an office of discount and deposit, in the city of Baltimore, in the State of Maryland, which has, from that time, until the first day of May 1818, ever since transacted and carried on business as a Bank, or office of discount and deposit, and as a branch of the said Bank of the United States, by issuing Bank notes and discounting promissory notes, and performing other operations usual and customary for Banks to do and perform, under the authority and by the direction of the said President, Directors and Company of the Bank of the United States, established at Philadelphia as aforesaid. It is further admitted, that the said President, Directors and Company of the said Bank, had no authority to establish the said branch, or office of discount and deposit, at the city of Baltimore, from the State of Maryland, otherwise than the said State having adopted the constitution of the United States and composing one of the States of the Union. It is further admitted, that James William McCulloch, the defendant below, being the cashier of the said branch, or office of discount and deposit, did, on the several days set forth in the declaration in this cause, issue the said respective Bank notes therein described, from the said branch or office, to a certain George Williams, in the city of Baltimore, in part payment of a promissory note of the said Williams, discounted by the said branch or office, which said respective Bank notes were not, nor was either of them, so issued, on stamped paper, in the manner prescribed by the act of assembly aforesaid. It is further admitted, that the said President, Directors and Company of the Bank of the United States, and the said branch, or office of discount and deposit, have not, nor has either of them, paid in advance, or otherwise, the sum of fifteen thousand dollars, to the treasurer of the Western Shore, for the use of the State of Maryland, before the issuing of the said notes, or any of them, nor since those periods. And it is further admitted, that the treasurer of the Western Shore of Maryland, under the direction of the governor and council of the said State, was ready, and offered to deliver to the said President, Directors and Company of the said Bank, and to the said branch, or office of discount

www.milestonedocuments.com

and deposit, stamped paper of the kind and denomination required and described in the said act of assembly.

The question submitted to the Court for their decision in this case, is, as to the validity of the said act of the general assembly of Maryland, on the ground of its being repugnant to the constitution of the United States, and the act of Congress aforesaid, or to one of them. Upon the foregoing statement of facts, and the pleadings in this cause (all errors in which are hereby agreed to be mutually released), if the Court should be of opinion, that the plaintiffs are entitled to recover, then judgment, it is agreed, shall be entered for the plaintiffs for twenty-five hundred dollars, and costs of suit. But if the Court should be of opinion, that the plaintiffs are not entitled to recover upon the statement and pleadings aforesaid, then judgment of *non pros* shall be entered, with costs to the defendant.

It is agreed, that either party may appeal from the decision of the County Court, to the Court of Appeals, and from the decision of the Court of Appeals to the Supreme Court of the United States, according to the modes and usages of law, and have the same benefit of this statement of facts, in the same manner as could be had, if a jury had been sworn and empanelled in this cause, and a special verdict had been found, or these facts had appeared and been stated in an exception taken to the opinion of the Court, and the Court's direction to the jury thereon.

Copy of the act of the Legislature of the State of Maryland, referred to in the preceding statement.

An Act to impose a Tax on all Banks or Branches thereof, in the State of Maryland, not chartered by the Legislature.

Be it enacted by the General Assembly of Maryland, that if any Bank has established, or shall, without authority from the State first had and obtained, establish any branch, office of discount and deposit, or office of pay and receipt in any part of this State, it shall not be lawful for the said branch, office of discount and deposit, or office of pay and receipt, to issue notes, in any manner, of any other denomination than five, ten, twenty, fifty, one hundred, five hundred and one thousand dollars, and no note shall be issued, except upon stamped paper of the following denominations; that is to say, every five dollar note shall be upon a stamp of ten cents; every ten dollar note, upon a stamp of twenty cents; every twenty dollar note, upon a stamp of thirty cents; every fifty dollar note, upon a stamp of fifty cents; every one hundred dollar note, upon a stamp of one dollar; every five hundred dollar note, upon a stamp of ten dollars; and every thousand dollar note, upon a stamp of twenty dollars; which paper shall be furnished by the treasurer of the Western Shore, under the direction of the governor and council, to be paid for upon delivery; *Provided always*, that any institution of the above description may relieve itself from the operation of the provisions aforesaid, by paying annually, in advance, to the treasurer of the Western Shore, for the use of State, the sum of fifteen thousand dollars.

And be it enacted, that the President, Cashier, each of the Directors and Officers of every institution established, or to be established as aforesaid, offending against the provisions aforesaid, shall forfeit a sum of five hundred dollars for each and every offence, and every person having any agency in circulating any note aforesaid, not stamped as aforesaid directed, shall forfeit a sum not exceeding one hundred dollars every penalty aforesaid, to be recovered by indictment, or action of debt, in the County Court of the county where the offence shall be committed, one-half to the informer, and the other half to the use of the State.

And be it enacted, that this act shall be in full force and effect from and after the first day of May next.

Mr. Chief Justice MARSHALL delivered the opinion of the Court.

In the case now to be determined, the defendant, a sovereign State, denies the obligation of a law enacted by the legislature of the Union, and the plaintiff, on his part, contests the validity of an act which has been passed by the legislature of that State. The constitution of our country, in its most interesting and vital parts, is to be considered; the conflicting powers of the government of the Union and of its members, as marked in that constitution, are to be discussed; and an opinion given, which may essentially influence the great operations of the government. No tribunal can approach such a question without a deep sense of its importance, and of the awful responsibility involved in its decision. But it must be decided peacefully, or remain a source of hostile legislation, perhaps, of hostility of a still more serious nature; and if it is to be so decided, by this tribunal alone can the decision be made. On the Supreme Court of the United States has the constitution of our country devolved this important duty.

The first question made in the cause is, has Congress power to incorporate a bank?

It has been truly said, that this can scarcely be considered as an open question, entirely unprejudiced by the former proceedings of the nation respecting it. The principle now contested was introduced at a very early period of our history, has been recognised by many successive legislatures, and has been acted upon by the judicial department, in cases of peculiar delicacy, as a law of undoubted obligation.

It will not be denied, that a bold and daring usurpation might be resisted, after an acquiescence still longer and more complete than this. But it is conceived, that a doubtful question, one on which human reason may pause, and the human judgment be suspended, in the decision of which the great principles of liberty are not concerned, but the respective powers of those who are equally the representatives of the people, are to be adjusted; if not put at rest by the practice of the government, ought to receive a considerable impression from that practice. An exposition of the constitution, deliberately established by legislative acts, on the faith of which an immense property has been advanced, ought not to be lightly disregarded.

The power now contested was exercised by the first Congress elected under the present constitution. The bill for incorporating the Bank of the United States did not steal upon an unsuspecting legislature, and pass unobserved. Its principle was completely understood, and was opposed with equal zeal and ability. After being resisted, first, in the fair and open field of debate, and afterwards, in the executive cabinet, with as much persevering talent as any measure has ever experienced, and being supported by arguments which convinced minds as pure and as intelligent as this country can boast, it became a law. The original act was permitted to expire; but a short experience of the embarrassments to which the refusal to revive it exposed the government, convinced those who were most prejudiced against the measure of its necessity, and induced the passage of the present law. It would require no ordinary share of intrepidity, to assert that a measure adopted under these circumstances, was a bold and plain usurpation, to which the constitution gave no countenance.

These observations belong to the cause; but they are not made under the impression, that, were the question entirely new, the law would be found irreconcilable with the constitution.

In discussing this question, the counsel for the State of Maryland have deemed it of some importance, in the construction of the constitution, to consider that instrument, not as emanating from the people, but as the act of sovereign and independent States. The powers of the general government, it has been said, are delegated by the States, who alone are truly sovereign; and must be exercised in subordination to the States, who alone possess supreme dominion.

It would be difficult to sustain this proposition. The convention which framed the constitution was indeed elected by the State legislatures. But the instrument, when it came from their hands, was a mere proposal, without obligation, or pretensions to it. It was reported to the then existing Congress of the United States, with a request that it might "be submitted to a convention of delegates, chosen in each State by the people thereof, under the recommendation of its legislature, for their assent and ratification." This mode of proceeding was adopted; and by the convention, by Congress, and by the State legislatures, the instrument was submitted to the people. They acted upon it in the only manner in which they can act safely, effectively and wisely, on such a subject, by assembling in convention. It is true, they assembled in their several States—and where else should they have assembled? No political dreamer was ever wild enough to think of breaking down the lines which separate the States, and of compounding the American people into one common mass. Of consequence, when they act, they act in their States. But the measures they adopt do not, on that account, cease to be the measures of the people themselves, or become the measures of the State governments.

From these conventions, the constitution derives its whole authority. The government proceeds directly from the people; is "ordained and established," in the name of the people; and is declared to be ordained, "in order to form a more perfect union, establish justice, insure domestic tranquillity, and secure the blessings of liberty to themselves and to their posterity." The assent of the States, in their sovereign capacity, is implied, in calling a convention, and thus submitting that instrument to the people. But the people were at perfect liberty to accept or reject it; and their act was final. It required not the affirmance, and could not be negatived, by the State governments. The constitution, when thus adopted, was of complete obligation, and bound the State sovereignties.

It has been said, that the people had already surrendered all their powers to the State sovereignties, and had nothing more to give. But, surely, the question whether they may resume and modify the powers granted to government, does not remain to be settled in this country. Much more might the legitimacy of the general government be doubted, had it been

www.milestonedocuments.com

Document Text

created by the States. The powers delegated to the State sovereignties were to be exercised by themselves, not by a distinct and independent sovereignty, created by themselves. To the formation of a league, such as was the confederation, the State sovereignties were certainly competent. But when, "in order to form a more perfect union," it was deemed necessary to change this alliance into an effective government, possessing great and sovereign powers, and acting directly on the people, the necessity of referring it to the people, and of deriving its powers directly from them, was felt and acknowledged by all.

The government of the Union, then (whatever may be the influence of this fact on the case), is, emphatically and truly, a government of the people. In form, and in substance, it emanates from them. Its powers are granted by them, and are to be exercised directly on them, and for their benefit.

This government is acknowledged by all, to be one of enumerated powers. The principle, that it can exercise only the powers granted to it, would seem too apparent, to have required to be enforced by all those arguments, which its enlightened friends, while it was depending before the people, found it necessary to urge; that principle is now universally admitted. But the question respecting the extent of the powers actually granted, is perpetually arising, and will probably continue to arise, so long as our system shall exist.

In discussing these questions, the conflicting powers of the general and State governments must be brought into view, and the supremacy of their respective laws, when they are in opposition, must be settled.

If any one proposition could command the universal assent of mankind, we might expect it would be this—that the government of the Union, though limited in its powers, is supreme within its sphere of action. This would seem to result, necessarily, from its nature. It is the government of all; its powers are delegated by all; it represents all, and acts for all. Though any one State may be willing to control its operations, no State is willing to allow others to control them. The nation, on those subjects on which it can act, must necessarily bind its component parts. But this question is not left to mere reason: the people have, in express terms, decided it, by saying, "this constitution, and the laws of the United States, which shall be made in pursuance thereof," "shall be the supreme law of the land," and by requiring that the members of the State legislatures, and the officers of the executive and judicial departments of the States, shall take the oath of fidelity to it.

The government of the United States, then, though limited in its powers, is supreme; and its laws, when made in pursuance of the constitution, form the supreme law of the land, "anything in the constitution or laws of any State to the contrary notwithstanding."

Among the enumerated powers, we do not find that of establishing a bank or creating a corporation. But there is no phrase in the instrument which, like the articles of confederation, excludes incidental or implied powers; and which requires that everything granted shall be expressly and minutely described. Even the 10th amendment, which was framed for the purpose of quieting the excessive jealousies which had been excited, omits the word "expressly," and declares only, that the powers "not delegated to the United States, nor prohibited to the States, are reserved to the States or to the people;" thus leaving the question, whether the particular power which may become the subject of contest, has been delegated to the one government, or prohibited to the other, to depend on a fair construction of the whole instrument. The men who drew and adopted this amendment had experienced the embarrassments resulting from the insertion of this word in the articles of confederation, and probably omitted it, to avoid those embarrassments. A constitution, to contain an accurate detail of all the subdivisions of which its great powers will admit, and of all the means by which they may be carried into execution, would partake of the prolixity of a legal code, and could scarcely be embraced by the human mind. It would, probably, never be understood by the public. Its nature, therefore, requires, that only its great outlines should be marked, its important objects designated, and the minor ingredients which compose those objects, be deduced from the nature of the objects themselves. That this idea was entertained by the framers of the American constitution, is not only to be inferred from the nature of the instrument, but from the language. Why else were some of the limitations, found in the 9th section of the 1st article, introduced? It is also, in some degree, warranted, by their having omitted to use any restrictive term which might prevent its receiving a fair and just interpretation. In considering this question, then, we must never forget that it is a constitution we are expounding.

Although, among the enumerated powers of government, we do not find the word "bank" or "incorporation," we find the great powers, to lay and collect taxes; to borrow money; to regulate commerce; to declare and conduct a war; and to raise and support

www.milestonedocuments.com

armies and navies. The sword and the purse, all the external relations, and no inconsiderable portion of the industry of the nation, are entrusted to its government. It can never be pretended, that these vast powers draw after them others of inferior importance, merely because they are inferior. Such an idea can never be advanced. But it may with great reason be contended, that a government, entrusted with such ample powers, on the due execution of which the happiness and prosperity of the nation so vitally depends, must also be entrusted with ample means for their execution. The power being given, it is the interest of the nation to facilitate its execution. It can never be their interest, and cannot be presumed to have been their intention, to clog and embarrass its execution, by withholding the most appropriate means. Throughout this vast republic, from the St. Croix to the Gulph of Mexico, from the Atlantic to the Pacific, revenue is to be collected and expended, armies are to be marched and supported. The exigencies of the nation may require, that the treasure raised in the north should be transported to the south, that raised in the east, conveyed to the west, or that this order should be reversed. Is that construction of the constitution to be preferred, which would render these operations difficult, hazardous and expensive? Can we adopt that construction (unless the words imperiously require it), which would impute to the framers of that instrument, when granting these powers for the public good, the intention of impeding their exercise, by withholding a choice of means? If, indeed, such be the mandate of the constitution, we have only to obey; but that instrument does not profess to enumerate the means by which the powers it confers may be executed; nor does it prohibit the creation of a corporation, if the existence of such a being be essential, to the beneficial exercise of those powers. It is, then, the subject of fair inquiry, how far such means may be employed.

It is not denied, that the powers given to the government imply the ordinary means of execution. That, for example, of raising revenue, and applying it to national purposes, is admitted to imply the power of conveying money from place to place, as the exigencies of the nation may require, and of employing the usual means of conveyance. But it is denied, that the government has its choice of means; or, that it may employ the most convenient means, if, to employ them, it be necessary to erect a corporation.

On what foundation does this argument rest? On this alone: the power of creating a corporation, is one appertaining to sovereignty, and is not expressly conferred on Congress. This is true. But all legislative powers appertain to sovereignty. The original power of giving the law on any subject whatever, is a sovereign power; and if the government of the Union is restrained from creating a corporation, as a means for performing its functions, on the single reason that the creation of a corporation is an act of sovereignty; if the sufficiency of this reason be acknowledged, there would be some difficulty in sustaining the authority of Congress to pass other laws for the accomplishment of the same objects.

The government which has a right to do an act, and has imposed on it, the duty of performing that act, must, according to the dictates of reason, be allowed to select the means; and those who contend that it may not select any appropriate means, that one particular mode of effecting the object is excepted, take upon themselves the burden of establishing that exception.

The creation of a corporation, it is said, appertains to sovereignty. This is admitted. But to what portion of sovereignty does it appertain? Does it belong to one more than to another? In America, the powers of sovereignty are divided between the government of the Union, and those of the States. They are each sovereign, with respect to the objects committed to it, and neither sovereign, with respect to the objects committed to the other. We cannot comprehend that train of reasoning, which would maintain, that the extent of power granted by the people is to be ascertained, not by the nature and terms of the grant, but by its date. Some State constitutions were formed *before*, some *since* that of the United States. We cannot believe, that their relation to each other is in any degree dependent upon this circumstance. Their respective powers must, we think, be precisely the same, as if they had been formed at the same time. Had they been formed at the same time, and had the people conferred on the general government the power contained in the constitution, and on the States the whole residuum of power, would it have been asserted, that the government of the Union was not sovereign, with respect to those objects which were entrusted to it, in relation to which its laws were declared to be supreme? If this could not have been asserted, we cannot well comprehend the process of reasoning which maintains, that a power appertaining to sovereignty cannot be connected with that vast portion of it which is granted to the general government, so far as it is calculated to subserve the legitimate objects of that government. The power of creating a corporation, though appertaining to sovereignty, is not, like the power of making war, or levying taxes, or of regulating commerce, a great substantive and independent power, which cannot be implied as incidental to other powers, or used as a means of executing them. It is never the end for which other powers are exercised, but a means by which other objects are accomplished. No contributions are made to charity, for the sake of an incorporation, but a corporation is created to administer the charity; no seminary of learning is instituted, in order to be incorporated, but the corporate character is conferred to subserve the purposes of education. No city was ever built, with the sole object of being incorporated, but is incorporated as affording the best means of being well governed. The power of creating a corporation is never used for its own sake, but for the purpose of effecting something else. No sufficient reason is, therefore, perceived, why it may not pass as incidental to those powers which are expressly given, if it be a direct mode of executing them.

But the constitution of the United States has not left the right of Congress to employ the necessary means, for the execution of the powers conferred on the government, to general reasoning. To its enumeration of powers is added, that of making "all laws which shall be necessary and proper, for carrying into execution the foregoing powers, and all other powers vested by this constitution, in the government of the United States, or in any department thereof."

The counsel for the State of Maryland have urged various arguments, to prove that this clause, though, in terms, a grant of power, is not so, in effect; but is really restrictive of the general right, which might otherwise be implied, of selecting means for executing the enumerated powers.

In support of this proposition, they have found it necessary to contend, that this clause was inserted for the purpose of conferring on Congress the power of making laws. That, without it, doubts might be entertained, whether Congress could exercise its powers in the form of legislation.

But could this be the object for which it was inserted? A government is created by the people, having legislative, executive and judicial powers. Its legislative powers are vested in a Congress, which is to consist of a Senate and House of Representatives. Each house may determine the rule of its proceedings; and it is declared, that every bill which shall have passed both houses, shall, before it becomes a law, be presented to the President of the United States. The 7th section describes the course of proceedings, by which a bill shall become a law; and, then, the 8th section enumerates the powers of Congress. Could it be necessary to say, that a legislature should exercise legislative powers, in the shape of legislation? After allowing each house to prescribe its own course of proceeding, after describing the manner in which a bill should become a law, would it have entered into the mind of a single member of the convention, that an express power to make laws was necessary, to enable the legislature to make them? That a legislature, endowed with legislative powers, can legislate, is a proposition too self-evident to have been questioned.

But the argument on which most reliance is placed, is drawn from that peculiar language of this clause. Congress is not empowered by it to make all laws, which may have relation to the powers conferred on the government, but such only as may be *"necessary and proper"* for carrying them into execution. The word *"necessary"* is considered as controlling the whole sentence, and as limiting the right to pass laws for the execution of the granted powers, to such as are indispensable, and without which the power would be nugatory. That it excludes the choice of means, and leaves to Congress, in each case, that only which is most direct and simple.

Is it true, that this is the sense in which the word "necessary" is always used? Does it always import an absolute physical necessity, so strong, that one thing to which another may be termed necessary, cannot exist without that other? We think it does not. If reference be had to its use, in the common affairs of the world, or in approved authors, we find that it frequently imports no more than that one thing is convenient, or useful, or essential to another. To employ the means necessary to an end, is generally understood as employing any means calculated to produce the end, and not as being confined to those single means, without which the end would be entirely unattainable. Such is the character of human language, that no word conveys to the mind, in all situations, one single definite idea; and nothing is more common than to use words in a figurative sense. Almost all compositions contain words, which, taken in a their rigorous sense, would convey a meaning different from that which is obviously intended. It is essential to just construction, that many words which import something excessive, should be understood in a more mitigated sense—in that sense which common usage justifies. The word "necessary" is of this description. It has not a fixed character, peculiar to itself. It admits of all degrees of comparison; and is often connected with other words, which increase

www.milestonedocuments.com

or diminish the impression the mind receives of the urgency it imports. A thing may be necessary, very necessary, absolutely or indispensably necessary. To no mind would the same idea be conveyed by these several phrases. The comment on the word is well illustrated by the passage cited at the bar, from the 10th section of the 1st article of the constitution. It is, we think, impossible to compare the sentence which prohibits a State from laying "imposts, or duties on imports or exports, except what may be *absolutely* necessary for executing its inspection laws," with that which authorizes Congress "to make all laws which shall be necessary and proper for carrying into execution" the powers of the general government, without feeling a conviction, that the convention understood itself to change materially the meaning of the word "necessary," by prefixing the word "absolutely." This word, then, like others, is used in various senses; and, in its construction, the subject, the context, the intention of the person using them, are all to be taken into view.

Let this be done in the case under consideration. The subject is the execution of those great powers on which the welfare of a nation essentially depends. It must have been the intention of those who gave these powers, to insure, so far as human prudence could insure, their beneficial execution. This could not be done, by confiding the choice of means to such narrow limits as not to leave it in the power of Congress to adopt any which might be appropriate, and which were conducive to the end. This provision is made in a constitution, intended to endure for ages to come, and consequently, to be adapted to the various *crises* of human affairs. To have prescribed the means by which government should, in all future time, execute its powers, would have been to change, entirely, the character of the instrument, and give it the properties of a legal code. It would have been an unwise attempt to provide, by immutable rules, for exigencies which, if foreseen at all, must have been seen dimly, and which can be best provided for as they occur. To have declared, that the best means shall not be used, but those alone, without which the power given would be nugatory, would have been to deprive the legislature of the capacity to avail itself of experience, to exercise its reason, and to accommodate its legislation to circumstances. If we apply this principle of construction to any of the powers of the government, we shall find it so pernicious in its operation that we shall be compelled to discard it. The powers vested in Congress may certainly be carried into execution, without prescribing an oath of office. The power to exact this security for the faithful performance of duty, is not given, nor is it indispensably necessary. The different departments may be established; taxes may be imposed and collected; armies and navies may be raised and maintained; and money may be borrowed, without requiring an oath of office. It might be argued, with as much plausibility as other incidental powers have been assailed, that the convention was not unmindful of this subject. The oath which might be exacted—that of fidelity to the constitution—is prescribed, and no other can be required. Yet, he would be charged with insanity, who should contend, that the legislature might not superadd, to the oath directed by the constitution, such other oath of office as its wisdom might suggest.

So, with respect to the whole penal code of the United States: whence arises the power to punish, in cases not prescribed by the constitution? All admit, that the government may, legitimately, punish any violation of its laws; and yet, this is not among the enumerated powers of Congress. The right to enforce the observance of law, by punishing its infraction, might be denied, with the more plausibility, because it is expressly given in some cases. Congress is empowered "to provide for the punishment of counterfeiting the securities and current coin of the United States," and "to define and punish piracies and felonies committed on the high seas, and offences against the law of nations." The several powers of Congress may exist, in a very imperfect State, to be sure, but they may exist and be carried into execution, although no punishment should be inflicted, in cases where the right to punish is not expressly given.

Take, for example, the power "to establish post-offices and post-roads." This power is executed, by the single act of making the establishment. But, from this has been inferred the power and duty of carrying the mail along the post-road, from one post-office to another. And from this implied power, has again been inferred the right to punish those who steal letters from the post-office, or rob the mail. It may be said, with some plausibility, that the right to carry the mail, and to punish those who rob it, is not indispensably necessary to the establishment of a post-office and post-road. This right is indeed essential to the beneficial exercise of the power, but not indispensably necessary to its existence. So, of the punishment of the crimes of stealing or falsifying a record or process of a Court of the United States, or of perjury in such Court. To punish these offences, is certainly con-

Document Text

ducive to the due administration of justice. But courts may exist, and may decide the causes brought before them, though such crimes escape punishment.

The baneful influence of this narrow construction on all the operations of the government, and the absolute impracticability of maintaining it, without rendering the government incompetent to its great objects, might be illustrated by numerous examples drawn from the constitution, and from our laws. The good sense of the public has pronounced, without hesitation, that the power of punishment appertains to sovereignty, and may be exercised, whenever the sovereign has a right to act, as incidental to his constitutional powers. It is a means for carrying into execution all sovereign powers, and may be used, although not indispensably necessary. It is a right incidental to the power, and conducive to its beneficial exercise.

If this limited construction of the word "necessary" must be abandoned, in order to punish, whence is derived the rule which would reinstate it, when the government would carry its powers into execution, by means not vindictive in their nature? If the word "necessary" means "needful," "requisite," "essential," "conducive to," in order to let in the power of punishment for the infraction of law; why is it not equally comprehensive, when required to authorize the use of means which facilitate the execution of the powers of government, without the infliction of punishment?

In ascertaining the sense in which the word "necessary" is used in this clause of the constitution, we may derive some aid from that with which it is associated. Congress shall have power "to make all laws which shall be necessary and *proper* to carry into execution" the powers of the government. If the word "necessary" was used in that strict and rigorous sense for which the counsel for the State of Maryland contend, it would be an extraordinary departure from the usual course of the human mind, as exhibited in composition, to add a word, the only possible effect of which is, to qualify that strict and rigorous meaning; to present to the mind the idea of some choice of means of legislation, not strained and compressed within the narrow limits for which gentlemen contend.

But the argument which most conclusively demonstrates the error of the construction contended for by the counsel for the State of Maryland, is founded on the intention of the convention, as manifested in the whole clause. To waste time and argument in proving that, without it, Congress might carry its powers into execution, would be not much less idle, than to hold a lighted taper to the sun. As little can it be required to prove, that in the absence of this clause, Congress would have some choice of means. That it might employ those which, in its judgment, would most advantageously effect the object to be accomplished. That any means adapted to the end, any means which tended directly to the execution of the constitutional powers of the government, were in themselves constitutional. This clause, as construed by the State of Maryland, would abridge, and almost annihilate, this useful and necessary right of the legislature to select its means. That this could not be intended, is, we should think, had it not been already controverted, too apparent for controversy. We think so for the following reasons:

1st. The clause is placed among the powers of Congress, not among the limitations on those powers.

2nd. Its terms purport to enlarge, not to diminish the powers vested in the government. It purports to be an additional power, not a restriction on those already granted. No reason has been, or can be assigned, for thus concealing an intention to narrow the discretion of the national legislature, under words which purport to enlarge it. The framers of the constitution wished its adoption, and well knew that it would be endangered by its strength, not by its weakness. Had they been capable of using language which would convey to the eye one idea, and, after deep reflection, impress on the mind, another, they would rather have disguised the grant of power, than its limitation. If, then, their intention had been, by this clause, to restrain the free use of means which might otherwise have been implied, that intention would have been inserted in another place, and would have been expressed in terms resembling these. "In carrying into execution the foregoing powers, and all others," &c., "no laws shall be passed but such as are necessary and proper." Had the intention been to make this clause restrictive, it would unquestionably have been so in form as well as in effect.

The result of the most careful and attentive consideration bestowed upon this clause is, that if it does not enlarge, it cannot be construed to restrain the powers of Congress, or to impair the right of the legislature to exercise its best judgment in the selection of measures to carry into execution the constitutional powers of the government. If no other motive for its insertion can be suggested, a sufficient one is found in the desire to remove all doubts respecting the right to legislate on that vast mass of incidental powers which must be involved in the constitution, if that instrument be not a splendid bauble.

We admit, as all must admit, that the powers of the government are limited, and that its limits are not to be transcended. But we think the sound construction of the constitution must allow to the national legislature that discretion, with respect to the means by which the powers it confers are to be carried into execution, which will enable that body to perform the high duties assigned to it, in the manner most beneficial to the people. Let the end be legitimate, let it be within the scope of the constitution, and all means which are appropriate, which are plainly adapted to that end, which are not prohibited, but consist with the letter and spirit of the constitution, are constitutional.

That a corporation must be considered as a means not less usual, not of higher dignity, not more requiring a particular specification than other means, has been sufficiently proved. If we look to the origin of corporations, to the manner in which they have been framed in that government from which we have derived most of our legal principles and ideas, or to the uses to which they have been applied, we find no reason to suppose, that a constitution, omitting, and wisely omitting, to enumerate all the means for carrying into execution the great powers vested in government, ought to have specified this. Had it been intended to grant this power, as one which should be distinct and independent, to be exercised in any case whatever, it would have found a place among the enumerated powers of the government. But being considered merely as a means, to be employed only for the purpose of carrying into execution the given powers, there could be no motive for particularly mentioning it.

The propriety of this remark would seem to be generally acknowledged, by the universal acquiescence in the construction which has been uniformly put on the 3rd section of the 4th article of the constitution. The power to "make all needful rules and regulations respecting the territory or other property belonging to the United States," is not more comprehensive, than the power "to make all laws which shall be necessary and proper for carrying into execution" the powers of the government. Yet all admit the constitutionality of a territorial government, which is a corporate body.

If a corporation may be employed, indiscriminately with other means, to carry into execution the powers of the government, no particular reason can be assigned for excluding the use of a bank, if required for its fiscal operations. To use one, must be within the discretion of Congress, if it be an appropriate mode of executing the powers of government. That it is a convenient, a useful, and essential instrument in the prosecution of its fiscal operations, is not now a subject of controversy. All those who have been concerned in the administration of our finances, have concurred in representing its importance and necessity; and so strongly have they been felt, that statesmen of the first class, whose previous opinions against it had been confirmed by every circumstance which can fix the human judgment, have yielded those opinions to the exigencies of the nation. Under the confederation, Congress, justifying the measure by its necessity, transcended, perhaps, its powers, to obtain the advantage of a bank; and our own legislation attests the universal conviction of the utility of this measure. The time has passed away, when it can be necessary to enter into any discussion, in order to prove the importance of this instrument, as a means to effect the legitimate objects of the government.

But, were its necessity less apparent, none can deny its being an appropriate measure; and if it is, the decree of its necessity, as has been very justly observed, is to be discussed in another place. Should Congress, in the execution of its powers, adopt measures which are prohibited by the constitution; or should Congress, under the pretext of executing its powers, pass laws for the accomplishment of objects not entrusted to the government; it would become the painful duty of this tribunal, should a case requiring such a decision come before it, to say, that such an act was not the law of the land. But where the law is not prohibited, and is really calculated to effect any of the objects entrusted to the government, to undertake here to inquire into the decree of its necessity, would be to pass the line which circumscribes the judicial department, and to tread on legislative ground. This Court disclaims all pretensions to such a power.

After this declaration, it can scarcely be necessary to say, that the existence of State banks can have no possible influence on the question. No trace is to be found in the constitution, of an intention to create a dependence of the government of the Union on those of the States, for the execution of the great powers assigned to it. Its means are adequate to its ends; and on those means alone was it expected to rely for the accomplishment of its ends. To impose on it the necessity of resorting to means which it cannot control, which another government may furnish or withhold, would render its course precarious, the result of its measures uncertain, and create a dependence on other governments, which might disappoint its most important designs, and is incompatible with the language of the constitution. But were

www.milestonedocuments.com

it otherwise, the choice of means implies a right to choose a national bank in preference to State banks, and Congress alone can make the election.

After the most deliberate consideration, it is the unanimous and decided opinion of this Court, that the act to incorporate the Bank of the United States is a law made in pursuance of the constitution, and is a part of the supreme law of the land.

The branches, proceeding from the same stock, and being conducive to the complete accomplishment of the object, are equally constitutional. It would have been unwise, to locate them in the charter, and it would be unnecessarily inconvenient, to employ the legislative power in making those subordinate arrangements. The great duties of the bank are prescribed; those duties require branches; and the bank itself may, we think, be safely trusted with the selection of places where those branches shall be fixed; reserving always to the government the right to require that a branch shall be located where it may be deemed necessary.

It being the opinion of the Court, that the act incorporating the bank is constitutional; and that the power of establishing a branch in the State of Maryland might be properly exercised by the bank itself, we proceed to inquire—

2. Whether the State of Maryland may, without violating the constitution, tax that branch?

That the power of taxation is one of vital importance; that it is retained by the States; that it is not abridged by the grant of a similar power to the government of the Union; that it is to be concurrently exercised by the two governments—are truths which have never been denied. But such is the paramount character of the constitution, that its capacity to withdraw any subject from the action of even this power, is admitted. The States are expressly forbidden to lay any duties on imports or exports, except what may be absolutely necessary for executing their inspection laws. If the obligation of this prohibition must be conceded—if it may restrain a State from the exercise of its taxing power on imports and exports—the same paramount character would seem to restrain, as it certainly may restrain, a State from such other exercise of this power, as is in its nature incompatible with, and repugnant to, the constitutional laws of the Union. A law, absolutely repugnant to another, as entirely repeals that other as if express terms of repeal were used.

On this ground, the counsel for the bank place its claim to be exempted from the power of a State to tax its operations. There is no express provision for the case, but the claim has been sustained on a principle which so entirely pervades the constitution, is so intermixed with the materials which compose it, so interwoven with its web, so blended with its texture, as to be incapable of being separated from it, without rending it into shreds.

This great principle is, that the constitution and the laws made in pursuance thereof are supreme; that they control the constitution and laws of the respective States, and cannot be controlled by them. From this, which may be almost termed an axiom, other propositions are deduced as corollaries, on the truth or error of which, and on their application to this case, the cause has been supposed to depend. These are, 1st. That a power to create implies a power to preserve: 2nd. That a power to destroy, if wielded by a different hand, is hostile to, and incompatible with these powers to create and to preserve: 3d. That where this repugnancy exists, that authority which is supreme must control, not yield to that over which it is supreme.

These propositions, as abstract truths, would, perhaps, never be controverted. Their application to this case, however, has been denied; and both in maintaining the affirmative and the negative, a splendor of eloquence, and strength of argument, seldom, if ever, surpassed, have been displayed.

The power of Congress to create, and of course, to continue, the bank, was the subject of the preceding part of this opinion; and is no longer to be considered as questionable.

That the power of taxing it by the States may be exercised so as to destroy it, is too obvious to be denied. But taxation is said to be an absolute power, which acknowledges no other limits than those expressly prescribed in the constitution, and like sovereign power of every other description, is entrusted to the discretion of those who use it. But the very terms of this argument admit, that the sovereignty of the State, in the article of taxation itself, is subordinate to, and may be controlled by the constitution of the United States. How far it has been controlled by that instrument, must be a question of construction. In making this construction, no principle, not declared, can be admissible, which would defeat the legitimate operations of a supreme government. It is of the very essence of supremacy, to remove all obstacles to its action within its own sphere, and so to modify every power vested in subordinate governments, as to exempt its own operations from their own influence. This effect need not be stated in terms. It is so involved in the declaration of supremacy, so necessarily implied in it, that the expression of it could not make it more certain. We must, therefore, keep it in view, while construing the constitution.

The argument on the part of the State of Maryland, is, not that the States may directly resist a law of Congress, but that they may exercise their acknowledged powers upon it, and that the constitution leaves them this right, in the confidence that they will not abuse it.

Before we proceed to examine this argument, and to subject it to test of the constitution, we must be permitted to bestow a few considerations on the nature and extent of this original right of taxation, which is acknowledged to remain with the States. It is admitted, that the power of taxing the people and their property, is essential to the very existence of government, and may be legitimately exercised on the objects to which it is applicable, to the utmost extent to which the government may choose to carry it. The only security against the abuse of this power, is found in the structure of the government itself. In imposing a tax, the legislature acts upon its constituents. This is, in general, a sufficient security against erroneous and oppressive taxation.

The people of a State, therefore, give to their government a right of taxing themselves and their property, and as the exigencies of government cannot be limited, they prescribe no limits to the exercise of this right, resting confidently on the interest of the legislator, and on the influence of the constituent over their representative, to guard them against its abuse. But the means employed by the government of the Union have no such security, nor is the right of a State to tax them sustained by the same theory. Those means are not given by the people of a particular State, not given by the constituents of the legislature, which claim the right to tax them, but by the people of all the States. They are given by all, for the benefit of all—and upon theory, should be subjected to that government only which belongs to all.

It may be objected to this definition, that the power of taxation is not confined to the people and property of a State. It may be exercised upon every object brought within its jurisdiction.

This is true. But to what source do we trace this right? It is obvious, that it is an incident of sovereignty, and is co-extensive with that to which it is an incident. All subjects over which the sovereign power of a State extends, are objects of taxation; but those over which it does not extend, are, upon the soundest principles, exempt from taxation. This proposition may almost be pronounced self-evident.

The sovereignty of a State extends to everything which exists by its own authority, or is introduced by its permission; but does it extend to those means which are employed by Congress to carry into execution powers conferred on that body by the people of the United States? We think it demonstrable, that it does not. Those powers are not given by the people of a single State. They are given by the people of the United States, to a government whose laws, made in pursuance of the constitution, are declared to be supreme. Consequently, the people of a single State cannot confer a sovereignty which will extend over them.

If we measure the power of taxation residing in a State, by the extent of sovereignty which the people of a single State possess, and can confer on its government, we have an intelligible standard, applicable to every case to which the power may be applied. We have a principle which leaves the power of taxing the people and property of a State unimpaired; which leaves to a State the command of all its resources, and which places beyond its reach, all those powers which are conferred by the people of the United States on the government of the Union, and all those means which are given for the purpose of carrying those powers into execution. We have a principle which is safe for the States, and safe for the Union. We are relieved, as we ought to be, from clashing sovereignty; from interfering powers; from a repugnancy between a right in one government to pull down, what there is an acknowledged right in another to build up; from the incompatibility of a right in one government to destroy, what there is a right in another to preserve. We are not driven to the perplexing inquiry, so unfit for the judicial department, what degree of taxation is the legitimate use, and what degree may amount to the abuse of the power. The attempt to use it on the means employed by the government of the Union, in pursuance of the constitution, is itself an abuse, because it is the usurpation of a power which the people of a single State cannot give.

We find, then, on just theory, a total failure of this original right to tax the means employed by the government of the Union, for the execution of its powers. The right never existed, and the question whether it has been surrendered, cannot arise.

But, waiving this theory for the present, let us resume the inquiry, whether this power can be exercised by the respective States, consistently with a fair construction of the constitution?

That the power to tax involves the power to destroy; that the power to destroy may defeat and render useless the power to create; that there is a

www.milestonedocuments.com

Document Text

plain repugnance in conferring on one government a power to control the constitutional measures of another, which other, with respect to those very measures, is declared to be supreme over that which exerts the control, are propositions not to be denied. But all inconsistencies are to be reconciled by the magic of the word CONFIDENCE. Taxation, it is said, does not necessarily and unavoidably destroy. To carry it to the excess of destruction, would be an abuse, to presume which, would banish that confidence which is essential to all government.

But is this a case of confidence? Would the people of any one State trust those of another with a power to control the most insignificant operations of their State government? We know they would not. Why, then, should we suppose, that the people of any one State should be willing to trust those of another with a power to control the operations of a government to which they have confided their most important and most valuable interests? In the legislature of the Union alone, are all represented. The legislature of the Union alone, therefore, can be trusted by the people with the power of controlling measures which concern all, in the confidence that it will not be abused. This, then, is not a case of confidence, and we must consider it is as it really is.

If we apply the principle for which the State of Maryland contends, to the constitution, generally, we shall find it capable of changing totally the character of that instrument. We shall find it capable of arresting all the measures of the government, and of prostrating it at the foot of the States. The American people have declared their constitution and the laws made in pursuance thereof, to be supreme; but this principle would transfer the supremacy, in fact, to the States.

If the States may tax one instrument, employed by the government in the execution of its powers, they may tax any and every other instrument. They may tax the mail; they may tax the mint; they may tax patent-rights; they may tax the papers of the custom-house; they may tax judicial process; they may tax all the means employed by the government, to an excess which would defeat all the ends of government. This was not intended by the American people. They did not design to make their government dependent on the States.

Gentlemen say, they do not claim the right to extend State taxation to these objects. They limit their pretensions to property. But on what principle, is this distinction made? Those who make it have furnished no reason for it, and the principle for which they contend denies it. They contend, that the power of taxation has no other limit than is found in the 10th section of the 1st article of the constitution; that, with respect to everything else, the power of the States is supreme, and admits of no control. If this be true, the distinction between property and other subjects to which the power of taxation is applicable, is merely arbitrary, and can never be sustained. This is not all. If the controlling power of the States be established; if their supremacy as to taxation be acknowledged; what is to restrain their exercising control in any shape they may please to give it? Their sovereignty is not confined to taxation; that is not the only mode in which it might be displayed. The question is, in truth, a question of supremacy; and if the right of the States to tax the means employed by the general government be conceded, the declaration that the constitution, and the laws made in pursuance thereof, shall be the supreme law of the land, is empty and unmeaning declamation.

In the course of the argument, the *Federalist* has been quoted; and the opinions expressed by the authors of that work have been justly supposed to be entitled to great respect in expounding the constitution. No tribute can be paid to them which exceeds their merit; but in applying their opinions to the cases which may arise in the progress of our government, a right to judge of their correctness must be retained; and to understand the argument, we must examine the proposition it maintains, and the objections against which it is directed. The subject of those numbers, from which passages have been cited, is the unlimited power of taxation which is vested in the general government. The objection to this unlimited power, which the argument seeks to remove, is stated with fullness and clearness. It is, "that an indefinite power of taxation in the latter (the government of the Union) might, and probably would, in time, deprive the former (the government of the States) of the means of providing for their own necessities; and would subject them entirely to the mercy of the national legislature. As the laws of the Union are to become the supreme law of the land; as it is to have power to pass all laws that may be necessary for carrying into execution the authorities with which it is proposed to vest it; the national government might, at any time, abolish the taxes imposed for State objects, upon the pretence of an interference with its own. It might allege a necessity for doing this, in order to give efficacy to the national revenues; and thus, all the resources of taxation might, by degrees, become the subjects of federal monopoly, to the entire exclusion and destruction of the State governments."

Document Text

The objections to the constitution which are noticed in these numbers, were to the undefined power of the government to tax, not to the incidental privilege of exempting its own measures from State taxation. The consequences apprehended from this undefined power were, that it would absorb all the objects of taxation, "to the exclusion and destruction of the State governments." The arguments of the *Federalist* are intended to prove the fallacy of these apprehensions; not to prove that the government was incapable of executing any of its powers, without exposing the means it employed to the embarrassments of State taxation. Arguments urged against these objections, and these apprehensions, are to be understood as relating to the points they mean to prove. Had the authors of those excellent essays been asked, whether they contended for that construction of the constitution, which would place within the reach of the States those measures which the government might adopt for the execution of its powers; no man, who has read their instructive pages, will hesitate to admit, that their answer must have been in the negative.

It has also been insisted, that, as the power of taxation in the general and State governments is acknowledged to be concurrent, every argument which would sustain the right of the general government to tax banks chartered by the States, will equally sustain the right of the States to tax banks chartered by the general government.

But the two cases are not on the same reason. The people of all the States have created the general government, and have conferred upon it the general power of taxation. The people of all the States, and the States themselves, are represented in Congress, and, by their representatives, exercise this power. When they tax the chartered institutions of the States, they tax their constituents; and these taxes must be uniform. But when a State taxes the operations of the government of the United States, it acts upon institutions created, not by their own constituents, but by people over whom they claim no control. It acts upon the measures of a government created by others as well as themselves, for the benefit of others in common with themselves. The difference is that which always exists, and always must exist, between the action of the whole on a part, and the action of a part on the whole—between the laws of a government declared to be supreme, and those of a government which, when in opposition to those laws, is not supreme.

But if the full application of this argument could be admitted, it might bring into question the right of Congress to tax the State banks, and could not prove the rights of the States to tax the Bank of the United States.

The Court has bestowed on this subject its most deliberate consideration. The result is a conviction that the States have no power, by taxation or otherwise, to retard, impede, burden, or in any manner control, the operations of the constitutional laws enacted by Congress to carry into execution the powers vested in the general government. This is, we think, the unavoidable consequence of that supremacy which the constitution has declared.

We are unanimously of opinion, that the law passed by the legislature of Maryland, imposing a tax on the Bank of the United States, is unconstitutional and void.

This opinion does not deprive the States of any resources which they originally possessed. It does not extend to a tax paid by the real property of the bank, in common with the other real property within the State, nor to a tax imposed on the interest which the citizens of Maryland may hold in this institution, in common with other property of the same description throughout the State. But this is a tax on the operations of the bank, and is, consequently, a tax on the operation of an instrument employed by the government of the Union to carry its powers into execution. Such a tax must be unconstitutional.

JUDGMENT. This cause came on to be heard, on the transcript of the record of the Court of Appeals of the State of Maryland, and was argued by counsel: on consideration whereof, it is the opinion of this Court, that the act of the legislature of Maryland is contrary to the constitution of the United States, and void; and therefore, that the said Court of Appeals of the State of Maryland erred, in affirming the judgment of the Baltimore County Court, in which judgment was rendered against James W. McCulloch; but that the said Court of Appeals of Maryland ought to have reversed the said judgment of the said Baltimore County Court, and ought to have given judgment for the said appellant, McCulloch: It is, therefore, adjudged and ordered, that the said judgment of the said Court of Appeals of the State of Maryland in this case, be, and the same hereby is, reversed and annulled. And this Court, proceeding to render such judgment as the said Court of Appeals should have rendered; it is further adjudged and ordered, that the judgment of the said Baltimore County Court be reversed and annulled, and that judgment be entered in the said Baltimore County Court for the said James W. McCulloch.

www.milestonedocuments.com

The Committee of Conference
the Senate and of the House of R
sentatives on the subject of the d
greeing votes of the Two Houses, upon
Bill entitled an "Act for the adm
of the State of Maine into the Unio

Report the following Resolution

Resolved.

1st That they recommend to th
Senate to recede from their amendm
to the said Bill

2d. That they recommend to the two Houses agree to
out of the fourth section of the Bill
the House of Representatives now p
ding in the Senate, entitled an "A
to authorise the people of the Missi
Territory to form a Constitution and S
Government and for the admission
such State into the Union upon an
footing with the original States" t
following proviso in the following word
and shall ordain and establish, tha
there shall be neither Slavery nor
luntary Servitude otherwise than in

The Missouri Compromise (National Archives and Records Administration)

Missouri Compromise

1820

"In all that territory ceded by France to the United States ... which lies north of thirty-six degrees and thirty minutes north latitude ... slavery ... shall be ... forever prohibited."

Overview

The legislation known as the Missouri Compromise passed Congress in 1820. The bill that President James Monroe signed into law actually embodied several compromises painstakingly worked out and often hotly debated over a period of months between the congressional representatives of states where slavery was legal and those where it was not, and the most important of its provisions concerned slavery. The immediate issue was the Missouri Territory and its admission to the Union as a new state. Would it be admitted as a slave state, or should it be kept out of the Union unless it declared itself free? The larger question was how (if at all) slavery would be allowed to expand in the United States, or how it was to be restricted. Proslavery legislators would have preferred unlimited admittance of new slave states. Legislators from free states wanted no expansion of slavery; many wanted it abolished in the states where it already existed.

The Missouri Compromise was an attempt to give something to both of these deeply opposed sides. The legislation allowed Missouri to enter the Union as a slave state, thus mollifying proslavery advocates. At the same time, however, it specifically stated that the act was intended *"to prohibit slavery in certain territories"*—wording that brought crucial support from some free-state members of Congress. Moreover, the new law did in fact set up a sharp geographical limitation on the spread of slavery in the vast new lands of the Louisiana Purchase: Besides Missouri itself, no new slave states would be admitted from this territory north of Missouri's main southern boundary. Of course, this provision also implied that new slave states could enter from *south* of that line, but far more of the Louisiana Purchase lay to the north.

The Missouri Compromise contained other features indicating the lawmakers' goal of cobbling together a bill that both sides could bring themselves to vote for. For instance, it stated that all citizens of the new state were to be treated equally under its laws and that free blacks were not to be treated as slaves—provisions that appealed to free-staters. On the other hand, it appeased slave-staters by limiting voting for Missouri's constitutional convention to "free white male citizens of the United States" in the territory. Even more important to the proslavery forces, the law provided that a fugitive slave escaping into any state or territory of the United States could be "lawfully reclaimed" by his or her owner.

The new law also dealt with several matters not related to slavery. For example, considering that the Mississippi River formed most of Missouri's eastern boundary, one clause proclaimed that travel on that river and all waters leading into it would be "for ever free" to all citizens of the United States. As important as such a provision might be, however, what most Americans, then and for decades to come, debated about the Missouri Compromise of 1820 was its treatment of slavery.

Context

The years 1819 and 1820 were terrible ones for many Americans. For the first time since the ratification of the Constitution the nation was in a deep economic depression, the so-called Panic of 1819. Amid fears of mass starvation and of riots by those who had lost their livelihoods, many citizens were probably disinclined to think about the country's foremost social and political problem, the issue of slavery. Two seemingly unrelated events in early 1819, however, led to a fierce national debate over that issue. One was a Supreme Court decision, the other the attachment of an amendment to a statehood bill pending in Congress.

On February 13, 1819, Congressman James Tallmadge of New York rose in the U.S. House of Representatives to offer an amendment to the enabling bill that would set forth the conditions for the territory of Missouri to meet in order to become a state. He proposed that all slaves who were then in Missouri remain slaves in the new state but that no slaves be imported into the state from anywhere else and that children born to the slaves who were already in Missouri be freed when teenagers. This was, to his mind, a balanced proposal that would inhibit the spread of slavery while not causing slave owners in the new state to lose money or the services of slaves they already owned. It is unlikely that Tallmadge foresaw the firestorm of controversy his seemingly moderate amendment would ignite.

Time Line

1819

- The Panic of 1819, an economic depression caused by a downturn in exports, strikes the United States and continues into following years.

- **February 13**
Representative James Tallmadge adds to the Missouri statehood bill an amendment that would allow slave owners in Missouri to keep their slaves but would forbid the importation of slaves into Missouri and would eventually free children born to slaves in Missouri.

- **February 17**
Tallmadge's amendment passes the House of Representatives. It later dies in the Senate.

- **June**
Maine agrees to allow its District of Maine to become a separate state, thus allowing the federal government to maintain an even split between free and slave states and a fifty-fifty split in the U.S. Senate.

- **December**
Leaders of the Senate link Maine's admission to the Union to the admission of Missouri, meaning that if one could not become a state, neither could the other.

- **December**
Admission of Alabama to the Union as a slave state threatens to upset the balance between slave states and free states.

1820

- Violence by Missouri's slave owners against antislavery Missourians threatens chances that the statehood bill will be ratified by Congress.

- **January 3**
The House of Representatives passes a bill allowing admission of Maine to the Union as free state.

- **January 28**
The House adds to the Missouri statehood bill an amendment by Representative John W. Taylor of New York that would allow Missouri to be a slave state.

By 1819, politicians in slave states had become split into two general camps. One faction viewed slavery as essential to economic prosperity and wanted to preserve it even at the cost of civil war. Many in this camp feared that freed African Americans would arm themselves and exact revenge on their former masters, starting a race war. This fear was particularly strong in parts of Virginia and the Carolinas where slaves were the majority of the population, and it was often invoked to rally citizens of slave states against proposals to free slaves. The strong supporters of slavery could also offer economic arguments for their stance. Even in the midst of an economic depression in which the value of northern industrial exports had fallen, the value of slaves had risen. A good field hand who had cost $400 in 1810 would sell for $800 in 1820. This was the case because there was demand for slaves in new American territories. Slaves by the thousands were marched westward to work on the plantations of Tennessee, Louisiana, Alabama, and Mississippi. Women slaves of childbearing age were looked upon as a particularly good long-term investment, as the children they produced would eventually be worth more than the cotton or other crops that a good field hand could cultivate.

Southerners of a more moderate faction, led by Thomas Jefferson, regretted the institution of slavery (even if, like Jefferson, they owned slaves) and viewed it as a social evil that should be allowed to gradually die out. Since this was exactly the process contemplated for Missouri in Tallmadge's amendment, these slave-state moderates might have been expected to support, or at least acquiesce in, passage of that amendment. Instead many reacted by becoming "Radicals," a term then applied to proslavery extremists. By the end of 1820 a South divided in its thinking had become solidly opposed to efforts to restrict slavery. Even Jefferson argued that Tallmadge's amendment and similar proposals represented too much government interference in private affairs and would enable the federal government's power to grow into tyranny. Secretary of War John C. Calhoun of South Carolina, a longtime advocate of a strong federal government, now argued just as eloquently for states' rights instead.

Contributing to this polarization of southern opinion was a decision by the U.S. Supreme Court barely a month after Tallmadge offered his amendment. On March 16, 1819, the Court ruled unanimously in the case of *McCulloch v. State of Maryland et al.*, with Chief Justice John Marshall writing the opinion. The case had no direct bearing on slavery, but at its center was the concept of *nullification*, the notion advanced by states' rights advocates that, within their boundaries, individual states had the right to nullify federal laws. In Maryland the state government had tried to tax the offices of the federally established Bank of the United States. In *McCulloch* the Supreme Court ruled not only that the federal government had the right to establish such a bank but also that, in Chief Justice Marshall's words, "The States have no power, by taxation or otherwise, to retard, impede, burden, or in any manner control, the operations of the constitutional laws enacted by Congress to carry into execution the powers vested in the general government" (*McCulloch v. Maryland*, 17 U.S. 316 [1819]). In other words, federal law overruled any contrary state law. This decision angered states'-rights advocates and seemed particularly ominous to slaveholders, who feared it meant the federal government could force them to give up their slaves. Thus it further fueled the debate started by Tallmadge with his amendment.

The enabling bill for Missouri statehood, complete with Tallmadge's amendment, passed the House of Representatives by a vote of 82 to 78. The Senate, however, was a different matter. The Senate for years had been roughly equally divided between senators from free states and those from slave states, and the desire of slave-state politicians to maintain this balance of power is one of the keys to understanding the debate that erupted over Tallmadge's amendment and eventually led to the Missouri Compromise. Alabama was about to be admitted to the Union and would certainly be a slave state, but Maine had also petitioned for statehood and would certainly be a free state. What happened with Missouri seemed crucial, especially since other new states undoubtedly would soon be formed out of the sprawling lands of the Louisiana Purchase.

The Senate allowed the Missouri statehood bill to die for the time being. The issue, however, did not die, and when Congress convened in a new session later in 1819, lawmakers in both houses began the arduous process that led to the compromise of 1820.

At the executive level, President Monroe had made it clear that he would veto any bill that had Tallmadge's amendment in it, but he also recognized the danger posed to America if the free states were not able to accept the eventual terms of Missouri's statehood. Thus, when the compromise of 1820 was proposed, he supported its balancing of free states against slave states and strove to have his cabinet vote in favor of it, even though the vote was only symbolic. He even persuaded Calhoun to vote in favor, delivering unanimous backing by his cabinet.

Although the Missouri Compromise temporarily maintained a shaky status quo, many Americans believed that it had set in motion ideas that would culminate in terrible tragedy. Representative Thomas W. Cobb of Georgia said to Tallmadge, "You have kindled a fire which all the waters of the ocean cannot put out, which seas of blood can only extinguish" (Howe, p. 148). Tallmadge responded to criticisms of his proposal by declaring, "If dissolution of the Union must take place, let it be so! If civil war, which gentlemen so much threaten, must come, I can only say, let it come!" (Howe, p. 148). John Quincy Adams thought the talk of seceding from the Union by some southern politicians was folly. He predicted that an independent nation of slave states would itself be torn apart by rebellion. He wrote in his diary for November 29, 1820,

> If slavery be the destined sword of the hand of the destroying angel which is to sever the ties of this Union, the same sword will cut in sunder the bonds of slavery itself. A dissolution of the Union for the cause of slavery would be followed by a servile war in the slave-holding States, combined with a war between the two severed portions of the Union. It seems to me it might result in the extirpation of slavery from this whole continent.... Calamitous and desolating as this course of events in its progress must be, I dare not say that it is not to be desired. (Howe, p. 160)

Adams was not alone in thinking this way. Many other Americans saw the Missouri Compromise as representing the moment when the two sides of the slavery issue solidified their positions in a way that eventually brought on the Civil War.

Time Line

1820

- **March 6**
President James Monroe signs the bill enabling Missouri to form a constitutional convention.

1847

- In violation of the Missouri Compromise of 1820, Missouri's government bans free African Americans from settling in Missouri.

1854

- **May 30**
President Franklin Pierce signs into law the Kansas-Nebraska Act, which repeals the Missouri Compromise of 1820.

1857

- **March 6**
In *Dred Scott v. Sandford* the Supreme Court rules that the Missouri Compromise is unconstitutional, while declaring it constitutional to deny free African Americans citizenship..

About the Author

There was no single author of the Missouri Compromise. Almost every U.S. senator and representative had a hand in creating it. Every senator and representative from states where slavery was legal wanted to participate in drafting the compromise in order to impress his constituents with how he was looking after their interests by blunting efforts by northern politicians to prevent the spread of slavery into new states. Although almost all of the politicians from slave states viewed the issues involved in drafting the final document as economic, most of the politicians from free states viewed the matter in terms of

www.milestonedocuments.com

morality and of peacefully putting to an end the most divisive social conflicts in America. Among the most important contributors to the Missouri Compromise were Representative James Tallmadge, Senator Jesse Thomas, Representative John W. Taylor, and Speaker of the House of Representatives Henry Clay.

James Tallmadge, Jr., was born in Stanfordville, New York, on January 28, 1778. After graduating from Brown University in 1798, he studied law and was admitted to the New York bar in 1802. He commanded a company of militia during the War of 1812. He was elected as a Democratic-Republican to the House of Representatives, serving from 1817 to 1819. In February 1819 he proposed an amendment to the bill that would enable Missouri to become a state. This amendment would have eventually resulted in Missouri's becoming a free state. Tallmadge served as president of New York University from 1830 to1846. He died in New York City on September 29, 1853.

Jesse Thomas was born in Shepherdstown, Virginia (in what is now West Virginia), in 1777. He studied law in Kentucky and was the clerk for Mason County in Kentucky until 1803, when he moved to the Indiana Territory to practice law. He was the territory's delegate to Congress from October 22, 1808, to March 3, 1809, when he moved to Illinois. In 1818 he presided over the constitutional convention for Illinois, a necessary step for Illinois to become a state. He was one of the state's first two U.S. senators, serving from 1818 to 1829. It was he who was primarily responsible for the wording of Section 8 of the Missouri Compromise of 1820, which was the heart of the compromise that temporarily resolved the dispute over slavery in new states. In 1829 he moved to live in Mount Vernon, Ohio, where he committed suicide on May 2, 1853.

John W. Taylor was born in Charlton, New York, on March 26, 1784. In 1803 he graduated from Union College in Schenectady. He was admitted to the New York bar in 1807. and practiced law in Ballston Spa, New York. He served several terms in the U.S. House of Representatives and was twice elected Speaker of the House. During his time in Congress he was notably sensitive to the interests of his African American constituents and tried to have Missouri admitted to the Union as a free state. He was a Democratic-Republican who was seen by southern members of his party as dividing the party into abolitionist and proslavery camps, but he helped bring the two sides together to agree on the compromise. He lost his reelection bid in 1832 and returned to practicing law. In 1843, he moved to Cleveland, Ohio, where he died on September 18, 1854.

Henry Clay was born in Hanover County, Virginia, on April 12, 1777. He became one of America's foremost statesmen, political philosophers, and orators. In 1797 he was admitted to the state bar in Virginia after studying law at the College of William and Mary. In November 1897 he relocated to Lexington, Kentucky, to practice law. He was elected to fill a vacancy in the U.S. Senate for a few months in 1806–1807 even though he was younger than the minimum age of thirty for a senator, set by the Constitution. He served in the House of Representatives from 1808 to 1809, including as Speaker of the House in 1809. From 1810 to 1811 he again filled a vacancy in the Senate. He then served as Speaker of the House of Representatives from 1811 to 1814. He resigned in 1814 to help negotiate a peace treaty with Great Britain to end the War of 1812. From 1815 to 1821 he again served as Speaker of the House of Representatives. His participation in the drafting of the Missouri Compromise of 1820 was crucial to persuading southern congressmen to support it. From 1825 to 1829 he was secretary of state in the administration of John Quincy Adams. He ran for his party's nomination for president three times—as a Democratic-Republican in 1824, a National Republican in 1832, and a Whig in 1844—but failed each time. He served in the Senate from 1849 to his death on July 1, 1852.

Explanation and Analysis of the Document

◆ Section 1

The Missouri Compromise legislation opens with an italicized preamble, a statement of purpose, a routine part of a bill. In this case it makes two statements crucial to the compromise reached among those who favored admitting Missouri as a slave state and those who did not. The phrase "and for the admission of such state into the Union on an equal footing with the original states" had been hotly debated in Congress. The underlying concept itself was not controversial, because all new states were admitted as equal to all previous states. However, advocates for slavery had been adamant about stating this principle plainly, because they wanted each state to be able to decide for itself whether slavery would be legal within its borders. Thus, by making the principle of Missouri's equality among the other states part of an explicit statement in the preamble, they hoped to give Missouri leverage to do as it wished once it was officially a state. The main paragraph of Section 1 emphasizes this principle: Missouri would be "admitted into the Union, upon an equal footing with the original states, in all respects whatsoever."

Many antislavery politicians had insisted that they would not allow Missouri into the Union as anything other than a free state. John W. Taylor and many others were prepared to deny Missouri statehood rather than permit it to enter with slavery being legal in it. They would have kept Missouri a federal territory, in which the federal government could dictate the laws. Although President Monroe would not have used the army to force an end to slavery in a federal territory, someone like John Quincy Adams, who did in fact succeed Monroe as president, might do exactly that. Thus the advocates of slavery needed to make a concession to get Missouri admitted to the Union as a slave state or face the possibility of a future president who might use the federal army to impose upon the western territories of the United States a settlement that would have left the slave states a permanent minority—with the possibility that federal troops would eventually be employed to force even the slave states to become free. The proslavery forces, after long and acrimonious debate, therefore accepted as part of the preamble the phrase "and to prohibit slavery in certain territories." This phrase also satisfied enough free-state members of Congress to get the votes needed for passage of the enabling bill for Missouri.

◆ Section 2

Section 2 of the bill is devoted almost entirely to legalities required for defining the future state of Missouri's borders. Deep amid the definitions is one defining the future state's main southern border as the "parallel of latitude of thirty-six degrees and thirty minutes," which became the dividing line for the purposes of the compromise. Although Missouri would be a slave state, all other new states north of that latitude would be free. (This section also cleared up the issue of who had access to the rivers that defined some of the borders of Missouri. Ever since the ratification of the Constitution, states had sniped at each other over land and water rights and had even tried to charge one another tariffs for goods crossing their borders. Section 2 declared flatly "that the river Mississippi, and the navigable rivers and waters leading into the same, shall be common highways, and for ever free, as well as to the inhabitants of the said state as to other citizens of the United States, without any tax, duty impost, or toll, therefor, imposed by the said state."

◆ Section 3

Of greater significance to modern readers, perhaps, than to Americans in 1820 is the phrase in the opening sentence of Section 3 declaring that "all free white male citizens of the United States" would have the right to vote on representatives to be sent to the future state's constitutional convention and would have the right to run for election as one of those representatives. This was a concession to slave states, although many free-state politicians would not have been bothered by it. In some states African Americans were accorded full rights of citizenship, including the right to vote. This was a sensitive issue to someone such as John W. Taylor, who had many African American constituents and tried hard to represent their interests in Congress. The specification of "males" may have signaled a recognition that there were Americans who thought women should have the right to vote.

◆ Section 4

This section explains how the members of the convention could go about their work. It states where the convention was first to meet, somewhat vaguely calling the place "the seat of government." It expressly allows the delegates to decide during their first meeting that they would wish to meet elsewhere and to then hold their next meeting in the place they chose. Further, the delegates could decide anything about a new constitution but to instead set up their own rules for electing delegates to the constitutional convention and hold a new election of representatives under those new rules.

Section 4 says that the constitution and laws of the new state must not be "repugnant to the constitution of the

Henry Clay was instrumental in securing congressional passage of the Missouri Compromise in 1820. (Library of Congress)

www.milestonedocuments.com

United States," a point made a year earlier in the Supreme Court ruling in *McCulloch v. Maryland*. This clause may have been a concession made by states' rights advocates and slavery advocates to advocates of federal supremacy and as antislavery advocates.

◆ Section 5

Although it is only one sentence in length, this section is more than a mere formality. It asserts Missouri's immediate right upon statehood to be represented in the House of Representatives by at least one elected official. After a census of the residents is made, the number of representatives from Missouri could rise if it had a sufficiently large population but could never drop below one.

◆ Section 6

This complex section promises that federal lands will be ceded to Missouri for certain purposes and that Missouri must take additional lands to meet its obligations to its citizens. It requires that land be set aside in townships for the building of schools and that taxes be leveed to pay for the schools and to pay the teachers of the schools. The issue of

Essential Quotes

"An Act to authorize the people of the Missouri territory to form a constitution and state government, and for the admission of such state into the Union on an equal footing with the original states, and to prohibit slavery in certain territories."

(Preamble)

"In all that territory ceded by France to the United States, under the name of Louisiana, which lies north of thirty-six degrees and thirty minutes north latitude, not included within the limits of [Missouri], ... slavery and involuntary servitude ... shall be, and is hereby, forever prohibited."

(Section 8)

salt springs may seem minor, but it was enough of an issue among people western territories that they would fight each other for access to them. Salt was a valuable commodity. Congress promises to give up to twelve salt springs on federal land within Missouri to the state of Missouri of Missouri's choice, but Missouri must choose the salt springs before 1825, when the offer would end. The state government would be forbidden to seize any privately owned salt springs. The new state government would be required to levee taxes for building roads and canals; Congress would tell Missouri how much it had spend. The federal government will give the new state federal land on which to build a state capital. A large tract of federal land would be given to the state of Missouri on which to build a state college or university, a "seminary of learning." This idea was probably inspired by Thomas Jefferson's efforts to create the University of Virginia, where Virginians could attend college. The lands given by the federal government to the state of Missouri were to be free from taxation for five years beginning the January after ratification of Missouri's constitution. Veterans of war were to be given tracts of land by the government that were to be free of state taxes for three years from the date that the veterans were given their land.

◆ Section 7

This section requires that the Missouri constitutional convention must send a copy of its proposed constitution to Congress.

◆ Section 8

The legislation comes to its main point in Section 8: Any new states created from the Louisiana Purchase "north of thirty-six degrees and thirty minutes north latitude, not included within the limits" of Missouri were to be free states. This seemingly straightforward statement on slavery was the result of months of arguing, threats of civil war, and eventually compromise. President Monroe put his administration on the line to support this section. Thomas Jefferson and John Quincy Adams viewed it as inadequate and fatally flawed. Others saw it as successfully ending the possibility of civil war by balancing the Senate evenly between slave states and free states.

In the same section the phrase "otherwise than in the punishment of crimes" means that criminals who have been properly convicted may be forced to work involuntarily, and such work is not to be considered slavery. The final statement in Section 8 was perceived in 1820 as a clear victory for the slave states. It says that escaped slaves must be returned to anyone who can prove ownership of them, even when the slaves have escaped into states or territories where slavery is against the law. A crucial phrase is "from whom labour or service is lawfully claimed." In spite of the common understanding that Section 8 required slaves living in free states to be returned to their masters, this phrase left open the opportunity for slaves to challenge the legality of their masters' ownership in court by asserting that their services were unlawfully claimed. Section 8 also left unresolved the matter of whether an American citizen from a slave state could move to a free state and keep his slaves while resident there. Finally, while other parts of the Missouri Compromise of 1820 seem to require that the rights of citizenship in one state be accepted in another, in practice Missouri ignored the requirement that American citizens of African ancestry be treated as free citizens with full rights to settle in Missouri. Whether to allow citizens from slave states to keep their slaves was a nettlesome problem that the Supreme Court seemed to resolve in *Dred Scott v. Sandford* in 1857.

Audience

The intended audience for the Missouri Compromise of 1820 was a broad one. Probably every member of the Senate and House of Representatives wanted to show his constituents that he was looking out for their interests.

The compromise was intended to satisfy as many Americans as possible, and therefore it was sometimes vague, avoiding direct statements of purpose that might offend any particular interest group. Further, it was meant to stave off threats of civil war by at least for the time being preventing free states from dominating the U.S. Senate. On the other hand, the compromise appeared to many northerners to be a first step toward enabling the federal government to require new states to be free states; they saw the compromise not as a federal recognition of the rights of some new states to allow slavery but as showing that the federal government had the right to regulate where and if slavery could be practiced, and they believed that this principle could eventually allow the federal government to abolish slavery.

Impact

John Quincy Adams, in his diary entry for February 24, 1820, said of the Missouri Compromise, "The Union might then be reorganized on the fundamental principle of emancipation. This object is vast in its compass, awful in its prospects, sublime and beautiful in its issue. A life devoted to it would be nobly spent or sacrificed" (Howe, p. 813). Thomas Jefferson had a somewhat different view of the effects of the compromise, saying that "like a fire bell in the night," it awakened and terrified him: "I considered it at once as the knell of the Union.... A geographical line, coinciding with a marked principle, moral and political, once conceived and held up to the angry passions of men, will never be obliterated; and every new irritation will mark it deeper and deeper" (Howe, p. 157).

One effect of the compromise was to do what Jefferson feared it would: divide America into two geographically distinct parts. Most of his southern colleagues, however, believed that they had gotten the better of the deal. For one thing, the compromise established that some new states would be admitted as slave states, which in effect meant that the federal government recognized slavery as an American institution. For another, the compromise would, at least for the immediate future, prevent the North from taking complete control of Congress by ensuring that there were enough slave states to keep the Senate evenly divided between antislavery northerners and proslavery southerners. For their part, some northern politicians agreed with a view expressed by Jefferson, that adding slave states to the Union would spread slave ownership more thinly, making it easier at some future time to abolish slavery gradually and peacefully, state by state.

Not all advocates of slavery were satisfied with the compromise. In Missouri proslavery factions began murdering antislavery Missourians. By the late 1850s atrocities were being committed by both sides. Thus, the Civil War had already begun in Missouri long before the official secession of the states that formed the Confederacy in 1861. Although Missouri was not supposed to prevent free African Americans who were citizens in other states from settling in Missouri, the state government, dominated by proslavery officials, passed laws prohibiting free African Americans from anywhere else to settle in Missouri. This law openly defied the Constitution, which said that the rights of citizens of one state had to be accepted in all other states.

In 1857 the U.S. Supreme Court ruled in the case *Dred Scott v. Sandford*. The slave Dred Scott had argued that when he was taken by his owner to a free state, he was automatically a free man because the free state's laws governed all within that state, including people visiting from outside the state. The Supreme Court ruled against him, allowing his owner to keep him as a slave. In the process, the Court ruled the Missouri Compromise of 1820 unconstitutional, voiding its restraints on practicing slavery in free states. This ruling resulted in many antislavery Americans believing that only by armed force would slavery by restrained.

Related Documents

Dred Scott v. Sandford, 60 U.S. 393 (1857). In this case the Supreme Court ruled that the slave Dred Scott had no constitutional protections from seizure, even in a free state; in the process, the Court ruled the Missouri Compromise unconstitutional, opening the possibility for all new states to become slave states. Decried by abolitionists in 1857, this ruling came to be seen during the Civil War as a national tragedy.

McCulloch v. State of Maryland, 17 U.S. 316 (1819). Although this case was not directly related to slavery, the Supreme Court's ruling in it alarmed slaveholders because the Court held that federal law overrode contrary state law, raising the possibility that the U.S. government might abolish slavery.

Bibliography

■ Books

Forbes, Robert Pierce. *The Missouri Compromise and Its Aftermath: Slavery and the Meaning of America*. Chapel Hill: University of North Carolina Press, 2007.

Freehling, William W. *The Road to Disunion*, Vol. 1: *Secessionists at Bay, 1776–1854*. New York: Oxford University Press, 1991.

Howe, Daniel Walker. *What Hath God Wrought: The Transformation of America, 1815–1848*. New York: Oxford University Press, 2007.

Remini, Robert V. *Henry Clay: Statesman for the Union*. New York: W. W. Norton, 1991.

www.milestonedocuments.com

Web Sites

"Clay, Henry." Biographical Directory of the United States Congress Web site.
http://bioguide.congress.gov/scripts/biodisplay.pl?index=C000482. Accessed on December 14, 2007.

"Tallmadge, James, Jr." Biographical Directory of the United States Congress Web site.
http://bioguide.congress.gov/scripts/biodisplay.pl?index=T000031. Accessed on December 14, 2007.

"Taylor, John W." Biographical Directory of the United States Congress Web site.
http://bioguide.congress.gov/scripts/biodisplay.pl?index=T000091. Accessed on December 14, 2007.

"Thomas, Jesse Burgess." Biographical Directory of the United States Congress Web site.
http://bioguide.congress.gov/scripts/biodisplay.pl?index=T000171. Accessed on December 14, 2007.

—By Kirk H. Beetz

Questions for Further Study

1. Why did many representatives of slave states view the Missouri Compromise as a victory?

2. Were those who predicted that the Missouri Compromise was a prelude to civil war correct? Explain your answer.

3. You are a justice of the Supreme Court deciding the constitutionality of the Missouri Compromise. Was it constitutional or not? Give reasons for your opinion.

4. Why did Thomas Jefferson and John Quincy Adams believe that the debate over the Missouri Compromise had made civil war more likely than before?

5. Jefferson and many other political philosophers in the early decades of the United States believed that slavery would fade away. Did passage of the Missouri Compromise make this possibility more likely or less so? Explain your answer.

Glossary

ceded	property given to someone else
contiguous	sharing a boundary
defraying	satisfying costs by payment
expedient	appropriate to the purpose
incident	caused by or required by
meridian	a north-south line envisioned as circumscribing the earth through both poles
parallel	an east-west line envisioned as circumscribing the earth a certain distance north or south of the equator
patents	government grants
patentees	recipients of government grants
salt springs	sources of dissolved salt, especially important to cattle ranchers

Missouri Compromise

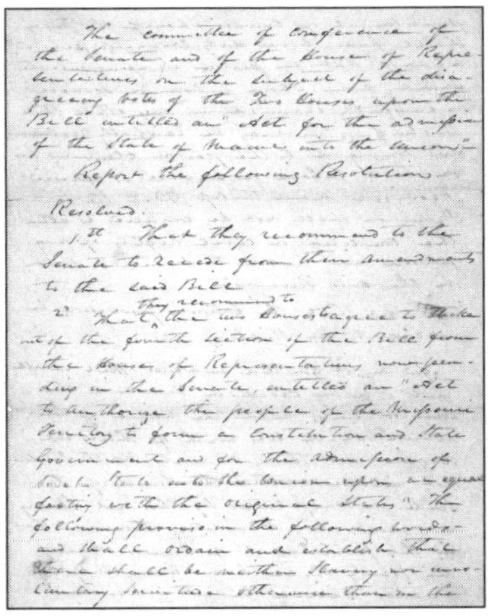

The committee of conference of the Senate and of the House of Representatives on the subject of the disagreeing votes of the two Houses upon the Bill entitled an "Act for the admission of the State of Maine into the Union"—
Report the following Resolutions

Resolved.
1st That they recommend to the Senate to recede from their amendments to the said Bill
2d That they recommend to the two Houses to agree to strike out of the fourth section of the Bill from the House of Representatives now pending in the Senate, entitled an "Act to authorize the people of the Missouri Territory to form a Constitution and State Government and for the admission of such State into the Union upon an equal footing with the original States", the following proviso in the following words— and shall ordain and establish that there shall be neither slavery nor involuntary servitude otherwise than in the

An Act to authorize the people of the Missouri territory to form a constitution and state government, and for the admission of such state into the Union on an equal footing with the original states, and to prohibit slavery in certain territories.

Be it enacted by the Senate and House of Representatives of the United States of America, in Congress assembled, That the inhabitants of that portion of the Missouri territory included within the boundaries herein after designated, be, and they are hereby, authorized to form for themselves a constitution and state government, and to assume such name as they shall deem proper; and the said state, when formed, shall be admitted into the Union, upon an equal footing with the original states, in all respects whatsoever.

SEC.2. And be it further enacted, That the said state shall consist of all the territory included within the following boundaries, to wit: Beginning in the middle of the Mississippi river, on the parallel of thirty-six degrees of north latitude; thence west, along that parallel of latitude, to the St. Francois river; thence up, and following the course of that river, in the middle of the main channel thereof, to the parallel of latitude of thirty-six degrees and thirty minutes; thence west, along the same, to a point where the said parallel is intersected by a meridian line passing through the middle of the mouth of the Kansas river, where the same empties into the Missouri river, thence, from the point aforesaid north, along the said meridian line, to the intersection of the parallel of latitude which passes through the rapids of the river Des Moines, making the said line to correspond with the Indian boundary line; thence east, from the point of intersection last aforesaid, along the said parallel of latitude, to the middle of the channel of the main fork of the said river Des Moines; thence down arid along the middle of the main channel of the said river Des Moines, to the mouth of the same, where it empties into the Mississippi river; thence, due east, to the middle of the main channel of the Mississippi river; thence down, and following the course of the Mississippi river, in the middle of the main channel thereof, to the place of beginning: Provided, The said state shall ratify the boundaries aforesaid. And provided also, That the said state shall have concurrent jurisdiction on the river Mississippi, and every other river bordering on the said state so far as the said rivers shall form a common boundary to the said state; and any other state or states, now or hereafter to be formed and bounded by the same, such rivers to be common to both; and that the river Mississippi, and the navigable rivers and waters leading into the same, shall be common highways, and for ever free, as well to the inhabitants of the said state as to other citizens of the United States, without any tax, duty impost, or toll, therefor, imposed by the said state.

SEC. 3. And be it further enacted, That all free white male citizens of the United States, who shall have arrived at the age of twenty-one years, and have resided in said territory: three months previous to the day of election, and all other persons qualified to vote for representatives to the general assembly of the said territory, shall be qualified to be elected and they are hereby qualified and authorized to vote, and choose representatives to form a convention, who shall be apportioned amongst the several counties as follows:

From the county of Howard, five representatives. From the county of Cooper, three representatives. From the county of Montgomery, two representatives. From the county of Pike, one representative. From the county of Lincoln, one representative. From the county of St. Charles, three representatives. From the county of Franklin, one representative. From the county of St. Louis, eight representatives. From the county of Jefferson, one representative. From the county of Washington, three representatives. From the county of St. Genevieve, four representatives. From the county of Madison, one representative. From the county of Cape Girardeau, five representatives. From the county of New Madrid, two representatives. From the county of

www.milestonedocuments.com

Wayne, and that portion of the county of Lawrence which falls within the boundaries herein designated, one representative.

And the election for the representatives aforesaid shall be holden on the first Monday, and two succeeding days of May next, throughout the several counties aforesaid in the said territory, and shall be, in every respect, held and conducted in the same manner, and under the same regulations as is prescribed by the laws of the said territory regulating elections therein for members of the general assembly, except that the returns of the election in that portion of Lawrence county included in the boundaries aforesaid, shall be made to the county of Wayne, as is provided in other cases under the laws of said territory.

SEC. 4. And be it further enacted, That the members of the convention thus duly elected, shall be, and they are hereby authorized to meet at the seat of government of said territory on the second Monday of the month of June next; and the said convention, when so assembled, shall have power and authority to adjourn to any other place in the said territory, which to them shall seem best for the convenient transaction of their business; and which convention, when so met, shall first determine by a majority of the whole number elected, whether it be, or be not, expedient at that time to form a constitution and state government for the people within the said territory, as included within the boundaries above designated; and if it be deemed expedient, the convention shall be, and hereby is, authorized to form a constitution and state government; or, if it be deemed more expedient, the said convention shall provide by ordinance for electing representatives to form a constitution or frame of government; which said representatives shall be chosen in such manner, and in such proportion as they shall designate; and shall meet at such time and place as shall be prescribed by the said ordinance; and shall then form for the people of said territory, within the boundaries aforesaid, a constitution and state government: Provided, That the same, whenever formed, shall be republican, and not repugnant to the constitution of the United States; and that the legislature of said state shall never interfere with the primary disposal of the soil by the United States, nor with any regulations Congress may find necessary for securing the title in such soil to the bona fide purchasers; and that no tax shall be imposed on lands the property of the United States; and in no case shall non-resident proprietors be taxed higher than residents.

SEC. 5. And be it further enacted, That until the next general census shall be taken, the said state shall be entitled to one representative in the House of Representatives of the United States.

SEC. 6. And be it further enacted, That the following propositions be, and the same are hereby, offered to the convention of the said territory of Missouri, when formed, for their free acceptance or rejection, which, if accepted by the convention, shall be obligatory upon the United States:

First. That section numbered sixteen in every township, and when such section has been sold, or otherwise disposed of, other lands equivalent thereto, and as contiguous as may be, shall be granted to the state for the use of the inhabitants of such township, for the use of schools.

Second. That all salt springs, not exceeding twelve in number, with six sections of land adjoining to each, shall be granted to the said state for the use of said state, the same to be selected by the legislature of the said state, on or before the first day of January, in the year one thousand eight hundred and twenty-five; and the same, when so selected, to be used under such terms, conditions, and regulations, as the legislature of said state shall direct: Provided, That no salt spring, the right whereof now is, or hereafter shall be, confirmed or adjudged to any individual or individuals, shall, by this section, be granted to the said state: And provided also, That the legislature shall never sell or lease the same, at anyone time, for a longer period than ten years, without the consent of Congress.

Third. That five per cent. of the net proceeds of the sale of lands lying within the said territory or state, and which shall be sold by Congress, from and after the first day of January next, after deducting all expenses incident to the same, shall be reserved for making public roads and canals, of which three fifths shall be applied to those objects within the state, under the direction of the legislature thereof; and the other two fifths in defraying, under the direction of Congress, the expenses to be incurred in making of a road or roads, canal or canals, leading to the said state.

Fourth. That four entire sections of land be, and the same are hereby, granted to the said state, for the purpose of fixing their seat of government thereon; which said sections shall, under the direction of the legislature of said state, be located, as near as may be, in one body, at any time, in such townships and ranges as the legislature aforesaid may select, on any of the public lands of the United States: Provided, That such locations shall be made prior to the public sale of the lands of the United States surrounding such location.

Fifth. That thirty-six sections, or one entire township, which shall be designated by the President of the United States, together with the other lands heretofore reserved for that purpose, shall be reserved for the use of a seminary of learning, and vested in the legislature of said state, to be appropriated solely to the use of such seminary by the said legislature: Provided, That the five foregoing propositions herein offered, are on the condition that the convention of the said state shall provide, by an ordinance, irrevocable without the consent or the United States, that every and each tract of land sold by the United States, from and after the firsl day of January next, shall remain exempt from any tax laid by order or under the authority of the state, whether for state, county, or township, or any other purpose whatever, for the term of five years from and after the day of sale; And further, That the bounty lands granted, or hereafter to be granted, for military services during the late war, shall, while they continue to be held by the patentees, or their heirs remain exempt as aforesaid from taxation for the term of three year; from and after the date of the patents respectively.

SEC. 7. And be it further enacted, That in case a constitution and state government shall be formed for the people of the said territory of Missouri, the said convention or representatives, as soon thereafter as may be, shall cause a true and attested copy of such constitution or frame of state government, as shall be formed or provided, to be transmitted to Congress.

SEC. 8. And be it further enacted. That in all that territory ceded by France to the United States, under the name of Louisiana, which lies north of thirty-six degrees and thirty minutes north latitude, not included within the limits of the state, contemplated by this act, slavery and involuntary servitude, otherwise than in the punishment of crimes, whereof the parties shall have been duly convicted, shall be, and is hereby, forever prohibited: Provided always, That any person escaping into the same, from whom labour or service is lawfully claimed, in any state or territory of the United States, such fugitive may be lawfully reclaimed and conveyed to the person claiming his or her labour or service as aforesaid.

APPROVED, March 6, 1820.

www.milestonedocuments.com

29.

It was stated at the commencement of
the last Session, that a great effort was then
making in Spain and Portugal, to improve
the condition of the people of those countries;
and that it appeared to be conducted
with extraordinary moderation. It need
scarcely be remarked, that the result has
been, so far, very different from what was
then anticipated. Of events in that quarter
of the Globe, with which we have so much
intercourse, and from which we derive our
origin, we have always been anxious and
interested spectators. The Citizens of the United
States cherish sentiments the most friendly,
in favor of the liberty and happiness of
their fellow men on that side of the Atlantic.
In the wars of the European powers, in matters
relating to themselves, we have never taken
any part, nor does it comport with our
policy, so to do. It is only when our rights are
invaded, or seriously menaced, that we
resent injuries, or make preparation for
our defence. With the movements in this
Hemisphere we are of necessity more imme-

The Monroe Doctrine (National Archives and Records Administration)

MONROE DOCTRINE

1823

"We should consider any attempt on their part to extend their system to any portion of this hemisphere as dangerous to our peace and safety."

Overview

On December 2, 1823, in his Annual Message to Congress, President James Monroe issued a bold statement on foreign policy that reaffirmed the nation's longstanding commitment to neutrality and offered an explicit warning to Europe that the entire Western Hemisphere was closed to further colonization. This pronouncement of American autonomy and hemispheric solidarity against European aggression is considered one of the most significant statements in American foreign policy and the greatest achievement of Monroe's two-term presidency. While Monroe discusses other issue in this presidential address, his statement on foreign policy is the most memorable.

Monroe's statement, originally known as the American System and later known as the Monroe Doctrine, contains four major principles. First, the political systems of the Americas are different from those in Europe. Second, the United States will continue to remain neutral in foreign affairs, unless these matters directly affect American security or interests. Third, the Western Hemisphere is no longer available for new colonization. If a former colony becomes independent, European powers should respect its new status and not try to intervene. If a colony in the Western Hemisphere remains under European control, the United States will not interfere. Finally, the United States will interpret any new effort by Europe to colonize the Western Hemisphere as a direct threat to its security.

Context

While President Monroe and his secretary of state, John Quincy Adams, deserve most of the credit for establishing this doctrine, a confluence of events, some old and some new, created the environment permitting its issuance.

Beginning with George Washington's presidency in 1789, the nation's foreign policy stressed neutrality unless American interests were directly affected, and the Monroe Doctrine represented both a continuation and a reaffirmation of this approach. Diplomatic triumphs that occurred several years before the Monroe Doctrine was issued also laid the groundwork for this statement. The successful resolution of the War of 1812 through the Treaty of Ghent and the acquisition of Florida from Spain permitted the United States to gain greater control over trade and territory. These accomplishments also allowed American negotiators to approach European countries from a position of strength rather than weakness. European countries were also undergoing great change with the end of the Napoleonic Wars and the peace treaty known as the Congress of Vienna, and South American countries were successfully challenging Spanish colonial regimes and declaring their independence. As Europe restored its monarchies and South American countries resisted colonization, Americans were reminded of their own colonial heritage. They realized that they had more in common with the "American system" of independence and equality than with the "European system" of absolutism and tyranny. The United States' identification with its southern neighbors also demonstrated its sense of vulnerability toward Europe, despite its recent diplomatic triumphs.

The final and most immediate impetus for the Monroe Doctrine came from the British foreign minister Stratford Canning in August 1823. Concerned about the renewed alliance between France and Spain, Britain invited the United States to join it in issuing an Anglo-American statement opposing further Spanish and French colonization in the Americas. Spain's intention to send troops into South America to put down rebellions gave the British proposal a particular sense of urgency. While Monroe gave the British offer serious consideration, including receiving favorable endorsements from both Thomas Jefferson and James Madison, he ultimately concluded that the United States should issue its own statement to demonstrate that America was truly independent and neutral and not merely an appendage of Britain.

The American System of the Monroe Doctrine should not be confused with Henry Clay's American System, an economic program consisting of tariffs, internal improvements and a national bank, originally proposed in 1824.

Time Line

1796	■ **September 17** President Washington warns Americans in his Farewell Address to "steer clear of permanent Alliances."
1803	■ **April 30** The Louisiana Purchase doubles the size of the United States.
1812	■ **Jun 18** The War of 1812 between United States and Britain begins.
1814	■ **December 24** The Treaty of Ghent ends the War of 1812.
1814–1815	■ **September 1814–June 1815** The Congress of Vienna ends the Napoleonic Wars.
1817	■ **March 4** James Monroe is inaugurated as president.
1818	■ **January–June** Andrew Jackson invades Spanish Florida.
1819	■ **February 22** The Transcontinental Treaty (also known as the Adams-Onis Treaty and more formally as the Treaty of Amity, Settlement, and Limits between the United States of America and His Catholic Majesty) between Spain and the United States is signed, resulting in the United States' acquisition of Florida and the resolution of the American-Spanish boundary west of the Mississippi River.
1820	■ **March** The Missouri Compromise admits Missouri as a slave state and Maine as a free one.

About the Author

The Monroe Doctrine has two principal authors, President James Monroe and Secretary of State John Quincy Adams. The best way to balance credit between these two men is a point of contention among historians. Most agree that Monroe was an advocate for the major principles of the doctrine—noncolonization, neutrality, and support for South American independence movements—but Adams's ideas and his diplomatic efforts created conditions enabling the successful pronouncement of the Monroe Doctrine. The doctrine's original name, the American System, reflects its shared authorship as well as its debt to longstanding practices in American foreign policy, which involved the work of many individuals.

James Monroe was born in Virginia in 1758 into a slaveholding family of the landed gentry, a class slightly below that of the exalted planters. As a young man, Monroe participated in the American Revolution, fighting in the battles of Trenton and Monmouth under the command of General George Washington. Monroe had hoped this experience would lead to a career in the military, but he was unable to raise a regiment and sought a professional future in law and politics instead. For more than three decades, Monroe amassed a successful political career that included terms as Virginia's senator and governor as well as diplomatic experience as minister to France during Washington's presidency. He served as secretary of state during the War of 1812. A founding member of the Democratic-Republican Party, Monroe enjoyed a close political and personal association with his presidential predecessors, Virginia neighbors, and fellow partisans Thomas Jefferson and James Madison. After completing his second term as president, Monroe retired to New York City, where he died on July 4, 1831, at the age of seventy-three.

John Quincy Adams, the son of President John Adams, was born in Massachusetts in 1767. The younger Adams enjoyed a distinguished public career that began in foreign affairs and culminated with his election to the presidency in 1824. Before becoming secretary of state, Adams had served as the American ambassador in a string of European capitals, including Holland, Portugal, Prussia, Russia, and Britain. He also participated in the Treaty of Ghent negotiations that ended the War of 1812. Breaking with tradition, Adams abandoned his postpresidential retirement to become a member of Congress from Massachusetts, where he emerged as a major opponent of slavery. Adams collapsed on the floor of the House of Representatives and died a few days later on February 23, 1848, at the age of eighty.

Explanation and Analysis of the Document

The Monroe Doctrine, issued by President James Monroe in his annual message to Congress in December 1823, offers a sweeping assertion of American autonomy in the southern and northern halves of the continent in the face of European colonization and aggression. This statement provides an elegant summation of the previous thirty years of American foreign policy, as it affirms the longstanding principles of neutrality and independence from European intervention.

◆ "Future Colonization by Any European Powers"

Because the Monroe Doctrine was issued as part of his annual presidential address to Congress, this speech deals with a wide variety of domestic and international issues in addition to this pronouncement. The first principle of the Monroe Doctrine appears separately from the other three and offers the boldest and most memorable statement of the doctrine: the American continents are "not to be considered as subjects for future colonization by any European powers." Noting a common heritage that involved colonization and then liberation, this statement recognizes the "free and independent condition" of the American continents. By issuing this statement, the United States was asserting its autonomy as well as that of its southern brethren from all forms of European intervention and control, particularly colonization.

This end of European colonization in the Western Hemisphere is the part of the Monroe Doctrine most often associated with the ideas of John Quincy Adams, who previously had expressed similar noncolonial sentiments in a Fourth of July address delivered in Washington in 1821. Adams had promoted this nonintervention position in July 1823 when he warned Russia that the United States would not tolerate its territorial claims in North America, particularly those in the Pacific Northwest.

Time Line

1822	**■ March** U.S. diplomatic recognition is offered to the newly independent states of Buenos Aires, Chile, Columbia, Mexico, and Peru.
1823	**■ December 2** The Monroe Doctrine is issued but is identified as the American System.
1824	**■ March 4** John Quincy Adams is elected president.
1852	■ The term *Monroe Doctrine* is coined to describe the 1823 proposal known as the American System.
1904–1905	**■ December 6, 1904 and December 5, 1905** Theodore Roosevelt proposes a corollary to the Monroe Doctrine.

◆ Neutrality

The second principle of the Monroe Doctrine reaffirms the nation's longstanding policy of neutrality, stating, "In the wars of the European powers in matters relating to themselves we have never taken any part, nor does it comport with our policy to do so." Later in this paragraph, the doctrine also stresses that the United States has not and will not interfere "with the existing colonies or dependencies of any European power" despite its opposition to further colonization in the Western Hemisphere. Both of these statements continue an American foreign policy that has stressed, since the government's establishment in 1789, the twin principles of neutrality and nonintervention in European affairs.

Despite its stated intention of remaining neutral, the United States had struggled to attain this goal, particularly during the 1790s, as Britain and France each sought the allegiance of the young nation in its long-running animosities with the other. While the French Revolution and the resulting Reign of Terror permitted the United States to distance itself from France, Britain remained an overbearing ally, particularly in the area of transatlantic trade. The Jay Treaty, ratified in 1796, represented an unsuccessful effort to achieve a diplomatic solution. Later, the more assertive Embargo Act of 1807 sought to curtail British trading access as a way to produce concessions. Neither approach worked, and the War of 1812 offered a military solution where diplomacy and economic pressure had failed. The two-year war was largely a stalemate, as each side enjoyed its share of military successes and failures, and the Treaty of Ghent mirrored these results by reaffirming the status quo of the prewar world. Nonetheless, the War of 1812 was a greater victory for the United States than the 1815 treaty indicated, because Britain finally recognized American autonomy by ceasing many of the aggressive trade policies that had led to the war. The world after the War of 1812 produced an environment in which the United States could issue a statement that reaffirmed its independence and increased its autonomy.

◆ "The Political System of the Allied Powers Is Essentially Different."

The third principle of the Monroe Doctrine concerns the historical and political similarities that exist among the sovereign nations of the American continents. Each country had once been a colony belonging to a European power and had fought to achieve its independence. The systems of government on each side of the Atlantic were also different—the United States had adopted a republican form of government that stressed popular sovereignty and representation, while European countries still embraced the monarchical government that the American Revolution had rejected. In fact, the aftermath of the Napoleonic Wars had witnessed the restoration of monarchy in France. As Monroe and Adams surveyed the post-1815 landscape, they realized that North and South America shared more than

www.milestonedocuments.com

James Monroe (Library of Congress)

geographic proximity; the two continents also shared a common history that abhorred European intrusions. America's newfound strength after the War of 1812 permitted the formulation of a new foreign policy that affirmed the common ground among the American nations that rendered them historically and politically separate from Europe. The diplomatic recognition that President Monroe and Congress extended to the newly independent South American states of Buenos Aires, Chile, Columbia, Mexico, and Peru in 1822 served as a significant step in an increasingly American-centered foreign policy. This recognition naturally paved the way for further expression of hemispheric solidarity in the Monroe Doctrine of 1823.

◆ "As Dangerous to Our Peace and Safety"

The fourth principle of the Monroe Doctrine deals with the consequences of Europe not respecting the statement's three principles: noncolonization, neutrality, and a shared tradition of independence and self-government. As the enforcement clause of the document, this fourth principle appears throughout the second section in various forms. Immediately following the declaration of the nation's long history of neutrality, the enforcement clause is then invoked to explain situations where the nation would get involved: "It is only when our rights are invaded or seriously menaced that we resent injuries or make preparation for our defense." A few sentences later, a similar warning appears, this time in relation to any efforts of new colonization or, a more pressing concern, recolonization through military force: "We owe it, therefore, to candor and to the amicable relations existing between the United States and those powers to declare that we should consider any attempt on their part to extend their system to any portion of this hemisphere as dangerous to our peace and safety." Finally, in the last portion of the speech devoted to this doctrine, Monroe warns that both European political systems and military interference in the Western Hemisphere would be seen as "endangering our peace and happiness." Explicitly mentioning Spain for the first time, he says that Spanish attempts to retake their colonies would be impractical because of the expense and the distance. Instead, these new states should be allowed to prosper on their own. Nonetheless, Monroe ends with a final warning: Any interposition by Europe will not be met with indifference by the United States. While military action is never explicitly stated, it is certainly implied throughout these sections, which are designed to enforce the three earlier provisions of the Monroe Doctrine.

Upon entering the presidency in 1817, Monroe encountered an international landscape that was substantially different from what had existed four years earlier when he had served as Madison's secretary of state. The 1815 Congress of Vienna had ended the Napoleonic Wars and had begun rebuilding Europe. In South America, independence movements were successfully overthrowing European colonial governments, particularly Spanish ones. As Europe regrouped and the Americas adopted an increasingly assertive approach to European incursions, the United States reoriented its foreign policy, which had been preoccupied with affairs in Europe and on the Atlantic, and looked to the West and the South. Building upon the successful outcome of the Treaty of Ghent as well as the acquisition of Florida from Spain through the Transcontinental Treaty of 1819, the United States was now in a position to assert a new approach to foreign policy that reflected strengthened American continents. The resulting pronouncement was the Monroe Doctrine, which boldly declares the Americas closed to colonization while also reiterating American neutrality. It also identifies a common political and historical heritage among the American continents that European countries did not and could not share. Finally, this doctrine warns that neutrality is not pacifism and that there would be consequences to any European attempt to interfere militarily or politically in the Western Hemisphere. Issued from a position of strength, the Monroe Doctrine serves as an enduring and effective statement of American autonomy and neutrality as well as hemispheric solidarity to warn against potential European incursions into the region's affairs.

Audience

The Monroe Doctrine was primarily aimed at the European powers that had colonial designs on the Americas.

Essential Quotes

"As a principle in which the rights and interests of the United States are involved, that the American continents, by the free and independent condition which they have assumed and maintain, are henceforth not to be considered as subjects for future colonization by any European powers."

(Paragraph 1)

"In the wars of the European powers in matters relating to themselves we have never taken any part, nor does it comport with our policy to do so. It is only when our rights are invaded or seriously menaced that we resent injuries or make preparation for our defense."

(Paragraph 2)

"The political system of the allied powers is essentially different in this respect from that of America."

(Paragraph 2)

"We owe it, therefore, to candor and to the amicable relations existing between the United States and those powers to declare that we should consider any attempt on their part to extend their system to any portion of this hemisphere as dangerous to our peace and safety."

(Paragraph 2)

"With the existing colonies or dependencies of any European power we have not interfered and shall not interfere. But with the Governments who have declared their independence and maintain it, and whose independence we have, on great consideration and on just principles, acknowledged, we could not view any interposition for the purpose of oppressing them, or controlling in any other manner their destiny, by any European power in any other light than as the manifestation of an unfriendly disposition toward the United States."

(Paragraph 2)

www.milestonedocuments.com

Spain was the immediate target of such warnings because of its desire to reclaim its former territories, despite the independence movements sweeping through South America. Russia, which had tentative claims in the Pacific Northwest, as well as France, which had ambitions in South and Central America, were also intended audiences. Britain, which wished to stop the expansion efforts of the Spanish and French, was a sympathetic recipient. Finally, the American public, the press, and Congress all responded enthusiastically to this declaration of American neutrality and European nonintervention.

Impact

The Monroe Doctrine of 1823 emerged from a series of diplomatic triumphs that increased American independence and lessened European involvement in national affairs. The Monroe Doctrine affirmed the nation's new autonomy after the War of 1812 and the Transcontinental Treaty by reiterating its neutrality, while also expanding its influence by forging alliances with newly independent South American states and warning Europe that these states were off limits to further colonization. As the United States continued to grow economically and territorially during the nineteenth century, the Monroe Doctrine served as an important warning to Europe to mind its own affairs. Issued at a time of unusual peace, the doctrine anticipated that this harmony would not last and acted as a unilateral warning to thwart any potential European invasions or interferences before they began. Although the United States was by no means a military powerhouse after 1815, it had enjoyed enough military successes in the recent War of 1812 to competently challenge a foreign invasion. This experience, coupled with the difficulty of launching a war from Europe, made the doctrine's threat of retaliation a credible one. For these reasons, the Monroe Doctrine succeeded in keeping Europe out of American affairs and allowed the country to expand and prosper.

When Theodore Roosevelt issued his Corollaries to the Monroe Doctrine in 1904 and 1905, the United States' prerogative to defend South America from a European invasion took on a more sinister aspect. By the early twentieth century, the United States was becoming an economic and military power, and its interventions in South America had more to do with economic interests than regional solidarity. In many ways, the United States had become the colonizer the Monroe Doctrine was supposed to ban from the Western Hemisphere.

The Monroe Doctrine was a powerful and enduring statement of American independence, neutrality, and nonintervention that was issued at a time when the young nation was finally able to assert itself against European encroachments. This doctrine successfully insulated America from outside intrusions and enabled it to prosper, although, later, the doctrine's imperialistic possibilities became more pronounced as the United States grew in power. Even as late as 1962, the Monroe Doctrine retained its original intent: thwarting a European invasion of the Western Hemisphere. During the Cuban Missile Crisis, John F. Kennedy invoked the doctrine to impose a naval blockade on Cuba to challenge the presence of Soviet missiles.

Related Documents

Ford, Worthlington C., ed. *The Writings of John Quincy Adams*. 7 vols. New York: Greenwood Press, 1968. The Monroe Doctrine was the culmination of a series of American diplomatic efforts, many of which involved Adams as the lead negotiator. Adams's writings are critical to understanding the environment and ideas that produced the Monroe Doctrine.

Hamilton, Stanislaus M., ed. *The Writings of James Monroe*. 7 vols. New York: G. P. Putnam's Sons, 1989–1903. Not to be overshadowed by the writings of John Quincy Adams, Monroe's writings about the formulation and drafting of the Monroe Doctrine deserve attention as well.

"Roosevelt Corollary of 1904, 1905." National Archives "Our Documents" Web site. http://www.ourdocuments.gov/doc.php?flash=true&doc=56. Issued by President Theodore Roosevelt in two consecutive annual addresses to Congress, this statement demonstrated an increasingly aggressive American policy toward the Western Hemisphere in the aftermath of the Spanish American War (1898) and the war in Philippines (1899–1902). Revising the Monroe Doctrine's warning to Europe to stay out of the Western Hemisphere, the Roosevelt Corollary unilaterally declared America's right to intervene in South and Central American affairs, if necessary, in cases of instability.

"Treaty of Amity, Settlement, and Limits between the United States of America and His Catholic Majesty, 1819." The Avalon Project at Yale Law School Web site. http://www.yale.edu/lawweb/avalon/diplomacy/spain/sp1819.htm. Accessed on September 25, 2007. This treaty was the direct antecedent of the Monroe Doctrine, and the resulting agreement with Spain offers insights into American expectations, Spain's strength, and John Quincy Adams's diplomatic goals for a more assertive American foreign policy.

Bibliography

■ Books

Ammon, Harry. *James Monroe, The Quest for National Identity*. Charlottesville: University Press of Virginia, 1990.

Bemis, Samuel Flagg. *John Quincy Adams and the Foundations of American Foreign Policy*. New York: Alfred A. Knopf, 1949.

Cunningham, Noble E., Jr. *The Presidency of James Monroe*. Lawrence: University Press of Kansas, 1996.

May, Ernest R. *The Making of the Monroe Doctrine*. Cambridge, Mass.: Belknap Press of Harvard University Press, 1975.

Nagel, Paul C. *John Quincy Adams: A Public Life, A Private Life*. New York: Alfred A. Knopf, 1997.

Perkins, Dexter. *A History of the Monroe Doctrine*. Boston: Little, Brown and Company, 1963.

———. *The Monroe Doctrine, 1823–1826*. Gloucester, Mass.: Peter Smith, 1965.

Russell, Greg. *John Quincy Adams and the Public Virtues of Diplomacy*. Columbia: University of Missouri Press, 1995.

Weeks, William Earl. *John Quincy Adams and American Global Empire*. Lexington: University Press of Kentucky, 1992.

■ **Web Sites**

"Monroe Doctrine." "The American Presidency" Web site. http://ap.grolier.com/article?assetid=0197260-0&templatename=/article/article.html. Accessed on September 25, 2007.

"The Monroe Doctrine: Origin and Early American Foreign Policy." National Endowment for the Humanities Web site. http://edsitement.neh.gov/view_lesson_plan.asp?id=574" Accessed on September 25, 2007.

"The Monroe Doctrine: Whose Doctrine Was It?" National Endowment for the Humanities Web site. http://edsitement.neh.gov/view_lesson_plan.asp?id=578. Accessed on September 25, 2007.

—By Sandy Moats

www.milestonedocuments.com

Questions for Further Study

1. How much credit should the Monroe Doctrine receive for promoting independence movements in the Western Hemisphere?

2. Compare and contrast the provisions of the Transcontinental Treaty with those of the Monroe Doctrine. Would the Monroe Doctrine have been possible without the successful negotiation of this 1819 treaty with Spain?

3. What are the negative, imperialistic aspects of the Monroe Doctrine?

4. Which events, both in Europe and in the Americas, were most instrumental in creating the Monroe Doctrine? What priority rank might you give the events listed in the chronology?

5. What is the appropriate balance of credit between Monroe and Adams in formulating the Monroe Doctrine?

Glossary

adduced cited as evidence or proof in an argument

disposition predominant temperament or inclination

interposition intervention

manifestation a public display or expression of power and intention

Monroe Doctrine

Note: The Monroe Doctrine was expressed during President Monroe's seventh annual message to Congress, December 2, 1823:

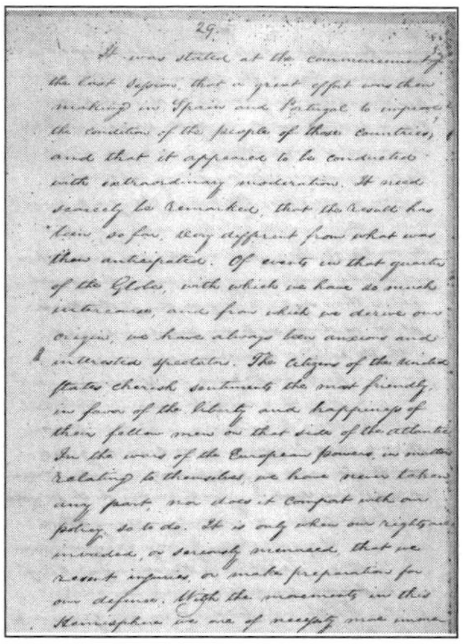
29.

It was stated at the commencement of the last session, that a great effort was then making in Spain and Portugal to improve the condition of the people of those Countries, and that it appeared to be conducted with extraordinary moderation. It need scarcely be remarked, that the result has been so far, very different from what was then anticipated. Of events in that quarter of the Globe, with which we have so much intercourse, and from which we derive our origin, we have always been anxious and interested spectators. The Citizens of the United States cherish sentiments the most friendly, in favor of the liberty and happiness of their fellow men on that side of the Atlantic. In the wars of the European powers, in matters relating to themselves we have never taken any part, nor does it comport with our policy, so to do. It is only when our rights are invaded, or seriously menaced, that we resent injuries, or make preparation for our defence. With the movements in this Hemisphere we are of necessity more more

…At the proposal of the Russian Imperial Government, made through the minister of the Emperor residing here, a full power and instructions have been transmitted to the minister of the United States at St. Petersburg to arrange by amicable negotiation the respective rights and interests of the two nations on the northwest coast of this continent. A similar proposal has been made by His Imperial Majesty to the Government of Great Britain, which has likewise been acceded to. The Government of the United States has been desirous by this friendly proceeding of manifesting the great value which they have invariably attached to the friendship of the Emperor and their solicitude to cultivate the best understanding with his Government. In the discussions to which this interest has given rise and in the arrangements by which they may terminate the occasion has been judged proper for asserting, as a principle in which the rights and interests of the United States are involved, that the American continents, by the free and independent condition which they have assumed and maintain, are henceforth not to be considered as subjects for future colonization by any European powers….

It was stated at the commencement of the last session that a great effort was then making in Spain and Portugal to improve the condition of the people of those countries, and that it appeared to be conducted with extraordinary moderation. It need scarcely be remarked that the results have been so far very different from what was then anticipated. Of events in that quarter of the globe, with which we have so much intercourse and from which we derive our origin, we have always been anxious and interested spectators. The citizens of the United States cherish sentiments the most friendly in favor of the liberty and happiness of their fellow-men on that side of the Atlantic. In the wars of the European powers in matters relating to themselves we have never taken any part, nor does it comport with our policy to do so. It is only when our rights are invaded or seriously menaced that we resent injuries or make preparation for our defense. With the movements in this hemisphere we are of necessity more immediately connected, and by causes which must be obvious to all enlightened and impartial observers. The political system of the allied powers is essentially different in this respect from that of America. This difference proceeds from that which exists in their respective Governments; and to the defense of our own, which has been achieved by the loss of so much blood and treasure, and matured by the wisdom of their most enlightened citizens, and under which we have enjoyed unexampled felicity, this whole nation is devoted. We owe it, therefore, to candor and to the amicable relations existing between the United States and those powers to declare that we should consider any attempt on their part to extend their system to any portion of this hemisphere as dangerous to our peace and safety. With the existing colonies or dependencies of any European power we have not interfered and shall not interfere. But with the Governments who have declared their independence and maintain it, and whose independence we have, on great consideration and on just principles, acknowledged, we could not view any interposition for the purpose of oppressing them, or controlling in any other manner their destiny, by any European power in any other light than as the manifestation of an unfriendly disposition toward the United States. In the war between those new Governments and Spain we declared our neutrality at the time of their recognition, and to this we have adhered, and shall continue to adhere, provided no change shall occur which, in the judgement of the competent authorities of this Government, shall make a corresponding change on the part of the United States indispensable to their security.

Document Text

The late events in Spain and Portugal show that Europe is still unsettled. Of this important fact no stronger proof can be adduced than that the allied powers should have thought it proper, on any principle satisfactory to themselves, to have interposed by force in the internal concerns of Spain. To what extent such interposition may be carried, on the same principle, is a question in which all independent powers whose governments differ from theirs are interested, even those most remote, and surely none of them more so than the United States. Our policy in regard to Europe, which was adopted at an early stage of the wars which have so long agitated that quarter of the globe, nevertheless remains the same, which is, not to interfere in the internal concerns of any of its powers; to consider the government de facto as the legitimate government for us; to cultivate friendly relations with it, and to preserve those relations by a frank, firm, and manly policy, meeting in all instances the just claims of every power, submitting to injuries from none. But in regard to those continents circumstances are eminently and conspicuously different.

It is impossible that the allied powers should extend their political system to any portion of either continent without endangering our peace and happiness; nor can anyone believe that our southern brethren, if left to themselves, would adopt it of their own accord. It is equally impossible, therefore, that we should behold such interposition in any form with indifference. If we look to the comparative strength and resources of Spain and those new Governments, and their distance from each other, it must be obvious that she can never subdue them. It is still the true policy of the United States to leave the parties to themselves, in hope that other powers will pursue the same course....

www.milestonedocuments.com